DOS USER'S
DESKTOP COMPANION

SYBEX
READY
REFERENCE
SERIES

DOS® User's Desktop Companion

Judd Robbins

SAN FRANCISCO · PARIS · DÜSSELDORF · LONDON

SYBEX Ready Reference Series
Editor-in-Chief: Rudolph S. Langer
Managing Editor: Barbara Gordon
Series Editor: James A. Compton
Editor: Judy Ziajka

Book and cover design by Thomas Ingalls + Associates
Cover photography by Casey Cartwright
Illustrations by Van Genderen Studio
Screen reproductions produced by XenoCopy

The tables on pages 906–910 are reproduced by permission from *Disk Operating System Version 3.3 Reference* ©1987 by International Business Machines Corporation.

AST and Six-Pack Plus are trademarks of AST Research, Inc.
Back-It and Q-DOS II are trademarks of Gazelle Systems.
Bernoulli Box is a trademark of Iomega Corporation.
CADVANCE is a trademark of ISICAD, Inc.
CompuServe is a trademark of CompuServe Information Services.
COPYIIPC is a trademark of Central Point Software.
Crosstalk XVI is a trademark of Digital Communcations Associates, Inc.
dBASE III PLUS, Framework II, and MultiMate are trademarks of Ashton-Tate.
Desqview is a trademark of Quarterdeck Office Systems.
Epson is a trademark of Epson America.
Freeway is a trademark of Kortek, Inc.
Imcap and Imshow are trademarks of ImageSet Corp.
IBM, IBM AT, IBM PC, IBM XT, IBM OS/2, PC DOS and PS/2 are trademarks or registered trademarks of International Business Machines Corporation.
Keyworks is a trademark of Alpha Software Corporation.
Lightning is a trademark of Personal Computer Support Group.
Lotus 1-2-3 and Symphony are trademarks of the Lotus Development Corporation.
Norton Utilities is a trademark of Peter Norton Computing.
Palantir is a trademark of Palantir Software.
Panasonic is a trademark of Matsushita Electric.
PreCursor is a trademark of The Aldridge Company.
Quadboard is a trademark of Quadram Corporation.
R-Doc/X is a trademark of Advanced Computer Innovations.
ReComm is a trademark of Computer Options
Samna is a trademark of Samna Corporation.
Scroll & Recall are trademarks of Opt-Tech Data Processing.
Sidekick is a trademark of Borland International.
Sideways is a trademark of Funk Software.
Squish is a trademark of SunDog Software Corporation.
UNIX is a trademark of Bell Laboratories.
WORD is a trademark, and Microsoft and MS-DOS are registered trademarks, of Microsoft Corporation.
WordPerfect is a trademark of WordPerfect Corporation.
WordStar and WordStar 2000 are trademarks of MicroPro International.
VOPT is a trademark of Golden Bow Systems.
XenoCopy is a trademark of XenoSoft.
XTREE is a trademark of Executive Systems.

SYBEX is a registered trademark of SYBEX, Inc.

SYBEX is not affiliated with any manufacturer.

Every effort has been made to supply complete and accurate information. However, SYBEX assumes no responsibility for its use, nor for any infringements of patents or other rights of third parties which would result.

Hardcover: Library of Congress Card Number: 88-60892
                ISBN 0-89588-459-3
Papercover: Library of Congress Card Number: 88-60890
                ISBN 0-89588-505-0
Manufactured in the United States of America
Printed by Haddon Craftsmen

10 9 8 7 6 5 4 3 2 1

To unseen realities,
And echoes in the darkness

TABLE OF CONTENTS

INTRODUCTION

Since its introduction with the first IBM PC computers in 1981, DOS has become the most popular operating system for personal computers. Millions of people now work with computers that use this system, and they will continue to do so for years to come, even as newer and more powerful operating systems, such as OS/2, are released. Among these millions of users, the level of involvement with, and knowledge of, the operating system varies enormously. Many DOS users almost never have to work directly with the operating system; they can perform all their routine tasks through their application software. Others are constantly tinkering with their systems, looking for ways to make them work more efficiently. Most users are somewhere on the broad middle ground between these extremes.

The *DOS User's Desktop Companion* is designed to meet the needs of the broadest possible range of DOS users. It will serve you in two different but overlapping ways. It provides both a progressive, step-by-step tutorial guide to the features of DOS and the tasks you can perform with it, and concise, accessible reference information about the individual commands that give you access to those features.

WHO SHOULD READ THIS BOOK

Nearly every DOS user can benefit from this book. The only class of user not specifically addressed here is the applications programmer. If you are writing programs in assembly language or C designed to run under DOS and to access its features directly, you should consult one of the many fine books available on that subject, such as Alan R. Miller's *DOS Assembly Language Programming* (SYBEX, 1988) or, for both C and assembly language techniques, Michael J. Young's *Performance Programming Under MS-DOS* (SYBEX, 1987). The DOS commands used exclusively in developing programs, such as DEBUG, EXE2BIN, and LINK, are not discussed in this book.

No previous knowledge of DOS, or even of the basics of working with computers, is assumed in the introductory chapters. If you are a first-time user, an infrequent user who has been away from the computer long enough to feel rusty, or someone moving beyond a single application program into direct involvement with DOS, you should start with this material. Then, as your computer work requires more sophisticated operations, you can consult the tables of contents (both for the entire book and for individual chapters) and the index to find the topic you need to know about.

Readers at the middle levels of experience with DOS can learn something from most chapters of this book. Each chapter is written with the assumption that any given topic is new to someone. Whatever aspect of DOS you need to learn about, you'll begin with an overview and move quickly into the practical steps for accomplishing the task at hand. If you belong to this category, you should begin by consulting the tables of contents or the index.

Advanced DOS users will probably find the later chapters to be of most interest. These chapters discuss refinements and extensions to the operating system rather than basic tasks.

DOS users at all levels of experience will want to consult the reference entries for particular commands; they appear at the end of the chapter in which a particular command is introduced.

VERSIONS OF DOS COVERED IN THIS BOOK

This book presents information about all versions of MS-DOS and PC-DOS up to 3.31. Appendix D outlines the enhancements Microsoft has made to DOS over the years. Because of these enhancements, the underlying assumption has been that nearly all readers will be using at least version 2.0, and that more than half will be using version 3.0 or later. Within this range, differences between versions are specifically noted wherever they occur.

Chapter 11 discusses DOS support for international use; these features are available only in version 3.3. and, to a lesser extent, in versions 3.0–3.2.

HOW TO USE THIS BOOK

The *DOS User's Desktop Companion* is written to allow two different approaches to the material. You can either work through the chapters in succession, trying all the examples as you go along, to learn the use of DOS in a systematic manner, or consult individual chapters and sections on an *ad hoc* basis as you need to learn about particular DOS features. The idea behind this book is simple: to provide a single source of information in which you, the DOS user, can find the answer to any question about the operating system that may arise in your work.

Most chapters are divided into two sections: a tutorial, task-oriented guide to some feature of DOS and a series of reference entries for the commands related to that feature and introduced in that chapter. If you are already broadly familiar with a topic, you should consult the chapter table of contents to find the specific aspect of interest to you. The book is thoroughly cross-referenced to help you follow any topic through all the discussions related to it.

Format of the Reference Entries

The reference entries that appear at the end of most chapters are designed to present the essential facts about each DOS command in a clear, highly accessible format. Each entry consists of the following sections:

- *Syntax*—a formal presentation of the exact format in which a command must be entered for DOS to interpret it correctly.
- *Type*—whether the command file (that is, the subprogram within DOS that carries out the command) is loaded into the computer's memory along with the rest of DOS (internal) or must be read from disk each time it is used (external).
- *Usage*—a discussion of the ways the command is most commonly used in practice. This discussion often presents a different aspect of the command's usage than is discussed in the main body of the chapter.
- *Restrictions*—where appropriate, a brief description of any limitations imposed on the use of the command by DOS or other commands.
- *Examples*—brief, annotated illustrations of the command in use.

The notation used in presenting command syntax can best be explained by considering an example:

[*D:path*] SELECT [[A: ¦ B:] *DestD:* [*DestPath*]]

Brackets indicate an optional part of the command. Here, only the command word SELECT and the *DestD:* parameter are required. *Italic* type marks a placeholder; when using the command you would substitute an actual value (here, drive letters and path specifications). The broken vertical bar (¦) indicates an either/or choice; here, you can enter A: or B: (or neither, as DOS assumes a default value of A:).

These conventions are used here purely for educational purposes; do not include brackets or vertical bars or attempt to reproduce italic type on the screen, and be sure to substitute an appropriate value for the placeholder of each parameter you intend to use.

ORGANIZATION OF THE BOOK

The book is organized into seven cohesive major sections. Within each section, each chapter represents an important topic. In Part I, "Preliminary Considerations," Chapters 1 and 2 are introductory and provide necessary background to the rest of the book's treatment of the latest developments in and features of DOS.

In Part II, "Disk and Directory Structures," Chapters 3, 4, and 5 explain the disk system in depth. You will learn how to use disks and how to manage files on multiple disks. You will also learn how to create, manage, and traverse complex DOS directory structures. Last, you will learn a variety of sophisticated techniques for working with hard disk directories and for running your application programs on hard disks.

In Part III, "Batch Files," Chapters 6 through 9 explain the powerful batch-file mechanism in DOS. First, you will learn the editing capabilities in the EDLIN program that allow you to create and modify your batch files. Then Chapter 7 introduces the fundamental batch-file mechanisms in DOS. Chapter 8 introduces the subcommands of this batch-file language. Chapter 9 presents a wealth of both simple and advanced examples of time and energy-saving batch files. Batch files represent an important and time-saving element of DOS.

In Part IV, "Custom Configurations," Chapters 10 and 11 describe the various sophisticated software devices available to you for customizing your computer system. These devices, such as RAM disks and ANSI escape sequences, not only can help you save time, but can also make computing with DOS a more rewarding and enjoyable experience. Chapter 11 concentrates on the particular customization necessary to set up your computer to accept, display, and print foreign character sets.

In Part V, "Communications," Chapters 12, 13, and 14 describe hardware devices and how the computer communicates with the outside world of peripherals. The first chapter in this section lays the groundwork for computer communications, and the second chapter concentrates on how DOS connects through its software ports with a variety of peripheral hardware devices. Chapter 14 describes DOS's connection with an area of computing that is increasingly important to business: local area networks.

In Part VI, "Printing Capabilities," Chapters 15 and 16 describe the techniques and programs under DOS available for outputting information to various printers. The basic techniques for printing your data are presented in Chapter 15, and the more advanced techniques for printer and spool control are presented in Chapter 16.

The final section is Part VII, "Advanced Features." Here, Chapter 17 describes the UNIX-like ability of DOS to reroute output to various internal and external destinations. Chapter 18 presents the important topic of backing up and restoring your important files and data. Chapter 19 discusses specialized commands that experienced users use to increase their control over the system. These sophisticated commands allow you to perform a variety of very interesting and useful techniques. You will learn how to manipulate your file and disk system in powerful and unique ways. Chapter 20 takes you on a tour of outside products, both hardware and software, that let you get the most out of your system. These products can ease computing tremendously, as well as offer you low-cost alternatives to high-priced purchases. You will learn how a range of available outside utility software can help you do some DOS chores more easily or more quickly.

You will also learn how some third-party software can provide you with significantly more control of your DOS system, offering more features and system extensions than DOS provides. Chapter 21 describes the options available to you should you want to program your computer directly. You will take a short look in this chapter at some of the internal setup of DOS, including such elements as the file-allocation table, the BIOS, and elements of the DOS kernel. The final chapter, Chapter 22, takes a close look at the visually attractive, mouse-based user interface offered by Microsoft's multitasking Windows program. You will learn what this program can do, why many people want and need to have it, and whether it will suit your purposes as an alternative to the typical DOS command prompt.

The appendices provide much supplemental information. Appendix A offers a comprehensive glossary of computer terms, particularly DOS and operating system terminology. System and information messages are clearly described in Appendix B, along with probable causes and possible corrective actions you can take. ASCII codes, code pages, and numbering systems are the focus of Appendix C. Appendix D summarizes various changes to DOS over the entire span of its history. Appendix E takes a new look at typical system problem areas and provides tips on troubleshooting these difficulties. You'll learn techniques for identifying and correcting certain common problems. Appendix F provides the most current information about expanded and extended memory, including the LIM EMS 4.0 specification.

ACKNOWLEDGMENTS

Writing a book is much more of a team effort than is indicated by the appearance on the cover of a sole author's name. I would like to thank Steve Mark in my office for his technical contributions to this book. And I would like to express my appreciation for the multifaceted support given to me by the many professionals at Sybex: Jim Compton, series editor; Judy Ziajka, editor; Robert Campbell, technical reviewer; Gina Jaber and Nancy O'Donnell, editorial assistants; Chris Mockel, Bob Myren, and Jocelyn Reynolds, word processors; Cheryl Vega, typesetter; Michelle Hoffman, Jeff Giese, and Sonja Schenk, screen producers; Suzanne Albertson, design coordinator and pasteup artist; Winnie Kelly, Maria Mart, and all their colleagues who pitched in to help, proofreaders; and Elinor Lindheimer, indexer.

I also wish to thank IBM for providing the copy of DOS 3.3 I used during the writing of this book.

PART

1

PRELIMINARY CONSIDERATIONS

What is DOS? What can it do for you? Why should you learn anything about it? These questions, and much more, are answered for you in this introductory section. You will learn the fundamentals of microcomputers and the basics of operating systems. You will learn why operating systems exist, and how they can help you successfully run application programs.

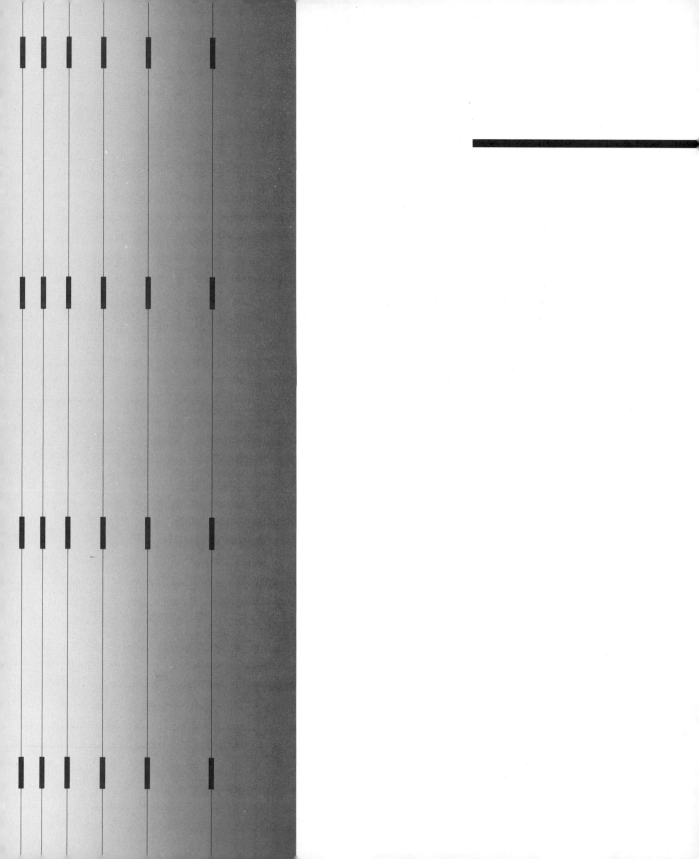

CHAPTER 1

DOS AND THE COMPUTER SYSTEM: AN OVERVIEW

DOS AND THE COMPUTER SYSTEM: AN OVERVIEW

Every computer that uses disks (hard or floppy) must have a master program that coordinates the flow of information from computer to disk and from disk to computer. This program is called the *disk operating system,* or DOS. In this book, you'll learn about the operating system used by the IBM PC and compatible microcomputers. This operating system is manufactured by Microsoft Corporation and licensed to IBM and other microcomputer manufacturers. The name of this system, when purchased from Microsoft, is *MS-DOS*— that is, *M*icrosoft *D*isk *O*perating *S*ystem. When it is purchased from IBM, it is called *PC-DOS.*

What does all this mean? Simply that the terms *DOS, MS-DOS,* and *PC-DOS* all refer to the same type of program and in fact are often used interchangeably. In this book, the term *DOS* refers to the disk operating system used by IBM microcomputers and the wide range of IBM-compatible microcomputers.

This chapter teaches you how DOS is used and the functions it can perform. You will also learn about the fundamental parts of the computer sitting on your desk and about a number of computer devices (peripherals) that you might not own yet but might be interested in acquiring. You'll learn the differences between input and output devices, as well as the purpose of these devices.

Most important, you'll acquire an understanding of what disks and diskettes are, how they're set up, and how DOS provides you with commands to manage them. You'll see how data is organized on disks, so you can make better decisions later about which disks are appropriate for you. You'll learn a host of good techniques for caring for your disks, so you can significantly reduce the odds of losing critical data through disk failure.

This chapter is addressed primarily to new users of DOS and personal computers. If you are already familiar with the material presented here, consult the table of contents to find the features of DOS that you want to know more about.

Variations among Versions of DOS

Because the manufacturer of each new computer may make minor adjustments to DOS before releasing the program for that machine, you may occasionally notice slight differences between your DOS messages and those in this book, which are based on DOS version 3.3. However, since DOS is virtually the same from machine to machine, you will probably never see any variation other than in the startup message. If you are interested in more information about distinctions between MS-DOS and PC-DOS, see Appendix D.

What DOS Does

The disk operating system performs the task of integrating the various devices that make up a computer system. The operating system must carry out three major tasks. It must

- Coordinate input and output devices, such as monitors, printers, disk drives, and modems
- Enable the user to load and execute programs
- Maintain an orderly system of files on the disk

Computer memory has one basic drawback. The area of memory in which your programs and data are stored, called *random-access memory* (*RAM*), cannot store information after the power has been turned off, even for a fraction of a second. To store information in the computer, you must have some means of recording it. The most common devices for this task are *disk drives,* which are devices that can read and write data on magnetic disks.

Magnetic disks fall generally into two categories: *hard disks* and *floppy disks,* or *diskettes.* On a hard disk the magnetic storage medium is rigid, or hard. Hard disks are called *fixed* or *nonremovable* disks if they are built into the drive itself; they are called *removable cartridges* if they can be inserted into and removed from the disk drive. Information is stored on disks as a collection of characters. Hard disks usually hold at least 10 million characters; larger models that hold 70 million characters are now available on the newest IBM Personal System/2 line of microcomputers. Each 10 megabytes is roughly equivalent to 5000 pages of typed text.

Diskettes usually store less information. The most flexible and common type, the 5¼-inch diskette, can store several hundred thousand characters of information, depending on the density of the magnetic material on the disk surface. A high-capacity 5¼-inch diskette can actually store 1.2 million characters. A less common but increasingly popular type, the 3½-inch diskette, is often called a *microfloppy* diskette. It owes its growing popularity to its higher storage densities;

it can hold up to 1.44 million characters, the largest storage capacity of any diskette. In addition, the microfloppy's small size makes it easier to store and transport than larger media.

Even though different types of disks store different amounts of information, all disks share information in the same way: as a collection of characters. You may have heard the term *byte;* it is generally interchangeable with the term *character*. Any keyboard character can be stored and represented by DOS as a series of 8 bits (of binary 0s and 1s), which together make a byte. (To transmit a character to another computer, however, DOS must add a few bits to the byte.) The 8 bits can be arranged in 256 different ways, thereby representing 256 different characters. Some of these characters are the ones you can type (A–Z, 0–9, and so on), and others are simply interpreted by DOS as *control* characters. This classification includes all special character codes that control special operations, such as sounding a computer's bell or performing a carriage return on a printer. See Appendix D for more information about character sets and numbering methods. See Chapter 12 for more information about the layout and uses of bits and bytes during data transmission.

Each complete collection of related characters is called a *file*. A disk can have many files that contain either instructions for the computer (*program files*) or data stored by the user (*data files*). A disk can contain both program files and data files. Each file must have a unique name so that the computer can later refer to the file and load it from the disk into the computer memory again.

DOS is responsible for managing this flow of information. As you will learn, DOS contains a host of commands and programs that enable it to store information on any disks connected to your computer. It also has full responsibility for arranging your files on these disks in ways that contribute to easy and efficient retrieval.

Fundamental Hardware

DOS is designed to manage the details of a variety of hardware connections and combinations. You should understand something about computer hardware before you use DOS.

A microcomputer system is composed of a *central system unit* and a variety of *peripheral devices*. The central system unit usually contains the primary processing chip (the *CPU,* or *central processing unit*), the main system memory (RAM), and usually one or more disk drives. In some IBM compatibles, particularly portable systems, the main unit may also contain the monitor and keyboard. These compatibles have everything housed together, but each device is treated by DOS as an independent unit. The following paragraphs describe the CPU and the memory, and the rest of the chapter discusses disk drives and other peripherals.

The Central Processing Unit: The Brains of the Beast

A computer is made of several thousand different circuits, all miniaturized to fit on a very small silicon chip. The main circuits coordinate the system, the routing of data, and the performance of all calculations; the circuitry for all of this processing is contained on one main chip, the CPU. The processor in the IBM PC-XT is called the 8088 or 8086, and the chip used in the IBM PC-AT is called the 80286; the newest microcomputers use the powerful and increasingly popular 80386 chip from Intel Corporation.

CLOCK SPEED

Every CPU has some speed at which it works. This speed is determined as much by how the chip was designed as by what kind of other circuits with which it needs to work in the rest of the computer system. A computer's speed is measured in cycles per second and is known as *clock speed.*

Every computer contains a special clock to govern the speed of operations and to help synchronize the processing of data and instructions in the computer system. How fast this clock actually "ticks" governs how rapidly your computer can process instructions and thereby complete program tasks. This is true both for application programs and for operating system (DOS) tasks.

The IBM PC runs at 4.77 MHz; one model of the Compaq 386 runs at 20 MHz. The abbreviation *MHz* stands for megahertz, or millions of cycles per second. Therefore, the IBM PC performs 4.77 million operations per second. This may seem fast, and indeed it is, but each of these operations is only a fundamental step in larger, more familiar operations. The fundamental sequence of steps in one electronic cycle consists of locating an instruction to process, fetching that instruction from memory, and actually activating that small yet essential computer operation. For example, adding two numbers requires several of these tiny steps, finding a square root requires hundreds of these steps, and locating a particular record in a data base may require thousands of separate operations. The fundamental sequence of steps that takes place during one electronic "cycle" consists of the locating of an instruction to process, the fetching of that instruction from memory, and the actual activation of that small yet essential computer operation.

Memory

A computer's ability to store information is just as important as its ability to process information. (If a computer couldn't store information, it couldn't process it, either.) Physically, the parts of the computer that store information are separate from the CPU, though they are also located in the system unit. Within the system unit are *memory chips,* and outside it are one or more external storage devices: *disks* and *disk drives.* Controlling the exchange of information between internal and external memory is one of the primary functions of a disk operating system.

You've seen that information is represented within a computer as binary digits (bits), each with a value of 1 or 0. These values take the physical form of electrical charges; +5 volts represents 1, and 0 volts represents 0. A memory chip consists of thousands of cells for holding these charges. A computer has two kinds of memory chips: RAM (random-access memory) chips and ROM (read-only memory) chips. It is important that you understand how the functions of RAM and ROM differ.

RANDOM-ACCESS MEMORY

Most of a computer's memory is RAM. RAM holds the information that the computer uses in performing particular tasks. While you are working with a computer, various parts of the operating system, the application program you are using, and the information you provide that program are all held in RAM. When your computer reads information from a disk, it is storing that information in RAM (and it is using DOS to do so). A disadvantage of RAM is that it is temporary. When you turn off the computer, all information in RAM is lost (unless you have saved it in an external, permanent storage medium, again using DOS).

READ-ONLY MEMORY

A much smaller part of your computer's memory is ROM. ROM storage is permanent. ROM therefore holds the kinds of information the computer needs no matter what task it performs. The instructions that tell a processor chip how to perform its fundamental operations are stored in ROM, as are the unchanging parts of the operating system. Although you cannot lose any information from ROM, you also cannot alter it in any way. This may seem like an inconvenience, but actually it is a vital safeguard to keep your computer operating properly.

UNITS OF MEASURE

Memory is measured in bytes. One byte is roughly equivalent to one character. A total of 1,024 bytes equals 1K (K stands for kilobyte, or 1 thousand bytes); 1K also equals 2^{10} bytes. A total of $1,024^2$ bytes, or 1,024K, equals 1,048,076 bytes, known as a megabyte (1M). This is precisely equal to 2^{20} bytes. Last, 1024M equals 2^{30}, or 1G (G stands for gigabyte, or 1 billion bytes).

Configuration of a Computer System

The *configuration* of a computer system is the arrangement of system components. Figure 1.1 shows a minimal configuration. As you can see, it consists of only the system unit (including disk drives), a video screen, and a keyboard.

DISK DRIVES

The disk drives in a basic configuration are usually diskette drives, although they may include a hard disk drive, especially as hardware prices continue to

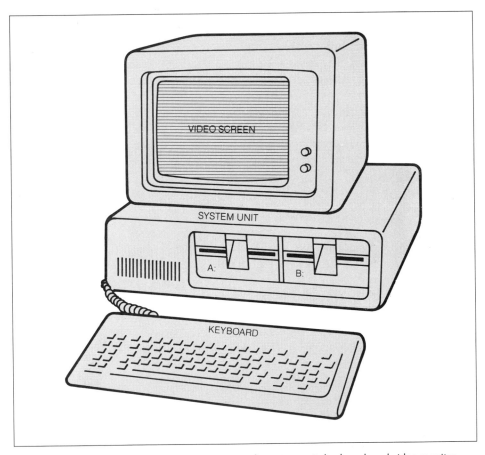

FIGURE 1.1: Basic microcomputer system consisting of a system unit, keyboard, and video monitor. Although all of these separate pieces may be housed in a single box, as in some portable computers, a typical system separates the keyboard and the monitor. The remaining rectangular unit contains the central processing unit (CPU) and one or two disk drives (usually drives for floppy disks in a basic configuration).

drop. As Figure 1.1 shows, systems that use diskettes refer to the drives as A: and B:. Systems that use one diskette drive and one hard disk drive refer to these drives as A: and C:, respectively. This book will refer to drives simply as A, B, and C. You will learn more about disks and disk drives throughout this book, but you may want to know a little about how they store information.

Both hard and floppy disks are rotating disks, coated with magnetized iron oxide. The particles on the disk are arranged so that they represent data, and when the data needs to be read, the part of DOS known as the disk device driver reinterprets the particle orientations into your data. This process is very fast and accurate, but it is understandably sensitive to magnetic interference and wear and tear; floppy disks don't last forever.

Hard disks are rigid disks permanently mounted and sealed in their own casing to prevent contamination. They record information very precisely and in a very high density, and if even the smallest particle of dust were to settle on a hard disk platter, data would be lost and the drive probably damaged. These disks can, at minimum, hold as much information as 35 floppy disks, and the highest-capacity hard disks can hold the equivalent of several hundred floppy disks.

The Keyboard

The keyboard of a personal computer is very similar to that of a typewriter, but it has a few extra keys. The 10 special keys located at the left or at the top, labeled F1, F2, ... F10, are called *function keys*. These keys are usually redefined for each specific application program, and you can define them too. Function keys are very handy for saving keystrokes. For example, you can program the F7 key to type "PC-DOS" so that every time you want to type PC-DOS, you can just press F7 (one keystroke) and "PC-DOS" (six keystrokes) will be printed. DOS has defined uses for six of these function keys: F1–F6; Chapter 2 discusses these keys.

In most programs, the Esc (escape) key lets you escape, or exit, from an operation (usually to the previous menu) or cancel a command. Depending on which version of DOS you are using, pressing Esc will either blank out the line on which you are typing or display a backslash and move the cursor down to the next line. In either case, it cancels what you were just typing and causes DOS to ignore that line.

The Ctrl (control) key is like a second shift key and is used in much the same way, except that its role is to control computer actions. For instance, pressing Ctrl-C usually causes the computer to completely stop what it's doing, and pressing Ctrl-S causes the computer to temporarily pause; other control-key combinations exist and will be presented in this book as appropriate.

The Alt (alternate) key is another shift key. It displays various graphics characters when used with the numeric keypad on the right side of your keyboard.

The NumLock (number lock) key makes the computer accept the numeric keypad keys as numbers. When NumLock is off (it is not lighted), pressing these keys will not print numbers, but rather will activate the cursor-control functions shown on the bottom of the face of each key. Some keyboards do not show a light, so you cannot easily determine which setting is in effect for the NumLock key.

Pressing the ScrollLock (scroll lock) key, in some programs, temporarily inhibits video scrolling. Pressing it again makes the computer resume scrolling. Pressing ScrollLock is equivalent to pressing Ctrl-S.

Pressing the Shift-PrtSc (shift print screen) key causes whatever is printed on the screen to be sent to the printer. This key is useful for taking a "snapshot" of the screen for immediate use or reference. If you invoke the GRAPHICS command, you can also send graphic images to the printer using Shift-PrtSc.

Most programs use the Ins (insert) key to toggle between the *insert* and *overwrite* modes. When your keyboard is in insert mode, any characters you type are inserted into the line of text at the position of the cursor. The right side of the line moves to the right one character for every character that you type. When your keyboard is in overwrite mode, any character you type replaces any existing character located under the cursor position.

The Del (delete) key moves the cursor back one character and deletes the character over which the cursor moved.

The keyboard usually has one of four layouts, depending upon whether it is designed to be compatible with an IBM PC-XT, the IBM PC-AT, the IBM Personal System/2, or the IBM Convertible. Chapter 2 shows these various keyboard layouts.

The Monitor

The monitor is simply the display screen, which shows you information. There are several possible video monitor formats; monochrome, color graphics, and enhanced graphics monitors are the most common. Higher-resolution monitors, although more expensive, are becoming more common in businesses using desktop publishing and computer-aided design (CAD) software.

Expanding the Range of Your System

There is virtually no limit to the range of additional devices that can be connected to a microcomputer. Most business microcomputer systems contain more than the minimal configuration, as Figure 1.2 shows. The various *connector ports* in the back of the computer, such as the *parallel* and *serial* ports, allow the straightforward (although not necessarily easy) connection of printers, plotters, digitizers, extra disk drives, and so on. The task of starting DOS so that it manages this

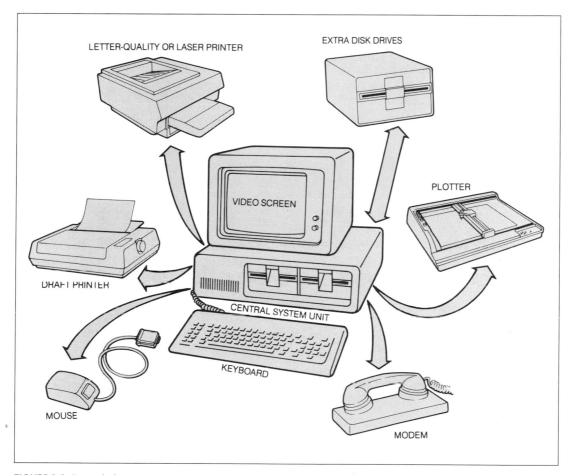

FIGURE 1.2: Expanded microcomputer system. Most business systems include more than just the basic hardware.

hardware is consistent, no matter what hardware configuration you have.

The most important device you can add to a system is a printer.

PRINTERS

Often you will want a printed copy of the work you entered on the computer, whether it is a letter you have typed with a word processor or a report produced by using a spreadsheet program. You will need a printer for this. The most common type of device is a line printer, which in most office or home personal computer systems prints up to 200 cps (characters per second). Line printers are usually *dot matrix* printers, in which any printed character is formed by printing a matrix of small dots in a well-defined pattern. Laser printers, as their cost decreases, are becoming increasingly common and popular because of their high output speed (6 to 12 complete pages per minute), variety of output layout options, and high print quality.

Expanding the Power of Your System

All the chips that control the computer, as well as some of the computer memory chips, are located on the *system board.* This main board, or *mother board,* is the circuit board that links all of these chips together.

If you want to add more power to your system, you can buy an *expansion board.* Expansion boards are actually small circuit boards that perform certain functions, such as adding more memory or providing a means to communicate with other devices. They fit into *slots* that hold the boards in place and electronically link each board to the circuitry on the motherboard. Different computers have different numbers of slots, thus allowing a different number of expansion boards to be installed in the system. Note that the more expansion slots you fill, the greater the drain on system power. You must be sure that your system's power supply can support all the expansion power that you purchase and install.

Input and Output Devices

Some of the devices connected to a personal computer handle information that is entered, or input, into the computer system, and others manage information output from the computer system. Some devices do both. Disk drives, for example, can be both input and output devices. Table 1.1 lists some input and output devices. Most DOS commands control the complex process of input from and output to the disk drives.

DEVICE	FUNCTION
Keyboard	Input only
Screen	Output only
Printer	Output only
Disks	Input and output

Table 1.1: Typical Input and Output Devices

SOFTWARE

Software comprises all the instructions that actually run your computer. Software is generally classified as either *systems* software or *application* software. Systems software is mostly concerned with a computer's internal "housekeeping," whereas application software is designed to perform real-world tasks. DOS is an example of systems software. It is simply a collection of programs that perform separate but related and well-defined tasks, all of which are necessary for the computer to carry out the instructions you give it. Using a computer would be impossibly tedious and complicated if you had to instruct the machine at this level of detail.

Programs

A program is a set of instructions the computer follows to perform a task. Programs can be written in any one of several *languages,* such as FORTRAN, COBOL, C, BASIC, a particular CPU chip's assembly language, or even the batch-file processing language available as part of DOS itself. Depending on the scope of the task it is intended to perform, a program can be as short as a few instructions or as long as several thousand instructions.

Commands

Commands are the building blocks of programs, the individual instructions you give the computer. Each one tells the computer to perform some action. Depending on the software you are using, commands may be either issued directly or combined into programs. DOS commands are generally issued directly, one at a time. This way of using the computer is sometimes called *immediate* or *interactive* mode, since when you give an instruction, the computer carries it out immediately, often requesting more instructions from you in the process. Because many of the tasks for which you use computers cannot be accomplished with single instructions, commands can be combined into programs. This mode is sometimes called *deferred* mode, as no commands are executed until the entire program is run.

Although the vast subject of programming is beyond the scope of this book, there is one small area of it that DOS users should know about: batch-file programming. DOS has a small subset of commands that can be combined into simple programs, called batch files, to help you work more efficiently. You'll learn about using batch files in Chapters 6 to 9.

Applications

Applications are the real-world purposes for which you use your computer. For example, setting up and maintaining a general ledger system are tasks a computer can handle; hence, these are applications of your computer system's power. By extension, the program that carries out an application is known as an *application program,* or simply an *application.* The most common general categories of application programs used today are *word processors, spreadsheets, database managers,* and *integrated packages,* which combine two or more functions. There are also more specialized professional applications; a general ledger program is an example of an accounting application.

CANNED VERSUS CUSTOM SOFTWARE

"Canned" software is the kind of program you buy from computer stores (or vendors). Its functions are strictly defined, and you cannot change any part of the actual program. DOS is a canned program, as are commercial applications such as WordPerfect and dBASE III PLUS.

Custom software is software written for you specifically or for a specific, customized application. You can modify custom software or have it changed to meet your specific needs. Custom software usually costs much more than canned software. You must pay a programmer to write it, usually just for you, whereas with canned software, development costs are spread among the many purchasers of the application.

Languages

Computer languages, like spoken languages, consist of a set of commands that can be grouped together in particular ways to complete tasks or applications. Certain languages are easier to use for certain applications. For example, BASIC is a good starting language, since it is easy to understand, yet it has a very limited set of commands. Standard Pascal, used mostly in academic circles, is very well structured, but its input/output structures, so necessary for flexible commercial applications, are limited. (Newer versions of the language, such as Turbo Pascal, have to some extent overcome this limitation, however.) FORTRAN is used mostly for engineering and scientific applications, and COBOL is used primarily for business jobs. C, one of the most recent and popular languages, is a cross between assembly language and Pascal. C is used by the majority of developers of complex applications, such as new operating systems and languages themselves. Each of these languages is a complete program in its own right.

How Disks are Set Up

When you buy a box of diskettes, the diskettes in that box are not yet ready to be used with your computer. To use them, you must prepare, or initialize, them with some of the special programs provided by DOS. Even hard disks must be prepared. Most users don't format and set up their own hard disk drives because computer dealers usually do this for them. This is not altogether an advantage, because users then never learn the basics of disk setup.

Preparing a disk for use by DOS requires essentially the same procedure whether you are formatting a floppy disk or a hard disk. Many computer users buy additional hard disks by mail and are therefore responsible for their own preparation and formatting. The basic steps you take in preparing floppy disks are presented in Chapter 2. The procedure for preparing a hard disk requires an extra step, *partitioning* the disk. This procedure is presented in Chapter 19.

Chapter 2 explains how to use disk-preparation programs. The techniques presented in Chapter 2 are some of the first steps you take with a new computer system. Before you take those steps, however, you should read this section, which explains what is really happening when you issue disk commands.

Disk Commands

The concept of DOS is confusing for two reasons:

1. A large part of DOS is invisible to the user. DOS has two parts: hidden files and a COMMAND.COM file. The *hidden files* are stored on the disk but do not appear on the disk directory. The COMMAND.COM file is visible on every diskette used to start (or *boot*) a computer system. In DOS 3.3, COMMAND.COM occupies 25,307 bytes, whereas the two hidden system files together occupy another 52,259 bytes. This 50K of disk space will be exacted from every system (boot) disk you create.

2. DOS performs two types of commands: internal commands and external commands. *Internal commands* are actions that DOS can always perform, no matter what disk happens to be in the computer. These commands are always resident in memory, and so they execute immediately whenever you call them. *External commands* are really small programs for special purposes. If you want to perform any of these actions, you must have the correct disk in the computer, or (as you'll see in Chapter 3) you must tell DOS where these programs are located on your disks. Since transient commands are brought into memory from a disk only when you request them, it is your responsibility to ensure that they are available when you need them.

Note that on floppy diskette systems, DOS command files must be accessible through one of the drives. Otherwise, DOS will display an error message indicating that it can't find the requested command.

Table 1.2 lists the internal and external DOS commands. You will learn more about these commands throughout this book. For now, you need be concerned only with the fundamental disk structure that stores these commands and makes them available whenever you need them.

INTERNAL COMMANDS		
BREAK	DEL	RMDIR
CHCP	DIR	SET
CHDIR	ERASE	TIME
CLS	MKDIR	TYPE
COPY	PATH	VER
CTTY	PROMPT	VERIFY
DATE	RENAME	VOL

EXTERNAL COMMANDS		
APPEND	FIND	RECOVER
ASSIGN	FORMAT	REPLACE
ATTRIB	GRAFTABL	RESTORE
BACKUP	GRAPHICS	SELECT
CHKDSK	JOIN	SHARE
COMP	KEYB	SORT
DISKCOMP	LABEL	SUBST
DISKCOPY	MODE	SYS
EXE2BIN	MORE	TREE
FASTOPEN	NLSFUNC	XCOPY
FDISK	PRINT	

Table 1.2: Internal and External DOS Commands

Disk Organization

When a floppy diskette is taken out of its box, it is totally blank. So, too, is a hard disk. The primary difference between diskettes and hard disks is in the arrangement of the magnetic material. This material can be arranged on one or both sides of a diskette, depending on whether the diskette is single sided or double sided. Diskettes can also have different densities. The more densely the magnetic material is written onto a diskette, the more information the diskette can hold. Hard disks, on the other hand, can have several layers of magnetic material, each with two sides, which means they can store even more information.

For a computer system to use any disk as a medium for storing information, the entire disk must be divided into sections organized so that every physical location on the disk has a unique address. This is the same concept as assigning

ZIP codes to towns and cities. Assigning addresses gives DOS an orderly way in which to store and then find various pieces of information.

DOS stores information magnetically in concentric rings (see Figure 1.3). Each ring is called a *track*. A double-sided, double-density diskette, for example, contains 40 tracks (numbered 0 to 39), and a high-capacity diskette contains twice as many tracks (numbered 0 to 79). Each track is divided into smaller parts called *sectors*. Tracks and sectors are created when a disk is formatted. It is DOS's job to assign addresses to each track and sector. You needn't be concerned about this addressing mechanism, because DOS manages it without your intervention

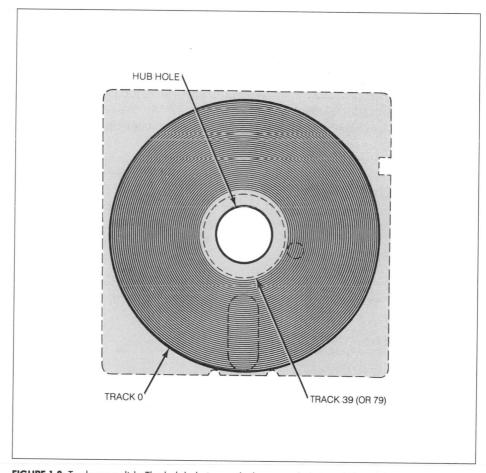

FIGURE 1.3: Tracks on a disk. The hub hole is merely the center hole in a disk or diskette, which fits onto the spindle of the disk drive. Like the hole in a record and the spindle on a turntable, this hole and spindle ensure that the disk spins in a true circular path. Data can then be read from and written to consistent places on the disk tracks.

and it is really only for DOS's benefit. DOS needs to know the actual disk location of your files; you need to know only their names. Such housekeeping capabilities as this are what make DOS such a valuable ally in running application software.

The exact number of sectors on a disk depends on the type of diskette being formatted. Standard double-sided, double-density diskettes have 9 sectors per track, whereas the high-capacity diskettes available for the IBM PC-AT and compatibles have 15 sectors per track. Each sector can hold 512 bytes. The newest $3\frac{1}{2}$-inch diskettes, containing 1.44Mb, have 80 tracks per side, each track holding 18 standard 512-byte sectors.

Table 1.3 outlines the amount of storage capacity provided when double-density and high-density diskettes are formatted. However, some of the formatted disk space is not available to you for storing data. When a disk is formatted, some of the sectors are set aside for keeping track of the information stored on that disk. Every formatted disk has these areas. Together they serve as a catalog of the contents of that disk. These areas are called the *file allocation table (FAT)*, the *boot record*, and the *directory table*.

You can learn much more about the mechanisms for disk management used by DOS by referring to Chapter 21. In this chapter, however, you should understand that the structural elements of each disk have variable impact on disk-space use. Table 1.3 presents the key space considerations for the most common types of diskettes used in DOS systems.

Note that standard double-density diskettes can store a maximum of 112 uniquely named files, whereas high-capacity diskettes can store 224 files. Hard disks can store significantly more individual files, depending on their size (10Mb, 20Mb, and so on).

DISK STRUCTURE	$3\frac{1}{2}$" DOUBLE DENSITY	$3\frac{1}{2}$" HIGH CAPACITY	$5\frac{1}{4}$" DOUBLE DENSITY	$5\frac{1}{4}$" HIGH CAPACITY
Number of tracks	80	80	40	80
Sectors per track	9	18	9	15
Characters per sector	512	512	512	512
Total number of sectors	1440	2880	720	2400
Total number of characters	720K	1.44M	360K	1.2M

Table 1.3: Diskette Organization

TAKING CARE OF YOUR DISKETTES

If you have never handled diskettes before, they may look and feel flimsy. They are not as flimsy as they appear, but they are also not as durable as many users believe. In many offices, computer users use diskettes like paperweights and store diskettes without the jackets they came in. These people are usually the ones who complain most vocally about their diskettes failing several times a year.

Mishandling diskettes can have serious consequences. An accident can destroy the contents of a diskette in seconds. A well-maintained diskette, however, can last for years, depending on how often it is used.

Here are some suggestions for handling diskettes. Keep in mind that experience lies behind every one of them.

- Store your diskettes in their jackets. You never know when they may fall on the floor or when something might fall or spill on them.

- Don't leave your diskettes in the disk drives, especially if the computer is going to be moved. Remember, others who clean around your computer may move it to clean the table top.

- Don't leave your diskettes in your car, where the temperature often gets high enough to warp them, making them unreadable for your computer. Also keep them away from any potential magnetic fields, such as motors, telephone bells, and magnetic card keys.

- Don't touch the magnetic surface of the disks—hold them by their covers. Fingerprints can damage data.

- Make backup copies of all original diskettes and keep current copies of all diskettes with important programs or data files.

- Keep your backup diskette copies in a different location from the original diskettes (for example, keep original diskettes at home if your computer is at the office, or at work if your computer is at home).

- Label all your diskettes, both electronically with a DOS command and with a printed, gummed label. Write on the label before you attach it to the diskette cover or use a soft, felt-tipped pen to write carefully on an existing label.

- Don't squeeze the last bit of space out of your diskettes. Always leave them slightly empty. This will allow you to later add new files to the diskette or to expand the size of some of the files on the diskette.

SUMMARY

This chapter has provided an overview of DOS and its role in your computer system. Since that role is to manage all the hardware and software components of a computer system, this chapter has briefly surveyed those components. Finally, since DOS is a *disk* operating system—disks are almost the only medium now used for storing and managing information on a computer—the chapter concluded with a discussion of how disks are set up and how you should take care of them.

For additional information about how disks are organized, see

- Chapter 4, "Understanding Directories and Subdirectories"

For additional information about installing application programs on your hard disk, see

- Chapter 5, "Working with Hard Disk Directories"

For additional information about printing with DOS, see

- Chapter 15, "Basic Printing Methods"
- Chapter 16, "Advanced Printing Techniques"

For additional information about expanding the power of your system with add-on software, see

- Chapter 20, "Extending DOS's Power with Utility Software"

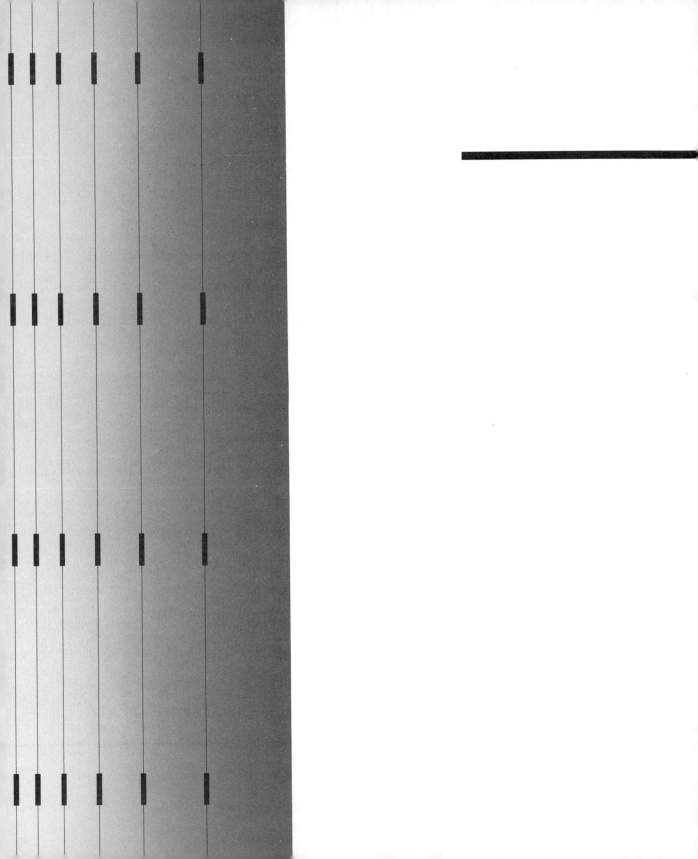

STARTING TO USE DOS

STARTING TO USE DOS

This chapter presents the basic operations anyone must master to begin using DOS and running application programs. It is addressed primarily to new computer users. More experienced users may want to skim the tutorial sections in the first part of the chapter for review and consult the reference sections at the end of the chapter when they need specific information about any of the DOS commands involved. Infrequent users of DOS will find a review of this chapter helpful when they have been away from the computer.

In the tutorial part of this chapter you will learn how to start your DOS system and, consequently, how to start any application program you will be running. You'll learn how to set the time and date correctly if your system doesn't have a built-in clock/calendar and how to change the time. You'll also learn how to enter DOS commands and how to quickly and efficiently correct errors or make changes in commands. You'll learn to prepare disks for storing your data and file information, as well as for booting up your system. Backing up your disks and exploring the status of a disk are necessary skills you'll also acquire here. In short, this part of the chapter will start "showing you the ropes" for operating DOS.

The second part of this chapter consists of reference entries for the DOS commands introduced in the first, tutorial part: DATE, TIME, CLS, FORMAT, DISKCOPY, CHKDSK, SYS, and VER. Following the format presented in the introduction to this book, these reference entries present the complete syntax of the command, including a description of each parameter or switch; the command type, whether internal (resident) or external (nonresident); a discussion of the most appropriate uses of the command, including any restrictions; and at least one example of the command in action. Readers at all levels of experience with DOS may sometimes find occasion to consult these entries.

GETTING STARTED

Your first task after turning on the computer is to load DOS into the computer. Place your DOS system diskette into drive A and close the door. (This drive is on the left side of most computers; however, some computers place it at the top when the drives are located one on top of the other.) If you have already loaded DOS onto a hard disk, all you need to do at this point is turn the power on. If you haven't prepared your hard disk or loaded DOS onto it, refer to your disk and DOS manuals for the proper procedures for your computer. Chapter 19 also offers instructions for this task.

The computer will go through a process called *booting* or *bootstrapping*. This process loads DOS into the memory of the computer and is necessary before the computer can actually be used. Once DOS is in memory, you can begin work.

The derivation of the term *bootstrapping* is an interesting one. In the minds of many, it is a mystery how an operating system like DOS gets started in memory since it is supposedly *disk* based. In fact, this process appears to be as paradoxical as a person being able to lift himself up by his own shoelaces, or bootstraps in earlier times. Actually, the read-only memory built into your computer contains the few instructions necessary to read the first sector on your boot disk into memory from the disk. DOS then finds in that sector the additional instructions necessary for continuing the power-up procedure, such as the instructions to read in more of the disk-based DOS management code, including the hidden operating system files.

Note that although this chapter focuses on the principal steps required to start your DOS system, certain information in the next several sections is not simply procedural. These sections present background information that will help you better use your keyboard, more easily enter and correct commands, and in general understand what DOS is doing when you use it.

Setting the Date and Time at Startup

Regardless of whether you use a hard disk or floppy diskettes, begin the startup process by placing the DOS system diskette in drive A. Then turn on the power to the computer. After the computer tests its internal hardware, it will display the following message:

Current date is Tue 1-01-1980
Enter new date (mm-dd-yy):_

January 1, 1980, is the default startup date each time you boot DOS on your system. Assuming you do not have an automatic clock in your system, you will see this message each time DOS starts. You'll be expected to enter the correct date at this point. However, if your system is one of the many that come already configured with hardware that includes a battery-backed clock, you won't have to enter this date each time. The additional hardware will come with instructions for avoiding the standard DOS request for correcting the date and for handling the subsequent request for the time of day, displayed as follows:

Current time is 0:02:47.82
Enter new time:_

DOS keeps track of time in standard military format, so if you want to enter the time 10:30 A.M., you simply enter 10:30. However, if you want to enter 3:30 P.M., you have to enter 15:30.

After you've entered the correct date and time, you're on your way. DOS will display a version of the following prompt (the actual wording will vary slightly from computer to computer; in some versions of DOS, you will receive these copyright notices *before* the date and time request):

> **DOS version 3.3**
> **Copyright Matsushita Electric Industrial Co., Ltd 1987**
> **Copyright Microsoft Corporation 1981, 1987**
> **A>_**

Since in this example the system diskette was loaded in drive A, the DOS A> prompt now appears. As you will see through much of the rest of the book, when DOS is installed on a hard disk, the typical "DOS is ready" prompt is C>, indicating that DOS is installed and operative on drive C and is awaiting your instructions.

How the DOS System Starts

You may wonder how DOS gets into the computer. A small part of DOS is already in the computer memory. Intelligent bootstrapping logic ensures that the rest of the disk operating system is loaded automatically from the disk when you turn on the computer. That is why *a diskette must always be present in drive A before you turn on the computer.* If you have a hard disk, then that disk is always ready and takes the place of the diskette in drive A. After loading, DOS shares the computer memory with the programs you run and the data those programs use (see Figure 2.1).

To let you know that DOS is active, the computer displays a prompt like this:

> **A>**

This DOS prompt (usually A> or C>) is a simple way of asking for your instructions. Unless you deliberately change this prompt (as you will learn to do in Chapter 4), it always has two characters: a letter and a greater-than sign (>). The letter indicates the currently active drive—unless otherwise specified, all commands affect data on that drive only. If you are using a two-drive system, the letter will be A (for the left drive) or B (for the right drive). Hard-disk users will usually see the letter C, indicating a standard hard disk drive.

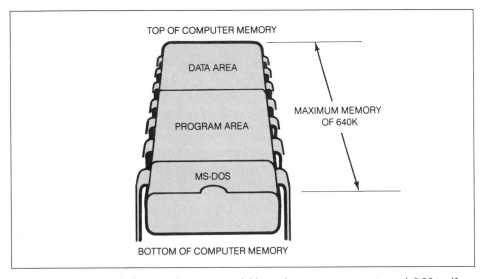

FIGURE 2.1: *Memory map* depicting how your available random-access memory is used. DOS itself occupies a small portion of memory, and your main application program takes up the lion's share of what is left. Each main program usually specifies how much memory is required for it alone, such as 256K or 384K or 512K. What remains after DOS and your main application program code become memory resident either is used for your program's data area or can be used by additional memory-resident software (see Chapter 20).

Whenever the A > (or C > for hard-disk users) prompt appears, DOS is ready to accept a command from you. This prompt also tells you that you are not working in any other program. Later, you will learn how to change the drive letter from A to B or C.

GIVING COMMANDS TO DOS

You can exercise complete control over what DOS does and when DOS does it. In this book, you will learn all of the instructions—commands—that you can give to DOS. Nearly all of the example commands must be entered at the DOS prompt. Unless DOS is prompting you for a command entry, you will be unable to enter any commands.

When the blinking cursor is positioned at the DOS prompt, all you need to do is type a valid DOS command and press the Return key. (The cursor always indicates the position of the next character to be typed.) Some computers label the Return key RETURN, others label it ENTER, and still others label it with the ⏎ symbol; all are equivalent. This book uses the term *Return key* (or *Return*).

You must press the Return key after almost every DOS command. This book will not specify Return after each command; instead, you should press the key automatically at the end of each command you enter. Should you *not* be required to press Return for a command, this book will clearly state so at the appropriate point.

Parameters

Pressing the Return key is necessary because some DOS commands require more entry information than the command word itself. Simple commands such as DIR (to obtain a directory listing) require only that you type the letters *DIR* and then press Return. Since even this simple command may be followed by additional specifications, such as the format of the resultant listing or the letter of the disk drive you want to use, DOS does not process your request until you press the Return key. Only then does it assume that you have completed your request.

The additional qualifications for command requests are called *parameters* or *arguments*. (This book uses the term *parameter*.) In writings about DOS and other command languages, parameters are conventionally represented by placeholders for the data that the user will type when entering the actual command. In DOS, this data most often consists of the names and locations of the files on which the command is to operate. The specific data itself is called the *value* of the parameter. When you actually enter a DOS command that requires parameters, you'll be expected to supply the parameter values. Parameters in this book will be represented in italic type—for example, *FileName*. You'll learn the most important examples of all of these modifiers in the context of the appropriate commands.

SWITCHES

With many DOS commands you can use a special type of parameter known as a *switch*. Whereas most parameters identify the *operands* of a command—the file names, numbers, or strings of text upon which it is to operate—a switch turns on or off some optional aspect of the command's operation. For example, you will soon learn to use the COPY command (if you haven't already). This DOS command requires you to identify both the disk or file you want to copy and the location to which you want that file copied; these parameters are represented by the placeholders *Source* or *SourceFile* and *Dest* or *DestFile*. But you can also include certain switches that tell DOS to do (or not to do) something extra with those files; for example, adding the /V (verify) switch instructs DOS to check that all the specified files were copied successfully.

As this example shows, switches also differ from other parameters in form. Each one is a literal pair of characters with a single meaning, predefined by DOS, that depends on the command (and sometimes the other parameters) with which it is used. Placeholders are never used to represent switches. All switches take the same general form as /V: a slash followed by a single letter. Whenever possible, this letter has been chosen for its *mnemonic* value to help you remember what the switch does.

The difference in function between switches and other parameters will be clearest if you think of a DOS command as an English sentence. The command word is always the verb, and DOS itself is always the implied subject; the form of the sentence is always "DOS, please do such-and-such." Most parameters function as nouns, the objects of the verb; the COPY command would be "DOS, please copy the contents of this source disk to that destination disk." Switches, by contrast, more nearly resemble adverbs or other verbs, modifying the main verb. With /V added, the sentence would read "DOS, please copy this source to that destination, with verification." (Incidentally, you should keep this analogy in mind whenever you issue commands to DOS. By using parameters and switches well in the DOS environment, you can produce results that are as aesthetically pleasing as a well-formed phrase in your native language.)

As you learn new commands in this book, you'll also learn the most important and useful switches available with each command. In some cases, other switches exist, but either their purpose is obscure or they are not frequently needed. The reference entry for each command lists all available parameters and switches for the command.

EDITING CONTROLS

Several keys on the keyboard perform special tasks. The location of these keys differs, depending on whether you are using a keyboard that is compatible with the IBM PC-XT, the PC-AT, the Personal System/2, or the PC Convertible. Figures 2.2, 2.3, 2.4, and 2.5 show the layouts of these keyboards. Several key combinations also are interpreted in special ways by programs like DOS. The following sections show you how to save energy and time by using these keys.

Correcting Mistakes

What happens if you make a mistake when entering a command? DOS supplies a few editing controls that you may find handy. The most common control is the Backspace key, which may appear as a large ⟵ on your keyboard just above the Return key. If you type

DIR B:∗.COM

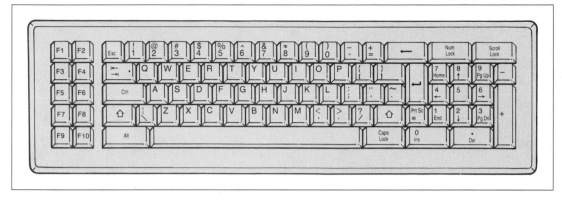

FIGURE 2.2: Keyboard layout for the IBM PC-XT and compatible computers. Notice the position of the 10 function keys at the left of the main keyboard and the backslash key to the left of the *Z* key.

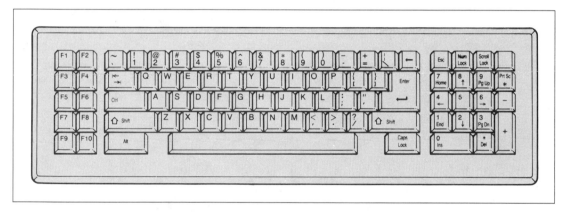

FIGURE 2.3: Keyboard layout for the IBM PC-AT and compatible computers. Notice the position of the 10 function keys at the left of the main keyboard and the backslash key above the Enter key. Also notice the position of the PrtSc key to the right of the numeric keypad.

but do not press Return, your cursor will be on the space just beyond the last character you typed. To erase that character, you press the Backspace key. The *M* disappears, and the cursor moves one space to the left. To erase the next character, the *O,* you again press the Backspace key. Continuing to press this key removes the entire command, keystroke by keystroke.

Canceling a Command

Suppose that you enter a command and decide before you press Return that you want to cancel it. One way to do this is to use the Backspace key to remove all the characters.

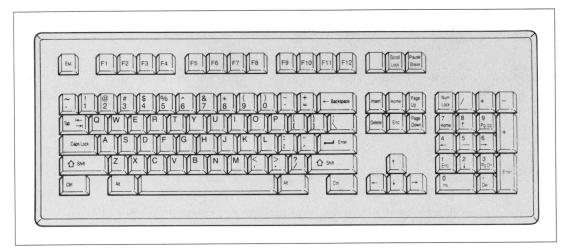

FIGURE 2.4: Keyboard layout for the IBM Personal System/2 and compatible computers. Notice the position of the 12 function keys at the top of the main keyboard and the backslash key above the Enter key. Also notice the separate key clusters for the cursor controls and the numeric keypad.

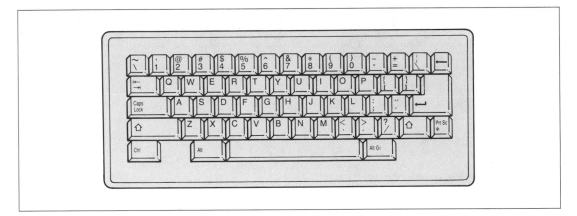

FIGURE 2.5: Keyboard layout for the IBM PC Convertible and compatible computers. Notice that the typical 10 function keys are missing, although they can be obtained via the AltGr key, located to the right of the space bar.

A better way, however, is to use the Esc key (short for Escape key) to cancel the entire line with a single keystroke. If you enter a typical command such as

DIR B:*.EXE

you can cancel the entire command by pressing Esc. A backslash mark (\) will appear on the line you typed, indicating that the entire command will be ignored, and the cursor will move to the next line, as follows:

DIR B:*.EXE

—

Note that the command is not erased from the screen—it is only ignored. The cursor moves to the next line, awaiting entry of your next DOS command.

Repeating a Command

DOS holds the last command you issued in a special place in memory. If you press one of the special function keys located usually on the left side or top of your keyboard, DOS will automatically retype your last command for you.

Suppose you need to locate a file called 88BUDGET.WK1 on one of several diskettes. You could place one of the diskettes in drive A or B and enter the command

DIR 88BUDGET.WK1

If you don't see the file listed, you could remove the diskette, place another diskette in the drive, and press function key number 3, referred to as F3. DOS retypes your original DIR command for you on the line; pressing Return again executes this DOS request for the second diskette.

Whenever you have to perform the same DOS request multiple times (whether for several diskettes, several files, or several directories), you can use the F3 key to retype the command line for you.

Correcting Part of a Command

Suppose you enter the command

DOR B:*.COM

DOS responds with the message "Bad command or file name." This makes sense: The command should have been entered as DIR, not DOR. You might think that the only way to correct this mistake is to retype the entire command. However, DOS provides a better way to edit the most recently entered command: Pressing the F1 key recalls the previous command one letter at a time. In this example, pressing F1 makes the *D* appear. Now you can type the correct letter, *I*. To recall the rest of the command line, which was entered correctly, you press F3. The entire corrected command is then ready to be executed. Pressing Return executes the line as if you had retyped it all.

The F1 and F3 keys are handy tools. Although other function keys can be used with DOS, you won't use them very often; you can explore these keys on your own. Special keys reserved for specific editing chores on your keyboard include the Ins, Del, Esc, and first six function keys. You can consider using a keyboard enhancement program (see Chapter 20) to assign additional special editing chores to the remaining function keys. Table 2.1 summarizes the editing keys and their functions for DOS.

KEY NAME	FUNCTION
F1	Retypes one character at a time from the last command entry
F2	Retypes all characters from the last command entry up to the one identical to your next keystroke
F3	Retypes all remaining characters from the last command entry
F4	Retypes all characters beginning at the first match with your next keystroke and ending with the last character from the last command entry
F5	Permits direct editing of all the characters from the entire last command
F6	Places a special end-of-file code at the end of the currently open file; sometimes referred to as a CTRL-Z or ⌃Z end-of-file code
Ins	Permits insertion of characters at the cursor
Del	Permits deletion of the character to the left of the cursor
Esc	Abandons the current command without executing it

Table 2.1: DOS Editing Keys

CLEARING THE DISPLAY

You may at times want to clear the current screen display and begin again with a clean screen. DOS provides a command to do this. Entering

CLS

and pressing Return clears the screen and then redisplays the current DOS prompt at the top of the screen with the cursor beside it awaiting your next command. Note that clearing the screen has no effect on either disk files or programs in memory. It simply clears the display of text or output left over from previous commands.

CHANGING THE SYSTEM DATE AND TIME

If your system does not have a built-in, battery-backed clock, you will automatically be prompted by DOS to enter the correct date and time each time you power up. However, even if your system does have the hardware for keeping track of the date and time, there may be times when you need to correct one or the other. For instance, twice a year in most of the United States, Daylight Savings Time requires you to adjust all clocks by one hour. Whenever you want to see the current system time or change it, you enter the TIME command at the DOS prompt:

> **C>TIME**
> **Current time is 11:09:14.05**
> **Enter new time:_**

At this point, you could press Return, which would make no changes to the current time, or you could enter a corrected time in the standard format hours:minutes:seconds.

> *Note:* Unless you are running DOS 3.3, the system retains the changed date or time of day only until DOS is rebooted or the system shuts down. DOS 3.3 improved the TIME and DATE commands so that they change the time and date on almost any built-in system clock until these commands are used to change the time and date again. Earlier versions of DOS require the Diagnostics program from the Utilities disk to change the time or date on a built-in clock. Systems containing add-on clock/calendar cards or boards also require you to run special utility programs supplied with the card or board.

Occasionally, you may want to run data that is date-stamped for some day other than the actual day it is run. For example, consider the case of the paymaster of a large computer company who wanted to run an end-of-quarter report two days early. The quarter ended on Sunday, and he wanted to go skiing that weekend. He changed the system date with the DATE command like this:

> **C>DATE**
> **Current date is Wed 4-08-1987**
> **Enter new date (mm-dd-yy):**

Then, after running the report dated for that coming Sunday, he changed the date back for the remainder of his Friday work. (His assumption was that no other transactions would be received and processed in the remaining days of the quarter.) Although his approach is not necessarily advisable, the DATE command does give you this capability.

In addition, the testing of newly developed financial programs, for example, often requires data to be 30, 60, or more than 90 days old. In lieu of creating different data, you can use the same test data and change the system date. This allows you to make your data *appear* to be 30, 60, and more than 90 days old so you can test the program.

PREPARING YOUR DISKS FOR USE

As you learned in Chapter 1, all disks—hard disks, regular and high-density diskettes, and microfloppy diskettes—must be prepared correctly before you can use them.

All disks, once formatted, can store any information you like. If you also want a disk to be able to start your system (in other words, to boot it), then you must include on that disk special DOS files, and you must prepare the disk in a special way. Once you've completed these steps, the disk is called a *system disk*. However, there is now less room remaining on the disk to store data for or from your application programs. If you don't need to boot your system from a particular disk, make that disk a *data disk*. All possible disk space is then available for your program and data storage, and none is consumed by DOS.

There are three main types of disk preparation processes:

- *Formatting a diskette.* You use this process to create a diskette that will operate in the computer but contains no information initially. Such diskettes are used to receive and store data.

- *Creating a blank system diskette.* You must often use this process when you receive a new software package. Most programs are not ready to run when purchased; you usually must create a blank system disk to get a working copy of the program.

- *Backing up an existing diskette.* You use this process to make an exact copy of another diskette. You use the DISKCOPY command to copy a diskette. This procedure is the fastest way in DOS to copy a complete diskette.

The next sections teach you how to perform these three processes. The FORMAT command is the primary means of preparing disks. As you'll see, you simply use different switches to tell DOS whether you want to create a blank data diskette or a system diskette. A number of other switches allow you to specify different diskette densities and layouts, as you will see in the reference entry for the FORMAT command. These are less frequently needed, so they won't be discussed here.

Formatting a Disk

Use a *scratch diskette*—that is, a diskette that is fresh out of the box from your local computer store, or any old diskette that contains information you no longer need—to try the following preparation commands. If you do not have a scratch diskette, you should get one before you continue.

Your computer screen should display the A> prompt (or the C> prompt if you are using a hard disk); as you learned before, this prompt is the computer's way of telling you that it is ready to accept a valid DOS command. Place the scratch diskette into drive B (or drive A, often the only diskette drive on a hard disk system). Now you are ready to format the diskette. For a dual-diskette system, enter the command

FORMAT B:

For a hard disk system, enter the command

FORMAT A:

The computer will then ask you to place a diskette in the drive you've specified. If you have not done so already, you can insert a diskette at this point. When you are ready to begin the formatting process, press Return. DOS will take over and completely erase any data from your diskette. DOS electronically lays down a pattern of marks, creating the tracks and sectors you learned about in Chapter 1.

> *Note:* When you format a disk, any information that might have been stored on that disk is destroyed. Before you format a disk, make sure that the disk does not contain any valuable information.

Diskettes can be formatted as many times as you like. You can even format some diskettes that were used previously by another computer. Of course, any information stored by the other computer on that diskette will be erased.

The number of seconds required to format a diskette varies, depending on the size of the diskette (double-density, high-capacity, or otherwise). When the process is complete, the diskette is ready to accept information. The computer will display the amount of space available for files on the diskette you have just formatted. This number will be 362,496 bytes on a double-sided, double-density diskette and 1,213,952 bytes on a high-capacity diskette.

The computer will then ask you if you want to format another diskette. If you enter Y, the process will begin again, and you will be asked to insert another diskette into your selected drive. If you are done, you enter N. The FORMAT command will end, and the system will return you to the DOS prompt. DOS is now ready for your next command.

> *Tip:* If a number of beginning users have access to your computer system, you might consider renaming your FORMAT command so that unauthorized users can't accidentally format any disks. This helps guarantee that your hard disk containing valid data will not accidentally be formatted (and valuable information deleted) by beginners experimenting with DOS commands.

See Chapter 9 for an example batch file that can be used to automate this protection.

Making a System Disk

A *system disk* contains three special files. Their most common names are listed in Table 2.2. If you want to boot the DOS system with a disk, that disk must have these system files stored in reserved sectors at the beginning of the first track. Only if this is true can the DOS bootup program find them, load them, and start DOS properly.

MS-DOS SYSTEMS	PC-DOS SYSTEMS
IO.SYS MSDOS.SYS COMMAND.COM	IBMBIO.COM IBMDOS.COM COMMAND.COM

Table 2.2: DOS System File Names

Only COMMAND.COM is visible to the user; the other two files, IO.SYS and MSDOS.SYS, are hidden. All MS-DOS systems name the two hidden files IO.SYS and MSDOS.SYS; IBM's proprietary version of DOS takes a proprietary approach to even the names of the comparable files. This does not mean that they do not take up space on the disk—they do. It means that their names do not appear on a normal DOS directory listing. These hidden files contain most of the information thought of as DOS. When you turn on the computer, one of its first operations is to seek the information in these files and read it into memory. The A> or C> prompt is an indicator that these files have been read and stored in the internal memory of the computer.

Note: The IO.SYS file contains the software programs that understand how to send data to and receive data from peripheral devices such as printers and disks. The MSDOS.SYS file contains the logic and routines for managing the data organization itself. In essence, the file system is controlled by logic in MSDOS.SYS, and the more nitty-gritty signal and data communications are handled by routines in IO.SYS.

What would happen if you turned on the computer and the diskette in drive A did not contain these system files? The computer would not load DOS and would therefore not be capable of using the disk drives. You would then receive a message requesting that a DOS system diskette be placed in the boot drive. To correct the situation, you would need to restart the system using a diskette with the DOS files on it.

You can see that having DOS on a disk is important. When you used the FORMAT command previously, you created a totally blank disk. This was not a system disk, because it did not have the three DOS files on it. Now you will learn how to format a disk and at the same time copy the system files onto it.

If you enter the command

FORMAT B:/S

the /S (the System switch) tells the computer to add the DOS files to the diskette in drive B when the formatting process ends. To begin this formatting process, you simply press Return after making sure the right diskette is in drive B.

> *Note:* The /S switch works by invoking a DOS command called SYS. You can also use the SYS command directly, when you need to add the system files to a disk that is not new. For example, you may have a data disk that you want to make into a system disk, or you may want to update a system disk that was formatted with an earlier version of DOS. In either case, you would enter the command
>
> **SYS** *DestD:*
>
> where *DestD* is the device to which the system will be copied.
>
> If you are not sure which version of DOS is installed on a system disk you are working with, you can find out by entering the VER command. Simply typing
>
> **VER**
>
> displays the number of the DOS version you are using.

When the process is complete, the computer tells you how much space is used by the DOS system and how much remains available for your use. The diskette in drive B is now a system disk. It is capable of starting the computer.

Why bother to set up a diskette with only the DOS files? The answer is that you can now transfer files from another disk onto this one. This is usually what you must do when you buy a new software program; most programs do not come on a system diskette. Although you can sometimes copy a DOS system onto your newly purchased application program diskette, it is usually preferable to follow these steps:

1. Format a system disk.
2. Transfer your new program files to that disk.
3. Use the resulting disk both to boot the computer and to run the application program.
4. Put your application software's original diskettes in a safe place.

Here's an example of a situation in which you might need to prepare a system disk. Imagine that you want to place BASICA.COM from your DOS supplementary diskette onto a self-booting disk. Your ultimate goal will be to initiate the BASICA program automatically when the system starts (see Chapter 9). A secondary goal of this and all the examples in this book is to teach good DOS work habits. To that end, you will also label the diskette, a valuable safety precaution that you should eventually take automatically. You can follow the steps presented here substituting an alternate application program, if you wish, for BASICA.COM.

First, select a scratch diskette and format it. Now follow the appropriate steps for your system.

For Dual-Diskette Systems

Format disks in dual-diskette systems as follows:

1. Place a scratch diskette in drive B and enter the command

    FORMAT B:/S /V

When the formatting is completed, you will receive the DOS messages

Format complete
System transferred

You will then be asked to enter a label for the disk you just formatted:

Volume label (11 characters, ENTER for none)? _

At this point, you can enter any meaningful sequence of characters—for example, CUSTOMERS—with which to label the disk to indicate the data to be stored on the disk. It's an excellent idea to include the /V switch each time you format any disk. If you know the intended use of a disk, you can choose a volume label that is meaningful and suggestive. If you are not sure of how a disk is to be used, you can skip this labeling step and use the LABEL command later to add an identifying volume label to the disk. Chapter 4 discusses this alternate labeling procedure using the LABEL command.

The FORMAT command will finish by reporting the disk status: the disk's total space, the amount of space used by the system, any bad sectors discovered, and the amount of space remaining for your files. For example, you might receive the following messages:

362496 bytes total disk space
78848 bytes used by system
283648 bytes available on disk

Format another (Y/N)?_

If you are formatting just one diskette, you can answer N and go on to step 2.

2. Enter the COPY command to copy the BASICA.COM file from drive A to the new system diskette in drive B.

COPY BASICA.COM B:

Your diskette is now prepared to receive any other application programs (through the COPY command) as well as to boot the DOS system at power-up time.

FOR HARD DISK SYSTEMS

To format a disk on a hard disk system, follow these procedures:

1. Place a scratch diskette in drive A and enter the command

FORMAT A:/S /V

When the formatting is completed, you will receive the DOS messages

Format complete
System transferred

You will then be asked to enter a label for the disk you just formatted:

Volume label (11 characters, ENTER for none)? _

At this point, you can enter any meaningful sequence of characters—for example, CUSTOMERS—with which to label the disk to indicate the data to be stored on the disk. It's an excellent idea to include the /V switch each time you format any disk. If you know the intended use of a disk, you can choose a volume label that is meaningful and suggestive. If you are not sure of how a disk is to be used, you can skip this labeling step and use the LABEL command later to add an identifying volume label to the disk. Chapter 4 discusses this alternate labeling procedure using the LABEL command.

The FORMAT command will finish by reporting the disk status: the disk's total space, the amount of space used by the system, any bad sectors discovered, and the amount of disk space remaining for your files. For example, you might receive the following messages:

362496 bytes total disk space
78848 bytes used by system
283648 bytes available on disk

Format another (Y/N)?_

If you are formatting just one diskette, you can answer N and go on to step 2.

2. Enter the COPY command to copy the BASICA.COM file from drive C to the new system diskette in drive A.

COPY BASICA.COM A:

Your diskette is now prepared to receive any other application programs (through the COPY command) as well as to boot the DOS system at power-up time.

In the preceding example, you were concerned only with preparing a diskette that could both hold files and be used to boot the system. At the beginning of Chapter 4, you'll learn how to name, or label, the entire diskette during this formatting process. You'll also learn how to display this label and change it when the diskette's contents change.

Backing Up an Existing Disk

The FORMAT command prepares a disk with tracks and sectors laid out in precise patterns. These patterns are required for DOS to store files of information on the disk. Now you will see how to use the DISKCOPY command to precisely duplicate the contents of one diskette onto another. Chapter 18 presents further examples and details of this command and other backup options.

The DISKCOPY command does not require you to format the target diskette before using it—DISKCOPY automatically formats the target diskette if necessary. DISKCOPY commands are the only DOS operations for which you can use an unformatted diskette.

COPY-PROTECTED DISKETTES

Diskettes that are *copy protected* cannot be copied accurately by DOS. DOS expects all diskettes to have the same basic setup in terms of tracks, sectors, directories, and so on. If a diskette is organized at all differently, then the DISKCOPY command will not work.

Copy protection was originally designed to prevent users from making inexpensive copies of expensive software. These cheap copies often prevented original manufacturers from receiving all the income from sales that they were due. However, after several legal battles (over the right of users to make legitimate backup copies for themselves) and several marketing battles (over large corporate accounts refusing to buy copy-protected products that could not be placed on hard disks without continued diskette handling), the current trend is away from copy-protected programs.

You can purchase special programs that can decipher most of the special codes used by copy-protected software, allowing purchasers of protected software to make backup or archival copies of their disks. Since DOS can't do this, such a package is a good investment if your software collection includes copy-protected software. An example of such a program is COPY II PC, from Central Point Software.

Backing Up Your DOS Diskettes

In this section you'll learn how to make duplicate (backup) copies of both of the DOS diskettes. You can then employ the backup diskettes, carefully storing and protecting the originals.

The procedure is slightly different, depending on whether you have a one-diskette or a two-diskette system. (You may have one diskette drive in your system because that is all you have, or you may have one diskette drive because your system has a hard disk.) In either case, you will use the DISKCOPY command to create an exact copy of each DOS diskette. You will need two double-sided, double-density blank diskettes for this purpose.

This section refers to the startup and operating diskettes contained in DOS 3.3. If you are using an earlier version of DOS, your two diskettes are labeled *System* and *Supplementary.* The instructions in this section will apply regardless of the DOS version you are using.

DOS produces several prompting messages during the disk-copying operation, in which your original diskette (which you are copying) is referred to as the *source* diskette, and the new, blank diskette (which you are copying onto) is referred to as the *target* or *destination* diskette (see Figure 2.6).

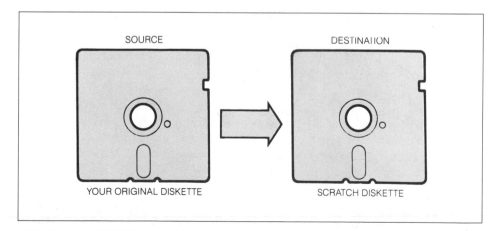

FIGURE 2.6: The DISKCOPY command makes an exact replica of any non-copy-protected diskette. The diskette you are copying is usually called the source diskette, and the new replica is created on a scratch diskette called the destination (or target) diskette.

FOR ONE-DISKETTE SYSTEMS

If you are using drive A, the single diskette drive of your system, type the following command:

DISKCOPY

When the DISKCOPY command executes, DOS prompts you as follows:

Insert source diskette in drive A:
Press any key when ready...

In this single-diskette environment, DOS asks you to place both source and destination diskettes, successively, into drive A (see Figure 2.7).

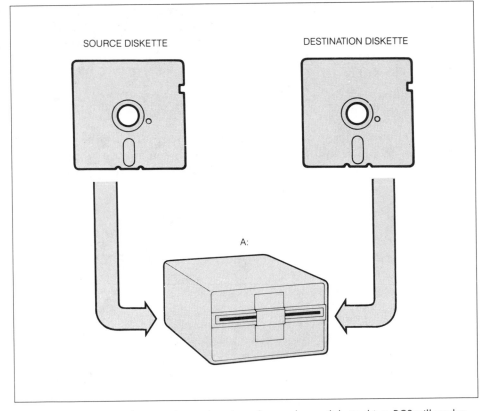

SOURCE DISKETTE   DESTINATION DISKETTE

A:

FIGURE 2.7: Diskettes can be copied even though you have only one diskette drive. DOS will read as much of the source diskette's contents into memory as it can fit and then prompt you to replace the source diskette with a destination diskette; then it will write the memory contents onto that destination diskette. This process will repeat until the source diskette is completely copied onto the destination diskette.

Assuming your DOS diskette is still in drive A, press the Return key to begin the DISKCOPY operation. DOS will display an informative message as it copies your diskette. This message varies, depending on the diskette's storage density and its number of sides, but it appears similar to the following:

Copying 40 tracks
9 Sectors/Track,2 Side(s)

When DOS has read as much as it can from the diskette, it prompts you as follows:

Insert target diskette in drive A:
Press any key when ready...

Write "DOS Startup Diskette" on a label and then place the label on a blank diskette. Place this blank diskette in drive A and press Return. DOS will then copy onto the blank diskette whatever part of the DOS system diskette it was able to read in its first pass. When it has finished copying this information onto your new diskette, it may prompt you to again place the original DOS system diskette in drive A. Whether this procedure repeats depends on the total size (in bytes) of your source diskette, and whether it can be completely read into memory and then copied in only one pass. If it can't, DOS prompts you as follows:

Insert source diskette in drive A:
Press any key when ready...

If this message appears, remove your blank diskette and reinsert the original DOS diskette so DOS can continue reading information from the source diskette. The system will then prompt you to again insert the destination diskette in drive A. This is your cue to remove the original diskette and place your newly labeled diskette in drive A. Depending on the amount of memory in your computer and the version of DOS you are using, this juggling of diskettes will continue until all of the information from the original diskette is read and written onto the destination diskette. Any existing volume label on the source disk will be copied onto the destination disk during this DISKCOPY operation.

At the end of this cycle, DOS asks if you would like to copy another diskette. You've copied only the first of the DOS diskettes, so you should answer with the letter Y (for yes). You will now repeat the entire cycle for your DOS operating diskette.

Prepare a label titled "DOS Operating Diskette" and place it on your second blank diskette. After you answer Y to the DOS prompt, you will again be prompted to insert a source diskette in drive A. Place your DOS supplementary diskette in drive A and begin the entire process again, this time using your blank, newly labeled DOS operating diskette as the target of the DISKCOPY procedure.

If your system has two diskette drives, the diskette-copying procedure progresses much faster because no juggling is required. Assuming your DOS diskette is in drive A, place a blank diskette, which you should label "DOS Startup Diskette," in drive B. Then type the following command at the DOS prompt:

DISKCOPY A: B:

This command tells DOS to read everything from drive A and write it onto the diskette in drive B (see Figure 2.8). DOS will prompt you as follows:

Insert source diskette in drive A:
Insert target diskette in drive B:
Press any key when ready . . .

At this point, before you press the Return key, make sure that your DOS system diskette is in drive A, and that your blank diskette, which is to become the copy of the DOS system diskette, is in drive B. Pressing Return will then initiate the operation to copy the complete contents of one diskette onto the other. While DOS makes the copy, it displays the type of diskette it believes it is copying (single- or double-sided, the number of sectors to a track, and so on):

Copying 40 tracks
9 Sectors/Track,2 Side(s)

When the copy operation ends, DOS asks you if you want to copy another diskette:

Copy another diskette (Y/N)?

At this point you should answer Y, indicating that you want to copy another diskette. You will see the same message, indicating that you should place the source diskette (your DOS operating diskette) in drive A and that you should insert the target diskette (your blank, newly labeled operating diskette) in drive B. Then—and only then—should you press the Return key to initiate the process of copying the operating programs onto your backup diskette.

You can now answer N (for no) to the question about copying another diskette. When the DOS prompt returns, you are ready to use DOS in earnest.

You can also use the procedure you have just followed to back up the DOS diskettes to create backup copies of most of your application software. However, certain copy-protected programs cannot be backed up in this fashion.

CHECKING A DISK FOR AVAILABLE SPACE

Your DOS system provides a very useful external command called CHKDSK. (All *external* commands are really programs stored in disk-resident

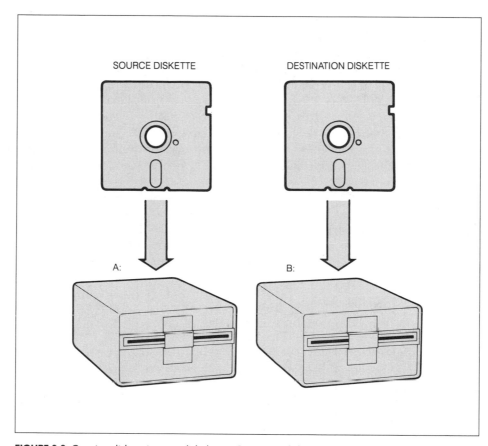

SOURCE DISKETTE   DESTINATION DISKETTE

A: B:

FIGURE 2.8: Copying disks using two disk drives. Copying a diskette is much easier and often faster when you can use two drives simultaneously. Both source and destination diskettes are available to DOS at any time, and no time is lost performing manual diskette switching, necessary for a single-drive DISKCOPY operation.

files; each has an extension of .COM or .EXE.) Simply entering CHKDSK and pressing Return allows you to check the amount of space, both used and unused, on a particular disk. One of DOS's drawbacks is that it does not pack information as densely on a disk as is possible. Files that contain large amounts of information will consume a significant amount of disk space. The CHKDSK command also displays detailed information about the files on your disk.

You can also use the CHKDSK command to find and fix file-allocation errors. DOS actually allocates space for files in groups of sectors called *clusters*. The number of sectors in a cluster varies according to the type of disk and the version of DOS you are using. This explains why you might run out of disk space, even though the sum of all your file sizes is much smaller than the disk you are using.

For example, if the cluster size is four sectors, then any data from 1 byte to 2K will be allocated all four sectors (2048 bytes) on your disk. If the cluster size is eight sectors, then all files will always require at least 4096 bytes. Even larger files may waste a number of bytes, since the last portion of these files will be allocated an entire cluster, even if only 1 additional byte is needed.

Note that DOS 3.2 reduced the cluster size for hard disks. If you're still using an earlier version of DOS, this feature in itself may be sufficient reason to upgrade to the latest version—and if you do, get DOS 3.3 (or a later implementation); it's faster, it offers a number of improved commands, and contains many features that improve efficiency. It supports the Personal System/2 series of computers as well.

The CHKDSK command displays a summary of the amount of space available on each disk. For instance, entering CHKDSK by itself displays information about the current default disk drive (as shown by the prompt). Typically, this is drive A in a dual-diskette system and drive C in a hard disk system, as shown in Figures 2.9 and 2.10. The same results could have been obtained by explicitly telling DOS which drives to check:

CHKDSK A:

or

CHKDSK C:

Note: You might notice after entering the CHKDSK command that the red light on the drive you specified turned on, indicating that the device was activated. Whenever you see the red light, you can assume that the system is reading from or writing to the disk. Unless you are instructed to, you should *never* remove a disk from a drive when the light is on.

CHKDSK displays the following information about disk space:

- *Bytes total disk space.* This value tells you the number of bytes of storage space available on the disk before any files were added.

- *Bytes in hidden files.* This value tells you the number of bytes in the special DOS files usually hidden from the user's view when a directory is listed.

- *Bytes in user files.* This value tells you the number of bytes in user-created files, which are listed on the directory.

- *Bytes in bad sectors.* This value indicates the number of bytes in bad sectors, which are usually sectors that have been removed from use because of some defect detected by the computer system. If all sectors are good, as in the disks displayed by CHKDSK in Figures 2.9 and 2.10, then no bad-sector display appears.

- *Bytes available on disk.* This value tells you the amount of space left for adding new files to the disk.

```
A>CHKDSK

   362496 bytes total disk space
    45056 bytes in 2 hidden files
   274432 bytes in 43 user files
    43008 bytes available on disk

   524288 bytes total memory
   443136 bytes free

A>_
```

FIGURE 2.9: CHKDSK output for a diskette (no volume label). The simplest possible report from CHKDSK includes the total disk space formatted (362496), the space taken up by DOS hidden system information (45056), the space in use by your files (274432), the disk space still available (43008), the total amount of installed memory (524288), and the number of bytes of memory currently unused by any memory-resident code (443136). This report is typical of many floppy diskettes that have not been electronically labeled with a volume ID.

```
C>CHKDSK
Volume ROBBINS        created Mar 22, 1987 4:43p

 21204992 bytes total disk space
    45056 bytes in 3 hidden files
   124928 bytes in 45 directories
 18618368 bytes in 1778 user files
  2416640 bytes available on disk

   524288 bytes total memory
   121920 bytes free

C>_
```

FIGURE 2.10: CHKDSK output for a hard disk (volume label ROBBINS). When CHKDSK is used with a typical hard disk, it provides standard information about memory use, total disk space, hidden file use, user file use, and available disk space. Since hard disks are usually defined as a hierarchy of directories, CHKDSK reports the space consumed by the administrative overhead of these directory structures as well.

The last two lines on the CHKDSK display are not specific to the disk drive. They tell you about the internal memory of the computer: How much total memory is installed in your system and how much is still free for use. Internal memory is usually an issue only if you are using many programs at once, or if you don't have the maximum physical memory available on your machine.

Programs can occasionally create problems in DOS's management area: the *file allocation table* (*FAT*) introduced in Chapter 1. Such problems often are the result of programs that begin to create files but stop because of some error condition.

The following special form of the CHKDSK command lists all FAT errors and also tells you whether the files are stored in contiguous clusters:

CHKDSK *.*

Contiguous, or adjacent, clusters are desirable because then disk heads must travel less distance to read or write the desired sector data; thus, disk operations occur faster. The symbol *.* is a *wildcard* specification. The asterisk (*) tells DOS to check all files on the disk. (You'll learn more about wildcard symbols in Chapter 3.) The results of this command might appear as in Figure 2.11, which shows you that on this disk, at this moment, there is only one file, SKN.COM, which is not stored in contiguous sectors.

```
A>chkdsk *.*

    362496 bytes total disk space
     10240 bytes in 2 hidden files
    236544 bytes in 41 user files
    115712 bytes available on disk

    655360 bytes total memory
    590128 bytes free

A:\SKN.COM
    Contains 3 non-contiguous blocks.

A>_
```

FIGURE 2.11: CHKDSK request for file-contiguity information. Use wildcards or specific file identifiers with CHKDSK to display the extent of file contiguity or fragmentation on a disk. CHKDSK reports the number of pieces each specified file is broken into on a disk. This number has a direct relationship to the speed at which the file's information can be accessed.

There is nothing inherently wrong with files in noncontiguous sectors. However, large files in noncontiguous sectors are processed more slowly than are files in contiguous sectors. (Chapter 20 provides more information about this issue and options for improvement.) Whenever possible, do not allow your disk to contain noncontiguous files.

If a CHKDSK command does list file allocation errors, you need to enter a special version of the CHKDSK command to correct the errors. The CHKDSK/F command collects lost or misallocated sectors into a series of files named FILE0000.CHK, FILE0001.CHK, FILE0002.CHK, and so on. These are ASCII text files; you can type their contents from DOS to see the data, or you can use your word processor to try to change the data. (See Appendix C for a more complete description of ASCII codes and files.) You are usually best advised simply to be pleased at recovering the disk space and to erase the "recovered" files. However, if the data a lost file contains is simple text that does not exist in any other form (perhaps it was lost during a power failure), you may use your word processor to try to recover as much of the file as possible. You can sometimes save much reentry time, especially if the lost data is all text and there was a good deal of it. See Chapter 20 for information about the Norton Utilities and advanced methods for more complete file-recovery methods.

DOS COMMANDS USED IN THE STARTUP PROCESS

Following are the reference entries for the commands used to start DOS and prepare diskettes. They are presented in alphabetical order.

CHKDSK

CHKDSK checks the formatted size and available space on a disk. It also indicates the amount of disk space consumed by system files, data files, and bad sectors, and indicates memory size and amount of memory available.

SYNTAX

[*D:Path*]CHKDSK [*FileSpec*][/F][/V]

D:Path	is the drive and path where the command file is located if it is not in the current directory.
FileSpec	is an optional drive and path, plus the file name and extension, of the file that is the object of the command. Wildcards are allowed.

/F	allows corrections on the disk.
/V	lists all files and their paths.

TYPE

External.

USAGE

CHKDSK shows the status of your disk and its use of file space. It is most often used to check the amount of available space on a disk. Sometimes, in situations where you are using memory-resident routines as well, CHKDSK is also used to assess the amount of available memory space.

EXAMPLES

The last two lines indicate the total memory space and the amount of memory that is free.

To check the status of your default disk drive, enter CHKDSK with no parameters:

CHKDSK

This command produces a report on your monitor like the following (assuming default drive D):

Volume DRIVE-D created Sep 26, 1987 6:02pm

22255616 bytes total disk space.
0 bytes in 1 hidden files.
112640 bytes in 45 directories.
17446912 bytes in 1552 user files.
4696064 bytes available on disk.

655328 bytes total storage
540208 bytes free

Checking the status of another disk drive requires only the addition of the disk drive identifier:

CHKDSK B:

If errors are reported on a disk, you can do nothing about them unless you run the CHKDSK command using the /F switch. Only when you use the /F switch can CHKDSK adjust the file allocation table, and this occurs only if you answer Y to the question posed by the CHKDSK command about fixing the error.

CLS

The CLS command completely erases your video screen and resets the position of the cursor to the upper-left corner.

SYNTAX

CLS

TYPE

Internal.

USAGE

When the screen becomes cluttered, or you have a batch file that does many different things and you no longer need to see everything on the screen, you may want to clear the screen. The CLS command clears the screen. After the screen erasure, the cursor is placed at the top left of the screen. You normally use the CLS command when you want succeeding output from any program or batch file to begin at the top line of a screen. It's the electronic equivalent of erasing a blackboard before doing any more work on it.

EXAMPLES

Entering

CLS

erases the screen and leaves the cursor at the top-left side of the screen. You can also use CLS during batch-file operations, when successive screenfuls of messages are displayed. It erases the screen between each set of messages or each block of text being displayed.

DATE

This command changes the date. Use it either to update or to simply find out what day of the week a certain date is. DATE also resets the date of a permanent clock, if one is installed.

SYNTAX

DATE [*mm-dd-yy* ¦ *dd-mm-yy* ¦ *yy-mm-dd*]

    mm   is the month (01 to 12).

    dd   is the day (01 to 31).

    yy   is the year, either 80 to 99 or 1980 to 1999.

If you do not specify the *mm-dd-yy* parameter, DOS will prompt you for it. The order of *mm, dd,* and *yy* depends on the country you have selected.

TYPE

Internal.

USAGE

When you enter the month, day, and year, you can separate each entry by dashes, slashes, or periods. The order of these entries depends on the setting of the COUNTRY command in your CONFIG.SYS file. (If you are using a code page other than 437—United States—the separator symbols for separating your numeric entries may also vary.)

The DATE command, like the related TIME command, has been enhanced in DOS version 3.3. In earlier versions, the system retains the changed date only until power is turned off or the system is rebooted. To reset a permanent clock in these versions, you must use the Diagnostics program on the Utilities disk.

Also note that if, on startup, DOS finds an AUTOEXEC.BAT file, it bypasses the normal date and time prompts. If you are using such a file and you need to reset the date and time values each time you start the computer, include the DATE and TIME commands in the file, and the prompts will appear. (See Chapter 9 for more information about AUTOEXEC.BAT files.)

EXAMPLES

You can set the date on your computer system by using the DATE command with one parameter equal to the desired date: for example,

DATE 2-3-89

This command calls up the date routine that permanently resets your internal computer clock to the date February 3, 1989. The DOS command prompt immediately returns.

If you wish to set the date from a batch file, as you might in AUTOEXEC-.BAT or STARTUP.CMD, simply enter the DATE command. DOS displays the current date and prompts you to enter a new date: For example,

Current Date is FRIDAY 2-3-89
Enter New Date (mm-dd-yy);_

DISKCOPY

The DISKCOPY command makes an exact copy of a diskette.

SYNTAX

[*D:Path*]DISKCOPY [*SourceD:DestD:*][/1]

D:Path	is the drive and path where the command file is located if it is not in the current directory.
SourceD	is the source drive to be copied.
DestD	is the destination drive to be copied onto.
/1	forces the computer to copy only the first side of the source diskette to the first side of the destination diskette as if they were both single sided, even if the disks are double sided.

TYPE

External.

USAGE

The DISKCOPY command permits you to make a precise replica of a floppy disk. The destination drive should contain either a new and unformatted floppy disk or an older formatted disk that contains data you no longer need. During the DISKCOPY operation, any existing data on the destination disk will be completely overwritten. As with DISKCOMP, a one-diskette system supports DISK-COPY operations. DOS will prompt you when you need to switch diskettes.

If DOS finds any errors on either disk, DISKCOPY indicates the drive, track, and side where the problems exist and proceeds with the copy operation. You can make your own assessment of the severity of the error. In general, it's better to use a new destination diskette if the one you are using contains hardware errors, since such errors call into question the validity of the copy. If the source disk contains hardware errors, you should determine the validity of your original data on that diskette before assuming that you are now protected with a backup diskette. Both the original and the backup diskette may contain questionable data.

RESTRICTIONS

You cannot use DISKCOPY with a hard disk; also, the command does not recognize an assigned or substituted drive and should not be used with JOIN. (The ASSIGN, SUBST, AND JOIN commands are discussed in Chapter 19.) DISKCOPY cannot reliably read a double-sided disk formatted in a high-capacity drive, and it will not work with network drives.

EXAMPLES

To copy a disk from drive A to drive B, enter

DISKCOPY A: B:

If you have only one drive, enter DISKCOPY with no parameters, and DOS will prompt you at appropriate times to switch your source and destination disks.

FORMAT

This command formats a disk for use with DOS.

Syntax

[*D:Path*]FORMAT *D1:*[/S][/1][/8][/V][/B][/4][/N:*xx*][/T:*yy*]

D:Path	is the drive and path where the command file is located if it is not in the current directory.
D1:	is the drive to be formatted.
/S	causes a system disk to be created.
/1	formats only one side of a disk. Version 1.X of DOS was originally designed to handle single-sided disks only.
/8	formats a disk with 8 sectors instead of 9. Version 1.X of DOS was originally designed to handle only 8 sectors per track. This was a conservative IBM decision to minimize the likelihood of errors appearing because of too much data being stored on one track.
/V	prompts you for a volume label after formatting is complete.

/B	formats a disk with 8 sectors and leaves room for the hidden system files, but it does *not* transfer the system to the diskette, thus allowing the use of the SYS command with any DOS version, especially the earlier versions, which expect only 8 sectors per track.
/4	causes a high-capacity drive to create a 360K, double-sided diskette.
/N:*xx*	formats a disk with *xx* sectors per track. This parameter is required if you use multiple machines, and you prepare disks on one for use on another.
/T:*yy*	formats a disk with *yy* tracks. This parameter is required if you use multiple machines, and you prepare disks on one for use on another.

TYPE

External.

USAGE

FORMAT is used regularly with all new diskettes fresh from the box. It is also used to reformat older, used diskettes; in addition to clearing the disk of all old data, using FORMAT with old disks helps protect you and your disks from the deleterious effects of possible bad sectors. During the formatting process, any bad sectors discovered are marked as such, and no new data is written to those places on the disk. Hence, reformatting disks in between major uses offers an additional level of data protection.

If you do not specify parameters, DOS formats the diskette as a standard data diskette according to the type of drive in which the diskette resides. A high-capacity drive produces an automatic 1.2MB formatted diskette, for instance, and a 5.25-inch double-density drive produces a 360KB diskette.

As the microcomputer industry develops, more and more different disk drives are making their way onto customer machines. The FORMAT command must be flexible enough to properly format a variety of different disks in a variety of different disk drives. In particular, DOS 3.3 makes available the /N and /T switches for managing similar sized diskettes (3.5-inch and 5.25-inch) which are designed for different volumes of information.

If you own a 1.44MB 3.5-inch disk drive, you can format a smaller volume diskette by using the /N and /T switches.

The /N switch specifies the number of sectors per track, while the /T switch specifies the number of tracks per side.

A similar capability is available in the 5.25-inch arena. You can downsize the formatting of a diskette in a high capacity (1.2MB) drive with the /N and /T switches.

As can be seen from the following examples a 320K diskette formats 40 tracks with 8 sectors per track, while a 360K diskette requires the formatting to prepare 40 tracks with 9 sectors per track. In each of these cases, the /N and /T switches are only required to format a diskette to a size which is not the default or standard for a particular drive.

RESTRICTIONS

FORMAT ignores assignments made with ASSIGN. You cannot use the /V switch to format a diskette for DOS 1.1. A 360KB diskette formatted in a high-capacity drive cannot be read reliably in single- or double-density drives. If you need a formatted 360KB diskette in another machine, format it in that other machine; it then *can* be reliably written on by a high-capacity drive.

EXAMPLES

As an extra protection, FORMAT requires you to enter the current volume label when you try to format a hard disk. If your hard disk does not have a volume label, press the Return key to begin the formatting. DOS will not format a disk if the volume label you enter does not match the label it finds on the disk. For instance, if you enter the command FORMAT D: for a hard disk and then enter a volume identifier different from the one DOS actually finds on the disk, DOS displays this message:

> **Invalid Volume ID**
> **Format Failure.**

If the volume labels match, DOS gives you a last chance to back out of this potentially disastrous procedure, in which all data on your disk will be lost:

> **WARNING!**
> **ALL DATA ON THE FIXED DISK DRIVE D: WILL BE LOST!**
> **PROCEED WITH FORMAT (Y/N)?**

A very simple and common use of the FORMAT command is to format a diskette in drive A to use as much space as the drive allows. To do this, enter

> **FORMAT A:**

To create a system diskette with a volume label, enter the following command:

> **FORMAT A: /S /V**

In this example, DOS formats the disk, copies the operating system files onto it, and prompts you to enter a volume label. This volume label identifies your disk; you should write a volume label each time you format a new disk. The label can contain up to 11 characters of any kinds, including spaces.

The following command will format a disk for 720KB in a 1.44MB drive:

FORMAT A: /N:9 /T:80

Formatting a 320KB diskette in a high capacity drive requires the following command:

FORMAT A: /N:8 /T:40

Similarly, formatting a 360KB diskette in the same 1.2MB drive requires the following variation:

FORMAT A: /N:9 /T:40

SYS

This command transfers the system files to the disk in the specified drive.

SYNTAX

[*D:Path*]SYS *DestD:*

D:Path	is the drive and path where the command file is located if it is not in the current directory.
DestD	is the drive to which the system files will be transferred.

TYPE

External.

USAGE

If you have a data diskette that you want to make into a system diskette, or if you want to transfer a new version of DOS to a diskette created with an older version DOS, the SYS command may be what you need. When you use FORMAT /S to format a disk, SYS is invoked automatically to transfer the system files. SYS does not transfer COMMAND.COM, but it does transfer the two hidden BIOS and DOS files.

RESTRICTIONS

The data diskette must not contain any files, because the two system files must be the first files on the disk. Also, you cannot use SYS on a network drive.

EXAMPLES

If you boot DOS from drive A and want to transfer the system files to your hard disk in drive C, enter

SYS C:

If your system files are already on C and you want to transfer them to a 1.44MB, 3.5-inch diskette in the drive F, you would enter

SYS F:

TIME

This command sets the system time. It also resets an internal clock.

SYNTAX

TIME [*hh:mm*[*:ss*[*.xx*]]]

hh	is the current hour, in 24-hour format. To translate from 12-hour to 24-hour format, if the time is between 1:00 P.M. and 12:00 A.M., add 12 to the hour (for example, 7:45 P.M. = 19:45).
mm	is the current number of minutes.
ss	is the current number of seconds.
xx	is the current number of hundredths of seconds.

TYPE

Internal.

USAGE

TIME is usually used simply to note the current system time, to correct it when the clock's battery wears down, or to adjust the system time for Daylight Savings Time.

The TIME command, like the related DATE command, has been enhanced in DOS version 3.3. In earlier versions, the system retains the changed time only until power is turned off or DOS is rebooted. To reset a permanent clock in these versions, you must use the Diagnostics program on the Utilities disk.

Also note that if, on startup, DOS finds an AUTOEXEC.BAT file, it bypasses the normal date and time prompts. If you are using such a file and you need to reset the date and time values each time you start the computer, include the DATE and TIME commands in the file, and the prompts will appear. (See Chapter 9 for more information about AUTOEXEC.BAT files.)

RESTRICTIONS

You cannot indicate a drive for this command. In addition, the command format used by TIME is influenced by the COUNTRY command in the CONFIG.SYS configuration file.

EXAMPLES

You can reset TIME on your computer's clock by entering the TIME command along with the new time in the form hours:minutes:seconds.hundredths, as follows:

TIME 7:58

This entry adjusts your computer's clock to the new time of 7:58 A.M. Remember that DOS maintains a 24-hour clock, so that hours numbered 1 to 11 are always A.M.

If you do not enter a new time as a parameter for the TIME command, DOS displays the current time recorded in its clock and gives you the opportunity to change it, as follows:

TIME
Current time is 7:58:27.16
Enter new time:_

VER

This command displays the current version of DOS you are using.

FORMAT

VER

TYPE

Internal

USAGE

Entering the VER command at the DOS prompt displays the current version number of the operating system. Typing VER might produce the result

MS Personal Computer DOS Version *vv.nn*

The characters *vv*, to the left of the decimal point, indicate the principal version number. The characters *nn*, to the right of the decimal point, indicate intermediate revisions of that version.

EXAMPLES

Entering VER at the DOS prompt on a Sperry computer currently running version 3.1 produces this display:

MS-DOS 3.10 version 1.20

SUMMARY

This chapter contained specific information to guide your first steps with your new operating system. You discovered many important facts about DOS.

For additional information about special configurations and the PROMPT command, see

- Chapter 10, "Configuration Possibilities"

For additional information about copying and backing up disks, see

- Chapter 18, "Backups and Restorations"

For additional information about preparing and partitioning your hard disk, see

- Chapter 19, "Other Advanced Commands"

For additional information about other memory-resident programs, see

- Chapter 20, "Extending DOS's Power with Utility Software"

In Chapter 3, you'll learn new commands and skills that will allow you to organize your programs and files.

PART

2

DISK AND DIRECTORY STRUCTURES

The disk system in DOS is the foundation for all the work you do on your microcomputer. In this section, you will learn how DOS manages files, and how you can instruct DOS to serve your application and file-management needs. You will learn what directories are, how they are set up, and how to use them efficiently when you run programs in a hard disk environment.

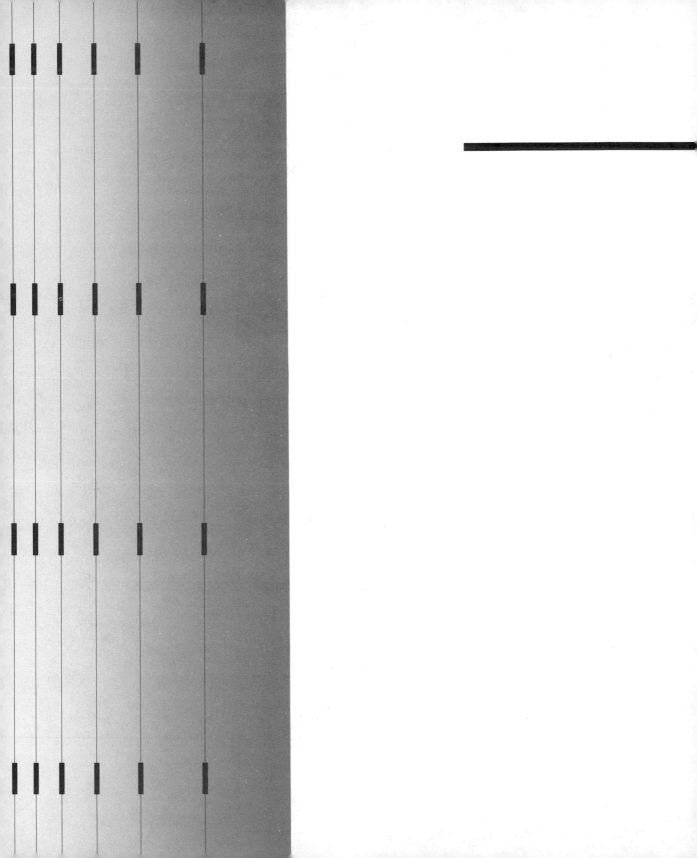

CHAPTER 3

The Disk System

THE DISK SYSTEM

T his chapter presents techniques used in manipulating files and defining directories. The tutorial sections discuss the following topics, which you may find useful, depending on your level of experience with DOS:

- The information available in a DOS directory listing
- Displaying a directory listing with the DIR command
- Using switches to modify the DIR command
- Using drive identifiers to access files on different disk drives
- Using wildcard characters in file names
- The various uses of the COPY command:
  - —to copy single or multiple files
  - —to transfer data between different physical devices
  - —to combine (*concatenate*) files
- Transferring files between disks and directories with the XCOPY command, available in DOS 3.2 and 3.3
- Typing the contents of text files with the TYPE command
- Changing the name of a file with the RENAME command
- Deleting a file with the ERASE command

The chapter concludes with reference entries for the DOS commands introduced here.

THE DISK DIRECTORY

How can you tell what files are stored on a disk? On diskettes, at least, you can read the printed disk label, although the label may be incorrect, and in any case it rarely contains all the information available electronically in DOS. The only way to know what is really on a disk is to have DOS display a *directory* of the files on that disk.

Tip: Just before storing each diskette you use, print a directory listing of its contents using the techniques described in Chapter 15. To make the information even more accessible, use the techniques in Chapter 17 to print a sorted listing.

Displaying a Directory with the DIR Command

The DIR (directory) command displays on the screen a list of all the files stored on a disk. If you enter the command

DIR

the computer will display a list of all the files on the currently active drive. Figure 3.1 shows a sample directory listing. Because DIR was entered with the

```
Volume in drive A has no label
Directory of  A:\

ANSI     SYS     1651   12-30-85   12:00p
ASSIGN   COM     1536   12-30-85   12:00p
ATTRIB   EXE     8247   12-30-85   12:00p
BACKUP   COM     6234   12-30-85   12:00p
BASIC    COM    19298   12-30-85   12:00p
BASICA   COM    36396   12-30-85   12:00p
CHKDSK   COM     9832   12-30-85   12:00p
COMMAND  COM    23791   12-30-85   12:00p
COMP     COM     4184   12-30-85   12:00p
DISKCOMP COM     5792   12-30-85   12:00p
DISKCOPY COM     6224   12-30-85   12:00p
DRIVER   SYS     1115   12-30-85   12:00p
EDLIN    COM     7508   12-30-85   12:00p
FDISK    COM     8173   12-30-85   12:00p
FIND     EXE     6416   12-30-85   12:00p
FORMAT   COM    11135   12-30-85   12:00p
GRAFTABL COM     1169   12-30-85   12:00p
GRAPHICS COM     3220   12-30-85   12:00p
JOIN     EXE     8955   12-30-85   12:00p
KEYBFR   COM     3291   12-30-85   12:00p
KEYBGR   COM     3274   12-30-85   12:00p
KEYBIT   COM     3060   12-30-85   12:00p
KEYBSP   COM     3187   12-30-85   12:00p
KEYBUK   COM     3036   12-30-85   12:00p
LABEL    COM     2346   12-30-85   12:00p
MODE     COM     6864   12-30-85   12:00p
MORE     COM      295   12-30-85   12:00p
PRINT    COM     8976   12-30-85   12:00p
RECOVER  COM     4297   12-30-85   12:00p
REPLACE  EXE    11650   12-30-85   12:00p
RESTORE  COM     6012   12-30-85   12:00p
SELECT   COM     3826   12-30-85   12:00p
SHARE    EXE     8580   12-30-85   12:00p
SORT     EXE     1911   12-30-85   12:00p
SUBST    EXE     9911   12-30-85   12:00p
SYS      COM     4620   12-30-85   12:00p
TREE     COM     3357   12-30-85   12:00p
VDISK    SYS     3307   12-30-85   12:00p
XCOPY    EXE    11200   12-30-85   12:00p
        39 File(s)       22528 bytes free
```

FIGURE 3.1: Sample directory listing. A typical listing specifies the base name and extension for each listed file. The letter of the drive to which the directory applies is first displayed, along with the disk label (volume ID) if one exists. The length of each file, in bytes, is also listed along with the date and time of file creation or last modification. Last, the number of files and the number of bytes remaining on the entire disk drive are listed at the bottom line of the display.

A> prompt, this directory is for a diskette in drive A. The list of files is scrolled automatically on the screen, since the list has too many lines to be seen at one time on a standard 25-line screen. (To control the list of files on the screen, use the key combination Ctrl-S, or ^S. This freezes the screen and stops the scrolling. The same combination restarts the screen scrolling. This type of key combination is called a *toggle*. Control-key combinations were introduced in Chapter 1.) The bottom of the display shows the amount of space left on the diskette for new files.

Contents of the Directory Listing

Each line in the directory represents a file stored on the disk. DOS displays four pieces of information about each file: the file name, the file size, and the date and time of the file's creation or last update: for example,

BACKUP COM   **6234**   **12-30-85**   **22:00p**
(File Name)   **(Size)**   **(Date)**   **(Time)**

Enter the DIR command now for each of the drives in your own system. Enter, as appropriate,

DIR A:
DIR B:
DIR C:

If you have other drives, enter the DIR command for them as well. If you accidentally enter DIR with the letter of a drive that doesn't exist, DOS will tell you so. You'll receive the error message "Invalid drive specification," and then DOS will display a new prompt. However, if you ask for a directory listing for a drive that *does* exist on your system, but the drive isn't ready (the drive door isn't closed or a diskette hasn't been inserted), you'll receive the "Abort, Retry, Fail" error message (or "Abort, Retry, Ignore" in versions of DOS earlier than 3.3). If you've really made a mistake, simply type the letter *A* to abort the request; if the diskette wasn't ready, prepare it properly and then type *R* to retry the DIR request. Select the FAIL option only if you are a DOS programmer, understand the nature of the internal system call that has failed, and know how to proceed in the program.

Elements of a File Name

The most important aspect of the directory display is the list of files. Each entry can have three parts:

1. A drive name (optional)
2. A base name
3. An extension (optional)

The general form of every DOS file name is as follows:

D:BaseName.Ext

where *D* represents an optional one-letter drive identifier (A, B, C, and so on), *BaseName* represents the base name, and *Ext* represents an optional three-character file-name extension. Figure 3.2 illustrates the general form.

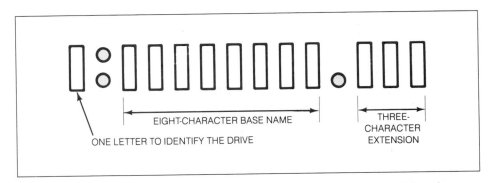

FIGURE 3.2: DOS file-name structure. DOS file names have a consistent structure, consisting of an optional drive identifier, a required base name, which can be nearly any combination of from one to eight characters, and an optional (though usually used) one- to three-character extension.

The drive name can be any letter from A to Z. However, a device corresponding to the drive designation must be connected to the computer. For example, two drives allow you to use A or B. Hard disks usually default to the drive identifier C. The drive name is separated from the base name by a colon.

When you enter a file name, you enter it in a manner different from that in which DOS displays it. In the example directory listing

BACKUP   COM6234   12-30-85 22:00p

the name appears as BACKUP   COM, but you must enter this name as BACKUP.COM, with a period between the name and the three-character extension. Note that DOS does not care whether letters are upper- or lowercase. However, you cannot enter spaces as part of a file name, even though spaces appear in the directory listing.

Valid and Invalid File Names   A file's base name can be from one to eight characters long. For the sake of readability as well as typeability, use only alphabetic and numeric characters in file names. However, you can use any sequence of characters except the following invalid ones:

. " / \ [ ] ¦ < > + : = ; ,

All DOS control codes (see Appendix C) also are invalid. DOS checks for invalid characters when you enter a base name.

The following base name would not be acceptable to DOS because it contains a space:

MY FILE

However, this name would be acceptable:

MY_FILE

The space has been replaced with an underscore, which is a legal character. Many people use this character to simulate a space, since it is visually unobtrusive. Use it if you like, but it always slows down the typing of the name; the name MYFILE, with neither a space nor an underscore, would be quicker and easier to enter.

An extension is limited to three characters. The rules regarding invalid characters in base names apply to extensions as well. Use a period to separate an extension from the base name.

Look at the following file names:

- A:LETTER.TXT
- SAMPLE DAT
- X
- MY:FILE
- msdos.les
- Sample.File
- C.test.doc
- b:user.fil

Do you know which of these are valid and which are not? If not, reread the preceding sections before proceeding. The valid file names are A:LETTER.TXT, X, msdos.les, and b:user.fil. The others are constructed incorrectly.

SAMPLE DAT is invalid because it contains a space. MY:FILE is unacceptable because two characters precede the colon. Colons cannot appear in a base name; they can *precede* the base name if a drive identifier begins the file name. However, a drive identifier can be only a single letter. The file name Sample.File is invalid because a file extension can contain only three characters. (In fact, DOS will accept this entry and treat it as if Sample.Fil had been typed; it will ignore the final *e*.) C.test.doc is invalid because a drive specification must be followed by a colon. Also, only one period can appear in a file name, and that can be used only to separate an extension from a base name.

USING CONVENTIONAL EXTENSIONS

As stated earlier, drive specifications and extensions are optional. The usual purpose of an extension is to group together files of the same type. Some file extensions, such as .BAS (for BASIC language programs), .COM (machine-language command files), and .DAT (data files), conventionally are used to identify certain types of files.

File extensions make it easier to see, group, and access all files of the same type. When you look at the files contained in any new application package, you can easily understand the use of many of them simply by noting the extensions (.HLP for help files, .TXT for text files, .OVL for overlay files, and so on). Table 3.1 lists commonly used extensions. Note, however, that every popular software package—from word processors to database managers to spreadsheets to specialized applications—typically uses and follows its own guidelines for naming extensions. Since conventions are by definition widely understood, following them makes it easier for others to work with your files.

Long Directory Lists

There are two alternative ways to list a directory that is too long to be displayed on a single screen. You can enter

DIR/W

The /W is an example of a switch; it modifies the way the DIR command executes. This command displays a directory like the one in Figure 3.3. This listing is called a *wide directory,* because the files are listed horizontally as well as vertically so that more names can fit on a single screen. Note that DOS no longer displays the size and creation or modification date and time of each file, which saves space on the display.

You can also enter the DIR command with the /P switch to obtain different results. If you enter

DIR/P

the screen fills, and the listing pauses until you press another key. If you then press Return again, the next screenful of file names is displayed. Using this command is somewhat akin to using the ^ S combination discussed earlier, except the listing breaks at precise places, depending on how many directory entries are required to fill the screen.

In summary, there are three styles of directory listings:

DIR   Complete listing of all files, including size and date and time of creation or modification

FILE EXTENSION	TYPE OF FILE
.BAK	Backup copies of files
.BAS	BASIC programs
.BAT	Batch files
.BIN	Binary object files
.COM	Simple executable programs (such as DOS commands)
.DAT or .DTA	Data files
.DBF	Database files
.DRV	Device driver files
.EXE	Executable programs, usually larger than 64K and more sophisticated than .COM programs
.NDX	Index files
.OVR or .OVL	Overlay files
.PRG	dBASE III PLUS program files
.SYS	DOS device drivers
.TXT	Plain ASCII text files
.WKS or .WK1	Worksheet (spreadsheet) files

TABLE 3.1: Commonly Used File-Name Extensions

```
A>DIR/W

 Volume in drive A has no label
 Directory of  A:\

ANSI     SYS    ASSIGN   COM    ATTRIB    EXE    BACKUP   COM    BASIC     COM
BASICA   COM    CHKDSK   COM    COMMAND   COM    COMP     COM    DISKCOMP  COM
DISKCOPY COM    DRIVER   SYS    EDLIN     COM    FDISK    COM    FIND      EXE
FORMAT   COM    GRAFTABL COM    GRAPHICS  COM    JOIN     EXE    KEYBFR    COM
KEYBGR   COM    KEYBIT   COM    KEYBSP    COM    KEYBUK   COM    LABEL     COM
MODE     COM    MORE     COM    PRINT     COM    RECOVER  COM    REPLACE   EXE
RESTORE  COM    SELECT   COM    SHARE     EXE    SORT     EXE    SUBST     EXE
SYS      COM    TREE     COM    VDISK     SYS    XCOPY    EXE
        39 File(s)     22528 bytes free

A>_
```

FIGURE 3.3: Wide directory listing. Such directory listings, which use the /W switch with the DIR command, present one of life's many tradeoffs. The wide listing enables DOS to display the names of five times as many files on a single screen; however, information about file size and date and time of file creation or last update is no longer displayed.

DIR/W   Wide directory listing, with file size, date, and time not shown

DIR/P   Directory listing by screenfuls, with listing pausing when one
screen is filled; size, date, and time are shown

Referencing Files on Other Drives

You can specify another drive's directory by following the DIR command with
the letter that indicates the drive. For example, on a dual-diskette system with a diskette in the second drive, if you type

DIR B:

the computer will display the list of files on the diskette in drive B. To get a wide
display of the drive B listing, enter

DIR B: /W

Changing the Default Drive

The A> prompt indicates that DOS will use the diskette in drive A unless you
specify otherwise. Thus, drive A is considered the *default* drive for all commands.
All commands will act on files located in the default drive unless you specifically
include another drive name as part of the command or file-name specification.
You can change the default drive simply by typing the letter of the desired new
default drive. For example, entering

B:

changes the A> prompt to B>. (Note that drive names are always followed by a
colon.) Entering the DIR command now will turn on the red light on drive B,
since drive B is now the default drive; DOS will change its prompt to B>. If you
want a listing of drive A, you now must enter

DIR A:

Limiting the Directory Display

Although the DIR command is useful for displaying the names of files, some
practical problems require other techniques. For example, suppose you want to
know whether the disk in the current drive contains a file called ASSIGN.COM.
If you simply enter the DIR command, you will have to locate visually the file
you want, which may be tedious, especially if you have scores of files (or hundreds of files, as you might on a hard disk). If you limit the display to just the files

that begin with the letter *A*, however, you will much more easily be able to determine whether the file you want is on the disk.

USING WILDCARD CHARACTERS

DOS allows you a certain degree of ambiguity in asking for files. This means that you can ask for a directory of files that meet certain criteria. You use an asterisk as a wildcard symbol to indicate your criteria. For example, if you want a list of all files that begin with the letter *A,* you enter

DIR A*

DOS will display a listing that looks something like this:

Volume in drive A has no label
Directory of A:
ASSIGN COM   1536   12-30-85 12:00p
AUTOEXEC BAT   34   4-01-87 6:27p
      2 File(s) 124928 bytes free

You can now much more easily determine whether ASSIGN.COM is on the disk, because DOS displays only files with names that begin with *A*.

Suppose you want to see whether the disk in drive A contains a file called WS.COM. You can enter

DIR W*

DOS will display a listing that looks like this:

Volume in drive A has no label
Directory of A:

File not found

This tells you that there are no files beginning with the letter *W* on the disk in drive A; therefore, the file WS.COM is not on the disk.

You can use wildcard characters to select files by their extensions as well as by their base names. Suppose that you want a list of all files on the disk in drive A that end with a .DAT extension. Since you do not care what the base name is, you can substitute an asterisk. If you enter

DIR *.DAT

DOS will list all files with the extension .DAT.

This discussion has presented the use of wildcards in the context of the DIR command. In fact, many of the commands you've already learned, as well as many of the ones you will learn later in this book, also permit the use of wildcards. Knowing which ones allow wildcards can make you a more productive user of DOS commands. The following DOS commands allow wildcards:

ATTRIB	COPY	FIND	REPLACE
BACKUP	DEL	PRINT	RESTORE
CHKDSK	DIR	RECOVER	XCOPY
COMP	ERASE	RENAME	

You can also use the ? symbol to search for names. The question mark is a wildcard symbol for one character, whereas the asterisk symbol can stand for multiple characters. For example, entering

DIR ????.COM

produces the display in Figure 3.4. The ????.COM specification told DOS to include any files with file names of four characters or less plus the .COM extension.

The following two commands combine the * and ? wildcard characters:

DIR ??S?????.*
DIR ??S*.*

```
A>DIR ????.COM

 Volume in drive A has no label
 Directory of  A:\

COMP     COM     4184  12-30-85   12:00p
MODE     COM     6864  12-30-85   12:00p
MORE     COM      295  12-30-85   12:00p
SYS      COM     4620  12-30-85   12:00p
TREE     COM     3357  12-30-85   12:00p
        5 File(s)      22528 bytes free

A>_
```

FIGURE 3.4: Directory searching with wildcards. Wildcards let you search directories selectively. Using the question mark wildcard four times, as was done here, selects only file names of four letters or less that end with the .COM extension.

Both of these commands have the same effect: They tell DOS to list only those files that contain the letter *S* as the third character in their names. (Remember that a DOS base name is limited to a maximum of eight characters plus an extension.)

You can direct DOS to search the disk in drive B by adding B: to the command. For example, to list all files on the disk in drive B that begin with *F,* you enter

DIR B:F*

Look at the following command. What files will it list?

DIR S???.COM

Enter this command on your DOS master disk. Is your prediction correct?

For additional practice, enter the commands to elicit the following lists of files:

1. All files on the active drive that begin with *M*
2. All files on the active drive that end in .COM
3. All files on drive B that begin with *S*

The solutions are as follows:

1. DIR M*
2. DIR *.COM
3. DIR B:S*

COPYING FILES

Making copies of files is an important capability to have in a computer system, especially a floppy diskette system. Although a double-density diskette holds about 360 kilobytes and a high-capacity diskette holds 1.2 megabytes, it is often necessary to transfer files from one diskette to another for organizational or backup purposes.

The COPY command copies files from one device to another. COPY has many uses. The first use discussed here is copying files from one disk to another. (A disk is only one type of device, but it is the most important and commonly used one.)

The general form of the COPY command is

COPY *Source Destination*

or

COPY *OldFile(s) NewFile(s)*

The first name is the name of the file(s) to copy. The second name is the name of the new file(s) to be created. When the copy operation is complete, both files (or sets of files) will contain the same information.

You will find many uses for the COPY command. You might want to make a secondary copy of a file you are working on, or you may want to make a back-up copy of a file on another disk as a precaution against data loss. You may want to make a replica of several files at the same time, perhaps from someone else's disk to yours. The following sections explore these and other uses of the COPY command.

Making Secondary Copies

You can easily make a second working copy of a file with the COPY command. You can then retain the original while working on and modifying the copy. For example, you can enter

COPY BUDGET.TXT BUDGET.BAK

A directory listing of your disk would then show two files where there had previously been only one, as you can see in Figure 3.5.

Making Backup Copies

Using COPY, you can make a backup copy on another disk. Suppose that you want to place a copy of your PHONES.DAT file on the diskette in drive B. You can do this by entering

COPY PHONES.DAT B:

The command will create a copy of PHONES.DAT on the diskette in drive B, using the same file name. Store this backup diskette to protect yourself against the time when your original file or disk is inadvertently lost.

Making Multiple Copies

Multiple files can be simultaneously copied by using wildcards with the COPY command. For example, to copy all files with the .SYM extension to a diskette in drive B, you can enter

COPY *.SYM B:

New users frequently ask if a disk can contain two copies of the same file if the file is copied twice to the same drive. The answer is no—a disk retains only one copy under any given file name. DOS will not allow two files to have exactly the same name on the same disk. If a file is copied to a disk that already has a file with

```
B>DIR

 Volume in drive B has no label
 Directory of  B:\

BUDGET86 TXT    15999   5-19-86   12:00p
BUDGET   TXT    13888   4-02-87    4:42p
        2 File(s)   286720 bytes free

B>COPY  BUDGET.TXT  BUDGET.BAK
        1 File(s) copied

B>DIR

 Volume in drive B has no label
 Directory of  B:\

BUDGET86 TXT    15999   5-19-86   12:00p
BUDGET   TXT    13888   4-02-87    4:42p
BUDGET   BAK    13888   4-02-87    4:42p
        3 File(s)    272384 bytes free

B>_
```

FIGURE 3.5: Creating a secondary or backup copy of any file. Copies are easily made by specifying the old file name as the COPY command *source* parameter and a new file name as the COPY command *destination* parameter. By convention, secondary copies are usually given the .BAK extension.

that name, DOS erases the old file and then writes the copy of the new file. *You receive no warning of this.* Thus, you can erase all the information contained in a file by accidentally copying another file of the same name to the same disk. When this happens, the old file is said to be *overwritten* by the new file, and you are said to be in big trouble! (However, as you will see in Chapter 4, when you learn about the possibility of different directories on a disk, a disk can contain two similarly named files if the two files are located in different directories.)

> *Tip:* When you're concerned that a wildcard COPY command may overwrite a file you want to retain, use a DIR command first with the same wildcard specification. Then you can check for duplicate file names before executing the copy operation. If a file that you want to retain has the same name as the file you want to copy, either change the file name on the destination drive or specify a unique name as the COPY command destination (COPY *OldFile* B:*NewName*).

Take a moment to practice using the COPY command. If a colleague or friend has some spreadsheet or database files or even games that you've been wanting, now's the time to copy them. Of course, never make a copy that violates a copyright.

Format a blank diskette and carefully copy the desired files from the original diskette to your new one. If your system has two diskette drives, you can specify a transfer from drive A to drive B by typing

COPY A:*FileNames* **B:***FileNames*

If you only have one diskette, you may have to first transfer the files to drive C by typing

COPY A:*FileNames* **C:***FileNames*

Then you can switch diskettes and transfer the files onto the new (destination) diskette by entering

COPY C:*FileNames* **A:***FileNames*

Copying Entire Disks

One of the most common uses of the COPY command is to copy all the files from one diskette to another. This is necessary because diskettes can become worn from use over a long period of time; copying the files onto a new diskette solves this problem. Also, keeping multiple copies of important files protects you against computer failures, human errors, and accidents such as fires.

You've already been introduced to the DISKCOPY command for copying all files from one disk onto another disk. Why should you consider using a version of the COPY command? The distinctions between the two commands are subtle. DISKCOPY copies the original disk exactly, *retaining all noncontiguity*. The following version of the COPY command usually rewrites files onto contiguous tracks and sectors on the new disk, improving future disk-access speed. The net result is probable improvement in the performance or responsiveness of your programs.

To copy all files on the diskette in drive A to the diskette in drive B, enter

COPY *.* B:

Warning: If the destination diskette (in drive B in this example) already contains some files, it may not have enough space to hold all the existing files from the disk in drive A as well. If this is the case, DOS will display the message "Insufficient Space." The best solution is to use a freshly formatted diskette or to erase files in advance on the destination diskette to ensure that enough space exists to receive the source diskette's files.

Copying Data to Other Devices

The COPY command can exchange information between the disk and other devices such as the screen and keyboard (CON) or the printer (LPT1). The following command sends the contents of a file named PHONES.DAT to the screen. The name of the destination device, CON, stands for console device (the monitor).

COPY PHONES.DAT CON:

COPY also allows the user to enter text into a file. If you use CON as the source device, you can use the keyboard to transfer information from the keyboard through the computer to a disk file.

If you enter the command

COPY CON: TEXT1.DAT

nothing seems to happen, except that the DOS A> prompt does not appear. This is an indication that you are no longer at the system level. DOS will now allow you to enter text directly from the keyboard, and anything that you type will eventually be stored in the file TEXT1.DAT. You could enter

**This is an example of keyboard entry
into a text file.**

or any other text lines, pressing Return after each line. You would then need to enter the character that DOS uses to mark the end of a file, Ctrl-Z (sometimes shown as ^ Z). You obtain this unusual character by holding down the Ctrl key and pressing the letter Z. The symbol ^ Z will then appear on the screen.

Note: The colon (:) after a device name (as in CON:) is not strictly necessary, since DOS will figure out what you mean. However, it's good form to enter the colon, if only for consistency with the way you enter drive identifiers (such as A: and C:).

To complete the file, press Return. The disk drive will spin, and all the lines of text that you typed at the keyboard will be saved as a file. To see the data, you simply reverse the items in the COPY command and enter

COPY TEXT1.DAT CON:

followed by Return. The text will be displayed just as you entered it. This is a convenient method for creating small text files quickly. Your alternative is to use a line editor (like EDLIN, which is contained in your DOS software and is described in Chapter 6) or a word processor (which offers many more text-manipulation facilities).

Combining File Copies

You can also use COPY to join two or more files together, which allows you to gather up small data files into a single, large file. This facility is sometimes useful when you have several small documents, all of which need to be word processed. To combine file copies, enter, for example,

**COPY CON: TEXT2.DAT
This is additional text that is stored
in another text file
^ Z**

pressing Return after each line. You then use the COPY command to join, or *concatenate,* these two files. The general form of this command is shown here. The + sign indicates the joining of text from two or more files.

> **COPY** *SourceFile(s) DestinationFile(s)*

or

> **COPY** *FirstFile* + *SecondFile* + *etc. CombinationFile*

To combine two existing files, for instance, TEXT1.DAT and TEXT2.DAT, you enter the following command:

> **COPY TEXT1.DAT + TEXT2.DAT COMBO.DAT**

To see the results, you enter

> **COPY COMBO.DAT CON:**

The resultant file, COMBO.DAT, will contain all the text lines from both of the two source files:

> **This is an example of keyboard entry**
> **into a text file.**
> **This is additional text that is stored**
> **in another text file.**

COMBINING FILES WITH WILDCARD CHARACTERS

You can also use wildcard characters to join text files. For example, if you want to join all the text files with the .DAT extension into a single file, you can enter this command:

> **COPY *.DAT ALL.TXT**

Using this form is simpler than typing "*file1* +*file2* +*file3* +..." if all the files have the same extension. This is another example of how wildcards can be helpful; it's also a good example of how to save time and effort by intelligently naming similar files with the same extension. You should be aware that in making a wildcard copy of this sort, the files will be copied in the order DOS finds them in the directory table.

Verifying Data Transfers Using the /V Switch

A useful switch with the COPY command is the /V switch. If you specify this switch in COPY operations, DOS checks the accuracy of the entire data transfer. Otherwise, the validity of the copy operation is not guaranteed.

Figure 3.6 illustrates a normal copy operation, in which COPY reads data from a source disk file into memory and then writes it to a destination-disk file. As the figure shows, a portion of memory acts as a *buffer* between the original source of the data (perhaps a disk file) and the destination of the data (perhaps another disk file). Chapter 12 describes DOS buffers in more detail. It's enough to know now that DOS reserves a portion of memory for the temporary storage of file information on its way to or from disk files.

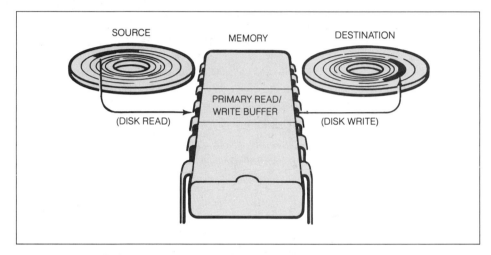

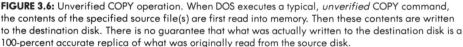

FIGURE 3.6: Unverified COPY operation. When DOS executes a typical, *unverified* COPY command, the contents of the specified source file(s) are first read into memory. Then these contents are written to the destination disk. There is no guarantee that what was actually written to the destination disk is a 100-percent accurate replica of what was originally read from the source disk.

Normally, DOS copies file information from a source file to a destination file by successively reading one buffer's worth of data into memory and then writing it to the destination drive. Usually, no problems occur. But if the destination drive has a hardware malfunction (unrecognized bad sectors, for example), the resulting destination file may not be an identical replica of the original, source file.

The /V switch eliminates this uncertainty about the success of a copy operation. Adding /V to the COPY command causes DOS to perform the steps depicted in Figure 3.7. In this verified copy operation, DOS undertakes an extra step. Each buffer's worth of information that is written to the destination file is also read back into memory. It is then reread to check for errors that may have occurred; if DOS discovers no errors, it assumes that the destination file has received the source file's data accurately. If the two files differ, DOS can try to rewrite the data again or simply report an error.

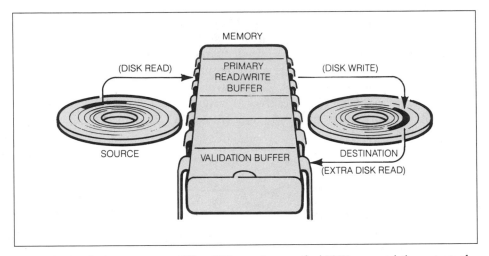

FIGURE 3.7: Verified copy operation. When DOS executes a *verified* COPY command, the contents of the specified source file(s) are first read into memory. Then these contents are written to the destination disk. Last, the data that was written is reread and compared to the data that was sent to be written. This extra step takes some time but ensures that any transmission errors are detected. When DOS finds an error, it retransmits the file data or issues an error message.

Since this validation procedure places an additional burden on your system, and since hardware malfunctions do not occur very often, you may want to add the /V switch only for especially important copy operations. The tradeoff is time versus security. However, if you want the security but don't want the bother of specifying /V all the time, DOS offers a special command. Entering VERIFY at the DOS prompt with the parameter ON (or OFF) appends (or does not append) a /V switch to all COPY commands. The command

VERIFY ON

followed by Return guarantees that all future COPY commands act like the one in Figure 3.7, using what is sometimes called *read-after-write* verification.

Using Ctrl-Z in ASCII and Binary File Copy Operations

You can use two other switches with the COPY command. Neither of them is used very frequently, but they are necessary in certain file-transfer situations. These switches are the /A, or ASCII, switch, and the /B, or binary, switch.

Since many of the files that you create and use are text, or ASCII, files, DOS assumes the /A switch whenever you copy file information to or from a character-oriented device. The reasoning here is quite straightforward. When receiving data character by character, an end-of-file mark (EOF) is critical to DOS being able to recognize when the end of the file is actually reached. Character-oriented devices require this mark as a necessary signal, so DOS assumes it will receive it (hence, the /A switch assumption) at the end of the file transmission.

Text files, by convention, are terminated by Ctrl-Z (a decimal-26 code) placed in the file. When source ASCII files are copied, DOS copies all data bytes in the file up to (but not including) the first Ctrl-Z encountered. At the other end of the transmission, when DOS creates the destination file(s), it adds Ctrl-Z to the file. This guarantees that the file is stored with a Ctrl-Z character, even if for some reason the source file lacked one.

Disk drives, on the other hand, are block-oriented devices. When data is transmitted to or from a block oriented device, the data is gathered into a transmission block of many characters at a time. Each block can consist of from one to several sectors (512 bytes). DOS obtains the actual file size from the directory entry and therefore has no real need for an EOF character.

For example, the following command copies the first.txt file to a first.bak file:

COPY /A FIRST.TXT FIRST.BAK

The first.txt file is read *up to* the Ctrl-Z, and the first.bak file is written with a trailing Ctrl-Z added to it.

The /B switch acts as the reverse of /A. This binary switch acts on files other than standard text files. Although usually thought of as applicable to program files, it in fact applies equally well to many other types of purely data files. In essence, this switch directs DOS to ignore the Ctrl-Z code during a transfer operation. It forces DOS to read the byte length of the source file(s) from the directory table and to transfer that many bytes from the source to the destination.

Many program and data files contain the decimal value of 26 as either plain data or an assembler instruction. Transferring such files as binary files eliminates the possibility of losing the end of the file. Erroneously transferring a program file with the /A switch almost always truncates the end of the file.

File transfer between disk drives always presumes binary transfer. Even when a file is a standard text file, the binary method still is used, even though more bytes than are necessary are transferred. The actual file's meaningful data may end in the middle of the final sector transmitted, but the entire final sector is nevertheless transferred.

Since the COPY command can copy data between devices as well as files, you can actually transfer information across communications lines. The following line accepts a transmission stream of bytes from the second serial port until the destination device receives a Ctrl-Z character, and it sends the received data to the file RESUME.DTA; no Ctrl-Z is added at the end of RESUME.DTA because the /B switch is specified.

COPY COM2: RESUME.DTA /B

As you can see in these examples, the placement of the /A or /B switch is important. Each switch applies to the file name just before it on the command line, as well as to succeeding file names, up to the next switch on the command line, if any other switches exist. Hence, the source data from COM2: is assumed to be ASCII data (the default assumption for nondisk sources), and the destination file RESUME.DTA is explicitly defined as binary, because of the /B switch that immediately follows the file name.

USING THE XCOPY COMMAND TO TRANSFER FILES

A special command called XCOPY (available only in DOS 3.2 or 3.3) allows more sophisticated file transfers between disks and directories. XCOPY is preferable for multifile transfers because it usually performs more quickly than COPY. XCOPY is also preferable for transferring files that exist in multiple directories, because XCOPY understands better than COPY how to select files located in *subdirectories,* which are subdivisions of existing directories on a disk. You'll learn more about subdirectories in Chapter 4.

Note: You cannot use XCOPY to transfer multiple files to a printer. XCOPY is designed for disk transfers only.

The general format of the XCOPY command is

XCOPY *SourceFile(s) DestinationFile(s) /Switches*

where *SourceFile(s)* and *DestinationFile(s)* are specified as they are with the COPY command. Using */Switches* properly can greatly expand the range of files encompassed. Try performing some sample operations using the files contained in three sections of a disk, as shown in Figure 3.8. Figures 3.9 and 3.10 show conventional directory listings of the files involved.

Here is a simple example of the XCOPY command:

XCOPY \HELP*.* A:

This command copies all files in the HELP directory to the disk in drive A. As you can see in Figure 3.11, DOS echoes the file names to the screen as they are copied.

The unique aspect of the XCOPY command is hidden behind the message "Reading source file(s)," which appears on the screen. The COPY command reads a source file and then writes a destination file. The XCOPY command first reads as many source files as possible into available memory; only then does it stop to write the destination files. Since memory operations occur much more rapidly than disk operations, the overall operation speed is increased. Simply said, less disk work and more memory work means files are transferred more rapidly.

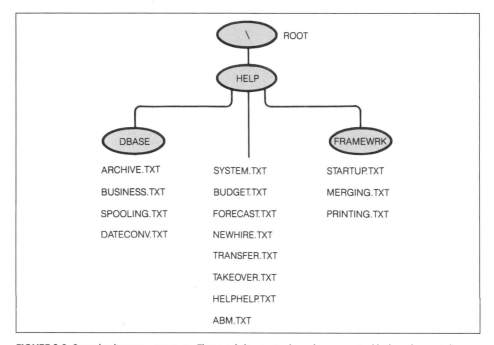

FIGURE 3.8: Sample directory structure. Three subdirectories have been created below the root directory. These subdirectories, called DBASE, HELP, and FRAMEWRK, each contain a separate set of .TXT files. In fact, the DBASE and FRAMEWRK subdirectories were created *within* the HELP directory.

```
C>DIR \HELP

  Volume in drive C is ROBBINS
  Directory of  C:\HELP

.              <DIR>       5-Ø3-87    8:16a
..             <DIR>       5-Ø3-87    8:16a
SYSTEM   TXT      328      1-13-87    7:5Øp
BUDGET   TXT     2186      1-22-87    6:Ø8p
FORECAST TXT      256      1-Ø2-87   12:25p
NEWHIRE  TXT     1781      2-26-87    6:39p
TRANSFER TXT     4429      1-19-87    2:55p
TAKEOVER TXT      621      1-Ø1-87   12:16p
HELPHELP TXT      258      1-14-87    2:41p
ABM      TXT      383      1-13-87    6:33p
DBASE          <DIR>       5-Ø3-87    8:24a
FRAMEWRK       <DIR>       5-Ø3-87    8:24a
      12 File(s)   113Ø496 bytes free

C>_
```

FIGURE 3.9: The HELP directory. This directory contains 12 separate entries. Eight of them are text entries, and the remaining 4 are DIR, or directory, entries. All 4 directory entries are dated 5/3/87, signifying that they were all created on the same date. The bottom line indicates that DOS views all of these entries as files, since they appear as directory entries in DOS's disk-management scheme.

```
     Volume in drive C is ROBBINS
     Directory of  C:\HELP\DBASE

     .            <DIR>        5-Ø3-87    8:24a
     ..           <DIR>        5-Ø3-87    8:24a
     ARCHIVE  TXT     1152   10-25-85    6:46p
     BUSINESS TXT      561    4-16-87   1Ø:Ø4p
     SPOOLING TXT     2816   10-25-85    6:38p
     DATECONV TXT     1536   10-25-85    6:41p
            6 File(s)   1124352 bytes free

  C>DIR \HELP\FRAMEWRK

     Volume in drive C is ROBBINS
     Directory of  C:\HELP\FRAMEWRK

     .            <DIR>        5-Ø3-87    8:24a
     ..           <DIR>        5-Ø3-87    8:24a
     STARTUP  TXT      195    3-Ø5-86    9:25a
     MERGING  TXT      638    2-19-86   1Ø:56a
     PRINTING TXT      147    2-19-86   1Ø:58a
            5 File(s)   1124352 bytes free

  C>_
```

FIGURE 3.10: The DBASE and FRAMEWRK directories. Both directories are located in the HELP directory, which itself is in the root (\) directory. Notice that the screen displays the number of free bytes on the disk, rather than the (possibly more useful) number of free bytes in each directory.

```
  C>XCOPY  \HELP\*.*  A:

  Reading source file(s)...
  \HELP\SYSTEM.TXT
  \HELP\BUDGET.TXT
  \HELP\FORECAST.TXT
  \HELP\NEWHIRE.TXT
  \HELP\TRANSFER.TXT
  \HELP\TAKEOVER.TXT
  \HELP\HELPHELP.TXT
  \HELP\ABM.TXT
          8 File(s) copied

  C>_
```

FIGURE 3.11: XCOPY reading files into memory and writing destination files. Unlike COPY, which reads each specified file and then writes it, the XCOPY command reads several files before it begins to write any data at all. The number of files read is only a function of how much free memory exists; this memory is used as a large input/output buffer by XCOPY. DOS displays the name of each file as it is read into memory.

Switches for the XCOPY Command

Now look at the XCOPY command's switches in order of their importance. These switches are listed in the reference entry for XCOPY at the end of this chapter.

THE /S SWITCH

The most powerful switch is /S, which allows you to select files located in the subdirectory structure. Notice in Figure 3.11 that the expected eight .TXT files in the HELP directory were copied. That's the same result as would have been obtained by using the COPY command, but the operation proceeded more quickly.

Figure 3.12 shows the direct effect of using the /S switch. The switch directs DOS to look in all subdirectories of HELP for file names that match the specified *.TXT wildcard. As simply as that, the additional four .TXT files in the HELP\DBASE subdirectory are copied, along with the additional three .TXT files in the HELP\FRAMEWRK subdirectory. If the respective directories do not already exist on the destination disk, DOS automatically creates them and then copies the files to them.

```
C>XCOPY  \HELP\*.*  A: /S

Reading source file(s)...
\HELP\SYSTEM.TXT
\HELP\BUDGET.TXT
\HELP\FORECAST.TXT
\HELP\NEWHIRE.TXT
\HELP\TRANSFER.TXT
\HELP\TAKEOVER.TXT
\HELP\HELPHELP.TXT
\HELP\ABM.TXT
\HELP\DBASE\ARCHIVE.TXT
\HELP\DBASE\BUSINESS.TXT
\HELP\DBASE\SPOOLING.TXT
\HELP\DBASE\DATECONV.TXT
\HELP\FRAMEWRK\STARTUP.TXT
\HELP\FRAMEWRK\MERGING.TXT
\HELP\FRAMEWRK\PRINTING.TXT
        15 File(s) copied

C>_
```

FIGURE 3.12: The /S switch. In this figure, /S searches all subdirectories for wildcard matches. Each file in the current directory and any subdirectory of the current directory that matches the wildcard specification is read and copied. The file's name is displayed as it is read.

THE /P SWITCH

You can further control the copy operation by employing the /P switch. This switch asks DOS to prompt you (hence, /P) to confirm the copy operation for each file whose name matches the wildcard specification, thus giving you control over whether to include each file name in the copy operation.

Look at the example of an XCOPY transfer in Figure 3.13, which uses the same /S switch as in the previous example but asks you to respond to a prompt for each file. In the figure, the prompt was answered affirmatively (Y) only four times. The destination drive consequently received copies of only the four selected files. These files were

- HELP\BUDGET.TXT
- HELP\FORECAST.TXT
- HELP\DBASE\BUSINESS.TXT
- HELP\FRAMEWRK\MERGING.TXT

Notice that two of these files are in subdirectories of the HELP directory. The /S switch also ensures that the same subdirectory structure is recreated on the destination disk (if it is not there already), as Figure 3.14 shows. Figure 3.15 verifies that the specified files are also copied accurately and into the proper subdirectories.

```
C>XCOPY  \HELP\*.*  B:  /S /P
\HELP\SYSTEM.TXT (Y/N)? N
\HELP\BUDGET.TXT (Y/N)? Y
\HELP\FORECAST.TXT (Y/N)? Y
\HELP\NEWHIRE.TXT (Y/N)? N
\HELP\TRANSFER.TXT (Y/N)? N
\HELP\TAKEOVER.TXT (Y/N)? N
\HELP\HELPHELP.TXT (Y/N)? N
\HELP\ABM.TXT (Y/N)? N
\HELP\DBASE\ARCHIVE.TXT (Y/N)? N
\HELP\DBASE\BUSINESS.TXT (Y/N)? Y
\HELP\DBASE\SPOOLING.TXT (Y/N)? N
\HELP\DBASE\DATECONV.TXT (Y/N)? N
\HELP\FRAMEWRK\STARTUP.TXT (Y/N)? N
\HELP\FRAMEWRK\MERGING.TXT (Y/N)? Y
\HELP\FRAMEWRK\PRINTING.TXT (Y/N)? N
        4 File(s) copied

C>_
```

FIGURE 3.13: The /P switch prompt before copying. Adding a /P switch to the XCOPY command forces DOS to pause whenever it finds a match for the file names specified. You are prompted as to whether you want to include each file in the XCOPY copy operation.

```
C>DIR B:

 Volume in drive B has no label
 Directory of  B:\

BUDGET   TXT     2186   1-22-87   6:08p
FORECAST TXT      256   1-02-87  12:25p
DBASE        <DIR>      5-03-87   9:20a
FRAMEWRK     <DIR>      5-03-87   9:20a
       4 File(s)    173568 bytes free

C>_
```

FIGURE 3.14: Destination drive after using /S and /P. In the previous figure, the HELP directory was the current directory, and the user responded Y only to the file prompts for budget.txt and forecast.txt. Since the transfer was to the B drive, only these two files were copied to the B drive's root directory.

```
C>DIR B:\DBASE

 Volume in drive B has no label
 Directory of  B:\DBASE

.            <DIR>      5-03-87   9:20a
..           <DIR>      5-03-87   9:20a
BUSINESS TXT      561   4-16-87  10:04p
       3 File(s)    173568 bytes free

C>DIR B:\FRAMEWRK

 Volume in drive B has no label
 Directory of  B:\FRAMEWRK

.            <DIR>      5-03-87   9:20a
..           <DIR>      5-03-87   9:20a
MERGING  TXT      638   2-19-86  10:56a
       3 File(s)    173568 bytes free

C>_
```

FIGURE 3.15: Accurately created destination subdirectories. The /S switch used in the previous prompted transfer accounted for the automatic creation of directories DBASE and FRAMEWRK on the B drive. The business.txt file was the only file from the former DBASE directory (in the C:\HELP directory) that received a Y answer to the Y/N prompt, and merging.txt was the only file in the former FRAMEWRK directory (in the C:\HELP directory) to receive the Y response.

THE /D SWITCH

Another important switch, /D, allows you to specify that all files be copied if their creation dates are the same as or later than a specified date. The format for this switch is /D:*mm-dd-yy* unless you have a DOS version with a different international date format (see Chapter 11). In that case, you can specify the date in whatever format your system recognizes. For example, in Figure 3.16 all files in the RESULTS directory that were created on or after October 1, 1988, are copied to drive A.

```
C>DIR \RESULTS

 Volume in drive C is ROBBINS
 Directory of  C:\RESULTS

                <DIR>      1-07-88    6:09p
      . .       <DIR>      1-07-88    6:09p
 TEST23    DTA     945    10-12-88    4:45a
 WEEK34    TXT     255     6-17-88    9:46a
 TEST467   DTA    1041    11-16-88    4:45a
 FIGURES   TXT   10555     1-07-88    6:17p
 RESULTS   DTA    3109     8-14-88    6:22p
 RESULTS   TXT    5266     7-04-88    4:43a
        8 File(s)   3907584 bytes free

C>XCOPY \RESULTS\*.* A: /D:10/1/88

 Reading source file(s)...
 \RESULTS\TEST23.DTA
 \RESULTS\TEST467.DTA
        2 File(s) copied

C>_
```

FIGURE 3.16: Specifying dates with XCOPY and /D. The /D switch allows you to specify a starting date for XCOPY transfers. In this example, only the two files (out of six total files) that were created or modified on or after October 1, 1988, are selected by XCOPY for transfer to drive A.

LESS COMMONLY USED SWITCHES

The remaining switches are of less practical importance. The /A switch selects files that are marked for backup (see Chapter 18 for a discussion of backup files). This switch does not change the archive attribute. The /M switch also copies files that are marked for backup, but it *does* change the archive attribute to indicate that the files have been backed up. For more information about the archive attribute, see the ATTRIB command in Chapter 19.

The /V switch performs the same task as it does with the COPY command: It requests the read-after-write verification step. The /W switch simply effects a brief pause and asks you to press any key to begin copying files.

OTHER FUNDAMENTAL FILE-MANAGEMENT ACTIVITIES

Typing text files, renaming files, and deleting files are fundamental file-management activities that you will perform often. This section discusses the commands used in these tasks. More advanced file-management commands are presented later in this book.

Typing Text Files

The TYPE command is similar to the COPY CON command. It can display the contents of any standard text or ASCII file. Using TYPE is also the best way to view the contents of *batch files,* which are simple ASCII text files. In both cases, the files consist solely of letters, numbers, and symbols that can be typed on a standard keyboard. Although you won't learn about DOS batch files in depth until Chapter 7, you should take note of the TYPE command now.

Many business application packages include a file called README.TXT or some similar name. This file usually contains information that arrived too late to be included in the printed user's manual. Using the TYPE command is the easiest way to read this file. Enter

TYPE README.TXT

Tip: Remember to use the Ctrl-S key combination to stop and start the display of the README.TXT file contents. You'll learn in Chapter 17 how to use the MORE command at the DOS prompt to display one screenful of information at a time.

Changing File Names

You can change the name of a file without affecting the contents of that file. You may, for instance, want to change some file names so that you can take advantage of the ? or * wildcard to deal with blocks of files. Consider the following example.

During the writing of this book, many screen images were captured and a number of text-file figures were created. The program that captures screen images gives these images such names as SCREEN01.CAP, SCREEN02.CAP, and so on—using a straight numerical sequence. But for both publisher and author, it is more convenient to name the images using chapter and figure numbers, since then all figures can be managed together using wildcard expressions. When someone needs to see the figures for Chapter 8, for example, it is much easier to look for FIG8*.* than to remember or look up the numbers for those figures.

Figure 3.17 shows a wide directory listing of a group of figures prepared for this book. At the bottom of the figure, the screen lists the file containing the most recently captured screen image, SCREEN03.CAP. Using the DOS RENAME command (see Figure 3.18), you can change the SCREEN03 file name without changing the data inside the file and still retain the extension by entering, for instance,

RENAME SCREEN03.CAP FIG8-12.CAP

This command changes SCREEN03.CAP to FIG8-12.CAP. Notice in Figure 3.18 that entering DIR SCREEN∗.CAP doesn't display any screen files, since the name of the only previously existing .CAP file was changed to FIG8-12.CAP.

The general format of the RENAME command is

RENAME *OldName NewName*

The first file name is the old name you want to change. The file name that follows is the new name the file will receive.

An important restriction on the RENAME command is that you can use it only for a single file on a single disk. You *cannot* use RENAME to simultaneously

```
C>DIR/W  FIG*.CAP

  Volume in drive C is ROBBINS
  Directory of  C:\PROGRAMS\FW\SYBEX

  FIG11-1   CAP      FIG11-2   CAP      FIG11-3   CAP      FIG11-5   CAP      FIG11-6B CAP
  FIG2-10   CAP      FIG2-11   CAP      FIG2-12   CAP      FIG2-6    CAP      FIG2-7    CAP
  FIG2-8A   CAP      FIG2-8B   CAP      FIG4-10A CAP      FIG4-10B CAP      FIG4-10C CAP
  FIG4-14   CAP      FIG4-15   CAP      FIG4-2    CAP      FIG4-3    CAP      FIG4-4    CAP
  FIG4-5    CAP      FIG4-6    CAP      FIG4-7    CAP      FIG4-8    CAP      FIG4-9    CAP
  FIG7-3    CAP      FIG7-4    CAP      FIG7-5    CAP
        28 File(s)   2293760 bytes free

C>DIR SCREEN*.CAP

  Volume in drive C is ROBBINS
  Directory of  C:\PROGRAMS\FW\SYBEX

  SCREEN03 CAP     4256   3-30-87   9:38a
        1 File(s)   2287616 bytes free

C>_
```

FIGURE 3.17: Listing of figure and screen files. When directories contain many different types of files, you can use the DIR command to present a more readable listing of the contents. When you have established a useful naming convention, you can use wildcards to separately list groups of similarly named files. In this figure, all file names beginning with FIG and having the extension .CAP are listed separately from the SCREEN∗.CAP files, even though all the files are located in the same SYBEX directory.

```
C>RENAME  SCREEN03.CAP  FIG8-12.CAP

C>DIR/W FIG*.CAP

 Volume in drive C is ROBBINS
 Directory of  C:\PROGRAMS\FW\SYBEX

FIG11-1   CAP     FIG11-2   CAP     FIG11-3   CAP     FIG11-5   CAP     FIG11-6B CAP
FIG2-10   CAP     FIG2-11   CAP     FIG2-12   CAP     FIG2-6    CAP     FIG2-7    CAP
FIG2-8A   CAP     FIG2-8B   CAP     FIG4-10A  CAP     FIG4-10B  CAP     FIG4-10C CAP
FIG4-14   CAP     FIG4-15   CAP     FIG4-2    CAP     FIG4-3    CAP     FIG4-4    CAP
FIG4-5    CAP     FIG4-6    CAP     FIG4-7    CAP     FIG4-8    CAP     FIG4-9    CAP
FIG7-3    CAP     FIG7-4    CAP     FIG7-5    CAP     FIG8-12   CAP
        29 File(s)   2281472 bytes free

C>DIR SCREEN*.CAP

 Volume in drive C is ROBBINS
 Directory of  C:\PROGRAMS\FW\SYBEX

File not found

C>_
```

FIGURE 3.18: Using the RENAME command. Using the RENAME command to change file names naturally affects the next listing of the directory contents. The SCREEN03.CAP file no longer appears, because its name was changed to FIG8-12.CAP (which now appears in the FIG*.CAP group's listing).

copy a file from one disk to another while renaming it—you use the COPY command for that particular chore. RENAME simply changes the name of a file, whereas COPY creates a new file entirely. With COPY, you begin with one file and end up with two; with RENAME, you begin with one file and end up with the same file, though it has a different name.

You can use the * and ? wildcards with the RENAME command. For example, if you want to rename all files with the extension .CMD so that the files instead use the extension .PRG, you can do so with one command:

RENAME *.CMD *.PRG

This sort of operation often is required when you switch from one system to another, or when a software manufacturer makes a major change in its naming conventions. For example, if you need to run programs written in Ashton-Tate's dBASE II under the auspices of your dBASE III PLUS, you would perform exactly this type of renaming task.

The RENAME command also helps you protect your files from unauthorized access. If you are not the only person with access to your computer and disks, you may desire a measure of security for some of your data files. You can change an obvious file name like BUDGET.WK1 to TEMP.NDX, a clearly misleading name, so that prying eyes will not be as likely to locate your sensitive budget file.

Take a moment now to try this renaming technique on any files for which you'd like to restrict access. But be careful: Don't forget the new file name you choose, and don't select a name (like TEMP.NDX) that makes a file sound dispensable if anyone else using your disk is at all likely to delete files.

Erasing Files

From time to time you will want to get rid of a file on a disk. The ERASE command will do this for you. The general form of the command is

ERASE *FileName(s)*

The following command will erase the file PHONES.DAT from drive A:

ERASE phones.dat

The ? and * wildcard characters also work with ERASE, so you can erase groups of related files with a single command. Be careful with ERASE—it erases files without asking for confirmation. The following command erases all .TXT files:

ERASE *.TXT

As you were advised in the section on the COPY command, *be certain* when you issue a command with wildcards that it will affect only the files you intend. You should always precede an ERASE request that uses wildcards with a DIR command, using the same wildcard specification, to ensure that you know which files will be deleted by the command.

The only time DOS will ask you to confirm an ERASE command is when you specify

ERASE *.*

This command erases all files. Be sure of your intention if you answer yes to that question. If you make a mistake and accidentally erase files you didn't mean to, *stop immediately.* Although you may shut your computer off, do nothing else until you buy a file recovery program. See Chapter 20 for more information.

The most common use for the ERASE command is to clean up disks that have been in use for a while. Old versions of data files often proliferate. When early copies of memos and other word processed documents consume needed space on a disk, you can use ERASE to get rid of these unnecessary files.

The DEL Command: A Warning

The DEL command works exactly the same as ERASE. However, you should avoid DEL—it's much closer in appearance to the commonly used DIR command, but devastatingly different in its effect. Too many people have typed

DEL *.* when they intended to type DIR *.*. To avoid making the same mistake, use the ERASE command when you want to remove files from your disks.

DOS COMMANDS USED IN FILE MANIPULATION

This section explains all of the DOS file-manipulation commands mentioned in this chapter.

COPY

The COPY command has three distinct uses. You can use it to duplicate files, to access devices, or to concatenate files.

SYNTAX

COPY [/A][/B]*SourceFile* [[/A][/B][*DestFile*][/A][/B][/V]]
COPY [/A][/B]*Source* [/A][/B][*Dest*][/A][/B][/V]
COPY [/A][/B]*SourceFile1* + *SourceFile2*[/A][/B] + ...[*ConcatFile*][/A][/B][/V]

/A	is used with *SourceFile, Source,* or *SourceFile1, SourceFile2* to read data up to but not including the first Ctrl-Z (end-of-file) character; the file is treated as an ASCII file. This is the default setting for concatenation (format 3).
/A	is used with with *DestFile, Dest,* or *ConcatFile* to write a Ctrl-Z character at the end of the file.
/B	the default setting for file duplication (format 1)—is used with *SourceFile, Source,* or *SourceFile1, SourceFile2* to copy a number of bytes equal to the number of bytes given as the length in the directory for the file.
/B	is used with *DestFile, Dest,* or *ConcatFile* to make sure that no Ctrl-Z character is written at the end of the file.
/V	causes DOS to check whether all files were copied successfully. It is used only with transfers to disk files.
SourceFile	is the drive, path, file name, and extension of the file to be copied.
DestFile	is the drive, path, file name, and extension of the file to which *SourceFile* will be copied.
Source and *Dest*	can be either device or file specifications, although DOS allows only ASCII files to be read from a device.

SourceFile1 and *SourceFile2*	are files to be added together (*SourceFile2* is added to the end of *SourceFile1,* and so on).
ConcatFile	is the file that contains the concatenation of the source files.

These switches affect the file immediately preceding the place where the switch is used, as well as all files following it, until the next time the switch is used.

TYPE

Internal.

USAGE

Duplicating files with COPY, using the first format of this command, allows you versatility in moving files around the disk system. You can copy the contents of entire directories and then move them to another disk. Without COPY, you could not transfer newly purchased programs from diskettes to your hard disk or copy files to a diskette for another system.

The second format of COPY is especially useful for printing multiple files at once, which cannot be done with the TYPE command.

The third format of the COPY command allows files to be concatenated; that is, ASCII-type files can be added to the end of one another to form one large file.

Note that copies of read-only files created with COPY will *not* be read-only files. Note also that if you do not specify a destination file in the third format of the COPY command, all source files will be appended to the end of the first source file.

EXAMPLES

To copy the file SK.COM, enter the following command:

COPY A:SK.COM B:

You can just as easily copy this file from drive A to drive C. For instance, to copy the file so that it appears in a drive C directory containing utility software, enter

COPY A:SK.COM C:\UTILITY

All copies placed under the utility directory have the same name as the original file on the diskette in drive A.

Copying all files from a new application program to a newly created directory on a hard disk is easy with the COPY command. The following sequence makes the DBMS directory the current default directory on drive C and then copies all files from the drive A diskette into that directory:

CD \DBMS
COPY A:*.*

You can also make a backup directory to house backup copies of all spreadsheet files, for example. The following command sequence creates a backup directory and then transfers all WK1 files into that directory, giving them new extensions (WKB) in the process. The base names of the files remain the same.

MD \LOTUS\BACKUPS
CD \LOTUS\DATA
COPY *.WK1 \LOTUS\BACKUPS*.WKB

You can also use COPY to consolidate a group of text files, so that you can more easily edit small files with a word processor, possibly to produce a consolidated report. The following example combines three separate text files into one.

COPY STUDY.TXT + RESULTS.TXT + ANALYSIS.TXT
SUMMARY.RPT

The separate text files—STUDT, REPORT, and ANALYSIS—are merged into a new file called SUMMARY.RPT. The new report file is created on the default drive with the current date and time. Be sure to specify a destination file such as SUMMARY.RPT. If you do not, DOS combines the files and places them in the first specified file of the collection. (You may sometimes want the files placed in the first specified file to avoid specifying a separate destination file.)

You can also use wildcards to combine several files. For example, you can combine all files with the .TXT extension into one complete report with the following command:

COPY *.TXT TOTAL.RPT

DEL

This command removes files from the directory. The files are still physically present on the disk and can be retrieved by using certain non-DOS disk utilities (such as Norton utilities), but they are not accessible using the directory structure.

SYNTAX

DEL *FileSpec*

FileSpec   is an optional drive and path, plus the file name and extension, of each file to be deleted. Wildcards are allowed.

TYPE

Internal.

USAGE

The DEL command is most often used to erase an individual file by specifying its name to free up space on a disk. The other most common use for this command, using wildcards, removes all files from a diskette or from a subdirectory of a hard disk.

An alternate command, ERASE, performs exactly the same function as DEL. Many users prefer the ERASE command because its letters are more distinct from the other three-letter command, DIR.

When you issue the command DEL *.*, which deletes all files in the current directory, DOS displays the warning "Are you sure (Y/N)?" to verify that you really wish to take such a drastic action. Issuing the DEL command with a subdirectory as the *FileSpec* parameter deletes all files in that subdirectory, but not the subdirectory itself. You must use the RD command to remove an empty subdirectory.

EXAMPLES

You can delete an individual file or use wildcards to delete multiple files at the same time. The following example deletes the file 1987.WK1:

    DEL 1987.WK1

You can use a wildcard to delete all backup files in any directory:

    DEL \DBMS*.BAK

This command deletes all backup files from the DBMS directory.

You can erase the complete contents of any particular directory by specifying the directory name itself as a parameter of this command. For example, to remove all files from the CAD\DATA directory, enter

    DEL \CAD\DATA

RESTRICTIONS

You cannot use DEL to delete read-only files or any subdirectory still containing files.

DIR

The DIR command offers several ways for you to see what files are on a disk. Without this command, it would be extremely difficult, if not impossible, to operate a computer system of any size.

SYNTAX

DIR [*FileSpec*][/P][/W]

> *FileSpec* is an optional drive and path, plus the file name and extension, of the file that is the object of the command.
>
> /P causes the computer to prompt you to continue listing directory entries if the listing is longer than one screen.
>
> /W causes the directory listing to be displayed in wide format (without listing the file size and date and time of creation or modification), with entries listed horizontally as well as vertically.

All DIR parameters represented by *FileSpec* are completely independent of one another. They can be used in any combination, either alone or together, to limit the directory listing.

TYPE

Internal.

USAGE

DIR is one of the most commonly used DOS commands. It displays status information about files on a disk. Its various forms display the names of files on different disks, information about a file's size and the date and time of file creation or last modification, the number of free bytes on the drive you are referencing, and the total number of files on a drive that meet a specified criterion.

RESTRICTIONS

The DIR command does not list hidden files.

EXAMPLES

Suppose you had created a new directory (in anticipation of your upcoming switch to a new operating system) called OS2. Entering

DIR C:\OS2

displays the label (volume) of the disk in drive C and the name, size, and date and time of last modification of each file in the OS2 directory on drive C.

You can compact the display by eliminating the size and date and time columns and displaying only file names in five parallel columns. The /W switch manages the creation of this wide display.

DIR C: /W

The command displays the same file names for the current working directory of drive C as the preceding command. This time, however, only the file names are displayed, in five columns.

ERASE

The ERASE command is identical to the DEL command. See DEL in this chapter for syntax and examples.

RENAME (REN)

The RENAME command (which can be shortened to REN) performs the very useful function of renaming a file.

SYNTAX

REN[AME] *OldFile NewFile*

OldFile   is the optional drive and path, plus the file name and extension, of the file that will be renamed. Wildcards are allowed.

NewFile   is a new file name and extension for *OldFile*. Wildcards are allowed. The *NewFile* parameter does not require or accept a prefixed drive and path.

TYPE

Internal.

USAGE

The RENAME command is often used simply to give an old file a more meaningful name, such as one that suggests the file's contents. Also, when data files are shared, a new owner may want to rename the files according to a different nomenclature. Last, you may want to rename individual files to hide them from the prying eyes of other users on systems that are shared.

RESTRICTIONS

You cannot use RENAME to give a subdirectory a new name. You cannot specify a drive for this command, and you can give a file on a particular drive a new name only on that same drive. Thus, you cannot type either a drive or a path in front of NewFile.

EXAMPLES

You can rename the BUDGET.TMP file as BUDGET.88 with the following command. (This example assumes that the original BUDGET file appears in the \LOTUS\DATA directory in drive D.)

REN D:\LOTUS\DATA\BUDGET.TMP BUDGET.88

BUDGET.88 still appears on the \LOTUS\DATA directory.

You cannot use the REN command to move a file from one directory or drive to another. A set of file names can all be changed at one time by using wildcards. For example, you can change all of the accounting files that begin with the letters ACC and have the extension .NEW so that they have the extension .OLD. To do so, enter the following command:

REN ACC*.NEW ACC*.OLD

TYPE

TYPE displays the contents of an ASCII file. ASCII files contain no control codes that affect the screen display; they appear as straight listings of data.

SYNTAX

TYPE *FileSpec*

> *FileSpec*   is the optional drive and path, plus the file name and extension, of the file to be displayed.

TYPE

Internal.

USAGE

The TYPE command is used principally to display, or type, a text file on your screen or on your printer. Using TYPE is a quick and easy way to view the contents of any text file or to obtain a quick hard copy of a small text file. (To print longer text files, use the PRINT command.)

Using TYPE with a non-ASCII file may have no effect, or it may display meaningless symbols on your screen. It can also lock up your system entirely. If this happens, reboot the system.

EXAMPLES

To type the file ANALYSIS.RPT on your screen, enter

TYPE ANALYSIS.RPT

To type the same file ANALYSIS.RPT on your printer, you would use redirection techniques. Enter

TYPE ANALYSIS.RPT > PRN

VERIFY

This command turns the DOS global verification feature on or off.

SYNTAX

VERIFY [ON | OFF]

ON   turns the VERIFY feature on.

OFF   turns VERIFY off. This is the default setting.

TYPE

Internal.

USAGE

When global verification is on, everything written to a file is checked buffer by buffer to ensure the accuracy of the transmission. This is a useful feature, but it decreases system speed. Use VERIFY ON when you must be completely sure of the validity of transferred file data—for example, during backup operations.

RESTRICTIONS

VERIFY will not work with network disks.

EXAMPLES

To invoke VERIFY, enter

VERIFY ON

This ensures that any files written to the disk are not corrupted by bad sectors. VERIFY remains in effect until you turn it off with the command

VERIFY OFF

If you enter VERIFY with no parameter, DOS displays the current value (on or off) of this switch.

XCOPY

This command copies one or more files.

SYNTAX

[*D:Path*]XCOPY [*FileSpec1*][*FileSpec2*][/A][/D:*mm-dd-yy*][/E][/M][/P]
[/S][/V][/W]

D:Path	is the drive and path where the command file is located if it is not in the current directory.
FileSpec1	is the necessary drive, path, and file-name specifications for the files to be copied. Wildcards are allowed.
FileSpec2	is the necessary drive, path, and file-name specifications for the files to be written to. Wildcards are allowed.
/A	copies only files with a set archive bit.
/D:*mm-dd-yy*	copies only files created or modified on or after the specified date; the date format depends on the COUNTRY specification.
/E	creates corresponding subdirectories on *FileSpec2* before copying (even if *FileSpec1* contains no files to transfer). When this switch is used, you must also select the /S

switch. The /E switch controls the output end of the procedure (writing), and the /S switch controls the input end of the same overall process (reading).

/M	copies files with a set archive bit and rescts the source file archive bit.
/P	prompts you before each file is copied.
/S	copies files from all subdirectories within the specified directory. Corresponding subdirectories will be created on *FileSpec2* for all *FileSpec1* directories that contain files.
/V	turns verification on during execution of this command only.
/W	causes XCOPY to prompt you to insert different disks before it executes.

TYPE

External.

USAGE

XCOPY works very quickly because it reads as many source files as it can fit into memory. Only then does it begin to write the files to the destination disk. In contrast, the COPY command reads and then writes files one after the other.

Because of its speed, XCOPY should become your command of choice for transferring groups of files between directories and drives. Unfortunately, you can use it effectively only with wildcards, as it is not sophisticated enough to allow you to specify a series of separately named files.

You can combine XCOPY's switches as well. The last example in the "Examples" section uses the /S switch to traverse the directory. If you want DOS to pause and ask you to verify the copying of *each* file, you can simply add the /P switch.

RESTRICTIONS

XCOPY does not copy to or from devices. It also does not copy hidden files from the source location and will not overwrite read-only files at the destination location.

EXAMPLES

To copy all files in the \LOTUS\DATA directory of drive C to a high-capacity diskette in drive A, enter

XCOPY C:\LOTUS\DATA A:

XCOPY also can copy files from a branch of a directory tree. This means that all batch files in all directories below the root of drive D can be backed up to a diskette in drive A with the following command:

XCOPY D:*.BAT A: /S

The /S switch starts at the directory specified in FILESPEC1 and works its way through all lower-level subdirectories, searching for files that meet the specification *.bat.

SUMMARY

To use your computer effectively, you need to understand how data, programs, and information of any sort is stored in files and how to properly manage these files. This chapter presented the principal commands and mechanisms in DOS for file management.

For additional information about viewing and editing batch and other text files, see

- Chapter 6, "EDLIN: The DOS Editor"

For additional information about backing up files and disks, see

- Chapter 18, "Backups and Restorations"

For additional information about a file's archive attributes, see

- Chapter 19, "Other Advanced Commands"

For additional information about recovering lost data from accidentally formatted disks, see

- Chapter 20, "Extending DOS's Power with Utility Software"

In the next chapter, you'll take a closer look at what goes on behind the scenes when you make any of these file-management requests. You'll see how the disk directory can be organized in special ways for efficiency and clarity. You'll learn how to set up your disk in the best way for your application plans, and you'll see how to maneuver quickly around your sophisticated organizational design.

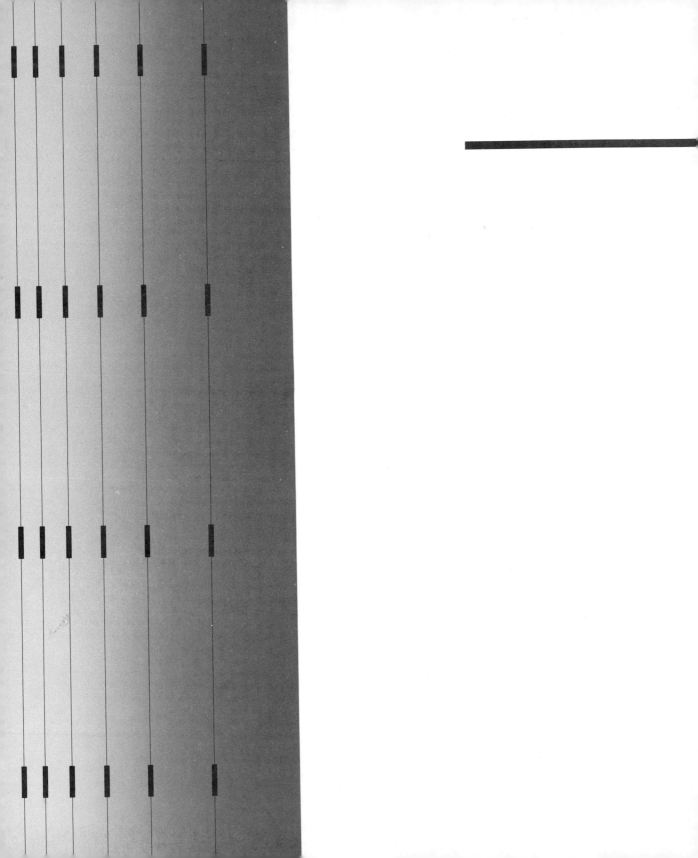

CHAPTER 4

UNDERSTANDING DIRECTORIES AND SUBDIRECTORIES

Understanding Directories and Subdirectories

hapter 3 presented the basic techniques for managing and manipulating files and introduced the concepts of directories and subdirectories. This chapter explores subdirectories in depth and shows you how to use them to organize your data and program files efficiently. If you have DOS version 2.X or a later implementation, every disk in your system can be logically split up into *directories* and *subdirectories*. This ability to create and maintain purposeful groupings of files is the most powerful organizational tool in DOS.

What Is a Subdirectory?

If directories are like separate drawers in a file cabinet, then subdirectories are like hanging folders—the further labeled categories within each drawer. Files are stored in subdirectories and isolated from other files. Just as a well-organized file cabinet promotes efficiency in the office, a well-organized set of DOS directories and subdirectories enables you to quickly and easily store and retrieve program and data files.

A hard disk stores many times the amount of data or number of files that a floppy disk does. For example, if the average size of your files is 20,000 bytes, then a 10-megabyte hard disk will hold approximately 500 uniquely named files. If the average size of your files is smaller (say, 10,000 bytes), then you can store 1000 different files on the disk. This multitude of files raises the problem of maintaining order. DOS allows you to create subdirectories—organizational units that divide the hard disk into sections—to solve this problem. Dividing the disk into these sections prevents any one directory, or group of files, from becoming excessively large. Root directories on different disks and under different versions of DOS have different capacities. However, if you group directories normally, you most likely will never reach the maximum capacity. A double-density diskette can hold over a hundred files, and a hard disk can hold several hundred files.

Table 4.1 provides rough approximations of the number of 20K files that can fit onto different-sized disks. A more exacting estimate would require that cluster size be considered. See Chapter 21 for additional details about this sophisticated internal concept.

TYPE OF DISK	TOTAL STORAGE (BYTES)	NUMBER OF 20K FILES
5¹/₄-inch floppy disk	360K	18
High-capacity 5¹/₄-inch floppy disk	1.2Mb	60
Double-sided 3¹/₂-inch floppy disk	1.44Mb	72
Hard disk	10Mb	500
Hard disk	20Mb	1000

TABLE 4.1: Potential Number of Files on Different-Sized Disks

If you've read much about DOS, you may have noticed that the words *directory* and *subdirectory* are often used interchangeably. Both are correct. *Subdirectory* is a relative term; any directory, except the root directory, is a subdirectory of another directory. In this book, the word *subdirectory* refers to any directory on a disk other than the *root* (main) directory. The word *directory* refers to either the root directory or any one of the many possible subdirectories extending from it.

The entire collection of directories and subdirectories on a disk forms a special structure called a *hierarchy* or a *directory tree*. This term describes the relationship each directory has to the directory within which it is located. This dependent relationship is also referred to as a parent-child (or father-son) relationship. Any directory created within another directory is called a child of the existing parent directory.

Although subdirectories are usually associated with hard disks, DOS can just as easily create subdirectories on floppy diskettes; they function exactly the same on diskettes as they do on hard disks, differing only in the volume of data they can hold. In this chapter, you'll explore the directory commands in the context of a diskette. In Chapter 5, you'll apply what you learn here to the more spacious realm of the hard disk. Read this chapter even if you have a hard disk system— this chapter presents many concepts and techniques applicable to hard disks as well. This chapter provides the basic information about disk structure within the relatively simple and limited confines of a floppy diskette. It also shows how the potential advantages of file grouping so commonly used on hard disks are just as available to you when transporting or storing data on a floppy diskette.

A First Look at a Disk's Directory Structure

Figure 4.1 shows the directory listing for a sample user diskette in drive B. (Hard disk users can try these methods on any diskette in drive A.) As the directory shows, five files are stored on the diskette.

```
B>DIR

 Volume in drive B has no label
 Directory of  B:\

IMCAP    COM    6114   6-20-85    1:09p
IMSHOW   EXE   20090   6-20-85   10:09a
QD2      EXE   74752  11-14-86   12:00p
SKN      COM   34009   8-05-85    6:14p
SR       COM    5356   1-01-85
         5 File(s)    175104 bytes free

B>_
```

FIGURE 4.1: Directory listing of sample diskette. The diskette contains five files that you will use in this chapter to learn about directory structures. Two of the files are .EXE files, and the remaining three are .COM files.

Look at the first line of the directory display:

Volume in drive B has no label

This line refers to the *volume label,* an 11-character name. If you have a label for your disk or diskette, it will appear at the top of the directory listing whenever you enter the DIR command. (The disk will also have an additional hidden file entry, which is inaccessible to you, to store the 11 characters in the label.)

Labeling Disks

The sample diskette in Figure 4.1 has no label because it was not prepared according to the instructions in Chapter 2. As was pointed out in Chapter 2, you should use the /V switch when formatting new disks to place an electronic identifying label on your disk. This label can help to identify the owner of the disk, the contents of the disk, and the intended use of the disk. Unfortunately, most users don't bother with labels, which were designed for the user's benefit. Labels are a simple but effective method of categorizing the files on a disk; when a file is labeled, anyone using the disk can quickly ascertain the nature or purpose of the disk's contents. When no label is entered, DOS displays the message "Volume in drive B has no label."

TIP: Always label your disks when formatting them. Use a name that describes the kind of data or files you intend to place on the disk. You can later use DOS's LABEL command (available in version 3.0 and later implementations) to modify the volume label if you wish.

To prepare a diskette for a volume label, you use the /V switch with the FOR-MAT command, which allows you to enter an 11-character name. Unlike file names, labels may contain spaces. Figure 4.2 shows a typical sequence used to prepare a diskette that will be able to boot the DOS system (/S) with a volume label (/V) that reads SYBEX BOOK.

```
A>FORMAT B: /S /V
Insert new diskette for drive B:
and strike ENTER when ready

Format complete
System transferred

Volume label (11 characters, ENTER for none)? SYBEX BOOK

    362496 bytes total disk space
     69632 bytes used by system
    292864 bytes available on disk

Format another (Y/N)?N
A>_
```

FIGURE 4.2: Formatting a diskette with a volume label. Using the /V (volume ID) switch with the FORMAT command is the easiest way to include a label at the time of initial disk preparation. After DOS writes the formatting marks onto the disk and transfers the system files to the disk, it pauses to let you enter a label of up to 11 characters.

LABELING DISKS AFTER FORMATTING

If you decide after you have formatted a diskette to add a volume label, or if you wish to modify an existing volume label, use the LABEL command, available in DOS version 3.0 and later implementations. Figure 4.3 shows the label BOOK SAMPLE placed on a previously unlabeled diskette.

If at any time you need to see the volume label of a disk, and you don't need any of the other information provided by a DIR display, use the VOL command. If the disk is in the default drive, simply type

VOL

If the disk is in another drive, you must add the appropriate drive letter.

```
A>LABEL B:

Volume in drive B has no label

Volume label (11 characters, ENTER for none)? BOOK SAMPLE

A>DIR  B:

 Volume in drive B is BOOK SAMPLE
 Directory of  B:\

IMCAP    COM     6114    6-20-85    1:09p
IMSHOW   EXE    20090    6-20-85   10:09a
QD2      EXE    74752   11-14-86   12:00p
SKN      COM    34009    8-05-85    6:14p
SR       COM     5356    1-01-85
         5 File(s)    220160 bytes free

A>■
```

FIGURE 4.3: DOS's LABEL command. This command enables you to change a label or define a new label on an existing disk. It will not work, however, on a disk previously formatted under DOS 1.X.

The second line of the initial directory display shown in Figure 4.1 indicates which directory is being listed. It reads

Directory of B:

A disk with no subdirectories has only a single directory. The backslash symbol (\) indicates a directory name. When DOS displays B:\, you are looking at the main or root directory of the disk. This root directory is created when a disk is formatted. Every disk has one—and only one—root directory. In the next section, you'll learn how to subdivide the root directory into smaller but more refined groupings: subdirectories.

CREATING A SUBDIRECTORY

In this section you will create a subdirectory called UTIL to store a group of related files. The UTIL subdirectory will hold some DOS utility programs selected from a DOS master disk. Without subdirectories, you would have to store all the files in the single, unorganized root directory.

Before you create this first subdirectory, log on to the disk drive with the sample diskette. If your machine has a hard disk drive and one floppy diskette drive, place your sample diskette in drive A and log on to that drive by typing A: at the DOS C> prompt:

C>A:

For dual-diskette systems, switch to drive B by typing B: at the DOS A>
prompt:

A>B:

To create a subdirectory you can use the make directory command—either
MKDIR or MD. (Both versions have the same effect, but the MD command is
easier to type.)

The command to create the UTIL subdirectory on your sample diskette is
as follows:

MD \UTIL

This command produces the new directory display shown in Figure 4.4.
Note that you use the left-slanting backslash character, not the right-slanting
slash character usually used to indicate arithmetic division. This backslash symbol is used in DOS to clarify the hierarchical directory structure. A backslash is a
delimiter that precedes any subdirectory's name, in part to specify the name as
representing a subdirectory, and in part to separate the name of the subdirectory
from that of the directory in which it can be found.

The directory in Figure 4.4 has a new type of entry. It is marked with the
<DIR> symbol, which tells you that UTIL is not a file but the name of a

```
B>MD \UTIL

B>DIR

 Volume in drive B is BOOK SAMPLE
 Directory of  B:\

 IMCAP     COM     6114    6-20-85    1:09p
 IMSHOW    EXE    20090    6-20-85   10:09a
 QD2       EXE    74752   11-14-86   12:00p
 SKN       COM    34009    8-05-85    6:14p
 SR        COM     5356    1-01-85
 UTIL            <DIR>              1-01-80   12:46a
        6 File(s)    219136 bytes free

 B>_
```

FIGURE 4.4: Listing of root directory containing new subdirectory. The MD command creates a new
directory by the name specified (UTIL). A DIR listing indicates which entries are directories with the
label <DIR>, which replaces the extension and file size entries used in a standard file.

subdirectory. Remember, directories contain only file names (or the names of other directories, as you'll soon see); the files themselves contain the actual data or programs.

ACCESSING FILES IN A SUBDIRECTORY

You can tell a command to work with a subdirectory other than the current default directory by using the name of the subdirectory preceded by the full path name to that directory. For example, entering the DIR command with a first argument of \UTIL produces the directory listing shown in Figure 4.5. This figure shows the directory of the files stored in the new subdirectory UTIL (located in the root directory). No files are listed because none have been created or copied into this subdirectory.

```
B>DIR  \UTIL

 Volume in drive B is BOOK SAMPLE
 Directory of  B:\UTIL

 .            <DIR>      1-Ø1-8Ø  12:46a
 ..           <DIR>      1-Ø1-8Ø  12:46a
        2 File(s)     219136 bytes free

B>_
```

FIGURE 4.5: Directory listing of new subdirectory. DOS creates each new directory with two special entries (marked . and ..), which provide a shorthand notation for the new directory itself (.) and for its parent directory (..). Later references to either of these directories will not require specification of the full path name; you can use the . or .. notation in place of the (much longer) path name.

You may wonder about the two entries that do appear: the single period (.) and the double period (..). They reflect DOS's understanding of your frequent need to reference files in the current directory or in the parent directory. The single-period directory entry is actually a shorthand notation for the full name of the path leading to the current directory. The double-period entry is actually a shorthand notation for the parent directory's full path name. In the example in Figure 4.5, the . entry is equivalent to \UTIL, and the .. entry is equivalent to the parent directory, which happens to be the root directory (\).

What happened to your two files? They are still on the disk, but they are in the root directory. To see them, you can explicitly request a directory listing of the root directory like this:

**DIR **

CHANGING THE DEFAULT DIRECTORY

Just as DOS allows you to select a default drive, it also allows you to select a default directory for a disk. Once you've created a new directory, you can tell the operating system that you want it, rather than the root, to be the default directory. This allows you to work with only the files contained in that subdirectory without entering the subdirectory name before each DOS command.

The command used to change directories is the CHDIR, or CD, command. (Again, CD is easier to type.) If you simply enter DIR, DOS displays the root directory; if you enter DIR followed by a backslash and a subdirectory name, DOS displays a listing of the specified subdirectory. If you enter the CD command, the DOS commands you enter will by default reference the subdirectory specified in that command. For example, entering

CD \UTIL

makes the UTIL subdirectory the current DOS default subdirectory whenever you reference files on the current disk drive.

Notice in Figure 4.6 that the same DIR command produces a different current default directory listing before and after the CD \UTIL command. The directory listing at the bottom of the figure is for the UTIL subdirectory. The CD command has reset the default directory to UTIL, so the DIR command lists only the files in that subdirectory.

COPYING FILES INTO A SUBDIRECTORY

Now that you have created a subdirectory, you can use it to store files. The basic DOS commands described in Chapter 3 (COPY, ERASE, RENAME, and so on) work with subdirectories. Since the default drive is the one you're working with (B: in this example), you'll need to specify the source drive for the files you're going to copy into the new UTIL subdirectory. First copy FOR-MAT.COM from drive A into the UTIL subdirectory by entering

COPY A:FORMAT.COM

```
B>DIR

 Volume in drive B is BOOK SAMPLE
 Directory of  B:\

IMCAP    COM     6114   6-20-85   1:09p
IMSHOW   EXE    20090   6-20-85  10:09a
QD2      EXE    74752  11-14-86  12:00p
SKN      COM    34009   8-05-85   6:14p
SR       COM     5356   1-01-85
UTIL            <DIR>            1-01-80  12:46a
        6 File(s)     219136 bytes free

B>CD \UTIL

B>DIR

 Volume in drive B is BOOK SAMPLE
 Directory of  B:\UTIL

.               <DIR>            1-01-80  12:46a
..              <DIR>            1-01-80  12:46a
        2 File(s)     219136 bytes free

B>_
```

FIGURE 4.6: Changing the current default directory. The CD command allows you to change the current directory. Succeeding DOS commands, as well as any application programs you run, look for referenced files in the current directory. Most commands, like DIR, perform their tasks for files in the current directory. As shown here, entering DIR first listed the six entries in the drive B root directory (B:\); after the CD command, DIR listed the two entries in the new current directory, B:\UTIL.

Notice that this command does not use a second argument to indicate the destination. When you don't specify a destination, the COPY command uses the current drive, subdirectory (UTIL), and file name as the path for the destination file. Copying another file into the UTIL subdirectory with

COPY A:CHKDSK.COM

and then entering DIR results in the listing shown in Figure 4.7. This listing confirms that the files have been copied from the source diskette to the UTIL subdirectory of the sample diskette.

RETURNING TO THE ROOT DIRECTORY

You can make the root directory the default directory again at any time by entering the CD command and using the root directory symbol (\) all by itself:

**CD **

Entering the DIR command now would produce the same results as in Figure 4.4, before you specified UTIL as the default subdirectory. Note that the files

```
B>COPY  A:FORMAT.COM
        1 File(s) copied

B>COPY A:CHKDSK.COM
        1 File(s) copied

B>DIR

 Volume in drive B is BOOK SAMPLE
 Directory of  B:\UTIL

 .            <DIR>      1-01-80  12:46a
 ..           <DIR>      1-01-80  12:46a
 FORMAT   COM    11135  12-30-85  12:00p
 CHKDSK   COM     9832  12-30-85  12:00p
        4 File(s)    197632 bytes free

B>_
```

FIGURE 4.7: Organizing files in a subdirectory. Users organize files in directory structures according to individual needs and purposes. The example in this figure uses the COPY command to group DOS .COM files in the specially created utility (UTIL) directory.

copied into UTIL do not appear in this directory. They can now be seen only by specifically referencing the UTIL subdirectory. Note that only one directory at a time can be active. If you use the CD command to make a directory active, it is implicit that all other directories are inactive, including, of course, the directory that was active immediately before you entered the CD command.

Note also that each drive on your system has an active directory. Thus,

COPY A:FORMAT.COM B:

or

COPY A:FORMAT.COM C:

copies the FORMAT.COM file on drive A to the active directory on drive B or C. In fact, the second parameter is sometimes not used; the default assumption is that the destination drive is the current drive. Thus,

COPY A:FORMAT.COM

copies the FORMAT.COM file from drive A to the current directory on the current drive. Any drive in your system can be the destination in this example— except drive A, since you cannot copy a file to itself.

HOW SUBDIRECTORIES WORK

DOS keeps track of the unique groupings of subdirectories by attaching a prefix, or *path name*, to every file in a subdirectory. Normally, the prefix is not displayed when you use the DIR command. However, a special form of the CHKDSK command reveals the prefixes attached to files. Entering

A:CHKDSK/V

results in a detailed display like that in Figure 4.8. This display shows the hierarchical structure of the disk. When you've created a number of directories and placed various files in them, remembering where everything is may be difficult. The CHKDSK command can help you manage your files and the disk structure you've created for them.

```
B>A:CHKDSK /V
Volume BOOK SAMPLE created Jan 1, 1980 12:06a
Directory B:\
        B:\IMCAP.COM
        B:\IMSHOW.EXE
        B:\QD2.EXE
        B:\SKN.COM
        B:\SR.COM
        B:\BOOK SAM.PLE
Directory B:\UTIL
        B:\UTIL\FORMAT.COM
        B:\UTIL\CHKDSK.COM
        B:\UTIL\FIG4-8.CAP

    362196 bytes total disk space
         0 bytes in 1 hidden files
      1024 bytes in 1 directories
    168960 bytes in 8 user files
    192512 bytes available on disk

    524288 bytes total memory
    435136 bytes free

B>_
```

FIGURE 4.8: Verbose output from the CHKDSK command. The /V switch on the CHKDSK command provides verbose output for the indicated drive. In this example, no drive was specified, so the default drive (B) is used. In addition to normal CHKDSK output, verbose output includes individual directories along with a list of their contents, including any other directories.

Remember from the discussion in Chapter 2 that CHKDSK is not an internal DOS command, so if CHKDSK is not on the current default drive (in this case, B), you must specify where it can be found. This is why you need to preface the command CHKDSK with A:, since in this simple dual-diskette configuration, the DOS master files are on the disk in drive A. The /V switch requests a *verbose* listing, which includes complete file names.

The display reveals first the disk drive prefix and then the directory prefix for every file. You can access the FORMAT.COM file in the UTIL subdirectory by using the path name B:\UTIL, and you can access the SKN.COM file in the root directory by preceding its name with the path-name prefix B:\.

Full path-name referencing of this type is a convenience available to DOS 3.X users. DOS 2.X can access only commands on the active directory of the specified drive.

MULTILEVEL DIRECTORIES

The DOS subdirectory path system allows you to create complex yet organized groupings. Using this system, you can create subdirectories of subdirectories. For example, you can create a subdirectory of UTIL called SPECIAL with the following command:

MD \UTIL\SPECIAL

However, if you used the DIR command to look at the entries in the root directory, you would see only the original files and the UTIL subdirectory (see Figure 4.9). Where is the new subdirectory? It does not appear in this listing because it is a subdirectory of UTIL. To see a listing of the new subdirectory, you must first log onto UTIL with the CD command, as shown in Figure 4.10.

```
B>MD \UTIL\SPECIAL

B>DIR \

 Volume in drive B is BOOK SAMPLE
 Directory of  B:\

IMCAP    COM     6114    6-20-85    1:09p
IMSHOW   EXE    20090    6-20-85   10:09a
QD2      EXE    74752   11-14-86   12:00p
SKN      COM    34009    8-05-85    6:14p
SR       COM     5356    1-01-85
UTIL           <DIR>     1-01-80   12:46a
        6 File(s)    196608 bytes free

B>_
```

FIGURE 4.9: Creating a multilevel directory. Here, the root directory is the current default directory. From this directory the MD command creates a subdirectory (SPECIAL) within the subdirectory UTIL, which already exists in the root directory.

```
B>CD \UTIL

B>DIR

 Volume in drive B is BOOK SAMPLE
 Directory of  B:\UTIL

 .            <DIR>      1-Ø1-8Ø  12:46a
 ..           <DIR>      1-Ø1-8Ø  12:46a
 FORMAT   COM    11135  12-3Ø-85  12:ØØp
 CHKDSK   COM     9832  12-3Ø-85  12:ØØp
 SPECIAL      <DIR>      1-Ø1-8Ø   4:19a
      5 File(s)    191488 bytes free

B>_
```

FIGURE 4.10: Display of a subdirectory within a subdirectory. The CD command makes UTIL the current default directory. Entering DIR displays the two .COM files that were copied into that directory, along with the newly created (using the MD command) SPECIAL directory.

Applying DOS Commands to Subdirectories

Many DOS commands allow you to specify the subdirectory in which the files occur or are to be placed. For example, the COPY command can accept this type of parameter. Suppose that you want to copy all the files from drive A that begin with the letter *M* into the subdirectory UTIL\SPECIAL. To do this, you enter

COPY A:M*.* \UTIL\SPECIAL

However, a directory listing now would not list the resulting files unless you first made the new SPECIAL subdirectory the default directory or unless you specified the complete path name for the desired subdirectory (see Figure 4.11).

The Concept of Paths

To reach the SPECIAL subdirectory, you must go through the UTIL subdirectory. Following a path to any particular file can be compared to climbing a tree. To get to any particular branch, you must first climb the larger branches leading to it. Any branch on the tree is analogous to a DOS directory or subdirectory.

Each branch of a tree can have new branches growing from it. Similarly, each subdirectory can have new subdirectories defined within it. And just as

```
B>COPY  A:M*.*   \UTIL\SPECIAL
A:MODE.COM
A:MORE.COM
        2 File(s) copied

B>DIR \UTIL\SPECIAL

 Volume in drive B is BOOK SAMPLE
 Directory of  B:\UTIL\SPECIAL
 .            <DIR>        1-01-80    4:19a
 ..           <DIR>        1-01-80    4:19a
 MODE     COM     6864  12-30-85   12:00p
 MORE     COM      295  12-30-85   12:00p
        4 File(s)     178176 bytes free

 B>_
```

FIGURE 4.11: SPECIAL subdirectory listing. The disk's hierarchical structure continues to branch here. The COPY command, using wildcards, copies two selected files to the SPECIAL directory.

each branch may also have fruit or leaves on it, each subdirectory may have program or data files stored in it.

The series of subdirectories that you link together is the path. You can see by the way the tree is structured that each subdirectory and each file within it follows a unique path from the root directory. The large arrows shown in Figures 4.12, 4.13, and 4.14 represent the current default directory in each of the three situations presented in Figures 4.9, 4.10, and 4.11, respectively. Use these figures to help you understand the concept of paths.

KEEPING TRACK OF YOUR DIRECTORY LOCATION

Forgetting where you are in the directory tree can often lead to difficult, if not disastrous, consequences. For example, you may be installing new software on your hard disk. Suppose you're in the root, having just used the MD command to create a NEWSTUFF directory for the new software, and then you enter the command COPY A:*.* in an attempt to copy all the files from the new software diskette to the NEWSTUFF directory. Having forgotten to change the current directory to NEWSTUFF first, you wind up with 87 new files merged into your existing 95 root directory files. At least that error only requires you to invest some time laboriously removing all the mistakenly copied files from your root directory. A more painful situation arises when you decide to delete all the files in

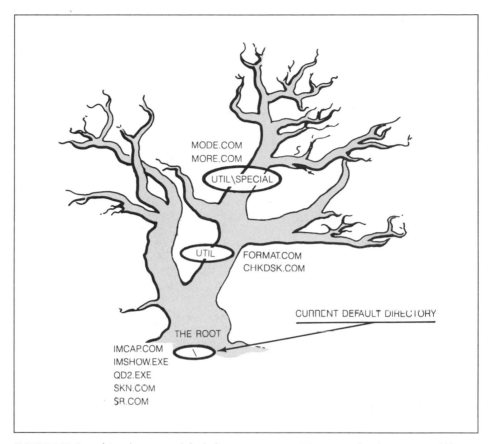

FIGURE 4.12: Root (\) as the current default directory. Issuing a DIR command at this point would list five files (IMCAP.COM, IMSHOW.EXE, QD2.EXE, SKN.COM, and SR.COM) and one directory entry (UTIL).

an older directory. Suppose that your software is a new revision of software you've been using for awhile and that the old versions of the files are in the OLD-STUFF directory. You plan to make OLDSTUFF the current directory, then delete all the files, and then remove that particular subdirectory. So you type CD, enter the ERASE *.* command, respond Y to the prompt, and type CD \ to return to the root to RD OLDSTUFF. DOS then tells you that OLDSTUFF still has files in it, and can't be removed. You realize too late that your CD command should have been CD \OLDSTUFF. In fact, since your current directory never changed from the root, you've erased all the root directory files, including those all-important and so carefully constructed AUTOEXEC.BAT and CON-FIG.SYS files. (These files are discussed in Chapters 9 and 10, respectively.)

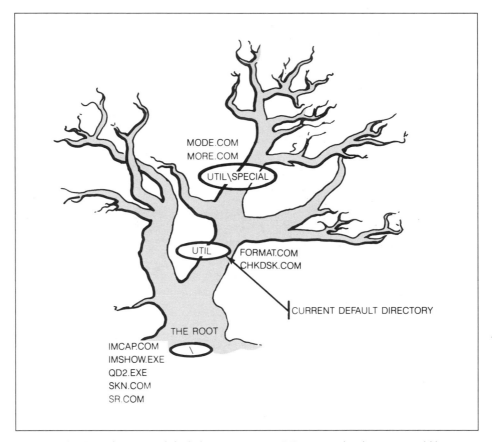

MODE.COM
MORE.COM

UTIL\SPECIAL

UTIL

FORMAT.COM
CHKDSK.COM

CURRENT DEFAULT DIRECTORY

THE ROOT

IMCAP.COM
IMSHOW.EXE
QD2.EXE
SKN.COM
SR.COM

FIGURE 4.13: UTIL as the current default directory. Issuing a DIR command at this point would list two files (format.com and chkdsk.com) and three directory entries (SPECIAL, . and ..).

Fortunately, DOS provides two quick, convenient ways to check your location in the directory tree. Simply typing

CD

with no parameters will display the current directory. The DIR command (again with no parameters) will do the same, but you may not want all the extra imformation its display provides.

EXTENDING THE PATH

You will now make one last subdirectory. Enter the command

MD \UTIL\SPECIAL\FINAL

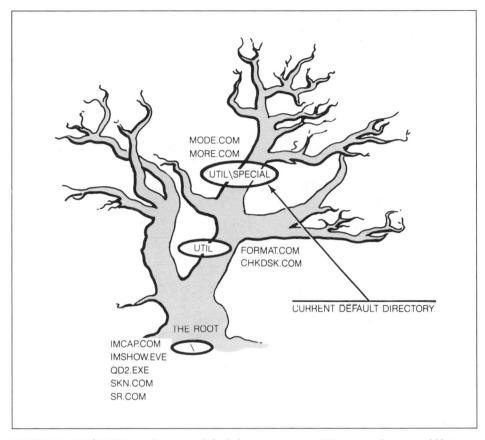

MODE.COM
MORE.COM

UTIL\SPECIAL

UTIL

FORMAT.COM
CHKDSK.COM

CURRENT DEFAULT DIRECTORY

THE ROOT

IMCAP.COM
IMSHOW.EVE
QD2.EXE
SKN.COM
SR.COM

\

FIGURE 4.14: UTIL\SPECIAL as the current default directory. Issuing a DIR command now would list two files (MODE.COM and MORE.COM) and two directory entries (. and ..).

This extends the disk structure another level. To see how well you've understood the methods and concepts of directories and subdirectories, create the tree of directories described so far in this chapter, ending with the SPECIAL directory. Then copy all .EXE files from your DOS master disk to the SPECIAL directory.

Verify that your creation and transfer operation worked properly by listing the contents of the SPECIAL directory. This listing should show the one- and two-period entries, along with all the .EXE files from your DOS master disk.

Moving Files between Directories

So far, you've copied files from drive A to subdirectories on drive B. But what if you want to transfer files from one subdirectory to another on the same diskette? For example, suppose you want to move the two utility programs, IMCAP.COM and IMSHOW.EXE in the root directory (see Figure 4.1) to the newly created SPECIAL directory. This requires two steps:

1. Use COPY to make a copy of each of the files in the new directory.
2. Use ERASE to erase the original copies of the files after verifying that the transfer took place correctly.

The key is to specify the correct path name when you enter the commands. Remember that you want to copy a file in the root directory (path name \) to a directory with the full path name of \UTIL\SPECIAL. Type

COPY \IMSHOW.EXE \UTIL\SPECIAL
COPY \IMCAP.COM \UTIL\SPECIAL

pressing Return after each command. Figure 4.15 shows this sequence followed by a DIR command to verify the transfer and an ERASE command to delete the old files from the root directory.

SOME FINE POINTS ABOUT COPYING FILES

In all of the examples presented so far, the new file created in the destination directory received the same name as the original file. When necessary, you

```
B>COPY \IMSHOW.EXE  \UTIL\SPECIAL
        1 File(s) copied

B>COPY \IMCAP.COM  \UTIL\SPECIAL
        1 File(s) copied

B>DIR   \UTIL\SPECIAL

 Volume in drive B is BOOK SAMPLE
 Directory of  B:\UTIL\SPECIAL

.              <DIR>      1-Ø1-8Ø    4:19a
..             <DIR>      1-Ø1-8Ø    4:19a
MODE    COM     6864   12-3Ø-85   12:ØØp
MORE    COM      295   12-3Ø-85   12:ØØp
IMSHOW  EXE    2ØØ9Ø    6-2Ø-85   1Ø:Ø9a
IMCAP   COM     6114    6-2Ø-85    1:Ø9p
        6 File(s)     151552 bytes free

B>ERASE \IMSHOW.EXE

B>ERASE \IMCAP.COM

B>_
```

FIGURE 4.15: Copying files between directories on the same disk. Files can be organized into subdirectories using this combination of a COPY command, which copies a file to a specified directory, and an ERASE command, to remove the original copy of the file. Notice the use of a DIR command in between COPY and ERASE to verify that the original files were successfully copied to the new location before they are removed from the old location.

can direct DOS to assign new names as part of the COPY procedure. For example, the command

COPY * .DBF \BACKUPS\ * .BAK

makes backup copies of all .DBF (database) files in the current directory. The new copies appear in the BACKUP directory with the extension .BAK.

Note that by using a first argument of * .DBF, you are assuming that all the .DBF files are on the current drive and in the current directory. In the second argument, in which you specify the desired directory (BACKUPS), you are assuming only the use of the current drive. To use a drive or directory other than the default, you must specify the drive or directory (or both).

MANEUVERING AROUND THE DOS DIRECTORY STRUCTURE

Although subdirectories are essential for good organization, their structure can become confusing very quickly. DOS offers some commands that help you navigate through the potentially complex tangle of directories.

Viewing a Disk's Directory Structure

The TREE command displays a summary of the directories and subdirectories on a disk. Unlike most DOS commands discussed in this book so far, TREE is not an internal command. This means that it will not work at all times or in every circumstance. TREE, like CHKDSK, is really a program file provided by DOS. This file, TREE.COM, must be present on one of the disks in your system, or you cannot execute the TREE command. Moreover, you must tell DOS, as part of the command, which drive to search to find the file.

Since TREE.COM is in drive A (the DOS system diskette) in the dual-diskette example, entering

A:TREE

lists the volume label of the diskette in the current default drive (BOOK SAMPLE) as well as all the directories on that diskette and any subdirectories within them. Prefixing the TREE file name with the drive identifier A: is necessary only because the current default drive is B (indicated by the DOS prompt B>). Since TREE.COM is an external, disk-resident command, DOS needs to know where to find it, if it doesn't exist in the default directory. See Figure 4.16.

You can also obtain a more detailed tree display that lists the specific files in each subdirectory. Entering

A:TREE/F

```
B>A:TREE
DIRECTORY PATH LISTING FOR VOLUME BOOK SAMPLE
Path: \UTIL
Sub-directories:   SPECIAL


Path: \UTIL\SPECIAL
Sub-directories:   None



B>_
```

FIGURE 4.16: DOS's TREE command. This command lists all directories on a disk and all subdirectories within those directories. It provides a textual representation of the disk hierarchy, rather than a more visual one. See Chapter 20 for information about add-on utility software that can provide graphical views of your disk directory structure.

produces the output shown in Figure 4.17. The /F switch asks DOS to include the file names of all files in each directory.

TREE listings usually are too long for one screen. If you have a printer, you can print the screen display by entering

A:TREE /F > PRN

The symbols at the end of this command line, > PRN, represent a special feature of DOS called *redirection*. This technique is discussed in much more depth in Chapter 17. For now, you can merely note that adding > PRN to the end of most DOS commands that otherwise produce output on your monitor causes that output to be printed. Usually, you should view the results first. When you find them satisfactory, you can then reenter the command including PRN to obtain hard, printed copy.

Searching Directory Paths

The main purpose of the subdirectory system is to separate groups of files. However, sometimes you may need a file in a directory other than the one you currently are using (that is, other than the default directory). For example, the sample diskette used so far now contains some files located in the root directory,

```
DIRECTORY PATH LISTING FOR VOLUME BOOK SAMPLE

Files:              QD2      .EXE
                    SKN      .COM
                    SR       .COM

Path: \UTIL

Sub-directories:  SPECIAL

Files:              FORMAT   .COM
                    CHKDSK   .COM


Path: \UTIL\SPECIAL

Sub-directories:  None

Files:              MODE     .COM
                    MORE     .COM
                    IMSHOW   .EXE
                    IMCAP    .COM


C>_
```

FIGURE 4.17: Detailed TREE listing using the /F switch. Using this switch with the TREE command provides an alternative to the CHKDSK/V command illustrated in Figure 4.8. Which command you select depends on personal preference, as well as whether you want to receive the additional disk and memory summary statistics offered by the CHKDSK command.

some in the UTIL directory, and some in the UTIL\SPECIAL directory. A copy of CHKDSK, for example, is located in the UTIL directory.

Assume you are currently back in the root directory (CD \). If you try to execute the CHKDSK command by typing

CHKDSK

and pressing Return, the computer will tell you that you have entered a bad command or file name. Why? You are currently logged onto the root directory, and the CHKDSK file is located in UTIL.

DOS offers a command that you can enter to specify where to look for files that are not located in the default directory. When this path is opened, the computer searches other directories to find the file you want. To create a path from the current working directory to the UTIL directory, for instance, you enter

PATH \UTIL

This command opens a path between the current working directory and the directory containing the desired file. Entering CHKDSK now produces the desired result; the CHKDSK program will execute because DOS followed the specified search path to the UTIL directory.

Note that the PATH command does not change the active directory. It simply tells DOS to search another directory when the desired program is not in the active directory.

Test your understanding of the PATH command now. If you have a directory structure set up with a program you normally use, change the current directory (CD) to some other directory. Then set the path properly so you can run a program that is not located in the current directory. Also try setting up a path with multiple directory entries, so you can run several different programs without having to change directories.

If your own system is not yet set up with any usable utility or application programs, look at the structure in Figure 4.17. Note the file named IMSHOW.EXE in the UTIL\SPECIAL directory. How would you set the path in DOS to run this program if your current default directory is the root directory? For example, would you enter

1. PATH \UTIL;\SPECIAL;\FINAL,
2. PATH \UTIL,
3. PATH \UTIL\SPECIAL, or
4. PATH UTIL\SPECIAL?

Many people are uncertain about the use of delimiters, which are simply characters that separate one part of a command from another. How and when they are used is always critical. In this example, three delimiters must all be used correctly. The backslash symbol separates directory names in a single path. The space symbol separates the PATH command from the list of directory names. The semicolon separates different directory names in the same path listing.

Choices 3 and 4 are both correct. PATH \UTIL\SPECIAL (choice 3) is the full name of the path from the root directory to the directory containing the desired program. The semicolons make choice 1 incorrect, since this path specifies the UTIL directory and the nonexistent SPECIAL directory. The SPECIAL directory does not exist in the root; it exists in the UTIL branch of the directory tree. Choice 2 is wrong, because UTIL is the branch of the directory tree that contains the subdirectory SPECIAL, not the desired program, IMSHOW.EXE.

Although it is correct here, choice 4 is incorrect if you execute the IMSHOW .EXE program while the current default directory is other than the root directory. The lack of a leading backslash indicates that the path branches off the current directory, which, except when the root is the default directory, yields an incorrect result.

Setting Up a Complex Path

You can open a path to several directories at once by entering a series of path names separated by semicolons. For example, if DOS can't find the program you ask for in the current default directory, you can ask it to search the UTIL directory first and then UTIL\SPECIAL by entering

PATH \UTIL;\UTIL\SPECIAL

Separate the name of each directory to be successively searched by a semicolon (and no space). Multiple paths allow you to access programs in several directories without having to constantly revise the PATH command.

When the PATH Command Isn't Enough

You can use the PATH command to search a directory only for files with the extensions .COM, .EXE, and .BAT. The first two types are executable programs, and the last is a DOS batch file. (Batch files are discussed in depth in Chapters 7 through 9; they are simple DOS programs that contain a set of DOS commands.) DOS will not search the path directories for files with other extensions.

Some programs require special *overlay* or *driver* files in order to load properly. These files have extensions such as .OVR, .OVL, and .DRV and contain additional program information that usually won't fit into memory because the main program consumes so much space. The PATH command enables DOS to locate and load the main program—for instance, WS.COM (WordStar)—but DOS will fail to locate WSOVLY1.OVR, the overlay program that WordStar requires.

Some of new programs, such as dBASE III PLUS, that require overlays can run because they are smart enough to use DOS's path information themselves to locate any required overlay files. Other programs, such as WordStar, that need these supporting files often cannot be run simply by opening a path to the directory in which they are stored. If you are using an older program, you may have to use the change directory command to run the program from within the directory that contains the main and overlay files. DOS 3.3 contains a new command, APPEND, that also provides a solution. This command is presented in depth in Chapter 19. In essence, APPEND gives you the ability to set up a path to overlay files and data files, effectively closing the former gap in DOS's ability to locate these files. You'll explore this issue again in the next chapter.

Checking the Path

Sometimes, after you have used several directories of your hard disk, you may not be sure which directory is current. You may also not be sure which path DOS will take to search for files not found in the current directory. If this is the case, you can ask DOS to show you the current path. To see what the current defined path is, enter

PATH

To close the path, enter the PATH command with the semicolon (;) alone. This indicates that the path is once again reset to the current working directory.

> **PATH;**

After you've entered this command, asking DOS for the current path will produce the message "No Path."

PRUNING THE TREE

There comes a time on many disks, as on many trees, when a branch must be cut back or cut off. You should use the ERASE command regularly to control the use of space on your diskette. Once in a while, you may also want to put files together and collapse two directories into one. Or, if you no longer need all the files in a directory, you may want to completely remove the directory they're in.

The following sequence moves all the files from the UTIL\SPECIAL directory into the UTIL directory. Keep in mind that the directory tree looks somewhat like Figure 4.18.

First you need to copy the files from UTIL\SPECIAL to the UTIL directory:

> **COPY \UTIL\SPECIAL*.* \UTIL**

```
Directory B:\

        B:\QD2.EXE
        B:\SKN.COM
        B:\SR.COM
        B:\BOOK SAM.PLE

Directory B:\UTIL

        B:\UTIL\FORMAT.COM
        B:\UTIL\CHKDSK.COM

Directory B:\UTIL\SPECIAL

        B:\UTIL\SPECIAL\MODE.COM
        B:\UTIL\SPECIAL\MORE.COM
        B:\UTIL\SPECIAL\IMSHOW.EXE
        B:\UTIL\SPECIAL\IMCAP.COM


C>_
```

FIGURE 4.18: Current directory tree. This listing was produced by using the /V switch with the CHKDSK command.

DOS displays the file names as they are copied:

B:\UTIL\SPECIAL\MODE.COM
B:\UTIL\SPECIAL\MORE.COM
B:\UTIL\SPECIAL\IMSHOW.EXE
B:\UTIL\SPECIAL\IMCAP.COM
4 File(s) copied

You should always verify that your new copies are in place before erasing the old copies (see Figure 4.19).

```
DIR \UTIL

Volume in drive B is BOOK SAMPLE
Directory of  B:\UTIL

.            <DIR>      1-01-80   12:46a
..           <DIR>      1-01-80   12:46a
FORMAT   COM    11135   12-30-85   12:00p
CHKDSK   COM     9832   12-30-85   12:00p
SPECIAL      <DIR>      1-01-80    4:19a
MODE     COM     6864   12-30-85   12:00p
MORE     COM      295   12-30-85   12:00p
IMSHOW   EXE    20090    6-20-85   10:09a
IMCAP    COM     6114    6-20-85    1:09p
         9 File(s)   149504 bytes free




C>_
```

FIGURE 4.19: Directory status of UTIL showing consolidated directory contents. The four files from the SPECIAL directory are first copied into the UTIL directory (actually, into SPECIAL's parent directory). Then the SPECIAL directory is removed with the RD command. Note that RD will not work until the file contents of the specified directory have been erased.

Since the files have been copied successfully, you can now use the RD (remove directory) command to remove the old directory:

RD \UTIL\SPECIAL

DOS will immediately respond with

Invalid path, not directory,
or directory not empty

This is DOS's way of protecting you from a major catastrophe—namely, the removal of an entire directory when there may still be useful but forgotten programs stored in it. In this case, you haven't made a mistake. You just need to erase the old files before removing the directory from the DOS tree with the RD command:

> **ERASE \UTIL\SPECIAL*.***
> **Are you sure (Y/N)?Y**
>
> **RD \UTIL\SPECIAL**

Figure 4.20 reveals the new directory structure.

Removing directories that are empty has the aesthetic benefit of cleaning up the directory structure. It is then easier to read and understand the remaining hierarchical structure of subdirectories. This makes file maintenance easier and saves you time and energy in later work with your system.

```
Directory B:\

        B:\JUNK1.TXT
        B:\QD2.EXE
        B:\SKN.COM
        B:\SR.COM
        B:\BOOK SAM.PLE

Directory B:\UTIL

        B:\UTIL\FORMAT.COM
        B:\UTIL\CHKDSK.COM
        B:\UTIL\MODE.COM
        B:\UTIL\MORE.COM
        B:\UTIL\IMSHOW.EXE
        B:\UTIL\IMCAP.COM




    C>_
```

FIGURE 4.20: Revised directory tree structure: the result of proper DOS commands. All files, formerly spread over three directories, are now organized into a more balanced and purposeful fashion.

DOS COMMANDS USED WITH DIRECTORIES AND SUBDIRECTORIES

The following reference entries explain in detail the DOS directory and sub-directory commands discussed in this chapter.

APPEND

The APPEND command causes the computer to search a predetermined set of directories for files with extensions other than .COM, .BAT, and .EXE.

SYNTAX

[*D:Path*]APPEND[*D1:Path1*][;*D2:Path2...*][/X][/E][;]

D:Path	is the drive and path where the command file is located if it is not in the current directory.
D1:Path1	is the first drive and directory searched after the default drive and directory.
D2:Path2...	is the second drive and directory searched after the default drive and directory, and so on.
/X	causes APPEND to process the searching methods SEARCH FIRST, FIND FIRST, and EXEC (used by programmers only).
/E	stores the paths in the DOS environment (paths can be changed with SET, but that they will be lost if a secondary processor exits). Secondary processors come into being only when the COMMAND command is used in DOS. Within the framework of your DOS, the COMMAND command provides, among other things, the opportunity to run DOS from within application programs. This switch enables you to change these APPEND path name entries with the SET command while the secondary command processor is active. Since these path values are stored in memory, in a special place called the DOS environment, they will be lost when the secondary command processor terminates (with the EXIT command) and returns control to the application program that invoked it. There are other possible ways in which a secondary command processor can be invoked and effectively used. See Chapter 19, for more details about the COMMAND command.
;	used alone nullifies the APPEND command by erasing the path list.

TYPE

External upon first execution; internal after first execution. Conventionally, this type of command is precisely called an external, terminate-and-stay-resident (TSR) program. It resides on disk until it is needed, thereby taking up no room in memory. When it is invoked for the first time, it comes into memory. When it is done, however, it does not free the memory space it used. Instead it stays resident in memory, continuing to provide service.

USAGE

The two most common uses of APPEND are to allow DOS to locate overlay files for sophisticated application programs and to allow DOS to locate data files for referencing by those programs. These types of files (.OVL, .DTA, and so on) cannot be located by using the PATH command. Earlier versions of DOS could not effectively find these support files unless they appeared in the current default directory.

The APPEND command tells DOS to open files to read from or write to. To tell DOS to find executable files, use the PATH command.

RESTRICTIONS

DOS provides 128 bytes of memory in which to specify paths. Do not use this command in conjunction with the APPEND command in the IBM PC Network program 1.00 or in the IBM PC LAN program 1.10.

Unless you specify otherwise, APPEND saves files in the default directory, not in the directory they were called from (unless that directory was the default directory). Suppose you edit a file with DOS's line editor, EDLIN (see Chapter 6). Suppose further that the file to be edited is not in the current directory, but *is* specified in the APPEND path list of directories. If you call the file (say TEST-.TXT) by its name only—for example,

EDLIN TEST.TXT

then the edited version of the file will be saved in your current default directory. Clearly, this is a quirk of the APPEND feature, since APPEND gave you access to a data file in one directory, but the changed data is saved in the current directory, not the directory from which the file was retrieved. The solution to this problem is to specify a full path name when referencing the file—for example,

EDLIN \FW\DATA\TEST.TXT

When the edited file is eventually saved, it will be saved correctly in the original directory, not in the current directory.

EXAMPLES

Suppose you want to execute a simple batch file you wrote for a menu management system. You want the file to reference and execute your database program in the DBMS directory, your computer-aided design program in the CAD directory, and your word processing program in the WP directory. You must enter the following command, which explicitly specifies that the DBMS and the WP directories are on drive C and the CAD directory is on drive D:

APPEND C:\DBMS;D:\CAD;C:\WP

This example assumes that any referenced data files also appear in those directories; if, in fact, any data files are located in subdirectories, you must add those subdirectory names to the APPEND path list.

Clearing the current path list for the APPEND command is one way to force DOS to limit its search to only the current working directory.

The APPEND command is also useful in a network environment to locate data files residing on computers other than your own (on other nodes on the network).

CHDIR (CD)

You can use CHDIR (or simply CD) to change directories as you move through the directory structure.

SYNTAX

C[H]D[IR] [*D:Path*]

> *D:Path*   is the optional drive and path specifying the directory you wish to make the default directory.

TYPE

Internal.

USAGE

The CHDIR (or CD for short) command allows you to change the current working directory. DOS looks for *executable files* in the current working directory before searching the path; it looks for *data files* in the current working directory before searching the APPEND list. It is therefore often desirable to work in the current directory. The CD command is most often used to make a particular directory the current directory.

Executing CHDIR .. puts you in the immediate parent directory of the directory you are in. (The double-period symbol denotes the particular parent directory.)

EXAMPLES

Suppose you want to make the data subdirectory within the CAD directory your current working directory. Enter

> **CD \CAD\DATA**

To reset the current working directory to the root of your current drive, enter

> **CD **

If you wish to make LOTUS\ACCOUNTS\JUDD the working directory, enter

CD \LOTUS\ACCOUNTS\JUDD

Entering CD with no parameters displays the current working directory for the default drive. To display the current working directory for any other drive, enter the drive name as a first parameter, as follows:

CD D:

This command displays the current working directory for drive D.

LABEL

LABEL allows you to label your disk volumes electronically. These disk names will appear each time you call up a directory.

SYNTAX

[*D:Path*]LABEL [*D1:*][*String*]

D:Path	is the drive and path where the command file is located if it is not listed in the current directory.
D1:	is the drive containing the disk whose label is to be changed or displayed.
String	when specified, becomes the label of the disk in *Drive2*.

TYPE

External.

USAGE

If you know the contents of a particular disk and want to give that disk a new electronic label, you can most quickly do so with the LABEL command. LABEL is most often used to assign volume identifiers to older disks that were not labeled during the formatting process. Note that disks formatted with the FORMAT program available in DOS version 1.X cannot accept volume labels, even those assigned with the LABEL command.

RESTRICTIONS

You cannot use LABEL with drives that have been substituted or joined.
You cannot use the following characters in a volume label: * ? / \ | . , ; : + = < > [ ] ( ) @ ^ .

EXAMPLES

Assume that you want to label the disk in drive B with the name "budgets." Enter

LABEL B: budgets

If you are not sure what is currently on a disk, you can use the LABEL command to display the current volume label. For example, entering

LABEL B:

produces the following results:

Volume in drive B is budgets
Type a volume label of up to 11 characters or
Press Enter for no volume label update: _

MKDIR (MD)

The MKDIR command (or MD for short) creates a new directory, either in the current working directory or at the specified path location in an existing tree.

SYNTAX

M[K]D[IR] [*D:Path*]

    D:Path   is the optional drive and path specifying the directory you wish to create.

TYPE

Internal.

USAGE

The MKDIR command enables you to make new directories, which helps you organize files on any disk. As with all other file references, you can specify a file name without entering the complete path, and DOS will assume that the reference is to the current working directory.

The new directory initially will be empty of files, but it is usable immediately.

EXAMPLES

No matter what directory you are using, you can also create a new subdirectory, called Data, within it by entering

MD Data

Assuming that your current working directory is \Symphony, you have effectively created a data directory with the full path name of \Symphony\Data.

You do not need to place the new subdirectory in the current directory. For example, your working directory can be located in drive A, and you can use the MD command to create a new INFO subdirectory within the SCHOOL directory, located in drive D:

MD D:\School\Info

PATH

The PATH Command sets or resets the sequence of directories (that is, the path) to be searched for executable files.

SYNTAX

PATH [*D1:Path1*][;*D2:Path2*...]

[*D1:Path1*]	is the first drive and directory searched.
[*D2:Path2*...]	is the second drive and directory searched, and so on.

TYPE

Internal.

USAGE

PATH is a command you are likely to use frequently. It sets or resets the sequence of directories to be searched for executable files, whether they be .COM, .EXE, or .BAT files. In the typical DOS application setup, you select a default directory for data files and then specify a PATH list to locate the executable file to run.

Use PATH when you need to access a program in a directory other than the current one. The PATH command gives DOS a list of drives and directories to search, in a specified order, until it finds the requested program file. Be careful when specifying a search sequence: If there are two different files with the same name in different directories along the path, DOS will use the first one it encounters.

RESTRICTIONS

PATH will not work with data files, overlay files, or other nonexecutable files (see APPEND).

EXAMPLES

The following simple example entry instructs DOS to search the root directory, then the 123 directory, and finally the UTILITY directory to locate any external commands or programs not in the current working directory:

PATH \;\123;\UTILITY

RMDIR (RD)

When you want to delete or remove a directory, you must delete all files or subdirectories in the directory and then use the RMDIR command.

SYNTAX

R[M]D[IR] [*D:Path*]

    D:Path   is the drive and path of the directory to be removed.

TYPE

Internal.

USAGE

You will probably use RMDIR only infrequently. Typically, you use this command only to clean up a messy hard disk directory structure. After you erase all files in an individual directory, that directory may no longer be needed and so can be removed from the hierarchy. Removing unnecessary directories makes the remaining structure clearer and easier to understand. In the conventional tree analogy, removing directories is comparable to pruning a tree.

RESTRICTIONS

You cannot remove a directory until all files and subdirectories within it have been deleted or removed by a separate operation.

EXAMPLES

To remove an empty directory, such as OLDSTUFF in the DBMS directory, enter

RD \DBMS\OLDSTUFF

If OLDSTUFF isn't empty, use DIR to display existing file names or to determine which subdirectories still exist within it. You can then use the ERASE command to delete the files in those directories or the RD command to remove an existing subdirectory.

If your current working directory is already DBMS, then you need only indicate OLDSTUFF as the object of RD:

RD OLDSTUFF

TREE

TREE displays a list of all of your directories and subdirectories and the files they contain. Such a list is especially useful for examining the directory structure to determine where pruning might improve efficiency.

SYNTAX

[*D:Path*]TREE [*D2:*][/F]

D:Path	is the drive and path where the command file is located if the file is not in the current directory.
D2	is the drive identifier of another drive you want TREE to affect.
/F	displays all paths and file names in the directories.

TYPE

External.

USAGE

The primary role of the TREE command is to display the hierarchical tree of directories and subdirectories for a particular disk drive.

EXAMPLES

To display each directory on a drive and each subdirectory within each directory, simply enter

TREE

Use the /F switch with this command to produce a log of all files, listed by directory, for your disk drive. Redirection in DOS allows you to send output to a printer, which normally would be displayed on your screen. Combining this TREE command with redirection allows you to produce a complete log of all files on a disk, store the log in a new file, and then later print this log file:

TREE D: /F > FILES.LOG

VOL

The VOL command shows the volume label of a disk in a specified drive.

SYNTAX

VOL [*D:*]

D   is a specified drive, if different from the default drive.

TYPE

Resident.

USAGE

Entering the VOL command alone causes DOS to display the label of the current working disk drive. It's quick, if that's all the information you need. Since the DIR command always displays the disk's volume ID, this command is not invoked very often.

EXAMPLES

Entering:

VOL

is likely to produce the simple result:

Volume in drive C is *drive ID*

SUMMARY

This chapter has examined the tree-like directory structure of DOS and shown you how to work with directories and subdirectories on floppy diskettes.

For additional information about using directories on hard disks, see

- Chapter 5, "Working with Hard Disk Directories"

For additional information about editing text files, see

- Chapter 6, "EDLIN: The DOS Editor"

For additional information about file output and redirection, see

- Chapter 17, "Pipes, Filters, and Redirection"

For additional information about pathing possibilities for data files, see the APPEND command; and, for additional information about secondary command processors, see the COMMAND command in

- Chapter 19, "Other Advanced Commands"

For additional information about graphic representation of your disk hierarchical directory structure, see

- Chapter 20, "Extending DOS's Power with Utility Software"

For additional information about disk clusters and DOS disk management methods, see

- Chapter 21, "A Closer Look behind the Scenes of DOS"

In the next chapter you will continue your study of DOS directories, but in the context of the more complex and eminently more useful environment of a hard disk.

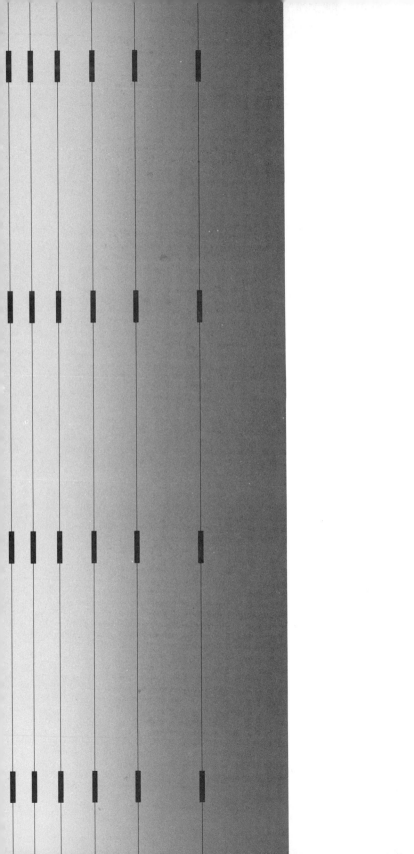

CHAPTER 5

Working with Hard Disk Directories

WORKING WITH
HARD DISK DIRECTORIES

Working with hard disks requires good organization and planning. This chapter presents some practical examples that will help you develop the requisite organizational skills. Chapter 4 presented the DOS directory structure and the commands necessary to set up and use that structure on your floppy diskettes. This chapter focuses on the directory structure of hard disks.

As the price of hard disks decreases, hard disks are increasingly likely to be a part of the typical computer system. Knowledge of DOS directory structures becomes even more important as the amount of hardware under your control grows. Knowing how to successfully manage all your disk space will make you more efficient and save you time; the manipulation of diskettes to run application programs can then be replaced by manipulation of DOS directories.

In this chapter, you'll format your hard disk or review the formatting process if your disk is already formatted. Then you'll use the appropriate directory commands to set up the hard disk for three common and very popular types of program: a spreadsheet, a word processor, and a database management system. The techniques you learn will be directly applicable to setting up a hard disk for any application software.

PREPARING YOUR DISK

Just like floppy diskettes, hard disks must be prepared before information can be stored on them. There are two major steps in preparing a hard disk for use with DOS: partitioning the disk and formatting it. *Partitioning* means allocating either all or part of the disk to DOS; this capability has been included to accommodate those users who also want to run other operating systems, such as UNIX, from the same disk. *Formatting*, as you saw in Chapter 2, means writing onto the disk certain information that DOS needs when using any disk. Both tasks are often performed by the computer dealer before a new machine leaves the shop, however, so you should consult your dealer for the status of your hard disk before trying out the instructions presented in this section. Since the FOR-MAT command erases any existing information on a disk, it should be used only once on a hard disk, when it is new. The following instructions, then, are for the DOS user whose hard disk has *not* received any advanced preparation. Other readers should begin with the section titled "A Place for the DOS Files."

Partitioning Your Disk

All DOS users must use the FDISK command (see Chapter 19) to partition their disk. Nearly all users follow the straightforward and simple procedure outlined in Chapter 19 for creating one *partition* out of the entire hard disk space. Since DOS is limited to a maximum partition size of 32MB, FDISK can create several drives out of one larger physical disk. Thus, you can split a large disk, such as a 70MB drive, into three virtual drives (say drives C, D, and E) of sizes 20MB, 20MB, and 30MB.

Formatting Your Disk

Place the DOS master diskette into drive A and close the door. Then enter the proper format command at the A> prompt. Remember that you want to use the hard disk as a system disk; therefore, you must use the form of the FORMAT command shown here. It will format the disk and copy the system information files at the same time. Since the hard disk drive is usually drive C, type

A>FORMAT C: /S

When formatting is complete, change the active drive to C:

A>C:

For the rest of this chapter, the default drive will be C, and you'll be moving around the directory tree on the hard disk.

A PLACE FOR THE DOS FILES

The DOS prompt on your screen now indicates that drive C is the active drive. The first command you should enter is the directory command, DIR. DIR reveals that you have one file on your drive, COMMAND.COM, and that you have over 10 million bytes of free space (or 20 or 30 million bytes, depending on the size of your hard disk). The display also tells you that COMMAND-.COM is in the root directory, indicated by the backslash (C:\). The COMMAND.COM file is part of the computer's basic operating system and must always appear in the root directory.

The DOS system has several special utility programs that can aid in the proper operation of your system. Right now these programs are stored on the DOS master diskettes, but they can be copied to your hard disk. If you have 5¼-inch floppy diskette drives, these utility files are separated onto two 360K floppy disks, labeled Startup and Operating (DOS 3.3) or System and Supplementary (DOS 3.2 and earlier implementations) disks; if you have the appropriate 3½-inch microfloppy drive, all DOS utility files are included on one diskette, labeled DOS Startup/Operating disk, also included with your DOS 3.3 package. These files include all disk-resident DOS commands: from CHKDSK to FORMAT to commands that support international-type keyboards. Performing any utility operations requires that the appropriate DOS support files be available on your hard disk. However, before you copy these files, you need to take an organizational step.

Creating New Directories

When adding files to a hard disk, it is always a good idea to create a special directory for all files that are related to one another. Grouping similar and related files together will make finding and using them easier and faster. In this example, you will copy all of the DOS files to a directory called DOS so that they are all grouped together.

To create the directory, you enter the make directory command, MD:

MD \DOS

On the screen, nothing seems to have happened, but in fact the computer has recorded a change. Entering a DIR request displays this information:

Volume in drive C is JUDDROBBINS
Directory of C:

COMMAND	COM	23791	12-30-85	12:00p
DOS		\<DIR\>	1-01-80	12:05a

1 File(s) 10565240 bytes free

The \<DIR\> symbol next to the name DOS indicates that DOS is not a file, but a directory. You can now store information in that directory.

Copying Files between Disks and Directories

The COPY command transfers copies of files from one disk to another and to subdirectories on the same or different disks. To transfer the DOS support files from the source diskette in drive A to the destination hard disk directory, C:\DOS (drive C, subdirectory DOS), enter

COPY A:*.* C:\DOS

DOS will list the files as they are copied. However, a directory listing now will still show only one file, COMMAND.COM. This is because the current directory listing is for the root directory; the files that were just copied were stored in the DOS directory.

To see the contents of this subdirectory, you can use one of two methods:

1. Specify the subdirectory name in the DIR command.
2. Change the default directory to the desired directory and enter the DIR command.

The following sections employ both methods.

Listing a Subdirectory

To list the contents of a directory other than the current default directory, you can add the name of the subdirectory to the DIR command:

DIR \DOS

If your current default disk were in a drive other than C, you could even explicitly ask for the DOS directory on drive C by typing

DIR C:\DOS

Tip: When entering commands, remember that you should always follow drive names with a colon—for example, A:, B:, C:—and you should always precede subdirectory names with a backslash character—for example, \DOS, \LOTUS, \DBASE.

Changing the Active Directory

The second method used to list the contents of a subdirectory requires you to tell the operating system that you want to work in a directory other than the root. When you issue a command to change the directory, you are telling the computer to assume that all succeeding commands should affect the files in that directory, not in the root directory.

If you enter a command that tells the computer to use the DOS directory and you then enter DIR, only the files in the DOS subdirectory will be listed. The advantage of changing the directory is that you do not have to type the directory prefix, \DOS, after each command and before each file name.

As you saw in Chapter 4, entering the change directory command (CD) allows you to perform a DIR operation without specifying any directory. You can type

CD \DOS
DIR

and press Return after each line. The desired directory is now the current default directory. The names of files in the DOS subdirectory will now be listed.

Returning to the Root Directory

You can use the CD command to make the root directory the default directory again. Enter the backslash character alone:

**CD **

The default directory is now reset to the root directory. A request for a directory listing will now produce a listing for the root directory.

You may need to use the CD command often. Each time you switch directories to run a different program such as 1-2-3 or dBASE III PLUS, you should reset the root directory as the default directory afterward. Doing so provides a consistent frame of reference for future processing—it's good hard disk management.

COPYING THE DOS FILES TO YOUR HARD DISK

You can use the techniques presented in the last few sections to copy all necessary DOS support files onto your hard disk. Issuing the MD command is the first step in this process. If your default drive is not your hard disk (usually drive C), precede the MD command with C:, as follows:

C:
MD \DOS

You could also simply create the DOS directory on the C drive by prefixing the directory name with the letter of the drive on which you want the DOS directory created:

MD C:\DOS

For users with PS/2 or compatible machines, the next step is to place your 3.5-inch DOS Startup/Operating diskette into drive A and then ask DOS to transfer the files:

COPY A:*.* C:\DOS

This command works independent of your default drive, as you are explicitly asking DOS to copy all files from the diskette in drive A to the DOS directory in drive C.

If your computer uses 5¼-inch diskette drives, your DOS system comes on two diskettes, either Startup and Operating (DOS 3.3) or System and Supplementary (DOS 3.2 and earlier implementations) diskettes. You can simply enter the same COPY command successively for each of the two diskettes, or, as discussed in Chapter 3, you can use the XCOPY command to speed up the copying operation:

XCOPY A:*.* C:\DOS

That's all there is to it. All your required disk-resident (external) DOS commands are now grouped neatly in one hard disk directory. Using the PATH command to properly make these commands available, no matter what your default directory is, will ensure smooth operations from now on:

PATH C:\;C:\DOS

You should augment this PATH command with other directory names containing other referenced application programs. See Chapter 4 for more information about the PATH command.

CHANGING THE PROMPT

As you know, the DOS prompt usually consists of two characters: a letter indicating the active drive plus the > character. The > character is not required, but it makes the display easier to read by separating the drive letter from any command you enter.

When you are working on a disk with more than one directory, it is useful to expand the prompt to include the directory name along with the drive identifier. The PROMPT command can be used to change the prompt displayed whenever DOS is active.

To change the prompt, enter

PROMPT pg

after the > character. PROMPT recognizes the argument $p as a command to display the directory, and it recognizes the argument $g as a command to tell DOS to display the > character. (The letters *p* and *g* can be entered in either upper- or lowercase.) This command changes the DOS prompt from the default display C > to C:\ >, which shows both the drive identifier (C:) and the current directory (the root \) followed by the > character. The DOS prompt will now reflect the current default directory. For example, if you enter the change directory command

>**CD \DOS**

after the C:\ prompt, DOS will change the prompt to

C:\DOS>

The prompt tells you that the active directory is now C:\DOS.

You can ask DOS to return to its normal prompt at any time by reentering the PROMPT command by itself:

C:\DOS>PROMPT

The prompt will return to

C>

You will explore more advanced uses of the PROMPT command in Chapter 10.

LOADING APPLICATION SOFTWARE ONTO YOUR HARD DISK

Hard disks are almost never used just for storing large files of data. You probably use or intend to use your hard disk for certain key application programs as well as for the data files created and used by those programs. In the sections that follow, you will learn how to use the directory structure efficiently to load and run any application program.

The instructions in these sections apply to any application package. The software selected as examples represent the three most popular types: word processing, spreadsheet, and data base management programs. You will learn how to set up a package that requires data and programs to be in the same directory, as well as packages that allow data files to be grouped separate from the main program files. You will also discover how to use the directory management commands to run the software from different places within the directory structure and why doing so can be helpful and can save you time.

Loading Your Word Processor onto Your Hard Disk

In this section, you'll set up your hard disk to store all your word processing files in a particular directory. To do this, you must have a copy of the program already on a floppy diskette. It is assumed that your word processor is *not* copy protected. If it is, you'll need to follow the special instructions in your software user's manual.

Although your word processor may be different from the described here, the process of setting up your hard disk will be similar. You'll still need to take the following steps:

1. Create a word processing subdirectory.
2. Copy the word processing files from the floppy diskette onto the correct subdirectory of the hard disk.
3. Make the word processing directory the default directory.
4. Run the program.

CREATING YOUR WORD PROCESSING DIRECTORY

To create a word processing directory, enter the MD (make directory) command:

MD \WP

To check that all went well, you can enter a DIR command. The root directory should show two entries with the <DIR> indicator: DOS and WP. There are now two directories branching from the root directory (see Figure 5.1). The next step is to copy the files from your word processing diskette(s) to the new WP directory.

COPYING WORD PROCESSING PROGRAMS TO THE NEW DIRECTORY

Your word processing program diskette may have a prewritten installation program to perform the following steps. If so, use it. In any case, the next step that either you or the installation program should take is to place the word processing master diskette into drive A and enter the COPY command:

COPY A:*.* C:\WP

When you press Return, the computer lists the names of the files as they are copied. If your word processor is on more than one diskette, repeat this step for each diskette.

RUNNING YOUR WORD PROCESSOR FROM THE NEW DIRECTORY

To run your word processor, you must change the default directory to WP and type the name of the main program. To do so, enter

CD \WP

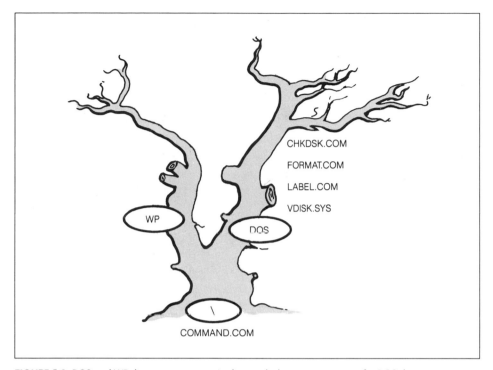

CHKDSK.COM

FORMAT.COM

LABEL.COM

VDISK.SYS

WP

DOS

\

COMMAND.COM

FIGURE 5.1: DOS and WP directory structure. In this symbolic representation of a DOS directory structure, the DOS subdirectory contains four files (VDISK.SYS, LABEL.COM, FORMAT.COM, and CHKDSK.COM), and the WP subdirectory contains all the program files from the word processor diskette(s) after you execute the COPY A:*.* C:\WP command.

Then enter

WS

for WordStar,

WP

for WordPerfect, or the name of whatever program you are using. The opening screen of your word processor will appear.

Now you can proceed to create and edit documents. When you finally exit the program, remember to return to the root directory by entering

**CD **

Now that your word processor has been copied to the hard disk, remember that you must set WP as the default directory each time you want to run the program again. The root directory now lists only the COMMAND.COM file and the primary DOS and WP directories, which themselves contain the bulk of your files. Keeping the root directory uncluttered makes finding your way around the hard disk much easier. Without subdirectories, the root directory would be a virtually unreadable list of hundreds of files.

Loading Your Spreadsheet Program onto Your Hard Disk

Loading a popular spreadsheet such as Lotus 1-2-3 onto a hard disk is not much different from working with a word processor such as WordStar or Word-Perfect. Although the procedure will be similar if you have a different spreadsheet program, the example presented here uses Lotus 1-2-3 because it contains a copy-protection mechanism (unlike the word processing example in the previous section). This special situation requires some discussion.

All the information necessary to run copy-protected programs such as 1-2-3 cannot be easily transferred to a hard disk. Because Lotus employs a copy-protection scheme on its program disks, if you simply transfer all the Lotus files to the hard disk with the COPY command, 1-2-3 still needs to access the original floppy diskette in order to run.

The most recent versions of 1-2-3 allow you to install the software onto the hard disk permanently. Even though the program is copy protected, copying the files to the hard disk is still worthwhile for two reasons:

- The program will load more quickly.
- All of the Lotus 1-2-3 system files can be placed in a single subdirectory; thus, you won't need to repeatedly juggle all the Lotus diskettes.

Tip: COPYIIPC is a useful utility program to own, even though there is some controversy over the legality of the way in which many people use this product. Its major selling point is that it gives you the ability to back up most copy-protected disks. However, it also enables you to load most copy-protected software onto a hard disk and avoid using the key diskette in drive A and following the manufacturer's restrictive installation procedures.

USING SUBDIRECTORIES FOR DATA

Most newer software packages such as 1-2-3 allow you to store work and access files in one of several directories. With earlier and still popular versions of programs such as WordStar, all of the data files you create occupy the same subdirectory as the program.

1-2-3 can switch from one data subdirectory to another while the program is operating. This allows you to group together related 1-2-3 program files and separate them from worksheet files. As you'll soon see, you can use the DOS directory structure more effectively by maintaining directories for groups of worksheets separate from the main LOTUS directory of program files.

The first step is to create a directory for all of the Lotus system files:

    MD \LOTUS

Then, for each of the original diskettes in the Lotus package, copy the necessary programs into that directory by entering

    COPY A:*.* C:\LOTUS

Now that the 1-2-3 files have been copied, you can run the program. First change the default directory to the LOTUS directory and then enter the name of the main program, pressing Return after each command:

    CD \LOTUS
    LOTUS

The screen will then prompt you to select a program. If you select the main 1-2-3 spreadsheet program, 1-2-3 will spin the diskette in drive A to check the copy-protection scheme if you have not installed it permanently according to the manufacturer's instructions. In either case, you no longer need to have the floppy diskette in drive A.

Configuring Programs

When you copy a program to a hard disk from a floppy diskette, the program is not necessarily *configured*. Configuration refers to those special settings in the software that give the program all of the information unique to your system, such as what type of screen display and printer are being used. In addition, some programs require you to specify the default data drive and directory. 1-2-3 is one of those programs.

Just because the program was copied to the hard disk, it does not follow that 1-2-3 knows what drive you want to use for data. Many times when 1-2-3 is copied onto a hard disk, the program still attempts to store data on drive B. To change the default disk and directory for any program like this, you usually must invoke some command in the software; refer to your application software's user's guide to discover it. In 1-2-3, this command is /wgdd.

Creating Multiple Subdirectories for Your Data Files

Since 1-2-3 allows you to change the subdirectory used to store program data, you can create a separate directory for your spreadsheet files. In fact, if you work in an office where more than one person uses the computer, each person's work can be stored in a different subdirectory. The same concept can be used to store work related to different projects in separate subdirectories.

To see how this procedure works, you must return to the operating system level. As you know, subdirectories are organized in a hierarchy. The root directory is the parent of all subdirectories. Each directory created in the root can in turn have its own children; for example, LOTUS is a subdirectory of the root. LOTUS can also have subdirectories of its own.

Suppose that in your office, three people—Sue, Harry, and Alice—will be working with 1-2-3. To keep their documents separate, you can group and store their files in unique subdirectories. Create individual directories for each of these people by entering the following:

MD \LOTUS\SUE
MD \LOTUS\HARRY
MD \LOTUS\ALICE

Drive C will then be structured as shown in Figure 5.2, which shows a tree view. Figure 5.3 shows another way to visualize the directory structure: a line view. In the remainder of this chapter, you'll use the line view.

RUNNING PROGRAMS FROM WITHIN SUBDIRECTORIES

You now have set up a directory that contains the main program files (the Lotus programs in this example, but it could just as well be one of the word processing programs in the last section). To run the program, you change the main directory to LOTUS with the CD command, bring up the program, and then tell the program in which subdirectory you wish to work. This type of request for changing the default directory from within a program varies with each program, but the concept—separating program and data files into separate directories, then making the desired data directory the default—remains the same.

In 1-2-3, you use the file directory (/FD) command to change default subdirectories. The program will first display the current directory setting. Because you started 1-2-3 from the main LOTUS directory, 1-2-3 automatically sets C:\LOTUS as the default directory. To change directories, you enter the full path name of the subdirectory that you want to use. If you were Alice, for instance, you would tell 1-2-3 that you want to use your specific directory. Including the drive letter as well, you would enter

C:\LOTUS\ALICE

All files would be saved in or retrieved from the subdirectory LOTUS\ALICE. In this way, Alice can separate her work from Harry's and Sue's. If Harry or Sue later log on, they can follow the same sequence to ensure that they have access to the files in their own subdirectories.

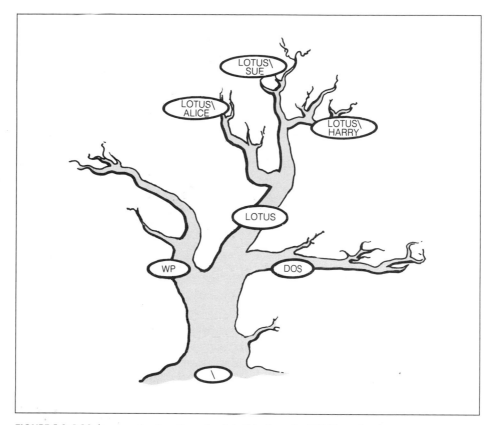

FIGURE 5.2: DOS directory structure (tree view). In this view of a DOS hierarchy, the tree grows new branches (named in the figure) as new subdirectories are created with the MD command. In this figure, after MD \LOTUS creates the LOTUS subdirectory in the root, the three succeeding MD commands create the subdirectories ALICE, SUE, and HARRY.

Tip: Because every program makes different assumptions about default directories, you may at times try to retrieve a file and not find it. Check the default directory setting. The solution to your problem may be as easy as changing the default directory to the directory that you usually use for file work.

Loading and Running Your Database Management System

As a last example, you will create a directory for a DBMS (database management system). Suppose you intend to use a package such as dBASE III PLUS for several purposes. You plan to write your own custom accounting program to

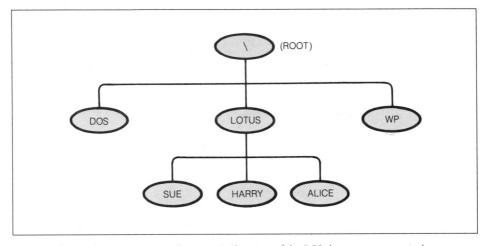

FIGURE 5.3: DOS directory structure (line view). This view of the DOS directory structure is the conventional representation of a disk hierarchy. In this view, the structure is represented by lines leading down from parent to child directories, with ellipses representing subdirectories. Directory names are placed within the ellipses.

manage your entire inventory system, and you also plan to manage your company's personnel records with the software.

With the following commands you can quickly visualize and then create the new directory structure:

MD \DBMS
MD \DBMS\ACCOUNTS
MD \DBMS\INVNTORY
MD \DBMS\PRSONNEL

The results are shown in Figure 5.4. As you can see, you've set up a directory structure organized by application purpose. Similarly, in the last section you set up several subdirectories: one for the data files of each user of the spreadsheet program. It's up to you to decide how to group your files.

You now probably want to run your DBMS program. If you are a dBASE III PLUS user, you could simply use the CD \DBMS command and then enter the program name:

DBASE

You could then change the default directory from within the program. However, you can conveniently set the default file directory *before* you execute the main program. The next section describes how.

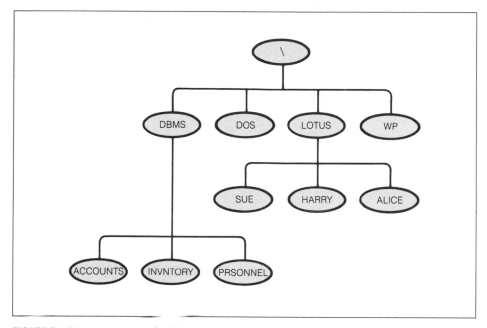

FIGURE 5.4: Directory structure for DBMS applications. This line view shows the structure after adding a DBMS subdirectory to the root and adding three application directories (ACCOUNTS, INVNTORY, and PRSONNEL) to the DBMS. The line view of the hierarchy continues to provide a clearer and more concise representation of the structure than a tree view.

RUNNING ANY PROGRAM ON YOUR HARD DISK

When you have set the working directory to the one you want to use, related files will be read from and written into that directory. Suppose, however, that you then want to run a utility program that is in another directory. For instance, suppose you want to run the CHKDSK program in the DOS directory, or a special hard disk management program such as QDOS II, located in the UTILITY\MISC directory.

It usually is preferable to remain in the current directory, if possible, rather than go to the trouble of changing to another directory. In fact, more and more programs are allowing users to run other programs while they are still active, so you most likely will be able to maintain the current working directory. You can do this by using the PATH and APPEND commands. (APPEND is available only to DOS 3.3 users.)

Assume that you've copied all the necessary database programs onto your hard disk and now you want to see how much space remains. Assume also that you are logged onto the DBMS directory. If you entered CHKDSK now to analyze the disk, you will get the message "Bad command or file name," indicating that DOS cannot run the CHKDSK program. DOS looks in only the current directory for this program. Because you are probably logged onto the DBMS directory, DOS reports that it cannot find the program you requested.

Opening a Path to Any Program

The CHKDSK program *is* on the hard disk, but it is stored in the DOS subdirectory. How can you tell DOS to check the DOS subdirectory if it can't find the requested program in the current directory? You can use the PATH command. The command tells DOS what subdirectories, in addition to the current one, to check when you specify a program to run.

To open a path to the DOS subdirectory, enter

PATH \DOS

The CHKDSK command now executes properly, because the path to the correct subdirectory is open.

As you saw in Chapter 4, you can open a more complex path by using a semicolon to separate a list of directory names. For this example, enter

PATH \DOS;\WP;\LOTUS;\DBMS

If DOS can't find the program name you enter in the current default directory, it will first look for that program in the DOS subdirectory. If it isn't there, DOS will then successively look in the WP, LOTUS, and DBMS subdirectories. Only if it doesn't find the command in any of these directories will it return the "Bad command or file name" message to you.

Warning: Do not leave any spaces between the entries on the path list. DOS stops reading the line as soon as it encounters a space.

By using the PATH command before you start your main program, you can set the path to enable DOS to find any requested program. Whenever your program reads or writes files, it will use the default directory. When it performs other tasks, such as database work using accounting files, it will use the appropriate alternate directory. For example, you can make the DBMS\ACCOUNTS directory the DOS default directory and set the path to DBMS; you can then invoke the database management program (in this case, dBASE III PLUS) by entering

CD \DBMS\ACCOUNTS
PATH \DBMS
DBASE

pressing Return after each line. The default directory is now ACCOUNTS, so dBASE will expect to find all databases and program (.PRG) files in that directory. It will hunt for its own management programs in the directories specified on the path, and it will find them in the DBMS directory.

Tip: Preface all entries in a path with a drive designator for that directory. Then you can execute the program in that directory from any logged drive.

LIMITATIONS OF THE PATH COMMAND

PATH opens a search channel for programs and batch files only—you can't use it to access data files in other subdirectories. In fact, some main programs, such as WordStar (through version 3.3), won't run properly if you use the PATH command. The reason is that WordStar, dBASE, 1-2-3, and most other sophisticated microcomputer programs occasionally need to load overlay files in addition to the main .COM or .EXE file. (Remember, overlay files contain additional program information that usually can't fit into memory along with the main program.) The PATH command searches only the designated directories for files that end with .COM, .EXE, or .BAT. The result is that although DOS may find WS.COM in the WP subdirectory, WordStar can't find the .OVR files that it needs to run.

Some programs, such as dBASE III PLUS, are smart enough to search the operating system path themselves. In such cases, you can set up a useful partitioned directory structure like the one in Figure 5.4. However, when the main program is *not* smart enough to use path information, you may have to put up with the limitation, placing all your data files along with the main program files in one large directory.

Another, better solution allows you the flexibility of using DOS's directory organization. If you are using DOS version 3.2 or an earlier implementation, you can use a separately purchased utility program called SMARTPATH, which extends the path concept to include other types of files besides .EXE, .COM, and .BAT files. In Chapter 20, you will read about several other useful utility programs, which you should seriously consider acquiring, that enable you to extend and more easily harness the capabilities of your operating system.

For now, you should consider using a single PATH command that enables DOS to hunt for and find all of your main programs:

PATH \DOS;\UTIL;\LOTUS;\DBMS;\WP

Tip: The SMARTPATH program is only one of many utility programs you can buy to significantly extend the power of DOS. In the likely event you begin to collect these add-on tools, it is a good idea to place them in their own utility directory. You can create this directory once and then copy your new utility programs to it. You can then add the UTIL directory name to the main path so that DOS can find the SMARTPATH program and any other utility programs when you ask for them.

Creating a Search Path for Nonexecutable Files

DOS 3.3 users can also use the APPEND command, whose syntax is similar to PATH, to create search paths. Just list the directory names containing the files (with extensions other than .COM, .EXE, or .BAT) you want DOS to find after the command name itself. For instance, entering

APPEND \WP;\DBMS\DATA

establishes a search path for DOS to follow to locate overlay files for a word processor or command and database files for a database management system. In fact, any file that does not have the extension .COM, .EXE, or .BAT can be found by including the directory name containing it in the APPEND list. See the simple example in the next section for further information.

Tip: Whether using the PATH or APPEND command, power users should consider redefining the directory path for certain applications. The more often DOS has to resort to the path to find files, the longer time processing takes and the slower the system's response time. In addition, since DOS searches the path in the order in which you list directory names, you should list the directories in the order most likely to succeed. List first the directories that contain the programs you use most frequently.

Working in More Than One Directory: An Example

Look at a simple but realistic example that requires APPEND. In many business environments, a menu program such as PreCursor (see Chapter 20) allows easy selection of different main programs, such as dBASE III PLUS (or Framework II or Lotus 1-2-3). The programming language of dBASE III PLUS offers the capability for further controlling menu choices to run different dBASE programs.

The main menu program typically can locate the directory containing the main application program, such as dBASE III PLUS. Once inside dBASE, however, you may want to create or access data files in several different directories, such as the ACCOUNTS, INVNTORY, or PRSONNEL directories in Figure 5.4. In addition, the main menu program itself may allow parameters, as does PreCursor, that represent data files located in other directories.

Setting up an APPEND command to follow the standard PATH command ensures that all files referenced by either your menu program or your main application program—here, dBASE III PLUS—are easily found:

PATH C:\;C:\DBASE
APPEND C:\;C:\DBASE\ACCOUNTS

In this example, the PATH command ensures that you can access the main modules of dBASE III PLUS from anywhere in your directory structure, and the APPEND command ensures that the data files in the ACCOUNTS directory can be accessed just as easily.

MAPPING YOUR HARD DISK

When you work with floppy diskettes, the DIR command usually provides a sufficient map of each diskette because you probably don't have anything but a root directory on most or all of your floppy diskettes. (Occasionally, however, you may receive a diskette containing files organized into directories. The companion diskette to one of my other books, *Expert dBASE III PLUS*, published by SYBEX in 1987, actually contains multiple directories. Each directory is named after a chapter in the book and contains the sample programs in that chapter. Understanding directory structures is obviously important for using a disk created in this way by someone else; it is just as valuable to you when you back up files or generate a diskette that you want to organize as carefully as your hard disk.)

When you are working with a hard disk that contains many directories, DIR is no longer adequate—it operates on only one directory at a time. The TREE and CHKDSK commands, however, allow you to get information about the hard disk as a whole.

As you saw in Chapter 4, you can use TREE to list all the directories and subdirectories on a disk. Figure 5.5 shows a TREE listing for the hard disk directory structure created in this chapter. Chapter 4 also discussed another option: the CHKDSK/V command. This command lists not only all directories, but the file names within them plus information about disk and memory use. If you don't need all of this information, you should use the TREE command. If you like the format of the TREE command but also want the file names listed (but not the disk and memory status information), you can use the /F switch with TREE.

Both CHKDSK/V and TREE/F usually display a listing much longer than one screenful of data. Since the information displayed by TREE is very valuable to have, you might want to print the TREE display. You do this by using the >PRN redirection command with the TREE command:

TREE/F > PRN

You will now get a complete printed listing of all the files on your hard disk. (You will learn more about the redirection capability in Chapter 17.) Like the TREE/F command, the CHKDSK/V command can also generate a printed copy if you use the redirection command:

CHKDSK/V > PRN

```
DIRECTORY PATH LISTING FOR VOLUME SYBEX_BOOK

Path: \DBMS
Sub-directories:    ACCOUNTS
                    INVNTORY
                    PRSONNEL

Path: \DBMS\ACCOUNTS
Sub-directories:    None

Path: \DBMS\INVNTORY
Sub-directories:    None

Path: \DBMS\PRSONNEL
Sub-directories:    None

Path: \DOS
Sub-directories:    None

Path: \LOTUS
Sub-directories:    SUE
                    HARRY
                    ALICE

Path: \LOTUS\SUE
Sub-directories:    None

Path: \LOTUS\HARRY
Sub-directories:    None

Path: \LOTUS\ALICE
Sub-directories:    None

Path: \WP
Sub-directories:    None
```

FIGURE 5.5: Output from the TREE command. The TREE command provides the usual list of directory path names along with any included subdirectories.

You have now seen two methods by which you can produce a complete listing of all the files on a hard disk. With these lists, you can figure out where on the hard disk various programs and files are stored. You can also use these lists to find lost files and identify files to be erased.

DOS COMMANDS USED IN WORKING WITH HARD DISK DIRECTORIES

This section describes in detail the DOS commands used for working with hard disk directories.

FDISK

This command divides a hard disk into *partitions*, so that the disk can contain more than one operating system.

SYNTAX

[*D:Path*]**FDISK**

    D:Path   is the drive and path where the command file is located if it is not in the current directory.

TYPE

External.

USAGE

FDISK allows you to create a new partition, delete an old partition, specify the active partition, display current partition information, partition multiple hard drives, and define new logical drives within extended partitions.

You can set up a hard disk to contain more than one type of operating system. For example, DOS 3.3 can manage one part of a disk, and UNIX can manage another. Each of these sections is called a *partition*. A disk can contain from one to four partitions (see Chapter 19).

Note that you must set up partitions *before* the disk is logically formatted. All data on your hard disk will be destroyed when you create partitions with FDISK. If your disk is already being used and you wish to create a partition, you will have to back up all of your data, run FDISK on the system diskette, and then reformat your disk.

You can set up two types of partitions for DOS: a primary partition and an extended partition. DOS needs only the primary partition, which can be as large as 32Mb. If you have more space available than that on one hard disk, you will need to create an extended partition, which you assign the next logical drive letter. You can also subdivide the extended partition into more logical drives, up to the letter Z. Partitioning is performed because DOS is limited to 32Mb per drive.

RESTRICTIONS

You can use FDISK only on hard disk systems. A disk must be reformatted logically after being partitioned. FDISK will not work if another process is accessing the disk.

EXAMPLES

See Chapter 19 for an extensive presentation on the FDISK command procedure.

PROMPT

This command changes the system prompt to whatever you like—it can display the time, the date, or a simple message. This command is useful for determining the current directory before you modify or delete any files.

SYNTAX

PROMPT [*String*]

    String   is a string of characters that can contain special-purpose entries. Possible values are shown in Table 5.1.

TYPE

Internal.

USAGE

The PROMPT command is frequently used to redefine the system prompt to include more useful information than just the default drive letter. Prior to each command entry, DOS can display a host of useful system information, such as drive letter, directory name, date, time, and even cursor and color values. Display of the default drive and directory are the most common uses of this command, although sophisticated users frequently display the other values as well. See Chapter 10 for a more detailed discussion of configuration possibilities using the PROMPT command.

The character sequences for creating special prompts are always two characters long, beginning with the dollar sign ($). You can combine any number of these sequences to create more complex and informative DOS prompts.

EXAMPLES

The standard adjustments to your prompt can be made with any two-character sequence shown in Table 5.1.

CHARACTERS	DESCRIPTION
$$	$ sign
$t	Time
$d	Date
$p	Current directory
$v	DOS version number
$n	Default drive identifier
$g	> symbol
$l	< symbol
$b	¦ symbol
$q	= symbol
$h	Erasing backspace
$e	Escape character
$_	Carriage return and line feed

TABLE 5.1: Special-Purpose PROMPT Codes (Meta Strings)

Each special result is obtained with a different character preceded by a $. The simplest and most common change in the default prompt causes the prompt to display *drive:current directory*. To effect this change, enter

PROMPT $P

If your current default directory were \Lotus, the prompt now would read

C:\Lotus _

If your monitor supports graphic functions or color and you have installed the ANSI escape sequence support function, then you can use the additional escape codes shown in Table 5.2. You make these available by including the symbols $e[p1;p2;...m in your prompt sequence. Use the values in Table 5.2 to select number codes for colors and screen attributes.

For example, the following PROMPT command results in a standard prompt of current *drive:directory*, nestled inside square brackets. This prompt is displayed as bold white letters on a red background.

PROMPT $e[1;37;41m[$P]$e[0m

	CODE		MEANING
Attributes	0		All attributes off
	1		Boldfacing
	4		Underlining (on IBM-compatible monochrome monitors only)
	5		Blinking
	7		Reverse video
Colors	**Foreground**	**Background**	
	30	40	Black
	31	41	Red
	32	42	Green
	33	43	Yellow
	34	44	Blue
	35	45	Magenta
	36	46	Cyan
	37	47	White

TABLE 5.2: Screen Attribute and Color Codes

SUMMARY

In this chapter, you have explored the DOS capabilities for setting up a complex but highly usable structure of directories on any hard disk. You learned how to set up your hard disk for a word processor, a spreadsheet, and a database management system. Using these examples, you should be able to set up a functioning directory structure for any application software system.

For additional information about the XCOPY command, see

- Chapter 3, "The Disk System"

For additional information about the PATH command, see

- Chapter 4, "Understanding Directories and Subdirectories"

For additional information about defining paths to data files, see the APPEND command in

- Chapter 19, "Other Advanced Commands"

For additional information about disk management and menu software, see

- Chapter 20, "Extending DOS's Power with Utility Software"

The next group of chapters, Part III, discusses batch files and the built-in DOS line editor, EDLIN. Batch files offer a convenient means of streamlining your work with DOS. Essentially, you can group together a sequence of commands into a single named file and then run the entire sequence at any time just by typing the sequence name. EDLIN is a small word processor, less powerful (and less friendly) than commercially available programs, but it comes free with DOS. Although creating and editing batch files is by no means the only use for EDLIN, many users consider it the most appropriate. For that reason, and because some readers may not have access to a more powerful add-on word processor, the use of EDLIN is presented as a kind of prologue to the use of batch files.

PART

3

BATCH FILES

Automating your work is an important goal of computerization. DOS provides a batch-file programming language that can save you time and energy by reducing the drudgery of repetitive command entry. In this section, you will learn about batch-file creation, the fundamental techniques for using batch files, and the built-in subcommand language DOS provides. This section also presents a host of useful example batch programs that you can copy and implement on your own computer system.

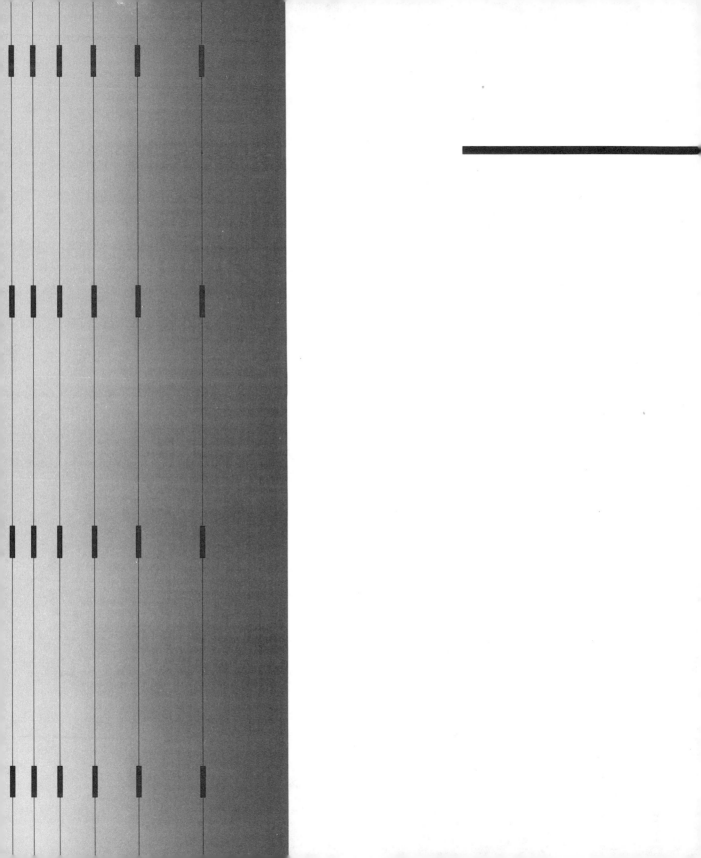

CHAPTER 6

EDLIN: THE DOS EDITOR

EDLIN: The DOS Editor

In addition to their ability to process numbers and large amounts of data, computers are exceptionally good at manipulating text. It comes as no surprise, then, that so many different programs are available to do this.

The advantages of using a computer instead of a typewriter are many. Computers allow text to be manipulated on the screen, changed, and corrected before it is printed. Computers also can store entire documents and reports on disk for later use. Thus, with a computer, you can type half a report, go away for a week, and then come back and finish your work. You can create a rough draft and later correct it in minutes, without having to retype the entire document.

Two primary kinds of program allow you to create and manipulate text. The first kind is a line editor like the DOS EDLIN editor. With a line editor, you work with a line of text at time. Line editors number each line and reference each line by these numbers. You can make changes in only one line at a time.

The second kind of program, a word processor, shows you a full screen of text. You can move the screen cursor to any character position on any line and make changes anywhere on the screen. Word processors usually support such features as multiple fonts, boldfacing, and underlining.

Naturally, it's up to you to choose the kind of program you want. You may want to use both, at different times. The DOS line editor consumes very little memory space (only 7526 bytes), and it comfortably fits on most application diskettes in diskette-based systems. This means that you won't need to juggle diskettes often. On the other hand, your work may require the more extensive set of commands available with most word processors. You may also prefer the full-screen mode of a typical word processor that allows you to edit any character on any line. Also, word processors are much more user friendly than line editors. Text manipulation is typically much easier with a word processor than with EDLIN. The cryptic one-letter commands of EDLIN have been attacked from all directions as inconvenient, annoying, and error inviting. There really is no comparison, from the standpoint of user friendliness, between EDLIN and full-screen word processors, with their comprehensible commands and easy-to-use menus.

User friendliness, however, is not always the only factor used in deciding whether to use EDLIN or another product. Full-screen word processors invariably require more RAM than does EDLIN and consume much more disk. These factors, of course, are irrelevant if you have more than enough space on your hard disk and plenty of RAM in your system.

Word processors also cost a lot more than EDLIN, which is included for free with DOS, so that may also be a factor in your decision. However, if you are a typical DOS user, you will likely use both EDLIN and a more powerful word processor.

Size and speed are two more factors to consider. Owing to its larger size, a powerful word processor usually takes longer to start up (sometimes as long as 15 seconds) than does EDLIN. If you're only making a simple correction, you may prefer the speedier route of using EDLIN. Also, the EDLIN program is so small that you can keep a copy of it on each of several diskettes for rapid and easy file editing. Most advanced word processors are too large to fit on diskettes that contain other sophisticated software.

DOS provides the EDLIN.COM program as part of your system. It is disk-resident and acts like any other external command. You can use EDLIN to create and edit ASCII text files, which are files that contain standard letters, numbers, and punctuation symbols. Besides the documents that we ordinarily think of as text, these files can consist of source code for programs that you will assemble and, most importantly for some users, DOS batch files, which are discussed in Chapters 7,8, and 9. Except for the special codes indicating carriage returns, line feeds, and the end of a file (Ctrl-Z), text files have no control codes for such features as underlining on a printer or high-intensity display on a screen. (You can easily display a text file on screen with the TYPE command.) In short, EDLIN works with whole lines of text, but you cannot use it to change fonts or to produce boldface or underlined text. EDLIN can, however, manipulate text files, and it contains search and replace functions and standard text-editing features.

STARTING EDLIN

Start EDLIN from the DOS prompt with the command

[*Drive*] [*Path*] **EDLIN** *FileSpec*

where *FileSpec* is the drive, path, file name, and extension of the file to be edited. You must enter the full file name, including any extension. *Drive* and *Path* indicate, as with all external commands, the source of the command file; they must be specified when that source is not the current drive or path. EDLIN must either be resident on the disk you are using, in the current default directory, or on the path to be searched by DOS.

> *Tip:* You can use the optional /B switch (short for binary) with the EDLIN command when the file you will be using contains Ctrl-Z markers other than the end-of-file marker. As you'll learn later in this chapter, you can use EDLIN to incorporate and then edit control characters in a text file.

Starting a New File

If you invoke EDLIN with a *FileSpec* value for a file that does not currently exist, EDLIN will respond with the following message and prompt:

New file
*_

EDLIN gives you a clean slate and awaits your commands. Table 6.1 summarizes the commands you can use with EDLIN, their actions, and their general formats. You will learn about each of these as you read this chapter. In addition, the reference section of this chapter provides more information about the EDLIN commands.

Changing an Existing File

Invoking EDLIN with the *FileSpec* of an existing file yields the following:

End of input file
*_

COMMAND	ACTION	GENERAL FORMAT
A	Appends lines	[*Num*]A
C	Copies lines	[*Line*],[*Line*],*Line*[,*Count*] C
D	Deletes lines	[*Line*][,*Line*]D
- -	Edits line	[*Line*]
E	Updates and exits document	E
I	Inserts lines	[*Line*]I
L	Lists lines	[*Line*][,*Line*] L
M	Moves lines	[*Line*],[*Line*],*Line*M
P	Displays full page	[*Line*][,*Line*] P
Q	Aborts changes and exits document	Q
R	Replaces globally	[*Line*][,*Line*] [?] R[*String*][^ Z*NewString*]
S	Searches globally	[*Line*][,*Line*] [?] S[*String*]
T	Merges files	[*Line*] T [*FileSpec*]
W	Writes lines	[*Num*] W

TABLE 6.1: EDLIN Commands

EDLIN tries to load your entire text file into available memory (RAM). When it tries to load a file that exceeds 75 percent of the currently available RAM, it loads only part of the file, using only 75 percent of the available memory. The message just shown will not appear, but the prompt will. You may then edit the lines that were loaded. When you are done editing these lines, you can use EDLIN commands to write the edited lines to a diskette and then display additional text lines to edit.

Bringing New Text into Memory

The Append command, abbreviated as the single character A, adds new, unedited lines of text from a disk file. Use this command only when you have loaded a file that is larger than 75 percent of current memory. Enter Append at the EDLIN * prompt, using this general format:

[*Num*]A

Note: The brackets around parameters in this chapter indicate EDLIN parameters that are optional for a command. Do not enter the brackets themselves as part of the command.

This command loads *Num* lines from the rest of the file (where *Num* is the number of lines to load), provided there is room. EDLIN will load as many lines into memory as it can fit. If there is insufficient room to load any more lines from your file, the command will not load anything. You must then use the W command (described shortly) to write some of your edited lines from EDLIN to disk.

If you successfully load the rest of the file into memory, the following message will appear:

End of input file

You can then continue editing using any of the EDLIN commands.

Combining Separate Text Files

The Transfer command (T) combines two text files: one in memory and another somewhere else. When you specify the file to be transferred to your current file (*FileSpec*), EDLIN reads in the whole file and inserts it before the line number specified by *Line:*

[*Line*] **T** *FileSpec*

If you have not specified *Line,* EDLIN inserts the file's contents before the current line.

The Transfer command can be quite useful. For example, suppose you have the following two files:

File1	**File2**
1: Line 1, File 1	1: Line 1, File 2
2: Line 2, File 1	2: Line 2, File 2
3: Line 3, File 1	3: Line 3, File 2
4: Line 4, File 1	4: Line 4, File 2

If File1 is the current file being edited in memory, and you enter the following command:

3 T FILE2

the result is a new, combined file that looks like this:

```
1:  Line 1, File 1
2:  Line 2, File 1
3:*Line 1, File 2
4:  Line 2, File 2
5:  Line 3, File 2
6:  Line 4, File 2
7:  Line 3, File 1
8:  Line 4, File 1
```

Note that the current line is now the first line of the transferred file, as indicated by the EDLIN * prompt.

Making Space for Large Files

You need the Write command (W), like the Append command, only when your file is too large to fit in 75 percent of available memory. In that situation, only as many lines of your file as can fit in that space (75 percent of available memory) will have been loaded. To edit the rest of the file, you need to make room. You must transfer lines from the file in memory to disk, thus freeing enough space to load more, if not all, of the file. The general format of the Write command is

[*Num*] **W**

where *Num* is the number of lines to be written. After you execute this command, you can load the rest of the file with the A command.

If you do not specify the number of lines to be written, the W command will keep writing lines to the disk, starting with line 1, until 75 percent of available memory is free. If 75 percent of available RAM is already freed for EDLIN text lines, then no lines will be written to disk. If, for example, the first 200 lines were written to disk, then line 201 of the total file would become line 1 of the memory portion being worked on by EDLIN. For example, the command

200 W

would cause the first 200 lines of the current file to be transferred to disk, and line 201 would be numbered line 1. You could then use the A command to read in additional text lines from the disk file.

DISPLAYING EDLIN FILES

Perhaps the task you'll most frequently ask your line editor to perform will be showing you the text in a file. EDLIN offers two commands for this purpose: the L command, for listing any range of lines, and the P command, for rapidly displaying complete screenfuls of your file.

Listing Your Text File

Since line numbers change each time you add or delete a line, the List command (L) will probably be the EDLIN command you use most frequently. You will always want to see the new numbers assigned to your text lines before you execute line-oriented commands.

You can list a block of lines in a variety of ways. If you don't provide explicit line starting and ending numbers, EDLIN will attempt to display 23 text lines: one screenful. The size of the display range can extend from 11 lines before the current line to 11 lines after the current line.

Most commonly you will specify the command using the precise line numbers at which to begin and end the listing. For example,

6,19L

displays lines 6 through 19 on your screen and then redisplays the EDLIN prompt.

Simply typing L with no line-number specification displays the 11 lines preceding the current line, then the current line, and then the 11 lines after the current line. If your file has less than 23 lines, EDLIN displays the entire file.

Listing Your Text File Rapidly

The Page command (P) works like the L command, except that it redefines the current line number as whatever line was last displayed on the screen. This command gives you a way to list rapidly all the lines in your text file a screenful at a time, and to move to a specific point in your file.

Entering a line number alone, such as

17 P

displays up to 23 lines, in this case starting with line 17. The last line listed becomes the current line. You can also display a specified range of lines and make the last line the current line; for example, you can enter

14,28 P

If you simply enter P, EDLIN will make its standard assumptions, displaying 23 lines starting with the line after the current line and making the last line displayed the new current line.

EDITING EDLIN FILES

As the previous sections of this chapter indicate, EDLIN is *command oriented;* that is, it does not display menus, but rather expects you to enter individual commands, just as DOS does. Because of this, you can move around and execute tasks in EDLIN much more quickly than you can with a menu system, but you must know the commands to execute them quickly and correctly.

The EDLIN prompt, as you have seen, is the asterisk symbol. Whenever the asterisk appears on the screen with a blinking cursor next to it, EDLIN is prompting you for a command. This prompt also shows you the current line of the file being edited, which is the default line being worked on. Any EDLIN command you enter will apply to the text on this particular line (and possibly others as well). You can use a variety of commands to edit lines in your file and to move a certain number of lines forward or backward from the current line, insert, edit, or delete text in relation to this current line.

Here are some useful tips to keep in mind as you work with EDLIN:

- You can enter most commands using just the first letter of the command. When you are performing an operation on a specific line or group of lines, specify the line numbers first. For example, to delete line 7 of your text file, you simply need to precede the deletion command (the letter D) with the line number (7):

    7D

- You can enter the EDLIN letter commands in uppercase, lowercase, or uppercase-lowercase format. For example, the command in the preceding example could just as easily have been entered as

    7d

When you enter command requests, you can use whatever case is most convenient.

- You must specify line numbers as whole numbers between 1 and 65529. When you enter more than one line number, you must separate the numbers with commas. If you enter a line number higher than the highest line number in memory and you then add a line, the line will be added after the highest line number. In other words, if you know that your file is approximately 25 lines long (assume that in fact it is precisely 22 lines long), entering the insertion request

    50i

inserts your new text directly after the actual last line in your file (after line 22 in this example).

- You can use the pound symbol (#) to refer to the line, as yet nonexistent, that will follow the highest line number currently in memory. Thus, you don't have to keep mental track of approximately how many lines exist in your file. You can just add new lines at the end of the file by specifying # as the line number as follows:

    #i

This entry has the same effect as the previous example. However, this method is preferable since it eliminates the possibility of error due to specifying a line number that actually lies within the range of existing line numbers.

- You can use a period to specify the current line. For example, suppose you had just edited line 12 in your file but then decided you wanted to reedit that line. Although you could reenter the number 12 at the asterisk prompt, you could also just enter the period symbol:

Line 12 would be redisplayed for editing.

- You can use the Plus and Minus keys to specify lines *relative* to the current line number. For example,

    – 20, + 5D

deletes the 20 lines preceding the current line number, the current line number, and 5 lines after the current line number. If the current line number is 50, the command will delete lines 30 through 55.

- You can enter more than one command on a line. Simply separate the commands with semicolons (;). For example, you can combine the command to delete lines 4 through 7 with a command to redisplay the remaining lines:

  4,7D;L

  As soon as it executes the deletion request, EDLIN looks for the next command submitted at the same time, based on the semicolon it finds after the D. These combined commands let you easily view line numbers and editing results to evaluate the effect of the editing operation.

- You can (although it is not often necessary) enter a control character into a file. Press Ctrl-V first and then the desired control character (in uppercase). For example, if you were entering a text file containing tabular information, you could align the text entries in colums by entering Ctrl-V followed by Ctrl-I just before you enter the text to be aligned.

- When you are displaying a lot of data, you can pause the screen output by pressing the Break key, Ctrl-ScrollLock. Press Ctrl-ScrollLock again to restart the output. Note that this command also stops the command processing.

- With some commands, you can enter optional parameters. Usually, these parameters take the place of the numbers indicating the line on which the command is to act. If you omit a parameter, EDLIN usually will assume a value. You must, however, hold the place of an omitted parameter with a comma. For example, if you have just edited line 3 in your file and you want to place a copy of lines 3, 4, and 5 just before line 15 in your file, you enter

  ,5,15C

  The first comma takes the place of the missing first parameter: namely, the starting line number for the copy operation.

Now let's look at the editing tasks EDLIN performs and the commands that execute them.

Inserting New Lines

The Insert command (I) inserts lines. Its general format is

[*Line*]I

Again, you can specify *Line* as either a specific or a relative line number. Not including *Line* will result in lines being added before the current line. If you created a new file called LINCOLN.TXT by calling EDLIN, you would use the I command to insert text for the first time at line 1. At the EDLIN * prompt, enter

> ***1I**

This command yields

> **1:*_**

which places you in insert mode. As Figure 6.1 shows, EDLIN displays each line number as you type it.

```
C>EDLIN  LINCOLN.TXT
New file
*1I
        1:*Four score and seven months ago (approximately),
        2:*DOS's forefathers brought forth upon this nation
        3:*a new operating system (more or less).
        4:*^C

*_
```

FIGURE 6.1: Inserting text for the first time. When you create a new text file, the first command (1I) facilitates entry of text lines beginning with line number 1. The ^C on line 4 terminates line entry mode and returns you to the EDLIN command prompt.

Notice the ^C on line 4. This is EDLIN's response when you press Ctrl-C during text insertion. Use the Ctrl-C key combination to exit from text insertion mode and return to the EDLIN prompt.

You can also use the I command to insert new text before any existing text line in a file. Simply specify the number of the line in the file before which you want the new text placed.

Tip: Inserting lines changes all line numbers after the insertion. For example, if you insert new text at line 3, remember that all line numbers after 3 have been changed. You should print a new listing (L) to see the new numbering before you issue any further commands.

Changing Existing Lines

Editing a line merely means that you are changing the information on the line, *not* adding or deleting a line. If you don't specify a line number (in other words, you have simply pressed Return), then EDLIN will let you edit the line after the current line. This may at first appear contrary to what you might expect, but EDLIN was purposely designed this way. This feature allows you more easily to edit a series of lines consecutively: You merely need to edit the first line in the series, press Return, and then press Return again to edit the next line; you don't need to enter the next line's number. If the current line is the last line in the file, pressing Return simply produces another * prompt. You can also enter any line number, or enter a relative line number, to activate edit mode for that line.

When you are in edit mode, the display looks something like this:

3:*a new operating system (more or less).
3:*_

The old line 3 is displayed, followed by a new line 3 displaying only the number of the line. The edited old line 3 will become the new line 3 after you complete your editing entries and press Return.

THE EDITING KEYS

The arrow keys and function keys work as they do at the DOS prompt. For instance, in the preceding example, pressing F3 will completely retype the original line 3 and move the cursor to the end of the line to await additional input, as follows:

3:*a new operating system (more or less).
3:*a new operating system (more or less)._

While you are editing any line, pressing the Right Arrow key moves the cursor one character to the right and displays the character the cursor was on (or under). Pressing Esc-Return or the Break key combination anywhere on the line cancels edit mode and leaves the line unchanged.

To add text to the end of a line, simply press F3 and start typing. EDLIN will automatically activate insert mode. However, if your cursor is located anywhere else on the line, you must press the Ins key to enter insert mode, and you must press it again to exit that mode. In Figure 6.2, you can see how line 3 of the example was changed. You press F3, use the Backspace key to erase the period, and then type the new characters

, dedicated

```
C>EDLIN LINCOLN.TXT
End of input file
*L
        1:*Four score and seven months ago (approximately),
        2: DOS's forefathers brought forth upon this nation
        3: a new operating system (more or less).
*3
        3:*a new operating system (more or less).
        3:*a new operating system (more or less), dedicated
*L
        1: Four score and seven months ago (approximately),
        2: DOS's forefathers brought forth upon this nation
        3:*a new operating system (more or less), dedicated
*■
```

FIGURE 6.2: Making corrections to a line. The three lines of the LINCOLN.TXT file are first displayed with the L command, then line 3 is edited by simply entering the number 3 as a command, and finally, the new version of the complete file is listed once again with the L command.

Both before and after the change, you enter the L command to display the current contents of the file.

The edit of line 3 is only the first step in a common sequence, as shown in Figure 6.3. You make a change, then list the file, then enter another editing change (in this case, new text inserted at the end of the file), and then enter another L command to verify the results of the edit. Continuing this process and adding still more text (with a correction to line 10 along the way) results in the 12-line text file shown in Figure 6.4.

Moving Lines: Cutting and Pasting

The Move command (M) allows you to move one line or a body of lines in a file to a new location in the file. (A group of lines to be moved is called a *block.*) For example, entering

9,12,6M
L

at the EDLIN prompt moves lines 9 through 12 in the file shown in Figure 6.4 to a new position—in front of line 6, as shown in Figure 6.5. This operation commonly is called *cutting and pasting.* When the operation is completed, all affected lines are renumbered. Notice that the new line 6 is now the current line, since this was the first line in the block that was moved.

```
C>EDLIN LINCOLN.TXT
End of input file
*L
        1:*Four score and seven months ago (approximately),
        2: DOS's forefathers brought forth upon this nation
        3: a new operating system (more or less).
*3

        3:*a new operating system (more or less).
        3:*a new operating system (more or less), dedicated
*L

        1: Four score and seven months ago (approximately),
        2: DOS's forefathers brought forth upon this nation
        3:*a new operating system (more or less), dedicated
*4I
        4:*to the proposition that all computers (with the same
        5:*microcomputer chip) are created equal.
        6:*^C

*L
        1: Four score and seven months ago (approximately),
        2: DOS's forefathers brought forth upon this nation
        3: a new operating system (more or less), dedicated
        4: to the proposition that all computers (with the same
        5: microcomputer chip) are created equal.

*▪
```

FIGURE 6.3: Adding new lines at the end of a file. The command 4I places you in a mode that allows the addition of new lines. Two lines (numbered 4 and 5) are added and then a Ctrl-C is typed to escape from the addition mode back to the asterisk prompt. An L command confirms that the two new lines have been correctly added to the existing three lines.

```
        5: microcomputer chip) are created equal.
        6: We are met today to chronicle a part of these DOS
        7: wars.  It is altogether fitting and proper (some may
        8: disagree) that we should do this.
        9: Now, we are engaged in a great computer war (more
       10: have fallen than have risen), testing whether this DOS
       11: or any other DOS so conceived and so dedicated, can
       12: long endure.
*10
       10:*have fallen than have risen), testing whether this DOS
       10:*have fallen than have risen), testing whether this DOS,
*L

        1: Four score and seven months ago (approximately),
        2: DOS's forefathers brought forth upon this nation
        3: a new operating system (more or less), dedicated
        4: to the proposition that all computers (with the same
        5: microcomputer chip) are created equal.
        6: We are met today to chronicle a part of these DOS
        7: wars.  It is altogether fitting and proper (some may
        8: disagree) that we should do this.
        9: Now, we are engaged in a great computer war (more
       10:*have fallen than have risen), testing whether this DOS,
       11: or any other DOS so conceived and so dedicated, can
       12: long endure.

*▪
```

FIGURE 6.4: Intermediate version of the text file. Continued additions to this file result in a new 12-line version. After a comma is inserted at the end of line 10, the current status of the file is displayed with the L command.

```
             3: a new operating system (more or less), dedicated
             4: to the proposition that all computers (with the same
             5: microcomputer chip) are created equal.
             6: We are met today to chronicle a part of these DOS
             7: wars.  It is altogether fitting and proper (some may
             8: disagree) that we should do this.
             9: Now, we are engaged in a great computer war (more
            10:*have fallen than have risen), testing whether this DOS,
            11: or any other DOS so conceived and so dedicated, can
            12: long endure.
         *9,12,6M
         *L
             1: Four score and seven months ago (approximately),
             2: DOS's forefathers brought forth upon this nation
             3: a new operating system (more or less), dedicated
             4: to the proposition that all computers (with the same
             5: microcomputer chip) are created equal.
             6:*Now, we are engaged in a great computer war (more
             7: have fallen than have risen), testing whether this DOS,
             8: or any other DOS so conceived and so dedicated, can
             9: long endure.
            10: We are met today to chronicle a part of these DOS
            11: wars.  It is altogether fitting and proper (some may
            12: disagree) that we should do this.
         *▄
```

FIGURE 6.5: Cutting and pasting text. In this example, the last sentence (lines 9 through 12) is moved to a new point just before the sentence that starts at the beginning of line 6.

Copying Lines

The Copy command (C) copies blocks of lines to other places in a file. It is similar to the M command, although not as frequently used. When you use the C command, the original lines are not moved to a new place in the file and deleted from the old place; instead, they are replicated in the new place, and the original lines are left intact. After the copy operation, all line numbers are recalculated, and the first line that was copied becomes the new current line.

The general format of the C command is

> **[*Line1*], [*Line2*], *Line3* [,*Count*] C**

Notice that the first two *line* parameters are optional, but the third is not. This third parameter represents the point before which the copied line(s) will be inserted. *Line1* and *Line2* define the line or range of lines to be copied; if they are omitted, the current line will be used. The optional *Count* parameter allows you to repeat the copy operation a specified number of times. Also notice the required commas. Remember that when you omit an optional parameter in an EDLIN command, you must mark its place with a comma. Likewise, when you include an optional parameter, you must also include a comma to separate it from the next parameter.

There are three versions of the C command. In the first, you can make a replica of the current text line anywhere else in the file. EDLIN will insert the copy of the current line in front of the line specified by *Line3:*

> **,,*Line3* [,*Count*] C**

Since you haven't entered values for *Line1* and *Line2*, EDLIN uses the default line (that is, the current line).

You can also copy multiple lines at once using the C command. The following format copies all lines from *Line1* through the current line to the position before *Line3*:

Line1,,Line3 [,Count] C

Note: In any EDLIN command that allows the specification of multiple lines, the beginning line number must be less than or equal to the ending line number. EDLIN cannot work backward.

The third C command format allows you to explicitly specify a range of lines to be copied:

Line1,Line2 [,count] C

Line1 represents the start of the range, and *Line2* represents the end. This version of the C command is similar to the previous version, except that you specify the last line number to be copied instead of using the EDLIN default value (the current line number).

The following example uses the *Count* parameter with the C command. While editing any text file of at least five lines, entering

*1,4,5,3 C

tells EDLIN to copy lines 1 through 4 in your file to a point just before line 5 and then to repeat this operation twice more (a total of 3 times). You can perform a repeating copy operation, for example, when you may have created a table of information and wish to generate several versions of the table, each slightly different than the others. A repeating copy operation like this one can provide the copied versions, each of which you can then separately modify. Repeating copy operations also are often useful in programs or batch files when you have created a block of programming code that you want to execute several times with slight modification. A programming loop or decision point that executes the same code, but under different conditions, is an example of such code.

Searching for Text Strings

The Search command (S) locates lines. You can specify the range for EDLIN to search in a variety of ways. The general format of the S command is

[Scope] [?] S[String]

You can define *Scope* as any of the following parameters:

- *Line* causes the search to start at *Line* and stop at the end of the file.
- *,Line* causes the search to start at the line after the current line and end at *Line.*

- *Line1,Line2* causes the search to cover only the lines within the block between *Line1* and *Line2*.

- Omitting the *Scope* parameter causes the search to start at the line after the current line and end at the last line in the file.

The *String* parameter specifies the text that you are seeking. The first character of this text should immediately follow the S. If you do not specify *String*, EDLIN uses the search string last used in a Search or Replace command. If you haven't yet used a Search or Replace command in the session, then EDLIN displays the message "Not found."

If you specify ? in the S command, EDLIN will stop each time it locates the specified string and ask you to confirm that the string is the correct one.

Warning: The Search and Replace commands are case sensitive—they look for *exactly* what you type. For example, the S command considers *Judd* and *judd* to be two different words because of their different capitalization.

To see the Search command in action, look for all occurrences of the word *is* in the following file:

1: This is the first line
2: of a test file to demonstrate
3: the use of the Search command.
4: It is included for your own
5: information.

You enter the following command:

*1,5 ? Sis

EDLIN then displays

1: This is the first line
O.K.? n
4: It is included for your own
O.K.? n
Not found
*_

In this example, the search string is the phrase *is*. When EDLIN finds the search string in line 1, it asks if this line is the one you are looking for. An answer of N here means that you want EDLIN to keep searching the file for other lines containing the search string. If you respond Y, EDLIN assumes that you want to do something with the text line it just found; it places you in edit mode and makes the line displayed the current line. You can see that line 4 has become the current line, because it was the last line to contain a match with *String*. Notice that

EDLIN displays line 1 only once in the search. This is because the search finds a *line* with a match on it. A line containing more than one match still is displayed only once.

Replacing a Text String

The Replace command (R), searches through any specified range of lines and replaces every occurrence of specific text (*String*) with new, replacement text (*NewString*).

The general format of the R command is

[*Scope*] [?] R[*String*][Ctrl-Z*NewString*]

The *Scope* and *String* parameters are the same as for the Search command. To enter replacement text (*NewString*), end *String* by pressing Ctrl-Z. (*String* is optional, because you may only want to remove the specified string EDLIN finds it.)

NewString is the text that will replace *String*. It does not need to be the same size as *String,* since it will be inserted after *String* has been deleted. If you do not specify *NewString*, then EDLIN deletes *String* in the specified block. If you also do not specify *String*, EDLIN will use the *String* value from the last Search or Replace command and the *NewString* value from the last Replace command. If you have not used the Search and Replace commands during the current session, EDLIN will display the message "Not found."

When you specify ? in the R command, EDLIN displays the replaced or modified line and asks whether you wish to confirm the changes that were made ("O.K.?"). Answer Y or press Return if you want a change to become permanent.

> *Note:* Once EDLIN finds an occurrence of *String* and you have accepted or not accepted the change, EDLIN continues the search in the specified block. EDLIN treats all occurrences of *String* on a single line in the same way; that is, if you want *String* replaced, EDLIN replaces all occurrence of *String* on the line.

Now try the R command with the example used earlier in this chapter. Ask EDLIN to search the file for each occurrence of the text string *DOS* and then replace *DOS* with *MS-DOS*, as shown in Figure 6.6.

In this example, you specified that all occurrences of the search string in lines 1 through 12 be replaced. You can see by the EDLIN prompt that line 10 has become the current line, since it was the last line changed. Notice also that EDLIN displayed each line that contained the search string (lines 2, 7, 8, and 10) after it changed the line. As shown in the figure, you usually execute the L command to verify the results of your command.

```
       7: have fallen than have risen), testing whether this DOS,
       8: or any other DOS so conceived and so dedicated, can
       9: long endure.
      1Ø: We are met today to chronicle a part of these DOS
      11: wars.  It is altogether fitting and proper (some may
      12:*disagree) that we should do this.
*1,12RDOS^ZMS-DOS
       2: MS-DOS's forefathers brought forth upon this nation
       7: have fallen than have risen), testing whether this MS-DOS,
       8: or any other MS-DOS so conceived and so dedicated, can
      1Ø: We are met today to chronicle a part of these MS-DOS
*L
       1: Four score and seven months ago (approximately),
       2: MS-DOS's forefathers brought forth upon this nation
       3: a new operating system (more or less), dedicated
       4: to the proposition that all computers (with the same
       5: microcomputer chip) are created equal.
       6: Now, we are engaged in a great computer war (more
       7: have fallen than have risen), testing whether this MS-DOS,
       8: or any other MS-DOS so conceived and so dedicated, can
       9: long endure.
      1Ø:*We are met today to chronicle a part of these MS-DOS
      11: wars.  It is altogether fitting and proper (some may
      12: disagree) that we should do this.
*▪
```

FIGURE 6.6: Search and replace operation. The R command is invoked here to replace all occurrences of the phrase *DOS* with the phrase *MS-DOS* in the range line 1 to line 12. Notice that the Ctrl-Z character is entered between the search phrase (DOS) and the replacement phrase (MS-DOS). EDLIN displays the four lines (2, 7, 8, and 10) containing the search phrase and therefore subject to the replacement operation.

Deleting Lines

The Delete command (D) deletes one or more lines from a file. Its general format is

[*Line1*],[*Line2*]D

The *Line* parameters specify the line or lines that you want to delete. If you omit the first parameter, *Line1*, EDLIN will start the D command at the current line. You should not omit the second parameter, *Line2* if you want to delete a range. If you do, EDLIN deletes only *Line1*, leaving all additional lines between *Line1* and the current line in the file.

Suppose you write some text and add it to the current file beginning at line 13 (see Figure 6.7), and then you decide (either immediately or later) to delete this new text with the D command. Figure 6.8 shows the results of deleting the lines and then listing the remaining file.

Warning: Deleting lines causes all line numbers after the deletion to be renumbered. Even if you do not request a listing of the lines (with L), they still are renumbered. For example, executing the command 1D twice deletes lines 1 and 2, and makes old line 3 the new line 1. Once again, it is a good idea to list the file after each insertion or deletion.

```
         8: or any other MS-DOS so conceived and so dedicated, can
         9: long endure.
        10: We are met today to chronicle a part of these MS-DOS
        11: wars.  It is altogether fitting and proper (some may
        12: disagree) that we should do this.
  *13I
        13:*The world will little note (not counting book reviewers,
        14:*of course) nor long remember what we say here, but you
        15:*can never forget what you learn here (who could possibly
        16:*forget such drama, not to mention irreverence?).
        17:*^C

  *L
         6: Now, we are engaged in a great computer war (more
         7: have fallen than have risen), testing whether this MS-DOS,
         8: or any other MS-DOS so conceived and so dedicated, can
         9: long endure.
        10: We are met today to chronicle a part of these MS-DOS
        11: wars.  It is altogether fitting and proper (some may
        12: disagree) that we should do this.
        13: The world will little note (not counting book reviewers,
        14: of course) nor long remember what we say here, but you
        15: can never forget what you learn here (who could possibly
        16: forget such drama, not to mention irreverence?).
  *_
```

FIGURE 6.7: Additional text entries. Several lines of text beginning at line 13 (with command 13I). The L command is invoked to ensure that the operation requested was performed as expected.

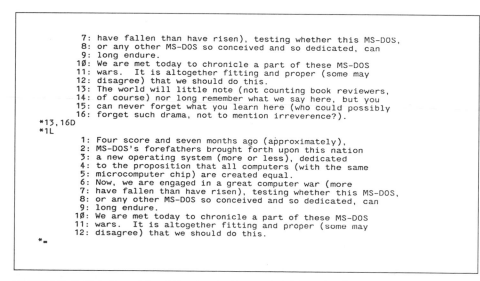

```
         7: have fallen than have risen), testing whether this MS-DOS,
         8: or any other MS-DOS so conceived and so dedicated, can
         9: long endure.
        10: We are met today to chronicle a part of these MS-DOS
        11: wars.  It is altogether fitting and proper (some may
        12: disagree) that we should do this.
        13: The world will little note (not counting book reviewers,
        14: of course) nor long remember what we say here, but you
        15: can never forget what you learn here (who could possibly
        16: forget such drama, not to mention irreverence?).
  *13,16D
  *1L
         1: Four score and seven months ago (approximately),
         2: MS-DOS's forefathers brought forth upon this nation
         3: a new operating system (more or less), dedicated
         4: to the proposition that all computers (with the same
         5: microcomputer chip) are created equal.
         6: Now, we are engaged in a great computer war (more
         7: have fallen than have risen), testing whether this MS-DOS,
         8: or any other MS-DOS so conceived and so dedicated, can
         9: long endure.
        10: We are met today to chronicle a part of these MS-DOS
        11: wars.  It is altogether fitting and proper (some may
        12: disagree) that we should do this.
  *_
```

FIGURE 6.8: Multiple lines deleted. Entering the D command deletes the range of lines from 13 through 16.

ENDING THE EDITING SESSION

There are two ways to exit EDLIN, depending on whether you want to save the changes you've made to the file. You can abort the entire editing operation and restore the file to its original condition, or you can save all your edits to the disk file, permanently engraving those changes in the original file.

Quitting the Editing Session without Saving

To leave EDLIN and return to DOS without saving the work you have just done, enter the Quit command (Q) all by itself. EDLIN will ask whether you are sure you wish to leave without saving your file. Any response other than Y will abort the Q command and return you to the EDLIN prompt.

You will usually use this exit path only when you have made a mistake. Suppose, for example, that you change your mind about the deletion of lines 13 to 16 performed in the last section, and you want to keep those lines in the text after all. You can enter them again or, if no other edits are at stake, you can abort the entire editing operation, return to DOS, and then call up the text file for editing once again. Figure 6.9 demonstrates this process. Using Q to abort the

```
          1Ø: We are met today to chronicle a part of these MS-DOS
          11: wars.  It is altogether fitting and proper (some may
          12: disagree) that we should do this.
 *Q
 Abort edit (Y/N)? Y
 C>EDLIN LINCOLN.TXT
 End of input file
 *L
          1:*Four score and seven months ago (approximately),
          2: MS-DOS's forefathers brought forth upon this nation
          3: a new operating system (more or less), dedicated
          4: to the proposition that all computers (with the same
          5: microcomputer chip) are created equal.
          6: Now, we are engaged in a great computer war (more
          7: have fallen than have risen), testing whether this MS-DOS,
          8: or any other MS-DOS so conceived and so dedicated, can
          9: long endure.
          1Ø: We are met today to chronicle a part of these MS-DOS
          11: wars.  It is altogether fitting and proper (some may
          12: disagree) that we should do this.
          13: The world will little note (not counting book reviewers,
          14: of course) nor long remember what we say here, but you
          15: can never forget what you learn here (who could possibly
          16: forget such drama, not to mention irreverence?).
 *▪
```

FIGURE 6.9: Aborting the editing process. After deleting a large block of text, as perhaps the four lines deleted in Figure 6.8, you may reconsider and decide that your original words should not have been discarded so lightly and quickly. If you entered the changes in the very last edit you performed, and if you entered no other significant edits during this editing session, you can enter the Q, or Quit, command. Entering that command, as in this figure, discards all edits performed during the session; calling up the same file again brings back the file as it appeared before you performed the last session's edits.

editing process, returning to DOS, and then immediately recalling the LINCOLN.TXT file returns the original text file to you unchanged.

Saving Your Work and Exiting to DOS

To exit EDLIN and save your changes, use the End command (E). When you issue the E command, EDLIN renames your original file with a .BAK extension and names the edited file with the original extension. If you created a completely new file, EDLIN will not assign a .BAK file.

> *Warning:* Make sure your disk contains enough room for the file to be saved. If it does not, EDLIN saves the part of the file that *will* fit with an extension of .$$$. It retains the original file on the disk, and does not create a new .BAK file. You will lose the part of the edited file not saved.

At the end of the file, EDLIN inserts a carriage return and line feed if the file does not already contain them. It also inserts a Ctrl-Z code as an end-of-file marker.

EDLIN will *not* prompt you to make sure you want to leave the program. Entering E followed by a press of the Return key is all you need do to save your editing changes and return to DOS (see Figure 6.10).

```
            12: disagree) that we should do this.
    *Q
    Abort edit (Y/N)? Y
    C>EDLIN LINCOLN.TXT
    End of input file
    *L
            1:*Four score and seven months ago (approximately),
            2: MS-DOS's forefathers brought forth upon this nation
            3: a new operating system (more or less), dedicated
            4: to the proposition that all computers (with the same
            5: microcomputer chip) are created equal.
            6: Now, we are engaged in a great computer war (more
            7: have fallen than have risen), testing whether this MS-DOS,
            8: or any other MS-DOS so conceived and so dedicated, can
            9: long endure.
           10: We are met today to chronicle a part of these MS-DOS
           11: wars.  It is altogether fitting and proper (some may
           12: disagree) that we should do this.
           13: The world will little note (not counting book reviewers,
           14: of course) nor long remember what we say here, but you
           15: can never forget what you learn here (who could possibly
           16: forget such drama, not to mention irreverence?).
    *E

    C>_
```

FIGURE 6.10: Normal EDLIN termination sequence. The proper way to end an editing session, retaining all edit operations and updating the text file on disk, is with the E command, shown as the last operation in this figure. After executing the E command, EDLIN returns you to the DOS prompt (C>).

THE EDLIN COMMAND LANGUAGE

This chapter has presented only one new DOS command, EDLIN. EDLIN is the DOS line editor. Unlike many word processors, it is not a full-screen editor. EDLIN has no formatting commands, and you must change data a line at a time. It is good for modifying short ASCII files and for creating and modifying simple batch files.

EDLIN itself contains a small "sublanguage" of 14 commands. Following are the reference entries for the EDLIN commands.

A (Append)

SYNTAX

[*Num*]A

>   *Num* is the number of lines to be appended

USAGE

The Append command brings into memory additional text lines from the disk file being edited. It is necessary only for large files that cannot completely fit into memory during the editing process.

EXAMPLE

Provided that enough space in memory is available (see the W or Write command below), you can load 20 lines of text from the rest of the file with the command:

>   **20A**

If there are 20 or less lines remaining in the file at the time you issue this command, you will receive the message:

>   **End of input file**

C (Copy)

SYNTAX

[*Line1*],[*Line2*],*Line3*[,*Count*] C

Line1   is the beginning of the range of lines to be copied

Line2   is the end of the range of lines to be copied

Line3   is the line before which the copied lines will be inserted

Count   is the number of times to copy the specified lines

USAGE

The Copy command enables you to make one or more replicas of text lines. It is often used to make copies of code segments which are then modified slightly to perform similar tasks, like logical tests.

EXAMPLE

Suppose you have a seven-line logical sequence of instructions to be used more than once in a program you are writing in a high-level language. Using EDLIN to write and edit this program, you want to copy and then slightly edit these seven lines located at line number 13 through 19. The following command will copy the seven lines four times into the file beginning just before line 20:

13,19,20,4C

D (Delete)

SYNTAX

[*Line1*][,*Line2*] D

Line1   is the beginning of the range of lines to be deleted

Line2   is the end of the range of lines to be deleted

USAGE

The Delete command is used to erase older lines of text from your file. Deleting lines is common when the text is out-of-date, or no longer necessary because of newly inserted text.

EXAMPLE

You can delete any one or more successive lines of text with this command. For instance, to delete line 16 from your file:

16D

To delete lines 20 through 24 from your file:

20,24D

(LineEdit)

SYNTAX

[Line]

USAGE

The LineEdit command, consisting of only the number of the line to be edited, allows you to make necessary changes to the contents of any existing line.

EXAMPLE

Suppose you wanted to correct the text on line 18 of your file. Entering 18 at the EDLIN prompt would display the current line 18, and a replacement line onto which you may type your corrected text:

```
*18
18:*DO WHILE .NOT. EOF( ) .AND. PAID
18:*do while .not. eof( ) .or. paid
```

E (End)

SYNTAX

E

USAGE

The End command is used to end an editing session normally. All edits during the session are saved in the disk file, and a backup version of the previous version of the file is prepared on disk as a .BAK file

EXAMPLE

When you have made all your editing changes and wish to apply them to the actual disk version of your file, simply enter:

E

I (Insert)

SYNTAX

[*Line*]I

USAGE

The Insert command enables you to selectively enter new text into your file before any chosen line number.

EXAMPLE

Entering the command 7I at the EDLIN prompt:

*7I

will result in:

7:*_

Whatever you enter now (even multiple lines) will be inserted into your text file beginning at line 7.

L (List)

SYNTAX

[*Line1*][,*Line2*] L

Line1	is the beginning of the range of lines to be listed
Line2	is the end of the range of lines to be listed

USAGE

The List command is used to display or list on your video monitor a portion of your file.

EXAMPLE

The most common use for the List command is to list the entire memory portion of the edited text:

L

If the file is more than one screenful, you can easily limit the display to the lines in which you are interested. To see only lines 15 through 25, you enter:

15,25L

M (Move)

SYNTAX

*[Line1],[Line2],Line3*M

    Line1   is the beginning of the range of lines to be moved

    Line2   is the end of the range of lines to be moved

    Line3   is the point before which the specified lines will be inserted

USAGE

The Move command enables you to remove a block of lines from any place in your file and to reinsert the entire block at another place in the file.

EXAMPLE

You can move the entire block of text consisting of lines 10 through 18 to a point just before line 25 by entering:

10,18,25M

P (Page)

SYNTAX

[Line][,Line] **P**

    Line1   is the beginning of the range of lines to be displayed

    Line2   is the end of the range of lines to be displayed

USAGE

The Page command facilitates rapid motion through your file. You can list any portion of lines, or list the whole file, one group at a time.

EXAMPLE

Like the List command, Page allows a display of a line number range:

15,25P

will display lines 15 through 25. However, unlike the List command, which does not change the current line being edited, the Page command redefines the current line to be the last one displayed. Successive entries of the Page command by itself:

P

will successively display the entire file, one screenful at a time.

Q (Quit)

SYNTAX

Q

USAGE

The Quit command is used to abort the editing session without saving any of your edits, or affecting the previous disk version of the file. It is typically used in two instances: first, when you mistype the name of the file to be edited and, realizing your mistake immediately, you want to abort any further editing; and second, when you have made several changes to a file and then decide that you want none of those changes to be made in the file.

EXAMPLE

Simply entering:

Q

will abort the current editing process. You will be asked by EDLIN if you really mean to discard any and all of your file entries and changes:

Abort edit (Y/N)?

R (Replace)

SYNTAX

[*Line1*][,*Line2*] [?] R[*String*][^ Z*NewString*]

Line1	is the beginning of the range of lines within which the replacement will be made
Line2	is the end of the range of lines within which the replacement will be made
String	is the text to be replaced
NewString	is the replacement text

USAGE

The Replace command is typically used when an error has been discovered after the entire file has been typed. This command allows you to make automatic corrections to all affected lines within your file.

EXAMPLE

Suppose you wrote a tongue-in-cheek commentary six years ago on the latest and greatest operating system for microcomputers. Now you wish to dust off that article, simply changing DOS to OS/2. The following Replace command will change the string DOS to the string OS/2 throughout your text file:

1RDOS ^ ZOS/2

S (Search)

SYNTAX

[*Line1*][,*Line2*] [?] S[*String*]

Line1	is the beginning of the range of lines to be searched
Line2	is the end of the range of lines to be searched
String	is the text to be searched for

USAGE

The Search command locates lines containing specified strings of characters. It can be constrained to search only within a specified portion of lines from the file.

EXAMPLE

You can locate all lines which contain references to OS/2 in your entire file by specifying line 1 as the starting line, then accepting the default end-of-file as the ending line of the range. Leaving out the *?* will allow the Search command to discover all lines that contain the search string *OS/2* without pausing to ask you which particular line you are interested in.

1SOS/2

T (Transfer)

SYNTAX

[*Line*] T [*FileSpec*]

   Line   is the point before which the transferred file will be inserted

   FileSpec   is the file to be copied into the current file

USAGE

The Transfer command enables you to merge two files. It does this by transferring the text contents of any specified disk file into the file being edited. The file is transferred into the current file before the *line* specified in the command.

EXAMPLE

Suppose you want to transfer a text file containing a spreadsheet's output (SPREAD.TXT) into the letter you are working on with EDLIN. To insert the spreadsheet information before line 15, you need only enter:

15T Spread.txt

W (Write)

SYNTAX

[*Num*] W

   Num   is the number of lines to be written to disk

USAGE

All of EDLIN's file edits take effect on lines of text held in memory. If the file is too large to completely fit into memory, you can edit a portion, then use the Write command to write the edited lines to the disk, thereby freeing up space for additional lines from the file (see the Append command).

EXAMPLE

Suppose you have been editing lines of your file, and want to explicitly write out to disk the first 20 lines of the edited text. Entering

20W

will free the memory space taken up by those 20 lines.

SUMMARY

This chapter has presented the set of commands available through the DOS line editor, EDLIN, and the techniques for using those commands. You've learned the major advantages and disadvantages of EDLIN as compared to page-oriented word processors, and you should now be able to decide where and how EDLIN meets your word processing needs. If you're like most DOS users, you'll leave the bigger jobs to a word processor, but you will often find EDLIN more convenient for working with small text files.

Although EDLIN has many potential applications (that is, you can use it to create and edit many types of text files), the most important and useful application of EDLIN is generally considered to be with batch files. Effective use of batch files can greatly streamline the work of anyone who works with DOS, beginners and experts alike. Now that you are familiar with the set of tools that DOS provides for working with batch files, you are ready to learn more about using them. The next three chapters discuss batch files in detail.

For additional information about the basic rules of batch files, see

- Chapter 7, "Fundamentals of Batch Processing"

For additional information about the command language used with batch files, see

- Chapter 8, "Batch-File Subcommands"

For examples of batch files that can be created with EDLIN, see

- Chapter 9, "Complete Batch-File Examples"

For additional information about DOS printing capabilities, see

- Chapter 15, "Basic Printing Methods" and Chapter 16, "Advanced Printing Techniques"

For additional information about using other word processors with DOS, see

- Chapter 5, "Working with Hard Disk Directories"

For additional information about exchanging text between files, see

- Chapter 17, "Pipes, Filters, and Redirection"

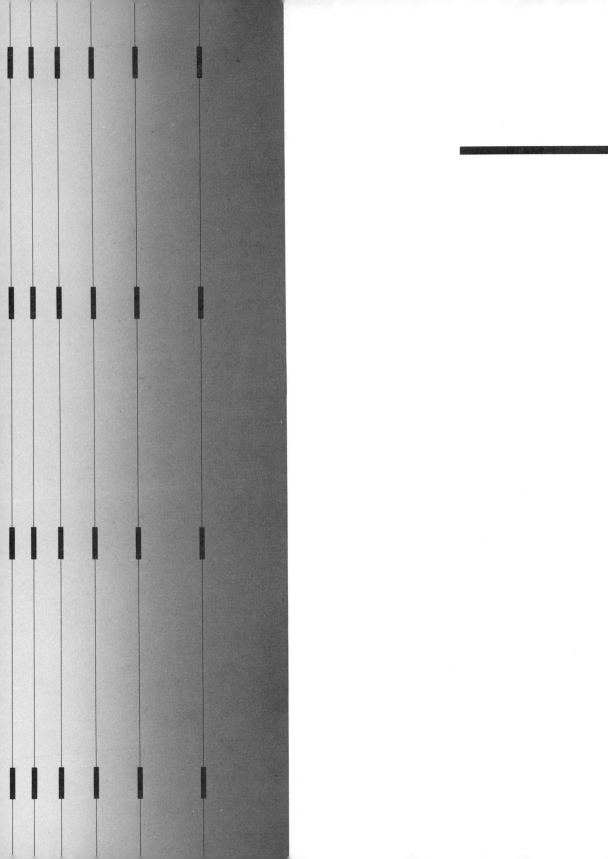

FUNDAMENTALS OF BATCH PROCESSING

Fundamentals of Batch Processing

The ability to combine a series of commands into a file for processing as a batch is one of the most powerful features of DOS, and one that every user should master. You create and edit batch files as ASCII text files, and so the previous chapter discussed the DOS text editor, EDLIN. This chapter discusses the rules for using batch files; presents a simple example involving the creation, editing, and execution of a batch file; and introduces the subject of batch-file programming. As you may know if you have programmed in other languages, writing a program to be used more than once with different data requires the use of *variables,* command parameters whose value is not specified until the program is run. This chapter also discusses the use of variables in batch files. The next chapter discusses the subject of batch-file programming in detail and presents the batch-file subcommands.

The approach of this chapter is primarily tutorial and introductory. Many DOS users who are well versed in the system's routine operations have little or no experience with batch files. If you are already using batch files in your work, however, you may still find it helpful to review the material in this chapter and the next, particularly the reference entries for the batch-file subcommands at the end of Chapter 8, but you will probably get the most out of the extended series of examples in Chapter 9.

Because this chapter introduces no new DOS commands, it contains no reference entries.

Why Use Batch Files?

If you've been reading the chapters of this book in sequence so far, you've learned quite a bit about individual DOS commands. (If you've been consulting it strictly as a reference, you presumably already know a good deal about using DOS.) You know that when you want to execute a DOS command, you just type the command at the prompt. When the command has completed its job, DOS displays the prompt again; then you can enter another command. You've seen that when you work with DOS, you must enter its commands one at a time.

Batch files allow you to enter a *group* of DOS commands automatically. A batch file is a series of ordinary DOS commands that the computer can execute automatically as a group (a *batch*) instead of one at a time.

You create batch files to automate DOS activities that require more than one DOS command. As you will see, this simple idea has some unexpected benefits. DOS's ability to understand simple batch files allows you to create sophisticated DOS programs, which are more complex batch files containing a series of commands and also special elements called variables, conditional statements, and subroutines.

BUILDING A BATCH FILE

Batch files can be as simple or complex as you want them to be. Look at a simple task first. Assume you're using a hard disk and would like to find out what .COM and .EXE files are available to you in the version of DOS installed on your disk. (Chapter 3 discusses .COM and .EXE files.) You first need to change the active directory to the directory that contains the DOS files. Then you might clear the screen (with CLS) before you enter the appropriate DIR commands. You might successively enter each of the following DOS commands to obtain the desired output:

CD \DOS
CLS
DIR/W *.COM
DIR/W *.EXE

The result of this sequence is the screen shown in Figure 7.1.

To complete this task, you had to issue four commands. If this were a task that you performed often, you could automate it with a batch file containing the commands. To do so, you need to know the rules for building batch files.

Rules for Batch Files

For DOS to properly recognize and process a file as a batch file, you must follow several rules regarding

- File type
- Naming conventions
- Limitations of the batch-file mechanism
- Running and stopping batch files

```
C>DIR/W *.COM

  Volume in drive C is ROBBINS
  Directory of  C:\DOS

ASSIGN    COM    BACKUP   COM    BASIC    COM    BASICA   COM    CHKDSK    COM
COMMAND   COM    COMP     COM    DEBUG    COM    DISKCOMP COM    DISKCOPY  COM
EDLIN     COM    FORMAT   COM    GRAFTABL COM    GRAPHICS COM    LABEL     COM
MORE      COM    PRINT    COM    RECOVER  COM    RESTORE  COM    TREE      COM
FDISK     COM    KEYB     COM    MODE     COM    SELECT   COM    SYS       COM
        25 File(s)   3799040 bytes free

C>DIR/W *.EXE

  Volume in drive C is ROBBINS
  Directory of  C:\DOS

APPEND    EXE    ATTRIB   EXE    FIND     EXE    JOIN     EXE    REPLACE   EXE
SHARE     EXE    SORT     EXE    SUBST    EXE    XCOPY    EXE    FASTOPEN  EXE
NLSFUNC   EXE
        11 File(s)   3799040 bytes free

C>
```

FIGURE 7.1: DOS program-file listings. As you can see, DOS itself uses both .COM and .EXE formats for its disk-resident commands. Although approximately two thirds of its external commands are of the .COM variety, that percentage is in transition. Most newer commands and programs use the more flexible and less restrictive .EXE format. (Chapter 21 discusses the differences between .COM and .EXE files.)

Batch Files Must Be Standard ASCII Text Files

Standard text files contain normal ASCII characters, and each line ends with a carriage return (CR) and a line feed (LF). Historically, high-level languages and command programs like operating systems have used special symbols called *separators* and *terminators*. A separator is a symbol placed between parameters, fields, or simply portions of a single command entry. A comma or a space is the most common separator used and seen in DOS command lines. A terminator is a special symbol or sequence of symbols indicating the end of a string of instructions or data. In DOS and its batch file system, each command is unique from every other command. The end of every DOS command is indicated by a special termination sequence consisting of these two special nonprinting characters: the carriage return (ASCII code decimal 13) and the line feed (ASCII code decimal 10). This code sequence not only terminates the preceding command, along with its parameters and switches, but visually separates it from the next command by ensuring that each appears on a different line.

You can create a batch file using the DOS COPY CON command (see Chapters 3 and 17), the EDLIN line editor (see Chapter 6), or a word processing program that can create an ASCII standard file or convert its files to ASCII standard. You can use the following word processing programs to produce

ASCII files directly:

- WordPerfect, using TEXT IN/OUT
- WordStar in nondocument mode
- WordStar 2000, using the UNFORM format
- Microsoft Word, saving the file as UNFORMATTED
- DisplayWrite III, using BLOCK ASCII SAVE
- Framework II, using DISK EXPORT ASCII

You can use the following programs to convert files to DOS standard text files after they have been saved as word processing files:

- MultiMate, running the CONVERT program
- Samna, using the DO TRANSLATE ASCII command
- Symphony, using the PRINT FILE command

For DOS users, the most convenient way to create and manipulate batch files is to use EDLIN, which has the advantage of being available with DOS. The EDLIN command set, which is limited compared to word processors, is genrally adequate for working with batch files. If you already work with one of the word processors, you may want to use it for batch files as well, because a word processor offers the greatest range of commands for manipulating text. The "least-best" way to work with batch files is to use COPY CON, because it allows only text entry; it does not permit manipulation of already entered text.

Because you may not have a word processor, this book assumes you are using EDLIN to create your batch files. If you need to refresh your memory regarding EDLIN, refer to Chapter 6.

BATCH FILES MUST FOLLOW CERTAIN NAMING CONVENTIONS

When you name batch files, you must include the .BAT extension after the base name and you must make each batch-file name unique.

As you learned in Chapter 3, your system contains certain classes of files: .COM and .EXE program files, .BAS BASIC language files, .WK1 spreadsheet files, .DBF database files, and probably many others. DOS must be able to distinguish a batch file from these other types of files on your system.

You can give a batch file almost any name you like, as long as you use the .BAT extension. Of course, the name must adhere to standard DOS file-naming rules, with no more than eight letters or numbers in the base name. SIMPLE.BAT and START.BAT are examples of acceptable batch-file names.

You also must be sure each batch-file name is unique. Never give a batch file the same base name as either a DOS command (for example, DIR.BAT or FORMAT.BAT) or a program name (that is, the name of an .EXE or .COM file). If you use the name of a DOS command, DOS could become confused as to whether you want to execute the DOS command with that name or the batch file with that name. DOS always assumes you want to execute a DOS command first; only if it can't find a DOS command (or any .EXE or .COM files) will it look for a batch file with the specified name. DOS expects you to enter the command or batch-file name without typing an extension. Thus, if you created a file named DIR.BAT, you could never use it—DOS would always assume when you entered it that you wanted the Directory command, not the DIR.BAT file.

Limitations of Batch Files

You can include only commands that work at the DOS prompt in a batch file. Commands you've used up to now at the DOS prompt, such as DIR and CHKDSK, fall into this category. You'll soon see that you can use some additional controlling commands (called subcommands) in a batch file; you can also use variable input parameters, which are discussed in detail later in this chapter. However, the main commands you use will look just as they do when they are typed at the DOS prompt.

Running and Stopping Batch Files

Executing all the instructions within a batch file is as simple as typing the name of the .BAT file containing those instructions. As with commands and programs, however, if you don't precede the batch-file name with a drive identifier or a directory name, DOS will assume you want to use the current drive and current directory.

You can stop batch-file execution at any time by pressing the Break key combination (Ctrl-ScrollLock). DOS will ask you if you want to terminate the batch job. If you do, you answer Y for yes. If you have a change of heart and answer N, DOS ignores your termination request and executes the rest of the commands.

Users of diskette systems should be aware that exchanging a diskette containing an executing batch file for another diskette will force DOS to stop after it completes the current instruction and prompt you to reinsert the original diskette. Only then can DOS execute the next instruction in the batch file properly. In other words, you should avoid placing a batch file on any disk that you know will have to be swapped during the course of the batch file's execution.

CREATING YOUR FIRST BATCH FILE

Take a moment now to create your first batch file. Create your own version of SIMPLE.BAT, including all the statements shown in Figure 7.2. Use the EDLIN program unless you are familiar with an available word processor and plan to use it for all your batch-file work.

```
CD \DOS
CLS
DIR/W *.COM
DIR/W *.EXE
```

FIGURE 7.2: The SIMPLE.BAT file. Your first batch file consists of the four simple steps entered separately to create the results shown in Figure 7.1. The CD command sets the default DOS directory, and CLS clears the screen for succeeding output. The two DIR commands display the group of .COM and .EXE files in this \DOS directory.

When you enter

EDLIN SIMPLE.BAT

DOS creates a file called SIMPLE.BAT. Remember that when you use EDLIN, you are entering text into a file. This means that nothing appears to happen when you type a command. Only after you have written the SIMPLE.BAT file can you tell DOS to read, process, and execute the instructions contained in it.

Write the file now using EDLIN's simple I (Insert) command. Leave insertion mode by pressing Ctrl-C and then enter E (to end the edit). The DOS prompt returns, and you are ready to execute the batch file by typing its name *without* the .BAT extension:

SIMPLE

The results of typing this one-word command are the same as those produced when you entered all four commands separately. DOS executes each of the commands automatically, one after the other, without further assistance from you.

Like programs or disk-resident DOS commands, batch files can be located on any disk and in any directory, and you can reference them simply by specifying the full path name to them. For example, if SIMPLE were located in a directory called UTILITY\MISC on drive C, you could execute it by entering

C:\UTILITY\MISC\SIMPLE

Remember, to prevent the batch instructions from continuing to execute, you need only press the Break key combination.

Editing a Batch File

You will notice that the batch file you just wrote displays the command lines contained in it as each one executes. This echoing of the commands to the screen is controlled by the batch-file subcommand ECHO. The default status of ECHO is on, which means that DOS commands executed from a batch file are displayed as they are executed. However, output results are sometimes more attractive or readable if the commands are *not* displayed, so add a line to the batch file that turns ECHO off.

Bring up EDLIN again, specifying the full name of the file you want to edit, SIMPLE.BAT. Use the I command to enter

ECHO OFF

as the new line 1. It is always a good idea to check your work whenever you have added or deleted lines. To list the resulting file, enter the L command and press Return. EDLIN will display the five lines of your batch file:

```
*L
    1: ECHO OFF
    2: CD\DOS
    3: CLS
    4: DIR/W *.COM
    5:*DIR/W *.EXE
```

You can then save the file and return to DOS with EDLIN's End command.

Now you can process the modified batch file. As before, just enter

SIMPLE

This single command executes all the individual DOS commands contained within the SIMPLE.BAT file. Note that since ECHO is off, only the results of the commands, not the commands themselves, displayed (see Figure 7.3).

Note: Notice the extra DOS prompt on your screen after batch-file processing ends. This second prompt appears because EDLIN has inserted a carriage return before the end-of-file marker in SIMPLE.BAT. Don't be concerned; it won't cause any harm.

VARIABLES IN BATCH FILES

Until now, you've seen only batch files that have been designed for a specific use: for example, a batch file that quickly and easily lists all the .COM and .EXE files in the DOS directory. In such cases, the batch file works with constant values

```
Volume in drive C is ROBBINS
Directory of  C:\DOS

ASSIGN    COM    BACKUP   COM    BASIC     COM    BASICA    COM    CHKDSK   COM
COMMAND   COM    COMP     COM    DEBUG     COM    DISKCOMP  COM    DISKCOPY COM
EDLIN     COM    FORMAT   COM    GRAFTABL  COM    GRAPHICS  COM    LABEL    COM
MORE      COM    PRINT    COM    RECOVER   COM    RESTORE   COM    TREE     COM
FDISK     COM    KEYB     COM    MODE      COM    SELECT    COM    SYS      COM
        25 File(s)    3725312 bytes free

Volume in drive C is ROBBINS
Directory of  C:\DOS

APPEND    EXE    ATTRIB   EXE    FIND      EXE    JOIN      EXE    REPLACE  EXE
SHARE     EXE    SORT     EXE    SUBST     EXE    XCOPY     EXE    FASTOPEN EXE
NLSFUNC   EXE
        11 File(s)    3725312 bytes free

C>
C>
```

FIGURE 7.3: Results of running SIMPLE.BAT. Running a batch file that essentially consists of the same commands as in Figure 7.1 produces a similar result. The additional ECHO OFF command eliminates the distracting appearance of the commands themselves between each group of output information.

(*.COM or *.EXE). If batch files could accept variables, as more sophisticated programming languages do, they could be much more flexible.

You can create DOS batch files that do just this. Variables in any language allow you to construct programs that differ in a well-defined way each time the program is run. In other words, the program stays the same, but the value used by the program to complete its tasks varies. You can consider the DOS batch-file feature as a simple programming language.

Replaceable Parameters

As you have seen throughout this book, many DOS commands accept a variety of parameters. These parameters are just additional pieces of information needed by DOS to clarify the task specified in the command. For example, the command

COPY REPORT.DOC FEBRUARY.DOC

contains the COPY command, and the REPORT and FEBRUARY documents are its respective source and destination parameters. Next month, however, you may want to run the COPY command again, with the REPORT.DOC file as the source and the MARCH.DOC file as the destination. Thus, the second parameter can be considered a variable, since it is subject to change. Batch files can accept variables as easily as they can accept DOS commands.

Numbered Variables

Variables always begin with a percent sign (%), which is followed by a number from 0 to 9. Thus, DOS allows variables named %0, %1, %2, and so on.

To see how this system works, create a simple batch file called DEMO.BAT, consisting of the following two lines:

CLS
DIR *.%1

This batch file clears the screen and then displays a directory of all file names that have similar extensions (.COM, .BAT, .EXE, .WP, and so on).

Note that instead of entering .EXE or some other extension, you used the variable %1. The batch file is not "locked in" to DIR *.EXE, DIR *.COM, or anything else. Instead, %1 can stand for anything you want.

Here's how the % character works. You know that to execute any available batch file, you simply type its name at the DOS command prompt. (Like any file, a batch file is available if it is in the current directory or on a defined path.) If your batch file uses variable parameters, you must include the value of each one as part of the command. As usual in DOS, you must separate the parameters from each other and from the command itself (the batch file name) with spaces. The space character tells DOS where one parameter ends and another begins.

When DOS reads your command, it automatically assigns one of its variable names to each parameter. The first parameter becomes %1, the second becomes %2, and so on up to %9. The name of the batch file is always assigned %0. Then, when DOS executes your batch file, it substitutes the parameter value you've just entered for the corresponding variable in the batch file. For example, if you enter

DEMO EXE

at the command prompt, DOS internally assigns %0 to the batch-file name (DEMO), %1 to the first parameter (EXE), and if there were other parameter entries on the line, % values up to %9. Since the DEMO batch file refers to %1,DOS actually uses whatever word follows DEMO (in this case, EXE) to complete the DIR command. Thus, DOS treats the command

DIR *.%1

as if you had originally typed

DIR *.EXE

and the batch file displays all files with an .EXE extension, as shown in Figure 7.4.

Running the batch file again with a different value for the first parameter generates a different result.

```
C>DIR *.exe

 Volume in drive C is ROBBINS
 Directory of  C:\DOS

 APPEND   EXE    5825   3-17-87  12:00p
 ATTRIB   EXE    9529   3-17-87  12:00p
 FIND     EXE    6434   3-17-87  12:00p
 JOIN     EXE    8969   3-17-87  12:00p
 REPLACE  EXE   11775   3-17-87  12:00p
 SHARE    EXE    8608   3-17-87  12:00p
 SORT     EXE    1977   3-17-87  12:00p
 SUBST    EXE    9909   3-17-87  12:00p
 XCOPY    EXE   11247   3-17-87  12:00p
 FASTOPEN EXE    3919   3-17-87  12:00p
 NLSFUNC  EXE    3060   3-17-87  12:00p
        11 File(s)   3715072 bytes free

C>
C>
```

FIGURE 7.4: Running DEMO.BAT with one variable parameter (EXE). This produces the expected result, listing all .EXE files in the current directory. In this example, the current directory is still \DOS on drive C.

DEMO COM

lists only the .COM files. You can refer to parameter %1 any number of times inside the batch file, even though DEMO.BAT referred to it only once.

Deferred Execution

Using a parameter submitted when the batch file is run is called *deferred execution,* since the decision as to what parameter will be used is deferred until the time of batch-file execution. In this example, a Directory command will be executed, but the decision as to what specific directory listing will be produced is deferred until the batch file has actually been called and the %1 parameter has been specified as the first parameter after the batch-file name.

With this in mind, you should be particularly careful when running batch files that use more than one variable parameter. As you'll now see, defining more than one deferred parameter requires you to exercise caution when running the batch file. The final order of your parameter values should be the same as that of the place-holder parameters you specified when you wrote the batch file.

Look at another example of a batch file, this one using multiple variable parameters. This time, you'll use a second variable to create MOVE.BAT, a batch file whose purpose will be to move files from one drive or directory to another. As you know, you must perform two operations to move a file:

1. Copy the file to the new drive or directory.
2. Erase the file from the old drive or directory.

Your task is to create a batch file that will issue all the necessary commands, so that you need to supply only the file names to be moved and the identifier of the new drive.

The batch file MOVE.BAT requires two variables: %1 and %2. The first variable is a file name or a wildcard to use for selecting a file or files. The second variable is the letter specifying the destination drive. For example, if you want to move all .EXE files from the current directory to drive B, you can enter the following four lines at the DOS prompt:

```
CLS
COPY *.EXE B:
ERASE *.EXE
DIR/W B:
```

Then again, if you want to move all .PRG files from your DBASE\TEST sub-directory on drive C to the ACTIVE directory on drive C, you can enter

```
CLS
COPY C:\DBASE\TEST\*.PRG C:\ACTIVE
ERASE C:\DBASE\TEST\*.PRG
DIR/W C:\ACTIVE
```

There will probably be many occasions when you need to perform this operation between drives, between directories, or both, so this is a perfect chance to use variables. Write a batch file called MOVE.BAT containing these lines:

```
CLS
COPY %1 %2
ERASE %1
DIR/W %2
```

This batch file issues the proper commands for you if you merely indicate the desired file source and destination. For example,

MOVE *.EXE B:

moves all the .EXE files from the current directory to drive B.

MOVE C:\DBASE\TEST*.PRG C:\ACTIVE

moves all the .PRG files from the DBASE\TEST subdirectory on drive C to the ACTIVE directory on drive C. The results are shown in Figure 7.5.

```
     Volume in drive C is ROBBINS
     Directory of  C:\ACTIVE

     .            ..             DB3BOOK  PRG    START    PRG    INVOICE  PRG
     CERTIF   PRG   RECOMM1  PRG   RECOMM2  PRG    PAYROLL  PRG    PAYROLL2 PRG
     EXPERT   PRG   EXPERT1  PRG   EXPERT2  PRG    EXPERT3  PRG    EXPERT4  PRG
     MESSAGE  PRG   LEDGER   PRG   INVOICE2 PRG    BOOKS2   PRG    DISKPREP PRG
          20 File(s)   1413120 bytes free

 C>_
 C>COPY \DBASE\TEST\*.PRG \ACTIVE
 C:\DBASE\TEST\DB3BOOK.PRG
 C:\DBASE\TEST\START.PRG
 C:\DBASE\TEST\INVOICE.PRG
 C:\DBASE\TEST\CERTIF.PRG
 C:\DBASE\TEST\RECOMM1.PRG
 C:\DBASE\TEST\RECOMM2.PRG
 C:\DBASE\TEST\PAYROLL.PRG
 C:\DBASE\TEST\PAYROLL2.PRG
 C:\DBASE\TEST\EXPERT.PRG
 C:\DBASE\TEST\EXPERT1.PRG
 C:\DBASE\TEST\EXPERT2.PRG
 C:\DBASE\TEST\EXPERT3.PRG
 C:\DBASE\TEST\EXPERT4.PRG
 C:\DBASE\TEST\MESSAGE.PRG
 C:\DBASE\TEST\LEDGER.PRG
 C:\DBASE\TEST\INVOICE2.PRG
 C:\DBASE\TEST\BOOKS2.PRG
 C:\DBASE\TEST\DISKPREP.PRG
          18 File(s) copied

 C>ERASE \DBASE\TEST\*.PRG

 C>DIR/W \ACTIVE
```

FIGURE 7.5: Running the MOVE.BAT file. The MOVE.BAT file can save a lot of work. It not only copies files from the source directory (%1) to the destination directory (%2), but it also automatically erases the original files and lists the new contents of the ACTIVE directory. This batch file is not as sophisticated as it can and should be, since any problems encountered during the transfer of source to destination files *may* leave you with no new files in the destination directory and erased old files in the source directory.

You can use the same batch file to move files in the opposite direction. Simply reverse the parameters. Entering

MOVE B:*.EXE C:

moves all the .EXE files from drive B to drive C. (Substitute A for C in this command if you are using a dual-diskette system.)

Note that the MOVE.BAT batch file includes a dangerous command, ERASE. Since this batch program has no automatic protection built into it, a mistake can have serious consequences. If the COPY command in the MOVE batch file fails—as it may if your destination disk becomes full or if your disk has a bad sector—the succeeding ERASE command will not allow you to effectively execute the MOVE command again, since the original files will have been deleted. Chapter 18 emphasizes the importance of making backup copies of your important files; the potential hazards of running a batch file such as MOVE.BAT reaffirm the need for backup procedures.

Using Batch Files with Variables—An Exercise

Variable parameters are a mainstay of batch files. You should stop here for a while and try out these new tools. Create a batch file called PARA.BAT that uses three variables: %1, %2, and %3. Have this program create a new directory (MD) using the first variable as the complete path name and directory name and the second variable as a wildcard file name. Then have it copy all file names meeting the wildcard specification in the current directory to the directory specified in %1. The batch file should execute a DIR/W command for this new directory after the transfer and should end with a CHKDSK command for the disk drive specified in the third variable, %3. For example, when you want the lines

MD \TRIAL
CD \TRIAL
COPY EX*.COM \TRIAL
DIR/W \TRIAL
CHKDSK B:

to be executed in your batch file, you should be able to invoke your batch file as follows:

PARA \TRIAL EX*.COM B:

SUMMARY

This chapter gave you your first look at the DOS batch-file mechanism, which extends the power of your operating system by allowing you to build your own set of commands. You can use this new set of commands just like any existing DOS command, except that it is your customized batch file that will execute when you specify a command, not a standard command provided by DOS.

For additional information about viewing and editing batch and other text files, see

- Chapter 6, "EDLIN: The DOS Editor"

For additional information about batch-file subcommands, see

- Chapter 8, "Batch-File Subcommands"

For additional information about examples of sophisticated batch files, see

- Chapter 9, "Complete Batch-File Examples"

For additional information about backing up files and disks, see

- Chapter 18, "Backups and Restorations"

The next chapter takes your batch-file construction skills one giant step further. You'll learn about the set of specialized subcommands designed to work only within the batch programming mechanism. You can incorporate these unique commands into any batch file, thus making DOS comparable to a high-level computer language.

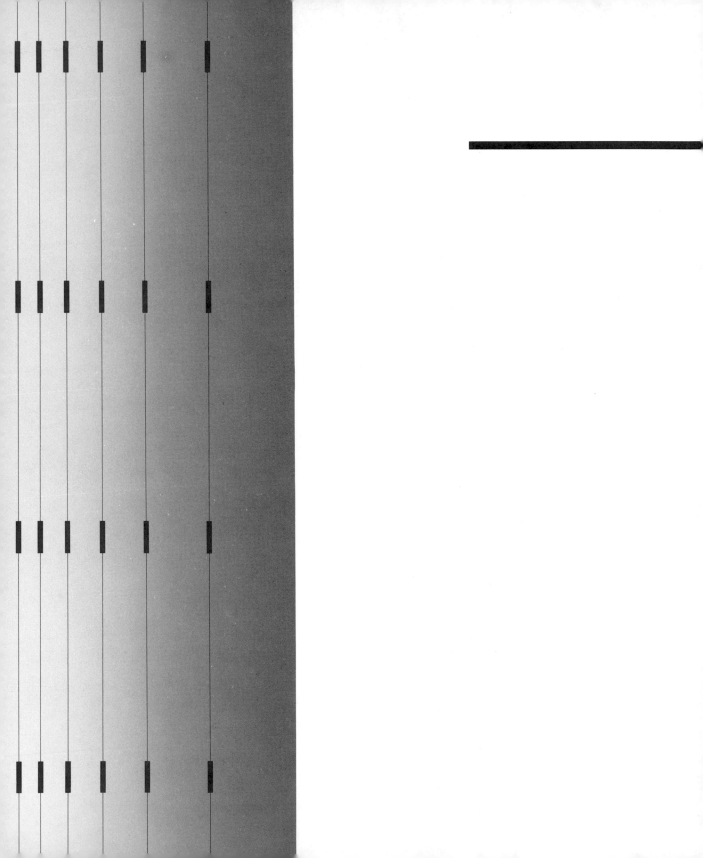

CHAPTER 8

BATCH-FILE SUBCOMMANDS

BATCH-FILE SUBCOMMANDS

Batch files have their own set of specialized support commands, known as *subcommands*. You don't need them to create simple batch files, but you greatly expand your possibilities when you learn them. You'll learn about these extra, built-in tools in this chapter. Depending on what type of batch program you write, you may need to use one or several subcommands.

Some subcommands will be commonplace in your batch files; for example, you will frequently use ECHO or REM to insert messages both in the batch file itself and on the screen. You'll use others only occasionally; for example, you'll use PAUSE only for batch files that must allow users sufficient time to read information on the screen. You will use still others in specific situations only. In this category are the FOR subcommand, which allows the repetition of operations, the IF subcommand, which provides decision making capabilities, and the GOTO subcommand, which manages the flow of control.

The preceding chapter presented some simple examples of batch files, in which each command was executed successively. DOS also allows you to execute these commands nonsequentially, according to your own specified order. Changing the order of command execution is known as modifying the flow of control, or, simply, branching.

This chapter focuses on the elements that make the DOS batch-file feature a simple but practical high-level programming language. A final tutorial section in the chapter discusses the distinction between creating a standard batch-file chain (which allows you to transfer execution control from one file to another) and emulating true programming subroutines.

The chapter concludes with reference entries for all the batch-file subcommands, including one whose usefulness is so specialized that it is not discussed elsewhere.

INCORPORATING MESSAGES INTO BATCH FILES

In the last chapter, you briefly used the ECHO subcommand to suppress the display of the commands themselves while a batch file was processing. ECHO has some other uses. If ECHO is followed by text instead of by ON or OFF, it will print the text. Thus, ECHO can be used to display information on the screen during batch file execution.

To see how this works, create a new batch file, called HELP1.BAT, containing several ECHO subcommands, each of which contains helpful information for a user (see Figure 8.1). This batch file will explain how to use the previously created MOVE.BAT file. (The figure contains a few sample lines of text to demonstrate the method of using the ECHO subcommand; the dots at the bottom indicate where you can add additional lines of text.) Running this batch file by typing

HELP1

at the DOS prompt results in Figure 8.2.

```
ECHO OFF
CLS
ECHO  The batch file MOVE.BAT is designed to
ECHO  transfer a file(s) from one drive or
ECHO  directory to any other drive/directory.
ECHO  =======================================
ECHO  MOVE first copies, then deletes the
ECHO  originals.  The general form is:
ECHO       MOVE  source  destination
.
.
.
```

FIGURE 8.1: The HELP1.BAT file. This batch file will echo a series of textual lines to the screen when run. Turning ECHO off ensures that the ECHO command itself is not displayed along with each message line. The CLS command minimizes distractions by erasing any preexisting information from the screen before the HELP1 messages are displayed.

```
The batch file MOVE.BAT is designed to
transfer a file(s) from one drive or
directory to any other drive/directory.
---------------------------------------
MOVE first copies, then deletes the
originals.  The general form is:
     MOVE  source  destination

C>_
```

FIGURE 8.2: Results of executing the HELP1.BAT file. The screen is erased; then the messages from the batch file are successively displayed on separate lines to form a coherent screenful of helpful information.

Notice that the first two commands turn ECHO off and clear the screen, so the remaining echoed messages appear without your seeing the actual ECHO subcommand for each line. Regardless of whether ECHO is on or off, the screen displays the text information on the ECHO line. ECHO OFF suppresses the display only of any succeeding DOS commands in the batch file.

One command line that is usually suppressed—and purposely so—is a REM statement. You will see many REM statements in batch-file listings. Here is an example:

REM This is a simple internal commenting line.
REM So is this... for the TYPICAL.BAT file

A REM (Remark) statement is used for internal documentation in a batch file. It usually contains notes to the programmer or to the future user of the batch program—anything from the file name to information about algorithms and techniques. Nearly all of the remaining batch files in this book have at least one REM statement containing the name of the batch file itself.

If ECHO is off, then the screen will now display the REM statements during program execution. The more complex or obscure your batch-file logic, the more you need to build REM lines into it.

As you can see, you can use batch files to provide system users with timely assistance and information. Many application programs, such as Lotus 1-2-3, provide help at the press of a key (usually function key 1). DOS provides no such help, so you must provide your own when necessary. Often you can use a batch facility such as described in this chapter to enable users to find information when they are using the system without having to search through (sometimes nonexistent) documentation for those answers. Additionally, helpful information provided through the batch file system is often easier and quicker to update than printed documentation.

INTERRUPTING BATCH-FILE EXECUTION

There are two kinds of interruptions in life: permanent and temporary. DOS provides batch-file equivalents of these types of interruptions with the PAUSE subcommand and with the Break key combination.

When you use a PAUSE subcommand in a batch file, the execution of the commands in the file stops temporarily, and DOS displays the message "Strike a key when ready...." When you press the Return key or the space bar (or virtually any other key), the next command in the batch file executes.

Tip: In a batch file such as HELP1.BAT, which displays text, it's a good idea to add PAUSE as a final command so that the screen information can be read. Information displayed for a user is usually only one part of a more complex batch file; pausing the execution allows the user to read the messages before continuing the program.

The PAUSE subcommand is not essential to the program, but it has a practical function. Filling the screen with a lot of instructions is a sure way to lose a user's attention. Instead, you can display a little information, pause the display, clear the screen, and display a little more information. This allows the user to absorb the information more easily.

HELP2.BAT, an expanded version of the batch file presented in the last section, represents a two-screen help system. It is listed in Figure 8.3. The display is divided into two screens by the commands PAUSE and CLS, inserted into the middle of the batch file. PAUSE temporarily interrupts the execution of the batch file, prompting you to press any key when you are ready to continue. CLS simply erases the messages you've already read, so that you can concentrate on the new messages displayed. When you run the HELP2.BAT program, the results will be like those shown in Figure 8.4.

Note: This batch file and its output illustrate a trick you can use in the construction of help files. Notice that the last line of Figure 8.14 contains a variable name (%2) as part of the explanatory text. In the original batch file in Figure 8.13, however, the name appears as % %2. Why the extra percent sign? When DOS encounters a variable name as it executes a batch file, it attempts to "expand" the variable, substituting its current value for the name. But %2 is

```
REM The HELP2.BAT File
ECHO  OFF
CLS
ECHO The batch file MOVE.BAT is designed to
ECHO transfer a file(s) from one drive or
ECHO directory to any other drive/directory.
ECHO .
ECHO MOVE first copies, then deletes the
ECHO originals.  The general form is:
ECHO      MOVE  source  destination
ECHO .
ECHO ****************************************************
ECHO Press Ctrl-BREAK key to terminate these messages, or
PAUSE
CLS
ECHO .
ECHO ****************************************************
ECHO Make sure you have a backup copy of all important files.
ECHO This batch file does an unconditional ERASE of
ECHO all the files requested to be moved.  It does this
ECHO even if the COPY command fails, and the files never
ECHO make it to the destination drive or directory (%%2)
```

FIGURE 8.3: The HELP2.BAT file. This file demonstrates a simple batch file technique for displaying multiple-screen help messages. The key to the technique is the PAUSE statement, which displays the screen message "Strike a key when ready . . ." and pauses the batch file until you strike a key. The immediately preceding ECHO statement is informational, telling you how to exit from the HELP2 batch file when you do not need to continue viewing the prepared message screens.

```
The batch file MOVE.BAT is designed to
transfer a file(s) from one drive or
directory to any other drive/directory.
.
MOVE first copies, then deletes the
originals.  The general form is:
     MOVE  source  destination
.
**********************************************************
Press Ctrl-BREAK key to terminate these messages, or
Strike a key when ready . . . ■
```

```
**********************************************************
Make sure you have a backup copy of all important files.
This batch file does an unconditional ERASE of
all the files requested to be moved.  It does this
even if the COPY command fails, and the files never
make it to the destination drive or directory (%2)
C>_
```

FIGURE 8.4: A two-screen help system created with PAUSE and CLS. The second screenful of text information displayed from the HELP2 batch file appears after the PAUSE statement. When this last screen completes its display, control is returned to DOS at the C> prompt.

not defined in this help file, so its value is null and there is nothing to display. You can see this for yourself by running the file with %2 substituted for %%2. The extra percent sign instructs DOS to treat the variable name as literal text and thus to display it. You can use this technique whenever you need to display a variable name within a help file.

After you issue a PAUSE subcommand, pressing almost any key will cause the batch-file processing to resume. One exception to this rule is Ctrl-ScrollLock,

```
The batch file MOVE.BAT is designed to
transfer a file(s) from one drive or
directory to any other drive/directory.
-----------------------------------------
^C

Terminate batch job (Y/N)? Y
C>_
```

FIGURE 8.5: Permanent batch-file interruption with the Break key combination. Pressing Ctrl-C or Ctrl-Break during the execution of any batch file forces DOS to interrupt the batch file. Its immediate response to your interruption is to ask if you wish the batch file to be permanently interrupted, or terminated. Responding Y to the question ends batch-file processing and returns control to the DOS prompt.

the Break key combination. Pressing Break interrupts batch-file processing. DOS first displays ^ C on the screen and then asks if you wish to terminate the batch job. Figures 8.5 and 8.6 demonstrate the screen results of your answer. In Figure 8.5, your Y answer causes the batch file to cease immediately and returns control to the DOS prompt. This interruption is permanent.

Notice in Figure 8.6 that the ^ C is displayed in the middle of the third ECHO statement's output. Because you answered N, the currently executing statement is not completed, and the batch file continues with the next line. In short, DOS's message gets in the way of normal batch-file output, which is a reason to avoid asking a batch file to continue after you interrupt it.

The Break key combination also works with DOS commands that have built-in pauses, such as FORMAT and DISKCOPY. When these commands display such messages as "strike ENTER when ready," the Break combination can cancel the command. You can also use Break to stop the execution of a batch file that is not working as you desire.

DECISION MAKING IN BATCH FILES

DOS can test the value of certain variables and parameters during batch file execution. Performing this test is known as *decision making,* or *logical testing.* A logical test allows branching within a program, which means that different actions will be performed based on the results of a test.

```
     The batch file MOVE.BAT is designed to
     transfer a file(s) from one drive or
     d^C

     Terminate batch job (Y/N)? N ----------------------------------------
     MOVE first copies, then deletes the
     originals.  The general form is:
          MOVE  source  destination

  C>_
```

FIGURE 8.6: Continuing a batch file after interrupting its execution. Interrupting a batch file with Ctrl-C or Ctrl-Break and then responding N to DOS's query cause the batch file to continue to its normal end. However, the line that was executing when DOS processed the interrupt is not completed properly.

A branching statement (also called a *conditional* statement) might look like this:

IF Something = Something Else Do This Otherwise Do That

A more formal way of stating the same thing is

IF A = B Then Perform Action C Otherwise Perform Action D

A = B is called a *logical expression.* As in any language, this expression can stand for such equations as Wage = 500 or Lastname = Robbins. In the example, if the statement A = B is true, then action C will occur. On the other hand, if A = B is false, then action D will take place. This branching ability allows you to create batch files that evaluate circumstances and perform different actions according to the conditions the file finds.

If you have programming experience, you will recognize these branching statements as the IF...THEN...ELSE type statements that appear in a variety of programming languages. This common implementation allows for one or two branches, based on the value of an A = B type of conditional expression. Unfortunately, DOS does not permit such convenience in its batch file system. It uses a more limited form of IF statement that allows only one operation to be performed if the conditional expression evaluates to true.

As experienced assembler and FORTRAN programmers know, you can create a two-way branch in this limiting situation by combining the limited IF statement with the GOTO statement (see the section "GOTO and the Flow of Control" later in this chapter). Although this works, it can easily lead to what is termed "spaghetti" code: code consisting of many interwoven instruction sequences, connected by GOTO statements. The more modern high-level languages employ two-way branching IF statements, as well as more sophisticated structured techniques, for both elegance and clarity.

A Branching Program Example

To see the usefulness of branching, create a batch file that uses branching along with the other features discussed so far in this chapter. This program's purpose will be to search a disk for a certain file and report whether the file is there.

After you've used your computer for a while, you probably will accumulate many diskettes with many files. When you need to locate one file among those diskettes, which diskette the file is on is often unclear. You can easily miss the file name on a complete disk directory listing, even if you print the listing and keep it with the disk.

A new batch file, LOCATE.BAT, is just what you need. Type the LOCATE-.BAT file as shown in Figure 8.7. (The line numbers are for your convenience only—don't enter them!) Once you have this batch file in memory, you can simply enter

LOCATE *FileName*

to learn whether the file is on the diskette.

Tip: You can also use the batch program presented here for diskettes to locate a file in a hard disk directory.

```
1    ECHO OFF
2    CLS
3    IF NOT EXIST %1 GOTO NOFIND
4    ECHO The file %1 has been located!
5    GOTO END
6    :NOFIND
7    ECHO The file %1 cannot be found.  Look elsewhere.
8    :END
9    ECHO ON
```

FIGURE 8.7: The LOCATE.BAT file. This file combines IF with GOTO to produce a two-way branching structure. DOS searches for the specified file name, %1, in line 3 with the IF NOT EXIST %1 clause. If the file does not exist, GOTO NOFIND transfers execution control to line 6 and displays the message on line 7. If the file does exist, the GOTO statement does not execute, and line 4 executes, informing you that the file has been found. Control is transferred to the end of the batch file with the GOTO END statement in line 5.

Figure 8.8 depicts the step-by-step flow of execution for the branching that occurs in the LOCATE.BAT file you just entered. The first two commands, ECHO OFF and CLS, are familiar to you by now. The next subcommand— IF—is new. IF tests a condition that the computer can evaluate as true or false.

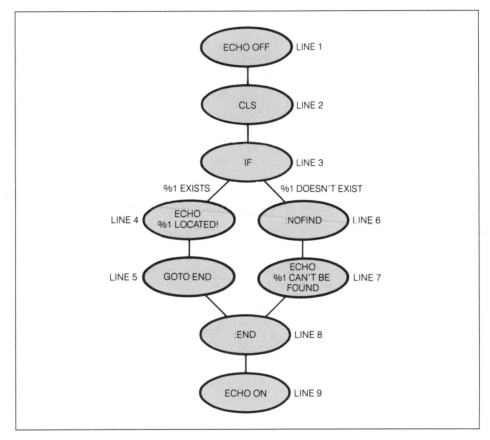

FIGURE 8.8: Flow of control in the LOCATE.BAT file. This visual representation makes the two-way branching structure more apparent. The IF statement clearly causes control to flow through either lines 4 and 5 or 6 and 7 before continuing, in either case, to lines 8 and 9 to end the program.

You can use the IF subcommand in three ways:

1. IF EXIST or IF NOT EXIST: Use this form of IF to test whether a file exists.

2. IF A == B or IF NOT A == B: Use this form to test the equality of A and B, where A and B represent character strings. Note that DOS uses == as the symbol for equality. The character strings can be literals or variables. A *literal* (also known as a constant) is any unchanging character string,

such as JUDD or END. A variable is one of the changing parameters %0 through %9, which you learned about in Chapter 7. For example, the command

IF %1 == END

tests whether the first variable parameter in the batch-file command %1 (a variable) is equal to the letters END (a literal). This is the most common use of the IF subcommand.

The IF subcommand is also used occasionally in testing for a missing input parameter. The equality test requires a string on either side of the equal sign to compare; and you may simply want to assure yourself that something has been entered before testing for a particular string. Therefore, you must provide yourself with a "dummy" string. You must use the following trick to determine whether an entry was made:

IF %1TRICK == TRICK *Command*

This version of the IF subcommand will execute the *Command* only if %1 is a null string (if the user entered nothing). Only in this way will the equality be true, since prefixing the characters TRICK with the parameter %1 (which in this case is a null string, or no string at all) will be equivalent to the characters TRICK alone. The *Command* can be logically designed to handle the case in which the user has not entered any value for the first parameter.

> *Warning:* DOS usually doesn't care whether you enter information in upper- or lowercase letters. However, when you are testing for the equality of groups of characters, as when you use the IF and the FIND subcommands, case *does* matter. If you enter the lowercase letters *end* as the first parameter in IF %1 == END, DOS will evaluate the IF statement as false. If you enter the uppercase letters *END*, DOS will evaluate the expression as true.

3. IF ERRORLEVEL #: Use this form to test whether the preceding command has terminated abnormally. DOS or any individual application program can set a return code equal to a number from 0 to 255. Usually, a value of 0 means that the preceding command ended successfully, and a value greater than 0 indicates a failure, with the particular number indicating the reason for the failure. Only the DOS commands BACKUP, FORMAT, and RESTORE affect this return-code value. (You can also write your own programs to set the return code, but that requires programming knowledge and goes beyond the scope of this book.) Note that ERRORLEVEL # indicates a return code of # *or greater*. If any of these three DOS commands fail, you can compare the error level to a particular

number, #, and act according to the severity of the error. The higher the return code, the more severe the error. The IF statement can use the error level to control which succeeding section of the batch file receives control.

GOTO and the Flow of Control   In the example batch file you are developing here you use the IF NOT EXIST form of the IF subcommand to test whether a certain file exists. Line 3 is

IF NOT EXIST %1 GOTO NOFIND

What does GOTO NOFIND mean? The GOTO subcommand tells DOS to continue executing the batch file at a new place. NOFIND is a special placeholder, or label, that you enter into the batch file to indicate that location. Where is NOFIND? Look again at Figure 8.7. You will see :NOFIND on line 6. If DOS cannot find the file name entered in the batch-file command line as %1 on the disk (in other words, if the file does not exist), then batch-file processing jumps from line 3 to line 6. The label line does nothing except facilitate this jumping, so the actual next line executed is line 7. This branching technique is referred to in programming languages as controlling the *flow of control.* (As you can see, this combination of IF and GOTO provides the same capability, mentioned earlier, as high-level programming languages using the IF...THEN...ELSE construct. Unfortunately, it is more difficult to follow this flow of control in a DOS batch file as it simulates the easier and cleaner structures of an IF...THEN...ELSE.)

If, however, the file does exist, then the next command to execute will be the next available one in the batch file, the one on line 4. This is just an ECHO subcommand, which states that DOS has loacted the sought-after file:

ECHO The file %1 has been located!

The displayed message will contain the actual file name specified: the name you assigned to %1, the first parameter on the command line.

Labels and Unconditional Branching   The next line, line 5, performs an *unconditional transfer of control.* It enables the processing sequence to skip over the :NOFIND section of the program. The label :END is again just a placeholder to mark where processing can continue. If DOS finds the desired file (line 4), then the flow of execution can skip over the :NOFIND section and proceed to line 9. Line 8 contains another label, called a *nonexecutable instruction* because it does not represent any steps that the processor takes but simply marks a place in the program. It can be compared to the address on your house, which is just a label that helps friends and the postman find their way to you.

RUNNING THE LOCATE.BAT FILE

Return to the LOCATE command. To see how it works, try it with a file on a diskette or in a directory. Assuming your DOS operating disk is in drive A, entering

LOCATE A:CHKDSK.COM

produces the message "The file A:CHKDSK.COM has been located!" The command

LOCATE A:TOPVIEW.EXE

will probably not find a file by that name. It will produce the message

The file A:TOPVIEW.EXE cannot be found. Look elsewhere.

If you want to search a large directory on your hard disk for the VTREE.COM file, you can enter

LOCATE C:\UTILITY\VTREE.COM

This might yield the message

The file C:\UTILITY\VTREE.COM has been located!

It's easy to see that the task performed by this batch file can be accomplished in other—perhaps simpler—ways. However, you've used an IF subcommand, a GOTO subcommand, the label mechanism, and variable parameters. That's the main point of this example batch file, not the actual job being performed. You can use these tools to create batch files that do meaningful work for you on your own system. Chapter 9 includes a number of sophisticated batch files that are more useful examples of these subcommand combinations.

USING LOOPING AND REPETITION IN BATCH FILES

The FOR subcommand is similar to commands in other programming languages that facilitate repetition. Often, one or more commands in a program need to be repeated, sometimes a fixed number of times and sometimes a variable number of times. In either situation, the FOR subcommand enables you to meet this need.

The general form of the FOR subcommand is

FOR *%%Letter* **IN** (*Possibilities*) **DO** *Command*

Letter is variable similar to the replaceable variable parameters, denoted by a single percent sign, discussed in Chapter 7. But the double percent sign here marks a significant difference. It tells DOS that you are referring to a batch-file variable in the looping FOR statement itself.

The *Possibilities* are a set of specific values, often file names, for the *Letter* variable. Wildcards are allowed in the specification of these *Possibilities*. The FOR statement is executed once for each item in the set of *Possibilities*. It is this repetition that makes using FOR loops a more economical form of coding than entering separate commands for each input value.

Command is the instruction you want the FOR loop to execute once for each of your specified *Possibilities*. It can be a standard DOS command or the file name of an executable program. As with all batch files, execution of the individual command is deferred until the entire batch file is run.

Examples of FOR Loops

A few examples will illustrate how the different forms of the FOR loop work.

Try all of the sample batch files in this section to affirm your understanding of the subcommands. In some cases, you will have to change the directory references to references that work on your system. Either in addition to or in place of the examples in this section, create a new batch file—for example, GYRO.BAT—that provides extra information to a user about your chosen topics. The batch file could be invoked as follows:

GYRO HEART

This command determines whether a text file called HEART.HLP exists. If it does, the screen clears and then displays the contents of the HEART.HLP file. If it does not, the screen displays the message "No help is available on subject HEART." Create your own sample .HLP text files to test your batch file.

FOR LOOP EXAMPLE 1: CALLING A PROGRAM REPEATEDLY

Suppose you have a program called QRTLY.EXE that generates a quarterly business report. This program requires only that you specify the desired quarter for the current fiscal year. Entering

QRTLY 3

at the DOS prompt produces a report for quarter 3.

At the end of the fiscal year, suppose you want to generate current copies of the quarterly reports for each quarter. You would enter

QRTLY 1
QRTLY 2
QRTLY 3
QRTLY 4

and press Return after each line. All four of these successive requests could be replaced by a batch file called REPORTS.BAT, with one automatic FOR subcommand, as shown in Figure 8.9. This batch file will generate all four quarterly reports when you enter simply

REPORTS

at the DOS prompt. The fourth line in the batch file, the FOR command, handles the repeated invocation of the QRTLY program for each successive quarter (1, 2, 3, then 4).

```
ECHO OFF
REM The REPORTS.BAT File
REM Produce the Four Quarterly Reports
FOR %%A IN (1 2 3 4) DO QRTLY %%A
ECHO ON
```

FIGURE 8.9: The REPORTS.BAT file. This file generates all four quarterly reports when you enter REPORTS at the DOS prompt. The fourth line in the batch file, the FOR command, handles the repeated invocation of the QRTLY program for each successive quarter (1, 2, 3, then 4).

Note: FOR is a batch-file subcommand. Thus, it can be executed only from within a batch file.

Using the following looping mechanism permits you to request all quarterly reports at once instead of having to wait for each to finish before you request the next.

FOR %%A IN (1 2 3 4) DO QRTLY %%A

Your first reaction might be that this is an awfully complicated-looking expression just to avoid entering four simple QRTLY report requests. Again, this example serves mainly to demonstrate the use of FOR. If you have a monthly report program called MONTHLY.EXE, you can just as easily request the printing of 12 monthly reports with

FOR %%A IN (1 2 3 4 5 6 7 8 9 10 11 12) DO MONTHLY %%A

Figure 8.10 shows the modified REPORTS file, REPORTS2.BAT.

```
ECHO OFF
REM The REPORTS2.BAT File
REM Produce the Twelve Monthly Reports
FOR %%A IN (1 2 3 4 5 6 7 8 9 10 11 12) DO MONTHLY %%
ECHO ON
```

FIGURE 8.10: The REPORTS2.BAT file. Batch files that use the FOR clause can do considerably more work with only slight changes in coding. In this file, the MONTHLY program is run for each of the 12 possible months (%%A ranges from 1 to 12).

In this example, a program was repeatedly invoked. In Chapter 9, the section entitled "Repeated Automatic Invocation" shows how to repeatedly execute even the batch program itself!

FOR Loop Example 2: Executing a DOS Command Repeatedly

As you've seen in the general form of the FOR subcommand, only one *Command* parameter can be executed after the DO portion of the command. It can be a program name, as has just been demonstrated, or it can be another DOS command, such as DIR or CHKDSK. Consider the following FOR subcommand:

FOR %%A IN (%1 %2 %3 %4) DO DIR %%A

This command performs a DIR command for each variable parameter (presumably, four different file names). If this FOR subcommand were in a batch file called HUNT.BAT, as shown in Figure 8.11, you could invoke HUNT in the following manner to determine whether any of the four specified files are located in the current directory:

HUNT HEART.EXE LUNGS.EXE LIVER.COM BRAIN.EXE

The result might look something like Figure 8.12. Even though you've suppressed the display of the DOS commands themselves with ECHO OFF, the remaining output still appears cluttered.

```
ECHO OFF
REM The HUNT.BAT File
FOR %%A IN (%1 %2 %3 %4) DO DIR %%A
ECHO OFF
```

FIGURE 8.11: The HUNT.BAT file. You can use the FOR...DO batch file subcommand to execute DOS commands repeatedly. In this, you can enter up to four separate file names as parameters in the HUNT command line. The FOR command ensures that a DIR command is executed successively for each file name to determine information about the file, if it exists in the current directory.

FOR Loop Example 3: Calling a Batch-File Subcommand

Using a batch subcommand as the object of DO can produce a more concise and attractive result than in the previous example. You can replace the DIR command with an IF subcommand:

FOR %%A IN (%1 %2 %3 %4) DO IF EXIST %%A ECHO %%A FOUND

```
C>HUNT HEART.EXE LUNGS.EXE LIVER.COM BRAIN.EXE

C>ECHO OFF

C>
C>_
```

```
     Volume in drive C is ROBBINS
     Directory of  C:\PROGRAMS\FW\CHAP11

HEART     EXE    186787    2-26-84   11:45a
          1 File(s)    1335296 bytes free

     Volume in drive C is ROBBINS
     Directory of  C:\PROGRAMS\FW\CHAP11

File not found

     Volume in drive C is ROBBINS
     Directory of  C:\PROGRAMS\FW\CHAP11

LIVER     COM    236398    1-13-86    9:55a
          1 File(s)    1335296 bytes free

     Volume in drive C is ROBBINS
     Directory of  C:\PROGRAMS\FW\CHAP11

File not found

C>
C>_
```

FIGURE 8.12: Executing HUNT.BAT to repeat a DOS command. Repeating the DIR command displays four successive outputs. Since ECHO is off, the DIR commands themselves do not appear on the screen between the command outputs.

The results are shown in Figure 8.13. The desired information about whether the files exist is not obscured by any additional DOS directory information. In this FOR subcommand, the actual command executed by DO is

IF EXIST %%A ECHO %%A FOUND

```
C>TYPE HUNT2.BAT
ECHO OFF
REM The HUNT2.BAT File
FOR %%A IN (%1 %2 %3 %4) DO IF EXIST %%A ECHO %%A FOUND
ECHO OFF

C>HUNT2 HEART.EXE LUNGS.EXE LIVER.COM BRAIN.EXE

C>ECHO OFF
HEART.EXE FOUND
LIVER.COM FOUND

C>_
```

FIGURE 8.13: Subcommands within subcommands. You can use batch-file subcommands as either stand-alone subcommands or as part of other commands, when syntactically correct. In this HUNT2.BAT file, the IF subcommand is contained (*nested*) within the FOR subcommand. Instead of the standard output of the DIR command, as seen in the preceding figure, the ECHO command displays a simple message for each file name found in the current directory.

Note, however, that the ECHO OFF command itself still is displayed, because the echoing feature is on until ECHO OFF shuts it off. DOS 3.3 users can surmount this limitation by preceding the command with the @ symbol.

@ECHO OFF

turns off the echoing feature for all succeeding commands, and the @ symbol suppresses the display of the command as well.

USING BATCH CHAINS AND BATCH SUBROUTINES

Since a batch file can execute any command that you could otherwise enter directly at the DOS prompt, a batch file can invoke another batch file. By simply entering the name of the second batch file, you can pass control from the first to the second file. Execution continues with the instructions in the second batch file and does not return to the first (calling) batch file through a process known as *chaining*. Chaining differs from the calling procedure familiar to programmers.

Look at the listings for the three batch files in Figures 8.14, 8.15, and 8.16. These three files together demonstrate both the capabilities and the limitations of chaining. Carefully read the steps in each of the three batch files while viewing the output results in Figure 8.17.

```
ECHO OFF
REM The FIRST.BAT File
ECHO Simulated Instruction 1 in First.bat
ECHO Simulated Instruction 2 in First.bat
ECHO Simulated Instruction 3 in First.bat
SECOND
```

FIGURE 8.14: The FIRST.BAT file. This extremely simple batch file contains a REM statement to clarify which batch file it is, three ECHO statements to simulate instructions that might exist if FIRST were doing more sophisticated work, and a final command that invokes the SECOND.BAT batch file.

```
ECHO OFF
REM The SECOND.BAT File
ECHO Simulated Instruction 1 in Second.bat
ECHO Simulated Instruction 2 in Second.bat
ECHO Simulated Instruction 3 in Second.bat
THIRD
ECHO Last Instruction in Second.bat
```

FIGURE 8.15: The SECOND.BAT file. This file simulates a second batch file demonstrating a chain of related executing batch programs. Note that the last instruction in this simulated program is not the invocation of a THIRD.BAT file. The final instruction here follows the invocation of THIRD and is merely an ECHO instruction demonstrating what can happen to your instructions if you chain programs incautiously.

```
ECHO OFF
REM The THIRD.BAT File
ECHO Simulated Instruction 1 in Third.bat
ECHO Simulated Instruction 2 in Third.bat
ECHO Simulated Instruction 3 in Third.bat
```

FIGURE 8.16: The THIRD.BAT file. When this final batch file in the demonstration chain shown in Figure 8.17 completes execution, execution ceases, and control returns to the DOS prompt.

The first batch file executes three simulated instructions and then invokes the second batch file as its last instruction. These simulated instructions are place-holders for any other successive batch-file commands that you might write. (You should focus on chaining here, rather than on other command lines; the simulated instructions are displayed merely to give you a context for the chaining technique.)

After FIRST finishes executing, it passes control to SECOND by invoking as its last instruction the name of the file (SECOND) to which control will be passed. Then batch file SECOND executes another three simulated instructions

```
C>FIRST

C>ECHO OFF
Simulated Instruction 1 in First.bat
Simulated Instruction 2 in First.bat
Simulated Instruction 3 in First.bat
Simulated Instruction 1 in Second.bat
Simulated Instruction 2 in Second.bat
Simulated Instruction 3 in Second.bat
Simulated Instruction 1 in Third.bat
Simulated Instruction 2 in Third.bat
Simulated Instruction 3 in Third.bat

C>_
```

FIGURE 8.17: Batch-file chaining. Simply invoke the batch file FIRST from the DOS prompt. When FIRST completes its instructions (three simulated ones here), it passes control (*chains*) to the SECOND batch file. This second link in the chain performs its three simulated instructions, and then passes control to the THIRD batch file; in the process, the file ignores the last instruction in the SECOND batch file, because it is located *after* the invocation of THIRD. When THIRD completes execution (of its three simulated instructions), control returns to the DOS prompt for further command processing.

before passing control to batch file THIRD. THIRD executes its own three simulated instructions before the chain process is complete. However, the line

> **Last instruction in Second.bat**

is never executed, because the third batch file was invoked *in the middle* of the second batch file.

> *Tip:* Proper chaining of batch files requires the new batch-file name to be the last instruction of the preceding batch file in the chain.

True subroutines let you write modular batch files that perform well-defined sequences of tasks, and temporarily leave one batch file to execute a sequence *without losing your place* in the first batch file. If you need to run a batch file while in the middle of another batch file, you can do so in two ways. If you are using DOS 3.3, you can use the CALL subcommand. If you are using an earlier version of DOS, you must invoke the COMMAND.COM program itself. The forms required are

> **CALL** *BatchFileName*

for DOS 3.3 users and

> **COMMAND/C** *BatchFileName*

for users of all earlier versions of DOS. Since under most circumstances DOS batch files can only chain, COMMAND/C brings into memory a completely separate copy of DOS for the express purpose of running the named batch file. This method is called a *secondary command processor* technique.

With either the CALL or COMMAND/C method, when the batch file has executed all its commands, control returns to the next line in the running batch file—the one *containing* the CALL or COMMAND/C instruction—and execution continues from there.

Look again at the THIRD.BAT file shown in Figure 8.16 and then look at FOURTH.BAT, shown in Figure 8.18. You can use these two files and the secondary command processor technique to invoke and run the instructions within the THIRD.BAT file, as shown in Figure 8.19. The results are different from the results of chaining.

```
@ECHO OFF
REM The FOURTH.BAT File
ECHO Simulated Instruction 1 in Fourth.bat
ECHO Simulated Instruction 2 in Fourth.bat
ECHO Simulated Instruction 3 in Fourth.bat
CALL THIRD
ECHO Last Instruction in Fourth.bat
```

FIGURE 8.18: The FOURTH.BAT file. Using the specialized DOS 3.3 subcommand CALL allows you to surmount the limitation of chaining. Equivalent in functionality to the true programming subroutine capability found in high-level programming languages, the CALL command allows the FOURTH.BAT file to *temporarily* pass control to batch file THIRD. When THIRD completes execution, control does not return to the DOS prompt, but instead returns to the next instruction (in this case, the last one) in the calling FOURTH.BAT file.

Running FOURTH with this method results in the same first three simulated instructions as with chaining. When those three instructions finish execution, control will be transferred to the THIRD batch file, at which point its three simulated instructions will execute. However, unlike in the previous chaining example, control returns to FOURTH, which can execute its last instruction. If there were another instruction in FOURTH, or another hundred instructions, they would then all execute. In this way, you can build sophisticated, structured application environments and systems by using only DOS commands and the batch-file mechanism.

THE BATCH-FILE SUBCOMMANDS

Following is a summary of the subcommands that make up the batch-file programming language. The most important difference between these commands

```
C>FOURTH
Simulated Instruction 1 in Fourth.bat
Simulated Instruction 2 in Fourth.bat
Simulated Instruction 3 in Fourth.bat
Simulated Instruction 1 in Third.bat
Simulated Instruction 2 in Third.bat
Simulated Instruction 3 in Third.bat
Last Instruction in Fourth.bat
C>_
```

FIGURE 8.19: DOS supports true subroutines. Running FOURTH at the DOS prompt verifies that the DOS 3.3 CALL command supports true subroutine capability in the batch-file mechanism. The instructions for FOURTH appear first, followed by the instructions for THIRD; then the final instruction of FOURTH executes, verifying that control has returned to the calling program rather than to the DOS prompt, as it would have had mere chaining been used.

and the standard DOS commands presented throughout the rest of this book is that, except as noted, you can use these commands only in batch files; you cannot invoke them from the DOS prompt.

CALL

This subcommand calls a second batch file as a subroutine, returning control to the calling program.

SYNTAX

CALL *FileSpec*

FileSpec   is the optional drive and path name, plus the file name, of the second batch file to be executed.

TYPE

Batch, internal.

USAGE

CALL allows a true subroutine capability in DOS 3.3. When you are executing a batch file, you may sometimes need to run a second batch file and then return to the first batch file at the place where the second file was called. In other words, you may want to run a second batch file without having to later completely restart the first one. You can do this with the CALL command.

RESTRICTIONS

Recursive calls are allowed, but you are responsible for ensuring that the call eventually ends.

EXAMPLES

Suppose you have written a simple batch file, called HEADER.BAT, whose only job is to display or print a consistent several lines of information identifying your Company name, the date, your name, and so forth. To use this file in any of your report or analysis programs, you need only enter

CALL HEADER

in your other batch files. The called file, HEADER.BAT, will perform its header writing chores and then return control to whichever other batch file called it at the instruction following the CALL HEADER line.

ECHO

This subcommand suppresses or restores the display of batch-file commands as they are executing.

SYNTAX

ECHO [ON ¦ OFF ¦ *String*]

ON	turns on the display of commands (the default).
OFF	turns off echoing.
String	is a message that will be displayed regardless of whether ECHO is on or off.

TYPE

Batch, internal (acceptable on a DOS command line).

USAGE

When you use a batch file, you may not want the executing commands to be displayed on the screen. ECHO suppresses the screen's presentation of batch-file command execution.

You can use ECHO to send a line of text to a printer or a file; for example

ECHO Hello >LPT1

prints "Hello." The greater-than symbol (>) is a *redirection* character; redirection is discussed in Chapter 17. This technique can be used to send control sequences through DOS to any peripheral device. Specifically, this combination of the ECHO command with redirection techniques can be used to send control sequences to your printer. The general form of such a command would be:

ECHO *Control Sequence* **> PRN**

In particular, you would simply enter the control characters into the command line with your word processor or EDLIN. For example, the control sequence to put an Epson printer into letter quality mode is *<esc>* followed by the small letter *x* followed by the digit *1*. In EDLIN, to obtain this control sequence, you would type ^ V followed by the left square bracket [, then followed by the characters *x1*. In many word processors, you would enter the Alt-027 sequence, followed by *x1*. You will then see the following line in a text file listing:

ECHO ^ [x1 > PRN

EXAMPLES

The most common use of ECHO is seen at the beginning of many batch programs. You can include a line such as

ECHO OFF

to ensure that all succeeding commands are not displayed, but rather, that only the output results from those commands are displayed. Command display will continue to be suppressed until you turn off this feature with

ECHO ON

In versions of DOS earlier than 3.3, the command ECHO OFF itself is always displayed, much to the dismay of DOS users who wanted to completely mask the batch file operation from the eyes of other users. DOS 3.3 includes a new capability that surmounts this difficulty. Placing the symbol @ in front of any command, such as ECHO OFF, suppresses the display of that command only. Thus, beginning a batch file program with the command

@ECHO OFF

suppresses *all* commands in the batch file, including this ECHO OFF command.

ECHO is also used in some batch files merely to display information to the user. If your batch file includes a series of instructions such as

ECHO This is a typical message line

then, assuming ECHO is off, the user would see the line

This is a typical message line

on the screen. Messages presented using the ECHO feature are the fundamental mechanism for providing on-line help to users of custom DOS systems. Both this chapter and Chapter 9 offer specific examples of batch files that accomplish this task.

FOR

FOR sets up a repeating loop in a batch file.

SYNTAX

FOR *%%Var* **IN** (*ComSet*) **DO** *Command*

Var   is a variable name, conventionally a single letter.

ComSet   is the set of values to be used successively by *Command*. These values can be any combination of character strings, batch file parameters, or environmental variables.

Command is the command to be executed using *%%Var* as a varying parameter (which uses the values given in *ComSet*).

TYPE

Batch, internal.

USAGE

Use FOR to repeat an operation using different parameters a specified number of times.

The FOR subcommand allows you to create a looping mechanism in a DOS batch file, very much like the loops and iterative structures found in high-level programming languages such as COBOL, FORTRAN, and C. This mechanism is not as powerful as the parallel ones found in these languages, but it is often sufficient.

As you can see in the "Syntax" section, the FOR command allows you to repeated any command the number of times specified in *ComSet*. Although this looping structure is limited to one command, you can in fact create quite powerful system structures by specifying the command to be repeated as the CALL (in DOS 3.3) or the COMMAND /C (in DOS 3.2 and earlier implementations) command. In this way, you can actually repeat blocks of code (see the "Examples" section) to approximate the more powerful block-structure capabilities of modern high-level languages.

RESTRICTIONS

You cannot use DOS reserved words as variable names in FOR commands.

EXAMPLES

You can repeat DOS commands, batch-file subcommands, and even other batch files. For example, suppose your system has five disk drives, labeled A through E. Your batch file could contain one line that performs a CHKDSK operation for each drive:

FOR %%R in (A B C D E) DO CHKDSK %%R

Suppose also that you have written a series of batch reporting program—called REP1, REP2, REP3, REP4, and REP5—whose order of execution has a direct impact on the resulting reports. You could invoke each report separately in the desired order, or you could create a simple batch program, called REPORT, consisting of this single FOR statement:

FOR %%X in (%1 %2 %3 %4 %5) DO CALL %%X

Now whenever you want to run your reports, you can simply run the REPORT batch file, specifying the individual reporting program file names in the order you want them executed. Entering

REPORT REP3 REP2 REP5 REP1 REP4

causes the FOR statement in REPORT.BAT to run the REP*x* batch files in the order 3, 2, 5, 1, and 4.

In fact, if you didn't care what order the reports were generated, you could simply enter

REPORT REP?

The reports would be printed in the order of their occurrence in DOS's directory table.

GOTO

This subcommand transfers control of a batch-file program to a point in the program indicated by a label.

SYNTAX

GOTO [:]*Label*

Label   is the line identifier used by the batch file to indicate the line to which GOTO will transfer control. The label line itself must always be preceded by a colon; this tells the batch file processor that the line is a label. The GOTO statement actually can work either with or without the colon, since the command itself tells the batch file processor that it will be looking for a label. The colon in this GOTO statement, therefore, is unnecessary, although it won't get in the way.

TYPE

Batch, internal.

USAGE

During a batch file's execution, it may be necessary to skip over some commands and execute others in a file or to jump back to another point in a file, perhaps for some logical looping. GOTO allows you to transfer execution.

Tip: Use descriptive labels in your GOTO commands.

EXAMPLES

The most common use of the GOTO command in batch files is the simple line

    GOTO END

or, with a colon,

    GOTO :END

No matter where DOS encounters this line in a batch file, it immediately transfers control to the label line :END, usually the final line in the program.

GOTO is also often used to jump around a block of code. See the example in the IF subcommand section.

IF

This subcommand allows conditional branching in a batch-file program.

SYNTAX

IF [NOT] *Condition Command*

NOT   inverts the truth of the condition. If NOT is included, a true condition would be regarded as false, and a false condition as true.

Condition   is the criterion for the execution of *Command*. *Condition* can be in one of the following formats:

ERRORLEVEL *Code*   determines whether the return code of the last-executed program or command equals or exceeds *Code*.

String1 == *String2*   specifies that *String1* must equal *String2* for the condition to be true.

EXIST *FileSpec*   causes the condition to be true if the file defined by *FileSpec* resides in the specified directory.

Command   is the action (usually a command) executed when *Condition* is true or not false.

TYPE

Batch, internal (acceptable on a DOS command line).

USAGE

Conditional statements play an important role in any type of programming. A conditional statement simply says "Do one thing if a certain condition is true; otherwise, do another thing." This allows branching, or decision making, in your programs.

In most high-level programming languages, conditionals are defined with the IF command. The statement IF A = B THEN GOTO :START is executed as "If A equals B, then transfer control to the line labeled :START; otherwise, just go on to the next instruction."

RESTRICTIONS

DOS is case-sensitive for *String* values.

EXAMPLES

You can implement a decision point in a batch file with the following code:

```
IF EXIST %2 GOTO :YES
GOTO :NEXT
```

```
:YES
COPY %2 A:
ERASE %2
:NEXT
```

In this example code, if the file name specified as parameter %2 exists, then the flow of execution is passed to the label :YES, after which the file name specified is copied to drive A and erased from the current drive and directory. Then the :NEXT code in the batch file is executed. If the specified file name does not exist, then GOTO :NEXT is executed immediately, rather than GOTO :YES. This batch-file structure is equivalent to the high-level programming language IF...THEN...ELSE construct.

PAUSE

PAUSE temporarily halts the execution of a batch file. A message appears on the screen telling you to strike a key when you are ready to continue.

SYNTAX

PAUSE [*String*]

    String   prints a specified string (a message) on the screen before "Strike any key when ready".

TYPE

Batch, internal (acceptable on a DOS command line).

USAGE

You typically use the PAUSE command in a batch file to temporarily interrupt the execution of the batch file's instructions. Usually, you insert a PAUSE statement whenever you want to give a user some time to think, decide, or simply read and absorb information displayed on the screen.

When ECHO is on, both the word PAUSE and the message *string* are displayed before the "Strike any key when ready" message. As this is not particularly desirable, you should consider the following combination when seeking an extra message with your pause. First, turn ECHO OFF to disable all messages except what you want to appear. Then, use the ECHO command (not the PAUSE command) to achieve your extra message. Lastly, use the PAUSE command solely to create the temporary pause in batch file execution:

```
@ECHO OFF
ECHO extra message
PAUSE
```

Note the use of the @ symbol to suppress the redisplay of the ECHO OFF command itself.

EXAMPLES

After sending a series of ECHO messages to the screen, you can insert

PAUSE

to provide a break before more ECHO messages appear. The user can then pause to read the first group of messages before striking a key to send the next series of messages to the screen.

You can also include an extra message at the point of the interruption. For instance, you may want to remind the user that pressing Ctrl-C or Ctrl-Break stops the batch file and returns control to the DOS prompt. Assuming ECHO is on, including the lines

PAUSE Press Ctrl-C to return to the DOS prompt, or

displays the following two lines on the screen:

PAUSE Press Ctrl-C to return to the DOS prompt, or
Strike any key when ready

REM

REM allows you to insert comments in a batch-file program.

SYNTAX

REM *String*

String   represents nonexecutable comments.

TYPE

Batch, internal (acceptable on a DOS command line).

USAGE

It is often helpful to place comments in your programs, so that when you return to those programs later, you can quickly and easily understand what the programs contain and how they work. In batch files, you insert comments with the REM command. The contents of a REM command line are not executed or displayed if ECHO is off, but you can read them if you look at the file itself.

RESTRICTIONS

Each REM statement can contain comments up to 123 characters long. Enclose characters that have special meanings to DOS (such as ¦) in double quotation marks (" ¦ ").

EXAMPLES

The beginning of every batch file should include one or more REM statements such as the following:

ECHO OFF
REM Batch file *filename*
REM The purpose of this batch program is ...
REM Input parameters accepted are:
REM %1 used for ...
REM %2 used for ...

Additionally, you should include REM lines in larger batch files to explain any nontrivial or nonobvious coding decisions or logic. For example, the following example includes REM lines explaining how and which lines are version dependent:

REM Next three lines valid for DOS 3.3 only.
REM Replace for earlier versions.
NLSFUNC
MODE CON CODEPAGE PREPARE =
  ((850,437) C:\DOS\EGA.CPI)
KEYB NL, 850, \DOS\KEYBOARD.SYS

SHIFT

This command shifts all variables down one number.

SYNTAX

SHIFT

TYPE

Batch, internal (acceptable on a DOS command line).

USAGE

Within any batch file, using the SHIFT command causes the % parameters to be shifted downwards by number. This means that after SHIFT, the second parameter on the batch file invocation line will no longer be accessible as %2, but rather as %1. Similarly, the third parameter will be accessible as %2, and so on. What this means, in practical terms, is that the tenth parameter on the invocation line (formerly inaccessible owing to the %9 limit on parameters) is now accessible to the batch file as %9. The flip side of this coin is that the former first parameter is no longer directly available to the batch file as variable %1. The usefulness of this capability is limited, as few batch files need to use more than ten variables. Nonetheless, as the following examples show, there are situations in which parameter-shifting can be a valuable technique.

EXAMPLES

Suppose your batch file RPT.BAT processes reports for months specified as parameters when the batch file is called:

RPT jan feb mar apr may jun jul aug sep oct nov dec

In the batch file, *jan* is available as %1, *feb* is available as %2, and so on up to *sep* as %9. If the batch file tries to deal directly with all the possible month entries, it will not be able to access the last three months. Instead, the SHIFT command can be used to allow the batch file to access any number of parameters:

```
:NEXT
IF %1TRICK == TRICK GOTO :END
REPORT %1
SHIFT
GOTO :NEXT
:END
```

This example combines the SHIFT command with the trick presented earlier in this chapter for testing for the existence of a null string. If the first parameter on the RPT.BAT command line is not null, that parameter is passed along to the REPORT.EXE program for report generation. Then the SHIFT command is executed, shifting all succeeding parameters down one in position: the second parameter becomes the new %1, and so forth.

The GOTO :NEXT continues execution at the trick IF statement. If there *was* a second parameter, then there is now a %1 (after the shift), and that value is now passed to the REPORT.EXE program, followed by another shift. When the last parameter (it could be twelve or fifteen or twenty or ...) is processed, the trick IF test passes execution control to the :END statement, and the batch file ends.

Another possibility for using the SHIFT command can be seen in the batch file CC.BAT seen in Figure 8.20. This real-life example illustrates a method used by programmers to afford themselves two different compilation possibilities based on the simple test for a particular switch on their batch file command line. A programmer can study all the complex options to a piece of software such as the Microsoft C language compiler once, and then enshrine his or her choice permanently in a batch file like CC.BAT. The programmer may have one set of compiler switches to use while developing a piece of software, and another set for compiling the finished code. The former set tells the compiler to prepare the program for debugging and to produce more comprehensive warning messages, whereas the latter set tells it to produce the smallest, fastest code possible. Now the programmer would like to have one switch to tell the batch file whether to call the compiler in its "developmental" mode or its "optimization" mode, without passing that switch on to the compiler itself. Line 7 of CC.BAT checks for a first switch /O, for "optimize." (Note that the test is case sensitive.) If the switch exists, control transfers to the label :OPTIM, and then the switch itself is shifted out and the compiler is called with optimization on. That is, the SHIFT command essentially strips off this first parameter, shifts down into accessibility the other possible parameters, and then sends them all to the Microsoft C compiler. (The exact function of each compiler switch is not our concern here.) If the first parameter is something else, line 8 transfers control to the label :DEV, and the compiler is called with switches to allow symbolic debugging using Microsoft CodeView. In either case, the compiler sees first a set of "default" switches included in the batch file and then arguments given on the batch file command line, which will be C source file names and, possibly, additional switches to supplement or overrule the "default" switches.

```
 1   ECHO OFF
 2
 3   REM Batch file to call Microsoft C compiler version 5.0
 4   REM Initial switch "/O" produces optimized code
 5   REM Otherwise developmental code is produced
 6
 7   IF %1==/O GOTO OPTIM
 8   GOTO DEV
 9   :OPTIM
10   SHIFT
11   CL /W1 /Oxn /FPi /Zp %1 %2 %3 %4 %5 %6 %7 %8 %9
12   GOTO OBJ
13   :DEV
14   CL /W2 /Od /FPi /Fa /Gs /Zi /Zp %1 %2 %3 %4 %5 %6 %7 %8 %9
15   :OBJ
16   FOR %%P IN (%1 %2 %3 %4 %5 %6 %7 %8 %9) DO IF %%P==c GOTO END
17   ERASE *.OBJ
18   :END
```

FIGURE 8.20: The CC.BAT file is designed to allow a C programmer to choose between two compilation possibilities—optimization, when the program is finished, and development, while it is still being debugged. The heart of the batch file lies in lines 7 and 10. DOS finds the switch /O (for optimize) as the first argument on the batch file command line, control passes to the label :OPTIM, and the SHIFT command shifts the first argument out and calls the compiler with optimization on.

SUMMARY

In this chapter, you extended your understanding of batch files. You learned about a variety of specialized commands that work only from within batch files. These subcommands provide DOS with many features normally reserved for high-level computer languages.

For additional information about the fundamentals of batch files, including variable parameters, see

- Chapter 7, "Fundamentals of Batch Processing"

For additional information about examples of sophisticated batch files, see

- Chapter 9, "Complete Batch-File Examples"

For additional information about DOS redirection, see

- Chapter 17, "Pipes, Filters, and Redirection"

For additional information about the Norton Utilities, see

- Chapter 20, "Extending DOS's Power with Utility Software"

Now you possess these fundamental batch-file construction skills; the next chapter will make you a more advanced batch-file user. You will learn many tricks and techniques that will allow you to develop fancy implementations and systems of your own.

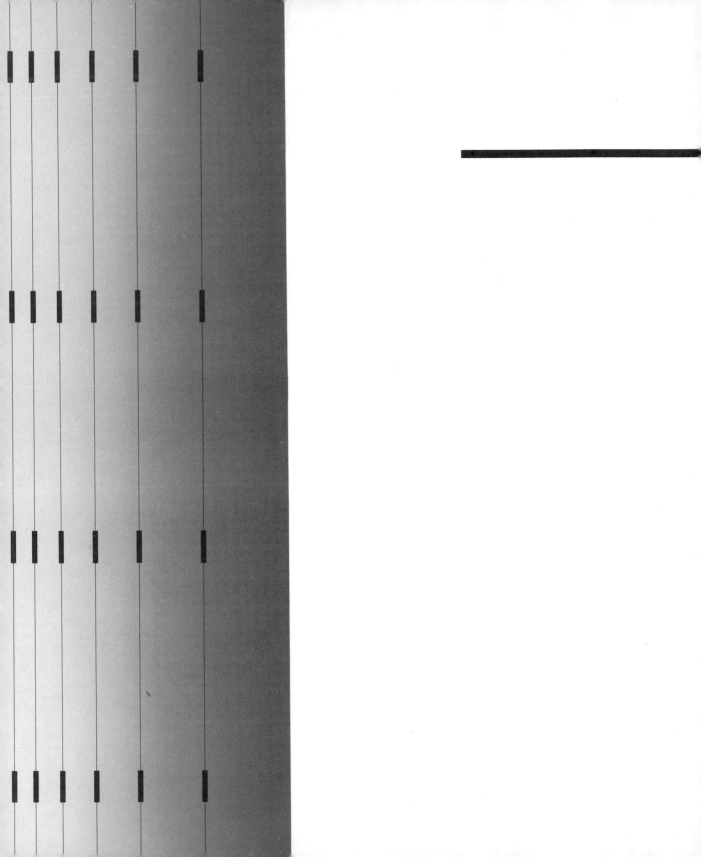

CHAPTER 9

COMPLETE BATCH-FILE EXAMPLES

COMPLETE BATCH-FILE EXAMPLES

You've seen in Chapter 7 that the primary role of batch files is to allow you to conveniently group together a collection of DOS commands, other programs, and other batch files. You've also seen how this entire collection of commands can be run by entering the batch-file name with any special parameters at the DOS prompt.

As you've learned in the last two chapters, there are several situations in which you should write batch files:

1. When you want to perform a time-consuming sequence of operations that don't require your attention during processing.

2. When you need to run a complex sequence of commands frequently, and you would like to ensure that they are performed consistently.

3. When you don't know any other programming language that might allow you to perform the same tasks.

4. When you want to minimize the maintenance requirements of the code that you write. Writing applications in the DOS batch-file system whenever possible will allow more future users to modify and maintain your code than if you had written the same logic in a high-level programming language.

This chapter presents a wide range of batch-file examples. These examples provide you with usable programs: You can enter them yourself, or you can send for a diskette with the files already on it (see the coupon at the end of this book). These examples will also give you ideas for creating similar programs for your own computer system.

> *Note:* If a batch file you write works, *it's right*. It may not be the fastest, most efficient, or most elegant file, but it's still right. That said, you can quickly move from questions of right and wrong to questions of good and better. Once you have designed and written a batch file that works properly, your next step often is to make that batch file run more quickly, work more efficiently, use a more elegant algorithm, or simply appear more aesthetically pleasing on paper. The batch files in this chapter provide you with a useful library of functions that you can call upon when developing your own DOS applications. These examples also demonstrate proper techniques, although you should recognize that personal style and the urgency and importance of the task all affect the quality and nature of the code you generate.

The batch files presented in this chapter offer a means of automating DOS operations and techniques ranging in complexity from the elementary to the relatively advanced. These operations are discussed in detail in various chapters throughout the book. If you are studying DOS by reading each chapter in succession, you will find many operations here that you have not encountered anywhere else yet. The introductory paragraphs for each of these operations provide some background, but you will always be able to find more information about the operation by referring to the appropriate chapter. Such cross-references are provided throughout. If, after reading the basic discussion, you decide to incorporate the operation in a batch file, you can then return to this chapter. (You will also find it useful to follow up these cross-references if you are consulting this book on a topical, need-to-know basis.)

AUTOMATING SYSTEM JOBS

When you turn on your computer and load DOS, DOS scans the root directory of the disk for a batch file called AUTOEXEC.BAT. If it finds that file, it executes the commands within it automatically.

Note: DOS does not supply a default AUTOEXEC.BAT file. However, many application programs do supply one on their system disks. When loading new application programs, be sure that the program's AUTOEXEC.BAT file does not overwrite an existing AUTOEXEC.BAT file that you carefully created.

AUTOEXEC.BAT is a valuable tool. In both diskette and hard disk systems, you can use it to execute any number of DOS commands or other programs. For example, you can set the time and date if you have a battery-powered clock in your computer, or you can configure your PROMPT and MODE commands for specific serial-port and video-screen requirements. There is no limit to the modifications you can make in your AUTOEXEC.BAT file.

Let's take a look at some of the uses for AUTOEXEC.BAT. You'll see first how to load and run a specific program automatically when you power up your computer. Then you'll see how to customize the PROMPT command. Finally, you'll explore some more complex uses for AUTOEXEC.BAT.

Warning: The AUTOEXEC.BAT file must be stored in the root directory of the boot disk. It will be ignored if it is stored in any other directory.

Automating System Startup

It's easy to add an automatic startup feature to your system disk. Then as soon as DOS is loaded, the computer will run a particular program. Assume you want to run the BASICA program each time you start your system. Since BASICA is totally self-contained, all you need to do is use the COPY command to place a copy of BASICA.COM on your new system disk.

Assuming your new system disk is in drive B (for dual-diskette systems) or in drive C (for hard disk systems), you enter the command

COPY BASICA.COM B:

(for a dual-diskette system) or the command

COPY BASICA.COM C:

(for a hard disk system).

A simple task your AUTOEXEC.BAT file can perform is entering the name of a particular application program you want to execute. The principle illustrated here applies to any program that you want to start automatically when you boot your system. In this example, you want to invoke BASICA.COM automatically upon start-up. Use whatever text-editing method you like to create an AUTOEXEC.BAT file containing the one line that invokes the BASICA program:

BASICA

If you'd like to try this method with another program such as a word processor—say, WP.COM—make sure you copy WP.COM to the new system disk. In this case, your AUTOEXEC.BAT file will contain one line:

WP

If the application program you are using includes overlay files, you must be sure to copy these files to your new system disk. For instance, suppose your word processor requires a file called WP.OVL. You need that file on the system disk containing your new AUTOEXEC.BAT file.

To see if your new setup works as planned, restart the computer from your system disk. You can do this in two ways. First, you can turn off the computer, wait a few seconds, and then turn the computer on again. When the disk spins, DOS should be loaded, and the program should run automatically.

Alternatively, you can use the keyboard rebooting procedure produced by the Ctrl-Alt-Del key combination. This also restarts the computer. However, it does not perform the same internal hardware and memory checks as an actual startup does.

Using the Ctrl-Alt-Del key combination is simple. If you have a hard disk system, remember to remove any disk currently in drive A, since the computer defaults to that drive automatically. Hold down the Ctrl and the Alt keys and press the Del key at the same time. Then release all of the keys. The system will be loaded, and your AUTOEXEC.BAT will be executed. This is called a *warm boot,* since the computer was already turned on. A *cold boot* occurs when you first turn on the computer's power; the same sequence takes place then, except that a cold boot activates several internal hardware tests.

Warning: Don't use the Ctrl-Alt-Del rebooting method casually. If you are in the middle of running a program such as a word processor, database manager, or spreadsheet, rebooting may destroy your current working file.

Either of these rebooting procedures can be used for most programs, and any main program can be run automatically at system startup. However, keep in mind that some copy-protected programs have their own instructions for automatic startup.

Changing the Default System Prompt

If you find yourself always changing your default system prompt, you can set a new prompt to appear automatically when you turn on the computer. You can use the AUTOEXEC.BAT file to accomplish this. Not only individual software programs, but also DOS commands themselves can be executed automatically during startup.

Create an AUTOEXEC.BAT file in the root directory that contains the single line

PROMPT pg

Even though this AUTOEXEC.BAT file contains only one command, the number of automatic commands you can have in this file is unlimited. To see how this particular command is activated, reboot your system.

Warning: Even though the number of command lines you can have in any batch file is unlimited, you should not write batch files with too many commands in them. The larger your files get, the harder to read, understand, modify, and debug they become.

Other Uses of AUTOEXEC.BAT

The number and types of useful instructions you can add to your AUTOEXEC.BAT file are limitless. Nearly every instruction discussed in this chapter could be included in it. For that matter, nearly every DOS activity discussed so far in this book—from customizing the prompt to initializing function keys—could be handled in your startup AUTOEXEC.BAT file.

For example, suppose that you want to press the function key F9 or F10 to generate a wide directory listing or a clean screen. As you will learn in Chapter 10, "Configuration Possibilities," the following two commands provide that setup:

PROMPT $e[0;67;"DIR/W";13p
PROMPT $e[0;68;"CLS";13p

Include these in your AUTOEXEC.BAT file—and your wish has become DOS's command. Use the more sophisticated versions of the PROMPT command presented in Chapter 10 if you'd like an even more useful prompt than this.

Use your own judgment and creativity in including commands in your AUTOEXEC.BAT file. The rest of this chapter contains a host of tips, tricks, and techniques that you can use with batch files. You'll want to include some of these in your AUTOEXEC.BAT file. The next section provides a good example of using batch files in AUTOEXEC.BAT.

CREATING YOUR OWN MENU SYSTEM

It's always helpful to set up a mechanism that makes it easy for you and others to run programs. Hard disk menu systems are designed to provide that very capability. Of course, you can always buy one; you'll read more about that in Chapter 20. However, an inexpensive way to set up a menu system is to use DOS's batch-file feature. A series of batch files stored on your hard disk can enable anyone to access the programs you have installed. You'll now see one possible design for such a series of batch files.

> *Note:* Remember that nearly everyone designs and programs differently, and that all of the batch files you see here are demonstrations. Feel free to add embellishments or to design the instruction sequences differently.

The first step in creating your own menu system is to create a file that contains a list of the programs available on your system. Put this display menu into a text file called MENU.SCR, as shown in Figure 9.1.

```
              MENU OF AVAILABLE HARD DISK PROGRAMS

     TO SELECT ONE, TYPE ITS NUMBER AND PRESS <RETURN>


     1  -  INVENTORY MANAGEMENT SYSTEM

     2  -  BUDGET ANALYSIS SYSTEM

     3  -  WORD PROCESSING

     4  -  SYSTEM UTILITIES



     ENTER YOUR CHOICE NOW, PLEASE:
```

FIGURE 9.1: Menu management file. This display is representative of many screen prompts that present menu choices. It happens to be a printout of a standard ASCII text file, MENU.SCR. To display this menu, simply type its name with DOS's TYPE command.

If you want this file displayed each time your system boots up, all you need to do is write an AUTOEXEC.BAT file containing these two simple commands:

CLS
TYPE MENU.SCR

To make this menu work, you must create other DOS batch files for each option listed on the menu. For example, to run your inventory management system, you need to create a batch file called 1.BAT. Because the file's base name is the number 1, and all batch files have the extension .BAT, typing 1 and pressing Return will execute the commands in that file.

A typical batch file for a menu system would contain a set of actions such as the following:

1. Changing the directory to the correct one: for example, C:\DBMS \INVNTORY

2. Running the program; for example, to run a dBASE III PLUS customized inventory program called INVENT.PRG, the batch file would execute the command DBASE INVENT

3. Returning to the root directory after the program has completed execution

4. Displaying the menu again, so that the user can make another choice

Of course, a file like 1.BAT could also perform many other tasks; for example, it could set a specialized path and then reset it at the end of the program. The rest of this chapter will focus on the many different operations you can include in any batch file.

Figure 9.2 shows the contents of example .BAT files that perform three steps. The three sets of commands shown in this figure perform the actions required for choices 1, 2, and 3 on the menu in Figure 9.1. The 1.BAT file brings up a database management program, the 2.BAT file brings up a spreadsheet program, and the 3.BAT file brings up a word processing program. The contents of each of these batch files are almost exactly the same, except that the directory and program differs in each.

The fourth choice on your sample menu, SYSTEM UTILITIES, is interesting because it suggests the possiblity of a flexible multilevel menu system. You could create a batch file called 4.BAT that would contain a new screen display, listing several utility choices. The utility operations could be safely nestled inside other batch files, and another entire set of menu choices could be automated.

At this point, you should write your own 4.BAT batch file and any necessary subordinate batch files to complete the menu example. Although you can use

```
CD \DBMS\INVNTORY
DBASE    INVENT
CD \
TYPE MENU.SCR

-----------------

CD \LOTUS
LOTUS
CD \
TYPE MENU.SCR

-----------------

CD \WP
WP
CD \
TYPE MENU.SCR
```

FIGURE 9.2: The 1.BAT, 2.BAT, and 3.BAT files. Each of the three batch files can be invoked by simply typing 1, 2, or 3 at the DOS prompt. They all parallel each other: First, they set the proper directory with the CD command and then they invoke the main program (data base, spreadsheet, or word processing) that will actually manage the main menu choice selected. When the main program ends, the root directory again becomes the default directory, and MENU.SCR is redisplayed so users can make other choices.

your imagination, start with the following simple tasks:

1. Clear the screen and display a file of new choices with TYPE. Call this file UTIL.SCR, and give the user these options:

   A. Display the current date and time
   B. Format a new diskette in drive A

   Remember that 1.BAT, 2.BAT, and so on are already used for your main menu, so your utility files will have to be named differently. For example, you might want the two options just presented to be contained in batch files named A.BAT and B.BAT. Or you could display the menu choices as 1 and 2 and then name the files U1.BAT and U2.BAT. (The latter method is preferable, since it presents a consistent appearance to any user; all choices are numbered 1, 2, 3, and so on.) In fact, you could even create new batch files called 1.BAT, 2.BAT, and so on, but you would have to place them in a separate directory and run them from there.

2. When you are done, display the main menu again (MENU.SCR).

   Tip: Remember to add REM statements to document all batch files that aren't transparently simple. Add them to help other users of your files, other programmers who must work with your files, and yourself—after all, *you* could be the one who, two months later, tries to figure out why a file includes a certain statement.

3. The final step is to create a new AUTOEXEC.BAT file that starts your menu system automatically when the computer is turned on. In the course of this chapter you may change this file, but for now create an AUTOEXEC.BAT file that looks like the one in Figure 9.3. This file contains commands that change the prompt, open a path, clear the screen, and display the menu.

```
ECHO OFF
PROMPT $P$G
PATH \;\DBMS;\WP;\LOTUS;\DOS
CLS
TYPE MENU.SCR
```

FIGURE 9.3: AUTOEXEC.BAT file for hard disk menu management. If you place this AUTOEXEC.BAT file in your boot disk's root directory, the PATH command will ensure that DOS finds the main program files, and the CLS and TYPE command lines will ensure that after your system starts, the current menu of choices (in MENU.SCR) will be displayed.

You are now ready to test the menu system you've created. Before you do, review the several files that make up your menu system:

- AUTOEXEC.BAT. This file executes when the computer is turned on or booted. It opens the path needed for hard disk operation and displays the menu for the user to read.
- MENU.SCR. This file contains the menu display. It has no DOS function. Its only purpose is to tell the user what options are available on the hard disk.
- 1.BAT, 2.BAT, 3.BAT, 4.BAT. These files execute the choices listed on the menu. You should create one batch file for each choice.
- If you completed the exercise, you also wrote UTIL.SCR and several other batch files.

To test the entire menu system, reboot your computer. When the computer starts, it should display your menu. Test each option on the main menu, as well as each option you programmed into the submenu. Be careful to use a new disk or scratch disk when testing the FORMAT choice on your Utility menu.

IMPROVING PERFORMANCE WITH BATCH FILES

There are many ways to improve processing performance using batch files. Some of these are ridiculously easy—what's hard is thinking of them at all. In this section, you'll learn a host of simple possibilities for batch files. Since the lines of code are few, you can implement these approaches quickly.

Simplifying Consistent Sequences

Whether you type poorly or well, you likely wouldn't mind reducing the number of keys you press in creating a document. In the music world, there is much debate on the value of pressing one button to obtain the sound of an entire rhythm section. No such debate rages in the PC world; anything that gets the same result with fewer keypresses receives a broad welcome.

ABBREVIATIONS

Any DOS command can be abbreviated to the ultimate in simplicity with a one-line batch file. For example, you can shorten the CHKDSK command to the letter C simply by creating a batch file called C.BAT and including in it the one instruction

CHKDSK

When you type C at the DOS prompt, the batch file C.BAT will be given control, and its one instruction will be executed as if you had typed it at the DOS prompt.

You can also use this technique with commands that normally take parameters, such as the RENAME and the XCOPY commands. You can easily create a batch file called R.BAT that only contains one executable instruction:

RENAME %1 %2

When you want to use this command, you can then type R instead of typing RENAME along with the variables. For instance, if you want to rename OLD.TXT to NEW.TXT, you can now type

R OLD.TXT NEW.TXT

DOS will quickly discover that R is a batch file and will handle the job through the batch-file invocation of the RENAME command, using the parameters represented as %1 and %2.

This simplification technique can be extended to commands with multiple lines. If you frequently execute CHKDSK commands on your A and C drives, your version of C.BAT could contain the following lines:

CHKDSK A:
CHKDSK C:

Now you can simply type C and press Return once. However, this C.BAT file is less flexible for other purposes, since it always issues the CHKDSK command for two disk drives, A and C.

SHORTHAND NOTATION FOR COMMAND SEQUENCES

You can also use batch files to simplify certain commands that perform fixed chores. For instance, you will learn in Chapter 12, "Computer Communications," how to use the MODE command to manage various aspects of different devices. If your system has both a color and a monochrome monitor, you can use a batch file to invoke the proper version of the MODE command. To switch output to the monochrome monitor, you can enter

MODE MONO

in a file called MONO.BAT. To switch output to the color monitor using 80 columns with color enabled, you can enter

MODE CO80

in a file called COLOR.BAT. Then, whenever you need to switch monitors, you have to enter only the simple batch name, MONO or COLOR, to obtain the desired result. With this method you don't have to remember (or even know) the actual DOS command or command and parameter sequence that produces a particular result.

Another good use of this technique is to turn on compressed printing mode for your Epson- or IBM-compatible printer, which you will learn about in Chapter 16, "Advanced Printing Techniques," as well. You can create a batch file called COMPRESS.BAT that contains one line:

MODE LPT1: 132

You can create another batch file called NORMAL.BAT that also contains only one line:

MODE LPT1: 80

Anyone now can type COMPRESS at the DOS prompt to send a wide spreadsheet or database information to the printer. When they are done, they can enter the command NORMAL to return the printer to its normal configuration.

Another benefit of this method is apparent if you acquire new printers at a later date. You can have a knowledgeable person change the batch file; everyone else using the system still only has to remember to type COMPRESS or NORMAL.

Repeated Automatic Invocation

The following technique is handy whenever you need to execute the same command repeatedly—for example, to find a text string in a series of files located in different directories or to obtain a directory listing of several diskettes successively. This method relies on the fact that %0, as a batch-file variable, represents the name of the batch file itself.

Take a look at the CONTENTS.BAT file shown in Figure 9.4. In this batch file, the PAUSE command prompts you to enter a new diskette in drive A and then waits for you to do so (see Figure 9.5).

If you press the Return key at this point, you will receive a directory listing of the diskette you placed in drive A, as shown in the top portion of Figure 9.5. However, this is also the point in the batch program at which you can terminate the otherwise unending sequence by pressing Ctrl-C. If you do not terminate the sequence, the batch file will retype its own name and the word "contents" and then will begin to execute again; it will prompt you to enter another diskette.

```
1   REM   CONTENTS.BAT
2
3   PAUSE Load diskette into drive A:
4   DIR   A: /P
5   %0
```

FIGURE 9.4: The CONTENTS.BAT file. This file demonstrates a form of programming recursion available in DOS batch files. Using the replaceable parameter known as %0 is a creative way to invoke the same batch file again. Line 5 (%0) is equivalent to typing CONTENTS on that line; the very same batch file is run again when control passes to line 5. The only way to end this batch file is to interrupt it by pressing Ctrl-C or the Break key.

```
COLORBAR BAS      1427   12-30-85   12:00p
COMM     BAS      4254   12-30-85   12:00p
DEBUG    COM     15799   12-30-85   12:00p
DONKEY   BAS      3572   12-30-85   12:00p
EXE2BIN  EXE      3063   12-30-85   12:00p
LINK     EXE     39076   12-30-85   12:00p
MORTGAGE BAS      6178   12-30-85   12:00p
MUSIC    BAS      8575   12-30-85   12:00p
MUSICA   BAS     13431   12-30-85   12:00p
PIECHART BAS      2180   12-30-85   12:00p
SAMPLES  BAS      2363   12-30-85   12:00p
SPACE    BAS      1851   12-30-85   12:00p
VDISK    LST    136315   12-30-85   12:00p
        18 File(s)    107520 bytes free

C>contents

C>REM   CONTENTS.BAT

C>
C>PAUSE Load diskette into drive A:
Strike a key when ready . . . ^C

Terminate batch job (Y/N)? y
C>_
```

FIGURE 9.5: Running the CONTENTS.BAT file. The results shown here highlight the recursive nature of the programming technique. After executing a DIR command on the diskette in drive A, %0 causes the batch program to automatically type its own name (CONTENTS) which reruns the CONTENTS.BAT program. When the batch file pauses, you can load a new diskette into drive A or press Ctrl-C to terminate the sequence.

The key to this repetitive behavior is in line 5 of the listing. The %0 is a variable parameter that substitutes for the original batch-file name typed at the DOS prompt. Using %0 is a better technique than hard coding the batch file name contents, as this allows the batch file to be used under a new name later, with no modification to the text lines inside the batch file itself.

Note: Remember that the line numbers in this batch file and in the other files listed in this chapter are for reference only. If you enter these batch programs for yourself, don't type the line numbers.

Program Setup and Restoration

This section offers several ways to start your own programs. You've already seen a typical small application in Figure 9.2. In that example, a main program was run (perhaps with initial parameters) after the proper directory was entered. Now you will see two more examples of how to use batch files to initiate programs.

INVOKING THE SAME SEQUENCE OF PROGRAMS

You likely often perform recurring series of steps in your computing tasks. For instance, whenever you run your word processor (WP.EXE) to create a new document, you may then, as a matter of course, run your grammar and style checker (STYLE.COM). You may also run a specialized spelling checker (SPELL.EXE) before you rerun your word processor to implement any suggested changes. The sequence, then, is as follows:

1. Word processor runs.
2. Style checker runs.
3. Spelling checker runs.
4. Word processor runs again.

If these programs do not allow parameter passing, you could write a batch file called WRITE.BAT, consisting of the following lines:

```
WP
STYLE
SPELL
WP
```

On the other hand, many programs now allow you to specify a parameter to indicate the name of a file to be selected. If a program allows such a specification, then a batch file can be even more useful. Suppose you are working on a proposal called PROPOSAL.DOC. Your WRITE.BAT file could do more work if it contained these lines:

WP PROPOSAL.DOC
STYLE PROPOSAL.DOC
SPELL PROPOSAL.DOC
WP PROPOSAL.DOC

Simply typing WRITE at the DOS prompt would successively invoke each of the four programs, with each one bringing in the specified PROPOSAL file.

Here's another example. Suppose you are working on the Great American Novel, and each chapter you write undergoes the same painstaking care and attention as the rest of your word processed documents. To simplify your work, you can add a variable parameter to the original WRITE.BAT file. Look at the following batch file:

WP CHAPTER%1
STYLE CHAPTER%1
SPELL CHAPTER%1
WP CHAPTER%1

If you've named your files CHAPTER1, CHAPTER2, and so on, you can then invoke your four-program sequence at the DOS prompt typing the chapter number as the parameter:

WRITE 5

Keep in mind that if your novel has more than nine chapters, you'll have to name them differently (for instance, as CHAP10 and so on) so that you don't exceed DOS's maximum limit of eight characters in a file name.

SETUP AND RESTORATION FOR TWO-DRIVE OPERATIONS

Some programs assume that the data they use is available on the default disk drive and directory. Since DOS allows you to run a program that isn't in the current drive and directory, you can first switch to the drive or directory containing your data and then run the program. After the program is done, you can return to your original drive or directory—usually the root directory in hard disk systems, and drive A in dual-diskette systems. The technique for returning to the root was shown in Figure 9.2. On a dual-diskette system, you can perform a similar sequence of steps.

Figure 9.6 shows a typical configuration in which programs reside on drive A and data files on drive B. Suppose you want to run a main program called ESTATE.EXE, which is on your program disk and which uses several real estate data files on the data disk in drive B. The following batch file, called

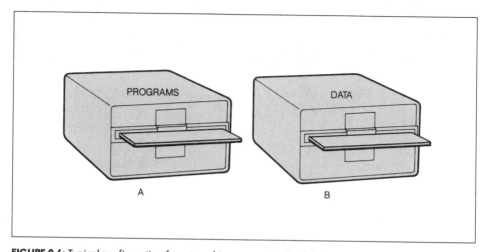

FIGURE 9.6: Typical configuration for a two-drive operation. Dual diskette computer systems typically use a design wherein disk A contains the main application programs (and sometimes the DOS system as well), and disk B contains a disk formatted solely for storing data.

SWITCH.BAT, will change the default drive to B for the duration of the execution of ESTATE.EXE, and then reset the default drive to A. DOS will look on drive B for any files referenced by the ESTATE program.

```
REM SWITCH.BAT
B:
A:ESTATE
A:
```

Chaining for Diskette-Switching Applications

Any batch file can contain references to other batch files. Those referenced batch files can also be on different drives, a feature you can use to develop sophisticated multidiskette applications. For example, you can have a batch file called FIRST.BAT in drive A. This batch file can include a number of instructions, ending with an invocation of a SECOND.BAT file, located in drive B. A segment of the FIRST.BAT file might look like Figure 9.7.

The SECOND.BAT file, which could control the backing up of your files onto a clean diskette, could be located on your data disk. SECOND.BAT might look like Figure 9.8. When control transfers to SECOND.BAT, its first instruction pauses the computer and prompts you to remove the main program diskette from drive A and replace it with a backup diskette. After performing the XCOPY backup sequence, the batch file pauses again so you can reinsert your original system diskette in drive A.

```
Instruction 1
Instruction 2
   .
   .
   .
Last instruction
B:
SECOND
```

FIGURE 9.7: Segment from the FIRST.BAT file. You can design a file, as this figure shows, to execute a series of instructions, change the default drive (to B in this example), and then pass control, through chaining, to another batch file on the diskette in the other drive (in this case, to SECOND.BAT in drive B.)

```
PAUSE Place your data backup diskette into drive A:
XCOPY *.*  A:
PAUSE Replace your original system diskette in drive A:
**** last line ****
```

FIGURE 9.8: Sample SECOND.BAT file. You invoke this file, located in drive B, from a batch file located in drive A (see Figure 9.7). Two-drive batch-file sequences can be executed simply by switching default drives at the proper times and making judicious use of the PAUSE command to enable users to switch disks as necessary.

The last statement in SECOND.BAT allows you to continue the execution chain. This "last line" can be the name of another batch file to execute in either drive A or B. You can even include a variable such as %1 in this last line, transferring it from the original FIRST.BAT file to a THIRD.BAT program. The %1 can also be a command that is executed as the last instruction of the SECOND.BAT file. In short, the last line in the SECOND.BAT file can contain A:FIRST, which would rerun the original starting program; %1, which would run a command passed from FIRST-.BAT to SECOND.BAT; or the name and location of any other batch file to continue the chain. If your last line uses %1, then you should modify the FIRST.BAT file to include a parameter in the final line.

Initializing Your RAM Disk

A batch file is an obvious place for the series of commands necessary to set up your RAM disk. If you use the VDISK or RAMDRIVE options of your CONFIG.SYS file (see Chapter 10), your RAM disk will already be created. However, some memory boards (such as AST boards) come with a program that can initialize a RAM disk whenever you choose. If this is the case on your system, you should invoke the program with a batch file.

Assume you have created a RAM disk called D. The following RAMINIT.BAT file can copy programs and files to it—for instance, commonly used batch files such as HELP.BAT and frequently used DOS programs such as CHKDSK.COM, SORT.EXE, and the command processor COMMAND.COM.

COPY HELP.BAT D:
COPY CHKDSK.COM D:
COPY SORT.EXE D:
COPY COMMAND.COM D:

Tip: Using redirection, and the special reserved device name NUL, you can avoid the DOS display of the file names as they are being copied by simply adding the characters >NUL to each of the above COPY commands. For example,

COPY HELP.BAT D: >NUL
COPY CHKDSK.COM D: >NUL

Redirection is a DOS technique discussed in Chapter 17.

You should also set the COMSPEC environment here to tell DOS where to find the command processor. (COMSPEC is a special DOS variable, designed to specify where a copy of COMMAND.COM can be found. You will learn more about this variable in Chapter 19).

Finally, you can reset the path to check the RAM disk for referenced files that are not in the default directory:

SET COMSPEC = D:\COMMAND.COM
PATH D:\;C:\LOTUS;C:\WP;C:\UTILITY;C:\DOS

In Chapter 10, you will learn a wide range of uses for a RAM disk. Placing all of the RAM disk setup commands in this RAMINIT.BAT file is a good idea, even if you eventually include a reference to RAMINIT.BAT in your AUTOEXEC.BAT file for automatic initialization of your RAM drive.

Tip: If you use this RAM disk method to improve your system's performance, remember to put the RAM disk on the path *before* any other references to directories that may contain the original copies of the files. Then DOS will find the fast-access RAM copy of the referenced file first, before the slower disk-resident version of the same file.

Initializing Your Color Monitor

You will learn in Chapter 10 how to use the PROMPT command to set up the foreground and background colors on a color monitor. Having to look up or remember the color codes can be tedious; this is a perfect opportunity to use a batch file. Create the batch file RGB.BAT. This file expects two parameters, each specifying what colors the monitor should use for the foreground and background. The calling sequence is

RGB *Foreground Background*

Entering the following sequence at the DOS prompt causes all future output to appear in blue letters on a white background:

RGB BLUE WHITE

Figure 9.9 shows the batch file itself.

This file demonstrates several interesting points:

- There are two major sections in the logical flow. The first section (lines 3–28) controls the setting of the foreground colors, according to the first color parameter specified after the batch-file name RGB. The second section (lines 30–58) controls the background color settings, based on the value of the second parameter on the batch-file line.

- This batch file is not case sensitive, as a batch program that relied on the IF subcommand would be. In other words, each of the following commands produces the same result:

  RGB BLUE WHITE
  rgb   blue   white

- If you don't specify a color for the foreground or background, you can use the IF ARG = = ARG%1 technique to test for the absence of a variable parameter. This IF test will be true only if the variable (either %1 or %2) is missing. This technique is the same as that shown in the previous chapter using the IF %1 TRICK = = TRICK\ command.

- The ECHO ON and OFF commands, followed by a screen clearing operation, are necessary between the setting of the foreground and background colors. The foreground prompt must take effect while ECHO is off and before the background color is set.

- As written, this RGB.BAT file requires you to enter both parameter values (foreground and background colors). If you enter only one color, the foreground will be set to that color, and the background will not be set at all. However, losing the background color also loses the pg portion of the prompt. This program, like all programs, could be improved by separating the setting of the background color from the pg. You could include PROMPT pg at the end of the batch file so it would always be

```
 1    REM   RGB.BAT
 2
 3    ECHO OFF
 4    IF ARG==ARG%1 GOTO BKGROUND
 5    GOTO %1
 6    :BLACK
 7    PROMPT $e[30m
 8    GOTO BKGROUND
 9    :WHITE
10    PROMPT $e[37m
11    GOTO BKGROUND
12    :RED
13    PROMPT $e[31m
14    GOTO BKGROUND
15    :GREEN
16    PROMPT $e[32m
17    GOTO BKGROUND
18    :BLUE
19    PROMPT $e[34m
20    GOTO BKGROUND
21    :MAGENTA
22    PROMPT $e[35m
23    GOTO BKGROUND
24    :CYAN
25    PROMPT $e[36m
26    GOTO BKGROUND
27    :BROWN
28    PROMPT $e[33m
29
30    :BKGROUND
31    ECHO ON
32    ECHO OFF
33    CLS
34    IF ARG==ARG%2 GOTO DONE
35    GOTO BK%2
36    :BKBLACK
37    PROMPT $p$g$e[40m
38    GOTO DONE
39    :BKWHITE
40    PROMPT $p$g$e[47m
41    GOTO DONE
42    :BKRED
43    PROMPT $p$g$e[41m
44    GOTO DONE
45    :BKGREEN
46    PROMPT $p$g$e[42m
47    GOTO DONE
48    :BKBLUE
49    PROMPT $p$g$e[44m
```

FIGURE 9.9: RGB.BAT sets foreground and background colors on a color monitor. The foreground color is %1, so the GOTO %1 transfers control to the label whose name is the color. This purposeful use of nomenclature for clarity is sometimes called *self-documenting code*. After the individual foreground color is set, a GOTO BKGROUND sends the flow of control to the :BKGROUND section, where a similar process occurs using the second parameter, %2, to direct the flow to the proper new PROMPT command, which sets the color. Notice the ECHO ON/OFF pair of commands between the foreground and background color settings; these necessary settings ensure that the foreground color takes hold before a new prompt is issued to set the background color.

```
50  GOTO DONE
51  :BKMAGENTA
52  PROMPT $p$g$e[45m
53  GOTO DONE
54  :BKCYAN
55  PROMPT $p$g$e[46m
56  GOTO DONE
57  :BKBROWN
58  PROMPT $p$g$e[43m
59  :DONE
60  ECHO ON
61  CLS
```

FIGURE 9.9: (continued).

executed (after line 59). Try this now as an exercise. Remember to include an ECHO ON, ECHO OFF sequence.

Figure 9.10 shows the overall flow of this program.

SOPHISTICATED BATCH FILES

This section discusses some specific batch files used by experienced DOS users. People's perceptions of advanced subjects differ dramatically; what one person views as sophisticated, another views as old hat. The batch-file techniques presented here are useful. If they're new to you, that's all the better. If they're old hat, perhaps you'll learn some new approaches by examining their implementation in these programs.

Customized System Help Screens

Some systems are used by many people at different times. A desirable feature for such a system is customizable help screens. You can use the batch-file mechanism in DOS to easily set up this capability. You can use the INFO.BAT file, shown in Figure 9.11.

Once you've installed this batch file in your path, you can use it from any directory. All you need to do is write a text file with the .HLP extension. This file should contain the text information you want displayed for anyone requesting help. The user, in turn, will need only to run the INFO.BAT file, specifying the first parameter as the topic for which help is desired.

For example, to provide users with helpful on-line information about a program named GOBBLEDY, place the information in a text file called GOBBLEDY .HLP. Then the user need only enter

INFO GOBBLEDY

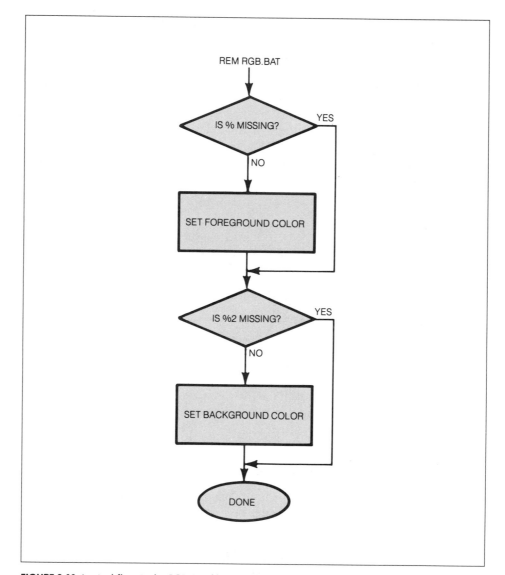

FIGURE 9.10: Logical flow in the RGB.BAT file. Using a flowchart to lay out the logical flow in the RGB.BAT file provides good documentation as well as clarifying the movement through the program. Viewing a flowchart like this before wading line by line through the actual code clarifies the operations shown in the preceding figure.

to display the predefined information (see Figure 9.12). If help is not available on your system (that is, a .HLP file does not exist for the subject), then a simple message to that effect is displayed (see Figure 9.13).

```
 1    REM   INFO.BAT
 2
 3    ECHO OFF
 4    IF EXIST %1.HLP   GOTO OK
 5    ECHO Sorry.  No help available for %1
 6    GOTO END
 7
 8    :OK
 9    TYPE %1.HLP
10    PAUSE
11
12    :END
```

FIGURE 9.11: Customizable help screens with INFO.BAT. You can implement a help feature for an entire system with this batch file alone. You can present each topic in a text file of the form *topic*.HLP. When a user enters INFO *topic* at the DOS prompt, the *topic*.HLP file will be displayed under control of this batch file. If the *topic*.HLP file does not exist, and therefore no help has been defined for a particular subject, the IF EXIST command in line 4 will determine this and pass control to the ECHO command in line 5.

```
C>INFO GOBBLEDY

C>REM  INFO.BAT

C>
C>ECHO OFF
GOBBLEDYGOOK is a specially coined phrase which means wordy and
generally unintelligible jargon.  It is symptomatic of many
computer textbooks.  No one believes that the phrase could
possibly apply to their writings or utterances.

Strike a key when ready . . . . ■
```

FIGURE 9.12: Running the INFO.BAT file with a sample first parameter of GOBBLEDY verifies that a *GOBBLEDY.HLP* file exists. This batch file displays the contents of the HLP file and then pauses to give you a chance to read the file before returning control to the DOS prompt.

Tip: In this example of a help file, no CLS instruction is executed. It was omitted so that Figures 9.10 and 9.11 could show the entire resulting sequences. If you were to write a similar INFO system for yourself, you might want to consider inserting CLS instructions before lines 5 and 9, the output lines in the INFO.BAT batch file.

```
C>INFO ARRAYS

C>REM  INFO.BAT

C>
C>ECHO OFF
Sorry.  No help available for ARRAYS

C>_
```

FIGURE 9.13: Screen display when help is not available. Running the INFO.BAT file with a request for information not yet prepared (no *ARRAYS.HLP* file exists) displays a message to that effect.

The program in Figure 9.11 can be understood quickly by looking at the logic-flow diagram in Figure 9.14. The heart of the batch program begins at line 4, after the initial REM and ECHO OFF statements. If a .HLP file exists for the subject (entered as %1), then the batch file continues executing at line 8. Line 8 is really only the label :OK, which is needed by the GOTO statement in line 4. The help information is presented to the user by the TYPE statement in line 9. The PAUSE statement ensures that the user will have time to read the information before anything else appears on the screen or before the screen is cleared.

If no help file exists, the IF statement in line 4 causes line 5 to be executed next. The ECHO statement displays a "Sorry ..." message to the user, and the batch program ends immediately. This operation is handled by the GOTO statement in line 6, which ensures that none of the instructions between lines 7 and 11 execute.

Now that you understand how a HELP system can be constructed, you should take this knowledge one step further. The .HLP files that are referenced in the above example must be located in the current directory (or on the APPEND list, as discussed in Chapter 19, "Other Advanced Commands"). You could use the method of full path names to make a useful generalized HELP system.

Rather than have a variety of application areas across your hard disk, each with their .HLP files in their respective directories, you could set up a special HELP directory:

MD C:\HELP

Then, the INFO.BAT file could be generalized to test for the existence of a HLP

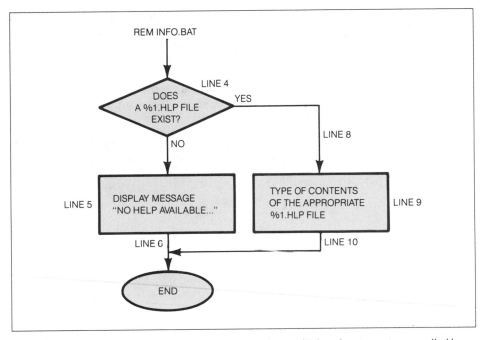

FIGURE 9.14: Logic flow for INFO.BAT. The logical flow relies on the key decision point controlled by the IF EXIST... command. Depending on the result of that conditional test in line 4, either the ECHO command in line 5 or the TYPE command in line 9 controls the primary remaining processing in this batch file.

file within that directory:

IF EXIST C:\HELP\%1.LP GOTO :OK

Similarly, when the specified file is to be typed, the TYPE command can reference the same entry in the HELP directory:

TYPE C:\HELP\%1.HLP

This more generalized approach groups all the possible .HLP files for various applications, and possibly various users, in one HELP directory. The only possible disadvantages to this approach are that the number of files may grow large and that file names may be duplicated, particularly if more than one person contributes .HLP files to the directory.

Appointment Reminder System

Some computer systems offer automatic appointment reminders. In addition, some utility packages, such as Sidekick, permit the entry and retrieval of date-oriented information (however, this is not automatic). The following example can mitigate the problem of forgetting to check your message or appointment log.

First include some reminders in your AUTOEXEC.BAT file. For instance, these three lines should jog your memory:

ECHO Remember to enter the following command to
ECHO get your messages for today (or any day).
ECHO TODAY mm-dd-yy

When you want to see the message or appointment file for, say, January 1, 1989, you only need enter

TODAY 01-01-89

Figure 9.15 shows the results of this sequence.

```
C>TODAY Ø1-Ø1-88

C>REM  TODAY.BAT

C>
C>ECHO OFF
Happy new year!
You probably shouldn't be at work today at all.
However, since you are, don't forget to start writing 1988
        on all your checks, memos, etc.
Also, don't forget the paperwork for the new tech writer
        beginning work tomorrow.

C>TODAY 1/1/88

C>REM  TODAY.BAT

C>
C>ECHO OFF
No messages for 1/1/88

C>_
```

FIGURE 9.15: Running the TODAY.BAT file. This file displays the entire contents of a text file whose name is entered as parameter %1 (in this case, 01-01-89). Notice the second attempt to run TODAY with a parameter equal to 1/1/89 fails to locate the desired file. In this situation, the parameter specified must have precisely the same spelling as the name of the file containing the messages.

Figure 9.16 shows the actual batch file that manages this simple operation. As you can see, this file is a variation on the help method discussed in the preceding section. The date files are text files, differing only in name and content from the .HLP files.

The way in which these text files are used (via the TYPE command) also reflects their similar batch-file approach. With the INFO method, all the files were similarly named with a .HLP extension, and their base names reflected the actual topic for which help was desired. In this appointment reminder system,

```
 1   REM   TODAY.BAT
 2
 3   ECHO OFF
 4   IF NOT EXIST %1 GOTO ERROR
 5
 6   TYPE %1
 7   GOTO END
 8
 9   :ERROR
10   ECHO No messages for %1
11
12   :END
```

FIGURE 9.16: The TODAY.BAT file. This file relies on the decision branch in line 4. If the specified file (%1) does not exist, the program branches to line 9, and the ECHO command in line 10 executes. If the specified file exists, then line 6 is executed next. This types the contents of file %1.

the actual file name is understood (via %1) to be the date itself, a simple-enough naming convention. The batch file types the text file with that precise name. Here you cannot assume that the batch-file code has the intelligence of the DOS DATE command; in other words, 01-01-89 could not be replaced by 1/1/89 or any other variation.

> *Warning:* The naming convention for date files must be adhered to precisely. If you use dashes or leading zeros to create the text files, then you must also use them in the TODAY.BAT file.

Figure 9.17 shows the logic flow for this batch file. You can see that it is only slightly different from the logic flow in the INFO.BAT file (see Figure 9.14).

One of many additions to this batch file could be the simple addition of the line

DATE %1

just before line 6 (the TYPE instruction). In systems that do not have a battery-backed clock/calendar, you usually have to execute the DATE command when you bring up the system. Since you must enter the date once for your appointment-making system, you can let the batch-parameter mechanism set the date as well. Programmers are always looking for ways to reduce user intervention time, system program time, or both. Minor improvements like this add up dramatically over time.

> *Tip:* Remember to erase your older date files when you no longer need them. Date files tend to proliferate quickly if they are not erased after use.

Broadcasting System Messages

The ANNOUNCE.BAT file in Figure 9.18 offers another means of increasing processing efficiency. This batch program uses an area in memory called the

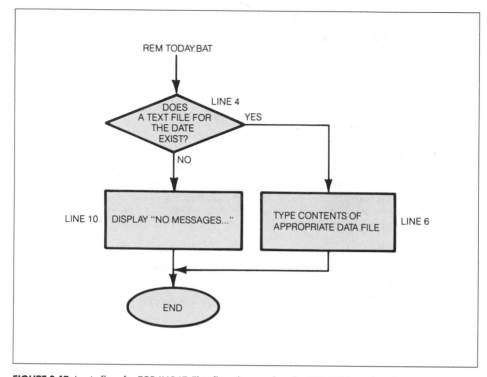

FIGURE 9.17: Logic flow for TODAY.BAT. This flowchart makes the YES/NO branch at line 4 clear. Either the "No messages" response in line 10 or the TYPE command in line 6 results, depending on the result of the decision in line 4.

```
1    REM ANNOUNCE.BAT
2
3    ECHO OFF
4    ECHO Current System Messages:
5    TYPE %message%
```

FIGURE 9.18: The ANNOUNCE.BAT file. The DOS environment lets you extend the numbered variables of the batch file system (%0, %1, ..., %9) to named variables using the surrounding percent sign. The variable %*message*% consists of a file name entered by a SET command at the DOS prompt. Invoking this ANNOUNCE.BAT file from the DOS prompt types the contents of the file whose name is contained in the variable %*message*%.

DOS environment, which contains a set of variables and the values assigned to them. The DOS environment always includes the COMSPEC variable and the values you assign to PATH and PROMPT variables, as well as other arbitrarily named variables used by some programs or by the batch files described here.

The little-known technique of referencing DOS environment variables from within batch files allows you to broadcast messages to your system's users. This technique is useful in systems with several users and perhaps one system operator. The goal is to have a simple command such as

ANNOUNCE

display for a user all current system messages (see Figure 9.19).

```
C>SET MESSAGE=WEEK34.TXT

C>TYPE WEEK34.TXT
Messages for Week 34 of FY88:
        Ted Bishop is on vacation.  Susanne Powers will be filling in.
        Next Saturday is the company picnic.  Mary has the tickets.
        Don't forget.  Backup, backup, backup.
        Time cards due on Thursday this week!

C>ANNOUNCE

C>REM ANNOUNCE.BAT

C>
C>ECHO OFF
Current System Messages:
Messages for Week 34 of FY88:
        Ted Bishop is on vacation.  Susanne Powers will be filling in.
        Next Saturday is the company picnic.  Mary has the tickets.
        Don't forget.  Backup, backup, backup.
        Time cards due on Thursday this week!

C>_
```

FIGURE 9.19: ANNOUNCE.BAT displays all current system messages. Assuming an operator has initialized the value of *message* to equal WEEK34.TXT, as shown in the SET command at the top of the screen, entering ANNOUNCE in the third line on the screen has the same result as typing the file name WEEK34.TXT.

In Figure 9.19, the first line is the key to the technique. You initialize a DOS environment variable (MESSAGE) to equal the name of this week's message file. In this case, the primary system operator has to assign WEEK34.TXT to MESSAGE only once, usually at the beginning of the day. For the rest of the time that the system is on, simply typing ANNOUNCE at the DOS prompt will display the current message file. Only the system operator needs to know the name of the actual message file; from week to week, the procedure for displaying system messages remains the same to the system users. Even the naming conventions can change, and only the system operator need be concerned.

You can modify this batch program slightly to allow for recurring messages that don't change from week to week. For instance, before line 5 you can insert another line, such as

TYPE ALWAYS.TXT

The ALWAYS.TXT file can contain any constant text that you want to display regardless of the week. Such text could include the operator's name and phone number, the service bureau's phone number, the security guard's extension, and so forth.

Using Batch-File Subroutines for Status Tracking

Programmers use a variety of techniques for debugging their code. One of those techniques is to place additional printing statements at critical points in the source code. These statements are like snapshots. When the execution flow reaches these points, various parameters and variable values are printed. The current program status can then be assessed and any problems discovered.

Programmers using this technique quickly learn the value of sending these debugging snapshots to a disk file instead of a printer. In this way, their program is not slowed down, and normal screen output is not compromised by debugging output.

You can borrow a page from the programmer's book for your own batch-file programming. Your batch files may at times become complicated, especially if you use the multifile technique of chaining. In writing any batch file, consider writing your own SNAPSHOT.BAT file. In a simple implementation, it can consist solely of the following two commands:

DIR   >> AUDIT.TXT
CHKDSK >> AUDIT.TXT

Whenever you invoke SNAPSHOP.BAT, the current directory and disk status will be noted, and the >> redirection symbol will ensure that the AUDIT.TXT file receives this information. You can peruse the contents of this tracking file later, at your convenience.

The CALL subcommand in DOS 3.3 (or the COMMAND/C feature of earlier DOS versions) is also critical to effective use of the snapshot method. You may want to note the current disk directory and memory status at various points during the execution of one of your batch files.

The ANYOLD1.BAT file shown in Figure 9.20 is representative of any batch file you might write; the vertical dots stand for your own instructions. The figure includes some example DOS commands: COPY, DIR, and ERASE. You take the snapshot by inserting a line that runs the SNAPSHOT.BAT file immediately.

In the figure, lines 8 and 18 use the CALL subcommand. If you're using a version of DOS earlier than 3.3, you can replace the CALL subcommand with

COMMAND/C SNAPSHOT

This command invokes a secondary copy of the command processor, which then runs the SNAPSHOT batch file before continuing with other statements in the batch program you are testing.

```
REM ANYOLD1.BAT

          .
          .
          .

COPY A:*.DBF  C:\DATABASE
CALL SNAPSHOT

          .
          .
          .

DIR C:\DATABASE
DIR A:
PAUSE Everything look OK? BREAK, if not.
ERASE A:\*.WK1
CALL SNAPSHOT
```

FIGURE 9.20: The ANYOLD1.BAT file. This file is representative of any batch file you write that doesn't do what you expect—in other words, a file that needs some debugging. At various points in the file, you can insert a subroutine (CALL SNAPSHOT) that invokes a debugging aid. The support routine traces the status of system variables at different points in your program to help you find the problems in the file.

When you are creating your batch file, you can insert as many of these secondary command processor lines as you need to assess the actual actions of your batch program. All of the snapshot results will be placed in the AUDIT.TXT file. You can erase this file at any time, since the >> redirection parameter recreates the AUDIT.TXT file if it does not exist. After your batch file is complete and working as you want it to, you can remove all of the snapshot lines.

Note the use of the PAUSE command in ANYOLD1.BAT. Since the next command is ERASE, you're giving the user of your batch program a last chance to stop the continuation of the batch file. This feature is made especially useful by the preceding display of the A and C directories in the ANYOLD1 program.

Several creative variations on this method are available to you. Look at the modified SNAPSHOT.BAT file in Figure 9.21. This version includes two additional lines before the DIR and CHKDSK lines. The DIR and CHKDSK commands are now executed for both of the disks affected by commands in ANYOLD1.BAT. Line 4 is an add-on utility program that displays the system date and time. It is one of the Norton Utilities (see Chapter 20), and it presents this information in an attractive and readable format.

You could, of course, use DOS's DATE and TIME commands instead of an additional utility, redirecting their output to the AUDIT.TXT file. However, doing this would require you to press the Return key twice because DOS places its normal request for any date and time changes in the AUDIT.TXT file instead

```
1   REM   SNAPSHOT.BAT
2
3   ECHO Snapshot at point %1  >> AUDIT.TXT
4   TM          >> AUDIT.TXT
5   DIR/W  A:   >> AUDIT.TXT
6   CHKDSK A:   >> AUDIT.TXT
7   DIR/W  C:   >> AUDIT.TXT
8   CHKDSK C:   >> AUDIT.TXT
```

FIGURE 9.21: The SNAPSHOT.BAT file. This file uses redirection to send the system time to the AUDIT-.TXT file. This batch file then sends to the same AUDIT.TXT file a wide directory listing and a CHKDSK output listing of both drives A and C. Notice that the first ECHO statement also uses redirection to indicate where succeeding output occurred. Each CALL statement uses a different first parameter value, which is echoed to the AUDIT.TXT file to indicate which snapshot is being viewed.

of on your video monitor. You won't see the requests, but DOS will wait for your response anyway.

> *Note:* You can, of course, modify the snapshot examples presented here to include any other utility program lines or DOS commands that provide you with useful information.

Line 3 is another useful variation. The AUDIT.TXT file expands to allow many entries, according to the complexity of your batch file and how often you invoke the COMMAND/C instruction. The file can tag each entry so that it indicates where the snapshot was taken.

Figure 9.22 shows the beginning of the AUDIT.TXT file. The first AUDIT entry sequence is labeled anyold1-A. Each time the secondary processor begins, it runs the SNAPSHOT program, passing the first parameter (%1) along. Line 3 causes the value of this parameter (anyold1-A) to appear in the output file AUDIT.TXT. You need only type a different string of characters each time you enter COMMAND/C in a batch file you want to trace.

TIPS, TRICKS, AND TECHNIQUES

The earlier part of this chapter presented several batch files that you can use in your system either directly or with slight modification. These stand-alone batch files can provide you and others with useful additional tools, such as the customized help screens and color-monitor initialization. This section presents several techniques that you can apply to your batch files. You can use these methods as you see them, or you can incorporate them into the more sophisticated batch programs you may write.

```
Snapshot at point anyold1-A
                                        5:16 am, Monday, September 26, 1988
 Volume in drive A has no label
 Directory of  A:\

COMMAND  COM    CONFIG   INT    FIG8-21  TXT    AUTOEXEC BAT    CONFIG   SYS
AUTOPARK COM
          6 File(s)    277504 bytes free

    362496 bytes total disk space
     53248 bytes in 2 hidden files
     31744 bytes in 6 user files
    277504 bytes available on disk

    655360 bytes total memory
    578480 bytes free

 Volume in drive C is ROBBINS
 Directory of  C:\SYBEX\DESKTOP

.                  ..             COMMANDS FW2    IMCAP           APPA     FW2
APPB     FW2    APPC     FW2    APPD     FW2    APPE     FW2    APPF     FW2
CHAP00   FW2    CHAP01   FW2    TBL15_1  FW2    FOR_JIM  FW2    CHAP13   FW2
CHAP14   FW2    CHAP15   FW2    CHAP16   FW2    CHAP17   FW2    CHAP19   FW2
-- More --_


-- More --

CHAP20   FW2    CHAP21   FW2    CHAP22   FW2    TITLEPRO FW2    REMIND2  FW2
INSERT01 FW2    REMIND1  FW2    REMIND3  FW2    REMIND4  FW2    REMIND5  FW2
REMIND6  FW2    REMIND7  FW2    INSERT06 FW2    DUPONT   FW2    JUDD10XX FW2
FOR_INFO FW2    MARGOT   FW2    INSERT07 FW2    INSERT08 FW2    INSERT09 FW2
AUDIT    TXT    ANYOLD1  BAT    INSERT02 FW2    INSERT03 FW2    INSERT04 FW2
INSERT05 FW2    1SUMMARY FW2    JUDD11XX FW2    INS-JUDD FW2    WSD
ICCL-2   FW2    ICCL     FW2    INSERT12 FW2    INSERT13 FW2    EARLYINS FW2
INS06NEW FW2    INS10NEW FW2    INS08NEW FW2    TBL11-XX FW2    INS11NEW FW2
INS09NEW FW2    TBL11-YY FW2    INSERT16 FW2    INS07NEW FW2    SYBEX    FW2
SYBEX2   FW2    DEBBIE   FW2
         67 File(s)    1544192 bytes free
Volume ROBBINS     created Sep 26, 1987 5:54p

  22124544 bytes total disk space
         0 bytes in 1 hidden files
    180224 bytes in 82 directories
  20400128 bytes in 1216 user files
   1544192 bytes available on disk

    655360 bytes total memory
    578480 bytes free

C:\SYBEX\DESKTOP>_
```

FIGURE 9.22: Contents of AUDIT.TXT after running ANYOLD1.BAT. The label *anyold1-A* indicates that this output resulted from the first CALL SNAPSHOT, which specified *anyold1-A* as the first parameter value. At the point of the PAUSE (see Figure 9.21), the user exited the batch file with Ctrl-C. Had processing continued, the AUDIT.TXT file would have received an entire new set of output results, labeled *anyold1-B*.

Using RAM Disks Effectively

RAM disks are discussed in Chapter 10. To initialize a RAM disk, you need only one of the following two lines in your CONFIG.SYS file:

DEVICE = VDISK.SYS 256

(for PC-DOS) or

>**DEVICE = RAMDRIVE.SYS 256**

(for MS-DOS). This creates a 256K RAM disk (the disk's size can vary depending on what you intend to use it for), and you can now transfer files to it.

>*Note:* These examples assume that you have previously transferred the correct main programs, help files, overlays, and so on to your RAM disk.

If you want your RAM disk to run a word processor, you can enter the lines

>**REM RAMWP.BAT**
>
>**CD\PROGRAMS\WORDPROC**
>**D:**
>**WP**
>**C:**
>**CD**

to create a file called RAMWP.BAT.

If you store the RAMWP.BAT file in some directory on your path, you can now switch to rapid RAM-based word processing easily and quickly by simply typing

>**RAMWP**

You can use the same technique for your database management program or for any other program for which normal disk-access speed is slow. A variation of the RAMWP.BAT file for a database management system might contain these lines:

>**REM RAMDBMS.BAT**
>
>**CD\PROGRAMS\DATABASE**
>**D:**
>**DBMS**
>**C:**
>**CD**

This batch file makes the C hard disk directory the one that holds your document or data files, and it makes D, the RAM disk, the current drive so that the WP or DBMS program that executes is the one on the RAM disk. Any references to C alone, with no directory path, will access the files in the current default directory on the C drive (in this case, either PROGRAMS\WORDPROC or PROGRAMS\DATABASE).

>*Note:* If you use this RAM drive technique to run more than one major program (for example, both a word processor and a DBMS), you must have

enough space reserved for both. If you do not, you may need to write a separate batch program to copy the required programs onto the RAM drive. Of course, you can use the IF and EXIST subcommands to check the RAM drive itself. They will do the work for you, determining what files are needed and whether any existing files need to be erased to make room for the new ones.

Controlling User Access

Entire books have been written on the subject of password protection. Even more advanced tomes discuss the subject of *resource allocation,* which involves usage as well as access. Resource allocation means controlling access to both the contents of data files and the running of program files. Here you will look at a simple but subtle form of password protection that you can implement with DOS alone.

The DOS environment gives you a special password feature. You can initialize a PASSWORD variable at the DOS prompt or in another batch file. For instance, you can enter

SET PASSWORD = EELS

If the batch file contains the code segment shown in Figure 9.23, access will be restricted to only those people who know the password. If PASSWORD was set correctly to EELS before a batch file containing this code was run, then PROGRAM will run. Otherwise, the invalid password message will be echoed, and the batch file will terminate. In short, only those users who know that the password is EELS and set it correctly will be able to run the particular program. The program could be contained in any .EXE or .COM file, and the batch file could reset the directory, if necessary, in the :RUN section.

```
IF %PASSWORD%==EELS GOTO RUN
IF %PASSWORD%==eels GOTO RUN

ECHO Sorry. That's an invalid password.
GOTO END

:RUN
PROGRAM
:END
```

FIGURE 9.23: Code segment for password protection. You can conceal a password in the DOS environment, using a simple SET PASSWORD = EELS, prior to running any other batch files. This batch-file code segment shows how the password set by a user in an environmental variable can be compared to a predetermined character string.

Note: This password code uses IF statements to check for entry of the password in uppercase and in lowercase. You never know what case a user's keyboard might be in when he or she tries to run your batch file or menu system.

You can easily extend the password feature by using several DOS environment variables, each containing different passwords. Your batch programs can check for the proper values. For instance, you can have three passwords controlling access to your inventory, personnel, and accounting programs. Doing this might require several blocks of code like the code just discussed and three passwords, PASS1, PASS2, and PASS3, controlling access to INVENTRY-.EXE, PRSONNEL.EXE, and ACCOUNTS.EXE.

You can also have a menu system that passes control to three batch files (see Figure 9.24) instead of directly to the three main programs. Only users who

```
        IF %PASS1%==STORE GOTO RUN
        IF %PASS1%==store GOTO RUN

        ECHO Sorry.  That's an invalid password.
        GOTO END

        :RUN
        INVENTRY


        :END


-------------------------------------------------

        IF %PASS1%==JOSHUA GOTO RUN
        IF %PASS1%==joshua GOTO RUN

        ECHO Sorry.  That's an invalid password.
        GOTO END

        :RUN
        PRSONNEL

        :END

-------------------------------------------------

        IF %PASS1%==1812 GOTO RUN

        ECHO Sorry.  That's an invalid password.
        GOTO END

        :RUN
        ACCOUNTS

        :END
```

FIGURE 9.24: Three batch files for a multiple password system. A multiple password system can be constructed using three separate batch files, or code segments, as in this figure. Only a user who knows that the password for the Inventory system is *store* will be able to run the INVENTRY program. Similarly, only a user who knows that *joshua* is the password for the Employee system can run the PRSONNEL program. Last, only someone who knows that *1812* is the password for the Accounting system will be able to run the ACCOUNTS program.

properly knew and set the appropriate DOS environment variable would be allowed access to the program they chose from the menu. Notice in the figure that the third password contains digits only, so IF tests for upper- and lowercase do not have to be performed.

Summary

For additional information about the fundamentals of batch files, including variable parameters, see

- Chapter 7, "Fundamentals of Batch Processing"

For additional information about subcommands in batch files, see

- Chapter 8, "Batch-File Subcommands"

For additional information about RAM disks and about customizing your system with the PROMPT command, see

- Chapter 10, "Configuration Possibilities"

For additional information about the MODE command and computer communications, see

- Chapter 12, "Computer Communications"

For additional information about standard printing methods and more advanced printing techniques, see

- Chapter 15, "Basic Printing Methods"
- Chapter 16, "Advanced Printing Techniques"

For additional information about redirection of both input and output data, see

- Chapter 17, "Pipes, Filters, and Redirection"

For additional information about the Norton Utilities and other utility software, see

- Chapter 20, "Extending DOS's Power with Utility Software"

PART

4

CUSTOM CONFIGURATIONS

Your computer system is unique to you. This section presents a range of specific DOS capabilites that allow you to customize your computer to meet your particular needs. You will learn how to influence the DOS configuration parameters to make your programs run faster and your screens appear more user friendly. You will also learn how to set up your DOS system for non-U.S. operations, using special monitors and printers designed to produce foreign-language character sets.

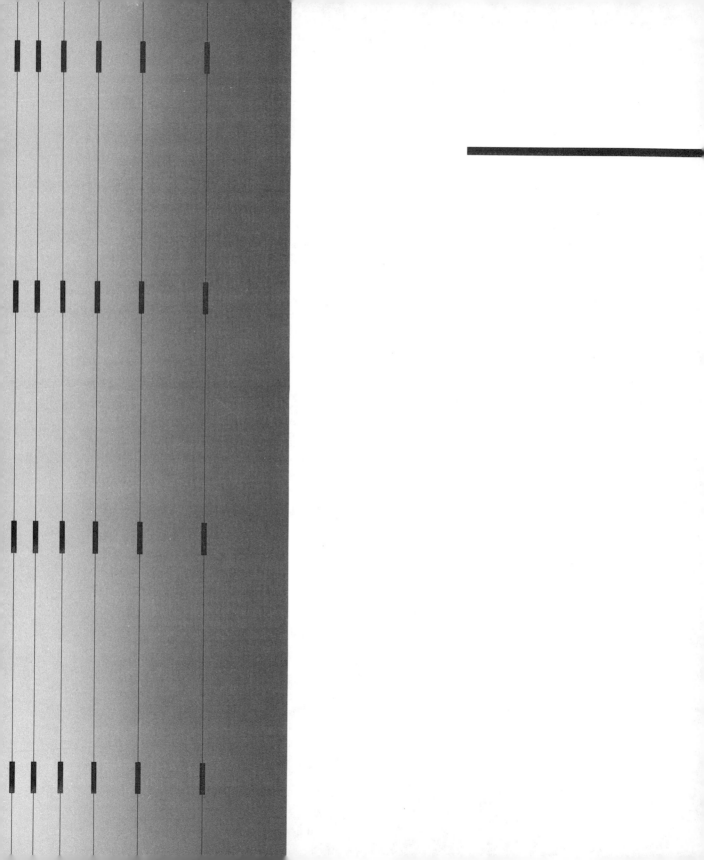

CONFIGURATION POSSIBILITIES

CONFIGURATION POSSIBILITIES

So far, everything you've seen about DOS has been clearly defined. Every feature has had a concrete definition and strict limits on how it could be used and what results you could expect. Behind the scenes, however, are several additional aspects to DOS itself that have considerable flexibility, and which you can control.

In DOS, you can customize your system in many ways. One of the most important ways is using the AUTOEXEC.BAT file, discussed in Chapters 9 and 11. DOS looks for this special type of batch file every time you start the computer, and so it provides a convenient place to record your startup preferences. Chapter 9 presents a series of examples of AUTOEXEC.BAT files and shows the different results of each one. Chapter 11 shows how you can include information about non-U.S. configurations of DOS in an AUTOEXEC.BAT file. Chapter 7 offers an introduction to batch files in general, and Chapter 8 discusses batch-file programming and presents the "sublanguage" of batch-file commands. Besides AUTOEXEC.BAT and the start-up customization it allows, batch files also provide a mechanism for customizing the operation of your system at any time after startup. Chapter 9 also illustrates some of these adjustments.

In this chapter, however, you'll focus on customizing some of the inner workings of DOS itself. Two principal mechanisms exist for the internal setups: the CONFIG.SYS file and the PROMPT command.

USING THE **CONFIG.SYS** FILE

When a microcomputer is turned on, it runs through a built-in bootstrap program. The time-consuming part of a typical bootstrap is a memory test. The more memory you have, the longer the test will take; if you expand the memory of your system, you will probably notice the difference.

Following the memory test, the bootstrap attempts to find the disk-resident portion of DOS on one of the drives in the system, usually beginning with drive A. That is why the light on drive A comes on before the hard drive is accessed, even if you have a hard disk. It is also why you can usually circumvent a menu system set up on your hard disk—you can place a DOS system disk in drive A, boot the system from that disk, and then access any files on the hard disk.

Note: Many people are concerned with security and protection of the files on their computer system. Entire books on the subject have appeared, each elaborating on one or more techniques. The hard disk menu method just mentioned relies on an AUTOEXEC.BAT file to automatically invoke the menu program. In general, anyone wishing to surmount this sort of protection method merely needs to search for an alternate path to the same information. Although many measures and countermeasures exist for protecting data, perhaps the best techniques are the simplest. Locking your computer with a key works up to a point, and simply placing your critical files on floppy disks and taking these disks with you when you leave the computer is even more effective. However, such a procedure can be cumbersome and time consuming if you have numerous, large files. The most sophisticated technique, and the one found to work the best, involves encrypting your files with a special algorithm.

Encryption is a procedure in which the computer accepts any string of characters from you (called the encrypting *key*) and uses this key to translate every character in your file to some other character. The result can typically be neither displayed nor printed and involves significant computer skills to decipher (without the key characters you entered and the original translating algorithm). Even if they can obtain physical access to the file, most computer experts cannot read and understand your file's data in this condition. Some utility programs, such as Keyworks and Superkey, provide encryption services among their many utility functions.

When the computer finds the system drive (the one that has a copy of the DOS files on it), the computer reads the information into its memory. DOS then scans the root directory of the drive from which it has read the DOS files for a special file called CONFIG.SYS. If this file is not present, DOS initializes your system according to built-in default values. Then, if an AUTOEXEC.BAT file exists, DOS proceeds with the instructions in that file and displays the DOS prompt (usually A> or C>, depending on which drive contained the system files).

If the root directory that DOS scans contains a CONFIG.SYS file, this file will contain a list of special statements that define a nonstandard system configuration. Figure 10.1 shows a sample CONFIG.SYS file actually used on a typical 640K DOS system. This system contains 640K of conventional memory, an expansion board to support a RAM disk, and a color video monitor. It runs data base software requiring multiple files to be simultaneously in use, and it runs sophisticated computer-aided design software. You'll learn in this chapter what each line of this file represents and how it relates to the hardware and software included with your system.

CONFIG.SYS is unique in the following ways:

- It can alter the size of internal DOS tables.
- It can be activated only by booting or rebooting the computer.
- It can contain only a limited set of commands.

```
FILES=20
BUFFERS=15
DEVICE=C:\DOS\ANSI.SYS
DEVICE=C:\DOS\VDISK.SYS 120
```

FIGURE 10.1: Typical CONFIG.SYS file for controlling several key startup features of your system. In this configuration, the FILES command ensures that a data base management system requiring multiple open files will run. The BUFFERS command improves the efficiency of DOS's handling of the increased data flow between memory and disk. The two DEVICE command lines bring into memory the ANSI.SYS driver (for special use of the color monitor by the PROMPT command later) and the VDISK.SYS driver (for special setup of a RAM disk for enhancing system performance).

Since the CONFIG.SYS file is a standard ASCII text file, you can create and modify it with a text editor such as EDLIN (see Chapter 6) or your own word processor. Each line in this file has the form

Command = Value

The commands you'll learn in this chapter are the most important and useful ones. They are FILES, BUFFERS, and DEVICE. You'll also learn a little about the SET and LASTDRIVE commands; SET, however, is discussed in much greater detail in Chapter 19, and its reference entry appears there.

Specifying the Number of Active Files

The first line of the CONFIG.SYS file in Figure 10.1 reads

FILES = 20

Why is this statement necessary? More and more frequently, users are running sophisticated programs such as WordStar 4.0, dBASE III PLUS, and Framework II. These programs can work with a number of files open at the same time, so they require the installation of a special CONFIG.SYS file. The FILES entry in the CONFIG.SYS file allows you to change the normal DOS default value for the maximum number of allowable files to be simultaneously in use.

The default value set by DOS is only eight files. This means that DOS reserves eight places inside its own memory space to track information about open files. DOS itself uses three of these places, and every running application program, overlay file, RAM-resident program, and so on may use additional places out of the eight.

Most popular application programs recommend that you set the FILES value to 20 in your CONFIG.SYS file, although some programs recommend higher or lower settings. Unless you're willing to run extensive performance tests in your system environment, just follow the software manufacturer's instructions for setting the value of FILES. However, if you are using several different software application packages—for example, you may be using a computer-aided design package that recommends the setting FILES = 20, and you may also be using a database management package that recommends FILES = 15—use the largest value. Although doing so will cost you some additional memory space when DOS boots up, the cost won't be much (48 bytes per open file). In nearly all cases, using the larger value will ensure that all of the application packages perform efficiently. Very occasionally, the extra table setting, say, of five files (20 – 15) will take up just enough memory to inhibit one of the application programs from running. When this happens (usually only in systems with less than 640K, or in systems using several additional memory-resident software programs), you will need to use a different version of your CONFIG.SYS file for each of the different application programs.

Specifying the Number of Internal DOS Buffers

The second line of the CONFIG.SYS file reads

BUFFERS = 15

The BUFFERS command refers to the way DOS manages the input and output of data to and from the disk drives. When a command is issued by a program to read information from a file, DOS really serves the role of an intermediary by loading the information into a reserved buffer area. Figure 10.2 presents a visual interpretation of this activity.

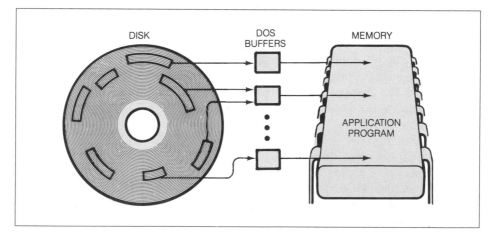

FIGURE 10.2: Disk data passing through DOS buffers. All data that flows either to (output data) or from (input data) the disk must flow briefly through DOS's internal buffers. These are temporary holding places in DOS's memory space. Each buffer is 512 bytes long, and the number of available buffers has a dramatic effect on the speed of data I/O during DOS file transfers. This speed has a direct bearing on the apparent speed of application programs, particularly sophisticated programs such as data base management systems.

Efficiency is the primary reason that operating systems use buffers at all. Imagine yourself in the role of an operating system. Then imagine that someone (an application program) wants to give you something, while someone else (a disk file) wants to get that same thing. If you act as a buffer by accepting the object with one hand and then hold it until you can locate the receiving person, the transaction will be fairly straightforward. However, if you try to do this procedure without using your hands or moving around, getting the giver together with the receiver in the same room, you've made your job much more difficult. In addition, you would not be able to do much else until the two-person operation was completed. DOS uses buffering to make transactions efficient.

When DOS receives a disk request, it checks the information in its buffer before it tries to read the disk. This step can sometimes eliminate the need for DOS to actually read the disk in order to satisfy an application program's file request; DOS may find that the requested file data is already in the buffer—for example, if the file was recently called by another program or by DOS. (This potential elimination of DOS work is in part the principle behind disk-buffering programs such as Lightning, discussed in Chapter 20). The result is that some programs perform certain operations faster.

Each buffer in DOS can hold 528 bytes. If you increase the number of buffers, the memory-resident requirements for DOS itself increase. This decreases the available memory for any application program, as well as for any memory-resident program you wish to use during your main program's execution. Sophisticated programs such as Framework II, which has its own buffer management and configuration file and therefore uses memory intensively, suffer greatly from too large a BUFFERS value.

A law of diminishing returns is at work here. Up to a point, more DOS buffers means faster performance for your system. On the other hand, too many buffers means DOS may spend more time looking through its buffers than it would spend going directly to the disk and reading the necessary data. Unless you have a good reason to do otherwise, use the software manufacturer's recommended setting for BUFFERS. A common setting is a value of 15.

Using Device Drivers to Customize DOS

The last two lines of the CONFIG.SYS file in Figure 10.1 read

DEVICE = C:\DOS\ANSI.SYS
DEVICE = C:\DOS\VDISK.SYS 120

These statements require more extensive discussion than the fairly straightforward FILES and BUFFERS commands.

The CONFIG.SYS file is also used to load additional software drivers into DOS. Software drivers are special-purpose programs whose only responsibility is to control specific peripheral devices (see Chapter 11 for an additional discussion of device drivers used in international processing). DOS can't be responsible for knowing all the control codes for all possible external devices; operating systems in general leave the details of communicating with and controlling these devices to the special driver programs.

Device drivers extend the command range of DOS. Naturally, they also take up more memory, which is one reason why they are optional. A special driver called ANSI.SYS extends the functions of DOS to include reprogramming or redefinition of keys and screen colors in DOS. You'll look at that feature more closely in the following paragraph.

Adding Power with the ANSI System Driver

The ANSI (American National Standards Institute) system allows you to modify the default setup of your screen and keyboard. For example, you can change the characteristics of the screen, including both the cursor position and screen colors (if you have a color monitor). You can also redefine the expected value of keys on your keyboard, so you can customize the function keys, as well as the effect of Ctrl, Shift, and Alt on them.

To obtain any of these customizing capabilities, the ANSI.SYS driver must be installed in your system. The third line of CONFIG.SYS (see Figure 10.1) does just that:

DEVICE = C:\DOS\ANSI.SYS

Some special-purpose application programs such as PreCursor, a hard disk management program, and SuperKey, a keyboard redefinition program, require you to include this type of command in your CONFIG.SYS specification. Of course, you should specify the full path name to the ANSI.SYS file; in this example, ANSI.SYS is located in directory DOS on drive C.

The command used to enter ANSI commands is PROMPT. This command is discussed at the end of this chapter, along with the changes you can make using the ANSI.SYS driver.

RAM DISKS

DOS also has a driver that is used to create a *RAM disk* (sometimes called a *virtual disk*). The RAM disk is not really a disk—it is an area in memory that simulates the operations of an additional disk drive. A critical aspect of this mechanism is that any files placed on the RAM disk are memory resident. They can therefore be retrieved at the speed of memory, which is usually microseconds or nanoseconds. Files on actual mechanical disk drives are retrieved more slowly, usually in the millisecond range.

You must perform some calculations to determine how much memory is available for your RAM disk. Simply subtract the memory required by your version of DOS from your total physical memory (640K, 512K, or whatever). Then subtract the memory requirements of your particular application program (for example, 378K for dBASE III PLUS or 512K for CADVANCE) from the remaining number. This tells you the maximum remaining memory space you can allocate for a RAM disk. For example, if the total physical memory of your system is 640K, the space required by your DOS 3.3 is 45K, and the space required by your application program is 384K, you have 211K remaining for your RAM disk (640 − 45 − 384 = 211).

There are a few other factors you must consider. The size of your version of DOS varies according to the values of FILES, BUFFERS, and any other CONFIG.SYS parameters. It also varies according to how many additional DOS programs you've run, which requires extra memory (see the MODE command in Chapter 12 and the KEYB command in Chapter 11). Naturally, if you run a memory-resident programs such as Sidekick, you need to subtract its memory requirements as well.

Use only as much memory for your RAM disk as you need. You should know in advance how you plan to use this space. Keep in mind that memory reserved for use as a RAM disk is no longer available for internal use by programs such as Framework II or Symphony. If a RAM disk or any other memory-resident software uses too much space, you may not have even enough remaining memory to load your main application software.

Creating a RAM Disk   You know that DOS maintains a directory and a file allocation table (a DAT and a FAT) on each disk, along with the actual data and program files. To simulate this structure in memory, a special piece of software is required. This software is included in DOS in a file called either VDISK.SYS (for PC-DOS) or RAMDRIVE.SYS (for MS-DOS).

The simulated RAM disk in Figure 10.3 can be implemented simply by including the following values in your DEVICE specification:

DEVICE = C:\DOS\VDISK.SYS 120

This DEVICE setting brings into memory the VDISK (virtual or RAM disk) driver.

> *Note:* If you are using a version of DOS for any machine other than an IBM computer, substitute RAMDRIVE.SYS wherever VDISK.SYS appears in this text.

In this example, the VDISK.SYS file itself is located on drive C in the DOS directory. The parameter value of 120 indicates that a total simulated disk of 120K should be created from the available physical memory (640K or whatever you have in your system).

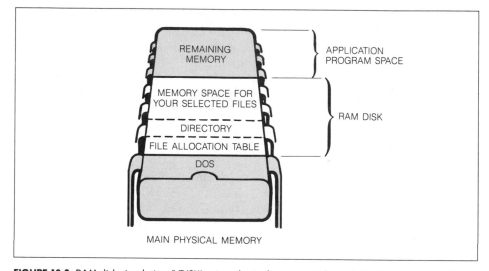

FIGURE 10.3: RAM disk simulation (VDISK) using physical memory. When physical memory is used to simulate a mechanical disk, the resulting apparent disk drive is called a RAM disk. Assuming your system has enough memory for both DOS and your main application program, the remaining memory can in theory (it usually must be a certain minimum number of bytes, such as 256) be arranged to mimic a real disk drive. A small number of memory bytes can be used to contain *directory* table information, an additional small number of bytes can be used for *file-allocation table* entries, and the remaining space can be used for file storage.

If you have an IBM PC-AT or a compatible computer, you should know about a switch you can use when you set up a RAM disk. The /E switch will use extended memory—extra memory above the conventional 1Mb of addressible memory—if your machine has this additional memory installed. The previous example could be modified like this to generate a 120K RAM disk in extended memory:

DEVICE = C:\DOS\VDISK.SYS 120 /E

DOS also allows you to use multiple RAM disks simultaneously, just as you can use different physical devices to protect files from one another by separating them on different drives. DOS will give each RAM disk a new single-character drive identifier.

All you need to do to create multiple RAM disks is enter multiple copies of the DEVICE command. DOS knows what physical drives exist in your system, and it creates the additional drives using the next available letters. For instance, if your system has two diskette drives and one hard disk drive, then adding the following two statements to your CONFIG.SYS file would create RAM disks D and E with sizes of 120K and 184K (see Figure 10.4):

DEVICE = C:\DOS\VDISK.SYS 120
DEVICE = C:\DOS\VDISK.SYS 184

```
C>CHKDSK D:
Volume VDISK   V3.3 created Dec 6, 1984 12:00p

    119168 bytes total disk space
         0 bytes in 1 hidden files
    119168 bytes available on disk

    524288 bytes total memory
    132208 bytes free

C>CHKDSK E:
Volume VDISK   V3.3 created Dec 6, 1984 12:00p

    183936 bytes total disk space
         0 bytes in 1 hidden files
    183936 bytes available on disk

    524288 bytes total memory
    132208 bytes free

C>_
```

FIGURE 10.4: Multiple RAM disks. Multiple RAM disks can be created and accessed if sufficient memory exists in your system. In this example, disk drives D and E are virtual disks (RAM disks) created by the MS DOS VDISK.SYS device driver. Two separate DEVICE command lines were used in the CONFIG.SYS file for this system.

Note: If you intend to create and use disk drives with drive identifiers beyond the letter E, DOS 3.2 and 3.3 will permit you to do so but will require another statement in your configuration file. This additional statement must be of the form LASTDRIVE = x, where x is the last valid alphabetic character DOS will use for a drive identifier.

There are other methods for creating RAM disks. These usually require software that comes with enhancement boards, such as AST's Six-Pak Plus or Quadram's Quadboard, or they require add-on boards that act as dedicated RAM disks. Some of these have their own power supplies and battery backup systems, which protect them from data loss during power outages. Another benefit of this type of add-on RAM disk is that no system memory is used by the device driver that manages the RAM disk. Installing a RAM disk with software packages or add-on boards requires a different procedure; you should follow the manufacturer's instructions.

An advantage of these other methods is that the RAM disk doesn't have to be carved out of memory at bootup time. Instead, you can first run your own programs, making use of all available memory. Then, at your convenience, you can run the special software to set up the RAM disk. Only then will you need to confront the problem of memory requirements. In Figure 10.4, the 512K machine with two RAM disks has only 132,208 bytes free in which to run programs. Having consumed so much memory with the two RAM disks, you would have to change the CONFIG.SYS file and reboot before you could reuse that memory space in any other way.

Note: None of the CONFIG.SYS file's settings take effect until the DOS system is booted. Remember this if you make any changes to your CONFIG.SYS file: You must reboot before the changes take effect.

Using a RAM Disk Now that you know how to create a RAM disk, you should also learn how to use what you've created to best advantage. Here are some suggestions for using your RAM disk.

Copy your DOS system's primary disk-resident program, COMMAND.COM, onto your RAM disk. Then employ the following special instructions to inform DOS that all future references to COMMAND.COM refer to the copy on the RAM disk, not on the boot disk. Assuming your RAM disk is in drive D (substitute the letter used by your system), enter the following command at the DOS prompt:

SET COMSPEC = D:\COMMAND.COM

This will speed up all programs that invoke DOS from within themselves, such as Framework II or QDOS II. These programs work by loading a second copy of the command processor (COMMAND.COM) from a RAM disk. This command will also speed up application software that overwrites the command-processor portion of DOS and then requires its reloading before the software can restore DOS and its prompt. For more information about the DOS environment and the SET COMSPEC command, see Chapter 19.

Load the files for frequently referenced external DOS commands such as CHKDSK.COM and FORMAT.COM onto your RAM disk; also load EDLIN.COM if you use EDLIN often to edit small text files (see Chapter 6). In fact, load any text files, such as batch files, that you run frequently.

Load any large support files (such as spelling dictionaries or a thesaurus file) that your word processor or integrated software may need. Also place index-type files (generated by many database management systems) on the RAM disk to much more rapidly access data records, especially if you must search through many records in large data files.

Place your favorite disk-resident utility programs (shareware, public domain, or purchased, such as the Norton Utilities) on the RAM disk if you use them frequently. Also place overlay files on your RAM disk for improved execution of your software. These overlays contain the portion of your application program that couldn't fit into memory and is normally read into a special part of memory only when it is needed. The overlay features of your software will operate at rapid RAM speeds if you place them on your RAM disk. Note that you will need to make your RAM disk the default DOS disk before invoking your application program so DOS will look for the overlay file on the RAM disk and not on the standard drive.

Remember to set your path properly so DOS can find main programs. Set the RAM disk near or at the front of the PATH specification so that DOS first accesses the file copies on the RAM drive, not the original files that may also be accessible from directories on the path.

Before you follow these suggestions for using your RAM disk effectively, you should learn how to use it safely. As you know, using a RAM disk is much faster than using real disks. Programs that formerly took hours to run may take minutes, those that took minutes may take seconds, and waiting time may disappear. When RAM disks are used improperly, however, hours of work can disappear in seconds.

Since a RAM disk is created in memory, any information stored on it will vanish when the computer is turned off. You gain great advantage by storing and accessing the right files on a RAM disk, but you must remember that these files are destroyed when you turn off the power or a power failure occurs, if your computer plug comes out of the wall, or if you reboot your system with Ctrl-Alt-Del.

If you place and update important data files on a RAM disk for the sake of rapid access, save copies of them on a real disk before you turn off the power. Also make backup copies of them on a real disk at frequent intervals to avoid losing all your work.

ANSI.SYS AND THE PROMPT COMMAND

Use the PROMPT command to enter ANSI commands. For example, the form of the PROMPT command used to change the color of the screen is

PROMPT $e[*aaaa*m

where *aaaa* represents screen attributes or colors (shown in Table 10.1). Separate these values with semicolons if you use more than one. The $e is a special symbol combination recognized by DOS as an equivalent of the Esc key. You invoke the ANSI driver whenever you enter an escape sequence, which is any series of keystrokes that begins with the Esc key; therefore, $e invokes the ANSI driver. There is no limit to the number of attributes you can enter between the left bracket [and the letter *m*.

Controlling the Screen Display

It's up to you to decide if you like the standard white letters on a black background (even if you've bought a color monitor), or if you prefer something else. Using the attribute and color codes shown in Table 10.1, along with the PROMPT command, you can customize the screen.

COLORS	FOREGROUND	BACKGROUND
Black	30	40
Red	31	41
Green	32	42
Yellow	33	43
Blue	34	44
Magenta	35	45
Cyan	36	46
White	37	47
ATTRIBUTES		
CODE	EFFECT	
0	All attributes off	
1	Boldfacing	
4	Underlining (on IBM-compatible monochrome monitors only)	
5	Blinking	
7	Reverse video	

TABLE 10.1: Screen Color and Attribute Codes

Note: The letter *m* in the PROMPT escape sequence signifies the end of your sequence of attribute settings. You must enter it in lowercase.

To switch the display to dark letters on a light background (see Figure 10.5), you use an attribute value of 7 for reverse video:

PROMPT $e[7m

All future output on your screen now appears in reverse video—black on white. Notice that in Figure 10.5, the DIR/W command itself is displayed in reverse video after the PROMPT command has been executed.

To return to normal video (see Figure 10.6), you use an attribute value of 0, which turns off all special attributes:

PROMPT $e[0m

Since video attributes settings are retained until they are changed or reset, you should issue the 0 resetting sequence first if you want to ensure that only the specified attribute holds. For example, if you wanted to turn reverse video on and all

```
SYS       COM    TREE      COM    VDISK     SYS    XCOPY     EXE    DEMO      BAK
AUTOEXEC  BAK    S-SAVE    COM    IMCAP     COM    SR        COM    VTREE     COM
DEMO      BAT    LOCATE    BAT    HELP      BAK    AUTOEXEC  BAT    CONFIG    SYS
          5Ø File(s)         2Ø48 bytes free

A>PROMPT $e[7m

DIR/W

Volume in drive A has no label
Directory of  A:\

ANSI      SYS    ASSIGN    COM    ATTRIB    EXE    BACKUP    COM    IMSHOW    EXE
SKN       COM    CHKDSK    COM    COMMAND   COM    COMP      COM    DISKCOMP  COM
DISKCOPY  COM    DRIVER    SYS    EDLIN     COM    FDISK     COM    FIND      EXE
FORMAT    COM    GRAFTABL  COM    GRAPHICS  COM    JOIN      EXE    KEYBFR    COM
KEYBGR    COM    KEYBIT    COM    KEYBSP    COM    KEYBUK    COM    LABEL     COM
MODE      COM    MORE      COM    PRINT     COM    RECOVER   COM    REPLACE   EXE
RESTORE   COM    SELECT    COM    SHARE     EXE    SORT      EXE    SUBST     EXE
SYS       COM    TREE      COM    VDISK     SYS    XCOPY     EXE    DEMO      BAK
AUTOEXEC  BAK    S-SAVE    COM    IMCAP     COM    SR        COM    VTREE     COM
DEMO      BAT    LOCATE    BAT    HELP      BAK    AUTOEXEC  BAT  . CONFIG    SYS
          5Ø File(s)         2Ø48 bytes free
```

FIGURE 10.5: Setting reverse video with PROMPT and ANSI.SYS. The ANSI.SYS screen driver allows you to modify the attributes of all positions on the screen. In this example, the PROMPT command invokes the ANSI.SYS attribute for reverse video (code = 7 from Table 10.1). All succeeding screen output appears in reverse video until you enter a countermanding PROMPT command.

```
SYS       COM    TREE      COM    VDISK     SYS    XCOPY     EXE    DEMO      BAK
AUTOEXEC  BAK    S-SAVE    COM    IMCAP     COM    SR        COM    VTREE     COM
DEMO      BAT    LOCATE    BAT    HELP      BAK    AUTOEXEC  BAT    CONFIG    SYS
          5Ø File(s)         2Ø48 bytes free

PROMPT $E[Øm

DIR/W

Volume in drive A has no label
Directory of  A:\

ANSI      SYS    ASSIGN    COM    ATTRIB    EXE    BACKUP    COM    IMSHOW    EXE
SKN       COM    CHKDSK    COM    COMMAND   COM    COMP      COM    DISKCOMP  COM
DISKCOPY  COM    DRIVER    SYS    EDLIN     COM    FDISK     COM    FIND      EXE
FORMAT    COM    GRAFTABL  COM    GRAPHICS  COM    JOIN      EXE    KEYBFR    COM
KEYBGR    COM    KEYBIT    COM    KEYBSP    COM    KEYBUK    COM    LABEL     COM
MODE      COM    MORE      COM    PRINT     COM    RECOVER   COM    REPLACE   EXE
RESTORE   COM    SELECT    COM    SHARE     EXE    SORT      EXE    SUBST     EXE
SYS       COM    TREE      COM    VDISK     SYS    XCOPY     EXE    DEMO      BAK
AUTOEXEC  BAK    S-SAVE    COM    IMCAP     COM    SR        COM    VTREE     COM
DEMO      BAT    LOCATE    BAT    HELP      BAK    AUTOEXEC  BAT    CONFIG    SYS
          5Ø File(s)         2Ø48 bytes free
```

FIGURE 10.6: Resetting to default video attributes. Resetting your screen to normal video output from the reversed output seen at the top of the screen is as simple as invoking the special resetting code (0) recognized by ANSI.SYS.

other attributes (like boldface) off, you would enter:

PROMPT $e[0;7m

Using Metasymbols

Notice that no visible prompt appears at the bottom of the screens in Figures 10.5 and 10.6. This is because the PROMPT command set video attributes only. Various other possibilities can be combined with these attributes by stringing them together. You can create a wide range of output possibilities by using symbolic replacements, called *metasymbols,* for the desired output result. Table 10.2 lists the single-character metasymbols that you can use in conjunction with the $ character to influence the output of the PROMPT command.

SYMBOL	MEANING
e	Esc key
p	Current directory of the default drive
g	> character
n	Default drive identifier
d	System date
t	System time
v	Version number
l	< character
b	¦ character
q	= character
h	Backspace
—	Carriage-return/line-feed sequence

TABLE 10.2: PROMPT Command Metasymbols

For instance, to display the current directory, you enter

PROMPT $p

To display the current directory and the > symbol, you enter

PROMPT pg

To display the current directory and the > symbol *and* to set to boldface all future video output, you enter

PROMPT pg$e[1m

Figure 10.7 shows the results of this command.

```
SYS       COM    TREE      COM    VDISK    SYS    XCOPY     EXE    DEMO     BAK
AUTOEXEC  BAK    S-SAVE    COM    IMCAP    COM    SR        COM    VTREE    COM
DEMO      BAT    LOCATE    BAT    HELP     BAK    AUTOEXEC  BAT    CONFIG   SYS
        5Ø File(s)         2Ø48 bytes free

A>PROMPT $P$G$E[1m

A:\>DIR/W

 Volume in drive A has no label
 Directory of  A:\

ANSI      SYS    ASSIGN    COM    ATTRIB    EXE    BACKUP    COM    IMSHOW    EXE
SKN       COM    CHKDSK    COM    COMMAND   COM    COMP      COM    DISKCOMP  COM
DISKCOPY  COM    DRIVER    SYS    EDLIN     COM    FDISK     COM    FIND      EXE
FORMAT    COM    GRAFTABL  COM    GRAPHICS  COM    JOIN      EXE    KEYBFR    COM
KEYBGR    COM    KEYBIT    COM    KEYBSP    COM    KEYBUK    COM    LABEL     COM
MODE      COM    MORE      COM    PRINT     COM    RECOVER   COM    REPLACE   EXE
RESTORE   COM    SELECT    COM    SHARE     EXE    SORT      EXE    SUBST     EXE
SYS       COM    TREE      COM    VDISK     SYS    XCOPY     EXE    DEMO      BAK
AUTOEXEC  BAK    S-SAVE    COM    IMCAP     COM    SR        COM    VTREE     COM
DEMO      BAT    LOCATE    BAT    HELP      BAK    AUTOEXEC  BAT    CONFIG    SYS
        5Ø File(s)         2Ø48 bytes free

A:\>_
```

FIGURE 10.7: Extending the PROMPT command. In addition to affecting screen attributes, the PROMPT command can change the default contents of the DOS system prompt. You can include the special symbols (metasymbols) in Table 10.2 in your PROMPT command to change or augment what DOS will display whenever it prompts you. The PROMPT command in this figure uses the $P symbols to obtain the current directory, the $G symbols to display the chevron (>) symbol, and the ANSI.SYS code sequence $E[1m to turn on the boldfacing attribute.

Combining Multiple Attributes

You can combine all of the preceding elements to create more complex prompt effects. The simplest combinations involve two attributes at once. For example, to create a reverse-video display that blinks, you can combine the codes for blinking (5) and reverse video (7):

PROMPT $e[5;7m

Future output will appear as black characters that blink on a light background. To return the screen to normal again, you enter

PROMPT $e[0m

You can enter text in your prompt by simply typing it, using no special metasymbols; you can also embed text between any special-purpose metasymbols. For example, you can change the prompting message to "Your Command?" and display it in high intensity by entering

PROMPT $e[1mYour Command?$e[0m

The beginning $e[1m turns on high intensity for the phrase "Your Command?" and the ending $e[0m turns it off.

> *Warning:* You can enter long screen prompts that wrap to a second screen line, but you must not press the Return key to get to the second line. The Return key terminates your prompt-string input; DOS wraps multiple-line commands on its own.

Color monitors present other interesting options. Using the color codes in Table 10.1 and the metasymbols in Table 10.2, you can easily set any desired combination of foreground and background colors. For example, the following command sets a three-line prompt. The first line contains the current directory (p). The carriage-return/line-feed sequence (_) ensures that the system date (d) appears on the next line. The time (t) and the > character (g) appear on the third line, and all succeeding text (including the future prompting strings) appears as blue characters on a yellow background. These colors are for a CGA monitor; different monitors may have slight variations in color. In this case, the same command issued to an EGA or VGA monitor would produce a brown background.

PROMPT p_d_tg$e[34;43m

A slight change in this command can display similar information, using reverse video for the text prompting information only. Thus, you can use essentially the same PROMPT command for both color and monochrome monitors. Notice in Figure 10.8 that the display of commands and output is in normal video, since the reverse-video code is reset immediately after the > symbol is output.

PROMPT $e[7m$p$_$d$_$tge[0m

If you do not like the multiline appearance of this information, you can easily put the same information on one line with the following variation:

PROMPT $e[7m$p $d tg$e[0m

The spaces in this command are critical to the separation of the directory name, date, and time. The space character is treated by the PROMPT command like any other keyboard character and will appear in the final DOS prompt line. The results are shown in Figure 10.9.

You can use the PROMPT command in many more fanciful ways to control the video display. The code required is beyond the scope of this book, but you can manipulate the cursor and its location in a variety of ways.

Use the PROMPT command now to redefine your DOS prompt to provide more information. Issue the proper command to display the DOS version number on one line, the system date on the next line, and the current directory on the third line of this multiline prompt. On a fourth line, generate the text string

Enter next command, please :

```
C>PROMPT $e[7m$p$_$d$_$t$g$e[Øm
C:\SYBEX
Mon  9-26-1988
 5:37:37.94>DIR/W

 Volume in drive C is ROBBINS
 Directory of   C:\SYBEX

              ..             DOSMASTR      ESSENTL      DESKTOP
        5 File(s)   152576Ø bytes free
C:\SYBEX
Mon  9-26-1988
 5:37:43.Ø5>VOL

 Volume in drive C is ROBBINS
C:\SYBEX
Mon  9-26-1988
 5:37:47.12>_
```

FIGURE 10.8: A three-line, reverse-video prompt. Using the underscore metasymbol ($_) generates a multiple-line prompt. Each time DOS prompts you in this figure, the screen displays the information requested by the PROMPT command in a group of three separate lines. The $e[7m turns boldface on at the beginning of this three-line prompt, and the $e[0m turns normal video back on at the end of the three-line prompt. Line 1 consists solely of the current directory ($p), line 2 contains the system date ($d), and line 3 combines the system time with the chevron symbol (tg).

```
C>PROMPT $e[7m$p     $d     $t$g$e[Øm
C:\SYBEX     Mon  9-26-1988        5:39:Ø2.2Ø>DIR/W

 Volume in drive C is ROBBINS
 Directory of   C:\SYBEX

              ..             DOSMASTR      ESSENTL      DESKTOP
NEW1Ø-8  CAP
        6 File(s)   1519616 bytes free
C:\SYBEX     Mon  9-26-1988        5:39:Ø7.25>VOL

 Volume in drive C is ROBBINS
C:\SYBEX     Mon  9-26-1988        5:39:1Ø.99>_
```

FIGURE 10.9: A one-line, reverse-video prompt. You can even use spaces in your PROMPT command to force spaces to appear in the actual DOS prompt later. The same information as displayed in three lines in Figure 10.8 can be combined, using spaces for separators, into a 1-line output prompt. Whether you use multiple-line or multiple-entry formats is merely a question of personal taste.

If you have a monochrome monitor, display this message in reverse video. Remember to reset the video attribute so that the rest of the display appears in normal video. If you have a color monitor, display this message in white letters on a rcd background.

Redefining Keys

In addition to changing screen colors, you can use the ANSI system to reprogram some of your keys to type commands or phrases. You can define any of the ASCII keys or the extended keyboard keys (F1–F10, Home, End, and so on). Some people have even used this technique to redefine individual keys to represent other individual keys, so that the keyboard assumed a different layout.

Like designing screen attributes, reassigning keys begins with the special symbol for the Esc key ($e) and continues with the left bracket ([). If you want to assign a new value to a regular key such as the *a* key or the = key, you enter the ASCII value of the key: for example, 96 for the letter *a* or 61 for = . However, to reassign values to the special keys on your keyboard (which is a more common goal), you must begin the key assignment with a zero and then follow it with the special code given the key by DOS (see Table 10.3).

For example, the reassignment code for F10 is 68. If you want the F10 key to automatically type the command DIR/W, you would enter

PROMPT $e[0;68;"DIR/W";13p

First, $e[tells DOS that an ANSI command is being entered. Next, 0 tells DOS that the key to be redefined is part of the extended keyboard. The code 68 selects F10 as the key to be redefined. "DIR/W" is the text of the command. (Note that these text characters are enclosed in quotation marks to indicate that they are not codes for ANSI.SYS to interpret.) The code 13 indicates the Return key, which is required after the DIR/W command, just as it would be if you typed DIR/W at the keyboard. The last character in a key redefinition is always *p*, just as the last character in the video redefinition was an *m*.

Try out this technique now. Use the ANSI.SYS system to program your F7 function key to perform a CHKDSK command. Be sure you have a CONFIG.SYS file in your root directory and that it contains a DEVICE specification that loads the ANSI.SYS driver.

Finally, you can set up some fancy custom menu systems simply with the PROMPT command and a well-thought-out group of function-key assignments. There are 10 function keys (F1–F10), 10 shifted function keys, 10 Ctrl-function-key combinations, and 10 Alt–function-key combinations, or a total of 40 assignment possibilities. Table 10.3 shows the code numbers for redefining all these keys.

FUNCTION KEY	REDEFINITION CODE	FUNCTION KEY	REDEFINITION CODE
F1	59	Ctrl-F1	94
F2	60	Ctrl-F2	95
F3	61	Ctrl-F3	96
F4	62	Ctrl-F4	7
F5	63	Ctrl-F5	98
F6	64	Ctrl-F6	99
F7	65	Ctrl-F7	100
F8	66	Ctrl-F8	101
F9	67	Ctrl-F9	102
F10	68	Ctrl-F10	103
Shift-F1	84	Alt-F1	104
Shift-F2	85	Alt-F2	105
Shift-F3	86	Alt-F3	106
Shift-F4	87	Alt-F4	107
Shift-F5	88	Alt-F5	108
Shift-F6	89	Alt-F6	109
Shift-F7	90	Alt-F7	110
Shift-F8	91	Alt-F8	111
Shift-F9	92	Alt-F9	112
Shift-F10	93	Alt-F10	113

TABLE 10.3: Function-Key Redefinition Codes

The following PROMPT commands redefine several keys. The first causes the shifted F4 key to type FORMAT A:. The second causes the Ctrl-F6 combination to type CHKDSK, and the third causes the Alt-F8 combination to type CD \.

```
PROMPT $e[0;87;"FORMAT A:";13p
PROMPT $e[0;99;"CHKDSK";13p
PROMPT $e[0;111;"CD \";13p
```

You must assign a key its original code value in order to reset it. The following sequence resets all three of the example function-key sequences:

```
PROMPT $e[0;87;0;87p$e[0;99;0;99p$e[0;111;0;111p
```

A nice feature of all these options is that they are cumulative—that is, you can issue any number of key redefinition requests, and they will accumulate. Until you reset each one, they retain their new definitions as long as you are at the DOS prompt level.

Warning: Some programs reset the function-key definitions when they begin, and you will not be able to use the PROMPT command for key redefinition. When you encounter such a situation, the best solution is to purchase and use a keyboard redefinition program such as Keyworks (see Chapter 20), which allows you to redefine any key while another program is operating.

DOS CONFIGURATION COMMANDS

Following are the reference entries for the DOS commands discussed in this chapter and used in tailoring DOS to particular configurations.

BUFFERS

This command causes a certain number of file-transfer buffers to be set aside in memory.

SYNTAX

BUFFERS = x

x is the number of buffers to be set up. If this command is not specified, DOS 3.3 will determine the number of buffers automatically, based on the current system memory.

TYPE

Configuration.

USAGE

While most programs only require a few buffers, remember that every disk access requires one. It is recommended that you set BUFFERS equal to the appropriate number, as shown in Table 10.4. Note that a value of three buffers for system RAM less than or equal to 128K is used only for high-capacity drives.

EXAMPLES

Including the following line in your CONFIG.SYS file:

BUFFERS = 20

BUFFERS VALUE	SYSTEM RAM (K)
2 or 3	< = 128
5	129–256
10	257–512
15	513 and up

TABLE 10.4: BUFFER Settings and System RAM sizes.

ensures that DOS will reserve twenty 512-byte memory areas to be used as temporary input/output buffers for DOS data transfers.

Entering

BUFFERS = 10

sets a more memory-conserving number of buffers, although it may not be sufficient for some sophisticated programs and operating environments.

DEVICE

This command loads a device driver.

SYNTAX

DEVICE = *FileSpec*[*Switches*]

    FileSpec   is the optional drive and path, plus the file name and extension, of the specified driver file.

    Switches   are the switches corresponding to the specific driver files.

TYPE

Configuration.

USAGE

A driver can be anything from a keyboard enhancement routine to a RAM disk specification. DEVICE can be used many times in the CONFIG.SYS file, limited only by how the drivers use the system's memory.

Entering

DEVICE = C:\DOS\VDISK.SYS 512 /E

will set up a RAM disk of 512 kilobytes in an IBM PC-DOS system. The /E switch enables DOS to use extended memory for this 512K RAM disk.

FILES

Just as the number of buffers to be used by DOS can be specified, so may the number of files open at any one time. The FILES command specifies the size of the file control area in which file control blocks are created.

SYNTAX

FILES = x

x is a number between 8 and 255 (8 is the default) specifying the number of files that can remain open at one time.

TYPE

Configuration.

Warning: When you are using the FILES command, keep in mind that the size of DOS increases by 48 bytes for each file beyond the eight default files.

USAGE

If you are using sophisticated software that can simultaneously maintain several files open at the same time, you must include the FILES command in your CONFIG.SYS file.

EXAMPLE

Entering

FILES = 25

will enable DOS to support such advanced programs, like data base management systems. Both DOS and the application software must be able to set up internal tables to understand multiple open files.

LASTDRIVE

This command allows you to specify up to 26 disk drives for access.

SYNTAX

LASTDRIVE = *D*

> *D*   is the last accessible drive; the default is E.

TYPE

Configuration.

RESTRICTIONS

If you specify a letter range that is not sufficient for the number of drives hooked up to the system, LASTDRIVE will not be accepted. For example, if you specify G as the final drive, and have eight drives hooked up to your system, LASTDRIVE will not work—you've assigned seven letters to cover your eight drives.

USAGE

If you have more than five drives hooked up to your system, or if you are using the SUBST command often and need to declare a drive name beyond E, you need this command. LASTDRIVE configures the system so that you can access drives up to the specified drive, which may even be Z.

EXAMPLES

Entering

LASTDRIVE = H

will allow three additional letters (F, G, and H) to be used in your system. These may either be actual additional hardware drives, or they may be RAM disks, or they may even be drives simulated with the SUBST command.

SUMMARY

In this chapter, you've learned some very powerful methods in DOS to customize your system for both power and convenience.

For additional information about viewing and editing the CONFIG.SYS and the AUTO-EXEC.BAT text files, see

- Chapter 6, "EDLIN: The DOS Editor"

For additional information about the DOS environment and the SET command, see

- Chapter 19, "Other Advanced Commands"

For additional information about memory-resident programs and about utility software that provides encryption capabilities, see

- Chapter 20, "Extending DOS's Power with Utility Software"

In the next chapter, you'll learn about another type of system configuration: initializing your keyboard and monitor to read and display international character sets.

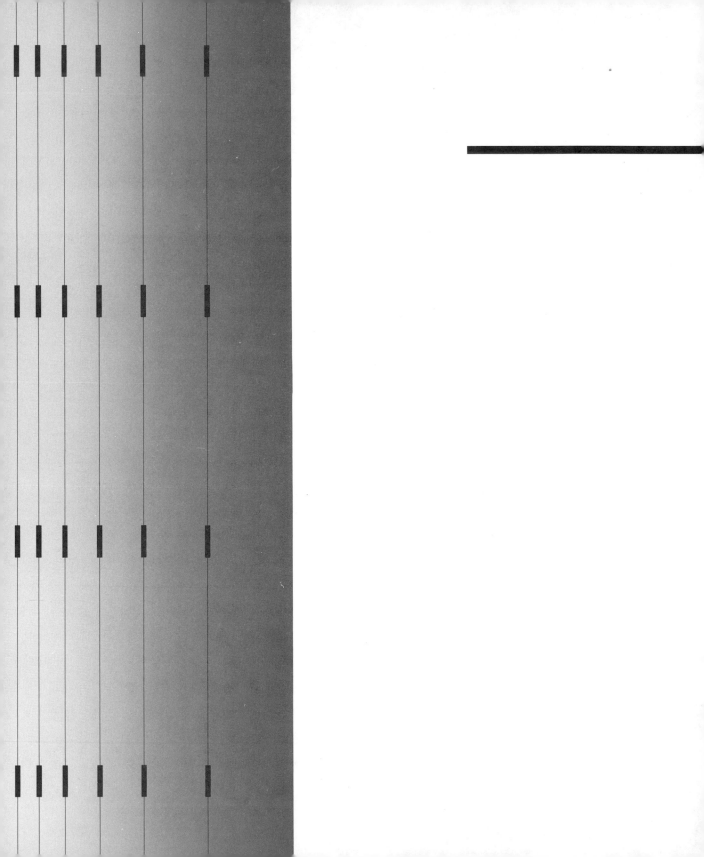

INTERNATIONAL SETUP

INTERNATIONAL SETUP OF DOS

The words and numbers that computer applications work with are made up of symbols, and different countries use different typographic symbols to represent various kinds of information. For example, currency symbols differ among countries—the $ in the USA, the DM in Germany, and the Fr in France. Time formats also vary: The separator symbol between the hour and minutes is a colon in the U.S., but a period in Norway. Decimal numbers are also punctuated differently; in the U.S., they contain a period, but in the Spanish-speaking world they contain a comma. You'll learn in this chapter how to set up your copy of DOS to understand the default values for symbols used in different countries.

Different countries also employ different keyboard layouts. If you learned to type in the U.S. and then try typing on a French typewriter or keyboard, you would type the letter *A* each time you meant to type a *Q*, and vice versa, because the positions of the *A* and *Q* keys on an American keyboard are reversed on a French keyboard. You'll also learn in this chapter about the differences between keyboard layouts in different countries and how you can easily ask DOS to redefine all the keys to suit you. In addition, you'll learn how to rapidly switch between the various possible layouts. If you're a foreigner in the U.S., you can easily switch between the U.S. default key values and your own. Thus, you don't need to learn the U.S. keyboard layout in order to use American computers. The same is true in reverse for Americans working abroad. The feature that allows you to do this is explained in detail later in this chapter.

This chapter concentrates primarily on the national language-support features found in DOS 3.3. The more limited support provided in versions 3.0 through 3.2 is discussed at the end of this chapter.

If you are using a CGA video adaptor, you may need to adjust your system to improve the display and printout of foreign characters; the required steps are presented later in this chapter.

CHARACTER SETS FOR DIFFERENT COUNTRIES

The *character set* of a given country or computer comprises the group of characters used in that country or on its computers. Most countries, like the United States and Great Britain, share a common set of characters. However, some countries have enough different characters and symbols to justify creating a special character set just for them. You instruct DOS which character set to use by supplying a number known as a *country code*.

Along with the different character sets comes different placement of the characters on a computer keyboard, which makes sense—commonly used elements must be easy to use. For example, on a French keyboard certain keys are reversed, and other keys facilitate the production of accented letters. You tell DOS which keyboard to use by supplying a *keyboard code*.

ASCII Codes

A computer does not interpret letters and other symbols as letters per se, but assigns a number to each symbol. These numbers range from 0 to 255, representing the 256 possible combinations of binary digits contained in an 8-bit byte. The whole set of number/symbol assignments is known as the American Standard Code for Information Interchange, or ASCII. Individual assignments are commonly known as *ASCII codes*. In spite of the name, the code has been adopted internationally and is only partly standard.

CONTROL CODES

Codes 0 through 31 are usually reserved for control codes, the codes that do not produce a visible character but perform some particular action. For example, sending code 7 to the console on most computers causes the computer to beep, and sending code 13 causes a carriage return. These codes control the hardware functions.

STANDARD ASCII CHARACTER SET

Codes 32 through 126 are standard characters and symbols (see Table 11.1). The capital alphabet starts at code 65, and the lowercase alphabet starts at code 97. Code 127 represents the deletion symbol. The control codes and the standard character codes together make up the entire set (from 0 to 127) of ASCII codes. The computer translates characters into these codes, and so does any other device using the characters. When a computer sends ASCII 65 to the printer, it expects an *A* to be printed, so the printer must also translate from code 65 to *A*. You can see why it is important for these codes to be standardized; many pieces of equipment rely on the same code.

EXTENDED ASCII SET

Codes 128 through 255 are computer or printer specific. IBM uses codes 128 through 255 for some graphics characters; some Epson printers use these codes for italics.

HEX DIGITS	1ST	0-	1-	2-	3-	4-	5-	6-	7-
2nd									
-0					0	@	P	'	p
-1				!	1	A	Q	a	q
-2				"	2	B	R	b	r
-3				#	3	C	S	c	s
-4				$	4	D	T	d	t
-5				%	5	E	U	e	u
-6				&	6	F	V	f	v
-7				'	7	G	W	g	w
-8				(	8	H	X	h	x
-9				)	9	I	Y	i	y
-A				*	:	J	Z	j	z
-B				+	;	K	[	k	{
-C				,	<	L	\	l	|
-D				-	=	M	]	m	}
-E				.	>	N	^	n	~
-F				/	?	O	_	o	

TABLE 11.1: Standard ASCII Characters and Symbols

The extended ASCII codes also represent certain specialized keys or key combinations, such as Alt-C and F1. These codes are defined by first sending an ASCII null character (code 0) to the device and then sending another code. For example, sending code 0 and then code 59 has the same effect as pressing the F1 key.

The combinations of all these codes produce the complete visual and printed output you are used to seeing. Depending on where you live and work, however, you may have altogether different characters in your language and keys on your keyboard.

What Country Do You Call Home?

When DOS boots up, the system date and time are queried. Everybody agrees that any given date has a month, a day, and a year, but not everyone agrees on that order. In the U.S., dates are shown with the month first, the day next, and the year last. In Europe, the day is shown first, the month next, and the year last. In the Far East, the year is first, the month next, and the day last. Hence, 11/04/07 can mean November 4, 1907; April 11, 1907; or April 7, 1911.

It depends on who's writing the date *and* who's reading it. Again, that's why standards are so important.

The DATE function in DOS displays the system date according to the accepted custom in a specific country. Table 11.2 shows the countries whose formats are currently known to DOS, along with their country and keyboard codes. You'll learn later in this chapter how to set up your version of DOS to understand which country or keyboard is in use.

The order of the month, day, and year fields is only one of many elements that differ among countries. Separator symbols between the month, day, and year values also vary from country to country. In fact, there are a host of special symbols that vary among countries: time separators (a colon or a period), list separators (a semicolon or a comma), decimal separators (a period or a comma),

COUNTRY	COUNTRY CODE	KEYBOARD CODE
Arabic	785	
Australia	061	US
Belgium	032	BE
Canada (Eng.)	001	US
Canada (Fr.)	002	CF
Denmark	045	DK
Finland	358	SU
France	033	FR
Germany	049	GR
Hebrew	972	
Italy	039	IT
Latin America	003	LA
Netherlands	031	NL
Norway	047	NO
Portugal	351	PO
Spain	034	SP
Sweden	046	SV
Switzerland (Fr.)	041	SF
Switzerland (Ger.)	041	SG
United Kingdom	044	UK
United States	001	US

TABLE 11.2: DOS International Country and Keyboard Codes

thousands separators (a comma or a period), and currency symbols ($, F, Fr, MK, DKR, and others). The U.S. shows time in 12-hour A.M./P.M. format, whereas most other countries use a 24-hour display. Most countries show two decimal places of accuracy in currency displays, whereas Italy shows none.

DOS maintains internal tables of these differing values according to which country is set up as the system default. If you do nothing, the U.S. will be assumed to be the standard. However, if you wish to customize the system for some other country, you can simply use the proper country code from Table 11.2 to add a line to your CONFIG.SYS file:

COUNTRY = *Code*

Figure 11.1 shows the results of DOS date and time requests after the system CONFIG.SYS file was changed to make Switzerland (code 041) the default country.

```
A:\>TYPE CONFIG.SYS
FILES=20
BUFFERS=15
DEVICE=C:\DOS\ANSI.SYS
COUNTRY=041,850,C:\DOS\COUNTRY.SYS

A:\>DATE
Current date is Sun 14.08.1988
Enter new date (dd-mm-yy):

A:\>TIME
Current time is  6.07.04.79
Enter new time:

A:\>
```

FIGURE 11.1: Date and time requests for COUNTRY = Switzerland. As a result of including the COUNTRY = 041 in your CONFIG.SYS file, subsequent requests for date and time show the results in the format customarily used in Switzerland. The date appears in the order day-month-year (August 14, 1988), with periods used as separators. The time appears in 24-hour format (6:07am), also with periods separating the hours.minutes.seconds.hundredths.

Finding the date and time was easy in this example. The real value of the COUNTRY code in CONFIG.SYS can be realized fully only by programmers using specialized assembly-language techniques. Thus, only a programmer can really obtain the specialized symbol and separator information necessary to customize an application program to the country it may run in. However, you can make many adjustments yourself.

Understanding Code Pages

A new feature in DOS 3.3, called *code pages,* gives DOS a complex ability to redefine its understanding of the keyboard you use. Code pages involve some complicated concepts, but with a little help and some extra knowledge, they can easily be understood. Let's start with the keyboard.

Keyboard Translation Table

The keyboard is simply a segregated group of buttons, monitored by a microprocessor, that sends a signal to DOS when any key is pressed. The signal that goes to DOS is called a *scan code.* A scan code is not a letter or an ASCII code, but simply a code that tells DOS which key has been pressed. It has nothing to do with what is printed on the physical key, but merely indicates the physical location of the key.

Whenever you press a key, whether DOS is busy or not, an event called an *interrupt* occurs inside the computer. One kind of interrupt occurs when a hardware device, such as a keyboard, asks for the attention of the CPU. The keyboard sends a small electrical signal—a scan code—to DOS, indicating which key was pressed. The part of DOS that receives and processes the interrupt is called a *device driver* (or sometimes an *interrupt handler*).

When the keyboard device driver receives a signal, it processes the scan code to determine which key was pressed *and* to convert the scan code back into an ASCII code. This translation is performed through a table in memory that compares scan codes and ASCII codes. Figure 11.2 diagrams this process.

> *Note:* During the entire process of handling each keyboard interrupt, DOS does not treat a scan code as any particular letter or symbol (such as the letter A), but simply as an ASCII code (such as 65).

Look at the different Personal System/2 keyboards used in the United States and France, shown in Figures 11.3 and 11.4. More than fifty other keyboard layouts are in use on different computers in different countries. DOS understands all of these; the complete layouts for these alternatives are displayed in your DOS user's manual.

On a U.S. keyboard, if you press *A*, its scan code will be translated into ASCII code 65. However, if you press the same key on a computer with a French keyboard translation routine embedded in the device driver, the same scan code will be converted to ASCII code 81, or the letter *Q*.

If you press a key combination such as Alt-Ctrl-2 with the U.S. translator installed, not much will happen, because the U.S. keyboard translator does not have an entry in its table for this scan code. However, if you press this key combination on a computer with the French keyboard translator in effect, the @ symbol will appear. The French translator understands this scan code and will match

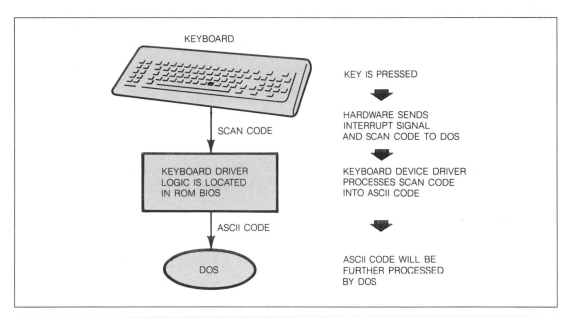

FIGURE 11.2: Processing keyboard interrupts. The logic for processing keyboard interrupts is contained in your computer's read-only memory (ROM). Because this logic is basic to a system's input and output functions, this portion of your system's code is called the Basic Input Output System (BIOS). The keyboard driver resides in the BIOS and translates the hardware signals (scan codes) into conventional ASCII codes for further processing by DOS and by your application programs.

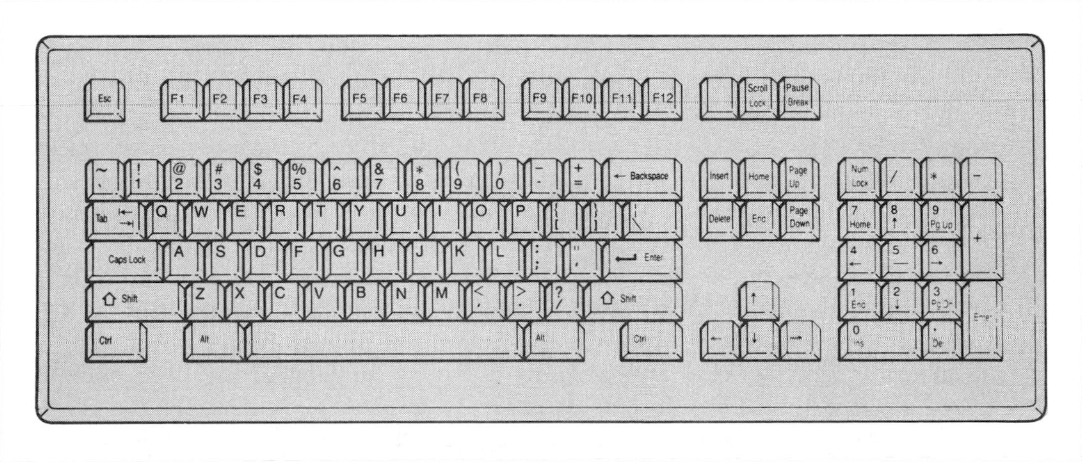

FIGURE 11.3: U.S. Personal System/2 keyboard. This keyboard has more function keys than earlier machines, more keys in general, and a different layout for some of the control keys, such as the cursor-control arrows and numeric keypad, than the French version.

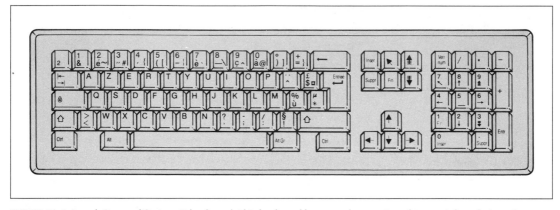

FIGURE 11.4: French Personal System/2 keyboard. This keyboard has more keys assigned to special symbols and accent marks used in the French language. It also has a different layout for some of the control keys, such as the cursor-control arrows and numeric keypad, than the U.S. version.

it up. The ASCII code generated will be 64, which is the same code generated by pressing Shift-2 with a U.S. keyboard translator. Both yield the same @ symbol. The two keyboard translation tables translate different keyboard scan codes to the same ASCII codes, allowing countries with different keyboards to use the same characters, even though the keys are labeled differently. Countries that have different keyboard layouts but still use the same character set are grouped into the same code page.

Code Pages

After determining what key was pressed on the keyboard and converting the scan code into an ASCII code by means of a translation table, DOS next determines where the ASCII code should go. If it goes to a disk drive, it is simply routed there and stored on the disk. If, however, it is destined for a monitor or printer, it is first processed by a *code page*. A code page is yet another translation table that converts an ASCII code into a printable or displayable character.

Five code pages are available in DOS 3.3. Table 11.3 shows the standard code page (numbered 437 in DOS) for the United States. (Refer to Appendix C for a complete explanation of the hexadecimal system shown in this table, as well as other number systems.) The other principal code page is the multilingual code page, numbered 850 (see Table 11.4). It contains a host of international characters.

You'll soon learn how to use and switch between these code pages, as well as the other three also available in DOS (Portugal, Norway, and Canadian French). See your DOS user's manual for the precise layouts of these other code pages.

Hex Digits 1st 2nd	0-	1-	2-	3-	4-	5-	6-	7-	8-	9-	A-	B-	C-	D-	E-	F-
0-		►		0	@	P	`	p	Ç	É	á	▓	└	╨	α	≡
1-	☺	◄	!	1	A	Q	a	q	ü	æ	í	▓	┴	╤	β	±
2-	●	↕	"	2	B	R	b	r	é	Æ	ó	▓	┬	╥	Γ	≥
3-	♥	‼	#	3	C	S	c	s	â	ô	ú	│	├	╙	π	≤
4-	♦	¶	$	4	D	T	d	t	ä	ö	ñ	┤	─	╘	Σ	⌠
5-	♣	§	%	5	E	U	e	u	à	ò	Ñ	╡	┼	╒	σ	⌡
6-	♠	▬	&	6	F	V	f	v	å	û	ª	╢	╞	╓	µ	÷
7-	•	↨	'	7	G	W	g	w	ç	ù	º	╖	╟	╫	τ	≈
8-	◘	↑	(	8	H	X	h	x	ê	ÿ	¿	╕	╚	╪	Φ	°
9-	○	↓	)	9	I	Y	i	y	ë	Ö	⌐	╣	╔	┘	Θ	∙
A-	◙	→	*	:	J	Z	j	z	è	Ü	¬	║	╩	┌	Ω	·
B-	♂	←	+	;	K	[	k	{	ï	¢	½	╗	╦	█	δ	√
C-	♀	∟	,	<	L	\	l	|	î	£	¼	╝	╠	▄	∞	ⁿ
D-	♪	↔	-	=	M	]	m	}	ì	¥	¡	╜	═	▌	φ	²
E-	♫	▲	.	>	N	^	n	~	Ä	Pt	«	╛	╬	▐	ε	■
F-	☼	▼	/	?	O	_	o	⌂	Å	ƒ	»	┐	╧	▄	∩	

TABLE 11.3: Code Page 437 for the United States

Code pages are simply character sets. As you saw in the last section, one character set (code page) can satisfy the needs of several different countries. Countries with significantly different character sets and keyboards are grouped into other code pages. The 21 different country codes (shown in Table 11.2) correlate altogether with at most 5 different character sets, so only 5 different code pages are needed. Remember, a code page has 256 entries, so even if in the U.S. you rarely use an accented *e*, it is included in one of the extra spaces in the U.S. character set. Figure 11.5 illustrates this relationship between code pages and country and keyboard codes. The keyboard code ensures that DOS knows what ASCII symbol was intended when a particular key is struck in any given country. The additional country code helps DOS decide what additional formatting information to merge with data during display and printing.

After the scan code has been translated into an ASCII code, it is matched to the currently active code page translation table. Now you're into the output side of DOS management. The device driver responsible for the output device now uses built-in logic to send a sequence of control instructions to the output device. These instructions describe precisely how to display the character that was

HEX DIGITS 1st / 2nd	0-	1-	2-	3-	4-	5-	6-	7-	8-	9-	A-	B-	C-	D-	E-	F-
0-		►		0	@	P	`	p	Ç	É	á	▓	└	ð	Ó	-
1-	☺	◄	!	1	A	Q	a	q	ü	æ	í	▓	┴	Ð	β	±
2-	☻	↕	"	2	B	R	b	r	é	Æ	ó	▓	┬	Ê	Ô	=
3-	♥	‼	#	3	C	S	c	s	â	ô	ú	│	├	Ë	Ò	¾
4-	♦	¶	$	4	D	T	d	t	ä	ö	ñ	┤	─	È	õ	¶
5-	♣	§	%	5	E	U	e	u	à	ò	Ñ	Á	┼	ı	Õ	§
6-	♠	—	&	6	F	V	f	v	å	û	ª	Â	ã	Í	µ	÷
7-	•	↨	'	7	G	W	g	w	ç	ù	º	À	Ã	Î	þ	¸
8-	◘	↑	(	8	H	X	h	x	ê	ÿ	¿	©	└	Ï	Þ	°
9-	○	↓	)	9	I	Y	i	y	ë	Ö	®	╣	╔	┘	Ú	¨
A-	◙	→	*	:	J	Z	j	z	è	Ü	¬	║	╩	┌	Û	·
B-	♂	←	+	;	K	[	k	{	ï	ø	½	╗	╦	■	Ù	¹
C-	♀	∟	,	<	L	\	l	|	î	£	¼	╝	╠	▬	ý	³
D-	♪	↔	-	=	M	]	m	}	ì	Ø	¡	═	=	¦	Ý	²
E-	♫	▲	.	>	N	^	n	~	Ä	×	«	¥	╬	Ì	´	■
F-	☼	▼	/	?	O	_	o	⌂	Å	ƒ	»	┐	¤	▬	'	■

TABLE 11.4: Code Page 850 for Multilingual Operations

represented by the ASCII code. The process by which DOS and the output device drivers convert the ASCII code to visual output is shown in Figure 11.6.

Devices and Their Drivers

All output consists of sequences of codes sent to an output device such as a monitor or printer. Unfortunately, not all monitors or printers act the same, have the same features, or can be controlled by the same device driver. In fact, sometimes the device driver consists of software instructions residing in your computer's main memory, and at other times these instructions reside in a special memory are built into the output device. Microsoft provides device drivers for two printers, the IBM Proprinter Model 4201 and the IBM Quietwriter III Printer Model 5202, as well as device drivers for the PC Convertible display (LCD) and the Enhanced Graphics Adapter used for the PC-XT, PC-AT, and Personal System/2 displays.

Each output device driver translates the requested output data into the specific commands needed to form the characters for each device. Figure 11.7 shows this

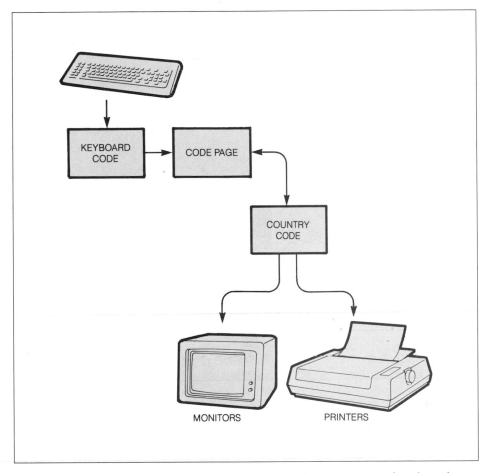

FIGURE 11.5: Keys pressed on a keyboard actually generate hardware interrupts and send signals to DOS called scan codes. The keyboard code that you select helps DOS interpret these scan codes and translate them into the appropriate ASCII code of the active code page. When displayed or printed, subsequent data is formatted on your monitor or printer using the country code value, which you can also specify.

part of the process. As the figure suggests, you must have one of the special monitors or printers to access any special additional symbols available in DOS 3.3's four code pages other than the U.S. page.

Translation Tables and Device Drivers

DOS 3.3 supports more than 50 different keyboard layouts and 11 languages. Microsoft supplies all of the necessary keyboard translation tables in a file called

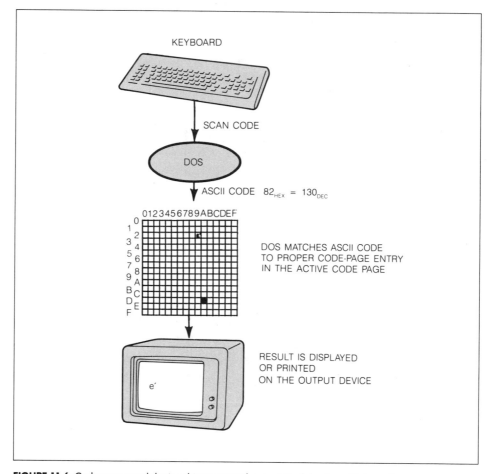

FIGURE 11.6: Code pages and device drivers control output. Each keyboard interrupt generates a hardware signal known as a scan code. The keyboard driver converts the scan code into an ASCII code that DOS looks up in the active code page. The appropriate symbol at that location in the table is then echoed to your monitor to visually confirm what you typed.

KEYBOARD.SYS, which you load into the computer by entering the KEYB command at the DOS prompt.

The output device drivers are loaded into memory from individual files. They are on the IBM startup disk in the files 4201.CPI, 5202.CPI, EGA.CPI, and LCD.CPI. *CPI* stands for code-page information; 4201 and 5202 refer to the IBM Proprinter and the IBM Quietwriter III Printer, respectively. EGA refers to both the standard Enhanced Graphics Adapter and the IBM Personal System/2 display types, and LCD drives the IBM Convertible's LCD screen.

As you know, a DOS device driver has five different code pages to choose from. Each of these is referred to by a unique number, as shown in Table 11.5.

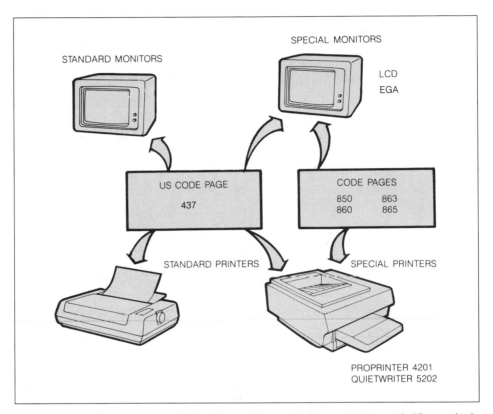

STANDARD MONITORS

SPECIAL MONITORS

LCD
EGA

US CODE PAGE

437

CODE PAGES

850   863
860   865

STANDARD PRINTERS

SPECIAL PRINTERS

PROPRINTER 4201
QUIETWRITER 5202

FIGURE 11.7: Sending output to standard and special devices. Code page 437 is provided for standard United States output to all monitors and printers. If your monitor or printer can display or print international symbols, you can also prepare and select up to four other code pages to obtain the special international sets of characters.

Since code page 437 is the standard U.S. code page that is used with any monitor, 437 is the default code page when DOS boots up. This is the only code page that can be used with devices other than the two printers and two monitors supported by the drivers included with DOS 3.3 (see Figure 11.7).

> *Note:* Some computers manufactured solely for foreign use have the foreign character set built in, as well as a keyboard with the appropriate key labels in place. These computers will not respond at all when you try to switch keyboard layouts with either the KEYB command or the Ctrl-Alt-function key combinations. No logic has been included to load additional keyboard tables, since the necessary non-U.S. tables are already there.

Figure 11.8 ties all of the preceding sections together. It shows the entire process of moving information from beginning to end—from the keyboard interrupt to the final display or printed output.

LANGUAGE	CODE PAGE
United States	437
Multilingual	850
Portuguese	860
Canadian French	863
Norwegian and Danish	865

TABLE 11.5: Code-Page Identification Numbers

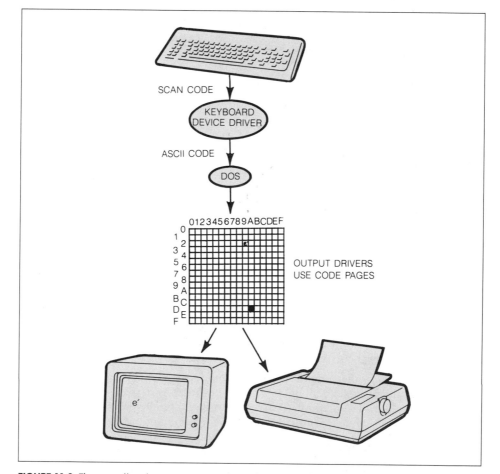

FIGURE 11.8: The overall code-page process. The code page mechanism uses code pages for both input and output. The keyboard device driver uses code pages to echo typed input to the screen, and later output of data and program results again uses the code pages to output the appropriate symbols to your printer and monitor.

Let's quickly review a last example of the process. Assume you've loaded the Canadian French keyboard translation table into the computer (you'll learn how to do this in the next section). You've also loaded code page 863 and the 4201.CPI device driver, as you wish to print a character on the Proprinter. The character you want to print is the 3/4 symbol, which is not included in the normal ASCII character set of U.S. computers or printers. The 3/4 symbol on the Canadian keyboard can be printed by using the key combination Alt-Shift- = .

When this key combination is pressed, DOS sends a scan code to the keyboard device driver, which routes the scan code to the keyboard translation table. Here, the scan code is matched against the ASCII table, and an ASCII code (in this case, 173) is sent back to DOS. DOS sees that this character was destined for the printer and sends it on its way. The code is now processed by the Proprinter, which uses the installed code page. The Proprinter's driver now translates ASCII 173 to a set of hardware instructions that describe how to print a 3/4 symbol.

WORKING WITH CODE PAGES

Now that you understand how code pages are used, you must learn the required sequence of DOS 3.3 commands necessary to implement them. You first need to learn how to tell DOS that you will be using the national language-support scheme (NLS), which is just another name for the code-page mechanism. You also need to learn how to prepare, select, and switch among the various code pages. The following sections will teach you the mechanics of the process. Figure 11.9 provides an overview of the DOS command sequences necessary for a complete international setup, which you will explore in this chapter.

After these startup steps shown in Figure 11.9 have been completed, you install an individual system by first bringing in some basic code required (NLS-FUNC does this). Next you must enter the MODE command to prepare any specialized output devices and then select the desired code page for sending output to that device. Last, you must enter a consistent KEYB command to ensure a correct match between keyboard entry and screen or printer output.

During the operation phase of international work, you can use the STATUS and REFRESH versions of the MODE command to determine current code page and output device connections, as well as to reestablish simple connections after a power failure. During operations, you can also change code pages (using CHCP) and adjust the quality of foreign language symbol output on a CGA screen (using GRAFTABL).

Loading Code-Page Support Routines

NLSFUNC (short for national language-support functions) is a DOS 3.3 command that permits the use of the new extended country information provided with DOS 3.3. This command loads all of the required country-specific

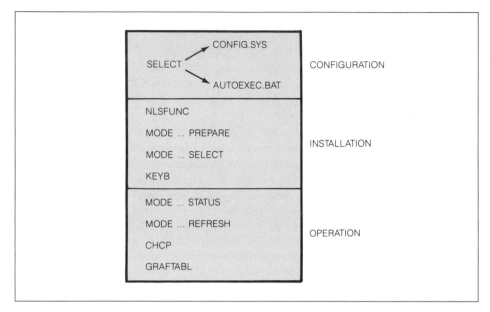

FIGURE 11.9: Command overview for international DOS operations. All necessary commands are grouped into three logical sections: configuration, installation, and operation. The SELECT command configures a disk for you with the required CONFIG.SYS and AUTOEXEC.BAT files.

information. It must be run *before* you attempt to select any code page other than the default (437). As part of the format for the NLSFUNC command, you must tell DOS where you've placed the COUNTRY.SYS file. This file contains information that defines the country standards, such as date and time formats, capitalization rules, and special symbol usage for each of the 21 available country codes (see Table 11.2). U.S. standards are assumed if you do not specify the location of the COUNTRY.SYS file.

Assuming you have created a DOS directory that contains COUNTRY.SYS, you can enter the command

NLSFUNC \DOS\COUNTRY.SYS

to load the code-page support routines into memory. No direct action or messages appears on the screen.

Loading Specific Code Pages

After preparing DOS for national language-support operations, you can select specific code pages to use. MODE is the primary command used for this purpose. In DOS 3.3 this command has several versions, all with a similar format:

MODE *DeviceName* **CODEPAGE** *Clause*

DeviceName is any valid DOS output reserved name, such as CON or LPT2. *Clause* represents a parameter you can use with several different values:

- Load the desired code pages with a PREPARE parameter; specify the number of code pages (one to five) available for output operations.
- Use the SELECT parameter to make one of the code pages active for a particular output device.
- Use the /STATUS parameter to display the status of all code pages and connected output devices supporting code-page operations.
- For advanced output devices that retain code-page information in memory located within the device itself (as opposed to main memory), use the REFRESH parameter to restore the information in case the device is turned off or loses power.

Let's consider the processing managed by the MODE command in more depth. You first use the PREPARE parameter to install the code-page information necessary for the output drivers to handle the special international characters. With the SELECT parameter you then select the code page to be activated on the specified device. This means you can have several code pages loaded into the device at once, but only one can be active at any one time. At any time, you can use the /STATUS parameter to display the active code page and all of the other code pages available. Finally, with REFRESH you can reinstall the currently active output driver in the specified device if it has been erased by a power failure.

With the PREPARE parameter, you can load one or several code pages for a device with one MODE command. This requires you to specify the device reserved name, the list of allowable code pages (one or more), and the file containing the output driver. Code page 437 is the default code page; it is automatically loaded into the device. Code page 437 is also the only code page that can access a nonspecified device (that is, one that IBM has not specifically written drivers for).

Essentially, a small buffer is set up for each device, and this buffer can contain up to five code-page specifications, one of which is active at a time. For example, entering

MODE CON CODEPAGE PREPARE = ((850,437) C:\DOS\EGA.CPI)

loads the code-page information file EGA.CPI, specifies that code pages 850 and 437 be selected for possible activation, and attaches these code-page values to the EGA display.

Tip: In all versions of the MODE command, you can enter CP instead of CODEPAGE. In addition, you can enter PREPARE as PREP, SELECT as SEL, REFRESH as REF, and STATUS as STA. You can reduce your typing burden by using these abbreviations, as well as save time and reduce the likelihood of errors. This chapter uses the full spelling for the sake of clarity only.

Suppose that later you decide to replace 850 with 863 and to make code page 865 available. You would enter

MODE CON CODEPAGE PREPARE = ((863,,865) C:\DOS\EGA.CPI)

The two commas hold the place of the second code page, thereby leaving 437 (the U.S. code page) as the second code page. If you had specified ((,850,437) instead, then the first code page would have been saved, and the second and third written over and reset to 850 and 437, respectively.

If you execute this command and the requested device is unavailable (not hooked up), you will get the message

Codepage operation not supported on this device

Assuming you really do have a device that supports code-page operations, check to see that it is connected properly to your system, that it is powered up, and that it is on line.

> *Warning:* If the device driver for your output device is resident in hardware (for example, like IBM Quietwriter III Printer Model 5202), using PREPARE is unnecessary, since it overwrites the hardware page. See your DOS user's manual for more information about hardware code pages.

You can use the next parameter for the international version of the MODE command only after you have properly prepared your code pages with PREPARE; the SELECT parameter works only if the requested code-page device driver has been loaded. SELECT activates the specified code page on the specified device. For example, entering

MODE CON CODEPAGE SELECT = 850

makes code page 850 the active code page for the console or the display device. Using this parameter in the previous MODE…PREPARE statement would prepare code page 850 for an EGA display.

When you want to see information on the currently active code page as well as a list of selectable code pages for a specific active device, you need enter only

MODE CON CODEPAGE /STATUS

DOS will display information about the current code page assigned to the monitor and keyboard.

The last parameter, REFRESH, is useful if you need to turn your printer off while you are printing with a code page that is not the default. The output device drivers stay resident inside the device they drive. The available code pages and their related information are available through DOS, which is resident in your computer. When a device driver is installed, DOS copies the code-page information in the computer and loaded into the memory of the device. If the device is turned off, then its memory—and hence its modified driver—is lost. However, the original copy is still in the computer's memory. Instead of having to load the code page again with PREPARE, REFRESH just makes another copy and sends it to the device's memory.

For example, suppose you've entered the following sequence of commands:

MODE LPT1 CODEPAGE PREPARE = ((850,437) \DOS\4201.CPI)
MODE LPT1 CODEPAGE SELECT = 850

These indicate that you have installed code-page information for the IBM 4201 Proprinter and that you have two code pages to choose from, with 850 the currently active code page. Selecting a code page (with SELECT) causes the code-page driver to be copied into the hardware device (in this case, the printer connected to LPT1). If you turn the Proprinter off and then back on (perhaps to reset some switches), it would lose its local memory copy of the code-page information. To reload the code-page driver without using system time to retrieve it from the disk, you can issue the command

MODE LPT1 CODEPAGE REFRESH

Loading a Keyboard Translation Table

You have properly prepared your system to use national language support with the NLSFUNC command. You have also correctly installed the desired code-page information with the MODE PREPARE parameter, and you have selected a specific code page to with the MODE SELECT parameter. Your next step involves the KEYB command. This command loads a new keyboard translation table for a specific country. In fact, it loads a complete replacement for the keyboard driver resident in your computer hardware (in ROM BIOS). You can now select from the 21 different country codes in Table 11.2.

If you were using alternate character sets in previous versions of DOS, then you need to use code page 850 in DOS 3.3, since the character sets and keyboard layouts of the previous versions are incompatible with those of this version (see Table 11.6).

Page 850 is the multilingual code page, which can support the primary character symbols used by all countries. If you switch between documents from different countries, you should load code page 850 in addition to your native-code page so that you can view these other documents.

Note: Versions of DOS earlier than 3.3 were significantly more limited in their support of national-language operations. In particular, foreign-country support was limited to only five alternatives to the United States keyboard and ASCII character set. The more general KEYB command discussed in this chapter was preceded in earlier versions with five specific commands that loaded into memory the code necessary to support the five acceptable keyboard layouts. The appropriate one-line command was typically included in

COUNTRY	KEYBOARD CODE	EXISTING CODE PAGE	NEW CODE PAGE
Australia	US	437	850
Belgium	BE	437	850
Canada—English	US	437	850
Canada—French	CF	863	850
Denmark	DK	865	850
Finland	SU	437	850
France	FR	437	850
Germany	GR	437	850
Italy	IT	437	850
Latin America	LA	437	850
Netherlands	NL	437	850
Norway	NO	865	850
Portugal	PO	860	850
Spain	SP	437	850
Sweden	SV	437	850
Switzerland—French	SF	437	850
Switzerland—German	SG	437	850
United Kingdom	UK	437	850
United States	US	437	850

TABLE 11.6: Converting between DOS Version 3.3 Code Pages and Earlier Versions

the AUTOEXEC.BAT file. These layouts were for Spain, Italy, United Kingdom, Germany, and France. The DOS commands which could be run to bring in the proper code were, respectively, KEYBSP, KEYBIT, KEYBUK, KEYBGR, and KEYBFR.

The general format for the KEYB command is

KEYB *KeyCode, CodePage, FileSpec*

where *KeyCode* is one of the two-letter country codes in Table 11.2, *CodePage* is one of the five three-digit code-page numbers, and *FileSpec* is the full path name to the keyboard definition file KEYBOARD.SYS. For example, entering the command

KEYB NL, 850, \DOS\KEYBOARD.SYS

loads the Netherlands keyboard translation table, based on code page 850, which is contained in the KEYBOARD.SYS file. Located in the DOS directory, the KEYBOARD.SYS file contains all of the keyboard translation tables.

Once you complete this initialization, pressing the keys on the keyboard will no longer necessarily result in the letter, number, or character shown on the key. The assumption is that you will be using one of the scores of different keyboard layouts, each with its own key labels. In fact, if you're taking advantage of the keyboard reconfiguration capability but are still using your original keyboard, you should get a new set of key labels, switch the key labels around, or at least put new labels on the keys that have been changed.

You can have up to two keyboard translation tables in memory at one time, but one of these must be the standard U.S. table. To switch between the U.S. and another translation table, use these key combinations:

- Ctrl-Alt-F1 for the standard U.S. translation table
- Ctrl-Alt-F2 for a non-U.S. translation table

Key Sequences for Accented Characters

Some languages supported by DOS require more accented characters than there are keys to assign. To accommodate these languages, DOS allows special two-key sequences to represent specially accented characters. For instance, certain foreign letters require a circumflex over them. On the French keyboard, this symbol looks like the control, or caret, symbol located above the 6 on the top row of a U.S. keyboard. To create this particular language-dependent effect, you press the lowercase key just to the right of the letter *p* and *then* press the letter you want to put the circumflex over. In other words, you must employ a two-keystroke sequence to generate the two-part character symbol.

These special keys that initiate a two-part character sequence are referred to as *dead keys* in DOS. If you make a mistake in typing the sequence, DOS will usually beep, display the erroneous result, and require you to erase the error and reenter the proper dead-key sequence. With dead keys, DOS provides yet another time-saving capability, saving you from having to add accents and other special marks to your text after it is output.

Switching between Available Code Pages

If you want to switch from one code page to another—for example, if you are switching between documents written by personnel either in or for different countries—you can use the CHCP command to change the currently loaded code page. CHCP is a very simple command to use. Its general format is

CHCP *CodePage*

By issuing the command

CHCP 850

you can replace the currently active code page with code page 850. You can use any of the other four possible code-page numbers if they have been properly prepared with the MODE command first.

The CHCP command does not have a parameter indicating which output device is being selected. That's because CHCP changes the active code page on all prepared output devices to the requested number.

> *Tip:* If you want to change only the code page on a particular device, use the MODE command with SELECT. Use the CHCP command to change all prepared code-page devices at once.

Displaying Extended ASCII Codes on a Color Graphics Adapter

A CGA monitor shows less detail than EGA, PGA, and VGA monitors because it has fewer pixels. When your CGA monitor is in graphics mode, you must use the GRAFTABL command to display the nonstandard characters with ASCII codes above 128. Entering

GRAFTABL 860

loads the Portugese code page and displays the following message:

Portugese Version of Graphic Character Set Table has just been Loaded.

This means that the characters—whether graphics symbols or national symbols—that occupy the ASCII codes higher than code 128 are accessible, and the ones displayed are those from the special Portuguese code page.

To dramatize the necessity of this command, Figure 11.10 shows the extended ASCII codes for the U.S. code page when a CGA monitor is in graphics mode. As you can see, the characters are indecipherable. After GRAFTABL 437 is executed, however, the codes are readable, as shown in Figure 11.11.

> *Note:* Use the GRAFTABL command only if you run programs that set the video mode to graphics. Otherwise, you lose the memory occupied by the alternate character set and gain nothing in return.

If you use GRAFTABL, make sure that the path is set properly so that DOS can find the command. Also be sure to run the GRAFTABL command *before* you invoke the programs that use the CGA graphics mode. If you need to use GRAFTABL often, you should add the GRAFTABL command to your AUTOEXEC.BAT file (you will learn how later in this chapter).

PREPARING AN INTERNATIONAL DOS SYSTEM DISK

DOS provides a special command, SELECT, which can help you if your principal goal is a system disk that supports code-page switching. With the following

```
129 =¢ 130 =¼ 131 =ª 132 =. 133 =% 134 =¼ 135 =¾ 136 =¼ 137 =& 138 =½ 139 =≈
140 =¼ 141 =¼ 142 =¾ 143 =⅛ 144 =¼ 145 =⊦ 146 =¼ 147 =¼ 148 =½ 149 =½ 150 =¾
151 =¼ 152 =¾ 153 =¾ 154 =⅝ 155 =½ 156 =½ 157 =¼ 158 =¼ 159 =½ 160 =¾ 161 =¾
162 =¼ 163 =¼ 164 =⅛ 165 =½ 166 =¼ 167 =¾ 168 =¼ 169 =½ 170 =½ 171 =½ 172 =½
173 =¼ 174 =¾ 175 =¼ 176 =¼ 177 =½ 178 =½ 179 =¾ 180 =¾ 181 =½ 182 =¼ 183 =¾
184 =¼ 185 =¼ 186 =½ 187 =½ 188 =½ 189 =¾ 190 =¼ 191 =¼ 192 =¼ 193 =¾ 194 =¾
195 =¼ 196 =¼ 197 =¼ 198 =½ 199 =¾ 200 =¾ 201 =¼ 202 =¾ 203 =¾ 204 =¾ 205 =½
206 =¾ 207 =¾ 208 =¾ 209 =¾ 210 =¾ 211 =¼ 212 =½ 213 =½ 214 =¾ 215 =½ 216 =½
217 =¾ 218 =½ 219 =½ 220 =½ 221 =½ 222 =¾ 223 =¾ 224 =¾ 225 =¾ 226 =½ 227 =½
228 =½ 229 =¼ 230 =½ 231 =½ 232 =¾ 233 =½ 234 =¼ 235 =½ 236 =¾ 237 =¾ 238 =¾
239 =¼ 240 =¼ 241 =½ 242 =¾ 243 =½ 244 =½ 245 =½ 246 =¾ 247 =¾ 248 =½ 249 =½
250 =½ 251 =½ 252 =¾ 253 =¾ 254 =¼ 255 =
```

FIGURE 11.10: Extended ASCII codes before executing GRAFTABL. On a CGA monitor, the resolution is insufficient under normal circumstances to display the more detailed characters with ASCII codes from 129 to 255. The GRAFTABL command enables these otherwise unreadable characters to be read on this monitor. This figure shows the unreadable view of the characters before using the GRAFTABL command. The next figure shows the results after invoking the command.

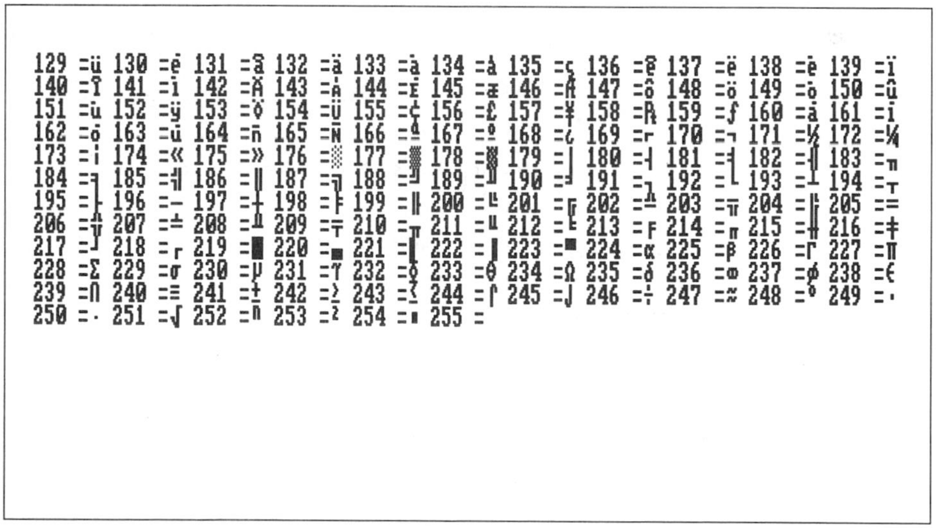

```
129 =ü 130 =é 131 =â 132 =ä 133 =à 134 =å 135 =ç 136 =ê 137 =ë 138 =è 139 =ï
140 =î 141 =ì 142 =Ä 143 =Å 144 =É 145 =æ 146 =Æ 147 =ô 148 =ö 149 =ò 150 =û
151 =ù 152 =ÿ 153 =Ö 154 =Ü 155 =¢ 156 =£ 157 =¥ 158 =₧ 159 =ƒ 160 =á 161 =í
162 =ó 163 =ú 164 =ñ 165 =Ñ 166 =ª 167 =º 168 =¿ 169 =⌐ 170 =¬ 171 =½ 172 =¼
173 =¡ 174 =« 175 =» 176 =░ 177 =▒ 178 =▓ 179 =│ 180 =┤ 181 =╡ 182 =╢ 183 =╖
184 =╕ 185 =╣ 186 =║ 187 =╗ 188 =╝ 189 =╜ 190 =╛ 191 =┐ 192 =└ 193 =┴ 194 =┬
195 =├ 196 =─ 197 =┼ 198 =╞ 199 =╟ 200 =╚ 201 =╔ 202 =╩ 203 =╦ 204 =╠ 205 ═
206 =╬ 207 =╧ 208 =╨ 209 =╤ 210 =╥ 211 =╙ 212 =╘ 213 =╒ 214 =╓ 215 =╫ 216 =╪
217 =┘ 218 =┌ 219 =█ 220 =▄ 221 =▌ 222 =▐ 223 =▀ 224 =α 225 =ß 226 =Γ 227 =π
228 =Σ 229 =σ 230 =µ 231 =τ 232 =Φ 233 =Θ 234 =Ω 235 =δ 236 =∞ 237 =φ 238 =ε
239 =∩ 240 =≡ 241 =± 242 =≥ 243 =≤ 244 =⌠ 245 =⌡ 246 =÷ 247 =≈ 248 =° 249 =·
250 =· 251 =√ 252 =ⁿ 253 =² 254 =■ 255 =
```

FIGURE 11.11: Extended ASCII codes after executing GRAFTABL. This figure shows clearly readable characters with ASCII codes 129 to 255 after the GRAFTABL command has been executed.

methods and commands, the delimiter format and keyboard information for each country can be installed permanently on a disk.

Installing Country and Keyboard Information

The SELECT command reads all the necessary DOS information from your startup and operating disks, now located on a diskette in drive A or B. It manages the formatting of the destination disk and the copying of all necessary DOS files onto this other disk. (The destination disk must not be the same as the source disk.) You must specify the desired three-digit country code and the two-letter keyboard code, both from the list in Table 11.2.

The required format of the SELECT command is

SELECT *Source Destination xxx yy*

Source is either A or B and is the drive containing KEYBOARD.SYS, COUNTRY.SYS, FORMAT.COM, and XCOPY.EXE. *Destination* is the drive and path to which the DOS command files will be copied. (The root directory is the default, but if you use the SELECT command to set up a hard disk, you would be advised to arrange a specialized subdirectory to hold the appropriate files.) The *xxx* is the country code, and the *yy* is the keyboard code. Since the U.S. keyboard file is resident in the computer's memory, it does not need to be on the source disk.

> *Warning:* If you are using a high-density drive as the destination drive for the SELECT command, you *must* use high-capacity diskettes. Also, since the SELECT command uses the FORMAT command, anything on the destination disk will be destroyed during the preparation of the disk. Since you can prepare a hard disk drive in this way, you must be careful.

When you first execute SELECT, the following message appears on the screen:

SELECT is used to install DOS the first time. SELECT erases everything on the specified target and then installs DOS.
Do you want to continue (Y/N)?

Entering Y starts the process and entering N aborts it.

Here is an example of the SELECT command. Entering

SELECT B: C:\JUDD 001 US

formats and copies the DOS command files to drive C, directory JUDD, executed from drive B, and installs with the U.S. rules for date, time, and so on in drive C.

The SELECT command also creates two files on the destination disk. These are an initial AUTOEXEC.BAT file, which contains

PATH \;\JUDD;
KEYB US 437 \JUDD\KEYBOARD.SYS
ECHO OFF
CLS
DATE
TIME
VER

and the CONFIG.SYS file, which contains

COUNTRY = 001,437,\JUDD\COUNTRY.SYS

The next section provides more details about these two files. SELECT also copies all of the contents of the source disk, including COMMAND.COM, into the specified directory. The six files that must be accessible on your source drive for this command to work are COMMAND.COM, FORMAT.COM, SELECT.COM, XCOPY.EXE, KEYBOARD.SYS, and COUNTRY.SYS.

MODIFYING THE REQUIRED SYSTEM FILES YOURSELF

The CONFIG.SYS and AUTOEXEC.BAT files can contain statements that will automate some of the processes for setting up an international DOS system disk if you don't want to rely on SELECT alone. CONFIG.SYS is discussed earlier in this chapter and in Chapter 10, and AUTOEXEC.BAT is discussed in more detail in Chapter 9. You can make these adjustments with your own word processor, with DOS's EDLIN editor, or by using the COPY command. You can use COPY to add a line (say, *FileName*) to any ASCII file in the following way. Typing the single command

COPY *FileName* **+ CON**

will allow you to enter as many lines as you like from the console. When you are done entering lines to be added, press Ctrl-Z and Return. You will return to the DOS prompt.

Updating the CONFIG.SYS File for International Support

You can use the DEVICE configuration command in CONFIG.SYS to load the various drivers needed for code-page switching. Assuming you have typed the preceding command or are using an editor and are creating or modifying a CONFIG.SYS file, adding the following lines will install the various

required drivers. In these cases, you need a different DEVICE line in your CONFIG.SYS for each different printer and display device.

The sample entry

DEVICE = *D:*\DISPLAY.SYS CON: = (*Type,Hwcp,x*)

in your CONFIG.SYS file loads the specialized display device drivers. *D* is the location of the DISPLAY.SYS file. *Type* is either LCD or EGA, depending on the display being used. *Hwcp* is the code-page number(s) supported directly by the hardware device, and *x* indicates the number of code pages to be added. The value for *x* should be 1 if 437 is the current code page, and 2 if it isn't.

This entry loads the specialized device drivers supporting the Proprinter and Quietwriter:

DEVICE = *D:*\PRINTER.SYS LPT1: = (*Type,Hwcp,x*)

The parameters are the same as those just described, except that *Type* can be 4201 or 5202.

The IBM Proprinter Model 4201 reserves a hardware memory area in its own read-only memory (ROM) specifically for code-page information. The IBM Quietwriter III Printer Model 5202 uses hardware font cartridges for the same support purpose.

As discussed in the section "Installing Country and Keyboard Information," you can also set the country automatically at the time your system boots up. The line to add to your CONFIG.SYS file is

COUNTRY = *xxx*

where *xxx* is the appropriate country code. This version, however, assumes that COUNTRY.SYS is available in the root directory, and that code page 437 will be used.

Updating Your AUTOEXEC.BAT File

You can add commands to the AUTOEXEC.BAT file in the same way as you can to the CONFIG.SYS file. Including the KEYB command in the AUTO-EXEC.BAT file loads the keyboard translation table and country codes automatically. For example, adding

KEYB FR 033

to your AUTOEXEC.BAT automatically loads the keyboard and country information for France.

You can also include versions of the NLSFUNC, MODE, and CHCP commands, which will work in conjunction with the CONFIG.SYS statements. For example, the following lines included in your AUTOEXEC.BAT file would initialize national language-support operations, prepare code pages 863, 437, and 850, load the keyboard information file for France, and then select 850 as the active code page for both output devices:

NLSFUNC
MODE CON: CP PREPARE = ((863,437,850) \DOS\EGA.CPI)
MODE CON: CP PREPARE = ((863,437,850) \DOS\4201.CPI)
KEYB FR 033
CHCP 850

INTERNATIONAL SETUP IN DOS VERSIONS 3.0–3.2

Versions of DOS earlier than 3.3 had markedly less international flexibility. The two principal requirements for international operations are to select a desired keyboard layout, and to specify a country. The latter is managed by entering one of five separate DOS commands that brings into memory the required foreign keyboard table.

The US keyboard table is always primary and is accessible by pressing the key combination Ctrl-Alt-F1. Once an alternate table has been loaded, that particular configuration is activated by pressing the key combination Ctrl-Alt-F2. Each of five alternate keyboard tables is accessible by simply entering the appropriate keyboard command from Table 11.7.

DOS COMMAND	COUNTRY
KEYBFR	France
KEYBGR	Germany
KEYBIT	Italy
KEYBSP	Spain
KEYBUK	United Kingdom

TABLE 11.7: Keyboard Layouts for DOS 3.0–3.2

For example, to load the arrangement of keys for a keyboard in Italy, you simply enter:

KEYBIT

Preparing the DOS internal tables for local currency symbols as well as decimal, time, and date separator symbols requires a COUNTRY command in the

CODE	COUNTRY
001	United States
031	Netherlands
032	Belgium
033	France
034	Spain
039	Italy
041	Switzerland
044	United Kingdom
045	Denmark
046	Sweden
047	Norway
049	Germany
061	Australia
358	Finland
972	Israel

TABLE 11.8: Country Codes for DOS 3.0–3.2

CONFIG.SYS file. In these earlier versions of DOS, however, the choice of country codes was somewhat smaller than in DOS 3.3. Table 11.8 lists the allowable country codes for use in the CONFIG.SYS file of a DOS 3.0, 3.1, or 3.2 system.

For example, to initialize your system for the local symbol and separator customs seen in Israel, you enter:

COUNTRY = 972

in your CONFIG.SYS system file.

DOS COMMANDS FOR INTERNATIONAL SETUP

This section presents reference entries for the DOS commands for international setup discussed in this chapter.

CHCP

This command allows you to change the currently loaded code page for all eligible installed devices.

SYNTAX

CHCP [*xxx*]

    xxx   is the code-page number.

TYPE

Internal.

USAGE

The NLSFUNC command must be loaded prior to using CHCP. Although this command is internal, it may need to access the COUNTRY.SYS file. Should this be the case, and should the COUNTRY.SYS file not be on the default drive, DOS will display the message ''File not found.''

RESTRICTIONS

The corresponding device drivers for the specified code page must be available. NLSFUNC must have been executed previous to this command.

EXAMPLE

Activating code page 850 for all installed devices only requires that you enter:

    CHCP 850

COUNTRY

This command specifies the nation whose date, currency, and other formats are to be used in DOS operations.

SYNTAX

COUNTRY = *xxx*,[*yyy*] [,*FileSpec*]

    xxx   is the three-digit international code of each country.

    yyy   is the specified code page.

    FileSpec   is the location and name of the file containing the country information; the default is \COUNTRY.SYS.

TYPE

Configuration.

USAGE

Since the format of such things as the date and time may change from country to country, your computer must be able to recognize and adapt to these different formats. The COUNTRY command has provisions for up to 21 country codes, and it will also call up a specified code page.

EXAMPLE

In order to specify Israel (country code 972) as the country of operations, using the international code page 850, you merely need to enter:

COUNTRY = 972,850

GRAFTABL

This command displays the ASCII character set for the code page specified.

SYNTAX

[*D:Path*]GRAFTABL [437¦860¦863¦865¦/STATUS]

D:Path	is the drive and path where the command file is located if it is not in the current directory.
437	loads the U.S. code page.
860	loads the Portugese code page.
863	loads the Canadian code page.
865	loads the Norwegian and Danish code page.
/STATUS	shows the number of the code page currently in use.

TYPE

External.

USAGE

It is nice to be able to display the full ASCII range of characters on the screen so that you can see exactly what you are dealing with. If you have a Color

Graphics Adapter, this command will enable you to display the ASCII characters that have codes from 128 to 255.

EXAMPLE

To read the Portuguese code page characters above ASCII 128 on a CGA monitor, you must enter:

GRAFTABL 860

KEYB

This command is used to load a new keyboard translation table for a specific country. There are 21 country codes to choose from.

SYNTAX

[*D:Path*]KEYB [*xx*[,[*yyy*],[*FileSpec*]]]

D:Path	is the drive and path where the command file is located if it is not in the current directory.
xx	is a keyboard code representing a country.
yyy	is the code page to be used.
FileSpec	is the drive, path, file name, and extension of the keyboard definition file (the default is \KEYBOARD.SYS).

USAGE

KEYB is only used when DOS version 3.3 is employed in the preparation or use of files for, in, or from countries other than the United States. Since keyboard layouts vary, as do the collections of special characters produced by application programs, this command becomes important for all international work under DOS.

EXAMPLE

Loading a keyboard table to be used in Sweden requires that you enter:

KEYB SV,850

Omitting the final parameter assumes that the KEYBOARD.SYS file is located in the root directory of the boot drive.

KEYB*XX*

The equivalent of KEYB in versions before 3.3, KEYB*XX* loads one of five keyboard translation tables.

SYNTAX

KEYB*XX*

    XX   is one of the five keyboard codes:

            FR   France
            GR   Germany
            IT   Italy
            SP   Spain
            UK   United Kingdom

TYPE

External.

USAGE

KEYB*xx* is only used when a DOS version earlier than 3.3 is employed in the preparation or use of files for, in, or from countries other than the United States. Since keyboard layouts vary, as do the collections of special characters produced by application programs, this command becomes important for all international work under DOS.

MODE

The MODE command controls and redirects output.

SYNTAX

(1)   *[D:Path]***MODE LPT***x:* **[***CPL***][,[***LPT***][,P]]**
(2)   *[D:Path]***MODE LPT***x:* = **COM***y*
(3)   *[D:Path]***MODE COM***y***[:]***Baud***[,[***Parity***][,[***Bits***][,P]]**
(4)   *[D:Path]***MODE** *Type*
(5)   *[D:Path]***MODE [***Type***],** *Shift* **[,T]**
(6)   *[D:Path]***MODE** *Device* **CODEPAGE PREPARE = ((***CP***)** *FileSpec***)**
(7)   *[D:Path]***MODE** *Device* **CODEPAGE PREPARE = ((***CPList***)***FileSpec***)**
(8)   *[D:Path]***MODE** *Device* **CODEPAGE SELECT = ***CP*

(9) **[D:Path]MODE** *Device* **CODEPAGE[/STATUS]**
(10) **[D:Path]MODE** *Device* **CODEPAGE REFRESH**

Note: The numbers in parentheses shown here are used only for reference to the accompanying discussion. Do *not* enter them as part of your MODE commands.

D:Path	is the drive and path where the command file is located if it is not in the current directory.
x	is a printer number.
CPL	is the number of characters per line.
LPI	is the number of lines per inch.
P	causes the computer to retry accessing the port continuously during time-out errors.
y	is a serial-port number.
Baud	is a baud rate for the COM port (110, 150, 300, 600, 1200, 2400, 4800, 9600, or 19200).
Parity	is a parity value for the COM port; it can be even, odd, or none (the default is even).
Bits	is combination of two parameters specifying the number of stop and data bits used.
Type	is the display type being used. It is specified as 40, 80, BW40, BW80, CO40, CO80, or MONO.
Shift	is the direction for a screen shift, either L or R.
T	puts a test pattern on the screen for checking the screen alignment when shifting.
Device	is a valid device name (CON, LPT1, and so on).
CP	is a code-page number (437, 850, 860, 863, or 865).
CPList	is a list of code-page numbers.
FileSpec	is the file containing the code-page data. Its value is 4201.CPI for the IBM Proprinter; 5202.CPI for the IBM Quietwriter III Printer; EGA.CPI for EGA displays; or LCD.CPI for LCD displays.
/STATUS	displays the active code page and the other available code pages for *Device*.

TYPE

External.

USAGE

There are ten formats for this useful command. The first selects various print modes on parallel printers, the second redirects output, and the third changes the parameters of the serial port. Format 4 changes the display type, and format 5 sets the video mode and, simultaneously, adjusts the horizontal alignment of the monitor.

The MODE command can also work with code pages. Formats 6 and 7 install code-page device drivers in the specified device. Format 8 selects the code page to be activated for the specified device. (You can have several code pages loaded into the device at once, but only one can be active at any one time.) Format 9 displays the active code page and then displays all of the code pages that can be activated for the specified device.

Format 10 reinstalls the currently active device driver in the specified device if it was erased. This comes in handy if for some reason you need to turn your printer off. Instead of using format 1 or 2 to reload the driver, which in fact is already in computer memory anyway, you can use format 10 to make another copy and place it into the device's memory.

EXAMPLES

As you can see from the syntax entries above, MODE performs many DOS tasks. In the international operations, its primary tasks are to prepare and select code pages for specific devices. Preparing code pages 860 and 850 for an EGA device, using the EGA.CPI file located in the directory \SYS requires that you enter:

MODE CON CODEPAGE PREPARE = ((860,850) C:\SYS\EGA.CPI)

Subsequently, to make code page 860 active on that device at any time requires:

MODE CON CODEPAGE SELECT = 860

A similar sequence is required to prepare the same two code pages for use on an IBM Quietwriter III printer, then to select code page 850:

MODE LPT1 CODEPAGE PREPARE = ((860,850) \DOS\5202.CPI)
MODE LPT1 CODEPAGE SELECT = 850

NLSFUNC

NLSFUNC supports national-language features and code-page switching.

SYNTAX

[*D:Path*]NLSFUNC [*FileSpec*]

D:Path	is the drive and path where the command file is located if it is not in the current directory.
FileSpec	specifies the location and name of the country-specific code file (the default is \COUNTRY.SYS).

TYPE

External.

USAGE

NLSFUNC uses the new extended country information provided with DOS 3.3 to load the part of the keyboard translation table containing the country-specific information.

EXAMPLE

DOS 3.3's national language support functions can be loaded into memory from the COUNTRY.SYS file by simply entering:

NLSFUNC \SYS\COUNTRY.SYS

This example assumes that the COUNTRY.SYS file is located in the \SYS directory.

SELECT

SELECT allows you to specify a new keyboard layout and country-specific date and time formats.

SYNTAX

[*D:Path*]SELECT [[A: ¦ B:]*DestD:*[*DestPath*]] *xxx yy*

D:Path	is an optional drive and path where the command file is located.
A: or B:	is the source drive that contains the command files and country information (A: is the default).

DestD:DestPath	is the drive and optional path of the disk to be formatted. The root directory is the default for an unspecified *DestPath*.
xxx	specifies the country code.
yy	specifies the keyboard code.

TYPE

External.

USAGE

This command is used extremely infrequently. When you need to prepare a DOS system diskette for use with a particular keyboard and different country information, the SELECT command will perform multiple steps for you automatically. In effect, this command is rather like a batch file that comes with DOS to do this infrequent chore.

RESTRICTIONS

Drives A and B are the only source drives, and the destination drive must not be the same as the source drive. The U.S. keyboard file is resident in the computer's memory, so it does not need to be on the source disk. CONFIG.SYS and AUTOEXEC.BAT files are created on *DestD*. High-capacity diskettes must be used in high-capacity drives.

Warning: SELECT uses FORMAT, so anything on the destination disk will be destroyed after this command is used. SELECT may be used on a hard disk, so be careful.

EXAMPLE

You can use the SELECT command to create a system disk that will have the necessary CONFIG.SYS and AUTOEXEC.BAT files for Spanish-language operations by entering:

SELECT B: C:\FOREIGN 034 SP

This entry will initialize the system disk in the B: drive, place the required international files in the \FOREIGN subdirectory, and generate the proper CONFIG.SYS and AUTOEXEC.BAT entries for Spanish operations.

SUMMARY

DOS and the PC family of computers are used worldwide. DOS thus provides features that allow you to customize your operating version by country. Although the specific commands and functions for national language support are used by only a small percentage of users, if you are among this group, this chapter is critical.

For additional information about device drivers and about the CONFIG.SYS file, see

- Chapter 10, "Configuration Possibilities"

For additional information about the MODE command, see

- Chapter 12, "Computer Communications"

For additional information on ASCII codes and numbering systems, see

- Appendix C, "ASCII Codes, Code Pages, and Numbering Systems"

PART

5

COMMUNICATIONS

Computers can do many marvelous things for you, but they must be able to output their results to be of any use. This section discusses how computers communicate. You will learn the fundamentals of serial and parallel data transmission, so you can make better choices and decisions about how to transmit data. You will also learn about DOS ports and the actual connections with peripheral devices. Finally, you learn about local area networks and how you can connect to a LAN from your DOS computer.

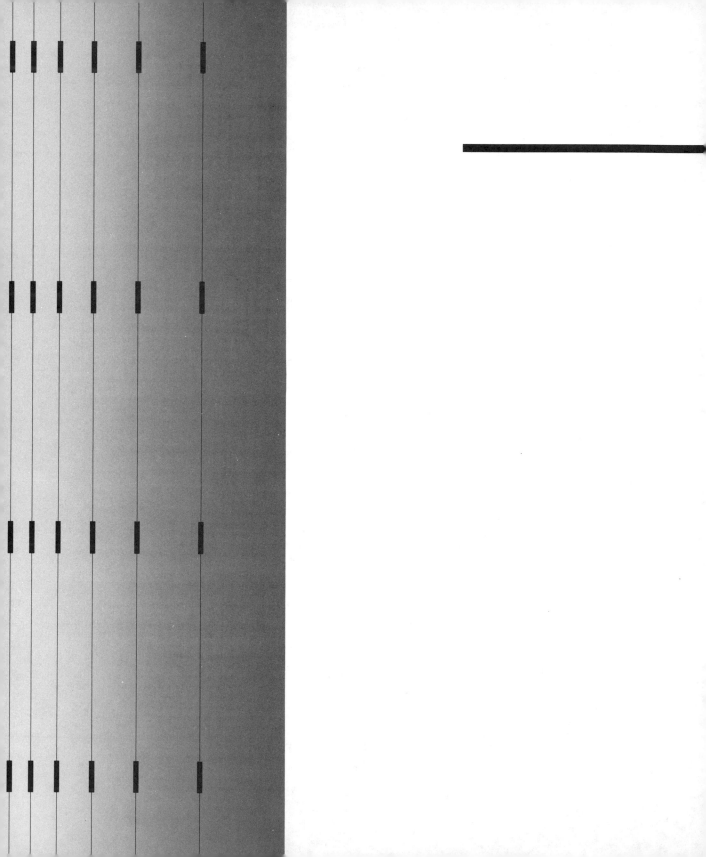

CHAPTER 12

COMPUTER COMMUNICATIONS

COMPUTER COMMUNICATIONS

A computer is a machine for processing information, and communication is an essential part of all computer use. When you press a key, the computer sends an electronic signal from the keyboard to the CPU chip. Likewise, a prompt appears on the screen because the computer sent information from the CPU to the video monitor. Without these and other peripheral devices, the computer (that is, the system unit) could do nothing. Moreover, you can greatly extend the power of a single computer by using it to exchange information with other computers. Local-area networks, in which computers are connected at close range by cable, are installed in many offices and businesses, and telecommunication, in which computers located farther apart are connected over telephone lines, has become a necessity in many industries. Even within the circuitry of the system unit, information is exchanged between the memory chip and the processor chip.

Broadly speaking, the term *computer communications* refers to all of these transfers of information. This chapter concentrates on the communication among the devices that make up a computer system. Beyond simply how to connect these devices, you will learn in this chapter how to get them started and how to transfer information to and from them. Learn this information well, and you will be able to confidently buy and connect new equipment.

This chapter discusses the difference between parallel and serial communication to help you make intelligent decisions about which is right for you. You will also learn enough about the various aspects of these two kinds of communication to use the DOS communications setup commands properly.

One major DOS command in particular, the MODE command, is central to an understanding of data transfer to printers, serial ports, and the video display. If you had to set up DOS for international use (as discussed in Chapter 11), you've already encountered some uses of MODE. Here, you'll learn what it can do for you in the context of communications and when to use it. The MODE command gives you control over

- Your printer (for improving the appearance of your hard-copy output)
- Your video screen (for enhancing all displayed information)
- Your keyboard (for getting more out of each key than simply what is printed on the keycap)

- Just about any additional device that connects to one of the communications ports (plugs) in the back of your computer, including such devices as plotters, modems, and digitizers

In addition to these topical discussions, a reference entry for the MODE command appears at the end of this chapter. The chapter begins with a background discussion of the binary option and its use in representing computer data. If this material is familiar to you, begin with the section "Parallel versus Serial Communications."

A BACKGROUND TO SYSTEM COMMUNICATIONS

To understand computer communications, you need to understand how computers represent information internally. This topic is briefly discussed in Chapter 1, but it is not a major concern throughout most of the book. Fortunately, DOS is designed so that the user need not bother with the computer's internal storage and transfer of information. It concerns us here because understanding the basics of how computers communicate makes using the many forms of the MODE command, the primary tool that DOS provides for controlling computer communications, much easier.

When you enter keyboard characters into programs, either as data or instructions, you enter them as numbers, letters, or punctuation marks, as represented on the face of the key. Each of these keystrokes is interpreted by the computer as a well-defined string of *binary digits,* the 0's and 1's discussed in Chapter 1. If you are familiar with the binary system and its use in representing data, you may want to skip ahead to the section "Control Codes."

Binary Representation of Data

A computer and all its connected devices (*peripheral* devices) can be thought of simply as a large collection of very tiny electronic parts—bits of magnetic material. Each of these parts can hold—or *not* hold—a small voltage, whose exact electrical value depends on the logic built into the computer. If a bit is energized with a small voltage, it has a value of 1. If it receives no voltage, it has a value of 0. The word *binary* means two; a single bit has two possible values: 0 and 1.

You may not realize it, but in communicating with others, you usually perform a variety of tasks based on simple yes/no answers or directives. Every task can be broken into smaller and smaller components, from hitting a baseball properly, to conducting an interview, to carrying out a superior's orders. Similarly, in a computer system, every operation can be broken into component bits. Complex logic and decision making are broken into sequences of bits that either receive voltage or do not receive voltage—values of 1 or 0. Perhaps the binary system does not offer as rich an alphabet as A through Z, but it serves the same purpose.

Communication between people is a sequence of sentences, which consist of a sequence of words, which in turn consist of a sequence of letters. These sequences are broken by verbal pauses or inflections, or written punctuation marks, intended to help the listener (or reader) better understand the speaker (or writer). Pauses and punctuation, therefore, help to *synchronize* the communication of information. To synchronize computer communications, each sequence of 0's and 1's is grouped into seven or eight data bits, each group representing a character. Characters can be letters (A–Z), numbers (0–9), or special symbols or codes (* # % " : > ? and so on).

To understand why some communications use seven data bits and others use eight, briefly consider the binary number system. One bit can have the value 0 or 1. Therefore, two bits in a row have four possible combinations of values, since each bit has two possible values:

- 0 followed by 0, or 00
- 0 followed by 1, or 01
- 1 followed by 0, or 10
- 1 followed by 1, or 11

Three bits in a row have eight possible combinations of values:

- 0 followed by 00, or 000
- 0 followed by 01, or 001
- 0 followed by 10, or 010
- 0 followed by 11, or 011
- 1 followed by 00, or 100
- 1 followed by 01, or 101
- 1 followed by 10, or 110
- 1 followed by 11, or 111

As you can see, the binary system is based on powers of the number 2. With one data bit, there are two possible values (2^1); with two data bits, there are four (2^2); and with three data bits, there are eight (2^3). Continuing this progression,

- Four data bits = 16 possible values (2^4)
- Five data bits = 32 possible values (2^5)
- Six data bits = 64 possible values (2^6)
- Seven data bits = 128 possible values (2^7)
- Eight data bits = 256 possible values (2^8)

The 128 possibilities contained in seven data bits are more than sufficient to represent the standard keyboard and ASCII character set. However, there are additional characters (graphics characters, foreign-language characters, and so on) that constitute what is called the *extended ASCII set*. When these additional characters must be transmitted, the eight-bit form of data communications is used. Chapter 11 and Appendix C discuss this issue more fully. You will usually see characters represented as eight bits and communicated as such. This conventional eight-bit unit is a byte, the fundamental storage and data unit used by DOS.

Control Codes

Groups of bits represent either data or controlling information. In a conversation, you gain someone's attention by saying the person's name or saying something like "Hey, you." Computer communications use special groups of bits to gain the attention of another device. Once attention is obtained with this special sequence of bits, or *control code,* the actual data transmission can begin.

You needn't be concerned with the minute details of data transmission; DOS takes care of them for you. However, as you'll learn in this chapter, you must use the MODE command to tell DOS something about the transmission connection. DOS must know, for instance, whether each character will be defined in seven or eight bits and how many bits will be used for the controlling information around the character bits. The MODE command even tells DOS how fast to send or receive the data bits through the actual connecting port at the rear of your computer.

Most users use a communications program, such as Crosstalk XVI or PC Talk to control data transmission, which handles the actual preparation of the string of bits. The final transmission of the character bits and control bits is handled by DOS. On the other end of the transmission, another copy of the communications program handles the interpretation of the bits, and DOS handles the mechanical reception of those bits through the other serial port.

Computers also use additional bits to ensure synchronization. *Stop bits* follow each unique character code (string of bits) to set it off from other transmitted information. To minimize transmission errors, a *parity bit* is also sent after the data bits. This bit is used by both the transmitting and receiving equipment, but how it is computed and used is beyond the scope of this book.

PARALLEL VERSUS SERIAL COMMUNICATIONS

Typing a capital *J* on the keyboard sends a code to the computer's input routines, which translate this code into the binary digits 01001010. The letter itself is echoed back to the video screen to confirm what you typed (see Figure 12.1).

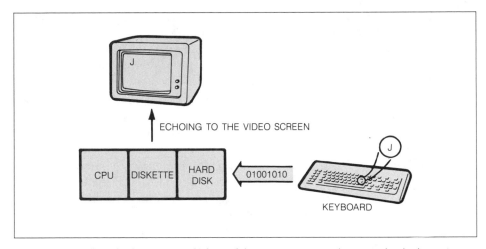

FIGURE 12.1: Keyboard echoing: a simple form of data transmission. In this example, the letter *J* is pressed on the keyboard. The keyboard driver obtains the ASCII code for *J* (01001010) and then sends this code to the video screen driver, which displays the letter *J* on the monitor.

Remember that the video screen is part of what the system calls its console; the keyboard is the input part of the console, and the video screen is the output part. The passing of information between these parts is called *data transmission*.

There are two methods of data transmission: parallel and serial. Nearly all DOS microcomputers are connected with peripheral devices using one of these communication techniques. Although most printers use the parallel method of data transmission, some use the serial method. Other peripheral devices, such as plotters, digitizers, modems, and mice, usually transmit data serially.

If a peripheral device is connected to a serial port and is designed for serial transmission, each bit will be sent to or received from the central processing unit one bit at a time, and only one transmission wire will be used. If the peripheral device is connected to a parallel port and is designed for parallel transmission, then eight separate bits will be transmitted simultaneously over eight separate wires. (In both cases, other wires are used for additional purposes, such as the synchronization of signals or grounding; however, it's sufficient in this context to understand serial versus parallel transmission in terms of one wire versus eight.)

Consider a simple analogy. Figure 12.2 shows an airport baggage terminal. The terminal has eight conveyor belts, and passengers' suitcases are unloaded from eight flights simultaneously. In Figure 12.3, however, the airport has only one conveyor belt. The baggage from all eight flights is unloaded onto this one belt. The passengers in this situation have to wait eight times as long as those in the first airport, and they probably won't be happy about it. Then again, the airline officials may not mind, since they spent approximately one-eighth the amount of money on the conveyor mechanism and ongoing maintenance and terminal space rental. The tradeoff is time versus money. In choosing between serial and parallel communications, you are the airline official. You make the decision about what equipment you buy and use: whether to spend more money on faster, parallel connections, or less money on serial connections, which require more waiting time for certain peripheral devices.

Return now to the example of keyboard data transmission. Suppose you type the word *JUDD* and you want the CPU to send it to a peripheral device. Your keystrokes will be translated into the ASCII character codes shown in Table 12.1.

Figure 12.4 shows a parallel transmission of these characters. As you can see, eight wires are used. A serial transmission of the same characters would require only one wire, as you can see in Figure 12.5. However, the transmission of data would be much slower. This explains why virtually all printers that print faster than several hundred characters per second *must* use parallel transmission and be connected to a computer correctly for parallel transmission.

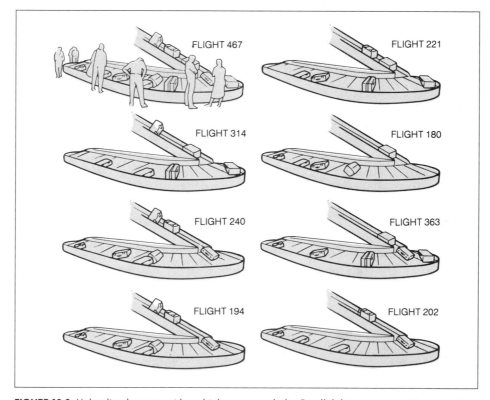

FIGURE 12.2: Unloading luggage with multiple conveyor belts. Parallel data communications permit much faster transmission of information than do serial communications. The analogy of an airport terminal dramatizes the difference. Eight separate luggage conveyor belts permit eight separate flights to be unloaded in the time otherwise required to unload only one.

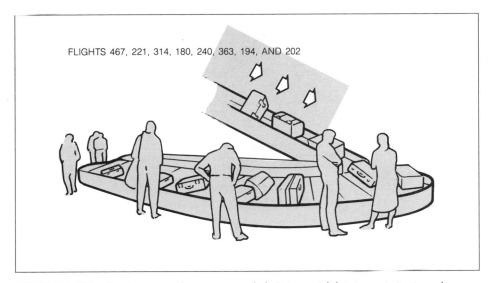

FLIGHTS 467, 221, 314, 180, 240, 363, 194, AND 202

FIGURE 12.3: Unloading luggage with one conveyor belt. Using serial data transmission is analogous to unloading baggage from multiple flights sequentially using only one conveyor belt. However, the hardware costs much less, and the price differential is often the deciding factor is selecting the slower (but often "fast enough") method of data transmission.

LETTER	BINARY DIGITS
J	01001010
U	01010101
D	01000100
D	01000100

TABLE 12.1: ASCII Codes for the Letters J, U, D, and D

A CLOSER LOOK AT COMPUTER COMMUNICATIONS

Computers communicate in a variety of ways. The modern personal computer uses a printed circuit board instead of the huge masses of wire characteristic of early computers or the cranks and shafts of computing machines before that. In the future, you can expect to see computers using light beams (*fiber optics*) for communications, which will greatly increase computer speed as well as facilitate further miniaturization of computer equipment.

As you've just learned, serial and parallel transmission are the two main modes of computer communications, and these are independent of the type of hardware used.

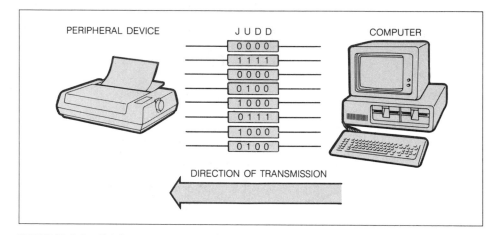

FIGURE 12.4: Parallel data transmission. Eight separate wires are available to carry the eight different bits of a character. In this example, the computer sends the eight bits for *J* (01001010), then the eight bits for *U* (01010101), and then the eight bits for *D* (01000100) twice to transmit the four characters *JUDD* to the peripheral device.

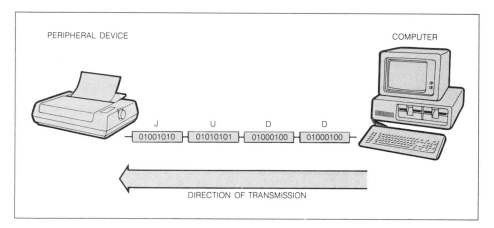

FIGURE 12.5: Serial data transmission. The sequences of bits for the letters *JUDD* are transmitted one after the other with appropriate control bits and codes interspersed between the character sequences.

Serial Communications Requirements

Serial communications acquired its name from the fact that data transmissions using this method transmit data one piece at a time, over a single line. Serial communication can be defined as communication through one channel.

For computers to communicate serially, the computers must exchange considerable information about how the data is to be sent. Both the sending and the receiving devices must agree on such attributes as the speed of data transmission and the control signals sent with the data. The next several sections address these transmission requirements.

COMMUNICATION SPEED

The speed at which the computer transmits and receives data is called the *baud rate. Baud* is defined as bits per second. Most modems now transmit data at 1200 baud. Compared to earlier microcomputer modems, which transmitted at 300 baud, this is rapid. However, the newest microcomputer modems in popular commercial use are capable of 2400-baud transmissions. Compare even this to that of a mainframe computer terminal, which transmits and receives data at 9600 baud, many times faster.

Computers transmit data bit by bit (a bit is one-eighth of a byte). This bit stream contains the character bits and control bits; a total of 10 bits, including bits of both types, are usually transmitted. Thus, a 1200-baud modem exchanges data at roughly 120 bytes (or characters) per second, and a 9600-baud terminal exchanges data at eight times that rate.

Because speed is essential to the communication process, it must be the same on both sides of the transmission. That is, if the transmitter sends data at 1200 baud, the receiver must receive data at 1200 baud. Matching speeds is one of the great hurdles in installing serial equipment on computer systems. If speeds are mismatched, then accurate data cannot be exchanged.

Note: Pay particular attention to the baud rate switch settings on your computer and serial peripheral equipment. Mismatched speeds are the most common reason for communication failure.

Synchronicity

There are two types of serial communication: synchronous and asynchronous. Both systems address the same basic problem: With each transmitted character consisting of more than one bit, how can the receiving computer tell when one character in the bit stream ends and another begins? *Synchronous* communication, as the name implies, depends on timing. If the transmitting device sends characters at a precisely fixed rate of speed, say 1000 characters per second, the receiving computer knows after each interval of 1/1000 second that a new character has begun. *Asynchronous* communication, by contrast, does not rely on a fixed transmission speed. Instead, it adds bits to mark the beginning and end of each character. The receiving device knows that a new character has begun when it recognizes these bits.

As you may have guessed, virtually all communication between microcomputer devices is asynchronous. Although synchronous communication is faster (adding bits to each character increases the total transmission time), it requires expensive, specialized communication lines or cables and is not feasible for most microcomputers. Virtually all microcomputer peripherals are designed to work asynchronously. Moreover, most computer communication begins with an individual typing at a keyboard, and people cannot type continuously at precisely the same rate of speed. Synchronous communication is used mainly with mainframes and minicomputers, in those situations where large amounts of data are begin sent and time is particularly important (that is, expensive).

ELEMENTS OF ASYNCHRONOUS COMMUNICATION

The individual bits that computers transmit and which form characters or pieces of data are called, appropriately, *data bits*. Each set of data bits is preceded by a start bit, which tells the receiver that data is coming. The data bits are followed by a *parity bit,* which is used to verify the accuracy of the data bits. The bits following the parity bit, which tell the receiver when the segment of data bits ends, are called *stop bits*.

In DOS, no start bits are used during data transmission. It is sufficient to include one or two stop bits to end each sequence of bits. The next sequence of bits begins immediately after the stop bit(s). However, start bits may be required by individual communications programs. Figures 12.6 and 12.7 illustrate four possible DOS transmission sequences.

In the first figure, seven data bits, one parity bit, and two stop bits are used. Here, *even parity* is achieved by making the parity bit equal to zero. This is necessary since the seven data bits already add up to an even number $(1 + 0 + 1 + 1 + 0 + 1 = 4)$. Even parity means that the data bits plus the parity bit add up to an even number. Thus, if the sum of the data bits had been odd, the parity bit would have been 1. *Odd parity* means that the data bits plus the parity bit add up to an odd number. Thus, when the data bits add up to an even number $(1 + 1 + 0 + 1 + 1 + 0 + 0)$, the parity bit must be 1.

In Figure 12.7, eight data bits are specified. Since both of these examples also add up to even numbers the parity bit must be set to 0 for even parity and to 1 for odd parity.

Space parity occurs when the parity bit is always set to 0. Space parity is useful for transmitting seven bits when eight are expected, as the parity bit will be used as the eighth bit, a procedure also known as *bit trimming*. *Mark* parity occurs when the parity bit is always set to 1; this is also known as *bit forcing*.

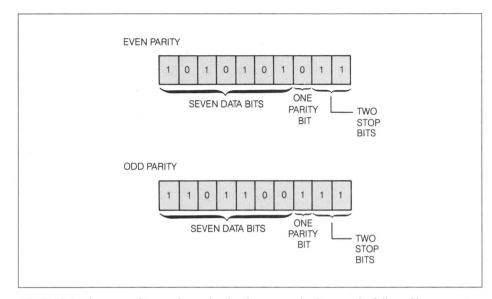

FIGURE 12.6: When seven bits are devoted to the character code, they may be followed by one parity bit and two stop bits. (No start bits are shown here because they are not required by DOS, but individual communication programs may require them.) The parity bit is automatically set by DOS to zero for even parity, as seen in the first example, if the sum of the data bits already equals an even number. In this illustration, the sum of the data bits is 4 (1 + 0 + 1 + 0 + 1 + 0 + 1). When odd parity has been requested during the MODE command setup and the data bits add up to an even number, as in the second example, then the parity bit is set to 1.

Full- and Half-Duplex Communications

In general, all computer communications are either full- or half-duplex transmissions. *Duplicity,* mainly used in telecommunications, refers to what you see on the screen. In *full-duplex* communications, if you type something, it first goes to the other computer; when that computer receives the data, it sends back an exact copy of it to your screen. This procedure shows you what the other computer has received. In half-duplex communications, on the other hand, what you type appears on your screen and then is sent to the other computer. You know what you sent, but you can't be sure what the other computer received. This method is less reliable than full-duplex transmission, but it's much less expensive.

If you are in half-duplex mode and the other computer is in full-duplex mode, your screen will display two copies of everything that is sent to the other computer. If you are in full-duplex mode and the other computer is in half-duplex mode, you will see nothing you send, since the other computer will not be sending back a copy of the data for your screen.

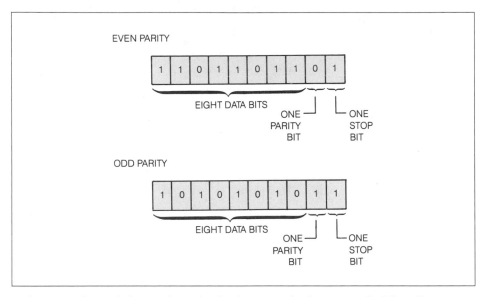

FIGURE 12.7: When eight bits are devoted to the character code, they are usually followed by one parity bit and only one stop bit. The one parity bit is automatically set by DOS to 0 for even parity, as seen in the first example, if the sum of the data bits equals an even number. In this illustration, the sum of the data bits is 6 (1 + 1 + 0 + 1 + 1 + 0 + 1 + 1). For the parity to be considered odd when the data bits add up to an even number, the parity bit is set to 1.

This issue of duplicity is of concern only during communication between computers. Although duplicity is not controlled by DOS, it is another factor that the software managing communications on each computer must coordinate.

Buffers and Handshaking

A *buffer* is an area in memory set aside to hold data for special purposes—for instance, data that arrives at a printer faster than the printer can process it. Suppose you execute a time-consuming command such as a COPY routine, and while the computer is executing this command, you enter DIR. You will not see ''DIR'' on the screen, and the command will not execute, until COPY command execution is complete. Where does the DIR go in the meantime? It goes into a *keyboard buffer* (usually only a few bytes long) that holds what you type until it can be processed.

Similarly, most printers have a small buffer, and some newer ones have buffers as larger as 16K. The buffer allows an entire document to be sent from the computer in perhaps 2 minutes, even though the document actually may take 15 minutes to print. The key advantage to using a buffer is that the computer will be free for other uses after just the transmission time; the actual printing time is irrelevant.

> *Note: Time-out errors* occur when the computer is expecting a response from a peripheral device and after a specified time does not get one. The amount of time can usually be changed when running specific applications, but it cannot be changed from DOS. A time-out error may occur when a slow printer cannot clear a sufficient space in its buffer in the time allotted by DOS. Usually, however, time-out is caused by such conditions as paper jams, ribbon failures (on letter-quality printers), and empty toner cartridges (on laser printers).

However, buffers do fill up; when they do, any additional incoming data must be handled. For instance, the computer may dump 250 bytes into a printer in one second, but the printer may require three seconds to print this data. So that no more data bytes are transmitted to the buffer, which is already full, the printer signals the computer to stop transmitting. When the printer is again ready to receive data, it signals the computer to send some more data. This signaling when ready and signaling when busy is referred to as handshaking.

Handshaking is, quite simply, the way that computers regulate the flow of information to each other. For example, a printer that accepts data at 1200 baud may not be able to print data that quickly. The printer may have a small amount of built-in memory (bigger if you buy a hardware buffer or use a software buffer) that it can use as a holding area for data to be printed. The process of handshaking ensures that no data is lost, and that the difference between transmission speed and printing speed does not cause any problems.

Figure 12.8 illustrates the handshaking process. In step 1, the computer transmits data at an agreed upon rate (see the MODE command later in this chapter) to the printer. Since the printer usually cannot print data at this same rate, it stores the characters to be printed in a buffer. While the characters are filling in one end of the buffer, the printer is taking characters out of the buffer from the other end and actually printing them.

The need for handshaking arises when the volume of data being transmitted is large, or when the buffer being used is small, and the buffer fills up with characters. Since the printer can't print characters as rapidly as the computer can continue to send them, without handshaking data will be lost. The solution is illustrated in step 2 of Figure 12.8. When the printer recognizes that its buffer is full, it immediately signals the computer to stop transmitting data. This signal takes several forms, but the most recognizable signal is the XOFF (transmission off) control code.

Once the computer receives this signal, it stops transmitting data until it receives another signal (XON) from the printer to resume transmission. The printer sends this signal when it has printed enough characters from the buffer to free a reasonable amount of space. The amount of space required to resume transmission varies, but a common value is one complete line of output.

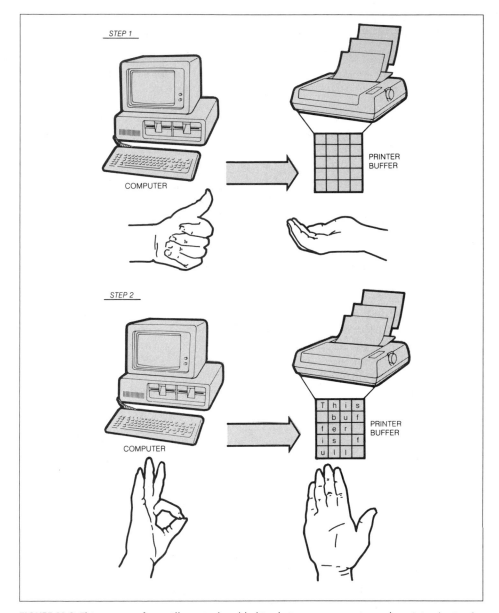

FIGURE 12.8: This two-step figure illustrates handshaking between a computer and a printer. In step 1, the computer sends data to be printed. The printer receives it and momentarily stores it in its internal buffer prior to printing it on paper. Step 2 illustrates what happens if the buffer fills up because the computer has sent data faster than the printer can both print and buffer it. The printer sends a signal to the computer to stop sending data (transmission OFF, or XOF), and the computer acknowledges (ACK) the request. When the buffer is cleared to the point of being usable again, the printer sends another signal (transmission ON, or XON) to request that data be sent again for printing. The process then returns to step 1 in the top diagram.

Protocols

All of the preceding methods for defining the characteristics of communicating are called *protocols*. For example, a communication protocol might consist of "even parity, 1 start bit, 7 data bits." In other words, a protocol is a format for computer communications, not unlike the protocols used for communicating in diplomatic circles. Of course, computers cannot bend the rules of protocol, as diplomats can. Modem users usually compare and set similar protocols before establishing an actual link, since computers using different protocols cannot communicate.

DOS DEVICES VERSUS FILES

Operating systems treat devices that are either data sources or destinations in a consistent manner. As you've seen many times already, you specify the source and destination of data in your software commands. The consistent ways in which you reference hardware devices (such as the console) or software "devices" (such as a disk file) make learning new commands and concepts easy. As you saw in Chapter 3, commands such as COPY work in precisely the same way for a data transfer from a CPU to a disk file as they do for a data transfer from a CPU to a printer.

DOS is designed to understand and permit you to reference certain peripheral devices. Unlike files, for which you can make up names yourself (obeying naming rules), devices are restricted to certain reserved names, shown in Figure 12.9. DOS allows only three specific parallel device names (LPT1, LPT2, and LPT3) and four serial device names (COM1, COM2, COM3, and COM4). Versions of DOS earlier than 3.3 allow only two serial device names, COM1 and COM2.

> *Note:* Like the drive names in previous chapters (A, B, C, and so on), reserved device names should be followed by a colon in your commands. The colon lets DOS know when the device name ends and the sequence of parameter values begins.

The additional device names in Figure 12.9, AUX and PRN, are called *standard* device names. They are used to communicate with the first-connected serial and parallel ports, respectively. You can use these nonspecific device names if you don't want to be bothered with the details of which communications port is connected to your printer or device. Programs don't necessarily have to know which device is connected to which port. They can simply reference PRN, and the output will be routed to the first-connected parallel port; or they can reference AUX, and the output will be routed to the first-connected auxiliary communications (serial) port.

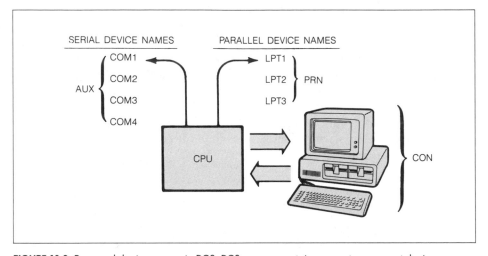

FIGURE 12.9: Reserved device names in DOS. DOS reserves certain names to represent devices connected to the serial and parallel ports. Up to three separate parallel devices may be connected to three parallel ports; data can be sent to those devices by referring to them as port LPT1, LPT2, or LPT3. If more than one port is active and connected, the first-connected port uses the special name PRN. DOS also reserves several names for up to four possible serial ports. These names are COM1, COM2, COM3, and COM4. The first-connected serial device is referred to as AUX.

> *Tip:* You can improve the flexibility of your system by using PRN and AUX as port device names. Use AUX to refer to any one of the four serial ports, COM1 to COM4. Then you can later easily change your hardware connections without having to change your software references.

Keep in mind that you must purchase the actual hardware to make the proper connections. In other words, DOS may understand what it means to send data to a serial port called COM1, but you must have a serial connector on your system, and it must be connected to a serial device, or the request is meaningless.

Even if you have purchased various pieces of peripheral equipment and sufficient add-on boards to connect them, DOS may not be able to address all of them. For instance, if your setup were like that in Table 12.2, you would have no more reserved names available if you wanted to add another serial device. In this case, you would have to buy some form of switch, connect this switch to one port (say, COM1), and then connect two peripherals (the mouse and the modem, for example) to the switch.

Once you have connected all this hardware, you must exercise great care to ensure that your software works. The key to this is ensuring that multiple devices connected to the same switch do not try to transmit data at the same time. Your first reaction may be that this isn't a complication you expect to confront often. On the other hand, if you have a computer with only one serial port (COM1) and you want

DOS RESERVED NAME	DEFINITION	EXAMPLE CONNECTION
LPT1	First parallel port	Fast draft printer
LPT2	Second parallel port	Letter-quality printer
LPT3	Third parallel port	Laser printer
COM1	First serial port	Modem
COM2	Second serial port	Plotter
COM3	Third serial port	Mouse
COM4	Fourth serial port	Digitizer

TABLE 12.2: Example Port Configuration

to use, say, a graphics package that requires a mouse for input and a plotter for output, you may have problems. If you run your software by using a switch for the two devices, you may become impatient with the slowness of the plotter, and long to regain control of the computer while the plot progresses independently. However, unless you add another serial port connector, you cannot do so.

Warning: When you are using the same serial line for two purposes, one operation must wait for the other to finish. If you are plotting, you cannot activate the mouse until all the plotting data has been transmitted to the plotter. When you are using the mouse to control cursor movement and menu selections, you cannot switch to the plotter for output until all mouse movements have been completed.

INITIALIZING DEVICES AND PORTS

Peripheral devices require special setup sequences when you connect them to the computer. The MODE command permits you to initialize aspects of your printers and your serial port devices, as well as to redirect output between parallel and serial ports and even to control some features of your video display. The MODE capabilities that support foreign-language characters were discussed in Chapter 11. Figure 12.10 depicts the four capabilities of the MODE command that this section explores.

In all four situations, you invoke the MODE command like any other disk-resident external DOS command. Simply typing MODE at the DOS prompt, preceded by any drive or path-name specification, initiates MODE operations. Assuming MODE is either in the current drive and directory or on the path you have specified, you enter

MODE *Parameters*

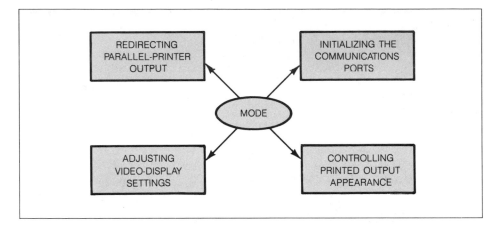

FIGURE 12.10: Four capabilities of the MODE command. In the context of communications between the computer and peripherals, the MODE command performs four separate chores. The text describes the syntax for each of these tasks.

Depending on what parameters you specify, one of the four versions of this command will be activated. The four versions of this command act almost as four separate commands.

Controlling the Printer

Wide spreadsheets and database records are often hard to read when the number of characters per line exceeds the standard number of characters. To make printouts more readable, you can often use *compressed print.*

Most printers assume a normal default setting of 80 characters per line, because most programs generate data using an 80-column video screen. Most printers also assume a default value of 6 lines per vertical inch. You can control both of these settings. The following version of MODE lets you instruct DOS to send the printer the control codes necessary to squeeze up to 132 characters on a line, or to squeeze up to 8 lines of output per vertical inch on the paper. The general form of this MODE command is

MODE *PrinterPort CharsPerLine LinesPerInch*

Warning: This version of the MODE command assumes you are using the most common kind of printer: an EPSON MX series printer, an IBM graphics printer, or a compatible printer. Any other printer requires different control codes. If you are using an incompatible printer this DOS command is useless to you.

Filling in the parameters with values, you could issue the following command to initialize the printer port to LPT1, the characters per line to 132, and the lines per inch to 8:

MODE LPT1: 132, 8

Figure 12.11 shows what a sample text file would look like printed after this command was executed. Figures 12.12 through 12.14 show other variations on the two parameters controlling characters per line and lines per inch.

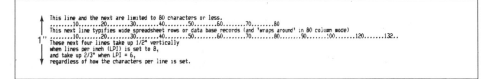

FIGURE 12.11: Output of MODE LPT1: 132,8. After you execute this command, succeeding output to the printer uses a line size of up to 132 characters with lines printed only 1/8 inch apart. In this figure, eight lines of text are printed in a vertical space of one inch, and up to 132 characters are printed on a line with no wraparound.

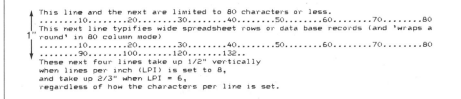

FIGURE 12.12: Output of MODE LPT1: 80,6 (the DOS default setting). After you execute this command, succeeding output to the printer uses a line size of up to 80 characters with lines printed only 1/6 inch apart. In this figure, six lines of text are printed in a vertical space of one inch, and up to 80 characters are printed on a line with no wraparound. This is the DOS default setting when your system starts.

FIGURE 12.13: Output of MODE LPT1: 132,6. After you execute this command, succeeding output to the printer uses a line size of up to 132 characters with lines printed only 1/6 inch apart. In this figure, six lines of text are printed in a vertical space of one inch, and up to 132 characters are printed on a line with no wraparound.

```
 ↑  This line and the next are limited to 80 characters or less.
 │  ........10........20........30........40........50........60........70........80
 │  This next line typifies wide spreadsheet rows or data base records (and 'wraps a
1"  round' in 80 column mode)
 │  ........10........20........30........40........50........60........70........80
 │  ........90........100.......120.......132...
 │  These next four lines take up 1/2" vertically
 ↓  when lines per inch (LPI) is set to 8,
    and take up 2/3" when LPI = 6,
    regardless of how the characters per line is set.
```

FIGURE 12.14: Output of MODE LPT1: 80,8. After you execute this command, succeeding output to the printer uses a line size of up to 80 characters with lines printed only 1/8 inch apart. In this figure, eight lines of text are printed in a vertical space of one inch, and up to 80 characters are printed on a line with no wraparound.

Tip: The MODE command has limited capability for sending control codes to printers. Some applications, such as Lotus 1-2-3 and Framework II, let you send control codes directly to a printer. In fact, you can use EDLIN or your own word processor to include a sequence of control codes in a file (say, CTRLCODE.TXT). You can then send the file and the control codes directly to a printer with the simple instruction COPY CTRLCODE.TXT PRN.

With these MODE commands for compressed print, DOS will respond to your command entry with statements similar to the following:

LPT1: not rerouted
LPT1: set for 132
Printer lines per inch set
No retry on parallel printer time-out

The first and fourth lines of these DOS messages refer to other versions of the MODE command, discussed shortly. The second and third lines indicate the horizontal and vertical printer settings, respectively.

Dot-matrix printers compress print horizontally by printing the dots closer together. Letter-quality printers create the same effect by leaving less space between characters. Compressing the print on letter-quality printers usually requires changing the print wheel or thimble to make the resulting squeezed printout readable.

Initializing the Serial Communications Port

Synchronization is difficult to accomplish when serial devices are connected to computers. For example, if a computer sends data to a serial port at a rate of 1200 baud, any printer connected to that port must be set (by means of hardware switches or software initialization) to receive this information at the same rate. This requirement also works in reverse.

A second version of the MODE command allows you to correctly set a number of parameters for this and other aspects of serial communications. The general form of this MODE command is

MODE *SerialPort BaudRate, Parity, DataBits, StopBits, DeviceType*

The parameters have the following meanings:

- *SerialPort* indicates which one of the four possible peripheral connectors DOS is using for a particular device.
- *BaudRate* sets the speed at which data bits are transmitted through the serial port.
- *Parity* represents the number of binary 1's, if any, that are used in a data transmission; parity is used to detect errors.
- *DataBits* specifies the number of bits used to represent actual transmitted data.
- *StopBits* represents the one or two bits used at the end of a set of data bits to indicate the end of that set of data bits.
- *DeviceType* indicates whether or not the port is being used by a serial printer.

Table 12.3 lists the valid values for these parameters.

PARAMETER	VALID VALUES
SerialPort	COM1, COM2, COM3, or COM4
BaudRate	110, 150, 300, 600, 1200, 2400, 4800, 9600, or 19200
Parity	N, O, or E (none, odd, or even)
DataBits	7 or 8
StopBits	1 or 2
DeviceType	P (if a serial printer); otherwise blank

TABLE 12.3: Valid Parameter Values for Serial Communications

Tip: Before using the MODE synchronization command, follow the initialization instructions in your software program's manual or in your serial device's instruction book. These instructions usually are sufficient for successful synchronization. Only if these procedures fail will you need to understand this version of MODE more fully.

For example, the following command issued at the DOS prompt sets the second serial port to transmit at 1200 baud, with no parity, using eight data bits and one stop bit:

MODE COM2: 1200, N, 8, 1, P

The last parameter value, P, asks DOS to automatically try again to send data to a busy communications port. This parameter facilitates communication when the initial transmission request is met by a control signal indicating the destination device is busy processing the last transmission. The P value is particularly useful with printers, which process data significantly more slowly than the computer's central processing unit.

The MODE synchronization command is disk resident, but it does require that a permanent part of physical memory be reserved for its processing and buffering chores. Thus, when you execute run the command for the first time, it will consume a small additional amount of memory, extending the memory requirements of the memory-resident portion of DOS. DOS issues a message to this effect at the same time as it confirms port settings:

Resident portion of MODE loaded
COM2: 1200,n,8,1,p

Normally, serial devices are accompanied by instruction manuals that describe their required settings. The best advice is to follow scrupulously the suggested connection settings. Switches often have to be set on or in the printer, as well as on the board that controls the serial port itself. In addition, the software product you are using may need to be initialized, since it may send its data directly to the port.

Unfortunately, there is no consistent standard for serial communications as there is for parallel communications, a situation that can lead easily to errors and frustration. You must determine the characteristics of your serial device and issue the proper MODE command before you can use the port in any way.

Connecting a Serial Printer to a COM Port

When the serial device connected to a COM port is a printer, you need to use another version of the MODE command. Printed output usually goes to a PRN device (usually a parallel port such as LPT1), so you must redirect that output to a COM port with the command

MODE LPT*Number:* = COM*Number*

The *Number* parameter should hold the specific number of your chosen port.

Assuming that you have first initialized the communications parameters for the port so that the device and the CPU are synchronized, as in the last section, you can redirect the LPT1 port to the COM2 port with

MODE LPT1: = COM2

DOS will confirm the redirection for all succeeding print output requests with the following message:

LPT1: rerouted to COM2:

Controlling the Video Display Mode

You can use one more version of the MODE command to control certain video characteristics. You will use this version of MODE most often when you purchase nonstandard equipment and when you connect multiple monitors to your computer. The command tells DOS which monitor is receiving a video display request; it also allows you to adjust the video image horizontally.

This MODE command has three parameters, of which the first is used most often:

MODE *VideoType, Direction, TestPattern*

Table 12.4 lists the valid values for the three parameters.

PARAMETER	VALID VALUES
VideoType	MONO (for IBM monochrome display) CO80 (for color 80-column display) CO40 (for color 40-column display) BW80 (for black-and-white, 80-column display; this specification disables color on a color monitor) BW40 (for black-and-white, 40-column display) 80 (adjusts to 80-column display; does not change the color status) 40 (adjusts to 40-column display; does not change the color status)
Direction	R (right) or L (left)
TestPattern	T (to display a test pattern)

TABLE 12.4: Valid Values for MODE Video-Display Parameters

The simplest form of this version of the MODE command uses only the *VideoType* parameter. Setting the display mode to 40 or 80 characters is as simple as entering

MODE 80

or

MODE 40

The 80-column mode is standard for business applications. Some games use 40-column mode. The 40-column mode produces larger, more legible characters on the video monitor. However, in the past, many simple microcomputers used inexpensive monitors with very low resolution. Even television sets often were used as displays; 40 characters were about the maximum that these monitors could readably display. The 40-column mode, and those early monitors, are seldom seen nowadays. Figures 12.15 and 12.16 show the same directory display in 80- and 40-column modes.

Entering a parameter value of 40 or 80 for *Video Type* does not affect the monitor color. Assuming that the monitor is controlled by a CGA (color graphics adapter) or an EGA (extended graphics adapter), you can explicitly enable or disable color by preceding the column number by CO (to enable color) or BW (to disable color, leaving a black-and-white image). If you have an IBM monochrome display, the proper parameter value is MONO. If your system has both a monochrome *and* a color graphics monitor, you can switch output between them. Enter

MODE MONO

to switch output to the monochrome monitor; enter

MODE CO80

to switch output to the color monitor, using 80 columns with color enabled.

Some monitors require some horizontal adjustment. You may not need to adjust your monitor often, but when you do, the *Direction* and *TestPattern* parameters will come in handy. You can shift the display to the right or to the left by entering R or L as the *Direction* parameter. In either case, you can enter T as the

```
C>DIR

 Volume in drive C is ROBBINS
 Directory of  C:\UTILITY\XENO

 .            <DIR>      5-02-86    1:17p
 ..           <DIR>      5-02-86    1:17p
 XENOCOPY EXE   83968    8-17-87    6:18p
 README          5067    8-21-87   12:35p
 XDEF     OPT     1221    8-25-87   10:06a
 SYBEX    OPT     1221    8-25-87   10:07a
         6 File(s)     634880 bytes free

C>_
```

FIGURE 12.15: Directory display after a MODE 80 command. The directory listing appears in its normal 80-column configuration.

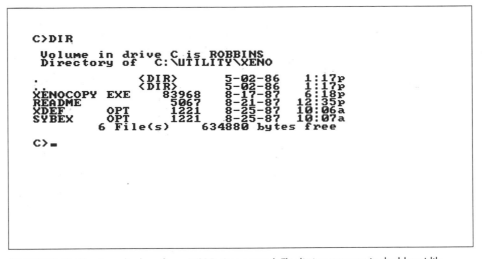

```
C>DIR
 Volume in drive C is ROBBINS
 Directory of  C:\UTILITY\XENO
 .              <DIR>       5-02-86    1:17p
 ..             <DIR>       5-02-86    1:17p
 XENOCOPY EXE      83968    8-17-87    6:18p
 README            5067     8-21-87   12:35p
 XDEF     OPT      1221     8-25-87   10:06a
 SYBEX    OPT      1221     8-25-87   10:07a
          6 File(s)       634880 bytes free

C>_
```

FIGURE 12.16: Directory display after a MODE 40 command. The listing appears in double-width format, an unusual configuration of up to 40 columns per line.

LastPattern parameter to display a test pattern on the screen to help you make adjustments. Entering

MODE 80, L, T

produces the screen shown in Figure 12.17.

If you respond N (for no) to the prompt asking whether you can see the right-most 9, DOS will shift the entire screen image to the left by one character (if the display mode is 40 columns) or by two characters (if it is 80 columns). The prompt will then reappear. You can continue to shift the display until you can see all 80 characters—until the rightmost 9 is visible.

MODE: THE DOS COMMUNICATION COMMAND

The MODE command controls and redirects output.

SYNTAX

(1) [*D:Path*]MODE LPT*x:* [*CPL*][,[*LPI*][,P]]
(2) [*D:Path*]MODE LPT*x:* = COM*y*
(3) [*D:Path*]MODE COM*y*[:]*Baud*[,[*Parity*][,[*Bits*][,P]]
(4) [*D:Path*]MODE *Type*
(5) [*D:Path*]MODE [*Type*], *Shift* [,T]

```
0123456789012345678901234567890123456789012345678901234567890123456789
Do you see the rightmost 9? (y/n)
▪
```

FIGURE 12.17: Shifting the video image left with MODE. This figure shows a test pattern of 0123456789 repeated eight times (four in 40-column mode). If you can't see the rightmost 9, you respond to the prompt with N; DOS then shifts the display to the left. The prompt reappears until you respond Y, indicating that you can see the entire display.

(6) *[D:Path]*MODE *Device* CODEPAGE PREPARE = *((CP)FileSpec)*
(7) *[D:Path]*MODE *Device* CODEPAGE PREPARE = *((CPList)FileSpec)*
(8) *[D:Path]*MODE *Device* CODEPAGE SELECT = *CP*
(9) *[D:Path]*MODE *Device* CODEPAGE[/STATUS]
(10) *[D:Path]*MODE *Device* CODEPAGE REFRESH

D:Path	is the drive and path where the command file is located if it is not in the current directory.
x	is a printer number.
CPL	is the number of characters per line.
LPI	is the number of lines per inch.
P	causes the computer to continuously retry accessing the port during time-out errors.
y	is a serial-port number.
Baud	is a baud rate for the COM port (110, 150, 300, 600, 1200, 2400, 4800, 9600, or 19200).
Parity	is a parity value for the COM port; it can be even, odd, or none (the default is even).
Bits	is a combination of two parameters specifying the number of stop and data bits used.

Type	is the display type being used. It is specified as 40, 80, BW40, BW80, CO40, CO80, or MONO.
Shift	is the direction for a screen shift, either L or R.
T	puts a test pattern on the screen for checking the screen alignment when shifting.
Device	is a valid device name (CON, LPT1, and so on).
CP	is a code-page number (437, 850, 860, 863, or 865).
CPList	is a list of code-page numbers.
FileSpec	is the file containing the code-page data. Its value is 4201.CPI for the IBM Proprinter; 5202.CPI for the IBM Quietwriter III Printer; EGA.CPI for EGA displays; or LCD.CPI for LCD displays.
/STATUS	displays the active code page and the other available code pages for *Device*.

TYPE

External.

USAGE

There are ten formats for this useful command, as shown in the SYNTAX section. The numbers in parentheses shown here are used only for reference to this discussion. Do *not* enter them as part of your MODE commands. The first format selects various print modes on parallel printers, the second redirects output, and the third changes the parameters of the serial port. Format 4 changes the display type, and format 5 sets the video mode and, simultaneously, adjusts the horizontal alignment of the monitor.

The MODE command can also work with code pages. Formats 6 and 7 install code-page device drivers in the specified device. Format 8 selects the code page to be activated for the specified device. (You can have several code pages loaded into the device at once, but only one can be active at any one time.) Format 9 displays the active code page and then displays all of the code pages that can be activated for the specified device.

Format 10 reinstalls the currently active device driver in the specified device if it was erased. This comes in handy if for some reason you need to turn your printer off. Instead of using format 1 or 2 to reload the driver, which in fact is already in computer memory anyway, you can use format 10 to make another copy and place it into the device's memory.

EXAMPLES

If you wish to connect COM2 (your second communications port) to an HP plotter, for instance, enter

MODE COM2:9600,N,8,1,P

This ensures that data is transmitted by DOS out of that second communications port at the rate of 9600 baud expected by the waiting plotter. Similarly, if you want to connect a 1200 baud printer to your first communications port, you can enter

MODE COM1:1200,N,8,1,P

The P parameter ensures that DOS will continue trying to print a file, even if the printer is not yet ready.

To change this setting, you can reenter the MODE command with adjusted parameters.

Standard parallel printer output must be redirected from LPT1 to COM1. Assuming that COM1 has just been set up with one of the appropriate preceding MODE commands, you can now control this redirection by entering

MODE LPT1: = COM1:

All succeeding output to the LPT1 port (the default PRN port) will now be sent out to the printer connected to the first serial communications port.

After outputting to a serial port, you may wish to use your parallel printer again. Redirection can be disabled by entering:

MODE LPT1:

These kinds of definitions, setups and redirections are usually done only once in a system. The AUTOEXEC.BAT file would then be the proper place to include these command lines.

SUMMARY

In this chapter, you learned the fundamentals of computer communications. You discovered what serial and parallel communications are and how they differ. You also saw how computers and peripheral devices such as printers use buffers and handshaking techniques to manage the transmission of information.

For a complete book discussing everything you need to know about serial processing, see

- *Mastering Serial Communications* by Peter W. Gofton (SYBEX, 1986)

For more information about displaying and printing foreign language characters and graphic symbols, see

- Chapter 11, "International Setup"

For more information about external devices, hardware buffers, and ports, see

- Chapter 13, "Software Ports and Hardware Devices"

For more information about redirecting output, see

- Chapter 17, "Pipes, Filters, and Redirecting Output"

The next two chapters will extend your understanding of communications in two very important areas. In Chapter 13, you will learn how DOS uses its parallel and serial software ports, as well as the MODE command, to establish communications with a variety of external hardware devices. In Chapter 14, you will learn more about local-area networks (LANs) and how DOS is designed to communicate with these networks.

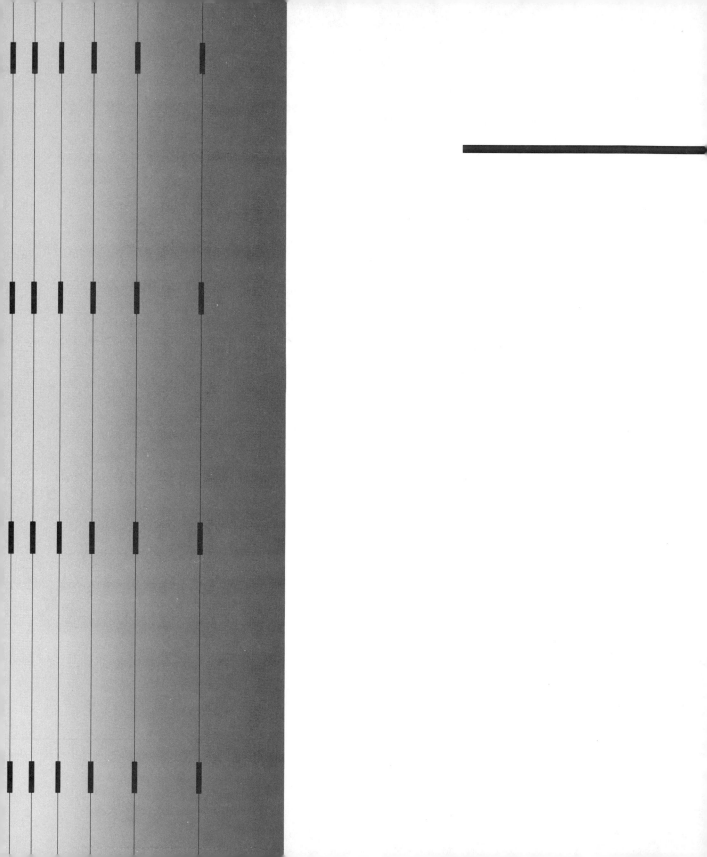

SOFTWARE PORTS AND HARDWARE DEVICES

CHAPTER 9

SOFTWARE PORTS
AND HARDWARE DEVICES

This chapter takes a closer look at the broad range of mechanical and electronic devices that you can connect to your computer. You are familiar with the most common of these already: printers, keyboards, monitors. Less common devices include touch screens and tapes.

In this chapter, you'll explore the array of hardware used in computing environments by focusing on example devices. You'll also look at some of the hardware necessary to connect these devices to your computer. Some of these devices may be useful to you in your business; their potential value to you will be pointed out as they are discussed.

First, you'll look at the point of connection—the software ports such as LPT1 or COM2 that connect your personal computer, DOS, and your extra hardware devices. In virtually all cases, you and your computer control these hardware devices via control signals sent over the cable or wire connections established by the serial or parallel port connectors (see Chapter 12). In addition, the MODE command (also presented in Chapter 12) is fundamental to establishing a correct connection between your computer and any peripheral device.

PORTS AND DEVICES

To accomplish useful results, computers must to be able to communicate with the outside world. They do this through *ports*. A port is the connection point where a computer interfaces with its peripherals, or add-on devices, such as printers and modems. The most common port is the video port. A cable of one sort or another usually makes the connection between computer and peripheral device. However, some devices interface by directly plugging into a board that contains the device.

Inside the system unit of most personal computers are several *expansion slots*. These are parts of the circuit board that can accommodate add-on cards, or small, printed circuit boards. Computers have different numbers of these slots, which allow you to connect additional equipment. Add-on cards fit into the expansion slots and automatically link up with the computer's internal processor, allowing you easily to add hardware semipermanently to your system. Add-on cards are accessed through the back of the system unit using *connectors*. Connectors are what cables plug into: they are actually part of the electronic cards.

Thus, just as the door to your house or apartment is a port to the outside world, a card is a port to other worlds for the computer. Data can travel electronically through this port, or door, into and out of your computer. The port is the interface between the computer and the connected device, the abstract line where the peripheral device becomes part of your computer system.

Sometime you may need direct access to the ports. For example, when sending data through a modem, you must be able to tell the computer to which port the modem is connected, and therefore to which port to send the data. Because of this, DOS provides names for the most common ports. These names are called *device names*, since DOS refers to the type of devices affected rather than the actual interfaces. Table 13.1 lists the valid DOS device names.

DEVICE NAME	DEVICE INFLUENCED	DIRECTION
CON	Keyboard/screen console	In/Out
AUX or COM1	Serial adapter 1	In/Out
COM2	Serial adapter 2	In/Out
COM3	Serial adapter 3	In/Out
COM4	Serial adapter 4	In/Out
LPT1 or PRN	Parallel printer 1	Out
LPT2	Parallel printer 2	Out
LPT3	Parallel printer 3	Out
NUL	Dummy device used for tests	In/Out

TABLE 13.1: Valid DOS Device Names

If, when you have only one printer connected to your computer, you print a file, the computer automatically sends data to the LPT1 port. For example, to print a file on the second parallel printer, you enter

TYPE *filename* >**LPT2**

which routes the output of the TYPE command to the LPT2 port (see Chapter 17).

CON is used by default for system input and output, but is particularly useful when creating a short file (see Chapter 6). The COM*x* ports are serial ports (see Chapter 12) and are used for two-way communication with serial devices, particularly modems or other computers that can transmit as well as receive data.

So now you know *how* the computer refers to the outside world. In the next section you will look at the different kinds of peripherals the computer uses to communicate with the outside world.

Some Devices and Precautions regarding Their Use

The computer uses various means to influence or communicate with peripheral devices. You are already familiar with some of these, such as disk drives, printers, and monitors; others are less common. This section introduces you to some of the many peripherals you can buy for your system.

BAR CODE READERS

Common first in supermarkets but now in widespread use on microcomputers are *bar code readers*. Bar codes are found on almost everything sold nowadays. A bar code is a white square with a series of parallel black lines of varying thicknesses printed on it. A bar code reader scans the order and thickness of the lines and translates them into numbers. Bar codes are extremely useful for managing inventory and controlling checkout purchases in stores.

Although many supermarkets use dedicated computer checkout systems, an increasing number of companies are using small, portable, DOS-based systems for inventory control. The bar code reader is attached to the portable computer either in place of the keyboard or to a serial port so that operators can enter bar code numbers without losing the option of regular keyboard entry.

CLOCKS AND CALENDARS

Many microcomputers have internal, software-driven clocks. However, when the power is turned off, this type of clock loses the contents of its memory. To eliminate this problem, peripheral manufacturers have created plug-in personal computer boards that contain a clock unit and a small battery that lasts several years. Using special software drivers (see Chapter 10), the computer can read the time of day from this board and use this value to initialize its own internal clock. Some of these boards come with extra options that allow you to display a calendar and a clock on the screen.

CONVERTERS

For a computer to operate or monitor some physiological or other real-world event, it must receive information in understandable digital form. For example, suppose you use a computer to measure the body temperature of a patient in a hospital. The computer needs a link to the temperature-sensing equipment. Each time the temperature is measured, a monitoring device connection is closed, creating an electric current. This current is represented by a voltage, not by a typical digital computer's 1 or 0. The computer needs some way to convert this voltage into a 1 or a 0 so it can manipulate the information. When the computer system translates temperature (or any other continuously varying event, such as sound, heat, or position) into voltage, the amount of voltage generated is directly proportional, or *analogous*, to the intensity of the physical phenomenon being measured. A 1 or a 0 is an abstract entity, with no physical meaning; it simply represents a physical entity, in this case voltage, in numeric, or *digital*, form.

Thus, the type of converter you need is called an *analog-to-digital converter* (abbreviated *a/d converter*). Its circuitry is usually a board that can be installed in the computer. It has a jack that tests for voltage, and when voltage is present, it sends a digital value to the computer. The computer then knows both the amount of voltage, and the analagous level of sound (or heat or temperature or whatever other factor) being measured by the probe.

For a computer to control equipment, commands must be turned into voltage to operate the machinery. For this process you use a *digital-to-analog converter* (abbreviated *d/a converter*), which functions exactly opposite an a/d converter.

The applications for converters are numerous: measuring frequencies, sampling pulmonary measurements, showing your car speed on a digital speedometer, measuring temperature, monitoring your heart rate, and more.

DIGITIZERS

Digitizers, or data scanners, are another powerful type of data input device. They are connected to microcomputers through a serial port and are synchronized as to speed and rate of data transmission by the MODE command. Typical data transmission rates are 9600 and 19,200 (only in DOS 3.3) baud; at these speeds digitizers are ideal for entering detailed drawings into the computer. Engineers, architects, and draftspeople make frequent use of digitizers to computerize hand-drawn images for future manipulation by computer-aided design (CAD) programs.

A typical digitizer has a scanning device mounted over a flat board. When the scanning device is moved over the board, the computer notes the device's position as the device passes over certain marks on the board, often a grid-like pattern of electrical wires. Any drawing can be mounted on the board, and any pattern in the drawing can be traced with the scanner's cross-hairs. Voltage signals are converted to digital numbers and sent over the serial line to DOS, which passes these digital numbers to the software that usually accompanies the digitizer.

The computer typically stores any data received from the scanner in a file for further processing. It sometimes stores the data in standard ASCII file format; at other times, it stores the data in a special format determined by the receiving program.

Optical scanning is a more limited, but increasingly popular form of digitization. Limited to the set of recognizable characters that can be typed or printed, optical recognition devices compare patterns on paper to predefined patterns for letters, numbers, and special symbols. The computer then stores the ASCII value of the recognized character in a file for later processing.

DISK DRIVES

On most microcomputers, the disk drives are built into the system unit, although external disk drives may be used for additional storage. The main system unit usually has room for several disk drives.

With the increasing popularity of lap-top computers, 3.5-inch drives are becoming common. These disks come in a hard plastic jacket, and the drive accesses the disk by sliding open a small aperture on the jacket. Because the disk itself is not as directly exposed to outside stresses, these disks are much more durable and resistant to damage than 5.25-inch floppy diskettes. They are also small enough to be carried in a shirt pocket, which makes them easily transportable.

Fixed disk drives are also becoming common as they become increasingly inexpensive. These drives can hold anywhere from 10 to over 200 megabytes. These disks are not floppies. Rather, the disk itself is a series of hard magnetic (oxide-coated) platters. The disk head literally glides on drafts of air less than the height of a fingerprint above the platter. One dust particle is all it takes to interrupt the air flow over the disk, to destroy the draft, and to cause the disk head to crash into the platter, making a furrow in the disk and destroying any data in its path.

The newest craze in mass storage is actually very small hard disks mounted onto add-on boards. These boards weigh little compared to a normal fixed disk and are usually more shock resistant. They appear to the system as normal drives, and one of their benefits is that they leave space open on the system unit for more regular drives. They do use a slot, but they are somewhat more portable (between machines) than a typical hard disk drive.

JOYSTICKS

A *joystick* (the term is a reference to the joysticks used in aircraft) allows the user to move the cursor around the screen in two dimensions (up, down, left, and right). Joysticks are mostly useful for games and computer-aided drawing, although mouse devices are increasingly being used for computer-aided design (CAD) work.

LIGHT PENS

Light pens have greatly increased the efficiency of creating drawings and entering data at a computer. A light pen is a wand used to point to positions or items on the screen. It works by detecting light emissions on the screen, and then determining the position on the screen of that emission. Using a light pen, you can easily point to choices on a menu or make drawings directly on the screen.

Mouse Devices

The *mouse* has become an enormously popular device. Mouse devices are virtually essential to an efficient desktop publishing system. A mouse is similar to a joystick but somewhat easier to use. One type of mouse is a simple box with a moving ball underneath it. Inside the box are optical sensors that can sense the direction of movement of the ball. On the top of the mouse are from one to three buttons.

After the computer positions a cursor on the screen, when you move the mouse, the cursor moves in the same direction. By modifying parameters, you can make the cursor move faster, slower, or at the same speed as the mouse, to achieve different levels of detail. Therefore, the mouse allows precise positioning of the cursor.

Many application programs now include *pull-down menus*. Such programs display a bar with several choices highlighted on it at the top of the screen. When you position the mouse (cursor) on an option and press the mouse button, a menu appears to drop down onto the screen (like a window shade). The menu lists choices you can make by repositioning the mouse and releasing the mouse button. Many computer users consider this method of choosing an option much faster than typing an option number on the keyboard.

Memory Options

Along with increasingly powerful computer programs have come demands for more memory. The 8086-based computers, such as the IBM PC/XT, can actually address more memory (one megabyte) than DOS itself, which can address only up to 640K of memory. For most users, and for most applications, that's enough. For others, additional memory means more memory-resident programs and additional RAM disks; in other words, power users are hungry for more usable memory.

To add more memory, Lotus, Intel, and Microsoft came up with a scheme to increase the amount of memory addressable by a system and by applications. This scheme, called the LIM specification, for Lotus, Intel, Microsoft specification, or the EMS, for expanded memory specification, bypasses DOS's standard addressability limitations. Using this scheme, you can increase the amount of memory in your system with relative ease.

The flaw in this scheme is that only software designed to use this extra memory can access it. Most software utilizes DOS to an extent, and such programs know about only the memory known to DOS. If DOS doesn't think there is any more memory in the system, then the typical application program also will think there is no more memory in the system.

Memory expansion and the LIM specification are discussed in Appendix F.

MODEMS

The word *modem* is derived from the term *mod*ulator/*dem*odulator, which refers to a function performed by a modem. A modem changes a digital or electric signal into an audible tone. Digital signals are either 1 or 0; thus, the computer uses two tones. The modem is plugged into the phone line, and a sequence of digital values (0 or 1) are converted into a string of audible tones through a process called *modulation*. This series of sounds is then sent over the phone to another modem, which, by sensing the tones, turns them back into a string of bits (0 or 1), a process called *demodulation* of the signal. In this way, data can be sent over telephone lines.

There are two different types of modems: acoustic-coupler and direct-connect. Acoustic couplers have two cups that a phone receiver fits into, and the tones go into and out of the phone through the mouth and ear pieces. Direct-connect modems connect directly to the phone line. Direct-connect modems are better than acoustic modems since fewer errors can creep into the signal transmission as a result of surrounding noise in the room. Also, digital electronics can provide additional features, such as automatic answering, dialing, and error correction. Most new modems are direct connect, but many acoustic couplers are still in use.

MONITORS

Monitor is another term for video display. A monitor has better resolution and color separation than a television set and only one channel. Having more than one monitor can be desirable because of the different features different monitors offer. For example, monochrome monitors often have better character definition than color monitors but comparatively poor graphic ability, so some systems have both a monochrome and a color monitor. Extra monitors are also desirable if you have a portable computer with a built-in monitor that does not support color or has a very small screen.

Research into alternative monitors is proceeding quickly. With the high demand for smaller systems and laptop models, smaller screens with better resolution are sorely needed. Plasma displays and the more common (and less expensive) liquid crystal displays are two alternatives to the standard picture currently in use.

Composite Monitors   Composite monitors work the same way as television sets. *Composite* refers to the way the image is displayed on the screen. In this case, each picture element (or pixel, or pel, or simply dot) on the screen is made of a dot that can change color. Composite cables are connected to the computer using an RCA jack (the same type of jack used on a stereo system).

Monochrome Monitors   Monochrome monitors, because they use only one color, have a high character resolution. The clarity or resolution of any character displayed on a video monitor depends directly on how many adjacent pixels are illuminated on the monitor to trace the shape of the character. In a monochrome monitor, pixels do not have to generate colors as well as shapes, so the monitor can assign more pixels to shaping an easily readable character. Monochrome monitors differ from composite monitors in that all dots display only one color (usually green or amber).

RGB Monitors   *RGB* stands for red, green, blue, the only colors these monitors support. All colors displayed on RGB monitors are formed from combinations of these three colors. RGB monitors are desirable for graphics applications and for applications that combine text and graphics. Different display adaptors are used to determine the overall resolution of the images an RGB monitor creates. A color graphics adaptor (CGA) yields the lowest resolution; an enhanced graphics adaptor (EGA), which yields better resolution, is the popular choice for combined text and graphics output. You can tell an RGB monitor from the back by its cable, which typically has a nine-pin connector to carry information to the monitor. Although monochrome monitors have exactly the same type of connector, connecting a monochrome monitor to a color monitor connector can destroy your hardware. The electronics on the circuit board for these two monitors are totally incompatible.

RGB monitors differ from composite monitors in that each pel on the screen is composed of three smaller pels; one that displays red, one that displays blue, and one that displays green. Since sub-pels are very small and will blend together, by turning any one of them on, or any combination of the three, you can display different colors.

Plasma Displays   Plasma is an increasingly popular alternative to monitors with large tubes. Plasma displays are made of a gas plasma contained in a flat glass and electrified to produce luminescence. In the search for a flatter and smaller screen, mostly for laptop computers, plasma is a major contender. Its display works quickly, and the screen has a high resolution.

Plasma displays are also highly valued for their high contrast and readability. In addition, this medium offers the widest readable viewing angle and is attractive to many users requiring portable machines for small-group presentations.

Liquid-Crystal Displays   Liquid-Crystal display (LCD) screens use inexpensive liquid-crystal technology. They are often slower and less readable than other types of monitors. LCDs are used for watches and calculators as well as computers. Improved LCD displays use backlighting to enhance the readability of the screen, as well as a new crystal pattern called *supertwisting* to produce crisper, more readable characters.

LCD technology has been attractive primarily because of several factors. The technique itself is based on the electrification of thin filaments running through an electrokinetic fluid. This approach lends itself to small, flat panel displays that are compact, portable, and importantly, very inexpensive to produce. Additionally, this medium is easy to power; computers that use LCD screens can run on battery power for up to several hours.

Compared to the flat panel gas plasma displays seen in a few competitive laptops, LCD portables win in the area of convenient portability (away from AC power) but lose in the area of readability (by one person) and viewability (by several people). Gas plasma screens also demand more power to run, so battery support is possible for a much shorter time (typically not much more than a single hour).

Optical Storage Devices

Optical storage is the new buzzword in computer information retrieval technology. In this technology, a laser burns holes in the coating on a disk; a laser beam is later used to read this information back. The benefits of this process are that the resulting information is stored permanently, since the disk is physically altered.

CD ROM Devices   Compact disks, or CDs, are optical disks about five inches in diameter. You've already seen them appearing in record stores. They store digital data as marks on the disk's surface. Because these marks are read by a laser, CDs are not subject to the same wear and tear as records and tapes.

CDs for computers are receiving attention because of their high storage density. They can store approximately 550 megabytes of data per disk. Their major drawback is the high cost of recording information onto them, a process that entails a special, clean computer room and a very expensive recording device. Owing to the great expense of proper production of CDs, they are currently designed only for playback by CD players and computers (when written with computer-readable data). Since they are typically read, and not written, by computer users, they are sometimes referred to as CD ROM, or compact disk read-only memory, devices. CDs are excellent for storing large amounts of information, such as an entire encyclopedia on a single disk or all the latest medical research for a specialty area. Currently, several CD players, in anticipation of future demand, come with jacks to connect them to computer systems.

WORM Devices   Brand new on the market, WORM, or write once, read many times, optical disks represent the revolution that CDs may not bring. That is, WORM drives will actually record on the disk surface using a laser. Again, since this process physically changes the disk, the data cannot later be changed. This mechanism can be perfect for archival storage or for storing permanent records such as audit trails or large-volume (and unchanging) data bases.

However, due to the relative newness and high cost of laser equipment, WORM drives currently cost several thousand dollars. Nevertheless, they may become more popular, owing to their ability to store business data. They can hold about as much data as a CD can, albeit in a slightly bigger package.

PRINTERS

Printers are devices that print information on paper; this information is usually textual, but on many printers it can be graphic as well. There are five primary types of microcomputer printers: *thermal*, *dot matrix*, *ink jet*, *letter quality*, and *laser*.

Regardless of which printer you use, the method of DOS connection will be the same. Either you use the default LPT1 output port (the first parallel port), or you use the MODE command described in Chapter 12 to redirect the output to one of the other ports. For example,

MODE LPT1: = COM1:

redirects all parallel output (to LPT1) to the first serial communication port (COM1). This then requires a second line to set up the serial port properly. The example line

MODE COM1:1200,N,8,1,P

prepares the port for DOS transmission at 1200 baud, with no parity, using eight data bits with one stop bit. It also specifies that DOS automatically try again to send data to a port if it is busy during the first attempt to transmit data.

Thermal Printers   *Thermal printers* use a heat application process to produce characters on specially coated paper, called *thermal paper*. Thermal printers are very quiet, since they do not use any pins, hammers, or mechanical impact. However, they are relatively slow. The print quality is not especially good, and the quality of thermal paper is not up to business standards. Also, because the paper is heat sensitive, it deteriorates and yellows rapidly. Thermal printers generally are used for draft-quality work in office environments where the noise of other types of printers would be distracting or discomforting.

Dot-Matrix Printers   *Dot-matrix printers* use an interesting process to form characters. Their printheads consist of an array of small pins. The head moves across the print line on the paper firing combinations of these pins to form parts of letters. The pins jump out of their holes and press against the ribbon, leaving a pattern of ink dots on the paper. These patterns form characters. The more dots (that is, the higher the dot density) the printer places per character, the crisper and clearer the characters appear and the easier they are to read. Because of the way they work, dot-matrix printers can be very good for printing graphics, since they have a moderately high resolution.

Ink-Jet Printers   *Ink-jet printers* form characters in the same way as dot-matrix printers do: by putting small dots of ink on the paper to form characters. However, the way they go about doing this is quite different. Instead of pins in the holes, the holes act as jets, from which very small bits of ink are sprayed on the paper. Ink-jet printers are much quieter and faster than dot-matrix printers; they also usually cost more. Drawbacks of ink-jet printers include their tending to clog and smear, and their use of special paper.

> *Note:* A hidden expense of ink-jet printers versus standard dot-matrix printers is their unusually high cost per printed character, owing to the expense of the ink cartridges, which require frequent replacement.

Letter-Quality Printers   *Letter-quality printers* have gone through many incarnations. The quality of a letter-quality printer is by definition the same as that of a good office typewriter. Early attempts at computerizing letter printing involved covering a typewriter keyboard with a special computer-controlled mechanism. Instead of interfacing directly with the typing mechanism, these keyboard covers used a series of small electromagnetic plungers that actually pressed the keys of the typewriter to print a document. Although this device was inventive, however, it was slow and prone to mechanical problems.

Many modern electronic typewriters also offer connections to computers, but this connection takes the form of either an RS-232 serial port or a Centronics parallel port. With the appropriate cable, you can then prepare text with your word processor, and send it to the typewriter for printing by using the DOS COPY or PRINT command.

If the typewriter does use the simpler parallel option, you only need to plug the cable into the typewriter and the computer and press some activating key on the typewriter (see your typewriter instruction manual). If your typewriter comes with a serial port connector, this connection requires you first to execute the appropriate version of the MODE command to set up the proper transmission parameters on your serial port.

Daisy-wheel printers use a flat wheel (see Figure 13.1) with the characters impressed on the outside spokes of the wheel.

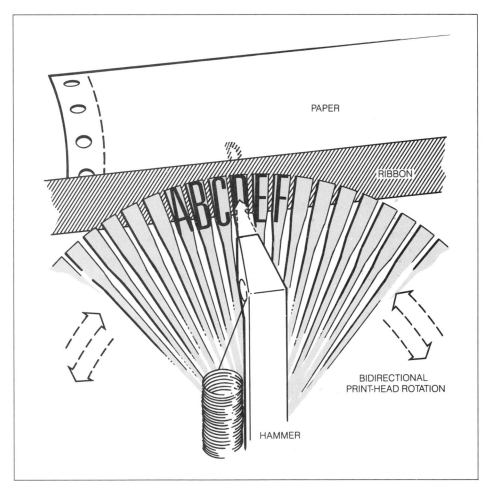

FIGURE 13.1: The wheel of a daisy-wheel printer rotates until the desired character comes into position beneath the hammer. The hammer strikes the tip of the wheel spoke, carrying the desired character into the ribbon and leaving an image on the paper behind the ribbon.

The wheel rotates, and a hammer presses the required letter against a ribbon to produce a high-quality, typewriter-like character. Some other letter-quality printers use a thimble-shaped mechanism with the individual characters located on the vertical prongs of the thimble. The problem with these types of printers is that they are often very large, very noisy, very slow, and very expensive. Yet they are quite durable, and the print quality is excellent. Their very existence is now being threatened by the influx of less expensive, equally high-quality, and considerably more flexible laser printers.

Laser Printers *Laser printers* offer excellent quality and a vast array of fonts. They can print a whole page at once, at dot densities several times those of dot-matrix printers. Whereas many dot-matrix printers use densities of 9 × 9 dots per character, a typical laser printer uses a density closer to 50 × 50 dots per character. A laser printer, linked with the proper software, enables you easily to print just about anything, including books, papers, magazines, and newsletters. The combination of the flexible output capabilities of a laser printer and the new generation of powerful software for merging text and graphics has given birth to the new field of *desktop publishing*. Using DOS, simply running an application program like Ventura Publisher on a system including a laser printer is all you need to enter the world of self-publishing. The main drawback of laser printers is their cost, which currently runs in the thousands of dollars.

PRINT SCANNERS

Print scanners (sometimes called optical character readers, or OCRs) although they still have a few bugs, offer an easy way to enter data. By running a scanner along a typed line of text, you can quickly enter vast amounts of printed text into your computer and save yourself significant typing time. In addition, since scanner technology is often used to reenter into a computer data printed by another computer, scanners reduce the likelihood of errors in the copied data.

Because scanner technology is relatively new on personal computers operating under DOS, scanners have had some difficulties in accurately identifying characters on the paper. For the most part, this potential problem means only that you should carefully try out a scanner with samples of the text you will be scanning before you actually buy the device. By and large, though, because of the typing time they can save you, optical scanners are still an excellent investment. Scanners also exist to scan graphics and create a bit-mapped, or pixel-based, image.

PLOTTERS

Plotters have been extremely popular for computer-aided design (CAD) applications of DOS computers. Rather than forming images from patterns of dots, plotters contain colored pens that are held above a piece of paper by a moving arm. On some plotters, the arm itself can move in two directions over a stationary piece of paper.

Instructions from your software are transmitted through a serial port to the plotter and control the direction of the pen. Instructions sent to the plotter also control when the pen should be moved down to contact the paper (to actually draw solid lines) and when the pen should be retracted above the paper (to reposition the pen before drawing again).

Some plotters, like the HP7475A, actually move the paper in one direction and move the pen in another direction to create the same X-Y effect of drawing in two directions. Plotters typically accept instructions at a fast rate, so a typical MODE command to set up the serial port for plotting might look like this:

MODE COM2:9600,N,8,1

TAPE DRIVES

If you are using a hard disk system, chances are you know the frustration of having to back up your data on floppy diskettes. Since a hard disk can hold more than 90 diskettes worth of data, performing a backup operation can be very time consuming. For this reason, manufacturers have seemingly taken a step backward and modified the conventional cassette player for data storage.

These new tape drives are considerably smaller than a standard cassette player; they are small enough to fit into a half-size diskette slot on the system unit. They use cassettes that measure about two inches by three inches. The tape itself is very small and thin, but very strong.

The tape is wound very tightly and moves through the drive very quickly in order to keep up with the speed of the data being sent. When you buy a tape backup system, you will usually receive some software with it to perform backup operations. The tape will copy all of the contents of a hard disk in about 15 minutes for a 10-megabyte drive. The tapes usually can hold 15 or 20 megabytes each. Tape backup copies can usually be made unattended; you will be notified when the backup is done, or if another tape is needed.

TOUCH SCREENS

Touch screens apply the same concept as light pens: the user points to information on the screen. With a touch screen, you directly point to (touch) the screen, and the computer responds. The computer knows where you are pointing because the screen is ringed with a series of diodes that emit light beams across the surface of the screen, similar to the beam of light used at the entry way of some stores. When you interrupt this grid of light, the computer knows where your finger is and easily interprets which displayed element (perhaps a menu choice or a graphic icon) you've selected.

Voice-Recognition Devices

Voice-recognition devices allow the computer to actually measure a spoken word for length, clarity, intonation, and so on to match it against a detailed "voice photo" in memory. Voice recognition has not been feasible on a large scale because of the enormous memory requirement, and because even the same person can speak one word in many different ways. However, sophisticated electronics and mathematical models are being developed now. Commercial use of this technology should be more common in the 1990s.

Summary

You can connect your computer to many different devices to accomplish many different tasks. This chapter has presented a sampling of the latest hardware being used and being developed commercially to allow your computer to communicate with and influence the outside world.

For additional information about editing text files, see

- Chapter 6, "EDLIN: The DOS Editor"

For additional information about device drivers, see

- Chapter 10, "Configuration Possibilities"

For additional information about serial data transmission and general computer communications, see

- Chapter 12, "Computer Communications"

For additional information about redirection of output, see

- Chapter 17, "Pipes, Filters, and Redirection"

Chapter 12 concentrated on standard communications between devices in your DOS environment. Chapter 13 extended the sphere of communications to include other hardware devices connected to your system through DOS's built-in ports. The next chapter in this section presents the next logical step in communications. Chapter 14 explains how computers can be connected to other computers through the sophisticated communications capabilities of local-area networks (LANs).

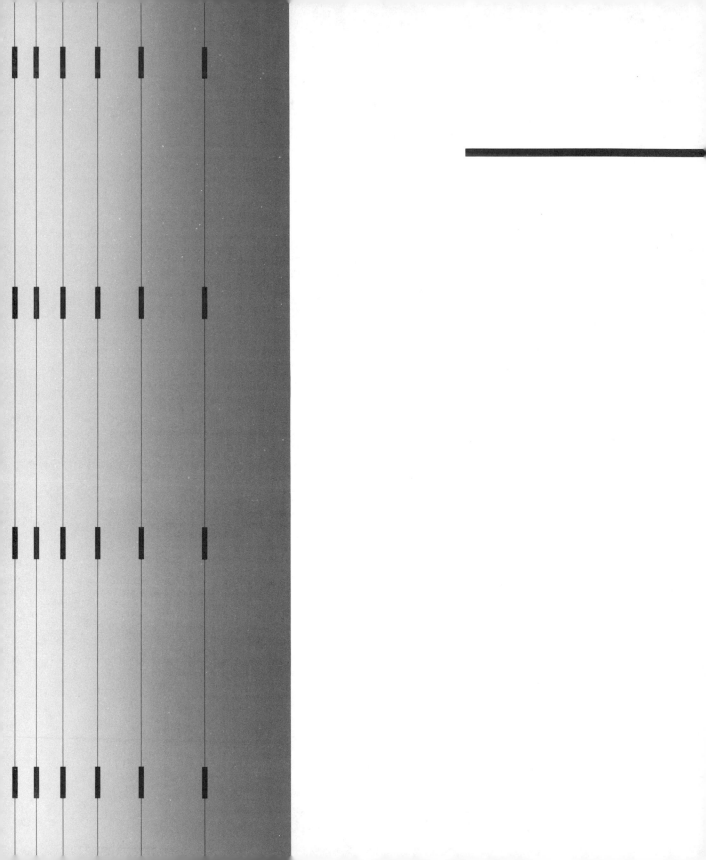

LOCAL AREA NETWORKS

LOCAL AREA NETWORKS

As computers become faster and capable of processing more data at once, they become more capable of performing several tasks at once. This power is most obvious when computers are used in multiuser systems. In a multiuser system, one computer contains the primary processing chip, disk storage, and memory; other computers act as terminals attached to that system. However, in some multiuser systems, the so-called terminals also can perform independent functions. For example, they can offer local memory and processing power for storing notes or handling some of the computational tasks of the main computer. They can also relieve the primary computer of the time-consuming task of monitoring input and output operations at individual stations. The main processing power, however, still is accessible at the primary, host computer.

As the power of these remote terminal computers increases and begins to rival the power of the original central computer, the primary-remote relationship begins to blur. The processing relationship becomes more analogous to a network of power, as opposed to a hierarchy. In fact, these networks of individually powerful computers are commonly referred to as *local area networks*, or *LAN*s. Each station in such a configuration often runs independently, relying on another station only for such processes as access to expensive single pieces of hardware (such as laser printers, E-sized plotters, and extremely large-volume data-storage devices).

Providing multiple users access to a single copyrighted program is a frequent application of networks. The main program can be stored on one computer and then accessed by multiple users at different workstations, or *nodes*. However, even though the LAN manages multiple-user access to the program, difficulties still can arise. Data corruption can easily occur if the application software package was written for only one user, yet is now being accessed by several users. The LAN provides only the mechanism for several users to gain access to the software package; the LAN cannot guarantee that simultaneous access by multiple users to the same spreadsheet or data file will not be mishandled by a software package designed for single-user use. Some companies therefore release multiuser versions of their software to avoid these problems.

> *Warning:* Software companies often sell extra licenses to use their software on different terminals of the same system. If you have a multiuser system, check with your software vendor to make sure that you do not violate copyright laws.

The first part of this chapter surveys the different types of networks, their hardware and software components, and the concepts and terminology involved in working with them. This information will serve as the background for the second part of the chapter, which discusses DOS support for local-area network operations. The last section presents reference entries for the DOS commands used exclusively with networks: CTTY, FCBS, and SHARE.

MAINFRAMES AND MINICOMPUTERS

The problem of multiuser access was first addressed by *mainframe* and *minicomputer* systems. Instead of linking individual computers, these systems link *terminals* to *host units*. A terminal is simply a screen and a keyboard, with little or no processing power or storage ability of its own. The central host unit does all the processing and holds all the memory. This method has both advantages and disadvantages. The first consideration for many potential users is cost.

Another problem with multiuser computer systems is the complete dependency of all users on the one central processing unit. Should the central unit malfunction, all processing on all terminals stops. The terminals, without their central processing unit, are useless, since they have no computing power of their own.

However, multiuser systems do have counterbalancing benefits. Mainframe CPU's execute tasks quickly, and adding terminals to expand multiuser systems is inexpensive. Also, a multiuser environment allows easy access to all data files in the system, making all files for all users resident and available on the one central machine. Electronic mail and document transmission among users is straightforward.

Upgrading a multiuser system is simple also: Only the central unit needs to be upgraded. System maintenance is limited to the main unit, with terminals requiring only secondary maintenance to keep them running. Terminals are also significantly less expensive than a complete, individual personal computer system.

SHARED ACCESS

Linking complete computer systems together, with each sharing the overall processing burden, represents an alternative solution to multiuser systems with shared access to system resources. These linked systems are called *networks*. In addition to various workstation computers, which perform the processing, a network consists of one or several computers, functioning as *servers*, which manage the system's storage and output devices, but do not necessarily process applications.

Processing is performed by the individual stations, each of which is a separate PC, complete with its own on-board processor and disk drives. Data can be sent from one user to another through the network, as in a mainframe system, and files can be accessed by all users using network commands.

NETWORKS

In general, a *network* is simply a connection of interacting components. One component of a network can talk to and work with another component of the network. There are many types of networks and many different ways in which they are set up and share information.

Wide-Area Networks

A *Wide-Area Network* (WAN for short) consists of terminals and computers linked to one main unit, with the accessing terminals spreading beyond the confines of a single building. Terminals can be located across the street or across an ocean from the main unit. WANs are used mostly in large, spread-out companies where employees need access to company-maintained files. However, these networks are extremely expensive, mostly because of the external linkups needed for terminals located outside of the main building. Wide-area networks usually use mainframe-type systems. However, they sometimes use personal computers placed in *terminal emulation* mode. The use of personal computers allows users access to a remote processor while being able to store data locally.

Local-Area Networks

A *local-area network* (LAN for short) is a network in which all processing is performed in one building or installation. Terminals access the main computer directly or from outside the building by using *modems* (devices that allow computers to talk over the phone lines by converting digital pulses into tones and back again; see Chapter 13).

Network Components

The remainder of this chapter concentrates on local-area networks, since DOS is sometimes used in this environment. Remember that the difference among personal computers, mainframe systems, and LANs is where the processing is performed.

NETWORKING TERMINOLOGY

Understanding networks will be easier if you are familiar with some of the basic terminology associated with these systems. A *channel* is simply a data path, or a connection between two elements, such as a workstation and a server. In contrast, a *gateway* is the interface between two networks that operate differently. When data of any sort is sent from one system to other, it must first pass through the gateway. At the gateway the data sequence is stripped of most control bits unique to the originating network. It is then repackaged with information that allows it to move around and be understood in the other network, and then it is passed to that network. The same process occurs in reverse when the other network sends a message back to the first network. A *bridge* is a gateway between two networks that operate the same way, and hence, that require little, if any, changes in the packaging of messages sent between the two systems.

The breaking of a channel, a bridge, or any type of communications link is called a *fault*. Faults are most evident in carrier-based networks (see the section "Information Transmission" later in this chapter), which treat a split-second break in the carrier wave as a fault.

Another term you should be familiar with is *node*. Each junction point, where one channel attaches to any other channel, is a *node*. The two endpoints of a channel are also nodes. Each network server and each network workstation thus are nodes, as are any peripheral devices connected to a network channel. Microcomputers are used as either network servers or workstations, depending on their hardware configuration, as well as the role assigned to them by whomever sets up the network.

WORKSTATIONS

LAN terminals that are linked to the central computer are called *workstations*. Workstations usually are fully capable personal computers with reduced storage capability. For instance, each workstation may only have one diskette drive, whereas the main station may have a large-capacity hard disk drive. Each of these workstations costs less than a fully equipped personal computer, yet it has access to whatever databases are stored on the central computer.

Workstations have their own processors and can also execute tasks without using the central computer. They can use the central computer for long-term storage of data and to route data to printers and other shared devices, such as modems. Thus, in a LAN many workstations perform individual functions, access stored data, and use a common set of peripherals.

Servers

A *server* is a central computer, or a computer that coordinates a network, handles network storage, or manages the spooling of multiple files submitted for printing. A system can have several servers, such as a *disk server*, a *printer server*, and a *network server*. In the context of a local-area network implemented on personal computers, a server is usually an ordinary PC that has been enabled to function as a server through the addition of network software and (usually) add-on cards.

Networking Software

The programs that actually manage the network are collectively called the *networking software*. This software coordinates the transfer of data within the system, from computer to computer, among peripherals, and so on. An example of network software commonly used with DOS is the IBM PC Network Program.

When establishing a personal computer as a node on a network, you must follow several steps. You must first make the appropriate hardware connections, which usually involves installing a network board in each computer, although some very low-cost networks are based on simple RS-232 connections using the serial ports of each networked computer. The software steps you must take are discussed later in this chapter, where network software is discussed in greater detail.

Media

The physical connections throughout a network are referred to as *media*. A medium can be a simple twisted wire, coaxial cable, or a fiber-optic cable. The medium connects the nodes on a network.

The media used affects the cost of networking. Coaxial cable, which consists of a single cable with two different wires in it, is expensive to install. Twisted-pair wire is two wires twisted or otherwise held together, such as phone line; it is easily installed and inexpensive. Fiber-optic cable can increase transmission speed by 1000 percent, but it is expensive to install and, due to a lack of qualified technicians, expensive to maintain. Most low-cost personal computer networks use twisted-pair wiring; they sometimes even use phone-line wiring already established between offices.

NETWORK INTERFACES

A *network interface* is what connects a workstation to the network. Most common interfaces are add-on circuit boards, also called *network adaptor cards*. There are also alternative interfaces that are less expensive, less flexible, and less powerful. These are usually software packages that allow computers to use a modem or a serial port to access the network, but because software consumes time on the workstation processor, such packages generally reduce network transmission speed.

Network Configurations

You can configure a network in several ways. Your configuration decision is extremely important and should be based on your specific needs. A network configuration is called a *topology*, or an arrangement of the component parts of the network. Selecting the best topology for your network is best done in concert with a consultant or staff member knowledgeable in network applications. The decision regarding which network topology is best often rests on what applications you intend to run, how much interaction (if any) you want among users, and where physical workstations are to be located. The following sections give you some sense of how workstation location affects your topology decision, but location is far from being the only criterion you should consider.

BUS NETWORKS

A *bus* network consists of a server connected to a line that runs through all of the workstations or to which the workstations are connected, as shown in Figures 14.1 and 14.2.

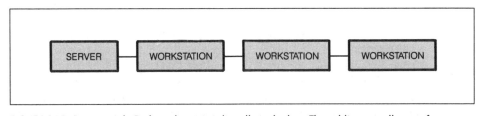

FIGURE 14.1: *Bus* network. Each workstation is literally in the bus. The cabling actually goes from one station, or node, into the next station on the bus. The next connection is made by a cable or wire which leads out of the station and then into the next station on the bus.

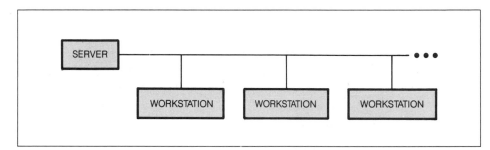

FIGURE 14.2: In this alternative bus implementation, the network provides special hardware for each station to plug into. In this way, each station actually is cabled individually from itself into the bus network. Topologically, each station is still in a particular order. One station precedes another, logically and physically; only the physical connection to the bus is changed.

RING NETWORKS

A *ring* network consists of the workstations and server being hooked up as in a bus network but with the two ends of the connecting cable attached to each other, as shown in Figures 14.3 and 14.4.

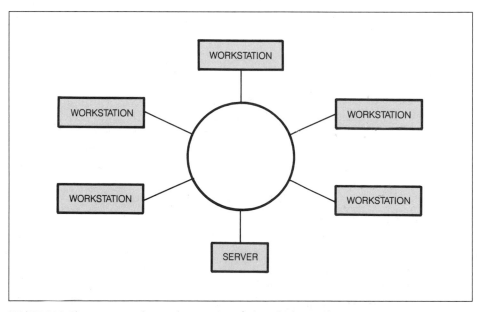

FIGURE 14.3: This ring network is Implemented similarly to the bus implementation in Figure 14.2. Each separate station is wired individually to the network cabling and hardware. In a ring network, there is no obvious beginning or end (for example, as in a bus configuration).

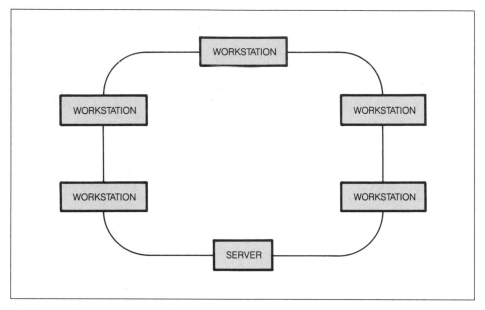

FIGURE 14.4: This ring network configuration looks most similar to the bus network of Figure 14.1; the beginning and end of the bus network are connected in this ring topology. This version of a ring network uses the less expensive technique of running the network cabling through each station, as opposed to running unique cables from each station to a network connector.

STAR NETWORKS

In a *star* network, the server is at the center of the system, and line runs from the server directly to each workstation, as shown in Figure 14.5.

Although they require extra wiring because of their configuration, star networks facilitate resolution of network problems. If something goes wrong with the system, you can easily unplug each workstation one by one until the problem disappears, thereby identifying the problem workstation. Although you can also unplug workstations in bus and ring configurations, doing so requires you to reroute the wiring around the unplugged terminal.

ETHER NETWORKS

In an *ether* network, the server and workstations all connect to a central area, or ether (named for the hypothetical upper region of space), and signals are broadcast into this area and picked up by the destination server or workstation. Figure 14.6 illustrates this type of network.

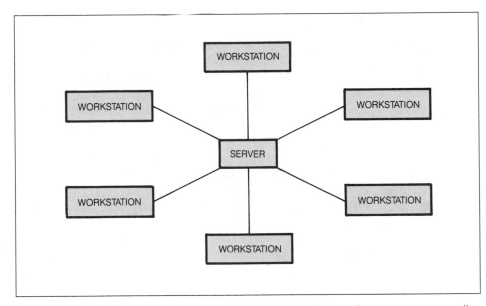

FIGURE 14.5: This star network gets its name from its design, which locates the server station centrally and then connects every other workstation to that star in radiating spokes.

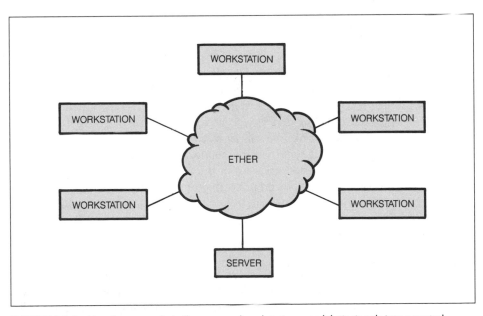

FIGURE 14.6: In this ether network, both server and workstations send their signals into a central hardware area which is responsible for making the messages and data available to the appropriate receiving station.

Information Transmission

Information is transmitted within a network via carrier waves. A *carrier wave* is a continuous tone whose pitch is modified to carry information. For instance, when two computers communicate using the phone system, they use a *modem* to transmit data. Common telephone lines are designed to carry sound, and cannot accept a purely electronic signal. The modem thus translates the digital coding used internally by the computer into a carrier wave, or audible tone. This tone is then retranslated on the other side of the telephone line.

Suppose that the carrier wave is a constant musical note of A. and you want to send the number 101 over the phone lines. To send the first 1, the modem changes the wave frequency to high C. To send the zero, it change the frequency to low C, and to send the last 1 it changes the frequency back to high C. When transmission is completed, the tone on the receiving station's end returns to A.

A network that uses this carrier wave to distribute information is called a *broadband network* (or a wideband network). A network that transmits information as a series of pulses not riding on a carrier wave is called a *baseband network*. Baseband networks are simpler than broadband networks because the pulses transmit signals at their original frequencies, unchanged by any sort of modulation. On the other hand, the use of pulses is inherently more limiting in the range of data and consequently the overall speed of transmission.

Network Protocols

For information to be accurately and successfully distributed within a network, certain rules must be adhered to and certain methods used. Several different sets of these rules and methods have been developed, and each of these sets is called a *protocol*, since each set defines a way of doing things.

A network can link several (from two to many hundred) workstations. Each time information is sent over the network, the data's destination must be known so that the information ends up at the right node. Also, steps must be taken so that two or more stations do not transmit at exactly the same time, with the result being a garbled transmission.

POLLING

In a polling system, a central station sends a message to each workstation asking whether it needs to transmit any information. The central station polls the workstations continuously until it receives a transmission request. The network software facilitates the transmission, and then the polling continues.

CSMA/CD AND CSMA/CA

CSMA protocol is the opposite of polling. CSMA/CA and CSMA/CD stand for carrier-sense multiple access with collision avoidance (CA) or collision detection (CD). In this protocol, before a transmission is introduced into a network, the sending station (workstation or server) listens first to see if any other station is transmitting. If any is, the station waits; otherwise, it sends its data. If two stations begin transmission at the same time, then a *collision* occurs. If *collision detection* is in effect, the transmitting stations stop transmitting, wait a random amount of time, and then start transmitting again. If *collision avoidance* is in effect, transmission continues with garbled information. The stations will know that a collision occurred when they receive an unsuccessful transmission response from the transmission destination.

TOKENS

Another way to regulate transmissions is to transfer a *token*, or code, from station to station. When a station receives the code (and therefore "owns" the token), it can transmit data.

NETWORK SOFTWARE

Assuming that you have connected all of the network hardware, you need to tell the computers how to deal with all the pieces of the network. The network software contains the instructions that govern data transfer throughout the system. Network software is really the most critical part of a network. Equipment surely matters, but the network software determines how the network works. Network software includes such management routines as security, system mail, interstation communications, and network diagnostics programs.

An example of network software that is commonly used with DOS and personal computers is the IBM PC Network Program. This bus network consists of software, add-on cards, and coaxial cables. Its interface to the user includes both a menu system and a command language. As we examine the various layers of network software, we'll see how they are implemented in this network.

Overall System Design

The network software is really a group of programs that work together, but on different levels. An understanding of network software entails an understanding of how the various programs are layered on top of each other, and thus how they interact.

Figure 14.7 shows the layers of a network software system.

When you instruct a workstation to save data on the system's disk drive or to access any of the other network functions, the commands or data traverse the program levels downward. When you recall data from the disk or receive it from the network, the data traverses the program levels upwards.

APPLICATIONS AND FILE LOCKING

An *application* is the particular program running on the workstation that is sending or receiving data from the network. Most programs today need no special software to execute on a network, but you must take certain precautions. In

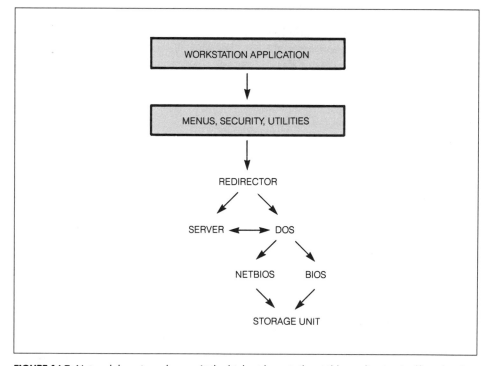

FIGURE 14.7: Network layering scheme. At the highest layer is the visible application itself, and at the lowest layer is the hardware responsible for final implementation of the application request. The network's job is to successively break down, interpret, and carry out the required steps. Various utility programs, complete with menus and security safeguards, provide the user interface at each station. The network redirector software sends necessary data and commands to either DOS or to an appropriate server station on the network. In the latter case, the DOS on the server station handles the serving tasks that will then be local to that station. In all cases, each station's version of DOS uses the local BIOS or NETBIOS to communicate directly to connected hardware.

particular, you must ensure that either DOS or the application program itself can prevent or successfully manage multiple access when several users attempt to access the same file at the same time. Usually, either the entire file or the particular record being accessed must be *locked*. No other user can simultaneously access a file when it is locked. This precludes the possibility of one user changing or deleting a file that another user is reading or modifying.

UTILITIES, SECURITY, AND MENUS

The next layer of software contains the routines for system utilities, data security, and system menus. Utilities perform many tasks, such as checking the status of network connections; sometimes, utilities perform such tasks automatically. Security routines protect your data from other users on the network. Menus display network functions for you to select and use.

In the IBM PC Network, the security scheme includes password protection and restrictions on access to directories. Utility functions, including exchanging messages with other computers, management of print requests, and access to information on other disk drives are available through a menu system that you call up with a hot key.

REDIRECTOR

The redirector part of the network software manages the connection between the workstation and the network and determines what information should be exchanged between the two. The redirector determines at each moment which instructions and data relate to which node on the network.

SERVER

The server layer is not a part of all network software, but it is often included. The server software basically allows the network (and thus everyone on the network) to use the peripheral devices local to any particular workstation, essentially making each workstation a potential server.

DOS

The higher layers just discussed call upon DOS to handle access to disk files and devices such as printers just as any other application programs do. DOS version 3 incorporates network support in many of its features but needs the additional support of the NETBIOS, described below, to implement network activity on the hardware level. DOS can direct requests to its original BIOS or to the NETBIOS as required.

NETBIOS

Computer systems need rules and guidelines to operate. The system software that handles all of the tasks inherent in sharing information and resources is called the *NETBIOS, network basic input/output system*. The NETBIOS handles the basic tasks of sending information to adaptor cards and getting information from them. The NETBIOS is normally included with your network hardware to meet its specific requirements.

BIOS

The BIOS, or basic input/output system, controls the flow of data to and from the disk drives used by the server. Data can either pass through the NETBIOS or straight to the BIOS on its way to the disk drives.

ESTABLISHING A PERSONAL COMPUTER AS A NETWORK NODE

Regardless of the type of hardware connection between your computer and the network, you must take several software steps. First you must issue the command to install memory-resident code to handle hardware-level input and output requests to and from the network. For example, entering

NETBIOS

in a batch file in the IBM network installs the network BIOS (basic input-output system) code in your microcomputer. Once this is done, the network itself can be initiated or begun with the primary IBM PC Network Program command NET. The following example uses the NET command to start the network on a particular workstation. This command also expands certain printer buffers to increase the efficiency of printer operations on the network (see Chapter 12 for more information about buffers):

NET start rdr user1 /PB1:8K

The /PB1 switch reserves an 8K buffer (the default value is only 1K) for the LPT1 printer channel.

Use a variation of this NET START command on the computer used as the printer server:

NET start srv server1 /prb:16K /pb1:8K

This command reserves 16K as a direct buffer for final print data as it is transferred to the actual printer (see Figure 14.8). If this command is not specified, the system uses the default buffer size of only 2K.

A further use of the NET command on the network is for defining the use of a shared hardware device such as a laser printer. When you specify that a workstation send data to the printer server through port LPT1, your startup batch file might contain a NET USE command:

NET USE lpt1: \\server1 \laser

This example recognizes that a command line such as the following has defined a server station:

NET SHARE laser = lpt1:

All of these command requests are means for you to connect individual DOS systems to local area networks. The use of various buffers in these examples hints

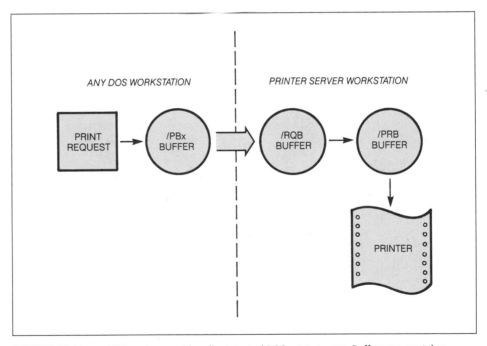

FIGURE 14.8: How a LAN environment handles a typical DOS print request. Buffers are crucial to efficient processing of print requests in all network situations and offer the best opportunity for improving the operating efficiency of printing. Here a print request from a workstation is being sent through the local /PBx buffer until the network enables the print data to be transmitted to the print server. When this happens, the system first stores the print request in the network request (/RQB) buffer until it can honor that particular request for printer service. The server's /PRB buffer holds the actual final output data as it is transmitted to the printer itself.

at the extensive analyses of printer efficiencies possible through parameter adjustments. Remember that at each computer station, your CONFIG.SYS file must define enough memory space for all network buffers. Define memory space with the BUFFERS = xx command (see Chapter 10).

DOS NETWORK SUPPORT

When your computer is part of a network, there are many new aspects to running programs. Communicating with other computers is easy, as is sharing certain expensive peripheral devices. To run DOS on your computer (on your node of the network), you need to know some specific setup requirements and some crucial limitations.

File Sharing using SHARE

The DOS SHARE command loads appropriate support logic for file sharing and protects against one user changing a diskette while another is using it. This logic, in conjunction with the INT 21H function calls 3DH and 5CH (see the *DOS Technical Reference* for programming details), enables you to lock a disk or all or part of a file so that it cannot be used by another process on the same computer. SHARE does not, however, prevent the use of a file by another computer when you are using the network. That level of protection is the responsibility of the network software.

What the SHARE command does is to validate all read or write requests against a special file-sharing logic. It also verifies that, during network operations, the drive door has not been opened and the diskette switched after I/O operations have commenced. The syntax for this external command is

[d:][path]SHARE [/L:*locks*][/F:*filespace*]

Because SHARE is an external command, you must specify the location of the SHARE.EXE file with the [*d:*][*path*] parameters. The /L switch allows you to specify how many unique locks you want for your system (the default value is 20). In any DOS system connected to a network, each individual computer's DOS is responsible through this SHARE command for limiting the number of shared files and simultaneous accesses to those files. Each file to be shared requires DOS to reserve 11 bytes in the *filespace* area plus up to 63 bytes for the full file name. The /F switch controls the amount of space reserved for this file-sharing information (that is, how many files can sustain shared access). The /L switch controls the number of these possible simultaneous accesses that the system will allow.

Each program that opens a file for access can inhibit simultaneous access by another program by *locking* the file against concurrent use. The SHARE command enables you to anticipate how many possible simultaneous accesses can occur and to protect certain files (up to /L:*locks* of them) from multiple shared access.

The /F switch reserves an area for file-sharing information. Although the default *filespace* setting is 2048 bytes, you can increase (and should) that value if you intend to have a large number of open files. The total space allocated should equal enough bytes for all shared filenames plus 11 bytes for each open file.

Configuring for File Sharing Using FCBS

Versions of DOS before 3.0 used a mechanism called a file control block (FCB) to track open files. In these versions, the FCBS command used during configuration (CONFIG.SYS) controls both the maximum number of open file control blocks and the minimum number that must always be kept open.

The syntax of this command is

FCBS = *Maxnum, Permnum*

Maxnum is the number of FCBs that may be opened concurrently (the default value is 4), and *Permnum* is the minimum number of FCBs that remain open when DOS tries to close files automatically (the default value is 0).

When file sharing is loaded (see the SHARE command), DOS keeps track of the least recently used FCB. If any program tries to open more than *Maxnum* files, DOS will close the least recently used file. DOS then opens the requested new file by reusing the now-available file-control block. Since DOS does not maintain the first *Permnum* files on the least recently used file list, these always remain open. The FCBS command is useful only when file sharing is loaded.

Command Restrictions during Network Operations

Some DOS commands make sense only when used on a single computer, and others can easily be garbled in a multicomputer network environment. Table 14.1 lists the DOS commands you cannot use in a network environment and any restrictions.

DOS COMMANDS USED IN NETWORK ENVIRONMENTS

This section describes the DOS commands you can use in a network.

CTTY

This command changes the current input and output device.

RESTRICTED COMMAND	LIMITATIONS
CHKDSK	Network access is not allowed.
DISKCOMP	Comparisons of disks on network devices is not feasible. You can, however, use the COMP command to compare files only.
DISKCOPY	Complete disk copy operations between network disk drives is not feasible. You can, however, use the COPY command to copy individual files.
FDISK	You can partition a hard disk at your own workstation, but not on any other network node location.
FORMAT	You can format a disk only on your own computer, not on any other network drive.
JOIN	You can't join a network drive to a local drive's directory.
LABEL	You can change the label only on a local disk, not on a disk on another network drive.
PRINT	PRINT spooling is a local capability and interferes with network print serving.
RECOVER	You can recover files only on your own workstation's disks. When attempting recovery, you should disconnect your workstation from the network.
SUBST	You can substitute a drive letter only for a local path at your own workstation.
SYS	You can transfer a copy of the DOS system only to a disk on your local disk drive.

TABLE 14.1: DOS Commands Restricted in a Network Environment

SYNTAX

CTTY *Device*

 Device   is a valid device name.

TYPE

Internal.

USAGE

If you use a special system configuration or if another workstation is connected to your workstation through one of the auxiliary serial ports (AUX, COM1, COM2, COM3, or COM4), CTTY can change the current input and output device (which is usually the keyboard and screen) to some other device connected to a serial port. You could, for example, specify a teletype as a console. You can also use the CTTY command to restore the keyboard and screen as the input and output devices after you have used some other device.

RESTRICTIONS

The keyboard and monitor are reset as the main console when you use BASIC and other programs that do not use DOS function calls.

Warning: Specifying a noninput device such as LPT1 in a CTTY command will halt the system. The computer will try to enter data from this port, an invalid operation.

EXAMPLES

Since DOS normally accepts commands from the console (CON:) device, you must invoke the CTTY command to permit command control from another device. For example, if you want to pass control of your computer to someone located remotely but connected to your machine via the modem installed on serial port 2 (COM2:), you enter the DOS command

CTTY COM2:

For you to regain control at your own workstation console, *the person at the remote device* (in this case, COM2:) must issue the command

CTTY CON:

FCBS

In DOS version 1, files were accessed via file control blocks (FCBs). These are approximately 40-byte sections in memory that tell DOS a file's name and other attributes. The FCBS command allows you to access FCBs.

SYNTAX

FCBS = *MaxNum, PermNum*

> *MaxNum* is the number of FCBs that may be opened concurrently (the default value is 4).
>
> *PermNum* is the minimum number of FCBs that will remain open when DOS tries to close files automatically (the default value is 0)

TYPE

Configuration.

RESTRICTIONS

If *PermNum* is less than *MaxNum*, DOS can close an FCB without alerting the program that is using the FCB, an operation that can cause major problems.

EXAMPLES

If your application program uses the older-style file control blocks to maintain status and structure for open files, you must include an FCBS command in your CONFIG.SYS file. For example,

FCBS = 10,6

initializes DOS to allow up to 10 files to be opened concurrently using the file control block method. Six of these files will be kept open at all times. If an application attempts to open 13 files, DOS will keep the first 6 open, and may close 3 of the next 4 that were opened in order to open the eleventh, twelfth, and thirteenth files referenced.

SHARE

This command loads routines that permit file sharing and allows you to lock a disk or all or part of a file so that it cannot be used simultaneously by another process.

SYNTAX

[*D:Path*]SHARE [/F:*FileMem*][/L:*Locks*]

    D:Path   is the drive and path where the command file is located if it is not in the current directory.

    /F:*FileMem*   sets aside the memory to be used for keeping track of file sharing (the default value is 2048 bytes).

    /L:*Locks*   specifies the number of locks that can be in effect at once (the default value is 20).

TYPE

External.

USAGE

In local area networks (LANs), several users often need to access the same file for reading or writing operations. The SHARE command facilitates the necessary file sharing and locking for correct multiple access operations. Users of a DOS system connected to a LAN must invoke SHARE once to load the required code into memory.

EXAMPLES

You must calculate the values for the /F and /L switches carefully. Change the default settings either to conserve space or to ensure that you have allocated enough space. Set the *Filemem* switch value to the sum of 11 bytes plus the number of bytes in the full path name of each file to be shared.

Suppose that your system needs to share 50 files, each with an average full path name requiring 13 bytes (for example, /NET/DTASET01 and /NET/DTASET50). You need to allocate at least 50 × 13, or 650 bytes; rounding that number up to the next sector size suggests this SHARE command:

SHARE /F:1024 /L:50

SHARE does not prevent the use of a file by another computer when you are using networks; that kind of protection should be provided with your network software.

RESTRICTIONS

You can load the SHARE command only once. Subsequent attempts at loading will yield an error message. You must reboot your computer to remove a SHARE command.

SUMMARY

You have learned much in this chapter. In addition to learning about how LANs and networks in general work, you have also seen how parts of DOS and computers themselves interact with other computers and you. You must know what kind of hardware and what kind of software you will need *before* you set up a network.

For additional information about special configurations and the PROMPT command, see

- Chapter 10, "Configuration Possibilities"

For additional information about computer communications, see

- Chapter 12, "Computer Communications"

For additional information about modems and other hardware connected to DOS through serial ports, see

- Chapter 13, "Software Ports and Hardware Devices"

The next two chapters will take you from the general to the specific: from this section's emphasis on generalized computer communications to the very specific output connections established between computers and printers. You will learn about the simplest and fastest methods of outputting data, both from your screen and from your files. You will also learn about print spooling, a sophisticated technique that enables you to continue running other programs and commands while printing at the same time.

PART

6

PRINTING CAPABILITIES

Printing is so critical to successful computing that this section focuses only on printing methods and techniques. These chapters span the range of printing options, from the simplest and fastest methods for outputting your data to paper to the most sophisticated approaches for simultaneous spooling of information to printers while other programs continue to run.

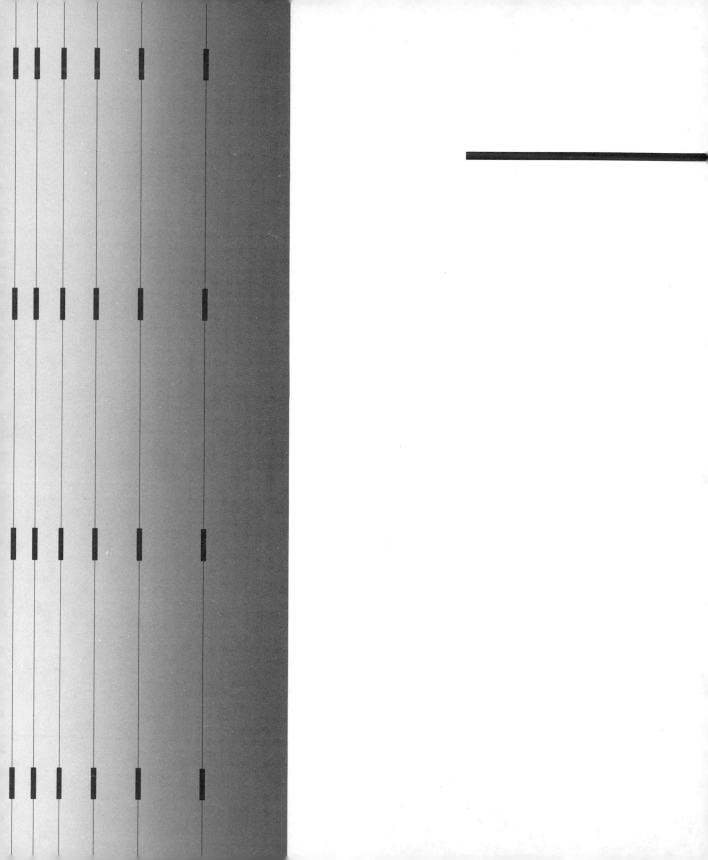

CHAPTER 15

BASIC PRINTING METHODS

BASIC PRINTING METHODS

Producing printed output is an essential final step in almost all computer applications. For this reason most of the powerful application programs offer their own printer commands or keystrokes, which may be quite flexible (particularly in the case of word processors). If you work only with those programs, you may never need to use the facilities that DOS provides for printing. Nonetheless, it is useful to know what kind of printing tasks you can accomplish with DOS commands alone.

This chapter presents the simplest techniques you can use to send output to a printer: printing screens with Ctrl-PrtSc and the GRAPHICS command and printing files with the COPY command. Chapter 16 discusses a more advanced technique called *spooling*. In addition, Chapter 17 shows how any DOS command that ordinarily sends output to the screen can be redirected so as to send its output to the printer instead. This chapter concludes with a complete reference entry for the GRAPHICS command and a partial entry for the COPY command that presents those forms of COPY used in printing. The complete entry for COPY appears in Chapter 3, where the command is introduced.

PRINTING SCREEN IMAGES

It's often easier to generate results on the video screen than on any other output device. However, as you'll learn in this chapter, anything that you can display on your video screen you can print with your printer.

All printers can create an exact replica of any text that appears on a screen. With DOS commands, you can easily obtain hard copies of any important data displayed on your monitor. These commands may be the only ones you ever need to obtain satisfactory printed output from your computer system. Note that to accurately replicate an image on the screen that was created in graphics mode instead of text mode, you must have a printer capable of creating graphics.

Note: A color graphics adaptor (CGA) monitor can generate graphics images using an array of pixels (dots) 640 pixels wide by 200 pixels high. This density—128,000 pixels—is acceptable for most applications, although many programs produce more pleasing and detailed results using denser output screens. An enhanced graphics adaptor (EGA) monitor has a density that is twice that of a CGA. Its graphics mode produces an array of 640 × 350 pixels, and its successors, the professional graphics adaptor (PGA) and the video graphics array (VGA), produce arrays 640 × 480 pixels. The VGA has several additional display modes; a popular one is 720 × 400 pixel resolution, with allows the screen to display more text lines. The top graphics capabilities currently available on IBM Personal System/2 computers feature a 1024 × 768 pixel addressibility.

For a printer to accurately reproduce a screen image, it must be capable of printing dots at the same density, or greater, as the video screen display. As the resolution of video monitors becomes higher, you will increasingly need to be concerned about the ability of your printer to accurately reproduce the high-resolution graphics images possible.

If neither you nor your dealer has yet connected your printer, you should do so now. If you need to do more than simply connect your printer and cable to the appropriate ports, consult Chapter 12, which discusses communications and the MODE command in detail.

Printing Text Screens

DOS requires you to press the keystroke combination Shift-PrtSc to print a copy of whatever is on the screen. The Shift-PrtSc key combination will work on any video monitor if the information being displayed uses standard text characters. To see how this print feature works, turn on your computer and display any document or enter a simple DOS directory command; then turn on your printer and press Shift-PrtSc. Your printer will print a hard copy of the data on the screen.

Printing Graphics Screens

Assuming you have a printer capable of generating graphics images, you can also create printed images of graphics by following a simple preparatory procedure. The GRAPHICS command in DOS is a disk-resident program that enables the same Shift-PrtSc combination to capture graphics screen images for printing if you have an IBM- or Epson-compatible printer. You must invoke this command *before* attempting to print a graphics screen.

The simplest form of the command is invoked by typing

GRAPHICS

This causes future presses of the Shift-PrtSc combination to reproduce on your printer all screen images, including graphics images. You cannot print graphics images from DOS without taking this crucial step.

If you have a graphics program or an integrated package that includes graphics, run it now and print one of the resulting graphics images. First try to print the graphic image without executing the GRAPHICS command. Then return to DOS and execute the GRAPHICS command. Return to your program and press Shift-PrtSc with the same graphics image displayed.

You can specify some of the characteristics of output generated by the GRAPHICS command. The general form of the GRAPHICS command is

GRAPHICS *PrinterType* /R /B

where *PrinterType* is one of the possible parameter values defining printer type, as shown in Table 15.1, and /R and /B are switches for setting background color and reverse video, as you will see shortly. If the GRAPHICS.COM file is not in the current directory, be sure to precede the GRAPHICS command with the names of the drive and directory where it can be found.

PARAMETER	PRINTER TYPE
COLOR1	For a color printer with a black ribbon (prints up to four shades of gray)
COLOR4	For a color printer with a red/green/blue ribbon
COLOR8	For a color printer with a cyan/magenta/yellow ribbon
COMPACT	For the IBM Personal Computer Compact printer
GRAPHICS	For the IBM Personal Graphics printer, or the IBM Proprinter (this is the default)
THERMAL	For the IBM PC Convertible printer

TABLE 15.1: GRAPHICS Command *PrinterType* Parameters

Figure 15.1 shows a typical graphics screen. If you do not execute the GRAPHICS command and simply try to print this screen with the Shift-PrtSc combination, the result will be unsatisfactory, as you can see in Figure 15.2. However, if you first type

GRAPHICS

with no parameters, and press Return before using Shift-PrtSc, the printed result will be what you want, as Figure 15.3 shows.

> *Note:* Printing a screen that contains only text with Shift-PrtSc is reasonably quick (under a minute for most microcomputer printers). Printing a screen containing graphics will require several minutes, depending on the graphics resolution and screen contents as well as the speed of your printer.

If you specify *PrinterType* as COLOR4 or COLOR8, you can print, the background screen color (assuming that your system has color capabilities). Use the /B switch when you invoke the command by typing, for example,

GRAPHICS COLOR4 /B

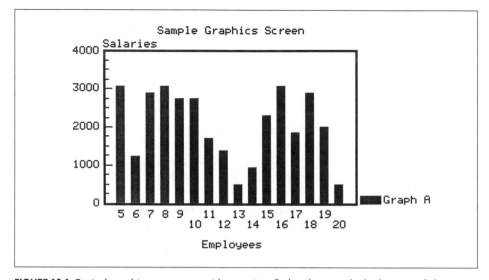

FIGURE 15.1: Typical graphics screen on a video monitor. Rather than simply display textual characters, a graphics screen uses all possible pixels to represent graphic elements such as the lines and bars
seen in this figure. Even the numbers and letters shown here are generated by a special pattern of
pixels, not the standard (usually smaller and less readable) character pattern used when the monitor is
in text mode.

--

FIGURE 15.2: Figure 15.1 printed with the Shift-PrtSc combination. The Shift-PrtSc method of reproduc-
ing a video monitor's image was designed to accurately reproduce only text characters. Without the
assistance of the GRAPHICS command, a printed image of Figure 15.1 might look like this screen. The
two dashes are all that erroneously appeared on this printout.

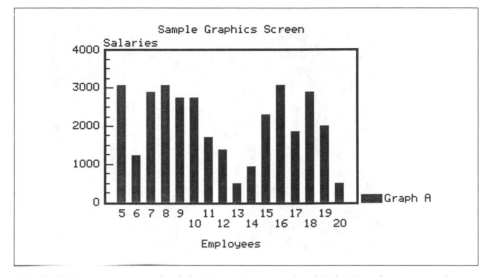

FIGURE 15.3: Figure 15.1 printed with the GRAPHICS command and Shift-PrtSc. After executing the GRAPHICS command at the DOS prompt, the video image seen in Figure 15.1 was accurately reproduced on the printer by using the Shift-PrtSc keypress.

Alternatively, using the /R switch with this command produces a *reverse-video* image (white letters on a black background). For example, typing

> **GRAPHICS COLOR4 /R**

produces the reverse-video output shown in Figure 15.4.

Note that the graphics mode of your video display affects the printed image. If your screen uses high-resolution mode (640 columns by 200 rows), then the printed image will be rotated 90 degrees on the paper to produce a *horizontal landscape* image. If the screen uses medium-resolution mode (320 columns by 200 rows), the printed image will be printed as you see it, producing a *vertical portrait* image. Resolution also affects color printouts; you can obtain four colors in medium-resolution mode, but only two colors in high-resolution mode.

PRINTING FILES

Creating exact replicas of displayed data with the Shift-PrtSc command and the GRAPHICS command is easy, but these commands can print only one screenful of information at a time, whereas often you will want to print an entire data file. Most files are created as standard ASCII files, which usually contain standard letters, numbers, and punctuation. In addition, each line of an ASCII

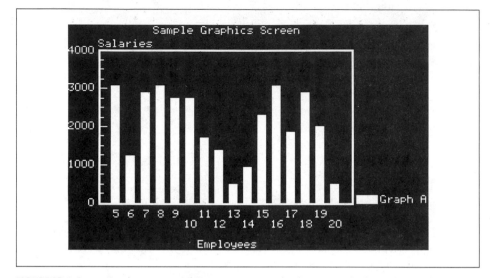

FIGURE 15.4: Reverse-video printout of Figure 15.1. Normal video output displays white characters on a black background. Normal printout generates black output on white paper. The GRAPHICS command has a reversing switch, /R, which, when used when the GRAPHICS command is invoked, causes all Shift-PrtSc images to appear reversed on paper: as letters white against a black background.

file has a carriage return and line feed (CR/LF) at the end of it, but no other special control characters are embedded in the file. An ASCII file can be printed in several ways, as you will see in the following sections.

Warning: Keep in mind that if a file is stored in some special format (as are the files of spreadsheet programs, DBMS programs, and many word-processing programs), you will need to follow procedures particular to that format to obtain a printed copy.

Printing Files with the COPY Command

You can readily copy files of any sort with the COPY command. Chapter 13 shows how to use this command to copy a file from one disk drive onto another. You can also use this same command to copy a file from any location (such as a disk file) to any other location (such as a printer).

DOS COMMANDS FOR BASIC PRINTING TECHNIQUES

Following are reference entries for the DOS commands used for the simple printing techniques described in this chapter. Note that only a partial entry for the COPY command appears here; this highly flexible command has 10 formats, of which four can be used to obtain printed output. A complete reference for COPY appears in Chapter 3.

COPY

The COPY command print functions copy a file from any location to any other location.

SYNTAX

(1) **COPY** *device1 device2*
(2) **COPY** *device filespec*
(3) **COPY** *filespec device*
(4) **COPY** *source[srcswitches] dest[destswitches]*

device, device1, device2	all refer to a valid device (COM*x*, where *x* = 1, 2, 3, or 4).
filespec	is an optional directory and path preceding a valid file name with an optional extension.
source and *dest*	can both be either a device or a file specification.
[*srcswitches*]	are optional switches used to specify different loading characteristics of the *source*. The following switches are available:
	/A tells DOS to copy using ASCII format.
	/B copies the *entire* file.
[*destswitches*]	are optional switches used to specify different copying characteristics of the *dest*. The switches are as follows:
	/A appends Ctrl-Z to the end of a file.
	/B does not add Ctrl-Z to the end of the *dest* file.
	/V tells DOS to verify data sent to *dest*.

TYPE

Internal.

USAGE

The forms of COPY that produce printed output are especially useful for printing multiple files simultaneously, a task that the TYPE command cannot accomplish. Using COPY is also the only way you can directly send information to a device from DOS. Use formats 1 and 2 to copy information from one device to another device or to a file. Use format 3 to directly transfer files to a device. Format 4 is the generic form of the command; it will be used here mainly to explain the use of switches /A and /B.

> *Note:* The COPY command enters data from a file only up to the *first* Ctrl-Z (a special character used as an end-of-file marker). In certain instances, however, this character may not mark the real end of the file, but may represent something to another program. Thus, the term *entire file* is used to refer to all data, up to and including the very *last* Ctrl-Z.

A *device* is a piece of external hardware physically attached to the computer. A *device name* is what the computer uses to refer to that device. The actual interface between the computer and the external, or *peripheral*, device is called a *port*. For example, when you send data to a parallel printer, the computer might send this data to the device named LPT1, routing the data through the first parallel port to the printer. You refer to ports by the type of interface they provide, such as parallel or serial port. You access these ports by using an appropriate device name. The name LPTx (x = 1, 2, or 3) refers to parallel ports, and COMy (y = 1, 2, 3, or 4) refers to serial ports.

If you use the COPY command to print one or more files and have not configured your system with some form of print spooler (see Chapter 16), you will not be able to use your system until the printing has finished. You can regain use of your system at the command prompt by interrupting the printing with a Ctrl-Z keypress.

RESTRICTION

You cannot use the /B switch with the source device connected to a COM or AUX port.

EXAMPLES

Format 1 of the COPY command transfers data, but only at the moment you execute the command and not continuously from one device to another.

To enter data from the keyboard directly to the first parallel printer, using format 1, for example, you can type

COPY CON: LPT1:

After you press Ctrl-Z, this data is sent to the first parallel port (LPT1), which sends it to the printer connected to this port. (You can similarly use other device names in the transfer of data.)

Format 2 of the COPY command copies data from a device into a file. For instance, you can change the command in the preceding example to

COPY CON: AUTOEXEC.BAT

In this case, COPY enters all the text lines that you type as the initial contents of a new AUTOEXEC.BAT file; you do not have to use EDLIN or any other word processor. This command is helpful for short files, but because it allows no editing except for backspacing, it is impractical for a long file.

Format 3 of the COPY command transfers data from a file to a port, thus allowing you to prepare a complete file before printing. This format also allows you to request the printing of multiple files simultaneously. For example, enter

COPY CHAPTER?.TXT LPT1:

to copy *all* files satisfying the wildcard specification to the printer. The computer will check the directory, and before sending a file to the printer, it will display the file's name on the screen.

The purpose of COPY format 4 is to focus your attention on the switches available for this command. Notice not only the effect of each switch, but also the location of each switch specification in the command. The switches perform different functions, depending on whether the switch specification follows the *source* or the *dest* parameter.

First look at what happens when you specify the switches after *source*. Since these switches influence files, you should use them in this location only when *source* is a file specification. The /A switch causes the file to be read as an ASCII file and copied up to but *not* including the first Ctrl-Z. Opposite in function is the /B switch, which copies the entire file, including any Ctrl-Z characters.

When used after *dest*, the switches change functions slightly. Now the /A switch causes a Ctrl-Z to be included at the end of the file, and the /B switch does not add a Ctrl-Z to the end of the file, even if one was sent. Again, when you use these switches with *dest*, *dest* must be a file specification.

You can use the last parameter, /V, with any format. By default, DOS copies its read buffer (when it is full of data entered from *source*) to *dest* and then discards the contents of this buffer, refilling it with succeeding data from *source*. When you use the /V switch, however, or execute the VERIFY command from DOS, DOS does not discard the buffer contents until it reads back in the data it just sent and compares the copy to the original. If the data differs, then DOS will resend the data to try to improve its accuracy. If the *source* and *dest* data match, DOS will reuse the buffer for the next data from *source*.

GRAPHICS

This command allows you to transfer graphics screens to your printer using the Shift-PrtSc key combination.

SYNTAX

[*D:Path*]**GRAPHICS** [*PrinterType*] [**/R**][**/B**][**/LCD**]

D:Path	is the drive and path where the command file is located if it is not in the current directory.
PrinterType	is an optional printer-type specification. Specify COLOR1, COLOR4, COLOR8, COMPACT, GRAPHICS, or THERMAL.
/R	prints a reverse-video image.
/B	prints the background color when *PrinterType* is COLOR4 or COLOR8.
/LCD	prints the image produced on a liquid crystal display.

TYPE

External.

USAGE

The GRAPHICS command enables DOS to accurately reproduce video screen graphics images on a printer using the Shift-PrtSc key combination. You can use several parameter options to tell DOS the type of printer being used and the type of image desired.

EXAMPLES

Suppose you are using the IBM PC Convertible printer for your graphics images. To reproduce a graphics screen on this printer, your GRAPHICS command must include the proper THERMAL parameter:

GRAPHICS thermal

If, in addition, you want to print a reversed white image against a black background, you must include the /R switch:

GRAPHICS thermal /R

Furthermore, if your monitor is an IBM PC Convertible liquid-crystal display, then your GRAPHICS command must also specify the /LCD switch:

GRAPHICS thermal /R /LCD

In these and other variations, the amount of printing time can vary dramatically according to whether reverse (/R) printing is requested. The video monitor mode also influences printing time. For example, when you use printer types GRAPHICS and COLOR1, the screen image is created on paper with up to four shades of gray. In the 640 × 200 color graphics mode, the screen image is printed sideways on the paper (landscape mode); this produces a larger printed image, which requires more time to print.

SUMMARY

In this chapter, you learned the fundamental DOS methods for printing information. You saw how to print screen images with the Shift-PrtSc key combination and how to print graphics images with the GRAPHICS command. You also learned the various ways in which the COPY command facilitates not only printing, but general file transfers between any peripheral devices.

For additional information about the COPY command, see

- Chapter 3, "The Disk System"

For additional information about computer communications, as well as about buffers and printing, see

- Chapter 12, "Computer Communications"

For additional information about buffers and spooling, see

- Chapter 16, "Advanced Printing Techniques"

The next chapter extends the fundamental skills presented in this chapter to include the more sophisticated DOS feature of spooling and simultaneous processing and printing.

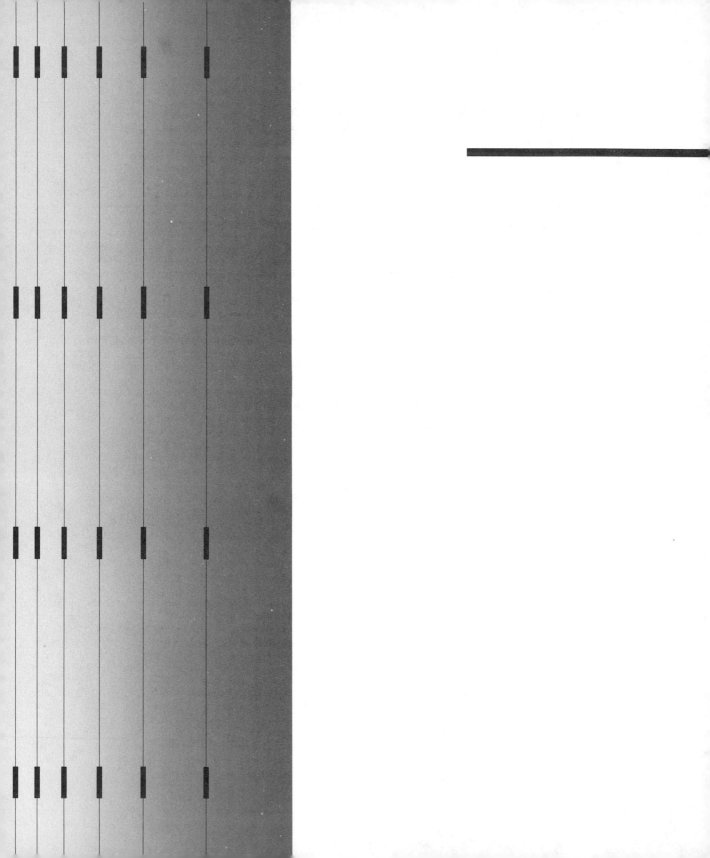

ADVANCED PRINTING TECHNIQUES

Advanced Printing Techniques

I n Part V you learned how the computer communicates with the outside world; that is, how data is transferred from one place to another, particularly between the computer and peripheral devices. One of the most universal of those devices is the printer, as producing printed output is an essential part of most applications. Chapter 15 presents the simplest and most direct methods of printing in a DOS system, based on the COPY command. In this chapter you learn additional methods to help you with your printing jobs. In particular, this chapter focuses on the powerful technique known as *print spooling* and the DOS command that enables you to use this technique, PRINT. As a background to print spooling, the chapter begins with a discussion of buffers.

In the last section of the chapter, we will briefly talk about drawing and plotting as another facet of computer printing. Formerly dominated by plotters, the new generation of dot-matrix and laser printers can provide very acceptable alternatives in plot quality and flexibility.

A Close Look at Buffers

A buffer is an area in memory where information is held temporarily on its way from one part of the computer system to another. Buffers are needed for various reasons. Chapter 11 briefly discusses the keyboard buffer in the context of setting up DOS for international operation; there, a buffer is a necessary step in the process of translating keyboard scan codes into ASCII codes. In printing, the most important reason we need to use buffers is speed. A printer is a machine with moving parts, and as such it cannot operate at the same speed as a purely electronic transfer of information. Without the use of buffers, a printer could never keep up with a computer.

DOS sets up a small area of memory called a printer buffer. DOS puts data into the buffer until the buffer is full, and then it waits until the buffer is empty before entering any more data for printing.

You have no direct control over the amount of memory buffer space DOS reserves for printing, although you can influence the total number of memory buffers DOS has available for miscellaneous operating system chores. See the discussion of the BUFFERS command in Chapter 10 for more information.

How does the print buffer become empty? Each DOS memory buffer actually is emptied by being transmitted to your printer. Each printer always has an internal buffer of its own, which can hold as little as one line or 64K or more. When the printer buffer fills up, the printer signals the computer to stop sending data temporarily. The printer then empties its buffer by printing the data contained in it. Figure 16.1 illustrates this complete sequence, beginning with a typical application program request for printing and ending with the actual printout. The almost invisible part of this procedure is the actual way in which the data passes through DOS buffers and printer buffers.

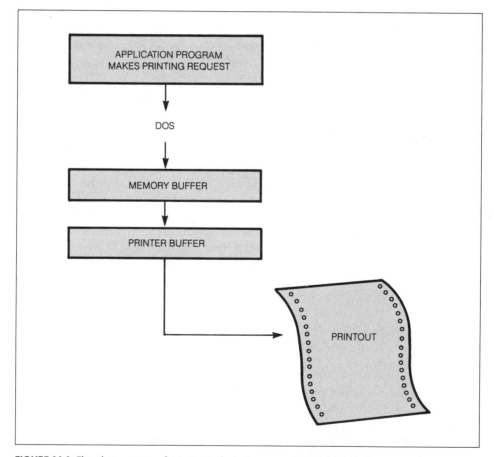

FIGURE 16.1: The obvious parts of printing include the request to print (made from an application program or by issuing the DOS COPY or PRINT command) and the actual printout on your printer. The invisible part of this process, shown in this figure, is the temporary transfer of all data to be printed to a DOS memory buffer and then the temporary transfer of this same data to the printer's internal buffer before printing occurs. Not shown in this figure are the control signals sent between computer and printer to ensure that transmission ceases when any buffer fills up and begins again when buffer space is free for reuse.

The following sections discuss two types of buffers: keyboard buffers and printer buffers.

Keyboard Buffers

You may have noticed that when the computer is performing some operation in DOS, such as copying files, if you type something, it does not appear on the screen until DOS finishes the operation. For example, if you type

COPY A:*.* B:*.*

and then, while DOS is copying all the files, you type DIR, you won't see the letters *DIR* appear on the screen right away. The computer will continue copying, and no directory listing will appear. Once the copying operation is complete, however, DIR will seemingly type itself on the screen, and the directory listing will follow. This process is called *typeahead*, since you are typing your request ahead of when the computer is ready to accept it.

What really happens is this: The computer was using most of its resources for its copy operations, but a small part (the keyboard handler) was watching the keyboard in case you should type something. Since the computer was copying and is not designed for multitasking, it could not perform both the copy and the DIR commands at the same time. Thus, it stored your DIR command until the processor could turn its undivided attention to that processing.

Where did the command go? It went into a small area of memory: another buffer. This buffer can store very little data (typically, only 15 bytes). If you type a command with too many characters, the computer beeps to tell you that the keyboard buffer is full and can store no more of what you are typing. The system discards each character exceeding the capacity of the keyboard buffer, alerting you to this fact by beeping. This process slows down the computer at its other task, since beeping takes considerably more time than storing a few keystrokes. However, the keyboard buffer does provide enough space for most common commands, and it allows you to enter commands efficiently.

Printer Buffers

A printer buffer is similar to a keyboard buffer, except that the computer itself usually feeds data to the buffer instead of you. The computer and the printer each have a buffer. These work in tandem, though printing still often takes considerable time.

To decrease printing time, increase the buffer size of the computer, the printer, or both. There are two ways to do this: by modifying the computer's and printer's hardware, or by using some of the computer's extra memory. This section focuses on how to increase the size of the buffer in the printer.

Note: Some programs set up their own buffers, handle their own direct printing, and will not acknowledge or use any software buffer other than their own.

HARDWARE PRINTER BUFFERS

A *hardware buffer* provides additional physical memory for either the computer or the printer. In a computer, a hardware buffer takes the form of an add-on board, which must usually be set up from DOS according to the procedure shown under the heading "Using a Printer Buffer." Sometimes, though, a computer uses an external hardware buffer that runs between the computer and the printer. A cable from the computer plugs into one end, and a cable to the printer plugs into the other end. This external buffer usually has memory ranging from 8K to 256K and additionally has its own small microprocessor to add some intelligence to the print data handling. Hardware buffers of these kinds require no adjustment in your normal printing commands or application program print sequences.

External buffers work by allowing the computer to send the data to be printed into the buffer at high speed. The buffer then, with its own independent processor, waits for the printer to print.

Some external buffers actually fit onto the control board of the printer. This feature eliminates some of the clutter on your desk, but such buffers require extra effort to install.

SOFTWARE PRINTER BUFFERS

There are several programs on the market that actually carve out a piece of memory (how big is up to you) and stay resident in the computer. That is, when data is sent to the printer, instead of sending it a byte at a time from memory into a small buffer, the computer moves it, a block of data at a time, into the carved-out chunk of memory. The software buffer then slowly feeds this data to the printer. This diversion of the processor's attention does not entail a significant reduction in speed for other tasks the processor is performing at the time.

USING A PRINTER BUFFER

Printer buffers thus allow two processes to occur at once in the computer. They allow your report to be printed, and at the same time they allow you to use the computer to do some other work. This feature can be very handy when you have only a short while to produce a report.

AST Research sells a memory board that serves as a printer buffer. Setting it up for use is not always easy, though, especially if your machine already includes several other add-on boards. On one of my office machines, an IBM PC-XT, I installed an AST Research RAMpage 2MB memory board. To use the memory on this board appropriately for applications in the office, I had to adjust the system's AUTOEXEC.BAT and CONFIG.SYS files.

The CONFIG.SYS file required three additional lines:

> **DEVICE = \REMM.SYS**
> **DEVICE = \REX.SYS 1884**
> **DEVICE = \FASTDISK.SYS 1384 512 25b/e**

The three .SYS driver files required were supplied with the hardware board by AST Research. REMM.SYS contained the expanded memory manager software, REX.SYS contained the instructions to configure extended memory (1884K bytes in this case), and FASTDISK.SYS provided a proprietary version of DOS's virtual disk (VDISK.SYS) software for this board and for the D: RAM disk.

Beyond this initial configuration, the AUTOEXEC.BAT file required additional instructions to make use of 400K bytes for spooling memory:

> **MODE LPT1:**
> **SUPERSPL LPT1:/M = 400/DL/EXTM**

The MODE command is necessary to AST's SUPERSPL (spooling) program setup.

Once the program is established with these two adjustments to CONFIG.SYS and AUTOEXEC.BAT, all normal output from any programs to LPT1 automatically is routed through the memory on the AST board and is managed by the electronic logic circuits on the board and by the management software supplied by the .SYS device files.

SPOOLING

Buffers can be very helpful, but what if you want to print *several* files? You would have to wait for one to finish, then issue a command to print the next, and so on. If you had, say, five reports to print and each require 10 minutes of printing time, you would repeatedly be interrupted from other tasks, or you might sit idle, feeling that 10 minutes is not enough time to get involved in any other task.

Spoolers solve this problem. The term *spool* stands for *s*imultaneous *p*eripheral *o*perations *on-l*ine. Spoolers are like buffers in that they constantly feed the buffers new files to print. These files form a queue. For example, at a busy restaurant, you often have to leave your name with a hostess or maitre d' and wait to be called for a table. Once you are seated at the table, you must still wait until the kitchen has prepared your order. Similarly, a spooler keeps track of files awaiting printing. Then, at an appropriate point, the spooler selects a file name and sends the file contents to the printer for processing.

Spoolers typically accept file names to be printed and then process them in the order that the files are ready to be printed. Some sophisticated spoolers offer special commands that allow the files to be printed in a different order from the order the file names are received. Sending the file to be printed, of course, just sends it on its way to the printer, via whatever buffers (DOS or other) are set up to improve the efficiency of printing operations.

Spoolers work in nearly the same way as buffers do, except they contain different data. In a spooler's memory are the names and locations of files to be printed. The spooler gets a new file as soon as the current job is done printing and dumps it into the buffer. Using a spooler can lead to much greater system availability and more efficiency.

Hardware Spoolers

Like buffers, hardware spoolers are physical devices, with their own processors and memory, that are connected to the computer or printer or between the computer and printer. Their built-in logic, however, manages the orderly transmission of up to several different files to one printer. More sophisticated spoolers can even manage the spooling of many files to different printers. The user effects this by defining special codes indicating which printer is to receive each of the print files. Each sequence of print jobs is maintained in a separate list, or *spool queue*.

Software Spoolers

Also like buffers, software spoolers carve out a chunk of memory and sap a little more of the processor's time to keep track of job progress and to transmit a little data at a time. Once the required installation process is complete, these programs are also *transparent* (you do not actively access spoolers or buffers; rather, they keep track of and change data as necessary).

Microsoft includes a software buffer with DOS. The PRINT command gives you access to this print buffering capability. A reference entry for the PRINT command appears at the end of this chapter. The following paragraphs discuss some of the most important uses for this command.

USING THE **PRINT** COMMAND

Unlike the COPY command, which directly prints to your printer, the PRINT command causes printing to occur indirectly. PRINT sends information to a disk file to indicate which data files are to be printed. Then later, while you are doing other work, DOS independently reads this disk file to discover which data files to print. The printing will occur simultaneously with other work you may then be doing with DOS and your computer system.

Indirect printing, as discussed, is often called spooling. Spooling is the only form of limited multitasking available in the current DOS operating system. (Multitasking is the apparent simultaneous operation of different programs or computer tasks.)

Switches and wildcards, when used intelligently, can also help you control the flow of information and files from one place to another—in this case, from a disk to a printer. The biggest complaint about system performance is the long waiting time for peripheral devices such as printers and plotters, which operate slowly compared to the computer itself; the PRINT command and switches help address this complaint.

Use the directory of .PRG text files in the DBASE\ADMIN\EXPERT directory in Figure 16.2 as you read the following sections.

```
C>DIR/W \DBASE\ADMIN\EXPERT\*.PRG

 Volume in drive C is ROBBINS
 Directory of  C:\DBASE\ADMIN\EXPERT

ARCHIVE  PRG     COLPRINT PRG     COMM     PRG     DATE     PRG     DELAY    PRG
DIR      PRG     DISKRPT  PRG     DUPLICAT PRG     GETSPACE PRG     LOWER    PRG
MAIL     PRG     MENU     PRG     MESSAGE  PRG     MODIFY   PRG     PRINT    PRG
PRINTER1 PRG     PRINTER2 PRG     PRINTER3 PRG     RUNDIR   PRG     SBENTRY  PRG
SBREPORT PRG     SBUPDAT2 PRG     SBUPDATE PRG     SNAP     PRG     STATS    PRG
STRIP    PRG     TIME     PRG     VALIDATE PRG     WASH     PRG     WINDEMO  PRG
WINDOW   PRG
        31 File(s)    1212416 bytes free

C>_
```

FIGURE 16.2: The DBASE\ADMIN\EXPERT directory. This listing shows 31 program (.PRG) files. You'll use some of these text files to explore the PRINT command.

Printing Files with the PRINT Command

The PRINT command is functionally similar to COPY. You could enter the following to print a file name or names on a standard system printer:

COPY *FileName(s)* **PRN:**

You could also just enter

PRINT *FileName(s)*

Unlike the COPY command, for which you must specify a printing destination such as PRN, PRINT *knows* that its job is to send the specified files to a printer. You can use one of the special switches, discussed later in this section, to indicate which printing device the files are to be printed on, but this is not necessary. If you don't specify a switch, DOS will ask you for a destination the first time you invoke the PRINT command:

Name of list device [PRN]:

At this point, you could press Return to accept the displayed default device name, PRN, or you could enter a specific reserved device name (such as COM2) for your system.

Stop now and use the PRINT command to print any text files (.TXT, .BAT, .DTA, and so on) you have on your system. Just enter the PRINT command at the DOS prompt followed by the names of the files you want to print. Use two or three names the first time; then, when DOS asks you for the name of the list device (the destination), just press Return.

Dual Tasking with PRINT

The major difference between PRINT and COPY is apparent immediately after you specify the file names to print and answer any questions PRINT asks you the first time you use it. The DOS prompt returns right after PRINT begins its work. You can invoke other programs or commands while PRINT prints your files. The effect is apparently simultaneous action: The CPU seems to be managing the printing job at the same time it is responding to your new requests at the DOS prompt for nonprinting work. The indirect printing, or spooling, is called a *background task,* and your principal new work (if any) is called the *foreground task.*

This dual-tasking technique is actually electronic chicanery—a silicon sleight-of-hand. A DOS computer has only one central processing chip (CPU), and it can really only do one thing at a time. However, it *can* do things very quickly. In any given period of time, a CPU can rapidly shift its processing attention from a slow printer to a slow typist to a not-really-so-fast disk drive.

If an operating system were advanced enough to manage all this shifting of attention from one operation to another and from one device to another, you would have a true multitasking environment. However, DOS is advanced enough only to play this juggling game between two tasks: printing and one other activity.

Figure 16.3 shows a request to print a single text file, MAIL.PRG, as a background task. In this example, the PRINT command has been invoked for the first time since DOS was started. The name of the desired printer was solicited (with DOS using the formal specification *list device*), and LPT1 was explicitly entered.

```
C>PRINT  \DBASE\ADMIN\EXPERT\MAIL.PRG
Name of list device [PRN]: LPT1:
Resident part of PRINT installed

    C:\DBASE\ADMIN\EXPERT\MAIL.PRG is currently being printed

C>_
```

FIGURE 16.3: First use of PRINT for background printing. As soon as the MAIL.PRG file is accepted for printing by PRINT and a message concerning PRINT's status (MAIL.PRG is currently being printed) is displayed, control is returned to you at the DOS C> prompt for further processing. The printing of MAIL.PRG will continue concurrently with whatever other operations you initiate at the DOS prompt.

Notice that a message appears informing you that the resident part of PRINT has been installed. PRINT expands the resident memory requirements of DOS when it runs. Although the extra memory requirement reduces the memory remaining for your primary application program, this cost is a small price to pay for the ability to continue using your computer while printing proceeds. PRINT also displays a message stating that the requested file is currently being printed. Then the standard DOS prompt reappears. If you now initiate any other command or program, DOS simply shifts its processing power back and forth between the new job and the currently running print job.

Depending on how much slack time exists in your new program (for example, how much keyboard or disk waiting time is built in), the new program may not noticeably slow down. Usually, however, the print job will not run as fast as it could if it were not competing with a foreground task for the processor's attention, though DOS will do its best to efficiently juggle the time spent on the two tasks.

Using Switches with PRINT

DOS provides performance-control switches for indirect printing. Detailed discussion of these switches is beyond the scope of this book. In fact, using these switches at all may be unnecessary for the average user. When future versions of DOS permit multitasking, these parameters will be more useful for fine-tuning DOS.

In the example shown in Figure 16.3, no switches were specified; DOS set its own initial values for the performance parameters. The memory-resident setup uses default settings unless you specify other values by switches. You can use some of these switches only the first time you invoke PRINT. Table 16.1 lists these switches and their parameters.

SWITCH AND PARAMETER	EFFECT
/D:*Device*	Specifies the device to which print output is to be sent (COM1, LPT2, and so on)
/Q:*QueueSize*	Specifies how many files can be accepted by the PRINT command at one time for background printing. Maximum number is 32, and the default value is 10
/M:*MaxTicks*	Specifies the maximum of CPU clock ticks to be used by the PRINT command each time it is given control by the CPU. Range of allowable values is 1 to 255, with a default value of 2
/B:*BufferSize*	Specifies the number of bytes in memory to be used for data to be printed. 512 bytes is standard, but it can be increased in 512-byte increments
/U:*BusyTicks*	Specifies how many clock ticks to wait for a printer that is still busy with earlier printing. Allowable range is 1 to 255, with a default value of 1
/S:*TimeSlice*	Specifies how long PRINT waits prior to getting its share of the CPU. Range is 1 to 255, with a default value of 8

TABLE 16.1: Switches and Parameters that Can Be Used Only in an Initial PRINT Command

Of the six initialization switches, the one you most likely may want to reset is /Q, the queue switch, which indicates how many separately named files the PRINT command can manage. A *queue* is just a waiting line, like a line of people waiting for a bus or for bank service. Here, a queue is a list of files to be printed. DOS allows 10 file names in the queue as the default maximum, but you can adjust this value with the /Q switch.

Figure 16.4 shows what happens if you try to ask DOS to queue more than 10 files when 10 is the maximum. Even though 31 files match the wildcard specification (*.PRG), only the first 10 are accepted for printing into the queue. Since you did not specify the /Q switch, PRINT used the default maximum of 10 slots.

In this situation, DOS displays several messages. It first indicates that the PRINT queue is full. Next, it indicates that the first file, ARCHIVE.PRG, is currently being printed. Messages also appear indicating that each of the other nine files is currently in the queue. Figure 16.5 portrays the way in which this queueing works.

```
C>PRINT  \DBASE\ADMIN\EXPERT\*.PRG
PRINT queue is full

    C:\DBASE\ADMIN\EXPERT\ARCHIVE.PRG is currently being printed
    C:\DBASE\ADMIN\EXPERT\COLPRINT.PRG is in queue
    C:\DBASE\ADMIN\EXPERT\COMM.PRG is in queue
    C:\DBASE\ADMIN\EXPERT\DATE.PRG is in queue
    C:\DBASE\ADMIN\EXPERT\DELAY.PRG is in queue
    C:\DBASE\ADMIN\EXPERT\DIR.PRG is in queue
    C:\DBASE\ADMIN\EXPERT\DISKRPT.PRG is in queue
    C:\DBASE\ADMIN\EXPERT\DUPLICAT.PRG is in queue
    C:\DBASE\ADMIN\EXPERT\GETSPACE.PRG is in queue
    C:\DBASE\ADMIN\EXPERT\LOWER.PRG is in queue

C>PRINT /T
PRINT queue is empty

C>_
```

FIGURE 16.4: Partial PRINT queue. Using the wildcard expression *.PRG normally defines all 31 files from the EXPERT directory. However, the /Q switch was not previously used to increase the number of queue entries from the default value of 10. Hence, only the first 10 files found in the directory table are queued for printing. Note the use of PRINT /T to remove all queued files from the PRINT queue; the file currently being printed, ARCHIVE.PRG, is interrupted, and a message is immediately printed.

The remaining 21 .PRG files that were not accepted into the queue for printing will have to be queued up with other PRINT commands after the first 10 finish printing. The total number of queued files can never exceed the maximum queue size. If you know that you will frequently need to queue more than 10 files at a time, you can type your first PRINT request as

PRINT *FileName(s)* **/Q:32**

Although each increase in queue size requires additional memory, you should use /Q if you frequently need to print many files.

Three other switches are always available to you for management of the queue and its entries. As Table 16.2 shows, they are /P (print), /C (cancel printing), and /T (terminate all spooling). You can use these each time you invoke PRINT, although you'll usually prefer to simply list the files you want to print.

SWITCH AND PARAMETER	EFFECT
/P:FileName(s)	Prints the file(s) specified; this is the default
/C:FileName(s)	Cancels the printing of the file(s) specified
/T:FileName(s)	Terminates the printing of all specified file(s) in the PRINT queue

TABLE 16.2: Switches and Parameters that Can Be Used in Any PRINT Command

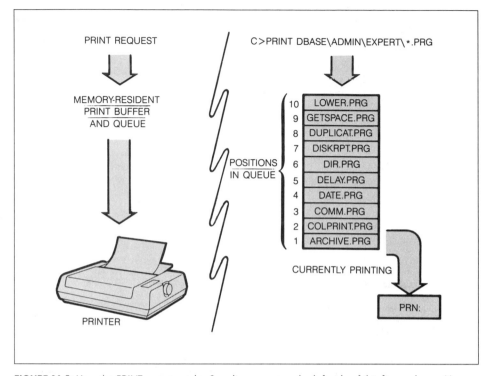

FIGURE 16.5: How the PRINT queue works. Spooling occurs as the left side of this figure shows: Your request generates memory-resident buffer and queue entries that eventually produce printed output. The right side of the figure clearly shows how a PRINT request actually results in queue entries. These queue entries consist of the file names to be printed. The entry names are taken in the order received, and the contents of the named disk files are transmitted to the PRN or some other output port.

You'll probably specify /P least often, since DOS sets it by system default. If you enter

CD \DBASE\ADMIN\EXPERT
PRINT STRIP.PRG SNAP.PRG WASH.PRG

DOS will queue the three text files specified, assuming that the queue has at least three available slots. DOS assumed the /P switch; you did not need to enter it specifically. You will need to use /P only when you construct more complicated PRINT requests.

Tip: When specifying file names in a PRINT command, you can list several different files on the same PRINT request line.

The /C switch cancels the printing of one or more files already in the queue. For instance, to remove the DIR.PRG and DATE.PRG entries from the queue, effectively canceling the former print request for those two files, enter

PRINT DIR.PRG /C DATE.PRG

Notice that the /C switch applies to the file name immediately preceding the switch in the command line and all files listed after it (up to the next switch). This allows a complex but useful construction in which you simultaneously add and remove queue entries. In the next example, LOWER.PRG and DUPLICAT-.PRG are removed from the queue with /C, and STATS.PRG is added with /P:

PRINT LOWER.PRG /C DUPLICAT.PRG STATS.PRG /P

Like the /C switch, the /P switch applies to the file name immediately preceding it on the command line.

If the file you wish to cancel is currently printing, the printing will stop, and you will receive a message to that effect. If the file you cancel is elsewhere in the queue, DOS will remove it, and your monitor will display the new status of the PRINT queue. In fact, you can always see the current queue status by simply entering the PRINT command at the DOS prompt with no parameters or switches. Figure 16.6 demonstrates a status request issued part way through the printing of the .PRG files.

```
C>PRINT
    C:\DBASE\ADMIN\EXPERT\DISKRPT.PRG is currently being printed
    C:\DBASE\ADMIN\EXPERT\DUPLICAT.PRG is in queue
    C:\DBASE\ADMIN\EXPERT\GETSPACE.PRG is in queue
    C:\DBASE\ADMIN\EXPERT\LOWER.PRG is in queue
C>_
```

FIGURE 16.6: Current status of the PRINT queue. You can obtain the current status at any time by simply entering the PRINT command with no parameters and no switches. This status display shows that PRINT is up to the seventh entry of the previous figure, DISKRPT.PRG, and that three files remain to be printed after this.

Finally, the /T switch cancels all file names in the queue. Perhaps the paper has jammed, or an ink-jet cartridge has run dry while the printing continues. In these cases, you may want to cancel all outstanding print requests and then restart the output spool, naming specific files in a particular order. Simply enter the command

PRINT /T

DOS will print the message "All files canceled by operator" on the printer. It will also display on the screen a message stating that the PRINT queue is empty.

> *Tip:* If you use a plotter and your software allows off-line plotting (that is, the software doesn't have to control the plotting process directly), you can use the PRINT command to queue several plots at once. Refer to your plotting program's documentation for further details.

PLOTTING AS A MAJOR SPOOLING APPLICATION

Plotters are in a different output class from printers. They connect to the computer in the same way and respond to spoolers and buffers in the same way, but they operate differently and serve a different function than a typical line or graphic printer.

Plotters have mechanisms for actually *drawing* images on paper using a ball-point or, more commonly, felt-tip pin. They are not good for printing documents since they usually form text characters considerably more slowly than conventional printers.

Plotters work by using a mechanical arm, implemented in several ways, to actually draw from point to point on paper. Contrast this with a dot-matrix printer mechanism, which lays down a matrix of dots to create both characters and graphics; the more dots per square inch, the greater the printer resolution. Or compare it to a letter-quality printer mechanism, which forms characters by striking a ribbon with a fully formed character image, much like a high-quality typewriter.

One way plotters manage their drawing is by using a sliding bar that moves up and down the page. The pen is in a holder that moves lengthwise across the sheet, as shown in Figure 16.7. The pen is lifted from the page when no printing is desired, such as when moving to a new spot, and put down to draw. These states of the pen are called *pen up* and *pen down*.

Because of the very slow drawing movements of a plotter, sometimes slowed down even further by pen changes, plotters benefit even more dramatically from spooling than do printers. You can use both hardware and software spooling to free your computer for other useful work. The ability to continue working with your plotting software application allows you to work on the next plot while the last one is still being drawn on your plotter. The most frequent beneficiaries of spooling are computer-aided design (CAD) programs and the business graphics application packages.

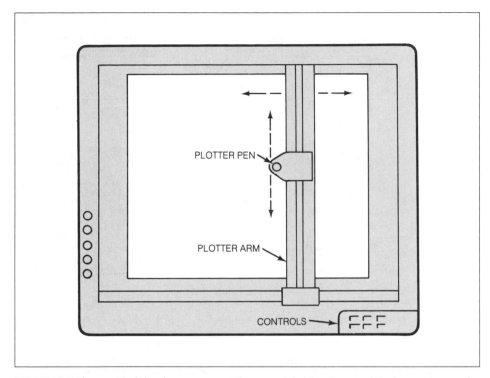

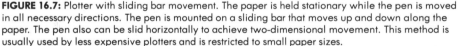

FIGURE 16.7: Plotter with sliding bar movement. The paper is held stationary while the pen is moved in all necessary directions. The pen is mounted on a sliding bar that moves up and down along the paper. The pen also can be slid horizontally to achieve two-dimensional movement. This method is usually used by less expensive plotters and is restricted to small paper sizes.

If you use a hardware spooler, then you needn't do anything special. If your hardware spooler has enough memory to store all the instructions for a particular plot, it will accept those instructions from DOS through the serial port as quickly as the port allows (see the MODE command in Chapter 12).

Another way plotters draw, usually used for high-volume plotting because of its speed and durability, is by moving the pen horizontally and moving the paper vertically. This method has the added advantage that the plotter can use continuous roll paper. Figure 16.8 illustrates this method.

If you have a software spooler in your system, then you similarly need to do nothing special to run your application. The software spooler will store the plot instructions in a disk file and then send those instructions out the serial port to the plotter while you continue to perform useful work with your application program.

CADVANCE is a typical computer-aided design application package. It has a direct plotting option that transmits plotter instructions directly to the serial port. It also has a second option that transmits all plotter instructions to a disk file

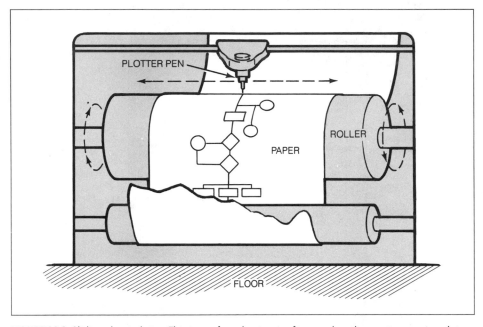

FIGURE 16.8: Sliding-sheet plotter. This type of mechanism is often used on the most expensive plotters. The pen can slide in one direction, while the paper itself is moved forward and backward in the other direction. Large paper sizes are usually managed in this way, and in fact, this plotter can be used with rolled paper, thereby allowing many engineering drawings to be created at full size (at least in one direction).

(named by the user from within the CADVANCE program). Using this second option (called the Utility/Plot option) allows the program to take advantage of the DOS PRINT spooling command.

Using CADVANCE, designers, architects, and engineers are freed from concern about plotting speeds and the size of hardware buffers. Each user can direct CADVANCE to prepare separate plot files during the day using the program's second plotting option. File names follow a carefully prescribed protocol; for example, D1012E19.PLT represents drawing 1012, an E-sized plot, and version 19 of that drawing.

During the course of a day, a user might prepare, for example, four different design variations. At the end of the day, when the user exits the CAD program, control returns to DOS. The following instruction then begins the plotting of all four drawings:

MODE COM2: 9600,N,8,1,P
PRINT D1012E19.PLT,D1012E20.PLT,D1012E21.PLT,
D1012E22.PLT

In this example, the MODE command sets up serial port number 2 to accept data transmission at 9600 baud and then sends the four prepared sets of plot instructions to the PRINT queue. The PRINT command then assumes control of the direct communication with the plotter through COM2. The computer is now free for other work—which is fortunate, because these four plots can often take up to six hours to complete.

THE DOS PRINT COMMAND

This section provides a reference entry for the PRINT command.

PRINT

The PRINT command is used to invoke, modify, and add files to an internal, software-based queue, so that you can automatically output multiple files in order.

SYNTAX

[*D:path*]PRINT [*parameters*][*switches*][*dest1*, ...]

D:path	is the drive and path where the command file is located if it is not in the current directory.
parameters	are optional redefinitions of the queue characteristics. You can enter these only the first time you set up a new print queue. They can be any of the following:

/D:*device*	specifies the output device. The default setting is PRN (or LPT1). If you specify / D, it must be the first parameter specified.
/B:*buffsize*	specifies the size of PRINT's output buffer in bytes. The default value is 512 bytes.
/U:*busyticks*	specifies how much time, measured in *ticks*, the spooler waits each cycle for a busy signal. The default setting is 1 tick. The higher value you assign to *busytick*, the slower the system will run, since the system must wait for the spooler you are requesting. You should increase the value of *busytick* only if you purposely want to maximize printer throughput, since increasing its value lends increased importance to printer output versus CPU processing.
/M:*maxticks*	specifies how much time, measured in *ticks*, the spooler has available for sending data to the printer before switching processing

control to another job. If this number is large, the spooler sends much data, but requires much computer time. If it is small, not much data can be sent, but the overall computer system runs faster. However, if the number is too small, your printer may slow down. The default setting is 2.

/S:*timeslice*   specifies how many time slices the computer allocates to the PRINT spooler every cycle. This value must be between 1 and 255, with 8 the default.

/Q:*queuesize*   specifies the maximum number of entries in the queue. This value may range from 1 to 32; the default value is 10.

switches   are optional settings that can be any of the following:

/C   cancels all previous and following entries on the command line. If you have queued files for printing and wish to selectively abort the queue, you issue a PRINT *filename* /C *filename2* ... command, which cancels the file specified before the /C and all files after it, up to the next switch.

/T   terminates the queue. All files queued are canceled from the queue. If a file is being printed, it is stopped, and DOS prints the message ''All files canceled by operator'' on the printer, sends a top-of-form command, and sounds the buzzer on the printer. DOS ignores anything entered on the line after a /T command.

/P   adds previous and all following entries on the command line to the queue. This switch works opposite to the /C switch. DOS adds the file specified immediately before the /P, and all files after it, to the print queue until it encounters a /T or /C.

[*dest1*, ...]   is an optional list of files with their respective paths, names, and extensions to be queued for printing.

TYPE

External.

USAGE

Since time is an important factor for defining the spooler, the amount of time the spooler needs to perform operations needs to be defined. This time is defined in *clock ticks*. Just as musicians use a metronome to tick off time and to adjust their music, a computer uses an internal clock, which ticks every fraction of a second.

A *time slice* is a very short amount of time, usually equal to a number of clock ticks. The computer allocates some time to one task and some time to another task. It does this by allocating a certain number of time slices to each task, as shown in Figure 16.9. Scheduling jobs by the larger time slice, rather than the smaller clock tick, is done to reduce the administrative overhead. The processing time within DOS's own code takes time away from your program; scheduling time slices rather than clock ticks is an operating system design element that attempts to enhance system performance.

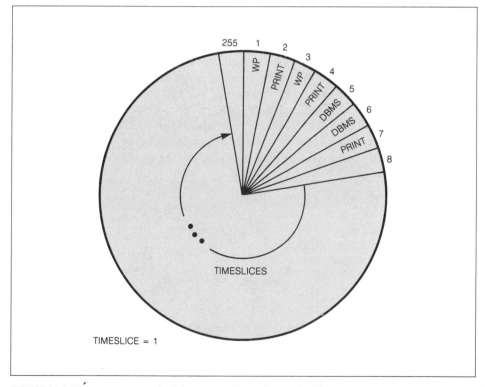

FIGURE 16.9: How a computer schedules time. DOS juggles its available processing time between the primary, or foreground, application program and the secondary, or background, print spooling job. The fundamental unit of time in a computer is the clock tick, a hardware-specific unit of time (usually ticking off nanoseconds or milliseconds). A user-specified group of clock ticks make up a *time slice*, which is the more manageable unit of time for which DOS programs and commands are scheduled.

This diagram shows a unit of time divided into 255 slices—hence, *time slices*. Each slice represents the time the CPU spends on a certain task. Operating systems have scheduling algorithms, or built-in logic that determines how many time slices are allocated to one task before the system moves on to another task. If the CPU allocates 200 time slices every cycle to the keyboard, there will be much idle time during which no effective processing is accomplished; during much of this time, the computer will simply wait for a user to enter new keyboard information or commands.

Thus, to give the illusion that it executes printing at the same time it executes another task, the computer spends one or more time slices on your printing job, and one or more time slices on your other keyboard requests. This explains why DOS seems to slow down slightly when printing occurs concurrently with other work. DOS is spending some of its total processing time and power elsewhere (on the printing) and devotes less attention to you during each total cycle.

The PRINT command follows certain rules, all specified by its parameters. For example, if you leave all default settings in effect, a sample operation would be as follows (see Figure 16.10): DOS allows the CPU to work on your word processor for 8 time slices; then it's the spooler's turn. If you just invoked PRINT, then DOS first checks to make sure the printer is connected and uses *maxticks* of time to spool data. When the spooler's time is used up, DOS switches the CPU to another task. At some future time, the spooler again regains processing control. When DOS returns to the printer, DOS checks whether the printer is still printing the previously transmitted data. If printing has finished, then the entire cycle is repeated. If the previously requested printing is still executing, the computer keeps testing the printer, and if it hasn't completed the printing task within

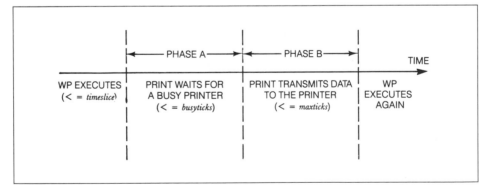

FIGURE 16.10: Flow of PRINT operations. Assuming that some foreground task (such as word processing, or WP) is processing, control will pass from WP to PRINT after a length of time (less than or equal to *timeslice*). When DOS passes control from a foreground application such as WP to the background PRINT task, PRINT first checks for printer availability. It waits up to the number of clock ticks specified in the *busyticks* parameter (phase A). Assuming the printer becomes available in that time, PRINT begins to transmit data to the printer for printing. It does this for a number of clock ticks equal to *maxticks* (phase B).

busytick ticks, PRINT forfeits its current time allocation, and DOS skips to the next task, returning to the printer later.

Figure 16.11 shows what happens when the printer is busy for too long a time period and *busyticks* is exceeded.

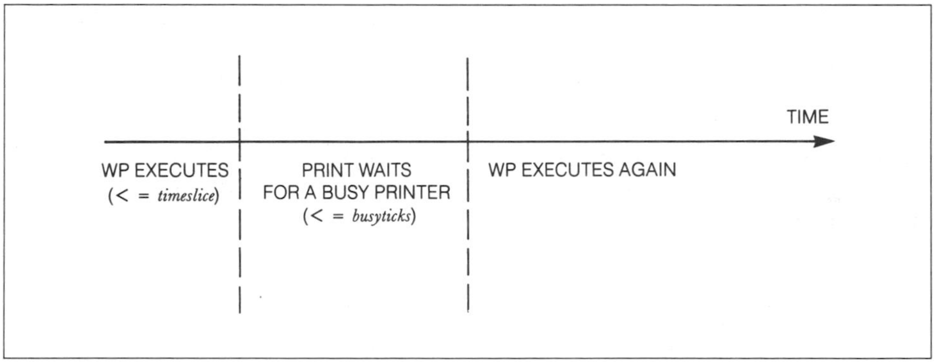

FIGURE 16.11: Flow of PRINT operations when the printer is busy. When PRINT first gains control, it checks for printer availability. If the printer remains unavailable or busy for a period of time longer than *busyticks*, control is passed immediately back to the foreground task (in this example, the word processing program). The print command forfeits the remaining time (*timeslice* minus *busyticks*).

RESTRICTIONS

You cannot use a printer without this PRINT command once any queue begins printing. You cannot use PRINT on a network. You cannot remove the disk where the files are located from the drive until the spooler is done.

> *Note:* The file name is queued, not the file data. Be careful when changing a file's contents after queueing it for printing, because DOS will print the changed file, not the previous version (the version existing when the printing request was made).

EXAMPLES

As Table 16.1 (presented earlier in this chapter) shows, you can set six switches the first time you invoke the PRINT command. For example, if you want to improve printing throughput by *maxticks*, you enter

PRINT /M:12

This command allows six times as much time as the default value for character transmission to the printer before DOS returns control to the foreground task.

Two examples follow. The first gives maximum print time to PRINT jobs:

PRINT /M:255 /S:1 /U:255

This command virtually halts other processing tasks whenever there is printer output to manage.

The second, opposite example gives foreground processing chores high priority over printing tasks:

PRINT /M:1 /S:255 /U:1

This command allocates very little time to printing and very little time to waiting for a busy printer; it implements the maximum delay for subordinating printing to any other task.

Table 16.2, presented earlier in this chapter, shows the three switches you can use any time you queue files for printing with the PRINT command. The following examples demonstrate their use.

Entering

PRINT FILE*.TXT

adds all the corresponding FILE*.TXT files to the print queue, with all of the default settings intact. The computer responds with

Name of list device [PRN]:

PRN is the default name, used here since you did not enter the **/D** parameter.
Entering

PRINT FILE2.TXT /C FILE3.TXT

cancels the files FILE2.TXT and FILE3.TXT from the queue.
Entering

PRINT FILEA.DAT FILE4.TXT /C FILE5.TXT FILE6.TXT /P

adds FILEA.DAT and FILE6.TXT to the queue and cancels FILE4.TXT and FILE5.TXT.

SUMMARY

This chapter showed you how computers manage the printing process and reduce the amount of time users must spend waiting for slow printers. Buffers and spoolers are becoming more popular as memory capacity increases. This chapter also showed you how to apply spooling to plotting to achieve benefits especially attractive in scientific, academic, and artistic environments.

For additional information about special configurations and the PROMPT command, see

- Chapter 10, "Configuration Possibilities"

For additional information about printers and buffers, see

- Chapter 12, "Computer Communications"

For additional information about hardware connected to DOS through serial ports, see

- Chapter 13, "Software Ports and Hardware Devices"

For additional information about standard printing methods, see

- Chapter 15, "Basic Printing Methods"

In the next section, "For Advanced Users," you will learn a host of sophisticated DOS techniques for managing your computer and your data. You will start in the next chapter with the capabilities of redirecting, connecting, and filtering your data.

PART **7**

ADVANCED FEATURES

This section presents the most advanced DOS comamnds, including specialized commands for unique situations and commands for performing advanced data manipulations that would be otherwise impossible. You will take a close look at DOS behind the scenes to discover how the system really works, knowledge you can put to use when you want to perform advanced data-management or file reconstructions. You will also learn how to extend and enhance the power of DOS by using additional, third-party software utilities. One particular extension of DOS is Microsoft's Windows program, a powerful and easy-to-use new multitasking operating environment for DOS programs. Windows is presented in Chapter 22.

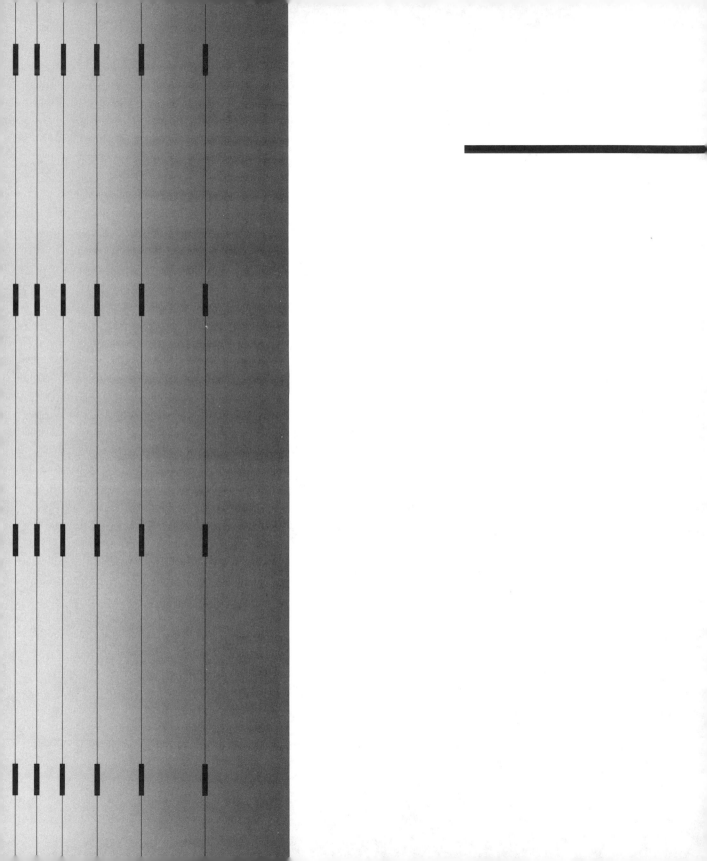

CHAPTER 17

PIPES, FILTERS, AND REDIRECTION

PIPES, FILTERS, AND REDIRECTION

This chapter concentrates on three related features: redirection, filters, and pipes. *Redirection* allows you to specify alternative input and output devices for DOS commands. *Pipes* enable you to direct the flow of information with precision from one command to another. *Filters* permit you to process data as it flows through your central processing unit under your direction. These features offer you additional ways to control input and output in your system, as well as new ways to process information. They are of great interest to programmers designing automated applications for DOS systems; they are also of practical value for anyone using DOS.

CONTROLLING THE FLOW OF INFORMATION BY REDIRECTION

Redirection refers to the ability of a program or a DOS command to choose an alternative device for input or output. Since DOS treats device names and file names as functionally equivalent, you can use either of these names in commands that specify source or destination names. Most programs and commands have a default device. For example, when you enter the DIR command, the computer assumes that you want a directory to be displayed on the screen. This is because the default device for DIR is the console (CON), which consists of the screen as the output device and the keyboard as the input device. Your normal interface with the microcomputer system is through the system console.

Sending Screen Output to the Printer

You often need a printout of the information that appears on your computer screen. As you learned in Chapter 15, the Ctrl-PrtSc key combination is limited to only one screenful of information at a time. However, it is often useful to send the complete output from a command such as DIR to another device, such as the printer. DOS has a simple way of redirecting the complete output, no matter how many screenfuls of data are involved.

Following a command with >PRN tells DOS to redirect the output to the printer. Think of the > sign as an arrow pointing to the destination. Entering the following command redirects the standard DOS directory listing to the printer

(PRN), instead of to the video screen:

DIR >PRN

The same principle of redirection applies to any DOS command that sends data to the screen. Entering

CHKDSK >PRN

generates disk and memory status information and sends it to the printer rather than to the video screen.

Storing Screen Output in a Disk File

DOS can also redirect the output of any command to a text file. This means that the information displayed on the screen can be sent to a file on the disk. Screen displays are temporary; if a directory display is captured and stored in a file, however, its information can be used later.

Redirection has many practical uses. If you're in a hurry and don't want to wait for printed output, you can quickly send the information to a disk file and then peruse it at your leisure. You can read it into your word processing program and then modify it or include it in reports. You can read it with a database management program and perform file management functions based on the information sent by DOS to the disk file.

REDIRECTION TO A DISK FILE: AN EXAMPLE

An excellent use of redirection to a file is to create a catalog of the contents of several diskettes. If you were working with a word processor or a database program, you could then get a master listing of all the files stored on all your working diskettes. If you were working with a hard disk, you could make a catalog of your backup disks.

The first step in creating your own diskette catalog is to decide where to place the master list. Assume that you want to place the data in a file called CATA-LOG. The CATALOG file will be created by DOS in the default directory on your default drive. The first cataloged directory will be that of the diskette in drive A. Entering

DIR A: > CATALOG

produces no visible result on the screen. You told DOS not to display the directory on the screen, but rather to store the information in a file called CATALOG. If you were watching, you would have seen the drive A light come on as the CATALOG file was being written.

To check the results of this command, you can ask DOS to type the contents of the CATALOG file:

TYPE CATALOG

The directory will be displayed just as if you had typed the DIR command. However, this printout represents the directory when the original CATALOG file was created by DOS; it is like a snapshot of the original directory. It contains only the directory information that existed when the file was created. If you continue to work with any of the files in CATALOG, the information contained in that file will not be current, since it will not be updated automatically to reflect any future changes in your system.

Try the following sequence now to reinforce your understanding of redirection. Redirect the output from the DIR and CHKDSK commands at the DOS prompt to a disk file. You can call this file CATALOG, or whatever name you prefer. Use the TYPE command to verify that the output was generated properly.

Later on, you can see that the contents of this file are unchanging. After doing some other work with the system, issue a DIR or CHKDSK command at the DOS prompt again. Compare the results to the snapshot contained in your CATALOG file.

Adding Output to an Existing File

Redirection also allows you to add the directory display of another drive to the CATALOG file. This requires a slightly different command. Look at the following two commands:

DIR A: > CATALOG
DIR A: >> CATALOG

They look quite similar. However, the first command has one > symbol, and the second has two. What is the difference?

The first command simply replaces the old CATALOG file with a new one. The second command, on the other hand, causes the CATALOG file to contain the directory listings of *both* of the diskettes. The >> symbol indicates that the output from the DIR command should be *appended* to (added to) the existing CATALOG file. The directory listing of the new diskette in drive A will be appended to the directory listing of the diskette previously in drive A.

You can continue this process by placing other diskettes in drive A and repeating the >> command. CATALOG will grow as you store your diskette directories on it. If you are a hard disk user, you can place your diskettes in A, and your CATALOG file will be updated on drive C.

To see the contents of this file, enter

TYPE CATALOG

The result will be a consolidated directory that includes the contents of several diskettes.

If you need a hard copy of the directories, you can redirect the data to your printer and use the TYPE command:

TYPE CATALOG > PRN

You can edit this command's output with your word processor, print the results on gummed labels, and attach them to your original diskettes. Some companies charge $50 for programs that perform this simple task.

Try the redirection feature yourself right now. Create your own CATALOG file, listing all the file names on several diskettes. If you're interested only in the names themselves and not in the size or date and time information, use a DIR/W command to direct the output to your CATALOG file. Remember to use a single > sign to create the file and a double >> sign to append new directory output to it. Dual-diskette users should place the diskettes to be cataloged in drive B and create the CATALOG file on drive A. Hard disk users should place their diskettes in drive A and create the CATALOG file on drive C.

Receiving Input from Text Files

DOS can receive input from a text file. This means that instead of waiting at the console to enter data, make responses, or otherwise generate input for a DOS command or a program, you can type your responses in advance. DOS will then take each response from the input file as it is needed. Let's look at a simple example.

> *Note:* Input from a file is more unusual than output. In the normal course of computer use, most users will not take advantage of the feature described here. However, it can be useful.

You may have noticed that some DOS commands require the user to enter additional keystrokes after the program has begun. For example, the FORMAT command always pauses to ask you to press any key before actually performing formatting operations. This safety precaution protects you from errors, giving you a moment to take a deep breath (and to check the disk in the drive) before actually committing yourself to the formatting process.

You can avoid that extra keystroke—and give up that protection—by creating an input file to be used with the FORMAT command. The input file can contain any keystrokes that you want typed while a program is running. In this case, a simple press of the Return key will do. To create a file containing a Return character, you can use a word processor, or you can create the KEYS file from the DOS prompt using the COPY command you saw earlier. Enter

COPY CON: KEYS

and press Return. Then press Return again. Enter

N

and press Return. Then enter

^Z

and press Return. The KEYS file now contains the keystroke for the Return key. It also contains the No response (N) to the FORMAT command's request "Do you want to format an additional diskette?"

To indicate that these responses are coming from a file and not from you at the keyboard, use the < symbol.

FORMAT B:/S < KEYS

When you enter this command, the formatting does not pause—the KEYS file enters Return keypress. When one disk is completely formatted, the N entry tells FORMAT you're done, and the DOS prompt reappears. As you can see, this kind of feature can save you time and effort and can be useful in many situations.

PROCESSING FILE INFORMATION WITH DOS FILTERS

Another powerful feature of DOS is its use of *filters* to process data directly. Just as a camera filter changes what you see through the lens, a DOS filter can process in unique ways any data that passes through it and can change what you see on the screen. DOS includes three filters: SORT, FIND, and MORE. They are stored on disk as the SORT.EXE, FIND.EXE, and MORE.COM files.

Arranging Data with the SORT Filter

Let's first examine one of the most useful filters: the SORT filter. As you will see, DOS's filter commands are equivalent to the simpler features of a data base management system (DBMS). Although SORT can't handle data records as powerfully as a full-featured DBMS, it does allow you to quickly and easily rearrange lines of data. For example, you can enter

SORT

at the DOS prompt, and all succeeding lines of data that you enter will be accepted until you press the ^Z key; then the SORT command will immediately rearrange and redisplay those lines.

judd
eli
joshua   } *Your input*
laura
^Z

eli
joshua
judd
laura

SORT's output

However, the SORT command is more commonly used in a different way. Look at the sample data files in Figures 17.1 and 17.2. These lists could have been prepared with a word processor, a database manager, a spreadsheet, or even with DOS itself. Lists like these usually grow in size, with the new entries added chronologically as your business acquires new clients or as you make new friends and acquaintances.

Every once in a while, you probably rewrite your own personal phone list. You usually want the list in last-name order, but you might want a special printout in nickname or first-name order. Even more often, businesses need to reprint their client list in some usable order. Perhaps the telephone receptionist needs an updated list in company-name order. The marketing department may need the same list printed in telephone-number order. Then again, the accounts payable department may want the list in customer-ID order. All of these sequences are easy to obtain with the SORT filter.

Using the redirection concept presented in the previous section, you can rearrange the data in each of these representative lists to suit your needs. The easiest

```
C>TYPE  BUSINESS.TXT
Cantonese Imports   134  Roberts   Joseph 212/656-2156
Brandenberg Gates   754  Bennett   Mary   415/612-5656
Sole Survivor,Inc.  237  Evans     Gail   415/222-3514
Presley Plastics    198  Presley   Robert 716/245-6119
Plymouth Granite Co 345  Williams  Peter  617/531-6145
Bucket Dance Wear   276  Lewis     Ann    415/635-2530
Intelli-Strategies  743  Griffiths Robert 415/362-9537
Benicia Balloons    983  Franklin  Marie  212/524-4157
Standard Shelters   690  Rucker    Sally  415/532-1107
Panama Rain Corp.   576  Cook      Freda  408/534-9739

C>
```

FIGURE 17.1: A business contact list. A contact list of clients or customers such as BUSINESS.TXT is maintained by most businesses; maintaining such a list is the single most common application of personal computers. In its simplest form, this list is an ASCII file of company names, ID numbers, contacts, and telephone numbers.

form of filtering involves entering the following command at the DOS prompt:

SORT < BUSINESS.TXT

The resulting screen displays the original lines of the file in company-name order (see Figure 17.3).

You can obtain a similar arrangement of your personal phone list by entering

SORT < PERSONAL.TXT

In this case, the arrangement is by last name (see Figure 17.4).

> *Note:* These lists are sorted by whatever data comes first on the line. Later in this chapter, you'll learn how to use SORT to arrange the data based on other information in each line.

In both examples just given, you *input* the .TXT files to the SORT command—the < arrowhead points to SORT. Since you did not specify *output* redirection, the sorted results appeared on the video screen. Each of these commands could also specify an output redirection that would place the sorted results in a disk file. You could then work with the sorted file as you liked, perhaps delaying the printing until a convenient time.

You can save the two sorted lists in the files CLIENTS.TXT and PHONES.TXT with the following commands:

SORT < BUSINESS.TXT > CLIENTS.TXT
SORT < PERSONAL.TXT > PHONES.TXT

```
C>TYPE PERSONAL.TXT
Klaar      Wim      213-968-2345   Ready
Torrance   Stan     415-567-4534   Stan
Quilling   Alan     415-526-4565   Al
Keepsake   Alice    415-249-3498   Jala
Bentley    Robert   415-654-4864   Speed
Hendley    Candice  415-212-3434   Candy

C>_
```

FIGURE 17.2: A personal phone list. This figure depicts a personal contact list maintained as an ASCII file of full names, phone numbers, and nicknames.

```
C>SORT  <  BUSINESS.TXT
Benicia Balloons    983  Franklin  Marie  212/524-4157
Brandenberg Gates   754  Bennett   Mary   415/612-5656
Bucket Dance Wear   276  Lewis     Ann    415/635-2530
Cantonese Imports   134  Roberts   Joseph 212/656-2156
Intelli-Strategies  743  Griffiths Robert 415/362-9537
Panama Rain Corp.   576  Cook      Freda  408/534-9739
Plymouth Granite Co 345  Williams  Peter  617/531-6145
Presley Plastics    198  Presley   Robert 716/245-6119
Sole Survivor,Inc.  237  Evans     Gail   415/222-3514
Standard Shelters   690  Rucker    Sally  415/532-1107

C>_
```

FIGURE 17.3: Sorting by company name. The SORT filter is most often used in DOS to rearrange the data in an ASCII file. In this figure, you use the input redirection operator (<) to redirect the lines of data from the BUSINESS.TXT file to the SORT command for reordering. The sorted output is sent from the SORT to the standard output device, your video monitor.

```
C>SORT  <  PERSONAL.TXT  ·
Bentley   Robert  415-654-4864  Speed
Hendley   Candice 415-212-3434  Candy
Keepsake  Alice   415-249-3498  Jala
Klaar     Wim     213-968-2345  Ready
Quilling  Alan    415-526-4565  Al
Torrance  Stan    415-567-4534  Stan

C>_
```

FIGURE 17.4: Sorting by last name. The SORT filter is most often used in DOS to rearrange the data in an ASCII file. In this figure, you use the input redirection operator (<) to redirect the lines of data from the PERSONAL.TXT file to the SORT command for reordering. The sorted output is sent from the SORT to the standard output device, your video monitor. In this example, notice that the default sequence is based on the first characters on each line.

Figures 17.5 and 17.6 show the verification of these results with the TYPE command. Figure 17.7 shows how the SORT filter works.

Performing Text Searches with the FIND Filter

Now look at another DOS filter: the FIND command. FIND permits you to scan any text file for a series of text characters and to locate any lines in the file that contain the specified characters. For instance, using the business contact list in Figure 17.1, you can use FIND to locate all clients with area code 415:

FIND "415" BUSINESS.TXT

This command locates all lines in the specified text file (the second argument) that contain the specified character string (the first argument). Figure 17.8 shows the results. Note that the first line of the output identifies the input text file.

Note: The quotation marks around the character strings are delimiters. You must use them. They help DOS distinguish a character string from the command line's other characters, which represent commands, file names, or parameters.

```
C>SORT  <  BUSINESS.TXT  >  CLIENTS.TXT

C>TYPE CLIENTS.TXT
Benicia Balloons      983  Franklin  Marie   212/524-4157
Brandenberg Gates     754  Bennett   Mary    415/612-5656
Bucket Dance Wear     276  Lewis     Ann     415/635-2530
Cantonese Imports     134  Roberts   Joseph  212/656-2156
Intelli-Strategies    743  Griffiths Robert  415/362-9537
Panama Rain Corp.     576  Cook      Freda   408/534-9739
Plymouth Granite Co   345  Williams  Peter   617/531-6145
Presley Plastics      198  Presley   Robert  716/245-6119
Sole Survivor,Inc.    237  Evans     Gail    415/222-3514
Standard Shelters     690  Rucker    Sally   415/532-1107

C>_
```

FIGURE 17.5: Sorted client list in text file. Redirection can be used for both input and output in the same command. In this figure, the data lines from BUSINESS.TXT are entered into the SORT command by using the input redirection operator (<). Then the sorted output of the SORT process is sent to a newly created file, CLIENTS.TXT, by using the output redirection operator (>). No output from this sequence appears on the video monitor; you use the TYPE command to view the resulting sorted CLIENTS.TXT file.

```
C>SORT  <  PERSONAL.TXT  >  PHONES.TXT

C>TYPE PHONES.TXT
Bentley   Robert   415-654-4864   Speed
Hendley   Candice  415-212-3434   Candy
Keepsake  Alice    415-249-3498   Jala
Klaar     Wim      213-968-2345   Ready
Quilling  Alan     415-526-4565   Al
Torrance  Stan     415-567-4534   Stan

C>_
```

FIGURE 17.6: Sorted phone list in text file. You can use redirection for both input and output in the same command. In this figure, the data lines from PERSONAL.TXT are entered into the SORT command by using the input redirection operator (<). Then the sorted output of the SORT process is sent to a newly created file, PHONES.TXT, by using the output redirection operator (>). No output from this sequence appears on the video monitor; you use the TYPE command to view the resulting sorted CLIENTS.TXT file.

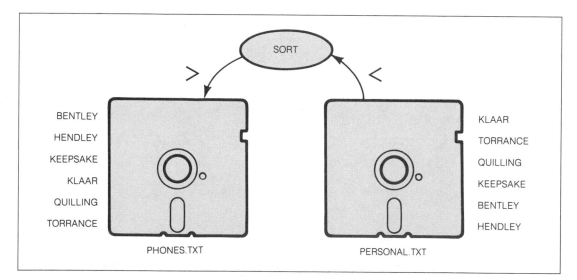

FIGURE 17.7: The SORT filter at work. This illustration depicts the six last names of the PERSONAL.TXT file being filtered by (that is, input to) the SORT command with the < operator. It then shows the six sorted names being output to the PHONES.TXT file with the > operator.

```
C>FIND  "415"  BUSINESS.TXT

---------- BUSINESS.TXT
Brandenberg Gates   754  Bennett   Mary    415/612-5656
Sole Survivor,Inc.  237  Evans     Gail    415/222-3514
Bucket Dance Wear   276  Lewis     Ann     415/635-2530
Intelli-Strategies  743  Griffiths Robert  415/362-9537
Benicia Balloons    983  Franklin  Marie   212/524-4157
Standard Shelters   690  Rucker    Sally   415/532-1107

C>_
```

FIGURE 17.8: Using the FIND filter to extract data that matches the specified string. In this figure, the specified string is "415", and FIND outputs the six lines from the BUSINESS.TXT file containing that string of characters. Notice that one of those lines, the line for Benicia Balloons, actually contains those three characters in the middle of the local phone number, rather than simply in the area code, as intended.

This FIND command is a typical database extraction request, and DOS has handled it *almost* satisfactorily. Notice that the results include the Benicia Balloons company, even though its area code is not 415. You asked DOS to find every line in the file that included 415 anywhere in the line, and 415 is in the last four digits of that company's telephone number: 524-4157. Therefore, the line was filtered into the resulting selection.

To avoid such a this problem, you can specify "415/" as the character string. By including the slash, you will be sure to extract only the telephone numbers that begin with the desired digits. Enter

FIND "415/" BUSINESS.TXT

Figure 17.9 shows the results. Your command has selected the correct lines from the file.

> *Tip:* Make sure your specified character string is limited enough to find only the data you want. The fewer characters in your string, the greater the likelihood that DOS will find lines containing those characters—in contexts other than the one you sought.

You can also name more than one file as input to the FIND filter. With the command shown in Figure 17.10, you can quickly also list any clients in the 212 area code that appear on your personal phone list.

```
C>FIND  "415/"  BUSINESS.TXT

--------- BUSINESS.TXT
Brandenberg Gates    754   Bennett    Mary    415/612-5656
Sole Survivor, Inc.  237   Evans      Gail    415/222-3514
Bucket Dance Wear    276   Lewis      Ann     415/635-2530
Intelli-Strategies   743   Griffiths  Robert  415/362-9537
Standard Shelters    690   Rucker     Sally   415/532-1107

C>_
```

FIGURE 17.9: Ensuring that your character string is sufficient. You use the FIND filter to extract data that matches the specified string. In this figure, the specified string is "415/", and FIND outputs the desired five lines from the BUSINESS.TXT file containing those characters. As intended, the addition of the slash character in the specified string ensures that only lines containing *415* as an area code are extracted.

```
C>FIND  "212"  BUSINESS.TXT  PERSONAL.TXT

--------- BUSINESS.TXT
Cantonese Imports    134   Roberts    Joseph  212/656-2156
Benicia Balloons     983   Franklin   Marie   212/524-4157

--------- PERSONAL.TXT
Hendley    Candice 415-212-3434    Candy

C>_
```

FIGURE 17.10: Filtering multiple files. The FIND command can search more than one file at a time for a specified string of characters. In this figure, FIND searches for the string "212" in both the BUSINESS.TXT and the PERSONAL.TXT files. The lines found in each file are shown separately. This example looks for commonality between business and personal contacts.

```
C>FIND  "617/"  BUSINESS.TXT  PROSPECT.TXT

---------- BUSINESS.TXT
Plymouth Granite Co 345  Williams  Peter  617/531-6145

---------- PROSPECT.TXT
Williams  Peter  Plymouth Granite Co 617/531-6145
Kingland  Benson Ranger Treadmills   617/222-4543
Brandeis  Judd   Scholar Support,Inc 617/298-4455

C>FIND  "415/"  BUSINESS.TXT  PROSPECT.TXT

---------- BUSINESS.TXT
Brandenberg Gates    754  Bennett    Mary   415/612-5656
Sole Survivor,Inc.   237  Evans      Gail   415/222-3514
Bucket Dance Wear    276  Lewis      Ann    415/635-2530
Intelli-Strategies   743  Griffiths Robert 415/362-9537
Standard Shelters    690  Rucker     Sally  415/532-1107

---------- PROSPECT.TXT
Simpson   Robert Wellington Services 415/446-2345

C>_
```

FIGURE 17.11: Finding duplicate entries in multiple lists. The FIND command can search more than one file at a time for a specified string of characters. In this figure, FIND searches first for the string "617/" and then next for the string "415/" in both the BUSINESS.TXT and the PROSPECT.TXT files. The lines with matching characters are shown separately. In an attempt, perhaps, to update the older prospect list, this example looks for overlap between the current client and former prospect lists.

In these sample situations, business and personal lives have been kept apart. The FIND command could just as easily have been used as in Figure 17.11, with two different business mailing lists, to identify duplicate entries that should be removed from the data lists.

The example in Figure 17.11 requires you to specify a FIND character string such as "415/" to locate a specific type of duplicate entry, in this case, for the 415 calling area; you must respecify more area codes to find all duplicate entries. Other tools that you've learned about can do the job even better. First use the COPY command to join the two business files into one temporary file, which you can delete later; then use SORT to filter the resultant file.

Using TYPE with the sorted file now shows you all duplicates. You can also find any record subset of interest (for example, the 415 calling area) with FIND. In both cases, you do not have to look back and forth between two lists. Duplicate entries appear one right after the other, like the two entries for Plymouth Granite Company in Figure 17.12.

Although Figure 17.12 shows the duplicates for the 415 calling area on the screen, remember that the TEMP2.TXT file still contains the sorted collection of *all* records from both the BUSINESS.TXT and the PROSPECT.TXT files. You can now erase this file, or you can use it in further processing.

Warning: When you are joining two files to create a third, or when you are creating any temporary file, make sure your disk has enough space for the operation.

```
C>COPY  BUSINESS.TXT + PROSPECT.TXT  TEMP1.TXT
BUSINESS.TXT
PROSPECT.TXT
        1 File(s) copied

C>SORT  < TEMP1.TXT  >  TEMP2.TXT

C>FIND  "617/"  TEMP2.TXT

---------- TEMP2.TXT
Brandeis  Judd    Scholar Support,Inc 617/298-4455
Kingland  Benson Ranger Treadmills   617/222-4543
Plymouth Granite Co 345  Williams  Peter  617/531-6145
Williams  Peter  Plymouth Granite Co 617/531-6145

C>_
```

FIGURE 17.12: Merging files before looking for duplicates. The previous two figures illustrate the difficulty in visually finding duplication, since if you specify separate file names, FIND separates the output lines. In this figure, however, the COPY command is first used to create a temporary file, TEMP1.TXT, containing all the lines from both the BUSINESS.TXT and PROSPECT.TXT files (using the + operator). These entries are then sorted to produce a TEMP2.TXT file, which becomes the single file processed by the FIND command that searches for lines containing the 617/ sequence of characters.

Controlling Screen Output

The last filter available in DOS is named MORE. This filter causes the screen display to pause, just as the /P switch does with the DIR command. Why not use the /P with the SORT filter? Try it and see what happens. Entering

> **DIR A:/P | SORT**

displays only a blinking cursor if your directory requires more than one screenful of information. This occurs because data to be filtered is stored in a temporary file (a pipe) for filtering; it's not sent to the screen. Thus, the DIR A:/P command forces the computer to pause when a screenful of information is sent *into* the pipe, which is not what you want.

The proper way to handle pauses with filters is to use the MORE filter, like this:

> **DIR A: | SORT | MORE**

The MORE filter pauses the output of the SORT filter, rather than pausing the input from the DIR command. The preceding sequence displays one screenful of the sorted directory listing at a time, signaling you with the "More" message that additional output remains to be viewed. Pressing Return displays the next screenful of information. The command

DIR ¦ MORE

creates a directory display like the one in Figure 17.13.

```
    Volume in drive C is ROBBINS
    Directory of   C:\SYBEX\REFERNCE

    .            <DIR>      3-06-88   10:03p
    ..           <DIR>      3-06-88   10:03p
    ICCL     FW2    12784   8-15-88    7:06a
    ICCL-2   FW2     3072   8-15-88   11:25a
    INSERT12 FW2     8832   8-16-88    2:24a
    CHAP14   FW2    34960   8-16-88    2:24a
    INSERT13 FW2    10496   8-16-88    4:24p
    EARLYINS FW2     2096   8-16-88    4:24p
    INS06NEW FW2     9680   8-16-88    8:05p
    INS08NEW FW2     7936   8-17-88    1:18a
    INS09NEW FW2     1728   8-17-88    4:34a
    INS10NEW FW2      752   8-17-88    5:10a
    INS11NEW FW2     6400   8-17-88    7:03a
    TBL11-XX FW2      512   8-17-88    7:03a
    TBL11-YY FW2      672   8-17-88    7:03a
    INS07NEW FW2      976   8-17-88    3:16p
    INSERT16 FW2    12896   8-17-88    3:23p
    SYBEX2   FW2      768   8-17-88    6:15p
    SYBEX    FW2     2000   8-17-88    6:17p
    DEBBIE   FW2     1056   8-18-88    4:23p
    -- More --_
```

FIGURE 17.13: The MORE filter. A directory listing that exceeds the capacity of a single screen normally will just scroll until it has displayed the complete directory. Entering a command such as DIR ¦ MORE filters the directory listing one screen at a time, displaying — More — at the bottom of the screen and waiting until you press any key to display additional filtered data.

CONNECTING DOS OPERATIONS WITH PIPES

You've seen how the SORT and FIND filters can work with data files as input. Now you'll explore how filters can work in connection with other programs or DOS commands. When these connections are made, they are called *pipes*. Earlier in this chapter, you saw how you could change DOS's default input and output devices using redirection. Pipes allow you to combine the power of redirection with that of filters. You can simultaneously change (filter) your data while it is being moved (redirected) from one location to another.

Even with the redirection techniques you have learned so far in this chapter, if you want to perform several operations in a row, you might still have quite a bit of work to do. You might need to run one program, send its results to a disk file, and then run another program to process the resulting data. Then you might have to take the next program's input from that disk file to continue the processing chain, perhaps creating several intermediate files before getting the final result. Piping allows you to use the output of one command or program as the input of another command or program. You can do this several times in a row. You can automate an entire series of programs that generate intermediate output for one another by using the sophisticated combination of filters and pipes.

Combining Piping and Sorting

As you know, you can use the SORT filter to create a sorted directory listing. By adding pipes, you can use any column in a directory listing as the criterion for the sort order. Sorting directory listings in this way is very helpful, because a normal directory display does not arrange the files in any particular order. Using the SORT filter, you can produce directory listings sorted by file name, file extension, file size, date of creation, or time of creation. As you'll see, you also can arrange any text file in any way you like.

You create pipes by entering the vertical bar symbol (¦) in a command. For instance,

DIR ¦ SORT

sends the output of a DIR command to the SORT filter before the output goes to the screen. The filtered result is a sorted directory display. Figure 17.14 shows a standard directory listing before sorting. Figure 17.15 illustrates the SORT processing operation, and Figure 17.16 presents the sorted results.

This procedure required only a single piping sequence. Previously, you would have had to redirect the results of the DIR command to a disk file and then redirect the disk file to make it the input for the SORT filter. Here, DOS created a pipe to handle the entire job.

Note that the first three lines have also been sorted:

> **17 File(s)   205824 bytes free**
> **Directory of A:**
> **Volume in drive A has no label**

The line "17 File(s)" is indented seven spaces beyond the "Directory" and "Volume" lines, which themselves are each indented one space. The file names that follow are not indented. This indentation is important to note because it makes it clear that the leading spaces on these lines (put there by DIR command formatting) are treated like any other characters by the SORT filter.

```
A>DIR

 Volume in drive A has no label
 Directory of  A:\

ANSI     SYS     1678   3-17-87   12:00p
RESTORE  COM    34643   3-17-87   12:00p
SORT     EXE     1977   3-17-87   12:00p
SUBST    EXE     9909   3-17-87   12:00p
XCOPY    EXE    11247   3-17-87   12:00p
DISPLAY  SYS    11290   3-17-87   12:00p
KEYBOARD SYS    19766   3-17-87   12:00p
PRINTER  SYS    13590   3-17-87   12:00p
VDISK    SYS     3455   3-17-87   12:00p
DRIVER   SYS     1196   3-17-87   12:00p
FIND     EXE     6434   3-17-87   12:00p
FORMAT   COM    11616   3-18-87   12:00p
JOIN     EXE     8969   3-17-87   12:00p
MORE     COM      313   3-17-87   12:00p
REPLACE  EXE    11775   3-17-87   12:00p
       15 File(s)    206848 bytes free

A>_
```

FIGURE 17.14: Unsorted directory listing. A simple DIR listing of a DOS system disk produces the output seen here. Notice the formatting performed by the DIR command: the Volume and Directory lines are indented by one space, and the 15 File(s) line is indented by seven spaces. Note carefully that there is an actual blank line between the Directory line and the ANSI.SYS line.

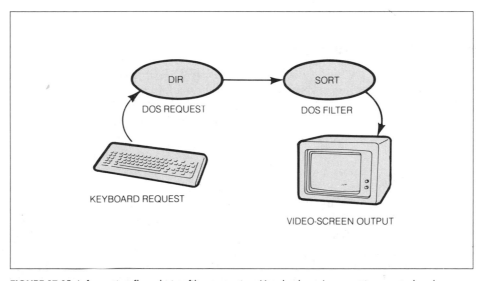

FIGURE 17.15: Information flow during filter operation. Your keyboard request is accepted and processed by DOS (in this case, a DIR command). Under normal unfiltered conditions, the output of the DIR command is sent to your video monitor. The directory listing here is sent to the SORT filter before the sorted results are sent to the video monitor for display.

```
A>DIR | SORT


        17 File(s)     2Ø5824 bytes free
 Directory of  A:\
 Volume in drive A has no label
ØA3BØ55Ø               Ø    7-26-87   1Ø:59a
ØA3BØ727               Ø    7-26-87   1Ø:59a
ANSI       SYS      1678    3-17-87   12:ØØp
DISPLAY    SYS     1129Ø    3-17-87   12:ØØp
DRIVER     SYS      1196    3-17-87   12:ØØp
FIND       EXE      6434    3-17-87   12:ØØp
FORMAT     COM     11616    3-18-87   12:ØØp
JOIN       EXE      8969    3-17-87   12:ØØp
KEYBOARD   SYS     19766    3-17-87   12:ØØp
MORE       COM       313    3-17-87   12:ØØp
PRINTER    SYS     1359Ø    3-17-87   12:ØØp
REPLACE    EXE     11775    3-17-87   12:ØØp
RESTORE    COM     34643    3-17-87   12:ØØp
SORT       EXE      1977    3-17-87   12:ØØp
SUBST      EXE      99Ø9    3-17-87   12:ØØp
VDISK      SYS      3455    3-17-87   12:ØØp
XCOPY      EXE     11247    3-17-87   12:ØØp

A>_
```

FIGURE 17.16: Sorted directory listing. In this figure, the output of the DIR command is piped into the SORT command, which outputs its results to the video monitor. Notice carefully that *all* the data lines in Figure 17.14, including the completely blank line, the seven space indented line (.......17 File...), and the one-space indented lines (Directory... and Volume...), are sorted before they are output. Notice also that the temporary files created by DOS to hold the piping information (0A3B0550 and 0A3B0727) are visible on the listing.

TEMPORARY FILES IN THE SORTING OPERATION

Two extra files, 0A3B0550 and 0A3B0727, appear in the sorted listing. These files are temporary work files created during the sort operation by DOS on the default drive. They are erased automatically when the piping operation is complete. Their obscure file names are based on the date and time of the actual SORT operation.

You can ignore these files completely if you wish. However, you may not want them to appear in your sorted output—their inclusion may confuse others who read your listing. To exclude these files, set the default drive to a drive other than the one you want to sort. Then use the PATH command to tell DOS where to find the SORT.EXE file. On a dual-diskette system, you might set the path to drive A; on a hard disk system, you might set the path to the DOS directory in drive C.

See Figure 17.17 for further clarification. In this example, you first make drive C the default drive. The temporary files will be written on this new default drive. Then you ask for a directory listing of drive A. Finally, you ask DOS to direct the DIR command output to the SORT command for filtering.

```
A>C:

C>DIR A: ¦ SORT


        15 File(s)    206848 bytes free
 Directory of  A:\
 Volume in drive A has no label
ANSI     SYS     1678    3-17-87   12:00p
DISPLAY  SYS    11290    3-17-87   12:00p
DRIVER   SYS     1196    3-17-87   12:00p
FIND     EXE     6434    3-17-87   12:00p
FORMAT   COM    11616    3-18-87   12:00p
JOIN     EXE     8969    3-17-87   12:00p
KEYBOARD SYS    19766    3-17-87   12:00p
MORE     COM      313    3-17-87   12:00p
PRINTER  SYS    13590    3-17-87   12:00p
REPLACE  EXE    11775    3-17-87   12:00p
RESTORE  COM    34643    3-17-87   12:00p
SORT     EXE     1977    3-17-87   12:00p
SUBST    EXE     9909    3-17-87   12:00p
VDISK    SYS     3455    3-17-87   12:00p
XCOPY    EXE    11247    3-17-87   12:00p

C>■
```

FIGURE 17.17: Creating automatic piping files on the default drive. To avoid having the temporary pipe files appear on your listing, you can change the default drive (from A to C here) and then specify the object of the DIR command (the A drive). In this case, then, the temporary files created as pipes are created on the default drive (now the C drive) and do not appear on the listing that represents the A drive.

Warning: The default drive must not be write protected because DOS needs to create temporary files while it performs filtering. In addition, the default drive must have sufficient available space for the temporary files. Otherwise, the automatic piping process will be unable to continue.

Customizing Your DOS Sort Operations

This section explores piping a little further and in the process, looks at some additional capabilities of DOS filters. The SORT filter lets you sort in several different ways. For example, the /R switch tells the program to sort in reverse (descending) order. Entering

DIR A: ¦ SORT /R

produces a directory listing in reverse alphabetical order (see Figure 17.18).

SORT also allows you to specify the column (that is, the character position on each data line) on which you want to sort. Normally, SORT begins with the first character in the line. However, you can tell SORT to sort from another position in the data line, which allows you to sort your directory in a variety of ways. The following command sorts by file extension rather than by file name (see Figure 17.19):

DIR A: ¦ SORT / + 9

```
C>DIR A: ¦ SORT /R
XCOPY     EXE    11247    3-17-87   12:00p
VDISK     SYS     3455    3-17-87   12:00p
SUBST     EXE     9909    3-17-87   12:00p
SORT      EXE     1977    3-17-87   12:00p
RESTORE   COM    34643    3-17-87   12:00p
REPLACE   EXE    11775    3-17-87   12:00p
PRINTER   SYS    13590    3-17-87   12:00p
MORE      COM      313    3-17-87   12:00p
KEYBOARD  SYS    19766    3-17-87   12:00p
JOIN      EXE     8969    3-17-87   12:00p
FORMAT    COM    11616    3-18-87   12:00p
FIND      EXE     6434    3-17-87   12:00p
DRIVER    SYS     1196    3-17-87   12:00p
DISPLAY   SYS    11290    3-17-87   12:00p
ANSI      SYS     1678    3-17-87   12:00p
 Volume in drive A has no label
 Directory of  A:\
      15 File(s)    206848 bytes free


C>_
```

FIGURE 17.18: Directory sorted in reverse alphabetical order. The /R reversing switch applies to the SORT command. In this figure, the directory listing of the A drive is sorted in reverse order before the final sorted results are output to the screen.

```
C>DIR A: ¦ SORT /+9

MORE      COM      313    3-17-87   12:00p
FORMAT    COM    11616    3-18-87   12:00p
RESTORE   COM    34643    3-17-87   12:00p
SORT      EXE     1977    3-17-87   12:00p
FIND      EXE     6434    3-17-87   12:00p
JOIN      EXE     8969    3-17-87   12:00p
SUBST     EXE     9909    3-17-87   12:00p
XCOPY     EXE    11247    3-17-87   12:00p
REPLACE   EXE    11775    3-17-87   12:00p
DRIVER    SYS     1196    3-17-87   12:00p
ANSI      SYS     1678    3-17-87   12:00p
VDISK     SYS     3455    3-17-87   12:00p
DISPLAY   SYS    11290    3-17-87   12:00p
PRINTER   SYS    13590    3-17-87   12:00p
KEYBOARD  SYS    19766    3-17-87   12:00p
      15 File(s)    206848 bytes free
 Volume in drive A has no label
 Directory of  A:\

C>_
```

FIGURE 17.19: Sorting by file extension. The / + n switch enables the SORT command to arrange the data lines beginning at the nth character in the lines. In this example, the file extension begins at the ninth position. Consequently, the directory listing is displayed in extension order (COM, then EXE, then SYS).

The 9 + in this command tells DOS to sort based on the ninth character space. Since DOS uses eight-character file names, the ninth character space is always blank (to separate the base name from the extension). Beginning the sort here sorts on the following three characters: the extension. Specifying sorting on the sixteenth character space in a directory listing, you can just as easily sort the directory by file size (see Figure 17.20). Character space 16 moves you past the base name and extension, allowing sorting on the file sizes.

DIR A: ¦ SORT / + 16

```
C>DIR A: ¦ SORT /+16

MORE     COM       313   3-17-87   12:00p
DRIVER   SYS      1196   3-17-87   12:00p
ANSI     SYS      1678   3-17-87   12:00p
SORT     EXE      1977   3-17-87   12:00p
VDISK    SYS      3455   3-17-87   12:00p
FIND     EXE      6434   3-17-87   12:00p
JOIN     EXE      8969   3-17-87   12:00p
SUBST    EXE      9909   3-17-87   12:00p
XCOPY    EXE     11247   3-17-87   12:00p
DISPLAY  SYS     11290   3-17-87   12:00p
FORMAT   COM     11616   3-18-87   12:00p
REPLACE  EXE     11775   3-17-87   12:00p
PRINTER  SYS     13590   3-17-87   12:00p
KEYBOARD SYS     19766   3-17-87   12:00p
RESTORE  COM     34643   3-17-87   12:00p
 Directory of  A:\
 Volume in drive A has no label
       15 File(s)     206848 bytes free

C>_
```

FIGURE 17.20: Sorting by file size. The / + n switch enables the SORT command to arrange the data lines beginning at the nth character in the lines. In this example, all the file sizes in this directory are displayed after the sixteenth position. Consequently, the directory listing is displayed in file-size order (from 313 to 34643).

In fact, using column number fourteen (/ + 14) instead of sixteen would ensure that this sorting would work at all times, even if the file sizes were very large. Column 16 works here since DOS's DIR command inserts leading space characters before the right justified file size numbers, and none of the file sizes in this directory are large enough to need an entry in column 14 or 15.

Combining Redirection with Filters and Pipes

To make your job easier and quicker, you can also combine a filter with a redirection command. To print a sorted directory listing, you can enter

DIR A: ¦ SORT > PRN

As Figure 17.21 shows, the output of the DIR command is piped forward to become the input for the SORT command; the SORT command output is then redirected from the screen to the printer.

In the next example, you create a text file containing a sorted directory listing. Enter

DIR A: ¦ SORT > SORTDIR

As Figure 17.22 shows, this example is similar to the previous one, except that the final sorted directory listing is not sent to the printer but is instead redirected to the SORTDIR disk file. To see the contents of the SORTDIR file, you enter

TYPE SORTDIR

Referencing Remotely Located Files

With pipes and filters, you can also reference files located elsewhere within the DOS directory structure. For example, Figure 17.23 shows a file called

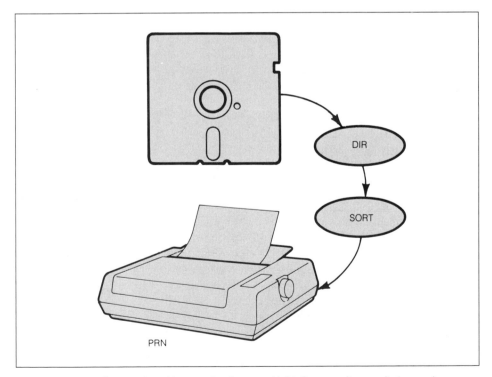

FIGURE 17.21: Combining pipes, filters, and redirection. In this figure, a directory listing can be sorted and then output to a printer for easy review and decision making, using a combination of these features.

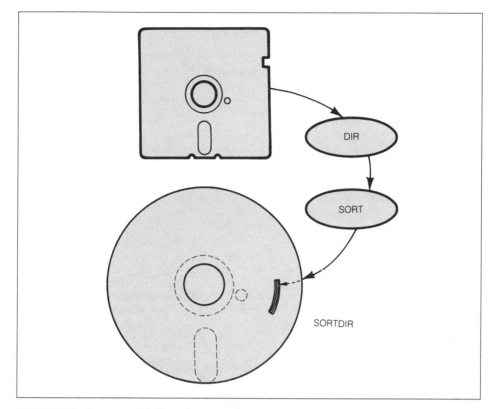

FIGURE 17.22: Creating a disk file with command combinations. In this figure, a directory listing can be sorted and then output to a new disk file (SORTDIR) for later review, text processing, or data base analysis using a combination of pipes, filters, and redirection.

CAD.KEY that is contained in the CAD\VWF directory. CAD.KEY lists the internal macros (miniprograms) of a computer-aided design (CAD) program. It contains three columns of information: the numeric key code, an ASCII indication of which key on the keyboard invokes the macro, and the name of the file containing the macro instructions.

The macro keys are listed in the order in which they were created during previous CAD program use. Even with only a handful of possibilities, it is difficult to see which keys are assigned and which are still available for macros. A simple SORT filter operation can rearrange the file lines within the same file, as shown in Figure 17.24. The command to use is

SORT < \CAD\VWF\CAD.KEY > \CAD\VWF\CAD.KEY

Figure 17.25 shows the results of this simple sorting.

```
C>TYPE \CAD\VWF\CAD.KEY
 316   F2  CLEARALL.MAC
  86    V  VERTSNAP.MAC
 318   F4  EXAMPLE2.MAC
  79    O  SNAPOFF.MAC
  71    G  SNAPGRID.MAC
  66    B  BACKUP.MAC
  76    L  LINE.MAC
  49    1  ALAN1.MAC
  65    A  ALAN2.MAC
  80    P  PLOTFIT.MAC
  51    3  ALAN3.MAC
  52    4  alan4.mac
 317   F3  EXAMPLE4.MAC

C>■
```

FIGURE 17.23: List of macro codes for a CAD program. The CAD.KEY file displayed here is a three-column ASCII file containing an internal key code, a visible keyboard indicator, and the file name of the macro to be invoked when this particular computer-aided design program (CADVANCE) is run.

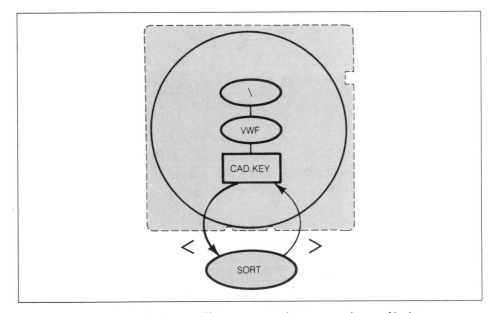

FIGURE 17.24: Sorting a file back into itself. You can use redirection to make your file data more readable. The CAD.KEY file in Figure 17.23 evolved over time, as different macro keys were assigned. Using the redirection operators and specifying the CAD.KEY file as both the input and the output file, you can sort this file by the key code. The sorted list simply replaces the older, unsorted list.

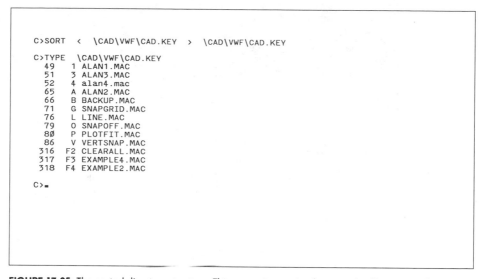

```
C>SORT   <   \CAD\VWF\CAD.KEY   >   \CAD\VWF\CAD.KEY

C>TYPE   \CAD\VWF\CAD.KEY
    49    1  ALAN1.MAC
    51    3  ALAN3.MAC
    52    4  alan4.mac
    65    A  ALAN2.MAC
    66    B  BACKUP.MAC
    71    G  SNAPGRID.MAC
    76    L  LINE.MAC
    79    O  SNAPOFF.MAC
    80    P  PLOTFIT.MAC
    86    V  VERTSNAP.MAC
   316   F2  CLEARALL.MAC
   317   F3  EXAMPLE4.MAC
   318   F4  EXAMPLE2.MAC

C>_
```

FIGURE 17.25: The sorted directory structure. This screen image implements the illustration of Figure 17.24. The CAD.KEY file, located in the \CAD\VWF directory, is both the input and the output file in the redirection and filtering example.

To test your understanding of filters, pipes, and redirection, select any subdirectory on your hard disk, or put any diskette into a disk drive; then construct and enter the proper command to ask DOS to produce a directory listing, sort the listing by file size, and print the results on your printer.

Sophisticated Text Searches Using Redirection

From the output of a command or program, FIND can select lines that contain a certain character or group of characters. You can combine this feature with a piping operation to conduct a sophisticated search operation. For example, the following command lists only those files that contain the letters OR:

DIR A: ¦ FIND "OR"

This command lists such files as MORE.COM and FORMAT.COM (see Figure 17.26), since they contain the letters *OR* somewhere in their file names. Because FIND includes a line if the search criterion is met anywhere in that line, this command also lists SYS.COM and ANSI.SYS.

> *Warning:* When you perform character searches in DOS or any other processing language, the case (upper or lower) of the characters is critical. You always must specify the character string *exactly* as you want to find it in the file.

```
C>DIR A: ¦ FIND "OR"
MORE      COM       313    3-17-87   12:00p
FORMAT    COM     11616    3-18-87   12:00p
RESTORE   COM     34643    3-17-87   12:00p
SORT      EXE      1977    3-17-87   12:00p

C>DIR A: ¦ FIND "SYS"
DRIVER    SYS      1196    3-17-87   12:00p
ANSI      SYS      1678    3-17-87   12:00p
COUNTRY   SYS     11285    3-17-87   12:00p
DISPLAY   SYS     11290    3-17-87   12:00p
PRINTER   SYS     13590    3-17-87   12:00p
KEYBOARD  SYS     19766    3-17-87   12:00p
SYS       COM      4766    3-17-87   12:00p

C>_
```

FIGURE 17.26: Searching capability with the FIND filter. You can use the FIND filter to search input data for a specified string. In this example, the input data is obtained from the pipe created to accommodate the output of the DIR A: command. First, DOS processes the DIR A: command. Then the FIND command displays any line containing the characters *OR* (first case in this figure) and *SYS* (second case).

You can use the FIND filter in reverse as well. For example, if you want to *exclude* all files that have an .EXE extension, you can use the /V switch, as shown in Figure 17.27. All files are found except those that have the letters *EXE* in their name.

The FIND filter can also assign line numbers to output. You request line numbers by adding the /N switch to a command: for example,

DIR A: ¦ FIND/N "EXE"

Figure 17.28 shows the results of this command. Lines 1 through 6 of the directory in drive A did not contain *EXE*, so these lines were discarded. The first line with an *EXE* in it was the seventh line input to the FIND filter; therefore, the /N switch put [7] in front of it. The next lines containing *EXE* were lines 8, 9, 15, 17, and 19.

You can combine switches in a FIND command to perform multiple operations. Figure 17.29 shows a file sorted by both numbering and exclusion using both the /N and the /V switch.

You can also use FIND to count the number of line matches by invoking the /C parameter. For example, suppose you want to know how many .EXE files are on a disk or in a directory. Assume for a moment that you have added the file AUTOEXEC.BAT to a disk in drive A. The command

DIR A: ¦ FIND/C "EXE"

```
C>DIR A: ¦ FIND/V "EXE"

 Volume in drive A has no label
 Directory of  A:\

ANSI     SYS     1678   3-17-87   12:00p
RESTORE  COM    34643   3-17-87   12:00p
DISPLAY  SYS    11290   3-17-87   12:00p
KEYBOARD SYS    19766   3-17-87   12:00p
PRINTER  SYS    13590   3-17-87   12:00p
VDISK    SYS     3455   3-17-87   12:00p
DRIVER   SYS     1196   3-17-87   12:00p
FORMAT   COM    11616   3-18-87   12:00p
MORE     COM      313   3-17-87   12:00p
        15 File(s)    206848 bytes free

C>_
```

FIGURE 17.27: Excluding files with the /V switch. Sometimes you need to locate data records or lines that *do not* contain a particular string. The /V switch enables you to exclude those lines. In this figure, all lines containing the character string "EXE" are excluded from the results.

```
C>DIR A: ¦ FIND/N "EXE"
[7]SORT     EXE     1977   3-17-87   12:00p
[8]SUBST    EXE     9909   3-17-87   12:00p
[9]XCOPY    EXE    11247   3-17-87   12:00p
[15]FIND    EXE     6434   3-17-87   12:00p
[17]JOIN    EXE     8969   3-17-87   12:00p
[19]REPLACE EXE    11775   3-17-87   12:00p
C>_
```

FIGURE 17.28: Using the /N numbering feature of the FIND filter. The /N switch on the FIND command enables you to learn the line numbers of the data lines that meet the specification criteria. In this figure, the six .EXE files found by the FIND command are numbered upon output. Their line numbers show that, in the original DIR A: directory listing, these six files occupied line numbers 7, 8, 9, 15, 17, and 19.

```
C>DIR A: ¦ FIND /N/V "EXE"
[1]
[2]  Volume in drive A has no label
[3]  Directory of   A:\
[4]
[5]ANSI     SYS     1678    3-17-87   12:00p
[6]RESTORE  COM    34643    3-17-87   12:00p
[10]DISPLAY  SYS   11290    3-17-87   12:00p
[11]KEYBOARD SYS   19766    3-17-87   12:00p
[12]PRINTER  SYS   13590    3-17-87   12:00p
[13]VDISK    SYS    3455    3-17-87   12:00p
[14]DRIVER   SYS    1196    3-17-87   12:00p
[16]FORMAT   COM   11616    3-18-87   12:00p
[18]MORE     COM     313    3-17-87   12:00p
[20]        15 File(s)    206848 bytes free

C>_
```

FIGURE 17.29: Combining FIND switches. All DOS commands allow you to combine command switches, whenever the combination is sensible. In this example, the /N and /V switches are combined to yield a numbered listing of all directory listing lines that *do not* contain the character string "EXE". Notice that, as expected, the six line numbers missing from this output listing are the six lines containing .EXE file names shown in Figure 17.28.

produces an answer of 7, as shown in Figure 17.30. This answer seems inaccurate, since only six files have the extension .EXE. However, remember that FIND locates *all* occurrences of the specified character string—and AUTO-EXEC.BAT contains these characters as well.

Once again, you need to specify a definitive character string. In this case, since the extension is always preceded by at least one space in the directory listing, the string " EXE" correctly identifies the six .EXE files, as Figure 17.31 shows.

Saving Time by Combining Filters

Once you are comfortable with DOS filters, you can save yourself both typing time and waiting time. You don't need to wait for the SORT filter to finish its work before you ask the FIND filter to begin. Since you can use the SORT and FIND filters together, you can tell DOS to execute both filters, one after the other. Enter

DIR A: ¦ SORT ¦ FIND "EXE"

to receive a sorted listing of the .EXE files (see Figure 17.32). The listing again includes AUTOEXEC.BAT.

```
C>DIR A: ¦ FIND/C "EXE"
7

C>DIR A: ¦ FIND "EXE"
AUTOEXEC BAT        152    7-Ø5-87   11:32a
SORT     EXE       1977    3-17-87   12:ØØp
SUBST    EXE       99Ø9    3-17-87   12:ØØp
XCOPY    EXE      11247    3-17-87   12:ØØp
FIND     EXE       6434    3-17-87   12:ØØp
JOIN     EXE       8969    3-17-87   12:ØØp
REPLACE  EXE      11775    3-17-87   12:ØØp

C>■
```

FIGURE 17.30: Counting occurrences with the /C switch. In this figure, the first command line uses the /C switch to discover that there are seven lines containing EXE. The second command actually displays those seven lines. Notice that AUTOEXEC.BAT meets the matching criterion and is dutifully included in the listing, even though its inclusion was probably not intended.

```
C>DIR A: ¦ FIND/C " EXE"
6

C>DIR A: ¦ FIND " EXE"
SORT     EXE       1977    3-17-87   12:ØØp
SUBST    EXE       99Ø9    3-17-87   12:ØØp
XCOPY    EXE      11247    3-17-87   12:ØØp
FIND     EXE       6434    3-17-87   12:ØØp
JOIN     EXE       8969    3-17-87   12:ØØp
REPLACE  EXE      11775    3-17-87   12:ØØp

C>■
```

FIGURE 17.31: Specifying a definitive character string. Here, the search string includes a space preceding the letters *EXE*, making a total character string of four characters (space, *E*, *X*, *E*). As you can see by comparing this result to that in the preceding figure, the desired six lines containing .EXE files are now the only results.

```
C>DIR A: ¦ SORT ¦ FIND "EXE"
AUTOEXEC BAT     152   7-05-87  11:32a
FIND     EXE    6434   3-17-87  12:00p
JOIN     EXE    8969   3-17-87  12:00p
REPLACE  EXE   11775   3-17-87  12:00p
SORT     EXE    1977   3-17-87  12:00p
SUBST    EXE    9909   3-17-87  12:00p
XCOPY    EXE   11247   3-17-87  12:00p

C>■
```

FIGURE 17.32: Combining SORT and FIND filters. There is no practical limit on the amount of combinations of pipes and filters. In this figure, the output of the DIR A: command is piped to the SORT command. The sorted results of this filter are then piped to the FIND command, which filters to the video screen only those lines containing the string "EXE".

You can now sort your files on any field using simple DOS commands. You've learned how to use switches with the SORT command to arrange your directory lines by categories other than the first category. You've also learned how to send the sorted results from one filter to another through piping.

To see another example of sophisticated DOS manipulation, you can now sort the original business contact list shown in Figure 17.1 by telephone number, pipe the results to the FIND filter to extract the 415 entries, and pipe the results back to the SORT command for alphabetical rearrangement. Enter

SORT / + 43 < BUSINESS.TXT ¦ FIND "415/" ¦ SORT

Figure 17.33 shows the results of this example. Notice that the first sort operation takes place using character space 43, the first space containing the phone number. If there were several contacts from the same company, their entries would appear in phone number order for each alphabetized company.

This example also shows how a well-written DOS command can save you the purchase of a functionally simple piece of additional software.

PIPES, FILTERS, AND REDIRECTION: AN EXAMPLE

Filters can help you overcome missing features in existing programs. One common problem is sorting a mailing list created by a word processor that does not contain a sorting feature. If you plan a bit, the SORT filter can help you.

```
C>SORT /+43  < BUSINESS.TXT ¦ FIND "415/" ¦ SORT
Brandenberg Gates   754  Bennett   Mary    415/612-5656
Bucket Dance Wear   276  Lewis     Ann     415/635-2530
Intelli-Strategies  743  Griffiths Robert  415/362-9537
Sole Survivor,Inc.  237  Evans     Gail    415/222-3514
Standard Shelters   690  Rucker    Sally   415/532-1107

C>_
```

FIGURE 17.33: Sorting, extracting, and sorting again. It is easy to produce sophisticated combinations of pipes, filters, and redirection operators. Here, the BUSINESS.TXT file is input to the SORT command, which arranges the contact data beginning in column 43. These results are then piped to the FIND command, which extracts all lines containing the string of four characters: *415/*. Finally, these extracted results are sent once more to the SORT command for final sorting by company name (default column 1) and display on the video monitor.

Following is a typical mailing list, which uses commas to separate the name, address, and city fields (categories of information). WordStar uses a file arranged like this to produce MailMerge letters.

> **Swampscott, Hillary, 14 Bains Court, Wellesley, MA 02181**
> **Gordon, Charles, 7 President's Lane, Washington, DC 10001**
> **O'Casey, Toshi, 1226 Sumner Avenue, Schenectady, NY 12309**

Assume that this information is stored in a file called NAMES.TXT. You could create this file using the text mode of a word processor; in WordStar, you would use nondocument mode to enter data for this special purpose. You could also enter the data using the COPY command, as you've seen earlier:

> **COPY CON: NAMES.TXT**
>
> **Swampscott, Hillary, 14 Bains Court, Wellesley, MA 02181**
> **Gordon, Charles, 7 President's Lane, Washington, DC 10001**
> **O'Casey, Toshi, 1226 Sumner Avenue, Schenectady, NY 12309**
> **^Z**

To sort this file by last name, you enter

> **TYPE NAMES.TXT ¦ SORT > LIST.TXT**

This creates a new file, called LIST.TXT, that contains the sorted list of names. To see the contents of LIST.TXT, you enter

TYPE LIST.TXT

Gordon, Charles, 7 President's Lane, Washington, DC 10001
O'Casey, Toshi, 1226 Sumner Avenue, Schenectady, NY 12309
Swampscott, Hillary, 14 Bains Court, Wellesley, MA 02181

Since the resulting LIST.TXT file is already sorted, it can now be used more readily by your word processing program or by any other application program.

You can also use the FIND filter to select entries based on some common text. For example, you can select all the people in your mailing list that live in a certain city. Look at the following command:

TYPE LIST.TXT ¦ FIND "Wellesley, MA" > P.TXT

This selects only those lines in LIST.TXT that contain the characters "Wellesley, MA". (Remember, you must enter the string of characters to be matched using the same case as the original text.) The results of this selection are then redirected to P.TXT, the output disk file. P.TXT will contain only one of the mailing list entries—the one containing "Wellesley, MA", as seen here:

TYPE P.TXT
Swampscott, Hillary, 14 Bains Court, Wellesley, MA 02181

As with the previous examples, this method is not a substitute for a real data management program.

DOS FILTER COMMANDS

Following are the reference entries for the DOS commands used in filtering data: FIND, MORE, and SORT.

FIND

FIND allows you to search through a file to locate any string of text characters.

SYNTAX

*[D:Path]***FIND [/V][/C][/N]***"String"* *[Filespec...]*

D:Path	is the drive and path where the command file is located if it is not in the current directory.
/V	causes FIND to display each line not containing *String*.

/C	counts the number of lines containing *String* and shows the total.
/N	shows the relative line number of each line containing *String*.
String	is the string of characters to be searched for.
Filespec	is the drive, path, file name, and extension of each file to be searched. Multiple files should be separated by a space.

TYPE

External.

USAGE

The FIND command searches for your specified *string* in one or more files. It displays any line that contains this string. You must enclose search strings with quotation marks. FIND is most often used to determine which lines in a file of one-line text entries contain a particular sequence of characters. It is DOS's simple equivalent to the record locator feature provided by file management programs.

RESTRICTIONS

This command does not allow wild cards. FIND ends its search at the first Ctrl-Z it encounters in a file.

EXAMPLES

The following command line displays all lines in the file CLIENTS.LST that contain "Ace Mfg":

FIND "Ace Mfg" CLIENTS.LST

If no file specification is made on the line, FIND acts as a filter. In this case, FIND takes input from the DOS standard input device (usually the keyboard), from a redirected input file, or from a temporary pipe.

MORE

The MORE command pauses the display after each screenful of data.

SYNTAX

[*D:Path*]MORE

D:Path   is the drive and path where the command file is located if it is not in the current directory.

TYPE

External.

USAGE

The MORE command is typically used as a filter to read information from standard input, from a pipe, or from a redirected file. It always displays a screenful of information at a time and usually is used to enable the easy perusal of long text files by displaying only one screen of information at a time.

This command is similar to the DIR/P command, which pauses the directory listing after each screenful of data and asks you to press a key to continue. MORE is a filter—that is, data is sent to it, and MORE processes the data and sends it out in a new format. In this case, the filter simply prints the data a screenful at a time and prints " – MORE – " at the bottom of the screen until you press a key.

EXAMPLES

You can look at a prepared text report by using the MORE command with redirection techniques:

MORE < ANALYSIS.RPT

With the SORT command, you can use MORE as a filter to provide a sorted display of the contents of any text file, one screenful at a time:

SORT ACCOUNTS.TXT ¦ MORE

SORT

This command receives input, sorts it, and then passes it on for display or further manipulation.

SYNTAX

[*D:Path*]SORT [/R][/ + *Col*]

D:Path   is the drive and path where the command file is located if it is not in the current directory.

/R	sorts in reverse alphabetical order
/ + *Col*	starts the sorting operation with column *Col* (the default setting is column 1).

TYPE

External.

USAGE

SORT is a filter command. Data is sent in, and depending on the parameters, sorted and displayed or routed to another file. SORT can display directories in a sorted format, but it does not physically sort files on the disk.

As with FIND and MORE, the SORT command can use the redirection features of DOS to arrange data in a file. If the /R switch is used, the data is arranged line by line and sorted in either ascending order (0-9 followed by A-Z) or descending order (9-0 followed by Z-A). Using standard redirection and filtering symbols, SORT filters data from the standard input device or from a file or a pipe.

EXAMPLES

The following sequence takes the data from the PERSON.TXT file and alphabetically sorts the lines in that file, sending the results to NEWPERS.TXT:

SORT < PERSON.TXT >NEWPERS.TXT

If the important key in your file is located in any column other than the first, the / + *Col* switch arranges the data according to that column. Combining / + *Col* with the pipes concept, the following command arranges the directory listing of the \CAD directory according to the file extension:

DIR ¦ SORT / + 10

Sorted results are displayed on the screen. This switch can be further combined with output redirection to send a sorted directory listing (by extension) to another file.

SUMMARY

In this chapter, you've learned about DOS's powerful ability to connect command sequences with pipes and to control the flow of both input and output information with redirection.

For additional information about both default and remote directories, see

- Chapter 4, "Understanding Directories and Subdirectories"

For additional information about alternative input source and output destination possibilities for command redirection, see

- Chapter 12, "Computer Communications"

For additional information about using redirection techniques to print to disk files, see

- Chapter 15, "Basic Printing Methods"

The next chapters all go beyond the basics. They will enable you to use your version of DOS to its fullest potential. Immediately following, you'll learn a host of sophisticated DOS features for backing up and then recovering files from your disks. Then, the remaining chapters will present a series of more advanced information about DOS, its advanced commands, and the possibilities for extending its power by using add-on software.

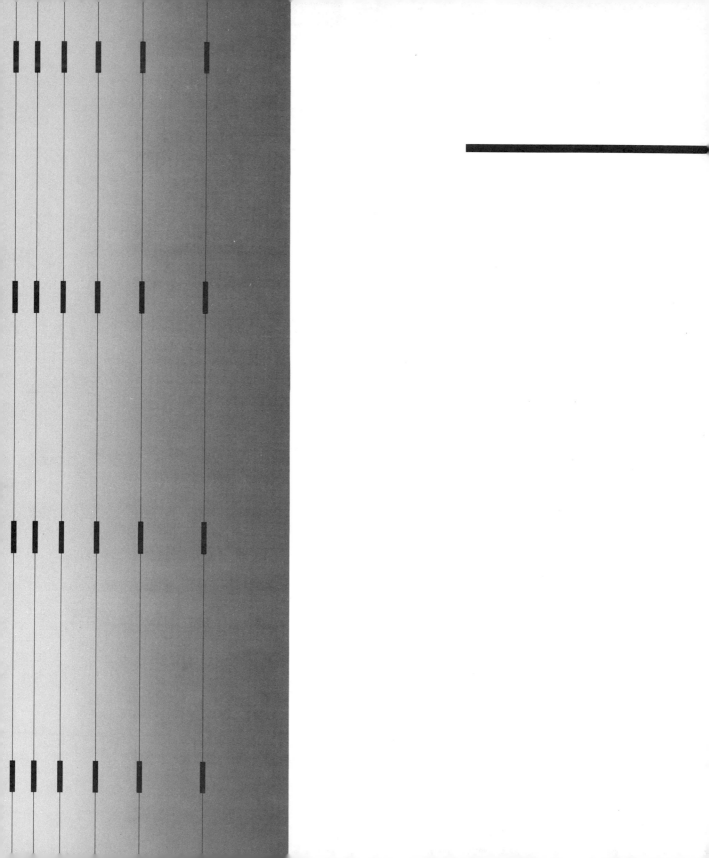

BACKUPS AND RESTORATIONS

BACKUPS AND RESTORATIONS

You can protect your investment in your computer hardware by buying a service contract. You can also protect your hardware by taking it down to your local dealer when it needs repair. Protecting your investment in computer software, however, requires a different approach.

No matter how high the quality of your hardware, the threat of data loss is always present with a computer. The cost of replacing or reentering lost programs or data can be very high. A loss can occur simply because the power goes out in the middle of a disk access operation, causing the software you're using to abandon your current data. Disks can also wear out or be bumped, destroying all of the data on them. Or you could be tired and instead of typing

FORMAT B:

you could type

FORMAT C:

and erase your hard disk. Even diskettes, although their storage capacities are much smaller than those of hard disks, can contain data or programs whose replacement can be expensive and time-consuming.

Any time you copy software for archival purposes, you are *backing it up*, or making *backup copies*.

This chapter discusses the facilities that DOS provides for safeguarding against loss of data or program files. It begins by considering the question of how often and under what circumstances you should make backup copies. Then it revisits three DOS commands introduced in earlier chapters—DISKCOPY, from Chapter 2, and COPY and XCOPY from Chapter 3—and introduces two new commands, COMP and DISKCOMP, in presenting the different methods you can use to back up diskettes. But since the consequences of losing the contents of a hard disk are much more serious, the greater part of this chapter discusses how to use the BACKUP command and the options provided by its switches to back up hard disks. The final tutorial section of the chapter presents the second half of the backup-and-restoration process: restoring backed-up files with the RECOVER command. The chapter concludes with reference entries for the DOS commands introduced in this chapter: BACKUP, COMP, DISKCOMP, and RECOVER. The reference entries for DISKCOPY, COPY, and XCOPY appear in Chapters 2 and 3.

WHEN TO MAKE BACKUP COPIES

Experience seems to be the best teacher in all things, and most people who back up files regularly do so because they have experienced an uncomfortable loss of data at some point. The more data they lost, the more frequently they now back up their work.

Although this section focuses on backing up hard disk data, you should also consider backing up your diskettes if you are using a diskette as the primary storage device for your file information. This could be the case if your computer is a dual-diskette machine, or if you are implementing a form of security by storing the original copy of a file on a diskette so you can remove it from your computer.

When you make a backup copy, you generate a current copy of your data. However, a week later, the backup data is a week old. Should the disk fail, you will have lost a week's worth of new data. If that one week had actually been one month, you could be in a lot of trouble.

It is a good idea to set a backup schedule. Once a week for the entire disk is usually sufficient, if you use your hard disk constantly. If you are entering very sensitive data and have no printouts or other records, you may wish to back up every day. You can configure the BACKUP command to back up only selected files, including only files that you have changed since the last backup. Thus, to make a complete backup copy, all you have to do is back up the data files that have changed since the last backup. This saves much time and space.

In addition to using BACKUP for these regular backup operations, there are four other times when you should run the BACKUP command:

1. Your computer is going to be moved. Especially if your computer will be traveling a long distance, in an airplane cargo hold or a shipping truck, you should back up your data before the trip. Your hard disk may not survive the physical handling (and potential abuse).

2. You are running out of space on your hard disk, and you decide to delete some files, consolidate some directories, and create new branches in your directory tree. For a job this massive, protect yourself against your own enthusiasm and possible fatigue by issuing a BACKUP command.

3. You are going to run a fragmentation-elimination program such as VOPT. (See Chapter 20 for information about how programs like this can reorganize all the files on your disk, providing improved system performance afterward.) Depending on the optimizing program you use—and many are sold commercially—your entire hard disk contents are open to loss in the event of a power failure *during the reorganization*. Back up the entire disk just prior to running such a program.

4. You are taking your computer in for servicing. If you are adding or removing a disk drive (doing anything involving changing the storage configuration), you should back up your data. In most cases, you should

have a current backup copy any time you or someone else opens the system cabinet.

BACKING UP DISKETTES

DOS provides three options for backing up files currently stored on diskette. You can copy one or more individual files to another diskette with the COPY command, you can do the same thing a little faster with the XCOPY command, or you can make an exact duplicate of the entire diskette using DISKCOPY. These methods have been discussed in earlier chapters, but they are presented here together in a somewhat abbreviated form for the sake of convenience and to help you choose among them. For more information about DISKCOPY, consult Chapter 2. For more information about COPY and XCOPY, consult Chapter 3.

Backing Up Diskettes using **DISKCOPY**

A simple DOS command allows you to make exact replicas of entire disks. DISKCOPY copies everything on one disk onto another, including bad or fragmented data. That is, unlike COPY, it simply copies the existing file structure as it exists at the time of the copy operation, with no attempt to rewrite files onto contiguous tracks and sectors, which might improve future disk-access speed. If the source disk is highly fragmented, use COPY or XCOPY.

DISKCOPY provides a very quick way to copy a diskette containing much data, an operation that would otherwise take much longer with the COPY command. DISKCOPY copies the raw data of the diskette, so if the diskette is a system disk, the new copy will also be a system disk. Likewise, if the source disk is not a system disk, then the destination copy will not be a system disk either, even it was one before being overwritten. The second disk will be an *exact* copy of the first disk. DISKCOPY also formats a nonformatted destination disk during the copy process.

The DISKCOPY command has few parameters, so it is easy to understand. When DISKCOPY copies a disk, it copies the *whole* disk, mistakes and all, by reading information from the disk sector by sector and track by track, rather than file by file. It literally reads a chunk of data from the source disk and then places it on the destination disk just as it read the data; therefore, you need *not* format the destination disk. Unlike the BACKUP command, DISKCOPY provides this ability to format as a standard feature; you need not activate it with a switch.

Note: If you formatted the destination disk, but with a different number of tracks or sectors per side than the source diskette, DISKCOPY will reformat it to conform to the source diskette.

The parameters you enter determine which drives DISKCOPY uses for source and destination drives. For example, entering

DISKCOPY

copies a disk using only the default drive (in this case, drive A). You will be prompted to switch your source and destination diskettes into and out of drive A. If you issue the command

DISKCOPY B:

the disk in drive B would be copied onto a disk in drive A. Thus, unless you specify two disks, the default drive (A) is always the destination drive. If you specify only one drive, then DISKCOPY uses the specified drive as the source drive and drive A as the destination drive. Table 18.1 shows these combinations, using drive A as the default drive.

COMMAND	SOURCE	DESTINATION
DISKCOPY	A	A
DISKCOPY A:	A	A
DISKCOPY B:	B	A
DISKCOPY A: B:	A	B
DISKCOPY B: A:	B	A

TABLE 18.1: DISKCOPY Commands Using Drive A as the Default

Including **/1** after any of the commands in this table causes the disks to be treated as single-sided; that is, only the first side of the disk will be copied.

Since DISKCOPY copies the entire disk, formatting is done automatically. Also, any hidden files (such as the DOS system files) are also copied. Thus, you can copy a DOS system diskette onto an unformatted diskette and get an exact copy that is bootable and works just like the original.

If, during the copy process, DISKCOPY comes across a bad part of the disk (one that it cannot read), it will display a message showing where this is, continue to copy, and then display a message informing you that the destination disk may be unusable due to the error (since any bad sectors may be important yet unusable).

When the DISKCOPY operation is done, the screen displays a message asking you whether you wish to make any more copies. You answer Y or N to indicate your choice.

LIMITATIONS OF THE DISKCOPY COMMAND

There are several significant restrictions on the use of DISKCOPY. First, you cannot use it with a hard disk. This command does not recognize a drive created with ASSIGN or SUBST, or a RAM drive, and you should not use it with JOIN in effect. DISKCOPY also will not work with network drives. The most important restriction, however, is that depending on the type of drive you use, you can copy only certain types of diskettes. Table 18.2 lists the drives that DISKCOPY supports.

Type A: 5.25 inch, single-sided, 160K/180K

Type B: 5.25 inch, double-sided, 320K/360K

Type C: 5.25 inch, high-capacity, 1.2M

Type D: 3.5 inch, double-sided, 720K

Type E: 3.5 inch, double-sided, 1.44M

TABLE 18.2: Drives Supported by DISKCOPY

The source and destination disks must be of the same type. For example, DISK-COPY will not copy a 5¼-inch diskette to a 3½-inch diskette. You must use the COPY command if you wish to copy files between different-sized media. In addition, each pair of drives used for copying can copy only certain types of diskettes. The various types of diskettes are the same as the drives (that is, type-A drives format type-1 diskettes). Table 18.3 shows the types of diskettes you can use for a given copy operation between two drives of the same type.

DRIVE PAIR	DISKETTE TYPES
A-A	A
B-B	A, B
C-C	A, B, C
D-D	D
E-E	D, E

TABLE 18.3: Valid Drive Combinations for DISKCOPY

When the DISKCOPY operation is done, the screen displays a message asking you whether you wish to make any more copies. You answer Y or N to indicate your choice.

Comparing Two Diskettes using DISKCOMP

To verify the results of a DISKCOPY operation, you can compare the copied version to the original, using the DISKCOMP command. You use this command and its parameters in much the same way as DISKCOPY. Use DISKCOMP after DISKCOPY only, as COPY and XCOPY *will* copy the diskette's data, but they will rearrange the data on the disk. Since DISKCOMP compares disks track by track, it notes errors and discrepancies with a message:

Compare error on side x, track y

DISKCOMP automatically determines the disk format, based on the first disk, if it is not specified with a /1 or /8 parameter. If the second disk is of a different format, the screen displays a different message.

Using COPY to Make Backups

The COPY command is sometimes used to back up a diskette's contents more efficiently. It works quite differently from the DISKCOPY command. DISKCOPY copies all sectors on all tracks from one diskette to the other, independent of what files reside on the diskette, and independent of where on the diskette they reside. Hence, the resulting diskette backup is truly an identical copy, sector for sector (see Figure 18.1).

When you use the COPY command to copy all the files from one diskette to another, as when you enter

COPY A:*.* B:

the diskette's data is written onto the new diskette file by file, rather than sector by sector. Hence, any file fragmentation is eliminated, and the resulting backup diskette contains all files written both sequentially and contiguously. Figure 18.2

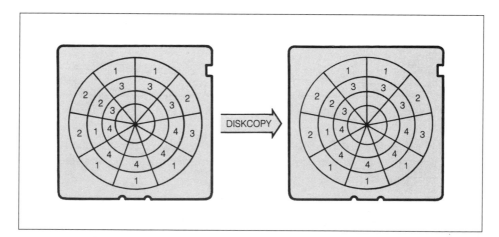

FIGURE 18.1: In this representative illustration, the DISKCOPY A: B: command exactly replicates the contents, sector by sector, of the original diskette. Each of the files, numbered 1 through 4, and the empty sectors are rewritten in precisely the same locations on the new diskette.

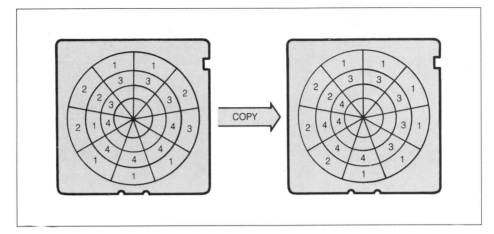

FIGURE 18.2: The same original diskette as shown in Figure 18.1, backed up using the COPY A:*.* B: command. The COPY command consolidates all files numbered 1 to 4 into contiguous locations at the beginning of the new backup diskette, thus eliminating fragmentation and allowing faster access.

illustrates this more efficient ordering of files. See Chapter 20 for more information about disk fragmentation.

Using XCOPY to Make Backups

The XCOPY command is even more powerful than the COPY command for making backup diskettes. It produces the same unfragmented layout as the COPY command, but XCOPY operates more efficiently. XCOPY uses all free memory to buffer specified files before writing them to the new backup diskette. Hence, the amount of disk reading and writing time is reduced, speeding up overall backup operations. Figures 18.3 illustrates this process.

Note that with both COPY and XCOPY, it is your responsibility to ensure that your destination diskette is either freshly formatted before you issue a command, or has had its former file contents erased to make room for the new backup files. The DISKCOPY command, on the other hand, formats a diskette as necessary during the backup operation.

Checking the Results of COPY or XCOPY

After a COPY or XCOPY operation, you can use the COMP command to compare individual files on two different diskettes to verify that the file copy operation was successful. For example,

COMP A:FILE1.TXT B:FILE1.TXT

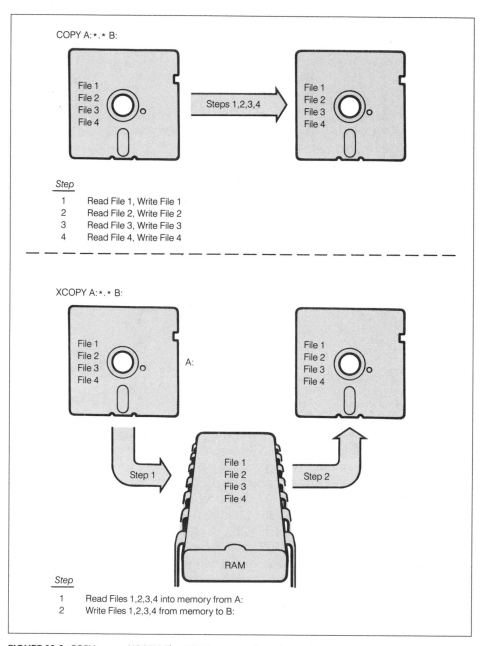

COPY A: *.* B:

Steps 1,2,3,4

File 1
File 2
File 3
File 4

Step

1	Read File 1, Write File 1
2	Read File 2, Write File 2
3	Read File 3, Write File 3
4	Read File 4, Write File 4

XCOPY A: *.* B:

File 1
File 2
File 3
File 4

A:

File 1
File 2
File 3
File 4

Step 1

File 1
File 2
File 3
File 4

Step 2

RAM

Step

| 1 | Read Files 1,2,3,4 into memory from A: |
| 2 | Write Files 1,2,3,4 from memory to B: |

FIGURE 18.3: COPY versus XCOPY. The COPY command reads and then writes the four example files on the original diskette one at at time. XCOPY first reads all disk data from the original diskette into available memory; only then does XCOPY begin to write file data to the backup diskette. This illustration assumes that available memory is larger than the sum of the sizes of the four example files on the original diskette.

compares FILE1.TXT on drive A with the backup copy FILE1.TXT on drive B. Wildcards are also possible:

COMP A:*.* B:*.*

compares each file by name on the original disk with each similarly named file on the backup disk.

BACKING UP HARD DISKS

Protecting yourself from the major trauma of losing an entire hard disk requires more effort than the simple procedures you can use to back up diskette files. DISKCOPY is designed for diskette copies, and the COPY and XCOPY commands have a fundamental weakness: The destination for your copied files is limited to the storage capacity of one drive. If the directory you want to back up contains more files than can fit on one destination diskette, or if it contains one large file that exceeds the capacity of the backup diskette, the COPY and XCOPY commands simply can't handle the job.

To allow you to back up files onto a series of floppy diskettes or another fixed (hard) disk, DOS provides the BACKUP command. With BACKUP you can copy the files on any of your disks. This command is usually used to back up the files from a hard disk and spread them, if necessary, over a series of floppy diskettes.

Note that the BACKUP command does not work for copy-protected diskettes. As you will learn in Chapter 20, utility programs such as COPY II PC allow you to back up diskettes that are copy protected.

How DOS Stores Backup Files

The files placed on a diskette by the BACKUP command are not stored as standard DOS files. Figure 18.4 shows the directory listing of the original files from a hard disk. Figure 18.5 shows the directory listing of the first backup diskette in drive A after the backup procedure has been completed. Compare these two figures. You'll see that your original files were not backed up in their original format.

Figure 18.6 illustrates how files are backed up. The original files are combined efficiently into a single file, called BACKUP.001, that contains only the original data. A separate control file, called CONTROL.001, contains the actual file names and their lengths, as well as the source directory from which these files were obtained. You can add up the file lengths for each of the source files in Figure 18.6 to verify that BACKUP.001 has efficiently combined all the bytes from each of the original files.

Note: The preceding discussion applies only to DOS 3.3 and later implementations. DOS versions prior to 3.3 store information differently. In addition, the

```
Volume in drive C is ROBBINS
Directory of  C:\DBASE\ADMIN

DB3BOOK   PRG     449   11-26-86    2:41a
START     PRG    2532   11-26-86    2:21a
INVOICE   PRG    3010    3-12-86    7:40a
CERTIF    PRG    1981   11-26-86    2:38a
RECOMM1   PRG     463   11-26-86    2:40a
RECOMM2   PRG     422   11-26-86    2:42a
PAYROLL   PRG    4224    4-28-86   12:57p
PAYROLL2  PRG    1792    3-12-86    9:17p
EXPERT    PRG    2432   10-24-85    6:48p
EXPERT1   PRG    2146    6-13-85    9:57p
EXPERT2   PRG    2944   10-18-85    8:11p
EXPERT3   PRG    3689   10-25-85   10:59a
EXPERT4   PRG    2176    7-30-86    9:08p
MESSAGE   PRG    1280    4-09-85    3:41p
LEDGER    PRG    2688   11-26-86   10:53a
INVOICE2  PRG    3200   11-26-86   11:16a
BOOKS2    PRG    2048   11-26-86   11:20a
DISKPREP  PRG     905   11-26-86    2:00a
       18 File(s)     880640 bytes free

C>_
```

FIGURE 18.4: The DBASE\ADMIN directory contains a set of program (.PRG) files that will be used in this chapter's examples for the BACKUP and RESTORE commands.

```
C>DIR A:

 Volume in drive A is BACKUP   001
 Directory of  A:\

BACKUP    001    38381    7-09-87   10:23a
CONTROL   001      821    7-09-87   10:23a
        2 File(s)    322560 bytes free

C>_
```

FIGURE 18.5: The BACKUP command places backup information onto diskettes in the form seen here. The file data being backed up is coalesced into a single file called BACKUP.*xxx*, where *xxx* is a sequential number to distinguish each diskette in a set of backup diskettes created during the same BACKUP command output. Additional information about the file data (for example, date, time, size) in BACKUP.*xxx* is stored in on each diskette a parallel file called CONTROL.*xxx*.

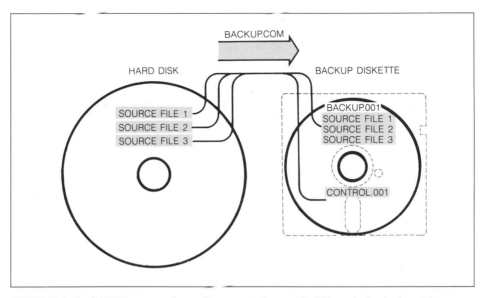

FIGURE 18.6: The BACKUP command actually compacts the specified files to be backed up. File contents are placed in a BACKUP.*xxx* file, and administrative information regarding the names, sizes, dates, and times are placed in a CONTROL.*xxx* file. The *xxx* is a sequencing number to identify different diskettes in a set of backup diskettes.

DOS 3.3 version of BACKUP is faster than previous versions and requires less disk space to store the original files. It requires less space primarily because each file does not waste extra disk cluster space during the storage process. The compaction technique uses both space and time more efficiently.

BACKUP-FILE STORAGE IN VERSION 3.2 AND EARLIER

If you have an earlier DOS version, your resulting backup diskette will be quite different. The syntax of the BACKUP command remains the same, however. It will have *file versions* (not replicas) of each of your original files, as well as an additional entry in the directory listing called BACKUP.@@@, with a length of 128 bytes. If you have a disk with this entry, the files stored on that disk were put there with an earlier version of the DOS BACKUP command.

Files stored with earlier versions of BACKUP *appear* to be independently accessible, but they cannot be read meaningfully with any of DOS's other commands, such as the COPY command. In earlier versions of DOS, BACKUP changes the actual file contents; whereas in version 3.3, it compacts the files into one file. You can reuse the files stored with earlier versions only by restoring them to their original condition with the RESTORE command.

Using the BACKUP Command

You can back up a hard disk either onto diskettes or onto another hard disk. When you back up a hard disk onto diskettes, you also need to format enough diskettes before you begin. If you are using DOS 3.3, you can format disks during the backup process. If you are using an earlier version of DOS, however, you should prepare in advance enough formatted destination diskettes to hold all of your data, since you cannot back up onto unformatted disks (except by using the DISKCOPY command). You will have to stop the backup process (or borrow someone else's computer) if you run out of formatted disks in the middle of backing up your files.

Backing up files from one hard disk to another is much faster than backing them up onto a collection of diskettes. It is also easier, since you don't have to insert and remove successive diskettes; the backup process between hard disks can proceed unattended.

> *Warning:* If your system has an extra hard disk for backup, make sure that it has enough space to hold all the backup files. If it doesn't, the entire process will terminate, and you'll have to make space on the backup disk by deleting some files.

Before you start backing up files, you should know how to use the VERIFY command. VERIFY controls the degree of error checking performed by DOS after all disk-write operations. Executing the command

VERIFY ON

turns the verification mode on. Each disk-write operation will be followed by a confirmation procedure verifying that the data just written can be read without error. You should execute this command just prior to making a backup copy; it increases the likelihood that your backup files will be written accurately. Although data errors occur only infrequently, a backup file is the worst place for such an error to occur. After your backup operation, you can enter

VERIFY OFF

at the DOS prompt to restore normal read and write operations. Note that using verification mode significantly slows down overall DOS operations.

A reference entry for the VERIFY command appears in Chapter 3.

Backing Up a Complete Directory

The general form of the BACKUP command is as follows:

BACKUP *SourceFile(s) DestinationDrive*

SourceFile(s) is the standard path name plus any specific file names you wish to select for backup. *DestinationDrive* is the letter identifier of the disk drive that is to receive the file copies.

Suppose you want to back up all the files in your DBASE\ADMIN directory. You simply specify the name of the desired directory as the first parameter. If you do not specify any files, DOS selects and copies all files in the directory to the backup drive (drive A).

BACKUP C:\DBASE\ADMIN A:

DOS displays the message

Insert backup diskette 01 in drive A:

Warning! Files in the target drive
A:\ root directory will be erased
Strike any key when ready

This warning gives you a chance to verify that drive A contains the correct diskette before DOS overwrites everything on that disk. The destination drive should contain a blank diskette or a previously used diskette containing files you don't mind overwriting.

Pressing Return at this point begins the backup process. All the files in the named directory will now be copied to your backup diskette (or your backup hard disk, if your destination drive is another hard disk). DOS lists all the files in this directory as they are being backed up to the specified disk drive.

Backing Up a Partial Directory

You can also perform selective backup operations—for example, you can back up only the .PRG files from the DBASE\ADMIN directory. Simply specify the names of the files you wish to back up. To back up all .PRG files in the DBASE\ADMIN directory, enter

BACKUP C:\DBASE\ADMIN*.PRG A:

Again, DOS lists the files while it writes the backup copies (see Figure 18.7). You *must* enter the leading drive identifier (in this example, C:). Otherwise, DOS will display the message "Invalid drive specification."

If DOS runs out of room on your first diskette, it will prompt you like this:

Insert backup diskette 02 in drive A:

Warning! Files in the target drive
A:\ root directory will be erased
Strike any key when ready

After you respond to this prompt, most likely by inserting a second diskette, DOS will continue to copy backup versions of your files. DOS will continue to prompt you for additional diskettes, as necessary, until it has copied all requested files.

```
Strike any key when ready

*** Backing up files to drive A: ***
Diskette Number: Ø1

\DBASE\ADMIN\DB3BOOK.PRG
\DBASE\ADMIN\START.PRG
\DBASE\ADMIN\INVOICE.PRG
\DBASE\ADMIN\CERTIF.PRG
\DBASE\ADMIN\RECOMM1.PRG
\DBASE\ADMIN\RECOMM2.PRG
\DBASE\ADMIN\PAYROLL.PRG
\DBASE\ADMIN\PAYROLL2.PRG
\DBASE\ADMIN\EXPERT.PRG
\DBASE\ADMIN\EXPERT1.PRG
\DBASE\ADMIN\EXPERT2.PRG
\DBASE\ADMIN\EXPERT3.PRG
\DBASE\ADMIN\EXPERT4.PRG
\DBASE\ADMIN\MESSAGE.PRG
\DBASE\ADMIN\LEDGER.PRG
\DBASE\ADMIN\INVOICE2.PRG
\DBASE\ADMIN\BOOKS2.PRG
\DBASE\ADMIN\DISKPREP.PRG

C>_
```

FIGURE 18.7: As the BACKUP command writes each file to the backup diskette, the video monitor displays the file's full path name. It displays the diskette number (of a possible set of diskettes) for you as well.

Note: You cannot delete files created by the BACKUP command; they are created with an attribute indicating that they are read-only files, which means that you cannot erase them (see the ATTRIB command in Chapter 19). To regain the disk space on this diskette, you will have to reformat the disk with the FORMAT command.

Other Types of Backup Processing

Sometimes you may need to do more than back up to a blank diskette all or some of the files in a DOS directory. For example, you might want to add additional files to a backup set to maintain some grouping and organization in your backup copies. You may also want to include files in the directory tree *below* the main directory you've just specified. Or you may want to combine these possibilities with selection criteria that go beyond simple wildcard specifications. You may want to back up files that have changed since the last backup operation, and not spend time backing up unchanged files that are already backed up. You may want to back up only those files created or modified since a certain date or even after a certain time on a certain day.

You can invoke all of these options by using one or more of the DOS switches for the BACKUP command (see Table 18.4). These switches are described in the following sections.

Warning: Do not have the commands SUBST, JOIN, APPEND, or ASSIGN active when you issue the BACKUP command. They're difficult to use

SWITCH	RESULT
/A	Adds files to a backup disk
/S	Backs up subdirectories
/M	Backs up modified files only
/D	Backs up files by date
/T	Backs up files by time on the date specified by /D
/F	Formats the destination diskette if necessary
/L	Creates a log file for the files contained in the compacted backup file

TABLE 18.4: Switches for the BACKUP Command

properly, and DOS cannot later restore files properly if these commands were active in a different way when you ran the BACKUP command. These commands are discussed in Chapter 19.

ADDING FILES TO AN EXISTING BACKUP COPY

The /A switch tells DOS not to erase (overwrite) any existing files stored on the floppy diskette, but to add the newly backed-up files to that disk. For example, Figure 18.8 shows the selective backup of all files in the CHAP07

```
C>BACKUP C:\PROGRAMS\FW\CHAPØ7 A:

Insert backup diskette Ø1 in drive A:

Warning! Files in the target drive
A:\ root directory will be erased
Strike any key when ready

*** Backing up files to drive A: ***
Diskette Number: Ø1

\PROGRAMS\FW\CHAPØ7\CHAPØ7.FW2
\PROGRAMS\FW\CHAPØ7\FIG7-14.CAP
\PROGRAMS\FW\CHAPØ7\FIG7-15.CAP
\PROGRAMS\FW\CHAPØ7\FIG7-16.CAP
\PROGRAMS\FW\CHAPØ7\SAMPLE.DTA
\PROGRAMS\FW\CHAPØ7\TBL7-1.TXT
\PROGRAMS\FW\CHAPØ7\TBL7-2.TXT
\PROGRAMS\FW\CHAPØ7\TBL7-3.TXT
\PROGRAMS\FW\CHAPØ7\TBL7-4.TXT
\PROGRAMS\FW\CHAPØ7\PART-3.FW2
\PROGRAMS\FW\CHAPØ7\TOC7.TXT

C>_
```

FIGURE 18.8: This example illustrates the creation of a backup diskette that selectively copies all the files from the CHAP07 directory into the BACKUP.001 file and places all administrative directory information about those files in the CONTROL.001 file.

subdirectory. The resulting backup-diskette directory is shown in Figure 18.9, with BACKUP.001 and CONTROL.001 files.

You may also want to back up the files in another directory (in this example, the CHAP09 directory). Although you can back them up to a separate diskette, you might want to add these additional files to the same backup set. You could do this—even if more than one diskette is required—by using the /A switch. Figure 18.10 shows the CHAP09 directory and the five files it contains. The figure also shows the form of the BACKUP command required:

BACKUP C:\PROGRAMS\FW\CHAP09 A: /A

This command adds the new files to the BACKUP.001 file on the diskette in drive A. It also updates the CONTROL.001 file with information about the newly added files. Figure 18.11 portrays this process. Compare this figure to Figure 18.3.

The resulting backup diskette (see Figure 18.12) now contains all the originally backed-up files, as well as the newly added ones. Notice the increase in size of the two files. As before, this increase represents the addition of the contents of the four CHAP09 files to the BACKUP.001 file and the addition of information about the files to the CONTROL.001 file.

If the existing backup copy required multiple diskettes, you would be prompted to insert the last backup diskette before DOS would write the actual

```
C>DIR A:

 Volume in drive A is BACKUP   001
 Directory of  A:\

BACKUP   001    52050   7-09-87   12:23p
CONTROL  001      583   7-09-87   12:23p
       2 File(s)    309248 bytes free

C>_
```

FIGURE 18.9: The backup diskette resulting from the backup operation in Figure 18.8 contains only the two files BACKUP.001 and CONTROL.001. The diskette has approximately 300KB free for later backup additions. The file size of BACKUP.001 is in fact precisely equal to the sum of the sizes of the 11 files selected from the CHAP07 directory in Figure 18.8.

```
C>BACKUP C:\PROGRAMS\FW\CHAP09 A: /A

Insert last backup diskette in drive A:
Strike any key when ready

*** Backing up files to drive A: ***
Diskette Number: 01

\PROGRAMS\FW\CHAP09\TBL9-1.TXT
\PROGRAMS\FW\CHAP09\FIG9-1.CAP
\PROGRAMS\FW\CHAP09\FIG9-14.TXT
\PROGRAMS\FW\CHAP09\CHAP09.FW2

C>_
```

FIGURE 18.10: The /A switch allows you to back up additional files and add them to an existing backup set. In this figure, all the files in the CHAP09 directory (four files) are added to the backup diskette in drive A. DOS manages the rewriting of the BACKUP.001 file to include the new file information, and it manages the rewriting of the CONTROL.001 file to include the details of the four new files.

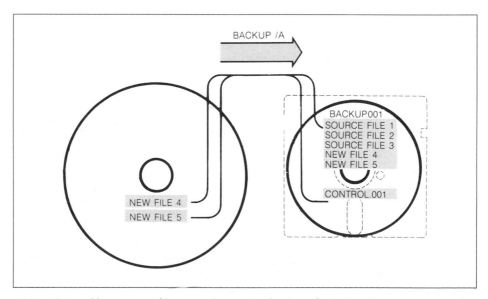

FIGURE 18.11: Adding any new files (New Files 4 and 5, for example) during a backup operation with the /A switch updates the two primary backup files. BACKUP.001 receives the contents of New File 4 and New File 5, and CONTROL.001 receives information about the names, path locations, sizes, and date and time of last update of those files.

```
C>DIR A:

 Volume in drive A is BACKUP   001
 Directory of  A:\

BACKUP   001     77655   7-09-87  12:13p
CONTROL  001       789   7-09-87  12:13p
        2 File(s)    283648 bytes free

C>_
```

FIGURE 18.12: You can compare the resulting BACKUP and CONTROL files, after the new additions of Figure 18.10, with the preceding values in Figure 18.9. Each backup file's size has been increased by the amount of information necessary to later reproduce the four new files backed up from the CHAP09 directory.

backup copies to the backup set:

Insert last backup diskette in drive A:
Strike any key when ready

Adding to Existing Backup Files: An Example   Now try some backup operations on your system. First, select two separate sets of files on your disk that need to be backed up. Choose files in two separate but important directories. Next, if you are using a DOS version earlier than 3.3, prepare several formatted diskettes to receive your selected files. If you are using version 3.3, you can include the /F switch, discussed later in this section, to format the destination diskettes during the copy operation.

To decide how many diskettes you need, use the DIR command to display the names of all the files you plan to back up. Add up all the file sizes for your selected files, and then divide this sum by the number of bytes on each of your backup diskettes. This value indicates the number of diskettes you'll need. Presented as an equation, the formula looks like this:

$$\text{Number of disks} = \frac{\text{Total Bytes to be Backed Up}}{\text{Disk Size (in bytes)}}$$

For example, if you were backing up onto double-density, double-sided diskettes (360K), your calculations might be as follows:

1. Total size of all selected files: 3MB
2. Number of bytes per diskette: 360K
3. 3,000,000 divided by 360,000: 9 diskettes

This calculation is only approximate for two reasons. First, 360K does not really equal 360,000 bytes. (Since a kilobyte equals 1024 bytes, 360K equals 360 × 1024, or 368,640 bytes.) The approximation is close enough, however, since the CONTROL.001 file consumes a variable number of bytes, depending largely on how many files are backed up. Second, using the same analysis, 3MB really equals 3,145,728 bytes, not 3,000,000. Performing the same type of calculation for the other types of diskettes supported by DOS 3.3 gives the results shown in Table 18.5.

Since backing up one diskette requires roughly one minute, (including write and handling time) backing up one hard disk can easily take you an hour (in reality, it takes longer).

Once you have calculated the correct number of diskettes and formatted them, issue the correct BACKUP command to back up all the files in your first selected directory. Then issue a second BACKUP command to append the files from the second directory you chose onto the first backup-diskette set. Use the /A switch.

Finally, issue one or more DIR commands for the backup diskettes to verify that all the original files were successfully copied. Add up the sizes of the original files to be sure that the backup diskette is complete.

BACKING UP SUBDIRECTORIES

The /S switch tells DOS to copy the files contained in any subdirectories of the directory being backed up. This switch is extremely powerful when used with the

DESCRIPTION	CAPACITY	DISKETTES REQUIRED TO BACK UP 10MB
5¼" single sided	160K	63
5¼" single sided	180K	56
5¼" double sided	320K	32
5¼" double sided	360K	28
5¼" high capacity	1.2MB	9
3½" double sided	720K	14
3½" double sided	1.44MB	7

TABLE 18.5: Calculating the Number of Backup Disks Required

BACKUP command, with capabilities on a par with the ability of the XCOPY command to move automatically through the directory tree structure. For example, if you start the backup operation in the root directory (C:\) and you use the /S option:

BACKUP C:\ A: /S

DOS attempts to back up the entire hard disk.

The /S switch tells DOS first to back up all data and program files in the root directory and then to go to each subdirectory in the root. DOS backs up all files in each subdirectory and then proceeds to do the same for each subdirectory of that subdirectory.

If you want to back up just a portion of your hard disk tree structure, you first specify the main branch. Assuming a tree structure like the one in Figure 18.13, you can back up all the files in the DBASE branch by entering

BACKUP C:\DBASE A: /S

DOS first backs up the files in the DBASE directory. Then it proceeds to the next directory in that portion of the tree (DB3PLUS) and copies the files located there. It then continues through each of the other subdirectories (CLASSES and ADMIN) in the tree structure, copying all the files in them. DOS prompts you to enter additional backup diskettes as each one is filled.

PERFORMING MULTIPLE OPERATIONS WITH ONE COMMAND

As with most DOS commands, you can use one or more switches to perform multiple operations with a single command. In addition, you can use several switches simultaneously as long as it makes sense to do so. For instance, the /A and /S switches can work together for some useful purposes. Suppose you want to locate and back up all the BASIC program files (*.BAS) on your entire disk. You can use the /S switch with the BACKUP command to look successively into each subdirectory you specify.

The following command locates and backs up all .BAS files anywhere on the disk:

BACKUP C:*.BAS A: /S

This command works because you've specified the root directory with which to begin (C:\), the wildcard for finding BASIC files only (*.BAS), and the subdirectory search switch (/S).

Changing the starting directory can limit the portion of the directory tree that is searched. The following command thus finds only .BAS files located in the UTILITY subdirectory and in all subdirectories below it in the directory structure (see Figure 18.14):

BACKUP C:\UTILITY*.BAS A: /S

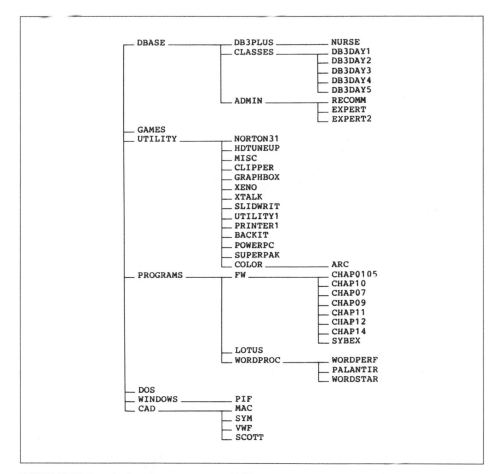

FIGURE 18.13: Sample directory structure on a 20MB computer. You may want to back up only major branches of this disk hierarchy. For instance, you may wish to produce only a backup set containing your utility files residing in the UTILITY directory and in a series of subordinate directories. The /S switch on the BACKUP command permits you to perform this operation.

Adding an /A switch in the preceding examples adds all the files found to the existing backup disk:

BACKUP C:\UTILITY\∗.BAS A: /S /A

BACKING UP MODIFIED OR NEW FILES

The /M option tells DOS to back up only files that have not already been backed up or that have been modified since the last backup operation. DOS can

```
C>BACKUP C:\UTILITY\*.BAS A: /S

Insert backup diskette Ø1 in drive A:

Warning! Files in the target drive
A:\ root directory will be erased
Strike any key when ready

*** Backing up files to drive A: ***
Diskette Number: Ø1

\UTILITY\MISC\POUNDS.BAS
\UTILITY\MISC\TREETOP.BAS
\UTILITY\MISC\OKIDATA.BAS
\UTILITY\BASMAIN\PARKIT.BAS
\UTILITY\BASMAIN\MENUONE.BAS
\UTILITY\BASMAIN\GAMESMNU.BAS

C>_
```

FIGURE 18.14: The /S switch directs the BACKUP command to search within the subdirectory structure for all files meeting the selection criteria. In this example, all files with a .BAS extension located in the UTILITY directory, or in any subdirectory under the UTILITY directory, are included in the backup set. The file names found, as well as their full path names, are displayed as the backup operation proceeds.

do this because it marks each file on the disk as it backs up the file. This mark—actually a bit stored by DOS for every file—is called the *archive bit*. Whenever a file is modified or a new file is created, DOS changes the mark to indicate that the file needs to be backed up. This archiving feature allows the backup process to skip files that have not been changed since the last backup operation. When any file is newly created in DOS, its archive bit is set to indicate that it should be treated like any other existing file that has undergone some changes.

For example, suppose that you keep your children's favorite computer games in a GAMES directory. Naturally, you need to safeguard your sanity in the event of a disk failure: you may suffer more if all these games are lost than you would if your business files were lost. Of course, neither situation will faze you if you've conscientously backed up your files.

Assume that you recently backed up all your files in this example directory. Your children then bring home two new games, HEADROOM.COM and MADMAX.EXE, which you can add to your existing GAMES backup set with the /M and /A switches (see Figure 18.15). The /A switch tells DOS to add all selected files to an existing backup copy, and the /M switch selects only the two new files from the much larger collection of unchanged files.

Immediately attempting to back up the very same files again would result in a message stating that no files were found to back up. This is because the archive bit was changed to indicate that the two files had already been backed up. Figure 18.15 also demonstrates this situation.

```
C>BACKUP C:\GAMES  A:  /M /A

Insert last backup diskette in drive A:
Strike any key when ready

*** Backing up files to drive A: ***
Diskette Number: 01

\GAMES\MADMAX.EXE
\GAMES\HEADROOM.EXE

C>BACKUP C:\GAMES  A:  /M /A

Warning! No files were found to back up

C>_
```

FIGURE 18.15: Combining switches to add only new files to an existing backup diskette. The /M switch selects only files created or modified since the last backup operation. In this figure, the /M switch discovers two new files in the GAMES directory (MADMAX.EXE and HEADROOM.EXE); the /A switch ensures that these are added to the existing backup set in drive A.

BACKING UP BY DATE AND TIME

DOS allows you to specify by date, and by time on that date, the files to be backed up. When you enter a date, DOS will back up only files that possess the same date or a more recent date.

Look at an example. The word processing directory PALANTIR contains thirty seven files (see Figure 18.16). Some of these are the word processor's system files, some are old document files, and others are more recent work. Assume that all the files dated earlier than November 4, 1988, are either on backup disks or on the original system disks. You can selectively back up only the 11 files created in this directory since November 4 by using the /D switch:

BACKUP C:\PROGRAMS\WORDPROC\PALANTIR A: /D:11/4/88

As usual, the first argument selects the directory or the set of desired files, the second argument indicates the destination drive, and the final entry on the line is the switch (see Figure 18.17). Notice that the /D switch is followed by a colon, which is followed immediately by the specific date on or after which you want the new and updated files to be selected for backup.

Note: If you are using a date format for a different country, as discussed in Chapter 11, you should revise the form of the date used here. For example, European countries usually use dates in the form *day/month/year,* so a selection

```
C>DIR/W \PROGRAMS\WORDPROC\PALANTIR

 Volume in drive C is ROBBINS
 Directory of  C:\PROGRAMS\WORDPROC\PALANTIR

.                  ..            ICCL     WP    ICCL-2   WP    INSERT12 WP
CHAP14   WP    INSERT13 WP    EARLYINS WP    INSØ6NEW WP    INSØ8NEW WP
INSØ9NEW WP    INS1ØNEW WP    INS11NEW WP    TBL11-XX WP    TBL11-YY WP
INSØ7NEW WP    INSERT16 WP    SYBEX2   WP    SYBEX    WP    DEBBIE   WP
AUDIT    TXT   NEW9-22A CAP   NEW9-22B CAP   NEW1Ø-8  CAP   NEW1Ø-9  CAP
HELP2    BAT   NEW8-4B  CAP   Ø2-14-88 WP    NEW14    WP    NEW13    WP
NEW12    WP    NEW15    WP    FOR_INFO WP    NEW16    WP    NAMES    TXT
LIST     TXT   INSERTØ3 WP
        37 File(s)   2185216 bytes free

C>_
```

FIGURE 18.16: A typical word processing directory has main system files, support files such as spelling checkers, and a group of document files and their backup versions. This figure displays all the files in the PALANTIR directory, which is only one of three main word processing subdirectories on this disk (see Figure 18.13).

```
C>BACKUP C:\PROGRAMS\WORDPROC\PALANTIR A: /D:11/4/88

Insert backup diskette Ø1 in drive A:

Warning! Files in the target drive
A:\ root directory will be erased
Strike any key when ready

*** Backing up files to drive A: ***
Diskette Number: Ø1

\PROGRAMS\WORDPROC\PALANTIR\ICCL.WP
\PROGRAMS\WORDPROC\PALANTIR\ICCL-2.WP
\PROGRAMS\WORDPROC\PALANTIR\CHAP14.WP
\PROGRAMS\WORDPROC\PALANTIR\INSERT13.WP
\PROGRAMS\WORDPROC\PALANTIR\INSERT16.WP
\PROGRAMS\WORDPROC\PALANTIR\DEBBIE.WP
\PROGRAMS\WORDPROC\PALANTIR\Ø2-14-88.WP
\PROGRAMS\WORDPROC\PALANTIR\INSERTØ3.WP

C>_
```

FIGURE 18.17: The /D switch lets you back up all files last updated on or after a certain date—in this case November 4, 1988. Those files meeting this date criterion (one .BAS, one .COM, two .CAP, six .WP, and one .TXT file) are displayed as they are written to the backup diskette set.

of files on or after November 4, 1988, would require you to enter /D:4/11/88 for the switch.

CREATING A LOG FILE OF THE FILES BACKED UP

Since all the files you back up are compacted into a single backup file, it's a good idea to simultaneously ask DOS to create a log file for you. This file will store the date and time of the backup, as well as the full path and file name of each backed-up file. It will have the extension .LOG. Also, DOS will indicate which of the possible backup diskettes stores each file.

To use this feature you need to add another switch to your BACKUP command. Using the /L switch alone causes DOS to create the log file under the name BACKUP.LOG; DOS stores this file in the root directory of your source drive. To give the log file another name, use the switch format

/L:*LogFileName*

For example, if you want to generate a log file for the word-processing backup files presented earlier, you add an /L switch to the complete BACKUP command:

**BACKUP C:\PROGRAMS\WORDPROC\PALANTIR A:
/D:11/4/88 /L**

If you prefer to store the log-file information in a file in the original source directory, you can do so by making the /L switch more specific:

**BACKUP C:\PROGRAMS\WORDPROC\PALANTIR A: /D:11/4/88
/L:\PROGRAMS\WORDPROC\PALANTIR\NOV4.LOG**

The results of using this BACKUP command switch are shown in Figure 18.18, which represents what DOS displays on the screen during the logging operation.

Figure 18.19 shows the contents of the log file (NOV4.LOG) itself. Using logging again during file-adding operations (/A) adds the newly backed-up files, along with their full path names, to this log file. This parallels the addition of file data and controlling information to the BACKUP and CONTROL files on the backup disk.

FORMATTING BACKUP DISKS AUTOMATICALLY

DOS 3.3 makes it easy for you to back up a variable amount of file information. If you add an /F switch to a BACKUP command, DOS will automatically format any diskette being used that is not already formatted. This relieves you from calculating how many diskettes you'll need and preparing sufficient formatted diskettes. Using this switch requires you first make the FORMAT.COM

```
C>BACKUP C:\PROGRAMS\WORDPROC\PALANTIR A: /D:11/4/88 /L:\PROGRAMS\WORDPROC\PALAN
TIR\NOV4.LOG

Logging to file \PROGRAMS\WORDPROC\PALANTIR\NOV4.LOG

Insert backup diskette Ø1 in drive A:

Warning! Files in the target drive
A:\ root directory will be erased
Strike any key when ready

*** Backing up files to drive A: ***
Diskette Number: Ø1

\PROGRAMS\WORDPROC\PALANTIR\ICCL.WP
\PROGRAMS\WORDPROC\PALANTIR\ICCL-2.WP
\PROGRAMS\WORDPROC\PALANTIR\CHAP14.WP
\PROGRAMS\WORDPROC\PALANTIR\INSERT13.WP
\PROGRAMS\WORDPROC\PALANTIR\INSERT16.WP
\PROGRAMS\WORDPROC\PALANTIR\DEBBIE.WP
\PROGRAMS\WORDPROC\PALANTIR\Ø2-14-88.WP
\PROGRAMS\WORDPROC\PALANTIR\INSERTØ3.WP

C>_
```

FIGURE 18.18: When you specify the /L switch, the video display during the backup operation shows one additional line at the top. This verifies that logging is occurring and indicates the name of the log file receiving information about the names and directory locations of each file being written to the backup diskette set.

```
C>TYPE \PROGRAMS\WORDPROC\PALANTIR\NOV4.LOG

12-9-1988  22:34:41
001   \PROGRAMS\WORDPROC\PALANTIR\ICCL.WP
001   \PROGRAMS\WORDPROC\PALANTIR\ICCL-2.WP
001   \PROGRAMS\WORDPROC\PALANTIR\CHAP14.WP
001   \PROGRAMS\WORDPROC\PALANTIR\INSERT13.WP
001   \PROGRAMS\WORDPROC\PALANTIR\INSERT16.WP
001   \PROGRAMS\WORDPROC\PALANTIR\DEBBIE.WP
001   \PROGRAMS\WORDPROC\PALANTIR\02-14-88.WP
001   \PROGRAMS\WORDPROC\PALANTIR\INSERT03.WP

C>
```

FIGURE 18.19: The log file produced by using the /L switch during the backup operation contains the date and time of the backup operation, and the full path names of each file in the backup set. The log file also contains a column indicating which diskette (of possibly many in the set) contains each individual backed up file.

command file available either in the current default directory or somewhere along the DOS path.

Backup Operations and the DOS Error-Level Code

When you are through backing up, the BACKUP command sets the DOS error-level code to one of the values listed in Table 18.6. The DOS error codes are primarily useful to you when you write batch files. Your batch file can use the IF ERRORLEVEL command (see Chapter 8) to test for the return code values in Table 18.6. If the code value equals 1, you will know that your backup diskette contains nothing. This may be all right, but if you had expected files to exist on the hard disk, you then will have to figure out why they did not. If your return code equals 2, you may have to rerun the BACKUP command after disassociating your workstation from the network to which it is connected. If the return code is 4, you will have to rerun the BACKUP command to try to avoid the unknown error situation that impeded the successful copying of your files.

CODE	DESCRIPTION
0	Normal completion
1	No files were backed up because none were found
2	Because of sharing, only some files were backed up
3	The user pressed Ctrl-Break to end the back up
4	An error occurred, ending the back up

TABLE 18.6: DOS Error-Level Codes for Backup Operations

OTHER BACKUP MEDIA

Although diskettes are by far the most commonly used medium for storing backup copies, other media—magnetic tape and hard disks—are also in common use.

Magnetic Tape

Magnetic tape (like cassette tape) helps combat the long time and large number of diskettes needed to perform backup operations. These tapes spin at a very high speed, are very small (about half the size of a cassette), and their drives can be added to almost any system, internally or externally. They can back up a 20MB disk in under 20 minutes.

Magnetic tape cartridge systems are relatively inexpensive, often costing less than $1000. The cartridges themselves are also inexpensive and easily stored, so you can create multiple backup copies at regular intervals. Many people, particularly in large corporations, use these systems to back up hard disks. The standard disadvantage, however, of tape backup media is that restoration operations must read through the tape sequentially to locate and reread individual files. A hard disk backup system, on the other hand, offers the obvious advantage of direct access to all files.

A Second Hard Disk

You can buy a second hard disk drive and use it solely for backup copies. Although hard disks are expensive, using them is much faster and easier than using floppy disks. You make backup copies in the same way as you do with floppy disks. However, be careful that your second hard disk has enough space to completely backup the entire first disk, because if you run out of space, the entire backup copy will become invalid and thus unusable.

Video Cassette Recorders

Video cassette recorders offer a very low-cost alternative to tape cartridges and second hard disks for mass backup operations. These devices use a special controller board and unique driver software and cost only a few hundred dollars. After adding a new DEVICE command line to your CONFIG.SYS file, as is also necessary with other special backup devices, you can write your hard disk data to a video cassette cartridge located in a standard video cassette recorder.

LABELING BACKUP DISKS

When you do make backup copies, you should use a labeling scheme to keep track of the backups. For example, labeling each series of backup disks with the labels shown in Figure 18.20 would tell you everything you need to know.

Affixing a label like the one in Figure 18.20 to each backup disk provides useful information. You should keep at least two sets of backup disks, alternating their use, so you always have the current and previous backup versions available. Add the new date, crossing off the date of the previous backup, each time you make a new backup version. Then if you lose your data and then find that one backup copy is no good, you can use the other set of backup copies.

Backup Disk No. _____ of _____   Set: _____

Computer: _____

Backup Command: _____

Backup Dates: _____

       _____

       _____

FIGURE 18.20: Typical diskette label containing identifying information. This sample label specifies an ID for the backup set that includes this diskette. It then gives the diskette a number and tells how many total diskettes are in the entire set. The label also indicates on which computer the backup was made, what command (including switches) was used, and the date of the last backup. Space is left for succeeding backup dates to be filled in (using felt-tipped pen, of course).

RESTORING FILES FROM A BACKUP DISK

The RESTORE command restores files from a backup-diskette set (or a fixed disk) back onto a hard drive. The drive can be the original source hard disk drive for the files, or it can be another hard disk drive onto which you want to place the files.

Note: Using the RESTORE command is the only way to properly copy files from a backup diskette. Neither the COPY nor the XCOPY command will accomplish this task correctly.

The general form of the RESTORE command is

RESTORE *BackupDrive Destination*

Restoring files is almost the reverse of backing them up, with fewer switches and options for restoration. However, RESTORE is not exactly the reverse of the BACKUP command. With BACKUP, you can specify a directory name alone, indicating you want to back up all files in the directory. Using RESTORE is not as easy. The second parameter, *Destination,* is the problem. If you do not specify a destination, the restoration is made to the current directory. However, in such a case, the current directory must be the same directory as the original source of the files on the backup disk. Otherwise, you'll receive the possibly misleading message "No files were found to restore." And, as Figure 18.21 shows, it isn't

```
C>RESTORE A: \PROGRAMS\WORDPROC\PALANTIR

Insert backup diskette Ø1 in drive A:
Strike any key when ready

*** Files were backed up 11-Ø2-1988 ***

*** Restoring files from drive A: ***
Diskette: Ø1

Warning! No files were found to restore

C>_
```

FIGURE 18.21: It is insufficient to simply specify the backup diskette drive name and the desired directory for RESTORE. Though doing so may seem to be intuitively correct, this syntax is unacceptable to the RESTORE command.

even enough to specify the correct directory as an argument in the RESTORE command.

The additional requirement for the *Destination* parameter is that you explicitly specify a file name, as in Figure 18.22, that simply adds the wildcard *.* specifier. You can also use the solution shown in Figure 18.23, which requires you to issue the CD command prior to RESTORE. In that case, specifying only drive C as the destination is sufficient, since the default directory is now the proper one—the one from which the files were originally backed up. Naturally, as with all DOS commands, the drive specifier C: is not strictly necessary since, in its absence, the current directory would be used by default anyway.

Restoring Only Some of Your Backed-Up Files

DOS provides a variety of very useful switches for RESTORE. The two principal switches presented here will be quite useful to you at various times. Other possible switches are presented in the reference entry at the end of this chapter.

Note: The ability to select the files you want restored can be very useful. It can also reduce the amount of time required to restore files because you restore only those files you actually need.

```
C>RESTORE A: \PROGRAMS\WORDPROC\PALANTIR\*.*

Insert backup diskette 01 in drive A:
Strike any key when ready


*** Files were backed up 11-02-1988 ***

*** Restoring files from drive A: ***
Diskette: 01
\PROGRAMS\WORDPROC\PALANTIR\ICCL.WP
\PROGRAMS\WORDPROC\PALANTIR\ICCL-2.WP
\PROGRAMS\WORDPROC\PALANTIR\CHAP14.WP
\PROGRAMS\WORDPROC\PALANTIR\INSERT13.WP
\PROGRAMS\WORDPROC\PALANTIR\INSERT16.WP
\PROGRAMS\WORDPROC\PALANTIR\DEBBIE.WP
\PROGRAMS\WORDPROC\PALANTIR\02-14-88.WP
\PROGRAMS\WORDPROC\PALANTIR\INSERT03.WP

C>_
```

FIGURE 18.22: RESTORE requires a complete path name when restoring from a backup set. In this case, the source drive is A, and the destination directory is PALANTIR, but the actual desired files are *.* (which must be specified here).

```
C>CD \PROGRAMS\WORDPROC\PALANTIR

C>RESTORE A: C:

Insert backup diskette 01 in drive A:
Strike any key when ready


*** Files were backed up 11-02-1988 ***

*** Restoring files from drive A: ***
Diskette: 01
\PROGRAMS\WORDPROC\PALANTIR\ICCL.WP
\PROGRAMS\WORDPROC\PALANTIR\ICCL-2.WP
\PROGRAMS\WORDPROC\PALANTIR\CHAP14.WP
\PROGRAMS\WORDPROC\PALANTIR\INSERT13.WP
\PROGRAMS\WORDPROC\PALANTIR\INSERT16.WP
\PROGRAMS\WORDPROC\PALANTIR\DEBBIE.WP
\PROGRAMS\WORDPROC\PALANTIR\02-14-88.WP
\PROGRAMS\WORDPROC\PALANTIR\INSERT03.WP

C>_
```

FIGURE 18.23: An alternate method for restoring a complete directory is to make the directory your default directory on the current drive. You can then specify the source for the restore operation as drive A, and the destination as the current drive (in this case, drive C).

If you have backed up an entire directory tree or any subdirectory tree, you will need to use the /S switch to restore the subdirectory tree structure. Also, if you have made changes to any of the previously backed up files, you should use the /P switch to ensure that the old version does not overwrite the new version.

RESTORING DIRECTORY STRUCTURES

The /S switch on the RESTORE command is the exact reverse of the /S switch on the BACKUP command. When used with BACKUP, /S allows you to search through a directory and all of its subdirectories for files to back up. When used with RESTORE, /S ensures that the backed-up files are restored to their proper subdirectories.

In fact, if DOS discovers that a subdirectory is missing during the restoration process, it will automatically recreate that subdirectory before copying the backed-up files to it. Your destination directory may be missing for a variety of reasons. Your entire disk may have failed or have been erased inadvertently. More likely, you may have erased the directory and file contents, after backing them up, in order to reclaim the disk space for other purposes. Or you may simply be restoring the directory structure and files to a different computer and hard disk.

> *Tip:* When you format a diskette for use during the backup process, you do not need to use the /S switch. In fact, it is inadvisable: Using /S will make less space available for backup files on floppy diskettes.

PROTECTING AGAINST ACCIDENTAL OVERWRITING

The /P switch is extremely useful if you're not completely sure of yourself or if much time has elapsed since the backup operation. When you specify /P, DOS asks you during the restoration if you really want to restore an old version and overwrite an existing disk file. DOS does this if the existing disk file has been updated since the earlier backup version, or if the disk file is marked as a read-only file. (The latter situation almost never occurs, so you needn't worry about it; you will learn about read-only files in Chapter 19.)

As a last example of RESTORE, use DOS's selective restoration capability to redo the example shown Figure 18.16. Instead of restoring all the files from the diskette in drive A, select only the document files (.WP):

RESTORE A: C:\PROGRAMS\WORDPROC\PALANTIR\ * .WP

Since the files UCSC.WP and STUFF.WP have been changed since the backup operation, make sure that they aren't accidentally overwritten:

RESTORE A: C:\PROGRAMS\WORDPROC\PALANTIR\ * .WP /P

The resultant protective sequence is shown in Figure 18.24.

The /P switch enabled RESTORE to note that two of the .WP files had been changed since they were backed up. The prompt allows you to inhibit overwriting and protect the changed version. Unfortunately, the display is somewhat confusing, since some but not all of the other restored files are interspersed between the warnings.

Now test your understanding of the restoration process. First back up any selected set of text files. If you completed the earlier exercises using BACKUP, you can use the resulting diskette if it contained text files. Otherwise, choose some files from your word processing (or other text-oriented) directory.

Make some textual change to one of the text files by using your word processor or DOS's EDLIN (see Chapter 6). Next, restore the backed-up files to their original directory. Use the /P switch so you do not overwrite the newly changed text files. Use your text-editing program to verify that the old versions of the changed files were not rewritten onto your disk.

File Restoration and the DOS Error-Level Code

When the RESTORE command ends, it sets the DOS error-level code to one of the values listed in Table 18.7.

```
C>RESTORE A: \PROGRAMS\WORDPROC\PALANTIR\*.WP /P

Insert backup diskette 01 in drive A:
Strike any key when ready


*** Files were backed up 11-02-1988 ***

*** Restoring files from drive A: ***
Diskette: 01
\PROGRAMS\WORDPROC\PALANTIR\ICCL.WP
\PROGRAMS\WORDPROC\PALANTIR\ICCL-2.WP
Warning! File CHAP14.WP
was changed after it was backed up
Replace the file (Y/N)?
N

\PROGRAMS\WORDPROC\PALANTIR\INSERT13.WP
\PROGRAMS\WORDPROC\PALANTIR\INSERT16.WP
\PROGRAMS\WORDPROC\PALANTIR\DEBBIE.WP
\PROGRAMS\WORDPROC\PALANTIR\02-14-88.WP
\PROGRAMS\WORDPROC\PALANTIR\INSERT03.WP

C>_
```

FIGURE 18.24: The /P switch helps to protect against accidental file overwriting during the restoration process. In this figure, the RESTORE command noted that SYBEX.WP and WKSHPS.WP had been changed on drive C since the previous backup operations. The prompts let you avoid having the earlier backup copies overwrite your more recent disk-resident (on drive C) work. The other three files (UCSC.WP, STUFF.WP, and CHICAGO.WP) are automatically restored since the hard disk contains no newer version.

CODE	DESCRIPTION
0	Normal completion
1	No files were restored because none were found
2	Because of sharing, only some files were restored
3	The user pressed Ctrl-Break or Esc to end the restoration
4	An error resulted, ending the restoration

TABLE 18.7: DOS Error-Level Codes for Restoration Operations

DOS COMMANDS USED IN BACKING UP AND RESTORING FILES

Following are the reference entries for the backup and restoration commands introduced in this chapter: BACKUP, COMP, DISKCOMP, and RESTORE. The DOS commands COPY, DISKCOPY, and XCOPY are also used in backing up diskettes. The reference entry for DISKCOPY appears in Chapter 2, and the reference entries for COPY and XCOPY appear in Chapter 3.

BACKUP

BACKUP selectively makes backup copies of specified files.

SYNTAX

*[D:path]*BACKUP *source dest switches*

D:path	is the drive and path where the command file is located if it is not in the current directory.
source	is the drive and optional file specification to be backed up.
dest	is the drive on which the backup will be made.
switches	are any number or combination of the following:

/S	backs up all subdirectories starting with the directory specified in *source*.
/M	backs up only those files that have been changed since the last backup.
/A	adds the files that will be backed up to those already on *dest*, thus not destroying existing files on *dest*.

/D:*mm-dd-yy*	backs up files changed on or after the date specified (the format depends on the country selected).
/T:*hh-mm-ss*	backs up files changed at or after the time specified (the format depends on the country selected).
/F	executes the program FORMAT.COM (which should be available) on any *dest* disk not already formatted.
/L[:*filespec*]	creates a log file with the given file name in the specified directory on a disk (the default name is BACKUP.LOG in the root directory of *source*).

TYPE

External.

USAGE

BACKUP is preferred over DISKCOPY and XCOPY for backing up your hard disk for several reasons. The most important reason is that XCOPY and DISKCOPY backup only onto one diskette. If a file takes up more space than is available on a diskette, as does a 5MB database file, for example, you cannot use any command other than BACKUP to back it up. BACKUP automatically breaks up large files and saves them on multiple diskettes (prompting you to insert a new diskette when necessary). BACKUP also saves long lists of files that together need more than one diskette for storage.

Make sure that you have the VERIFY command ON for doing backups. It's worth the extra time for the peace of mind that the backup copies are 100% accurate.

RESTRICTIONS

You cannot back up files that you are sharing but do not have access to. Do not use BACKUP with JOIN, SUBST, APPEND, or ASSIGN in effect. FORMAT must be available for use (in the same directory as BACKUP or on the path) as it may be used to format the target disk. Unless you use the /A parameter, BACKUP will erase all the files on the destination disk. The target disk will be formatted according to the capacity of the drive. Mismatches in capacity or formatting are not allowed.

EXAMPLES

A common and simple backup technique is writing copies of all files on a hard disk to a set of backup diskettes:

BACKUP C:\ B: /S

In this example command, the source directory on drive C is the root (\), the destination drive is drive B, and the /S switch ensures that all subordinate directories on drive C are similarly copied during the backup operation.

Another common backup operation is backing up all files within a single hard disk directory to a set of floppy disks. Entering

BACKUP C:\WP*.WP B:

backs up word processing files with extension .WSD from the WP directory. All files are written to successive diskettes on drive B.

COMP

COMP compares two or more files to see if they are the same.

SYNTAX

[*D:Path*]COMP [*FileSpec1*] [*FileSpec2*]

D:Path	is the drive and path where the command file is located if it is not in the current directory.
FileSpec1	is the optional drive and path, plus the file names and extensions, of the first set of files to be compared. Wildcards are allowed.
FileSpec2	is the optional drive and path, plus the file names and extensions, of the second set of files to be compared. Wildcards are allowed.

TYPE

External.

USAGE

The COMP command is used to compare the contents of two or more files. A common application is to compare whether two files located in two separate directories arc identical copies. COMP is also used to verify whether two programs on different disks with different dates are simply replicas of one another, acquired or created at different times.

EXAMPLES

The following command line verifies whether the version of BUDGET.TXT in the accounts directory is a duplicate of the file of the same name located in the budget directory:

COMP C:\LOTUS\BUDGET\BUDGET.TXT BUDGET.TXT

This example assumes that the second parameter, BUDGET.TXT, is located in the current working directory (presumably the accounts directory).

You can also use wildcards to compare multiple files with different extensions. In the following example, all word processing files with a .WP extension are compared with all word processing files with a .WPB extension to determine which files are identical to their backup versions (no changes were made in the most recent edit):

COMP \WP\ * .WP\WP* .WP

This command is most useful for verifying that the contents of two files are the same, but it is less useful to most users for determining exactly what the differences are. This is because the results of COMP are presented using hexadecimal notation, not the original source code. COMP returns values for the bytes that are different and for the offset into the files. For nonprogrammers, this information is of little or no use.

DISKCOMP

DISKCOMP compares the results of a DISKCOPY operation to the original file.

SYNTAX

[*D:path*]DISKCOMP [*drive1* [*drive2*]] [/1][/8]

D:path	is the drive and path where the command file is located if it is not in the current directory.
drive1 and *drive2*	are the two drives containing disks to be compared.
/1	causes only the first side of the diskettes to be compared.

/8 causes DOS to compare diskettes as if they were formatted 8 sectors per track, no matter what their current number of sectors per track.

TYPE

External.

USAGE

You typically use the DISKCOMP command after a diskette DISKCOPY operation to verify that the new diskette copy is identical to the original diskette.

EXAMPLES

After making a diskette copy with DISKCOPY, you can place the original version in the drive A and the copy in drive B and then enter

DISKCOMP A: B:

If the diskettes are exactly the same, DISKCOMP tells you so. If you know that the diskettes were originally one sided (160K) or formatted only for 8 sectors per track (320K), you can save time during the DISKCOMP operation by using, respectively, the /1 or /8 switch.

RESTRICTIONS

DISKCOMP will not work on a hard disk or with the JOIN and SUBST commands. DISKCOMP sees right through assignments.

RESTORE

RESTORE returns the original versions of files to your disks if you have properly created backup disks.

SYNTAX

[*D:path*] RESTORE *source filespec* [*switches*]

D:path   is the drive and path where the command file is located if it is not in the current directory.

source   is the drive containing the backed up files to be restored.

filespec	is an optional drive, path, file name, and extension of the files on the source disk to be restored. Wildcards are allowed.
switches	are any one or combination of the following:

/S	restores files in subdirectories specified in *filespec*
/P	prompts you before restoring each file, if that file was modified since it was backed up.
/B:*mm-dd-yy*	restores all backed-up files that were modified on or before *mm-dd-yy*.
/A:*mm-dd-yy*	restores all backed-up files that were modified on or after *mm-dd-yy*.
/M	compares the backed-up files and the files on the destination disk and restores those files that have changed or been erased since the last backup operation.
/N	restores files that no longer exist on the destination disk.
/L:*hh-mm-ss*	restores all files changed since *hh-mm-ss*.
/E:*hh-mm-ss*	restores all files changed prior to *hh-mm-ss*.

TYPE

External.

USAGE

The RESTORE command brings files from BACKUP disks (diskettes or fixed disks) back onto a hard drive. This drive can be the original source hard drive for the files, or it can be another hard drive onto which you want to place the files.

Two switches will be useful to you at various times. If you have backed up an entire directory tree, or any subtree, you will need to use the /S switch to restore the subdirectory tree structure. Also, if you have made changes to any of the previously backed up files, you should use the /P switch to ensure that the old version does not overwrite the new version.

The /S switch performs a function similar to the /S switch the BACKUP command. With the BACKUP command, the /S switch allows you to search through a directory and all its subdirectories for file names to back up. When used with RESTORE, /S ensures that the backed up files are restored to their proper subdirectories. In fact, if DOS discovers that a subdirectory is missing during the restoration process, it will automatically recreate that directory before copying the backed-up files to it.

The /P switch is extremely important to use, especially if you're not completely sure of yourself or if much time has elapsed since the backup operation. When you specify /P, DOS will ask you during the restoration process whether you really want to restore an old version and overwrite an existing disk file. DOS will do this if the existing disk file has been updated since the earlier backup version, and if the disk file has been marked as a read-only file.

The /A and /B switches work side by side, but not together. The /B switch specifies the *latest* date by which a file can have been modified and still be eligible for restoration; the /A switch specifies the *earliest* date. In other words, /B restores all files changed *before* a certain date, while /A restores all files modified *after* a certain date.

The /M switch restores only files that were changed or deleted since they were backed up. For example, suppose you back up the file FILE.DAT. If you later accidentally delete it, you can restore it by specifying FILE.DAT as the name and using the /M parameter.

The /N switch is similar to /M, except that it restores only files that have been deleted since they were backed up.

The /E and /L switches work the same as /A and /B, respectively, except /E and /L refer to time, not dates.

EXAMPLES

Restoring your backed-up files is essentially the reverse of backing them up. For instance, to restore an entire hard disk from a backup set created with the *BACKUP C:\ B: /S* command, you enter

RESTORE B: C:*.* /S

Similarly, to restore all the word processing files backed up with the BACKUP *C:\WP*.WP B:* command, you enter

RESTORE B: C:\WP*.WP

RESTRICTIONS

Warning: RESTORE overwrites files with the same name if they are in the specified directory. Use the /P switch or REPLACE to avoid rewriting a file.

Only backup files are restored. You can restore only your own shared files. Do not use RESTORE if SUBST, JOIN, or ASSIGN was invoked when a backup operation was performed.

SUMMARY

This chapter has taught you how to back up your disks. Power failures do occur in businesses, brownouts occur even more frequently, and a multitude of other incidents can cause the intermittent loss or corruption of important files. Therefore, making backups is of critical importance for avoiding disaster.

For additional information about the DISKCOPY command, see

- Chapter 2, "Starting to Use DOS"

For additional information about the COPY and XCOPY commands, see

- Chapter 3, "The Disk System"

For additional information about batch-file subcommands, see

- Chapter 8, "Batch File Subcommands"

For additional information about the ATTRIB command, see

- Chapter 19, "Other Advanced Commands"

For additional information about disk fragmentation and utility backup programs, see

- Chapter 20, "Extending DOS's Power with Utility Software"

In the next chapter, you will learn a series of even more advanced DOS commands. These commands are particularly sophisticated and are used only for special purposes. However, they allow you to perform certain advanced tasks that would not otherwise be possible with any combination of the standard DOS commands you have learned so far.

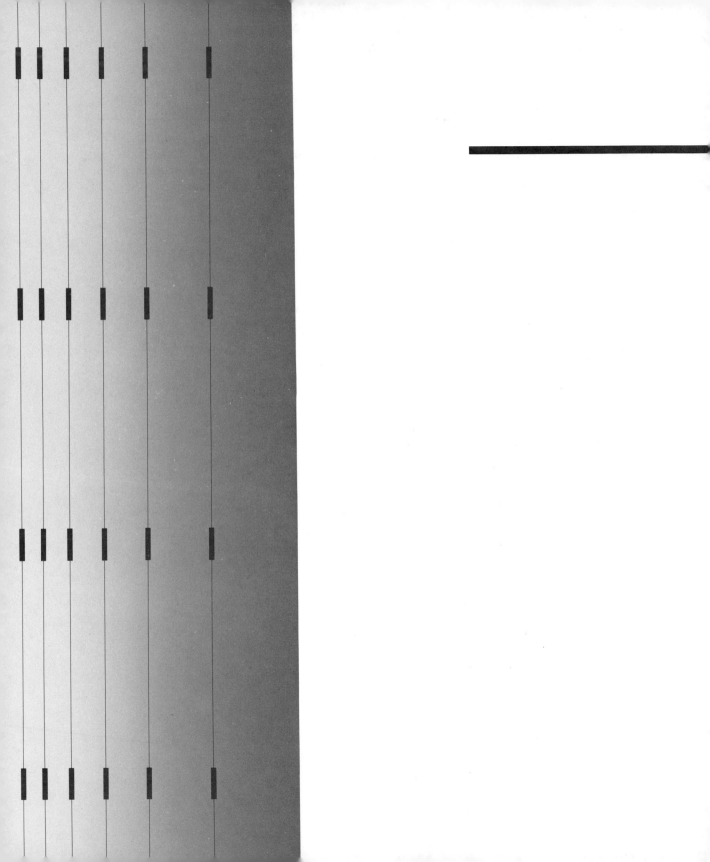

CHAPTER 19

ADVANCED DOS COMMANDS

ADVANCED DOS COMMANDS

The commands presented in this chapter extend the control of your computer system that DOS provides. The first group—ATTRIB, REPLACE, and RECOVER—allows you to expand the range of ways in which you manage and manipulate files. A second group consisting of JOIN, SUBST, ASSIGN, and FASTOPEN, enables you to use and traverse your directory and disk structures more easily and more quickly. The commands SET and COMMAND help you get more mileage from the main DOS controlling program, COMMAND.COM. Finally, the FDISK command allows you to create both primary and extended partitions on a hard disk. Every hard disk needs a primary partition; many DOS users can make effective use of extended partitions.

The chapter concludes with reference entries for the commands presented here.

ADVANCED FILE MANIPULATION

A file attribute is a characteristic of that file. Height is an attribute of a person; disk storage space is an attribute of a file. Another attribute of a file is its archive bit, which indicates whether the file has been changed since it was last backed up with the BACKUP command. Yet another attribute is the read/write bit, which indicates whether you are allowed to change the file. Several advanced DOS commands work specifically with files and with attributes such as these.

Changing a File's Attributes

Note: Most files can be read from and written to; they are said to be *read/write* files and to have an attribute of − R. Some files are restricted, permitting data to be read from them but not written to them. These files are called *read-only* files and have an attribute of + R.

ATTRIB, a DOS disk-resident command, changes the read/write and archive file attributes. This command can be very useful; since you can change a file's read/write attribute bit to read-only, you can block the deletion of the file, thus preventing accidental erasure of or changes to a file or group of files.

Influencing the archive bit allows you to control which files are backed up. If you are using many temporary files, for example, you can reset their archive bits to 0 (off). The BACKUP /M and XCOPY /M commands will then ignore those files.

No backup or copy operation will take place; as a result, the backup and copy operations for the rest of your files will be faster and will require less disk space.

One version of the ATTRIB command affects the attributes of one or more files. A second, simpler version displays the current attributes of one or more files. The format of the command is

ATTRIB *Switches FileNames*

The *Switches* parameter controls the on/off status of the two file attributes. If *Switches* is not specified, the screen displays the current attribute values of the specified files. *FileNames* is any standard file name. Wildcards are allowed, as well as drive and path-name prefixes.

Figure 19.1 shows the ATTRIB command applied to the root directory on drive C of a sample system. This display shows that three files have the A (archive attribute) bit set (COMMAND.COM, AUTOEXEC.BAT, and QD2.LOG), and only one file has the R (read/write attribute) bit set to read-only (COMMAND.COM). The CONFIG.SYS file has no attributes set, which means that it does not need to be backed up, and it can be read from and written to with no restrictions.

If the ATTRIB command includes switches, you can modify the archive and read/write attributes simultaneously with one command. Specify the first switch, which affects the read/write bit, either as +R for read-only or −R for

```
C>DIR

 Volume in drive C is ROBBINS
 Directory of  C:\

COMMAND   COM    25307    3-17-87   12:00p
CONFIG    SYS      160    8-10-87    6:03p
WP             <DIR>      8-10-87    9:44p
FW             <DIR>      8-10-87    9:45p
AUTOEXEC  BAT      276    8-10-87    6:08p
QD2       LOG     3206    8-11-87    4:46p
DBASE          <DIR>      1-01-80   12:06a
DOS            <DIR>      1-01-80   12:10a
UTILITY        <DIR>      1-01-80   12:14a
        9 File(s)    3715072 bytes free

C>ATTRIB *.*
   A    R   C:\COMMAND.COM
            C:\CONFIG.SYS
   A        C:\AUTOEXEC.BAT
   A        C:\QD2.LOG

C>▪
```

FIGURE 19.1: Attribute status of sample root files. The ATTRIB command displays current attributes for all specified files (in this case, *.*). An *A* is displayed for each file whose archive bit is set, indicating that the file should be included in the next backup operation. An *R* is displayed for each file whose read/write bit is set, indicating that that file can only be read from and cannot be changed at all.

read/write. If you set read-only status (+R), then the file may not be deleted or modified in any way.

> *Warning:* If you set read-only status, you may sometimes be puzzled about why later operations are difficult. Trying to use EDLIN on a read-only file, for example, produces the understandable message "File is READ-ONLY," but trying to erase such a file produces "Access denied," a less than obvious message. An application program, such as dBASE III PLUS, may display only the cryptic message "File cannot be accessed!"

The second switch affects the archive bit. You specify it either as +A, which sets the archive bit, or −A, which resets the archive bit. You normally set the archive bit whenever a file is rewritten to disk (after it has been changed). When you issue a BACKUP command, DOS checks the archive bit. If the archive bit is set, BACKUP will back up the file; otherwise, it won't. After BACKUP has scanned a file and either backed it up or not, DOS resets the archive bit to 0. Using the −A switch forces the archive bit to be reset, so that a file will be skipped over during a backup operation. This allows you some measure of control over which files are backed up.

Table 19.1 shows the different states of a file's attributes when you use different combinations of these two switches. Remember that 1 in a binary system indicates that the attribute bit is on, and 0 indicates that it is off.

COMMAND	READ/WRITE BIT	ARCHIVE BIT
ATTRIB +R +A SAMPLE.TXT	1	1
ATTRIB +R −A SAMPLE.TXT	1	0
ATTRIB −R +A SAMPLE.TXT	0	1
ATTRIB −R −A SAMPLE.TXT	0	0

TABLE 19.1: Attribute Status of Sample Root Files

As Figure 19.1 showed, you can determine the current status of a file by using the ATTRIB command without switches. Using the switches, however, lets you control those attribute values yourself. If you use the command

ATTRIB +R −A SAMPLE.TXT

to set the read/write attribute to read-only (on) and the archive attribute to off, the command

ATTRIB SAMPLE.TXT

produces the following result:

R   A:\SAMPLE.TXT

These results show that the read/write bit is set to read-only for the SAMPLE .TXT file, and that the archive bit is not set—no A indicator appeared.

Updating Sets of Files

If you work with a specific application program (for example, a word processor or a spreadsheet), you might want a backup disk to contain only copies of the most recently modified files. REPLACE allows you to selectively back up files without using the BACKUP command. It can replace (update) the files on the backup disk that were recently changed or newly created on your working disk. It can also ignore any of your older and unchanged files.

Tip: The REPLACE command is simply an advanced, selective version of the COPY command. It is most commonly used when you change versions of DOS and need to update system files. You can also use REPLACE to update an entire DOS directory on your hard disk when you upgrade your version of DOS. It comes in handy, too, when you regularly back up a small set of files at the end of each workday, adding new files or updating modified files on your designated backup diskette.

The format of the REPLACE command is

REPLACE *Source Destination Switches*

You can optionally prefix the command with a drive and path name indicating where the REPLACE command file is located. *Source* represents the changed or newly created files that are to be written to the destination disk. *Destination* is optional; it specifies the destination drive and path to receive the copies of the specified files. If you don't specify a destination path, DOS uses the default destination, which is the current directory.

The *Switches* parameter indicates one or more switches: /A, /P, /R, /S, or /W. Because the REPLACE command is defined primarily by these switches, some of them cannot be used together. Look at the two directories SOURCE and DEST in Figure 19.2 to see how the switches affect the REPLACE command.

The /A switch allows you to add files to the destination directory. DOS copies only source files that are not in the destination directory. The /P (prompt) switch instructs DOS to pause and ask you if it is all right to copy each file that meets the criteria of *any other* switch that you use.

Use the /A and /P switches together. If you issue the command

C> REPLACE \SOURCE*.* \DEST /A /P

for the files shown in Figure 19.2, your screen displays

Add C:\DEST\FILE2.TXT? (Y/N) Y
Adding C:\DEST\FILE2.TXT

1 file(s) added

```
C>DIR

 Volume in drive C is ROBBINS
 Directory of  C:\SOURCE

 .               <DIR>      3-05-88    3:00p
 ..              <DIR>      3-05-88    3:00p
 FILE3            12176   11-16-88   10:30a
 FILE1             1056    8-18-88    4:23p
 FILE2             3616    9-26-88    6:42a
        5 File(s)   2535424 bytes free

C>DIR \DEST

 Volume in drive C is ROBBINS
 Directory of  C:\DEST

 .               <DIR>      3-05-88    3:00p
 ..              <DIR>      3-05-88    3:00p
 FILE3            12784    8-15-88    7:06a
 FILE1             1040    1-08-88    4:57p
        4 File(s)   2535424 bytes free

C>_
```

FIGURE 19.2: Example directories. These two directories, SOURCE and DEST, are used in the following figures to demonstrate the REPLACE command. Files in the SOURCE directory are used to update files in the DEST directory using the REPLACE command.

As Figure 19.3 shows, REPLACE added the one file in the source directory (FILE2.TXT) that did not already exist by name in the destination directory; it left FILE1.TXT and FILE3.TXT as they were.

The /R switch overrides the read/write attributes of read-only files on the destination directory. It allows you to replace read-only files without generating an error message, so you will not be denied the implicit file update performed by REPLACE. You should use the /R switch with caution, since you or someone else may have set the read/write attribute bit to read-only for a good reason.

The /S switch replaces or updates only old files; it does not add new ones. Therefore, you cannot use it with the /A switch. Be careful when you use the /S switch with a wildcard character—it will replace *all* files matching the source specification, including those in any subdirectories of the destination directory.

Figure 19.4 shows how the /S switch works. This example uses the original destination directory from Figure 19.2, which contained only FILE1.TXT and FILE3.TXT. The command in the figure tells DOS to use files in the source directory to replace any files they match in the destination directory. Since only FILE1.TXT and FILE3.TXT are common to both directories, only they are replaced in the destination directory.

> *Warning:* Be careful to enter the source and destination directories in the correct order in your command. Performing a REPLACE backward could copy your old data over your new versions.

```
C>DIR \DEST

 Volume in drive C is ROBBINS
 Directory of  C:\DEST
 .            <DIR>      3-Ø5-88     3:ØØp
 ..           <DIR>      3-Ø5-88     3:ØØp
 FILE3         12784     8-15-88     7:Ø6a
 FILE1          1Ø4Ø     1-Ø8-88     4:57p
 FILE2          3616     9-26-88     6:42a
      5 File(s)   2525184 bytes free

C>_
```

FIGURE 19.3: Using the /A switch to add files in the destination directory. Since FILE1 and FILE3 already existed in the DEST directory, only the new file (FILE2) was added to the directory with the *REPLACE \SOURCE\ *. * \DEST /A /P* command.

```
C>REPLACE  \SOURCE\*.*  \DEST  /S
Replacing C:\DEST\FILE3 file.
Replacing C:\DEST\FILE1 file.
2 files were replaced.

C>DIR \DEST

 Volume in drive C is ROBBINS
 Directory of  C:\DEST
 .            <DIR>      3-Ø5-88     3:ØØp
 ..           <DIR>      3-Ø5-88     3:ØØp
 FILE3         12176    11-16-88    1Ø:3Øa
 FILE1          1Ø56     8-18-88     4:23p
      4 File(s)   2525184 bytes free

C>_
```

FIGURE 19.4: Updating matching files with REPLACE. The /S switch directs REPLACE to replace or update files that already exist in the destination directory. This replacement process does not include new files in the source directory (such as, FILE2).

The /W switch causes DOS to pause to allow you time to insert a new source diskette before the replacement process begins. For example, you can execute a REPLACE command from a DOS diskette in drive A, replace that disk with the correct source disk, and then replace files on drive B with files from the newly inserted source diskette in drive A.

Rescuing Lost Files

RECOVER puts a file or a complete disk back together again. For instance, if a file becomes unreadable and access to that file is denied (a problem usually stemming from the deterioration of the magnetic disk surface, rather than from the simple attribute modification discussed in the last section), you can use RECOVER to try to restore the file.

> *Note:* File loss may also be due to corruption of the file allocation table (FAT). Even RECOVER is not likely to help you much in this instance.

The RECOVER command reads a file part by part (actually, disk cluster by disk cluster), skipping over the parts that have gone bad. This command rewrites the file without the bad data and allows you to access what's left. The format to recover specific files is

RECOVER *FileNames*

The format to recover an entire disk is

RECOVER *DriveName*

Like all DOS commands, RECOVER can be prefixed with a drive and path name to indicate where the disk-resident DOS command file is located. In the first format, the file names to be recovered can also be prefixed with their directory locations.

> *Warning:* RECOVER will not work properly on a network disk. Disengage your disk completely from any network before you try to recover files with this command.

Recovering all files on a disk is necessary when the directory or file allocation table of the disk has been damaged. After you use the second version of this command, the directory will be made up of files of the form FILE*nnnn*.REC, where *nnnn* is a number. All of the recovered files will be numbered sequentially in the order in which they were recovered. Note that this is not necessarily the order in which they appeared in the directory before the damage was done.

> *Note:* Try to recover an entire drive only when your disk's directory has been damaged completely. RECOVER does not distinguish between normally

accessible and inaccessible files; it renames all files in the directory in the RECOVER command format.

When you try to recover all files on a disk, you are limited to the maximum number of files that can fit into the root directory of the disk. If your disk has a subdirectory structure that contains more than this maximum, you'll have to invoke RECOVER several times, clearing the recovered files from the root directory in between invocations.

In theory, entering

RECOVER C:

on a typical fixed disk will recover up to 512 files (the maximum number of root directory file entries). In practice, when an entire disk has been scrambled or garbled you can recover only several score or several hundred files at a time. If you can recover more than 512 files, you will have to offload the first 512 onto a diskette to free the root directory's file allocation table entries (see Chapter 21). You could then enter RECOVER C: again to continue the recovery process.

When you have finished recovering your text files, you will probably need to review each one and edit the end of the recovered files, since the recovery process is likely to capture meaningless data at the end of the last disk cluster occupied by your original file.

IMPROVING DISK AND DIRECTORY REFERENCING

The commands discussed in this section—JOIN, SUBST, ASSIGN, and FASTOPEN—influence the way that DOS looks at its disk drives and disk-directory structures. These commands can be very useful when you are running older programs that make fixed assumptions about drives, when your programs do not contain a changeable path specification, or when a path name simply is too long. These commands also make referencing your DOS application easier and faster.

Treating Disks as Directories

JOIN makes DOS treat an entire disk drive as if it were a subdirectory on another drive. This extraordinary command allows individual DOS commands to treat files on multiple disk drives as if they were part of one sophisticated directory on a single drive.

> *Note:* The JOIN command can be especially helpful when you use it with a directory management program such as XTREE. Each time XTREE switches disks, it totals all of the files to determine the amounts of used and of available disk space. This process requires considerable time and can be a burden to power users. Switching a new disk with JOIN switches the current directory rather than current drive and is a significantly faster operation.

There are three versions of the JOIN command. All of them allow you to precede the command itself with a drive and path name specifying where DOS can find the JOIN.EXE file. Entering JOIN with no parameters at the command prompt displays all the current directory and disk names that have been joined. Entering JOIN with two parameters specifies what directory and drive are to be joined. Entering JOIN with only one parameter (a drive identifier) and the /D switch *disjoins* the drive from a directory to which it had been joined.

Executing the following JOIN command connects the two drives internally:

JOIN D: C:\ACCOUNT

You can read this command as "Join the entire drive *D* to the C:\ACCOUNT directory." You can substitute any disk drive identifier for D and any empty directory of files for C:\ACCOUNT. To see how this command works, look at Figure 19.5, which shows two disk directory structures. Figure 19.6 shows the new directory structure after this JOIN command was executed. Drive D appears to be a subdirectory on drive C.

> *Warning:* The JOIN command applies only to root directories and the first level of subdirectories beyond root directories. You'll receive an "invalid parameter" message if you try to join to a directory any further into your hierarchical structure.

When you invoke JOIN with no parameters, DOS displays the results of any joining. The screen displays the joined drives and the directories to which they have been attached. For example, entering

JOIN

produces

D: = > C:\ACCOUNT

This display tells you that you can now access the root directory of drive D only through the ACCOUNT directory on drive C. In effect, C:\ACCOUNT is the new root directory of drive D, and all of drive D's subdirectories are now subdirectories of C:\ACCOUNT.

When you use the primary form of the JOIN command, in which you specify a drive and a directory to be joined, DOS will simply respond with a new prompt if everything went well. You won't receive any notice that the join operation occurred—and in this case, no news is good news. For example, if ACCOUNT is an empty directory, the command

JOIN D: C:\ACCOUNT

produces no obvious result.

If the proposed root directory (C:\ACCOUNT) had contained files, you would have received the error message "Directory not empty," and the JOIN

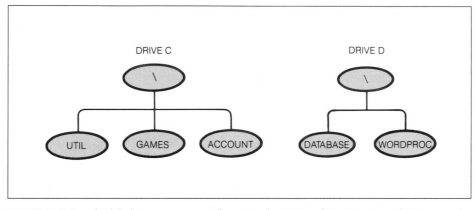

FIGURE 19.5: Sample disk directory structures illustrating the JOIN and SUBST commands. You can ask DOS to treat disks as if they were directories, or directories as if they were stand-alone disks.

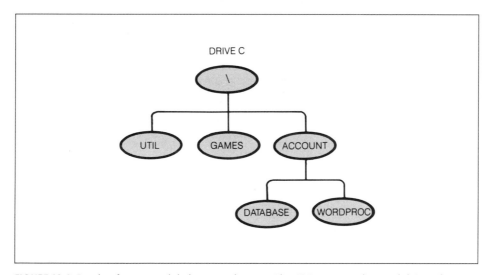

FIGURE 19.6: Results of joining a disk drive to a directory. The JOIN command treats disk D as if it were part of the directory structure of drive C. DOS now views the root directory of drive D, containing subdirectories DATABASE and WORDPROC, as the ACCOUNT directory of drive C. Former drive D files and path names can now be referenced as simply a long path name on drive C.

command would have failed. Although a proposed root directory *may* have subdirectories when the JOIN command is executed, JOIN will suppress temporarily any subdirectories until the drive and directory are disjoined. You won't be able to access any information in that part of your directory structure.

Note: You must use a completely empty directory when you join another disk drive to it.

Continuing with this example, if you execute a DIR command on drive C after the join operation has occurred, the remaining amount of disk storage space shown will be that of drive C, not of drive D. If you save anything in the ACCOUNT subdirectory (actually, drive D), DOS will use disk storage on drive D, not on C. Thus, you can save in ACCOUNT (drive D) a file that is larger than the apparent amount of disk storage space left. In addition, access to drive D will be denied, so any command using drive D explicitly (such as DIR D:) will generate the error message "Invalid drive specification."

The last version of the JOIN command cancels the effects of a previous JOIN command. You must specify the JOIN command you wish to disengage (you may have issued many). The following command disengages the JOIN command just executed in the preceding example:

JOIN D: /D

If you don't specify the destination drive (that is, the proposed root directory of the JOIN command in question), with the intention of undoing all joinings, the error message "Incorrect number of parameters" will appear. Similarly, disjoining a drive that has not been joined will generate the error message "Invalid parameter."

Now examine an actual session with the JOIN command. The following sequence shows the use of JOIN when you are using drives A and B on a dual-diskette system. The drives contain the directories shown in Figure 19.7. The first JOIN command in Figure 19.8 appends the root directory of drive B to the

```
A:\> DIR A:

 Volume in drive A has no label
 Directory of  A:\

UTIL          <DIR>       6-04-87    2:12p
GAMES         <DIR>       6-04-87    2:12p
ACCOUNT       <DIR>       6-04-87    2:12p
JOIN     EXE   8955   12-30-85   12:00p
SUBST    EXE   9911   12-30-85   12:00p
       5 File(s)      339968 bytes free

A:\> DIR B:

 Volume in drive B has no label
 Directory of  B:\

WORDPROC      <DIR>       6-04-87    2:12p
DATABASE      <DIR>       6-04-87    2:12p
       2 File(s)      359424 bytes free

A:\> ▪
```

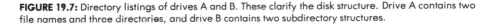

FIGURE 19.7: Directory listings of drives A and B. These clarify the disk structure. Drive A contains two file names and three directories, and drive B contains two subdirectory structures.

```
A:\> JOIN B: A:\ACCOUNT
A:\> DIR A:\ACCOUNT

 Volume in drive A has no label
 Directory of  A:\ACCOUNT

WORDPROC     <DIR>       6-Ø4-87    2:12p
DATABASE     <DIR>       6-Ø4-87    2:12p
       2 File(s)     339968 bytes free
A:\> ▪
```

FIGURE 19.8: Joining drive B to the ACCOUNT directory on drive A. A directory request for A:\ACCOUNT after the entire drive B has been joined to this directory reveals that A:\ACCOUNT appears to have the same subdirectory structure as formerly existed only on drive B.

directory A:\ACCOUNT, as a DIR command shows. A:\ACCOUNT has become the root directory of drive B.

The two commands in Figure 19.9 change the active directory and then create a file in that directory; this file is actually being created in drive B. To see that the file is actually on drive B, you need to disjoin the directories and look at the files on drive B (see Figure 19.10).

Treating Directories as Disks

The SUBST (substitute) command is the opposite of the JOIN command: It creates a new disk drive out of any existing directory. To visualize this, look at Figure 19.6 first and then at Figure 19.5. You can make any existing directory (in this case, ACCOUNT) and all of its subdirectories the root directory of a new drive.

A frequent use for this command is in running older software packages that cannot reference files in a hierarchical directory structure. By fooling these packages into thinking they are simply addressing files on a disk drive, you can still use the DOS directory structure for file storage.

Tip: You can also use the SUBST command to reduce your typing burden. You can redefine any directory, no matter how deep in your hierarchical structure, and then reference that drive with a single-letter drive identifier. All

```
A:\> CD \ACCOUNT
A:\ACCOUNT> COPY CON: TEST.TXT
This is a test file.  This will be saved in the
\ACCOUNT directory which is actually the root directory
of drive B.  Therefore, the available storage space
shown with the DIR command will be that remaining on
drive A.  When this file is saved, it will actually use
space on drive B, so the available storage space shown
on the screen (for A:) will not change.  However, it
will be decreasing the available disk space on drive B.
^Z
         1 File(s) copied

A:\ACCOUNT> DIR

 Volume in drive A has no label
 Directory of  A:\ACCOUNT

WORDPROC     <DIR>       6-04-87    2:12p
DATABASE     <DIR>       6-04-87    2:12p
TEST     TXT      380    6-04-87    2:58p
        3 File(s)     339968 bytes free

A:\ACCOUNT>
```

FIGURE 19.9: Directory files as files on another drive. When a JOIN is in effect, all file creations and modifications really occur on the joined physical drive. In this example, the file TEST.TXT is created on drive B. The reference to the file appears to be A:\ACCOUNT\TEST.TXT, but the available space on drive A (339968 bytes) is not affected by the creation of the 380-byte TEST.TXT file. As you can see in Figure 19.8, the amount of space available on drive A *before* the file was created does not change.

```
A:\ACCOUNT> CD \
A:\> JOIN B: /D
A:\> DIR B:

 Volume in drive B has no label
 Directory of  B:\

WORDPROC     <DIR>       6-04-87    2:12p
DATABASE     <DIR>       6-04-87    2:12p
TEST     TXT      380    6-04-87    2:58p
        3 File(s)     358400 bytes free

A:\>
```

FIGURE 19.10: Undoing the effect of a JOIN command. This operation requires you to specify the name of the drive (B:) to be detached and the /D switch. The actual physical structure of drive B is now available for viewing and referencing again through the identifier B rather than through the pseudo-specifier A:\ACCOUNT.

future command references then will be shorter, faster, and less likely to contain typing errors.

The SUBST command is handy in another common situation. If you have a hard disk with a directory structure containing many levels of subdirectories, SUBST allows you to avoid typing long path names. For the same reason, it is useful when a program requests a file name and path but allows you to enter only a limited number of characters. WordPerfect is an example of this type of program.

Like the JOIN command, SUBST has three versions. The first performs a substitution, the second displays all current substitutions, and the third cancels a previous substitution.

Note: A substituted drive is really only a portion of another drive. Don't mistake a substituted drive for a RAM drive; SUBST offers convenience, not increased performance.

Look at the following example. Specify a directory structure, as shown in Figure 19.11. Suppose you need to run an older general ledger program that needs the files in ACCOUNT\GL, but the older program does not support paths. You can issue the following command:

SUBST F: C:\ACCOUNT\GL

This command makes DOS assume that there is a disk drive F, and that the contents of this drive are the contents of the ACCOUNT\GL subdirectory on drive C. Drive F now includes all of the directory's subdirectories (in this example, however, there are no subdirectories).

You can refer to the directory just as you would a normal disk drive. If you type

DIR F:

DOS returns the same result as if you had typed

DIR C:\ACCOUNT\GL

Unlike the JOIN command, the SUBST command allows you to access the specified subdirectory directly after you issue the SUBST command. If you save a file on drive F (or in the subdirectory), the file will also be saved in the subdirectory (or on drive F), because both access the same part of the disk (see Figure 19.12). In effect, this command opens up another window into a directory, and you can access that directory's contents through the window simply by using a drive specifier.

Note: By default, DOS supports only drives lettered A through E (LAST-DRIVE = E). To create and access drives lettered beyond E, you must include in your CONFIG.SYS file the command LASTDRIVE = n, where n is the last letter allowed for a drive. For example, LASTDRIVE = Z allows drives labeled A through Z.

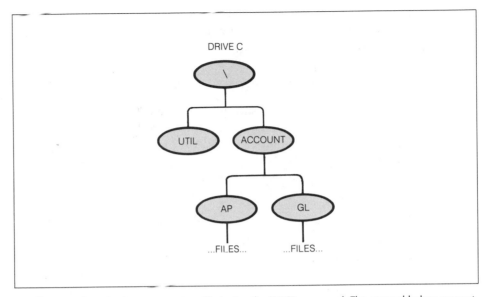

FIGURE 19.11: Sample directory structure illustrating the SUBST command. The general ledger accounting files are currently available only through the long pathname C:\ACCOUNT\GL*filename.*

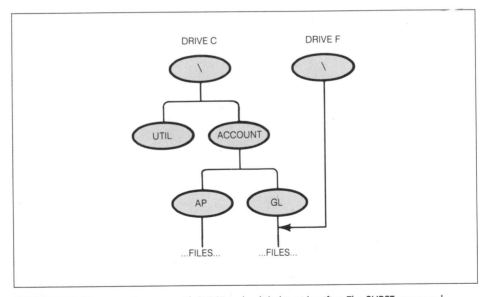

FIGURE 19.12: Directory references with SUBST and a disk drive identifier. The SUBST command enables DOS to use a fictitious drive identifier (F:) as a shorthand method of referencing the files located in the GL subdirectory. In fact, after changing the default drive to drive F, all the files located In the GL directory will appear to be in the root directory of this pseudo drive.

The second version of SUBST displays all currently active substitutions. DOS displays the created drive identifier and the drive and directory to which it is linked. For example,

C:\ > SUBST
F: = > C:\ACCOUNT\GL

tells you that drive F is being substituted for ACCOUNT\GL on drive C. As a result, you can access the ACCOUNT\GL directory normally (on drive C) or through its substitute (on the created drive F).

The final version of SUBST undoes a substitution. To undo the SUBST command shown in the previous example, you type

SUBST F: /D

The /D switch disjoins, or disassociates, the directory from the created drive F.

Now look at an example that uses all three versions of this command. Your first step is to examine the root directory on drive A to verify that no drive F exists (see Figure 19.13). Next, issue the SUBST command to create drive F, as shown in Figure 19.14. Then activate the windowing feature of this command by creating a file on drive F and verifying that it actually resides in the linked subdirectory (see Figure 19.15).

Finally, you can undo the SUBST command to restore the system back to its original state by issuing this command:

A:\ > SUBST F: /D

```
A>DIR

 Volume in drive A is DEMO
 Directory of  A:\

UTIL         <DIR>      3-05-88    2:40p
ACCOUNT      <DIR>      3-05-88    2:40p
        2 File(s)    358400 bytes free

A>DIR ACCOUNT

 Volume in drive A is DEMO
 Directory of  A:\ACCOUNT

.            <DIR>      3-05-88    2:40p
..           <DIR>      3-05-88    2:40p
GL           <DIR>      3-05-88    3:35p
AP           <DIR>      3-05-88    3:35p
        4 File(s)    358400 bytes free

A>_
```

FIGURE 19.13: Root directory of drive A. There is presently no drive F on this DOS system. A directory request produces the message "Invalid drive specification."

```
A>SUBST F: \ACCOUNT\GL

A>DIR F:

 Volume in drive F is DEMO
 Directory of  F:\

.              <DIR>       3-05-88    3:35p
..             <DIR>       3-05-88    3:35p
        2 File(s)     353280 bytes free

A>_
```

FIGURE 19.14: A directory treated as a disk drive. The SUBST command can generate a pseudo drive as far as DOS is concerned. Drive F will now exist; its root directory files will be the same as those in A:\ACCOUNT\GL. In fact, any new files created in or copied to drive F will actually be written to the A:\ACCOUNT\GL directory.

```
A>COPY CON: F:TEST.TXT
This file should appear in both F: and \ACCOUNT\GL^Z
        1 File(s) copied

A>DIR F:

 Volume in drive F is DEMO
 Directory of  F:\

.              <DIR>       3-05-88    3:35p
..             <DIR>       3-05-88    3:35p
TEST    TXT       50       3-05-88    4:31p
        3 File(s)     347136 bytes free

A>DIR \ACCOUNT\GL

 Volume in drive A is DEMO
 Directory of  A:\ACCOUNT\GL

.              <DIR>       3-05-88    3:35p
..             <DIR>       3-05-88    3:35p
TEST    TXT       50       3-05-88    4:31p
        3 File(s)     347136 bytes free

A>_
```

FIGURE 19.15: Substituted and original drive. A pseudo-drive identifier created by the SUBST command does not mask the original directory path. A directory listing of drive F shows the same contents as a directory listing of A:\ACCOUNT\GL.

Trying to use the DIR command on drive F will now result in the following message:

A:\ > DIR F:
Invalid drive specification

Rerouting Disk Input and Output

Some older programs have hard-coded drive references, which means they are internally frozen, with no way for you to make use of a hard disk. The ASSIGN command can help you overcome this restriction. ASSIGN causes any requests for one drive to be carried out on another drive. ASSIGN is very useful with older software packages designed to work only with drives A and B. Even though your files are actually in a directory on your hard disk, you can trick the older program into thinking it is accessing the files on a single drive without any hierarchical structure.

ASSIGN has two versions. The first makes or breaks assignations, and the second cancels all assignations currently in effect. The first version is the most frequently used:

ASSIGN *DriveX = BigDrive*

In this version, DOS treats all future references to files and directories on *DriveX* as if they had been made to *BigDrive*. As with all DOS external commands, you can prefix the command name with a drive identifier and a path name.

Warning: Do not use ASSIGN with BACKUP, RESTORE, LABEL, JOIN, SUBST, or PRINT. These commands act on the contents of drives and directories; serious problems can result if your intended destination drive has previously been reassigned to another drive. For your protection, DOS ignores reassignments when you invoke the potentially even more dangerous FORMAT, DISKCOPY, and DISKCOMP commands.

A simple example of ASSIGN involves assigning to drive C any references to the files on drive A.

ASSIGN A = C

can be read as "Let the current working directory on drive C handle all tasks requested of drive A." When you execute the command DIR A:, the screen displays a directory of drive C. To undo ASSIGN commands, use ASSIGN by itself without any drive assignments:

ASSIGN

Speeding Up Disk Access

When your directory structure contains many levels of subdirectories, DOS can take a very long time to search for a file or directory. To combat this problem, you can use the FASTOPEN command (available in DOS 3.3), which maintains a list of the most recently accessed directory and file locations. Thus, if you repeatedly reference a directory or file, DOS will be able to locate it more quickly on the disk. The FASTOPEN memory buffer will contain the disk location of that directory or file; DOS can then access it without having to check the disk directory structure itself.

The general format of the FASTOPEN command is

FASTOPEN *Drive:* **=** *Size*

Drive is the drive you want FASTOPEN to work for. You must repeat the *Drive:* and *=Size* parts of the command for each drive you want FASTOPEN to affect. *Size,* an optional parameter, represents the number of directory or file entries that FASTOPEN remembers.

Make sure that the FASTOPEN command file is available on the current directory or path. As with all DOS 3.3 commands, you can precede the command name with the full path name leading to it.

Warning: You cannot use FASTOPEN on a drive defined by the JOIN, SUBST, or ASSIGN command. You also cannot use it on network drives.

The most common use of the FASTOPEN command is simply to specify the disk drive whose performance you want to improve. For example, entering

FASTOPEN C:

enables DOS to remember the last 34 directories and files accessed (the default) and thus to be able to go right to them on the disk.

You can use FASTOPEN only once per boot session. FASTOPEN reserves 35 bytes per entry. A buffer size of 100 (FASTOPEN C: = 100) therefore consumes about 3500 bytes of memory. It is recommended that *Size* be at least as great as the highest number of levels in the directory structure, so that DOS can find quickly any file in the directory. In fact, unless you are working only with one file, *Size* should be larger. The default value thus is reasonable, unless you have special use requirements and want to perform timing tests.

INFLUENCING THE COMMAND PROCESSOR AND ITS ENVIRONMENT

The command processor on your system disk, COMMAND.COM, is the program that interprets all of the commands you type from the keyboard. It has been primarily responsible for interpreting all the commands you've learned so far. When it receives your command, it first scans its own internal command list to see if it can handle your request without going to the disk. If the command is an internal command, then the way in which that command will work is defined somewhere in COMMAND.COM. If it is an external command, COM-MAND.COM will check the current directory and then the PATH directories to see if the command file is present. If it is not, and your command is not in a batch file, the screen will display an error message. However, if the command processor does find the command file, it transfers control to that file.

Now look at some examples. TYPE is an internal command used to display the contents of ASCII files. When COMMAND.COM is ready to accept a command, it displays the DOS prompt. Suppose you type the command TYPE OUTLINE.TXT. COMMAND.COM first determines that TYPE is an internal command. It then looks internally for the instructions that tell it what to do when the TYPE command is used. Following these instructions, it gets the file name you typed and displays the file.

External commands are not really commands at all—each external command request actually runs a program contained in a separate file. These files are called .COM or .EXE files. For example, a file named ASSIGN.COM contains the program that performs an ASSIGN command. Suppose you issue the command ASSIGN A = B. COMMAND.COM first checks that this is not an internal command. After first checking the current working directory, it then finds the file called ASSIGN.COM somewhere along the specified path and transfers control of the system to that file. When ASSIGN has finished assigning, control returns to COMMAND.COM. Of course, this procedure assumes you've set the path properly (PATH \DOS).

When COMMAND.COM is doing all of this, it must access not only those parts of itself that contain definitions and instructions, but it also must access the DOS *environment*. The DOS environment is simply a reserved portion of memory containing a series of named character strings. Some of these strings are used for standard DOS jobs, such as the PATH and the LASTDRIVE definitions. Other strings are created by you in your batch files, or at the DOS command prompt, and used for miscellaneous chores such as system password protection and named batch program variables (see Chapter 9). The SET command gives you direct control over the contents of the DOS environment.

Renaming Commands

The SET command changes character strings and definitions within the DOS environment. Both you and DOS can set aside named areas of this environment for character strings. You can use them for anything you like—for example, individual path names for future commands, file names for later DOS operations, or variable values used by several batch files.

The SET command with no parameters

SET

displays the current DOS environment settings. A modified format erases any existing entry. For example,

SET *Name* =

erases the DOS environment variable *Name*. To create a completely new DOS environment string or to change one that already exists, use the format

SET *Name* = *String*

where *Name* is either a variable name defined by you or one of the system's pre-defined names such as PROMPT, PATH, LASTDRIVE, or COMSPEC.

> *Note:* You are limited by default to 127 bytes of total available DOS environment space, although you can increase this value by using the /E switch of the SHELL command.

The following sample sequence demonstrates the SET command. First, you can display the existing DOS environment, which includes all externally defined system default settings and user definitions. For example, issuing the SET command

A:\ > SET

at the DOS prompt displays the following:

```
COMSPEC = A:\COMMAND.COM
PATH = \
PROMPT = $p$g
LASTDRIVE = Z
FILES = \WORDPROC\WORDPERF\FILES
```

The first four of these environment names are predefined and have special meaning to the system. You've seen all of these except for COMSPEC, which is modified only infrequently, when you've relocated your command processor to some drive or directory other than the boot-disk root directory. COMSPEC is usually used when you place COMMAND.COM on a RAM disk to speed up applications that frequently invoke the command processor.

The next version of the SET command removes an entire string definition from the DOS environment. With the DOS environment defined as just shown, executing the command

SET PATH =

clears the value of the PATH variable. If you then execute the SET command, you will see that the PATH variable has been removed:

```
A:\ > SET
COMSPEC = A:\COMMAND.COM
PROMPT = $p$g
LASTDRIVE = Z
FILES = \WORDPROC\WORDPERF\FILES
```

environment exists only temporarily, and you can exit from it only by using DOS's EXIT command. The /P switch is handy if you are using a modified command processor for security reasons.

The /C *String* parameter tells the new processor to execute the command in *String* when it is invoked. If you don't specify /C *String*, the new command processor will prompt you for commands when it is invoked. For example, the normal processor that is run every time you start the computer, COMMAND.COM, has a built-in *String* value of AUTOEXEC.BAT, which causes the AUTOEXEC.BAT file to be run when the system starts.

The /E:*xxxx* parameter defines a new DOS environment size to permit extensive use of the SET command. This parameter is necessary only when you want to perform advanced commands in your batch files (as discussed in Chapter 9) or your application programs.

Following is an example of COMMAND use. Suppose the ERASE command has not been defined for a command processor in the UTILITY directory. You would like 500 bytes of DOS environment, and you would like this processor to supplant the COMMAND.COM processor permanently. The following command will do all of this:

COMMAND \UTILITY /P /E:500

COMMAND is the command name, and UTILITY is the directory containing the new command processor. The /P switch makes the newly active command processor (the secondary command processor) the permanent primary processor, and /E:500 tells the computer to allow half a kilobyte of DOS environmental memory.

Invoking a secondary processor without the /P parameter causes the DOS environment to appear as in Figure 19.16. You can terminate a secondary processor invoked without /P by using the DOS EXIT command. This will deactivate the secondary DOS environment and reactivate the main processor. On exiting from the secondary processor, the computer will reenter the DOS environment of the first processor. Therefore, any changes you make to any of the DOS environment variables of the secondary command processor will be lost when you exit to the primary DOS environment.

Although when you exit to the primary processor you will lose any changes you make to the DOS environment while running the secondary processor, any other operation you have performed—such as changing drives and deleting files—will be permanent.

COMMAND is handy in a number of instances. The most common use of this command in earlier versions of DOS (previous to version 3.3) was to simulate true subprogram linkage. See Chapter 8 for more information about this capability. You can even use this command to expand the available DOS environment. Simply reinvoking the original command processor with

COMMAND \ /P /E:5000

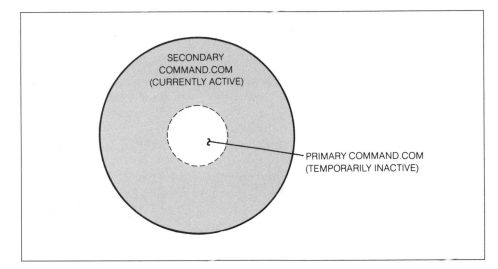

FIGURE 19.16: Invoking a secondary command processor. Using COMMAND to invoke a new version of the command interpreter temporarily deactivates the original (primary) command processor. This new program actually takes over all user interface chores, accepting and interpreting all new user commands.

activates a new copy of the original processor, expands the DOS environment to 5000 bytes, and makes the new copy the primary processor for the remainder of your DOS processing.

Do not invoke a secondary command processor lightly, since each new invocation of COMMAND.COM requires allocation of additional physical memory, which is a limited resource. Permanent attachment of a secondary processor is better used as a technique for customization or security, rather than simply to expand the DOS environment.

PARTITIONING YOUR HARD DISK

Hard disks are usually so large that they can contain more than one type of operating system. For example, you can have DOS 3.3 manage one part of a disk and UNIX manage another. Each of these sections is called a *partition*. A disk can contain from one to four partitions.

Partitions make a hard disk, especially a very large one, a more economical investment. They allow you effectively to have up to four completely different computer systems resident in one set of hardware. However, since they do not share a common software environment, they cannot share data.

You can set up two types of partitions for DOS: a *primary DOS partition* and an *extended DOS partition*. The primary DOS partition is the partition that contains DOS and is the first partition on the disk. This is the only partition that must be on the disk if your disk is no larger than 32MB. The extended DOS partition is a separate partition that you cannot use for booting, but which you can divide into separate logical drives.

If you have more than 32MB available on one hard disk, you will need to create an extended DOS partition, which is assigned the next logical drive letter. For example, if you have a 60MB hard disk drive and want access to all of it, you can create a 32MB primary partition and a 28MB extended partition. You could then access the primary partition as drive C and the extended partition as drive D. You could also subdivide the extended partition into more logical drives (up to the letter Z).

You must create partitions before using a hard disk drive. You will probably usually take the easiest route of using one primary partition for the entire disk. The FDISK program presented here, however, is necessary when you want to perform advanced operations. For example, if you want to use multiple operating systems from the same disk, FDISK will let you set up unique partitions for each system. (Each of these would be a primary partition, but only one can be designated the active partition: the one that gains control at startup.) Or if you are using a very large hard disk (40–70MB), you'll need to partition the physical drive into multiple logical drives since DOS can access a logical drive of only 32MB or less. Only by doing so can you store and retrieve information on such a large hard disk.

Note: If your disk is already being used and you want to create a new partition, you will first have to back up all of your data and then run FDISK from a system diskette. Finally, you'll need to reformat your disk before restoring your files to it.

Configuring a DOS Partition

In this section, you will see exactly how to use the FDISK command. Following this procedure is very important because using FDISK incorrectly can have serious consequences. Used correctly, however, FDISK can make your system more efficient. You can use FDISK only on hard disk systems.

Invoke the FDISK command by typing

FDISK

and pressing Return. (Remember to have your path set properly to include the directory containing the FDISK command file.) After this command creates the appropriate partitions, you must then logically format the disk.

Warning: Any data on your disk will be destroyed when you create partitions with FDISK.

When you first execute FDISK, the screen will clear and the FDISK Options screen will appear. This contains the menu of FDISK options (see Figure 19.17).

```
FDISK Options

Current Fixed Disk Drive: 1

Choose one of the following:

    1. Create DOS partition
    2. Change Active Partition
    3. Delete DOS partition
    4. Display Partition Information



Enter choice: [1]




Press ESC to return to DOS
```

FIGURE 19.17: The main FDISK Options menu. Four primary tasks may be selected: the creation or the deletion of a DOS partition, the specification of the active partition for default bootstrapping, and the display of all current partition information.

The menu presents four choices. If you have a system with more than one hard disk drive, the number in the "Current Fixed Disk Drive: 1" line would be the number of drives in your system. Also, your screen would display a fifth option, "Select Next Fixed Disk Drive." You can work on only one hard disk drive at a time, but you can switch from the drive you are working on to another drive. For now, assume you have one hard disk drive and that the screen in Figure 19.17 matches yours.

CREATING A PARTITION

The first option on the FDISK Options menu creates a DOS partition. Since you are using DOS and not another operating system such as UNIX, you can create only DOS partitions. Should you wish to add another operating system to the disk, that system would have its own version of FDISK and could then create its own partitions next to those of DOS. If you plan to use your hard disk to support another operating system, do not partition the whole disk. Leave some room so that another system can be loaded onto the disk.

Creating the Primary Partition   Choosing the first option to create a DOS partition results in Figure 19.18. If you select option 2 at this point, to create an extended DOS partition *before* creating a primary partition, DOS will display a message indicating that you cannot do so and will suggest that you press Esc to return to the main FDISK Options menu. Assuming you are starting from scratch, you would select option 1 to create the primary DOS partition. You will then see the screen shown in Figure 19.19.

If you want to use the whole disk for DOS, answer Y on this screen. The computer will allocate the entire disk and then return with the message

System will now restart

Insert DOS diskette in drive A:
Press any key when ready . . .

Since you just created the partition, there is still nothing on the hard disk. You must reboot the system from the disk drive. You can now format the entire hard disk just as you would a floppy diskette.

If you answer N, as shown in Figure 19.19, you have the opportunity to create a smaller partition, as shown in Figure 19.20. As you can see, there are 305 *cylinders* available on the total disk. A hard disk consists of several platters, each similar to a diskette; each platter consists of a series of concentric tracks made up of sectors. Each platter lies above another and is read by a different disk head. A series of tracks (with the same track number, but on different platters) located one above the other constitute a cylinder. The brackets on the screen in Figure 19.20 indicate where you can enter a number of cylinders less than the default maximum (305 on this disk).

```
Create DOS Partition

Current Fixed Disk Drive: 1


     1.  Create Primary DOS partition
     2.  Create Extended DOS partition




Enter choice: [1]



Press ESC to return to FDISK Options
```

FIGURE 19.18: The Create DOS Partition menu. For the specified fixed disk, you can create a primary DOS partition of up to 32MB, or you can create an extended DOS partition. The extended partition can itself be split into one or more logical drives.

```
Create Primary DOS Partition

Current Fixed Disk Drive: 1

Do you wish to use the maximum size
for a DOS partition and make the DOS
partition active (Y/N).........? [n]




Press ESC to return to FDISK Options
```

FIGURE 19.19: Creating the primary DOS partition. By simply entering a Y response, you can easily accept the default specifications: The maximum partition size is used, and this partition is made the active one. Booting operations on this disk will use the system resident on this drive.

```
Create Primary DOS Partition

Current Fixed Disk Drive: 1




Total disk space is  305 cylinders.
Maximum space available for partition
is  305 cylinders.

Enter partition size...........: [ 200]


No partitions defined

Press ESC to return to FDISK Options
```

FIGURE 19.20: Defining the size of the primary DOS partition. If you do not wish to accept the default maximum size, you can answer N to the question in Figure 19.19. The total number of cylinders on your disk will be displayed, and you can specify how many of those cylinders should be allocated for your partition. In this example, only 200 cylinders have been entered, thereby leaving 105 unused cylinders.

Notice that the second-to-last line on the screen says that no partitions have been defined yet. If you are using your disk for DOS alone, you should accept the default maximum cylinder value. All disk space will then be available for DOS and your DOS files. If you plan on splitting your disk between DOS and another operating system, however, you'll have to decide for yourself what percentage of total disk space the other operating system needs. The goal of this example is to create an extended DOS partition, so 200 was entered for the number of cylinders in the primary DOS partition.

Entering 200 results in the screen shown in Figure 19.21. This screen tells you that the first partition on drive C is a primary DOS partition (PRI DOS) that starts at cylinder 0 and ends at cylinder 199, constituting a total of 200 cylinders. Pressing Esc at this point returns you to the FDISK Options menu. If you again try to create a primary partition, DOS displays the following message on your screen:

Primary DOS partition already exists.
Press ESC to return to FDISK Options

Note: There can only be one primary DOS partition. When you start DOS, the system files from this partition are loaded into memory for your operations.

Creating Extended Partitions   In this example, you have used only 200 cylinders out of a possible 305, so you can create an extended DOS partition. To do so, you

```
Create Primary DOS Partition

Current Fixed Disk Drive: 1

Partition Status    Type  Start  End Size
   C: 1             PRI DOS    Ø   199  2ØØ









Primary DOS partition created

Press ESC to return to FDISK Options ▪
```

FIGURE 19.21: After the user specifies the number of cylinders to be used as a nondefault partition size, FDISK redisplays the Creation screen, indicating that the primary DOS partition has been created. The starting and ending cylinder numbers are displayed, along with the allocated size.

select choice 1 on the FDISK Options menu (see Figure 19.17) and then select choice 2 on the Create DOS Partition menu (see Figure 19.18).

The resulting screen, shown in Figure 19.22, allows you to create an extended DOS partition. This screen displays the current partition information—that is, that 305 total cylinders are available for use—and also tells you that 105 cylinders remain unused. Your system uses the 105 value as the default entry at this stage; you need only type a number over 105 to override this value. In Figure 19.22, a value of 55 was entered for the desired extended DOS partition, leaving 50 cylinders unused on the disk for another operating system.

```
Create Extended DOS Partition

Current Fixed Disk Drive: 1

Partition Status   Type  Start  End Size
   C: 1             PRI DOS    Ø   199  2ØØ




Total disk space is  3Ø5 cylinders.
Maximum space available for partition
is  1Ø5 cylinders.

Enter partition size...........: [  55]




Press ESC to return to FDISK Options
```

FIGURE 19.22: Creating an extended DOS partition. Selecting choice 2 in Figure 19.18 displays this screen. Current disk allocations are displayed, and you can enter the size to be used for your extended partition. In this case, only 55 of the remaining 105 cylinders are specified. This leaves 50 cylinders available for later use by another operating system.

The screen now clears, redisplays the partition information (including that for the new extended DOS partition), and prints the message

Extended DOS Partition created.
Press ESC to return to FDISK Options

near the bottom of the screen. Pressing Esc starts the next step of the process (see Figure 19.23).

Since you have just created an extended DOS partition, DOS wants to know if you want to create logical drives within this new partition. It tells you the total available cylinders in the partition and asks you to enter a size for the logical drive. In this example, you enter 45. The resulting screen displays

```
Create Logical DOS Drive(s)




No logical drives defined



Total partition size is    55 cylinders.

Maximum space available for logical
drive is    55 cylinders.

Enter logical drive size........: [   45]


Press ESC to return to FDISK Options
```

FIGURE 19.23: Within the extended partition, you can specify logical drives. They will be created using sequential letters. In this example, the extended partition contains 55 cylinders. A logical-drive size of 45 cylinders has been entered. It will be assigned the drive letter D.

the logical drive information (drive name, starting cylinder, ending cylinder, and total cylinders used).

Suppose you want to create another logical drive, drive E, using the remaining 10 cylinders. You could again choose option 1 on the FDISK Options menu. This again displays the Create DOS Partition menu, but the menu now offers one new choice:

3. Create logical DOS drive(s) in the Extended DOS partition

Choosing this option returns you to the screen for defining logical drives, where you can then enter the information for drive E. Going through this same sequence again to use the remaining 10 cylinders results in Figure 19.24. Notice that the cylinder numbers are within the bounds of the extended DOS partition. You are told that DOS created two logical drives, D and E, with sizes of 45 and 10 cylinders. Furthermore, you're reminded that no more available space remains for any other logical drives. Press Esc, and you will once again be back at the FDISK Options menu.

If you try to create another extended partition, the screen displays a partition information screen and the message

Extended DOS partition already exists.
Press ESC to return to FDISK Options

```
Create Logical DOS Drive(s)

Drv Start End  Size
  D:  200  244   45
  E:  245  254   10




All available space in the Extended DOS
partition is assigned to logical drives.

Logical DOS drive created, drive letters
changed or added
Press ESC to return to FDISK Options ▪
```

FIGURE 19.24: After processing the screen in Figure 19.23 twice (first to allocate a logical drive of 45 cylinders and again for another drive of 10 cylinders), FDISK displays the message that all available space has been used in this extended partition. You are also shown precisely how those cylinders have been allocated. Drives D and E have been created and are located on the disk drive contiguous to the cylinders previously reserved for drive C, the primary DOS partition.

You can create up to four separate operating system partitions on a single fixed disk, and you can subdivide the DOS partition itself into a primary and an extended partition. You can subdivide the extended partition further into several logical drives.

CHANGING THE ACTIVE PARTITION

The *active* partition is the partition that boots the system. It is the default partition. Choosing option 2 on the main FDISK Options menu displays a menu like that shown in Figure 19.25, in which partition information is displayed along with the total number of cylinders available on the disk. FDISK now wants to know the number of the partition that you wish to make active.

If you enter the number 2, as shown in the figure, DOS will inform you that you can make only the primary DOS partition (1) active. Type the number 1 so that the primary DOS partition has control when the system starts up. Pressing Return results in the adjusted partition information display shown in Figure 19.26.

Notice the letter A on the first line of this display. An A under "Status" tells you that partition 1 is the active partition. Pressing Esc returns you to the FDISK Options menu.

```
Change Active Partition

Current Fixed Disk Drive: 1

Partition Status    Type  Start  End Size
  C: 1               PRI DOS    0  199  200
     2               EXT DOS  200  254   55


Total disk space is  305 cylinders.

Enter the number of the partition you
want to make active...............: [2]


Partition selected (2) is not bootable,
active partition not changed.
Press ESC to return to FDISK Options
```

FIGURE 19.25: The Change Active Partition menu. Although the default boot drive is usually drive C, where the primary DOS partition is located, you can change this default setting with this screen. Selecting choice 2 here means that the next time the system is booted, system startup information is read from drive D.

```
Change Active Partition

Current Fixed Disk Drive: 1

Partition Status    Type  Start  End Size
  C: 1          A    PRI DOS    0  199  200
     2               EXT DOS  200  254   55


Total disk space is  305 cylinders.




Partition 1 made active

Press ESC to return to FDISK Options ▪
```

FIGURE 19.26: After changing the active partition, FDISK always shows you the current specification before returning to the main FDISK Options menu. In this case, after entering choice 2 to switch active partitions, choice 1 was again selected to respecify the primary partition as the default drive.

DISPLAYING PARTITION INFORMATION

Option 4 on the FDISK Options menu simply displays information about the partitions. Choosing option 4 yields the screen shown in Figure 19.27.

The information at the top of the screen is familiar by now. But what if you want to see information about the logical drives that have been defined? Look at the bottom half of the screen, where you are asked if you want to see this information. Replying Y results in a display of information about these logical drives (see Figure 19.28). Pressing Esc from this screen returns you to the FDISK Options menu.

```
Display Partition Information

Current Fixed Disk Drive: 1

Partition Status   Type  Start  End  Size
  C: 1       A    PRI DOS     0   199  200
     2            EXT DOS   200   254   55


Total disk space is  305 cylinders.


The Extended DOS partition contains
logical DOS drives. Do you want to
display logical drive information?  [Y]


Press ESC to return to FDISK Options
```

FIGURE 19.27: Select choice 4 from the main FDISK Options menu (see Figure 19.17) to obtain a current status display of all partition information. Primary and extended partition sizes and locations are displayed, as well as whether any logical disk drives have been created in the extended partition. You need only enter Y to obtain an additional display showing the specifications of these logical drives (see Figure 19.28).

DELETING DOS PARTITIONS

What DOS giveth, DOS can taketh away—with a little prodding from you. Selecting choice 3 on the FDISK Options menu produces the Delete DOS Partition menu, shown in Figure 19.29.

Using this menu, you can delete any of the information you've already set up. You may want to expand or contract some partitions, or you may no longer want to use a partition in the way you did originally. When you delete partitions, you

```
Display Logical DOS Drive Information

Drv Start End  Size
 D:   200  244   45
 E:   245  254   10












Press ESC to return to FDISK Options ▪
```

FIGURE 19.28: Logical drive information. When logical DOS drives exist within the extended DOS partition, you can ask FDISK to display the specifications of those drives. Two drives were created earlier on this disk, with cylinder sizes 45 and 10. DOS assigned them automatically the drive letters C and D.

```
Delete DOS Partition

Current Fixed Disk Drive: 1

Choose one of the following:

     1.   Delete Primary DOS partition
     2.   Delete Extended DOS partition
     3.   Delete logical DOS drive(s) in
          the Extended DOS Partition



Enter choice: [ ]




Press ESC to return to FDISK Options ▪
```

FIGURE 19.29: The Delete DOS Partition menu. You can remove the specifications for a partition with this menu. When deleting partition information, you must make your selections in the reverse order from the order in which they were created. Thus, in this demonstration sequence you must enter choice 3 first; this lets you remove the contents of the extended partition before you remove the extended partition itself.

follow a set order. Before you delete the primary DOS partition, you must first delete the extended DOS partition. Otherwise, DOS displays this message:

**Cannot delete Primary DOS partition on
drive 1 when Extended partition exists**

Press ESC to return to FDISK Options

In addition, before you delete an extended DOS partition, you must first "undefine" (delete) the logical drives in that partition. Trying to delete the extended DOS partition before deleting the drives in it simply displays the current partition information with the message

**Cannot delete Extended DOS partition
while logical drives exist.
Press ESC to return to FDISK options**

Choice 3 in the Delete DOS Partition menu is probably the first selection you will need to make; you work your way backward through the order in which you created elements. (Actually, you will find that this is a natural sequence.) Selecting choice 3 produces the screen shown in Figure 19.30, which contains logical drive information and the size of the extended DOS partition in which the drives reside. You are also warned that any data in the logical disk drive to be deleted will also be deleted.

If you still want to delete the drive, enter the drive identifier. You will then be asked to confirm this step. In Figure 19.30, drive E is to be to deleted first, a choice confirmed by the Y response. If N had been entered instead, DOS would have redisplayed the FDISK Options menu.

Once FDISK deletes the logical drive, it updates the display at the top of the screen and asks for another drive to delete. If you want to regain all the space used by this partition, you next specify drive D and confirm your entry; the result is the screen shown in Figure 19.31. Pressing Esc twice at this point returns you through the menu screens to the main FDISK Options menu.

Now that the logical drives are gone, you can delete the extended DOS partition itself. Choosing option 2 on the Delete DOS Partition menu results in the familiar form of an FDISK screen (see Figure 19.32). Again, the partition information display appears (as in Figure 19.27), and you are warned that data will be lost and asked if you really want to delete the extended DOS partition. If you reply Y, the screen will be updated to show only the primary DOS partition and the message

Extended DOS partition deleted

Press ESC to return to FDISK Options

Press Esc to return once again to the FDISK Options menu.

```
Delete Logical DOS Drive

Drv Start End  Size
 D:  200  244   45
 E:  245  254   10




Total partition size is   55 cylinders.

Warning! Data in the logical DOS drive
will be lost. What drive do you wish
to delete.......................? [e]

Are you sure....................? [y]


Press ESC to return to FDISK Options
```

FIGURE 19.30: Selecting choice 3 from Figure 19.29 displays this screen, which shows the defined logical drives. You specify a logical drive to delete and then confirm the selection. Performing this sequence twice for drives D and E results in the screen shown in Figure 19.31.

```
Delete Logical DOS Drive

Drv Start End  Size
 D: drive deleted
 E: drive deleted




Total partition size is   55 cylinders.
All logical drives deleted in the
Extended DOS partition



Press ESC to return to FDISK Options.
```

FIGURE 19.31: After deleting logical drives in the extended partition, FDISK displays the current status. This shows which drives have been deleted; restates the available space in the extended partition; and shows which drives, if any, remain undeleted.

```
Delete Extended DOS Partition

Current Fixed Disk Drive: 1

Partition Status   Type  Start  End Size
  C: 1        A   PRI DOS    Ø  199 2ØØ
     2            EXT DOS  2ØØ  254  55




Warning! Data in the Extended DOS
partition will be lost. Do you wish
to continue.....................? [y]



Press ESC to return to FDISK Options
```

FIGURE 19.32: Deleting the extended DOS partition. You can delete an extended partition only if it contains no logical drives. In this case, you can delete partition 2 (an extended DOS partition) because drives D and E are no longer defined within it. As in most computer operations that delete data, you are prompted to confirm that this choice is indeed the one you want to make.

ADVANCED DOS COMMANDS

Following are the reference entries for the advanced DOS commands discussed in this chapter.

ASSIGN

ASSIGN redefines the actual drive identifier that handles specific disk requests.

SYNTAX

[*D:path*]ASSIGN [*Drive1 = BigDrive1*] [*Drive2 = BigDrive2*] [...]

D:path	is the drive and path where the command file is located if it is not in the current directory.
Drive1	is the original drive to be rerouted.
BigDrive1	is the drive assigned to handle all of *Drive1*'s requests.
Drive2, *BigDrive2,...*	are drives used for other assignments.

TYPE

External.

USAGE

Use the ASSIGN command for specialized redirection of file requests. The parameter list allows you to assign drive references from one drive to another. With no parameters, ASSIGN cancels all current assignments.

ASSIGN is used most frequently to run older applications that are restricted to specific drives, typically A or B diskette drives. Because practical use of DOS requires a hard disk, the most convenient use of an older program is to place both program and data files in a hard disk directory or directories. This command makes that feasible.

RESTRICTIONS

Do not use ASSIGN with BACKUP, RESTORE, LABEL, JOIN, SUBST, or PRINT. FORMAT, DISKCOPY, and DISKCOMP ignore ASSIGN.

EXAMPLES

As already noted, ASSIGN is most commonly used in older programs that require you either to place your program disk in the A drive or your data disk in the B drive, or both. For instance, if you have copied all of your program and data files to a directory on the C drive and then made that directory the current directory, you might enter

ASSIGN A = C B = C

This forces all program references to A and B to be handled from the current working directory on the C drive.

You can apply the same principle if you have multiple disk drives and wish to use any other letters to represent diskette or hard disk alternatives to the diskette drive identifiers originally specified by the application program.

The SUBST command is a more flexible alternative that allows you to work with multiple directories on a hard disk. For instance, if you are running a program called OLDSTUFF, you can copy all program diskette files to a directory called \OLDSTUFF and all of the former data disk files to a directory called \OLDSTUFF\DATA. Then you could issue the following command:

SUBST A: C:\OLDSTUFF
SUBST B: C:\OLDSTUFF\DATA

See the SUBST command for further details and examples.

ATTRIB

The ATTRIB command changes the read/write and archive file attributes. When used with parameters, ATTRIB changes the attributes of a file. When used without parameters, ATTRIB displays the attributes.

SYNTAX

[*D:Path*]ATTRIB [+ R | − R][+ A | − A][*FileSpec*][/S]

D:Path	is the drive and path where the command file is located if it is not in the current directory.
+ R	makes *FileSpec* a read-only file.
− R	makes *FileSpec* read/write operations possible.
+ A	sets the archive bit of *FileSpec*.
− A	resets the archive bit of *FileSpec*.
FileSpec	is an optional drive and path, plus the file name and extension, of the file that is the object of the command. Wildcards are allowed.
/S	causes all files in the directory and its subdirectories to be modified.

TYPE

External.

USAGE

The ATTRIB command is most commonly used to set one or more files to read-only status. This prevents a file from being accidentally or purposely deleted and also inhibits any editing or modification of the file. In addition to this read-only (+ R) capability, the /S switch lets you easily protect files located in various places within the disk hierarchy with a single command.

ATTRIB also is used in network applications. It enforces read-only status of files intended to be shared by multiple users across the network.

EXAMPLES

To set read-only status for the BUDGET.WK1 file, you enter:

ATTRIB + R BUDGET.WK1

Since wildcards are allowed, you can just as easily turn on read-only status for all personnel data files in the PERSONEL directory, including .TXT, .WK1, .DBF, files:

ATTRIB + R personel.*

The /S switch adjusts the attributes of all files in the entire directory tree starting with the specified directory. For example, you can remove all read-only statuses from an entire disk with the following command:

ATTRIB – R C:\ /s

The A (archive) attribute controls the archival status of a file. Since the BACKUP, RESTORE, and XCOPY commands use this archive attribute, you can influence their operation by presetting the +A or –A status of a file prior to executing any of these three commands. See the individual commands for examples of how they treat archive attributes with /M and /A switches.

COMMAND

COMMAND runs a secondary copy of the DOS command interpreter.

SYNTAX

COMMAND [*D:path*][*switches*]

[*D:path*]	is an optional drive and path where the command processor to be invoked is located.
switches	any of the following:

/P	makes the new processor the primary processor.
/C *string*	executes *string* upon invocation.
/E:*xxxxx*	determines the environment size.

TYPE

Internal.

USAGE

Starting a new command processor with this command copies the environment from the existing, or parent, command processor. You can make any changes you like to the environmental parameters without affecting the old environment.

Note that you should invoke the /E switch to set the environment size *prior to* invoking any other DOS command that may increase the resident size of DOS. The space reserved for environmental parameters cannot be expanded once that resident area has been taken over for other DOS purposes.

As indicated in the "Examples" section, the /C switch is important during batch processing for DOS versions 3.2 and earlier as a means of simulating true programming subroutines.

EXAMPLES

The required syntax for invoking a permanent secondary real-mode command processor is

COMMAND /P

This invokes another command processor and keeps it in memory, returning to the parent COMMAND.COM only after you enter the EXIT command at the prompt.

To invoke a secondary processor for the temporary invocation of a single command, use the /C switch. For example, enter

COMMAND /C BATMAN

to invoke a batch file called BATMAN.BAT. This file could be a special batch-management program. Users of DOS versions prior to 3.3 used this approach to run one batch program from within another. DOS 3.3 introduced the CALL command to facilitate true programming subroutine capability. See the discussion of that command in Chapter 8 for more details about this feature.

FASTOPEN

FASTOPEN speeds up disk access by maintaining a memory-resident table of the most recently used file and directory names.

SYNTAX

[*D:path*]FASTOPEN *drive*:[= *size*]

D:path	is the drive and path where the command file is located if it is not in the current directory.
drive	is the drive to which FASTOPEN will be attached (the command can be issued for each drive separately).
size	is the number of file or directory entries that FASTOPEN will remember.

TYPE

External.

USAGE

FASTOPEN is normally used to ensure more rapid disk access to the most frequently referenced sectors. These include the actual files commonly accessed, as well as the sectors containing the directory entries for those files. Ideally, you should set the value for FASTOPEN on each referenced drive equal to the minimum number of frequently referenced file names plus the number of directory entries in the full path names leading to those files.

RESTRICTIONS

FASTOPEN will not work with JOIN, SUBST, or ASSIGN in effect on *drive*. It also will not work with network drives.

EXAMPLES

The FASTOPEN command is easy to use. Simply typing

FASTOPEN C: = 100

enables the computer to remember the last 100 directories and files accessed on drive C and thus to be able to go right to them on the disk. If, for example, *size* was specified as 5 rather than 100, and the list contained the information

DIR1   FILE1   DIR2   FILE2   FILE3

if you accessed another FILE4 in directory DIR3, the list would look like this:

FILE4   DIR3   DIR1   FILE1   DIR2

FILE2 and FILE3 were the least-recent entries in the list, so they were dropped off the end to accommodate the two new entries.

You can use FASTOPEN only once per drive (per session). It reserves 35 bytes per entry. Thus, a size of 100 would consume about 3.5K (3,500) bytes of memory.

Specify *size* as a value at least as great as the highest number of levels in the directory structure, so DOS can quickly locate any directory specification.

FDISK

FDISK partitions fixed disks for use by DOS. It also prepares logical drives with a part of the partitioned space.

SYNTAX

[*D:Path*]**FDISK**

[*D:Path*]   is the drive and path where the command file is located if it is not in the current directory.

TYPE

External.

USAGE

FDISK allows you to create a new partition, delete an existing partition, specify the active partition, display current partition information, partition multiple hard drives, and define new logical drives within extended partitions.

RESTRICTIONS

You can use FDISK only on hard disk systems. A disk must be reformatted logically after being partitioned. FDISK will not work if another process is accessing the disk.

Warning: Any data on your hard disk will be destroyed when you create partitions with FDISK.

EXAMPLES

Preparing your hard disk requires you simply to enter

FDISK

at the DOS prompt. This external DOS command displays the screen in Figure 19.33. You can select from among several possibilities on this main FDISK menu screen.

The FDISK main menu is a full-screen display, as are all of the FDISK subordinate-menu and data-entry screens. Selecting choice 1 brings up the Creation menu screen shown in Figure 19.34.

Selecting choice 4 on the FDISK main menu screen (see Figure 19.33) displays the screen in Figure 19.35.

JOIN

JOIN permits an entirely separate disk drive and all its contents to be perceived and referenced as if they were a branch of the directory structure on a second drive.

```
IBM Personal Computer
Fixed Disk Setup Program Version 3.30
(C)Copyright IBM Corp. 1983,1987

FDISK Options

Current Fixed Disk Drive: 1

Choose one of the following:

        1. Create DOS partition
        2. Change Active Partition
        3. Delete DOS partition
        4. Display Partition Information



Enter choice: [1]



Press ESC to return to DOS
```

FIGURE 19.33: The FDISK main menu screen. Choice 1 lets you create a DOS partition, choice 2 allows you to specify which DOS partition is to be activated during system bootstrapping, choice 3 controls the deletion of an existing partition, and choice 4 merely displays the current partitioning status of your disk.

```
Create DOS Partition

Current Fixed Disk Drive: 1


        1. Create Primary DOS partition
        2. Create Extended DOS partition
        3. Create logical DOS drive(s) in
            the Extended DOS partition



Enter choice: [1]



Press ESC to return to FDISK Options
```

FIGURE 19.34: This menu screen controls the creation of both partitions and logical drives. Choice 1 creates the primary DOS partition, and choice 2 creates the secondary (extended) DOS partition. Additional logical drives may be created from within this extended DOS partition.

```
Display Partition Information

Current Fixed Disk Drive: 1

Partition Status   Type  Start  End  Size
  C: 1        A    PRI DOS    Ø   5Ø9  51Ø
     2             EXT DOS  51Ø 1Ø22  513


Total disk space is 1Ø23 cylinders.


The Extended DOS partition contains
logical DOS drives. Do you want to
display logical drive information?  [Y]


Press ESC to return to FDISK Options
```

FIGURE 19.35: Selecting choice 4 on the main FDISK menu screen displays this Partition Information Display screen. In this example, the total disk space of 1023 cylinders is split into a primary partition (C), which will be the default boot drive, and an extended partition. To see how this extended partition is further split into logical drives, you need only press Return in response to the question displayed near the bottom of this screen.

SYNTAX

(1) *[D:path]* **JOIN**
(2) *[D:path]* **JOIN** *object source*
(3) *[D:path]* **JOIN** *object* **/D**

> *D:path*   is the drive and path where the command file is located if it is not in the current directory.
>
> *object*   is the drive to which a directory will be attached or released.
>
> *source*   is the drive and path of the directory to be joined.

TYPE

External.

USAGE

JOIN is used primarily to transmit data to or from a file on a diskette when a program tries to transfer data to or from a directory. It is used to fool older programs into using hierarchical disk structures when they were designed to understand only individual disk drives (usually drives A and B).

RESTRICTIONS

You can use JOIN only on multidisk systems. You cannot use this command to join a drive created with SUBST.

EXAMPLES

The JOIN command is used primarily in two ways. If a program is sending information to a fixed subdirectory on your C drive, such as C:\CAD\data, and you wish to send this information directly to a diskette in drive A, enter

JOIN A: C:\CAD\data

On the other hand, if you want the output of a program designed to send data to the root directory of drive B sent to the current working directory of drive C and you have changed (with CR) the working directory to that desired subdirectory on the drive C before running the program, enter:

JOIN C: B:\

to join drive C to the root directory of drive B.

To restore normalcy and nullify a previously defined JOIN, use the /D switch. For example, to disconnect drive C from the root directory of drive B, enter

JOIN C: /D

RECOVER

RECOVER lets DOS reconstruct a file, or an entire diskful of files, that have become damaged or corrupted.

SYNTAX

(1) **[*D:path*]RECOVER [*location*]*object***
(2) **[*D:path*]RECOVER [*drive*]**

    D:path   is the drive and path where the command file is located if it is not in the current directory.

    location   is an optional drive and path where the file *object* is located.

    object   is the file name, with an optional extension, of the file to be manipulated (wildcard characters may be used).

TYPE

External.

USAGE

You can recover an individual file from a disk by specifying it as the parameter of the RECOVER command. You can also use RECOVER to attempt to recover all files on an entire disk that has gone bad. Unfortunately, results with this command are not always completely satisfactory since many files can not be recovered so that they can be effectively reused.

RESTRICTIONS

You cannot use RECOVER on a network disk.

EXAMPLES

Assume that your SALARY.DTA file is corrupted because of bad sectors on the disk. Use the following command to ask DOS to recover as much of the file as possible:

RECOVER SALARY.DTA

If much of the disk has gone bad, you can still ask DOS to recover as much as possible by specifying the drive letter itself:

RECOVER C:

In this example, all former file names on the disk will be replaced by a sequentially numbered series of new file names. In addition, the amount of data successfully recovered will depend on how badly your disk is damaged. Executable files are usually useless after recovery; text files usually can be at least partially reconstructed with your word processor.

REPLACE

REPLACE allows easy updating of a set of files in one directory with another set (usually newer versions) in another directory or drive.

SYNTAX

*[D:path]*REPLACE *source [destination] [switches]*

D:path	is the drive and path where the command file is located if it is not in the current directory.
source	is the optional drive and path with a mandatory file name and optional extension of the source files that will be the replacement files.

destination   is the optional drive and path of the files to be replaced.

switches   is one or more of the following:

/A   adds files.

/P   prompts you before replacing a file.

/R   replaces only read-only files on *destination*.

/S   replaces files with matching filenames.

/W   waits for you to insert a diskette.

TYPE

External.

USAGE

The REPLACE command is most often used for two reasons:

- To find the locations of all directories containing a particular piece of software and to replace the old versions of that software with the latest version.
- To find all of the different files in a particular directory and update each of these individual files to their latest version.

EXAMPLES

Suppose you have acquired several software packages over the years, each of which may include its own version of COMMAND.COM. These COMMAND.COM versions may still be buried in the individual software application package directories, while your root directory contains the most current version of the DOS command interpreter.

You can upgrade all versions of the command interpreter at one time by asking DOS to replace occurrences of each version throughout the directory structure (using the /S switch) with the latest version from the system disk in drive A:

REPLACE A:\COMMAND.COM C:\ /S

Another application of REPLACE is upgrading your existing set of files with a new set from an application or system disk. For example, you might leave all current SYS files alone in your device driver directory \SYS, but add new sytem device drivers with the following command:

REPLACE A:*.SYS C:\SYS /A

This command leaves untouched all existing files in the SYS directory of drive C, while adding any new .SYS files from drive A to the SYS directory.

SET

The SET command creates or modifies named character strings stored in the DOS memory-resident environment area.

SYNTAX

(1) **SET**
(2) **SET** *name* =
(3) **SET** *name* = *parameter*

name	is a user-specified string used in place of *parameter*. It can also be one of the environment strings PROMPT, PATH, LASTDRIVE, or COMSPEC.
parameter	is what *name* will represent. It can also be the new setting of one of the environment strings.

TYPE

Internal.

USAGE

The SET command initializes the value of variables in one batch file that you will use in another batch file. You can also use it at the command prompt to set the value of those variables you will later use for testing a batch file.

EXAMPLES

DOS programmers might use the variable *lib* to specify the path name of the directory containing their library modules for compilation. DOS programmers might also use the variable *include* to specify the directory containing their high-level language code modules for inclusion during compiliation. The following command lines initialize those variables:

SET include = C:\include
SET lib = C:\lib

Batch files can also use named parameters during processing. This capability circumvents the limitation of nine numbered parameters and makes the batch program easier to read, debug, and maintain. For example, you can set up a password mechanism in your batch file that tests for the value of a variable called *password*. You can initialize this variable at the command prompt or in an initialization batch file with the following command:

SET password = 020346

With this command, the batch file tests whether a password entered by a user matches the string of digits "020346" stored in the DOS environment. See Chapter 9 for further information about using batch files for password protection, resource management, and named environmental parameters.

SUBST

SUBST enables you to access files using either their complete path name or a shorthand notation.

SYNTAX

(1) **[*D:path*]SUBST**
(2) **[*D:path*]SUBST** *newdrive source*
(3) **[*D:path*]SUBST** *object* **/D**

D:path	is the drive and path where the command file is located if it is not in the current directory.
newdrive	is the drive to be created to correspond to the *source* directory.
source	is the directory to be made into drive *newdrive*.
object	is the pseudo-drive identifier used as *newdrive* and now to be discarded.

TYPE

External.

USAGE

The SUBST command is often used to cut down on the typing needed to refer to file names located within a complex directory structure. It is easier to type a single letter and a colon than a complete path name.

You can substitute a single letter identifier, a pseudo-disk drive letter, for a complete directory path name leading to a particular file.

EXAMPLES

The following example creates a virtual drive, G, as a substitute for D:\PROGRAMS\WORDPROC\WORDPERF, the complete path name:

SUBST G: D:\PROGRAMS\WORDPROC\WORDPERF

All succeeding references to files in the WORDPERF subdirectory can now use either the full path name or the simpler G: designation.

You can also use this technique to fool older programs that understand only disk drives without a directory structure. For example, suppose you have a geometric analysis program called GEOMETRY.EXE. This program requires its own system and support files to be on drive A and all of its data files to exist or be created on drive B. You can create subdirectories within your disk hierarchy called \GEOMETRY and \GEOMETRY\DATA and then use SUBST to trick your original programs into accessing program files from the GEOME-TRY directory and data files from the DATA directory:

SUBST A: \GEOMETRY
SUBST B: \GEOMETRY\DATA

SUMMARY

You have now mastered some of the most advanced features of DOS. The sophisticated capabilities you've seen in this chapter often lie buried under unreadable documentation. In this chapter, however, you've seen how these advanced features can be used to your advantage.

For additional information about the batch file parameters, both fixed and variable, see

- Chapter 7, "Fundamentals of Batch Processing"

For additional information about subprogram linkage, see

- Chapter 8, "Batch-File Subcommands"

For additional information about advanced batch file examples, see

- Chapter 9, "Complete Batch File Examples"

For additional information about disk clusters and DOS disk management methods, see

- Chapter 21, "A Closer Look behind the Scenes of DOS"

You now have a complete picture of DOS, and you can see that it is a very useful operating system. However, software developers have created a vast body of new software designed to extend and enhance the power of DOS. The next chapter presents the best examples of add-on and add-in software that you should consider acquiring to make even more effective use of DOS.

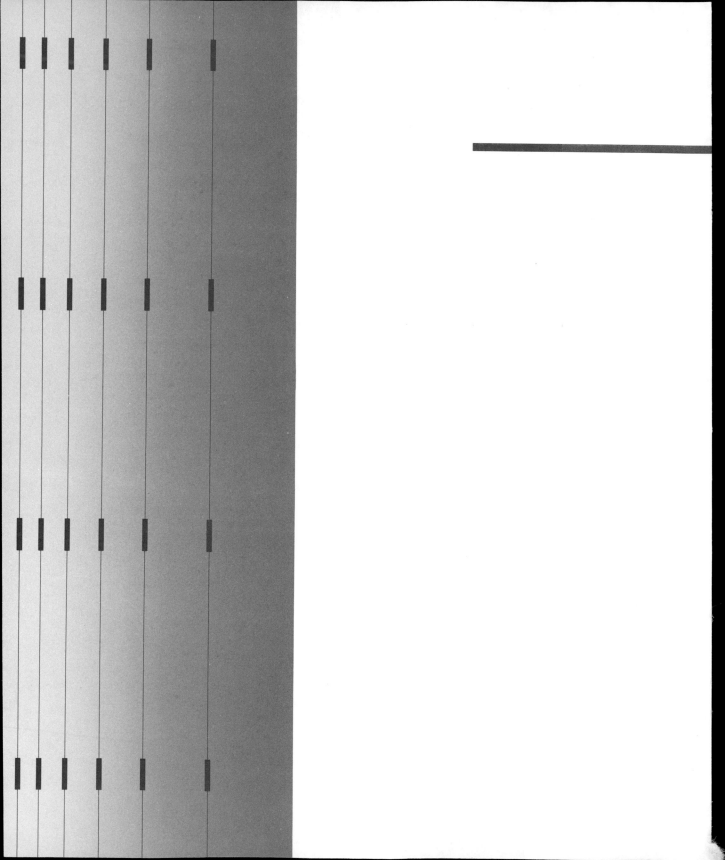

CHAPTER 20

EXTENDING DOS'S POWER WITH UTILITY SOFTWARE

EXTENDING DOS'S POWER
WITH UTILITY SOFTWARE

Microsoft supplies many useful programs with DOS; as with all things, however, there is still room for improvement. For instance, when you back up a hard disk, DOS does not tell you how many diskettes you will need. In this chapter, you will learn about a program that provides this feature and about other programs that fill some gaps in DOS's operations.

You will also learn about a number of programs that provide functionality well beyond the current scope of DOS. For example, different computers often have different disk formats, and different word processors often have different internal file-storage formats. Offices with several computers and different types of word processors can benefit from the special-purpose *conversion programs* that work with DOS. Because they provide you with added utility features, these programs are usually known as *utility programs*.

Thousands of utility programs are available today; advertisements for such products appear in the backs of all major personal computer magazines. In this chapter you will see how some programs improve the performance of hard disks, and how others speed up your keyboard and screen. You'll see utilities designed to enhance your printed output, to organize your desktop functions, and to make hard disk file management easier. This chapter presents only a few examples of the most useful types of utility programs; keep in mind that there are many excellent alternatives to the programs discussed here.

TYPES OF UTILITIES—ADDING *ON* VERSUS ADDING *IN*

Some utility programs are similar to the external (disk-resident) commands of DOS, such as CHKDSK and FORMAT. You can execute them whenever you choose, as long as they are accessible in the current directory or on the path. They require a certain amount of memory to run, but they release it back to DOS when they are done. Some people refer to these disk-resident enhancement programs as *add-on* utilities.

Other utility programs are similar to the internal, memory-resident commands of DOS, such as DIR and ERASE. This second type of utility is called a *memory-resident* or *terminate-and-stay-resident* (*TSR*) program. A memory-resident program is loaded from disk only once, as part of its required setup phase. It is read into a certain area of memory that will not be used later by any other program. It then terminates, but stays resident for rapid activation at some later time. Some people refer to these memory-resident programs as *add-in* utilities.

Most memory-resident software will do nothing—not even offer a command prompt—until you type a unique key combination, called a *hot key,* to call it into action. For instance, Sidekick leaps into action when you press the Ctrl-Alt key combination. Keyworks presents its own menu of options when you summon it with the gray Plus key (on the right side of most keyboards). The appealing aspect of these memory-resident programs is that their complete capabilities are instantaneously available when you need them, even during the execution of another program.

> *Note:* Memory-resident utility programs are fast; however, the cost for this responsiveness is that part of the physical memory on your machine must be allocated to them. That reduces the amount remaining for your main programs, and even for other memory-resident software.

In some cases, you can make more than one memory-resident program available simultaneously. If you do load one or more memory-resident programs, however, you should use the CHKDSK command afterward to determine whether enough memory is still free to run your main application program.

Some memory-resident programs and main application programs will not work together, because each will try to use the same area of memory. This can result in many problems, from the memory-resident program or main program simply not working correctly, to having to reboot a frozen system, to having your entire hard disk erased. To be sure a program is compatible with your current software, check its documentation before you begin.

> *Warning:* Back up your data files before running any new memory-resident utility in conjunction with existing software. You should protect yourself in the event of an unexpected memory conflict or a system failure. Techniques and options for backing up files are presented in Chapter 18.

IMPROVING YOUR HARD DISK MANAGEMENT

Managing many directories on a hard disk can require great effort and care. However, a class of utility programs can relieve your burdens. In this section, you'll look at Q-DOS II, a hard disk file manager; PreCursor, a hard disk menu system; the Norton Utilities, a wide-ranging file- and directory-support tool; and Back-It, a powerful substitute for DOS's BACKUP and RESTORE commands.

Managing Your Files and Directories with Q-DOS II

Q-DOS II makes standard DOS features much easier to use. Many of DOS's functions, such as displaying directories and listing and copying files, are implemented in Q-DOS II. Some commands that are not directly available in DOS, such as file moves, can be executed easily from within Q-DOS II. Figure 20.1 shows the main menu of Q-DOS II.

As you can see from the main menu line at the top of Figure 20.1, Q-DOS II offers you much more convenience in implementing many standard DOS commands. For example, instead of having to type a complete COPY command, specifying file names and path names, you use a more visual technique. You *tag*, or graphically select, which directories and files you want copied and where they should be copied to. You can easily see directories by moving along the directory tree (see Figure 20.2) and pressing Return, which displays a sorted list of files that reside in the selected directory.

You can sort directory entries by name, extension, size, or date. Although you see the files sorted in the Q-DOS II directory window, they will not be physically rearranged on the disk. Although the screens may appear crowded at first glance, they are quite comfortable in actual use.

Q-DOS II is available from

Gazelle Systems
42 North University Avenue, Suite 10
Provo, Utah 84601
(800) 233-0383
(801) 377-1288

```
┌────────────────────────────────────────────────────────────────────┐
│ ▌Directory▐ Tag  View  Copy  Move  Find  Erase  Rename  Space  Attribute  Print │
│ Change current directory, make or remove directory, see directory tree │
│                                                                        │
│ PATH  >> C:\TYPESET                                                     │
│ ┌────────┬──────────────┐  ┌──────────┬────────┬─────────┬───────┐      │
│ │ Count  │ Total Size   │  │ File Name│ Size   │ Date    │ Time  │      │
│ │ ┌──┐   │              │  │&BOOK-P1.CAP│   156│ 7-29-86 │ 5:44p │      │
│ │ │99│Files│ 323,228    │  │&BOOK-P1.CHP│ 1,862│ 7-29-86 │ 5:44p │      │
│ │ └──┘   │              │  │&BOOK-P1.STY│ 3,868│ 1- 1-80 │ 1:22a │      │
│ │ ┌──┐   │              │  │&BOOK-P2.CAP│   156│ 7-29-86 │ 5:44p │      │
│ │ │Ø │Directories│      │  │&BOOK-P2.CHP│ 1,848│ 7-29-86 │ 5:44p │      │
│ │ └──┘   │              │  │&BOOK-P2.STY│ 4,068│ 7-29-86 │ 2:44p │      │
│ │ ┌──┐   │              │  │&BRO-L2 .CHP│   844│ 7-29-86 │ 5:44p │      │
│ │ │Ø │Tagged│        Ø  │  │&BRO-L2 .STY│ 2,868│ 7-29-86 │ 5:44p │      │
│ │ └──┘   │              │  │&BRO-L3 .CHP│ 1,178│ 7-29-86 │ 5:44p │      │
│ │        │              │  │&BRO-L3 .STY│ 2,868│ 9- 1-86 │ 3:22p │      │
│ │F1- Help      F2- Status│  │&BRO-P3 .CHP│ 1,178│ 7-29-86 │ 5:44p │      │
│ │F3- Chg Drive F4- Prev Dir│&BRO-P3 .STY│ 2,668│ 9- 1-86 │ 3:22p │      │
│ │F5- Chg Dir   F6- DOS Cmd│  │&EXAMPLE.PUB│   732│ 9-19-86 │11:44a │      │
│ │F7- Srch Spec F8- Sort  │  │&INV-P1 .CHP│   824│ 9-19-86 │11:33a │      │
│ │F9- Edit      F1Ø- Quit │  │&INV-P1 .STY│ 2,468│ 9- 1-86 │ 3:22p │      │
│ │  SPACE BAR- Tag file   │  │&LSTG-P2.CHP│ 1,097│ 7-29-86 │ 5:55p │      │
│ │  ESC- Abort Command    │  │&LSTG-P2.STY│ 1,868│ 9- 1-86 │ 3:33p │      │
│ │                        │  └──────────┴────────┴─────────┴───────┘      │
│ │ Q-DOS II -- Version 2.ØØ │                                             │
│ │   Copyright (c) 1986   │                                               │
│ │ GAZELLE SYSTEMS - Provo, Utah │                                        │
│ └────────┴──────────────┘                                              │
└────────────────────────────────────────────────────────────────────┘
```

FIGURE 20.1: Q-DOS II main menu. The top line of the screen displays a horizontal menu of primary options, from the standard directory manipulation option to the option to print a file. A scrolling window of the files in the current directory being viewed through Q DOS II also appears. A list of powerful function-key options is displayed at the left of the screen.

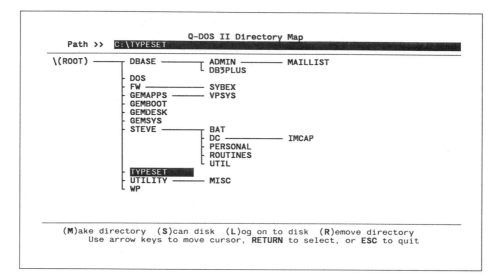

FIGURE 20.2: Q-DOS II displays a visual tree representing the disk's directory structure. Using a menu of choices at the bottom of the screen, you can create or delete directories, scan other disks to assess their directory structure, and set Q-DOS II's default drive.

Setting Up Menu Systems with PreCursor

A menu system for a DOS installation enables you to predefine paths and program names and to present to a user a simple and familiar list of choices. No commands need be entered at the DOS prompt, since all required DOS commands will have been incorporated into the menu system setup.

Some users prefer to enter commands at the DOS prompt because they run only one simple application, and they are more comfortable entering individual commands. Others feel that a menu system is too slow or restrictive, or that they simply cannot give up the memory required for the menu program itself. For most users, however, understanding and using DOS at the command level is unnecessary. This is especially true if the operations performed are repetitive and require little variation.

If the set of programs you run on your machine is fairly constant, a menu program can be a definite convenience. It can save you the trouble of changing directories or remembering where a particular program is located on your hard disk. This is particularly convenient in a large office environment, where it may not be feasible to teach all users enough about DOS to enable them to get on with their jobs. Once a menu system is set up by a knowledgeable user, individual users need make only simple, one-key selections to implement commands.

PreCursor is an excellent menu program. Beyond offering a menu system, it provides most of the key DOS functions on its own special DOS menu. You can do most things from PreCursor that you can do from DOS, without having to remember or know as much about formats and restrictions. The main menu of PreCursor is cleanly laid out and shows you exactly what you can do and where to go. It is shown in Figure 20.3.

The program is organized into menus and submenus. Menu systems are popular because it is much easier to select a desired program or task from a prepared list of choices. Although the resulting programs are each available at the DOS prompt, this direct approach requires greater knowledge of the DOS directory structure and the program invocation sequence.

Many menu systems are set up by one knowledgeable system user for the use of less knowledgeable users. Without such a menu mechanism, each user would have to enter a correct sequence of commands at the DOS prompt. However, some would argue correctly that a menu system is inherently limited by the possibilities designed into the menus, whereas a command prompt approach, such as that taken by DOS, provides unlimited access to all possible commands and all aspects of the program and operating system environment.

You can categorize your programs, placing them on different menus by function. By choosing an option, you can execute a DOS program, a batch file, or a DOS command, or you can go to another menu of predetermined choices. You use the DOS function keys to obtain special PreCursor services, such as menu screen creation and editing, program parameter initialization, and password

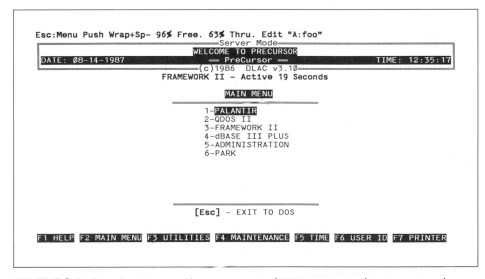

FIGURE 20.3: PreCursor's main menu. You can customize this menu; you can also set up nine submenus. You can apply passwords both to entire menu lists and to individual program names. You also can control DOS utility operations and printer control code transmission from this main menu screen.

set-up The PreCursor maintenance menu makes these features avaialable and is shown in Figure 20.4.

Menu systems can be set up for a large number of users, and access can be restricted by a powerful password mechanism. Separate passwords can be created for each individual menu choice, as well as for entire menus.

PreCursor is available from

The Aldridge Company
2500 City West Blvd., Suite 575
Houston, Texas 77042

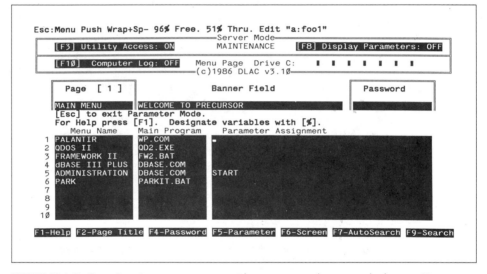

FIGURE 20.4: PreCursor's maintenance menu provides access to each menu and submenu. You specify the actual main program name to execute, as well as the menu name that appears for user selection. When necessary, you can specify parameters to be passed to the program when it is later run by PreCursor.

Investigating Disk Contents with the Norton Utilities

The Norton Utilities is a group of programs designed to increase your control over the data that is actually stored on your disk. For example, you can look at specific parts of a disk and modify the data you find there. You can also recover files that have been accidentally erased; you can even recover entire hard disks that have been formatted. Utilities of this kind come in very handy when you've made a major blunder. Even if things are going smoothly, the Norton Utilities can provide you with a greater understanding of how your system is set up, as well as an insider's glimpse into previously inaccessible disk files.

The latest version of the Norton Utilities features a menu-driven system. The system shows you various screens of information. For example, by requesting file information, you can see a screen of all the files on the disk, including hidden files, system files, and those that have been deleted but not yet overwritten since their deletion. You can change the attributes of any file, controlling even more attributes than you can with the DOS ATTRIB command. You can even change any individual byte in any file anywhere on the disk. For the technical user, detailed data about specific files and the hard disk as a whole is also available on another screen.

Included in the Norton Utilities are many individual utility programs that are both simple in form and powerful in function (see Table 20.1). For example, the DS (Directory Sort) program displays your current directory on the screen. You

UTILITY NAME	PROGRAM DESCRIPTION
ASK	Creates interactive batch files
BEEP	Controls the computer's speaker
DS	Sorts a directory's file names
DT	Tests disks for physical errors
FA	Sets, resets, and scans file attributes
FF	Finds disk files by name
FI	Assigns and retrieves file comments
FR	Recovers an accidentally formatted hard disk
FS	Lists and totals file sizes
LD	Creates a graphic view of directory structure
LP	Prints files with line numbers and headers
NCD	Allows fast directory navigation
NI	Integrates all utilities for easy selection
NU	Allows detailed disk and file exploration
QU	Allows quick unerase capability
SA	Sets screen colors and attributes
SD	Reorganizes disks to remove fragmentation
SI	Reports system information
TM	Displays time and offers stopwatch capability
TS	Searches text in files and disks
UD	Recovers removed directories
VL	Views, adds, removes, or changes disk labels
WIPEDISK	Completely blanks out disk contents
WIPEFILE	Completely blanks out file contents

TABLE 20.1: The Norton Utilities, Advanced Edition (4.0)

can then specify how you want to sort the directory's files, using several levels of sorting. DS then displays the sorted directory and allows you to re-sort it differently or write it to the disk.

The main hub of the utilities is the NI (Norton Integrator) program. Its menu is shown in Figure 20.5. This program brings information about all of the other Norton programs onto one screen, where you can choose which program to execute. When you select a program, the screen highlights it and displays a format and a functional description at the right side. At the bottom of the screen is a command line that changes whenever you highlight a different program. It allows you to enter parameters for a specific command. The right half of the screen explains the highlighted command and its possible switches.

Although all of these utility programs are useful, one of the most powerful is NU, perhaps the primary utility program on the Integrator menu. This utility allows you to view and edit any area of the disk directly, as well as to restore deleted files. Most important, NU also provides you with effective means for recovering lost file data and for repairing damaged disks with minimum data loss. The procedure for recovering deleted files with NU is discussed in Chapter 21.

The Norton Utilities are available from

Peter Norton Computing, Inc.
2210 Wilshire Boulevard
Santa Monica, California 90403
(213) 453-2361

Making Backup Copies with Back-It

Making backup copies can sometimes be very complicated, especially if you don't want or need to back up an entire disk. They can also take a long time to make and can be subject to simple mistakes, such as inserting the wrong diskette or forgetting a group of files. Back-It provides a way to back up and restore files easily on your hard disk. You can use it in place of DOS's BACKUP and RESTORE commands.

Back-It's main menu, shown in Figure 20.6, presents a well-grouped approach to its chores. The top line provides all desired options. When you are ready to back up, Back-It lets you choose exactly which directories to back up, by showing you the directory tree and letting you move around in it, tagging the directories you want or don't want backed up.

The program is very easy to use. It will even tell you how many diskettes you will need for the backup operation. You move around the menu screen by using the arrow keys. You can select different functions from the menu bar at the top of the screen and then modify the parameters that accompany each function on the main screen. Back-It is fast and truly user friendly, offering you many additional

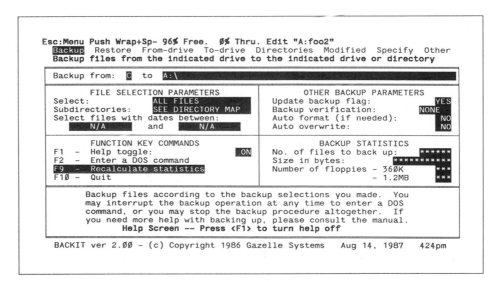

```
┌─────────────────────────────────────────────────────────────────────┐
│                        ┌ The Norton Integrator ┐                     │
│  ASK                                                                  │
│  BEEP                    Format Recover              FR [d:][/SAVE]   │
│  DS  Directory Sort        Undo an accidental formatting of a hard    │
│  DT  Disk Test             disk, thereby making the data accessible   │
│  FA  File Attributes       again.                                     │
│  FF  File Find                                                        │
│  FI  File Info             Format Recover is a preventive program     │
│ ▓FR  Format Recover▓       with two parts: one to save the            │
│  FS  File Size             information necessary for restoring the     │
│  LD  List Directories      original format of an accidentally         │
│  LP  Line Print            formatted hard disk (/SAVE) and one to     │
│  NCD Norton CD             reformat, using the saved information.      │
│  NU  Norton Utility                                                   │
│  QU  Quick UnErase       FR c: /SAVE                                  │
│  SA  Screen Attributes     Save the information necessary for         │
│  SD  Speed Disk            recovering the C: drive. You will          │
│  SI  System Information    probably want to put this command in       │
│  TM  Time Mark            the Autoexec.bat file.                      │
│  TS  Text Search                                                      │
│  UD  UnRemove Directory  FR c:                                        │
│                 more...    Recover the accidentally formatted C:      │
│                            drive.                                     │
│                                                                       │
│                          Switch                                      │
│ ┌───────────────────────┐  /SAVE  Save format recovery information    │
│ │FR c: /SAVE▄           │                                            │
│ └───────────────────────┘                        Press F1 for Help   │
└─────────────────────────────────────────────────────────────────────┘
```

FIGURE 20.5: The Norton Integrator menu makes it easy to run any of the many useful utility programs included in the Norton Utilities. Simply move the cursor to the desired utility program. All possible parameter and switch entries are displayed at the right of the screen; you can adjust the windowed command at the bottom of the screen before executing it by pressing Return.

```
┌─────────────────────────────────────────────────────────────────────┐
│ Esc:Menu Push Wrap+Sp- 96% Free.  0% Thru. Edit "A:foo2"              │
│ ▓Backup▓ Restore From-drive To-drive Directories Modified Specify Other│
│ Backup files from the indicated drive to the indicated drive or dir.  │
│                                                                       │
│ ┌───────────────────────────────────────────────────────────────┐    │
│ │ Backup from: ▓C▓ to ▓A:\▓                                      │    │
│ └───────────────────────────────────────────────────────────────┘    │
│ ┌──── FILE SELECTION PARAMETERS ────┐ ┌── OTHER BACKUP PARAMETERS ──┐ │
│ │ Select:        ▓ALL FILES▓        │ │ Update backup flag:    ▓YES▓│ │
│ │ Subdirectories:▓SEE DIRECTORY MAP▓│ │ Backup verification: ▓NONE▓ │ │
│ │ Select files with dates between:  │ │ Auto format (if needed): ▓NO▓│ │
│ │ ▓  N/A  ▓  and  ▓  N/A  ▓          │ │ Auto overwrite:        ▓NO▓ │ │
│ └───────────────────────────────────┘ └─────────────────────────────┘ │
│ ┌──── FUNCTION KEY COMMANDS ────────┐ ┌──── BACKUP STATISTICS ─────┐  │
│ │ F1 - Help toggle:         ▓ON▓    │ │ No. of files to back up: ▓*****▓│
│ │ F2 - Enter a DOS command          │ │ Size in bytes:      ▓********▓│
│ │▓F9 - Recalculate statistics▓      │ │ Number of floppies - 360K ▓***▓│
│ │ F10- Quit                         │ │                  - 1.2MB ▓***▓│
│ └───────────────────────────────────┘ └─────────────────────────────┘ │
│ ┌───────────────────────────────────────────────────────────────┐    │
│ │   Backup files according to the backup selections you made. You│    │
│ │   may interrupt the backup operation at any time to enter a DOS│    │
│ │   command, or you may stop the backup procedure altogether. If │    │
│ │   you need more help with backing up, please consult the manual.│   │
│ │       Help Screen -- Press <F1> to turn help off              │    │
│ └───────────────────────────────────────────────────────────────┘    │
│ BACKIT ver 2.00 - (c) Copyright 1986 Gazelle Systems  Aug 14, 1987  424pm│
└─────────────────────────────────────────────────────────────────────┘
```

FIGURE 20.6: Back-It's main menu. All possible main menu choices are visible in the menu line at the top of the screen. You can specify individual backup parameters using the middle sections of the screen. Function-key capabilities are shown in the lower section. The screen also displays dynamically updated statistics. A useful statistic this screen displays is the number of floppy diskettes needed for the backup operation.

options such as several standard backup sets, variable levels of data verification, and automatic formatting of target diskettes.

Back-It is available from

Gazelle Systems
42 North University Avenue, Suite 10
Provo, Utah 84601
(800) 233-0383
(801) 377-1288

Backing Up Copy-Protected Disks with COPYIIPC

Although Back-It improves on the DOS BACKUP command, it does not provide the specialized capability available with COPYIIPC. This software package prepares a working backup copy of most copy-protected software. Naturally, this backup copy is to be used for archival purposes only, and a notice to this effect is displayed on the first screen this product displays.

It is very simple to back up most software packages with COPYIIPC. On a two-diskette system, you simply enter

COPYIIPC A: B:

On a single-diskette system, you enter

COPYIIPC A:

In each case, you will be prompted as to when and where to place your original and target diskettes. It's a good idea to place a write-protect tab on your original diskette before this (and any other backup) procedure. That way, you will not accidentally destroy your original diskette, even if you place the original in the wrong drive at the wrong time.

Since different software vendors use different copy-protection schemes, the makers of COPYIIPC have incorporated a number of techniques for surmounting these protection mechanisms. At times, you are required to take additional steps to ensure that the backup copies you prepare with COPYIIPC will work correctly.

Some software programs require that your original diskette be in drive A at all times. Central Point Software includes an additional program, called NOKEY, on their distribution diskette. Running NOKEY before running your backup diskette created by COPYIIPC is often all that you need do to enable the backup copy to run. Trying this is the next step to take, if the backup copy does not run without the original diskette first place in drive A.

You should also run NOKEY if you have placed a copy of an original copy-protected diskette's files on your hard disk, and the program still asks that the original diskette be placed in drive A. However, some programs, such as

Lotus 1-2-3, have special install/uninstall sequences that you supposedly must follow to run them from a hard disk. Many a user has suffered greatly when a hard disk failed and the original diskette would not run because it had already been installed on a hard disk. Software that does this keeps an installation counter on the original diskette. Depending on the responsiveness of the software vendor, you could be without your copy-protected software for many weeks or even months.

NOGUARD is another program included on the COPYIIPC disk that specifically handles software with install/uninstall requirements. After you have created a nonworking backup copy, you can run NOGUARD, which will take you through a sequence that reads the original diskette and makes specific adjustments on the backup diskette to allow it to run without hesitation from your hard disk.

In fact, NOGUARD also allows you to produce a working diskette version of software requiring this special installation. This feature is useful if you decide to run your single licensed version of software on your diskette-based computer out of your office. Of course, some software is licensed to run only on a single computer, and other software is licensed to run on only one computer at a time.

COPYIIPC is available from

Central Point Software, Inc.
9700 SW Capitol Highway
Suite 100
Portland, Oregon 97219
(503) 244-5782

Controlling Data on Your Disk with the Mace Utilities

The Mace Utilities is a group of programs designed to increase your control over the data stored on your disk. For example, you can undelete files, look at specific parts of the disk, and modify the data you find there. These kinds of utilities can be very useful if your disk starts having problems. You can run some of these utilities for diagnosing and then actually fixing the disk problems found.

The Mace Utilities includes the following: a directory sorter, a PATH speed enhancer, a disk defragmentation program, several types of disk-caching software, and a keyboard accelerator. The package also includes several hard disk formatting programs, an undelete program, an (innovative) unformat program, and a dBASE file-fixing program.

The programs run in text mode and are different than The Norton Utilities; they also do not include a built-in help screen. The main menu program that integrates all of the programs is simple, using only the function keys (see Figure 20.7). Should a program not be able to be loaded (that is, if there is not enough memory), the program simply will not run and will tell you why.

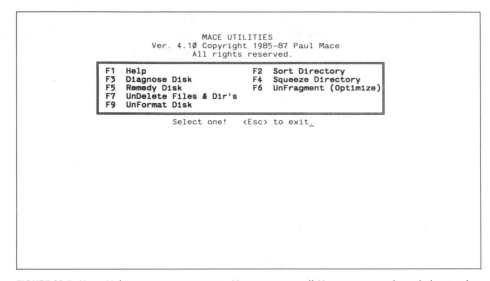

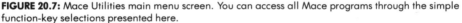

FIGURE 20.7: Mace Utilities main menu screen. You can access all Mace programs through the simple function-key selections presented here.

The Mace Utilities is available from

Paul Mace Software
400 Williamson Way
Ashland, Oregon 97520

Maintaining Hard Disk Data with Disk Technician

The Disk Technician program is a remarkable product that should be in every hard disk owner's utility collection. Simply put, the program claims to do what DOS should do but does not: corrects and maintains your hard disk data.

As described briefly in Chapter 1 and in greater depth in Chapter 21, data is stored on disks in tracks and divided into clusters and sectors. Being mechanical, disks are subject to their environment. For example, when cold, most materials shrink somewhat, and when hot, most materials expand. Thus, if you start your system when it is cold, early in the morning, then data you write to your hard disk may be written out of alignment with the other tracks. At first, this may not be a problem, but after subsequent write operations, the tracks could become significantly out of alignment, thereby making subsequent reading or writing of data unreliable, if not nearly impossible. This may account for many of the unrecoverable disk errors that occur in your system. Disk Technician can recover these errors.

When you first install (installation takes just a few moments) and run Disk Technician, it performs a complete test of all bits on all tracks in all cylinders of your disk, reading each bit and checking it. It compiles a file of possibly bad areas and refers to this as it operates. This checking process takes about two hours on a 10MB disk running on a PC-XT.

From then on, you can run a one- to five-minute daily test that checks the questionable areas of your disk and fixes any problems. It fixes a track by copying its data into RAM, executing a low-level formatting of the track, and re-copying the data back onto the track. Should the track prove to be defective, Disk Technician will block it from further use by the system and move the data elsewhere.

A part of the Disk Technician package is the program SafePark. This TSR program is loaded every time you use Disk Technician (if you so specify). It automatically parks the drive heads over a certain part of the disk if there has been no activity for 7 seconds. You can change the 7-second time interval to anywhere from 1 and 15 seconds. The area of the disk used for parking is a 34K block set aside the first time you use the program.

Disk Technician is copy protected and must be used from its own diskette (you cannot transfer it to a hard disk). It is compatible with DOS 2.1 through 3.3. Version 1.0 will *not* work on non-IBM standard track configurations, such as those with RLL-type controllers. Version 2.0 will, however.

Disk Technician is available from

Prime Solutions Inc.
1940 Garnet Avenue
San Diego, California 92109
(619) 274-5000

Speeding Up Your Hard Disk

If you have a hard disk system, the efficient operation of the disk is crucial to the efficient use of your entire computer system. As the number of files on your hard disk gets larger, the time required to access a file increases, slowing down your system. There are several reasons for this slowdown.

Fragmentation

When DOS writes a file on a disk, it writes it in groups of sectors called clusters. The number of 512-byte sectors in each cluster does vary by the version of DOS you are using, but the process of cluster writing creates the speed problem. For example, suppose that you write a first file to a disk, and it consumes a full cluster. Then you write another file to the disk, and it uses up the next (contiguous) cluster. Your disk looks like this:

Cluster	Contents
1	File 1 (first cluster of file 1)
2	File 2 (first cluster of file 2)

Then you double the size of the first file, perhaps by expanding a database or adding a new page of text with your word processor; you then save it again.

Instead of pushing the second file up to make room for the two clusters of the first file, DOS saves the additional information for the first file in cluster 3, leaving cluster 2, which contains the second file, untouched. If you were to expand the second file next and then add a third file, the disk would look like this:

Cluster	Contents
1	File 1 (first cluster of file 1)
2	File 2 (first cluster of file 2)
3	File 1 (second cluster of file 1)
4	File 2 (second cluster of file 2)
5	File 2 (third cluster of file 2)
6	File 3 (first cluster of file 3)
.	.
.	.
.	.

As you can see, files get broken up as you work on them. The time it takes to move the disk's read/write head can increase dramatically as the number of your files increases and as your files become more and more fragmented. *Fragmentation* occurs when pieces of the same file are stored in nonadjacent clusters on a disk. As this condition evolves, the first half of a file could be on an outside track, whereas the second half could be on an inside track. Head movement across the disk would take a lot more time than it would with sequential clusters.

Reducing or eliminating fragmentation speeds up the disk. The way to do this is to go through the whole disk and rearrange the clusters so that all clusters for every file are contiguous. With a great deal of effort, you can actually do this yourself. All you need to do is copy all files in all directories onto backup disks, reformat the entire disk, and then rewrite the files back onto the disk. An easier procedure is to buy one of the utilities, such as VOPT, described in this section.

Disk Access

A less obvious solution to speeding up the disk, which relieves the symptoms but does not really solve the problem, is to reduce disk access. Lightning, a memory-resident program, will actually remember disk-sector data every time it is used, so that continued access of the same sector will, instead of accessing the disk drive, access a memory area (called a *cache*) that already contains the data. This is much faster than accessing the disk, but it does cost you a certain amount of memory for both the Lightning program and the memory cache.

> *Warning:* File sizes and numbers always seem to expand to fill whatever amount of space your hard disk has. Be sure you regularly take the time to delete older files or early versions of files.

Memory Space

Another problem with disks of all sizes is that they can run out of space. This is especially true if you use large databases or manage hundreds or thousands of files. A creative solution to the problem of space availability is to shrink your existing files to a much smaller size. This is sometimes called *data compression.* When you need to use the files, you can expand them back to their normal size and then compress them again when you're through. This provides extra disk space, and your files are available for use when necessary. The utility program Squish provides this capability for your system.

Rapid File Reorganization with VOPT

VOPT is an interesting package of utilities from Golden Bow Systems. It features a hard disk optimizer that can optimize a badly fragmented disk in only a few minutes. It is so fast that it can be used in your AUTOEXEC.BAT file to optimize the disk every time you boot up; this maintenance mode takes only a few seconds.

The algorithms used in disk optimization differ among the various programs performing this function. VOPT's algorithm minimizes the time required by the optimization algorithm itself. Other programs, like Norton and Mace discussed earlier in this chapter, use logic that takes more time because more files are moved around the disk. The intention of such programs is not only to reduce fragmentation by compacting (and eliminating) unused sectors, but also to relocate files. By placing files near the directory entries that reference them, Norton and Mace expect to reduce eventual disk-head movement experienced in obtaining access to those files.

In practice, however, VOPT's approach represents a more attractive compromise solution. Fragmentation is reduced, so performance is enhanced, although it is perhaps not improved as much as it would be by another algorithmic approach. Many users, however, do not use Norton or Mace on as regular a basis as they might use VOPT, precisely because these programs take so much time to run.

The VOPT program itself is very easy to use: Just issue the VOPT command at the prompt. First the program uses its own version of CHKDSK to make sure there are no lost clusters or disk errors. Should there be any, VOPT will end, and you will be instructed to use the DOS command CHKDSK/F to correct the problem. Once this is done, or if no errors are found, optimization begins. Figure 20.8 shows a map of the disk space before optimization; the map was created by another utility program (VMAP) included on the VOPT diskette.

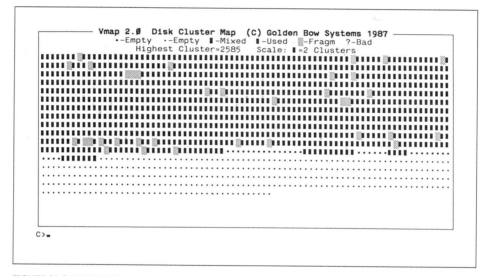

FIGURE 20.8: VMAP disk space display before optimization. Fragmentation is clearly visible in the scattering of used clusters mixed with empty clusters. Bad sectors, if any exist, show up on this display as ? symbols.

VOPT itself displays a version of this disk map, which changes during the optimization process. When the process is complete, you are shown statistics about the overall effort, as shown in Figure 20.9. The cluster display is more colorful than necessary, but flair and drama are always attractive in a good program.

Note: The probability of a utility package containing extra utility programs is directly proportional to the pizzazz and usefulness of its first utility.

VOPT is available from

Golden Bow Systems
2870 Fifth Avenue, Suite 201
San Diego, California 92103
(619) 298-9349

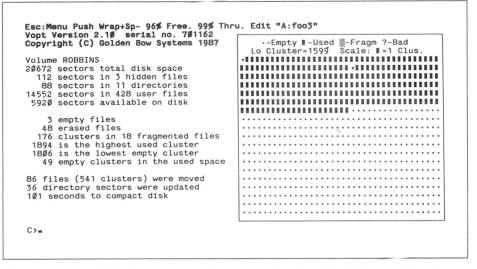

```
Esc:Menu Push Wrap+Sp- 96% Free. 99% Thru. Edit "A:foo3"
Vopt Version 2.10  serial no. 701162
Copyright (C) Golden Bow Systems 1987       .-Empty ∎-Used ▓-Fragm ?-Bad
                                            Lo Cluster=1599  Scale: ∎=1 Clus.
  Volume ROBBINS                          ·∎∎∎∎∎∎∎∎∎∎∎∎∎∎∎∎∎∎∎∎∎∎∎∎∎∎∎∎∎∎∎∎∎∎∎∎
  20672 sectors total disk space          ∎∎∎∎∎∎∎∎∎∎∎∎∎∎∎∎∎∎∎∎∎·∎∎∎∎∎∎∎∎∎∎∎∎∎∎∎
    112 sectors in 3 hidden files         ∎∎∎∎∎∎∎∎∎∎∎∎∎∎∎∎∎∎∎∎∎∎∎∎∎∎∎∎∎∎∎∎∎∎∎∎∎
     88 sectors in 11 directories         ∎∎∎∎∎∎∎∎∎∎∎∎∎∎∎∎∎∎∎∎∎∎∎∎∎∎∎∎∎∎∎∎∎∎∎∎∎
  14552 sectors in 428 user files         ∎∎∎∎∎∎∎∎∎∎∎∎∎∎∎∎∎∎∎∎∎∎∎∎∎∎∎∎∎∎∎∎∎∎∎∎∎
   5920 sectors available on disk         ∎∎∎∎∎∎∎∎∎∎∎∎∎∎∎∎∎∎∎∎∎∎∎∎∎∎∎∎∎∎∎∎∎∎∎∎∎
                                          ∎∎∎∎∎∎∎∎∎∎∎∎∎∎∎∎∎∎∎∎∎∎∎·............
      3 empty files                       ....................................
     48 erased files                      ....................................
    176 clusters in 18 fragmented files   ....................................
   1894 is the highest used cluster       ....................................
   1806 is the lowest empty cluster       ....................................
     49 empty clusters in the used space  ....................................
                                          ....................................
   86 files (541 clusters) were moved     ....................................
   36 directory sectors were updated      ....................................
   101 seconds to compact disk            ....................................
                                          ....................................
                                          ....................................
   C>_
```

FIGURE 20.9: VOPT display after optimization shows a more densely packed disk space. All used clusters are near the beginning of the disk; all empty clusters are in the latter sections of the disk. This screen also displays statistical information regarding this most recent execution of VOPT.

Installing a Memory Cache with Lightning

The Lightning program remembers the information stored in disk sectors. For example, you may need to access file information contained in disk sectors 1 and 2. The actual data stored in the sectors is placed in a memory buffer, or cache. If you need to access the data again, Lightning locates it in memory, eliminating the need for DOS to reaccess the disk.

You can execute Lightning only once at the command prompt (or from a batch file), along with all parameters. Lightning then becomes memory-resident, the memory cache is set up, and no further intervention on your part is required. It uses a default memory cache of 60K, but you can expand that (even to extended memory, if it exists in your system). Lightning can also display statistics on speed improvement, by disk, in your system.

Lightning is available from

The Personal Computer Support Group
11035 Harry Hines Blvd., Suite 206
Dallas, Texas 75229
(214) 351-0564

Compressing Files with ARC

ARC is handy if you use your modem frequently. It selectively compresses and decompresses files. For instance, if you regularly hook up to a bulletin board system and download files, you will probably be able to download ARC versions of the files. These versions take up much less room on the host system and therefore download much more quickly, saving you phone costs and time.

ARC is a public-domain package (see "Public Domain Software" later in this chapter), so you can get it for no cost from many bulletin board systems or from one of the reputable public-domain diskette supply firms. If you purchase a diskette with ARC on it, you will usually receive on the same disk other software that has been compressed using ARC. You can decompress the programs with ARC, thereby effectively acquiring more software on a diskette than the diskette nominally can store.

ARC is available from

Public Brand Software
P. O. Box 51315
Indianapolis, IN 46251

Compressing Data with Squish

Squish is one of those programs that may, with its first use, save you hundreds of dollars by eliminating your need to purchase a new hard disk, not to mention reducing the time required to create backup diskettes. DOS usually stores files on a disk with much unused space. For example, all the blank characters and lines in your word processing files and all those empty fields in your database files unnecessarily consume disk space. In other words, many files are stored inefficiently, taking up more room than they need on both your hard disk and your backup diskettes.

To reduce this inefficiency, Squish "runs interference" between your disk drive and DOS. When you save a file, Squish intercepts the request, compresses the file into the least amount of space possible, and then writes the "squished" file to a disk. For example, a single Pascal program that originally uses over 36K can be compressed to less than 27K, an improvement of 25 percent.

Squish runs invisibly—that is, you do not know that it is running, but it is there. This is the key difference between Squish and ARC. Once Squish is installed, it automatically compresses and decompresses files to save you disk storage space. ARC, on the other hand, compresses files into an archive format only at your explicit request. The files are not available in that compressed format; they must be decompressed to their original size and format before you can access the data in them.

Hence, ARC doesn't provide immediate disk storage benefits. Its value is typically seen in two instances: when a large amount of file data is to be transmitted over expensive communications lines, and when a very large collection of files (exceeding the space on a single diskette) is to be squeezed onto a single diskette.

Squish has a memory-resident portion (about 40K), which is activated not by a hot key, but by any request to DOS for a task requiring disk access. It converts files automatically when you access them; if you save a file, Squish automatically compresses it. Your only indication that the file has been compressed will be that it takes up less space than it normally would.

To decompress a file, just load it as usual. Squish will intercept the load command, get the file, decompress it, and send it on to your application. It does all of this in memory, so you don't need to budget extra disk space for decompressed files. Again, there will be no indication that the file is being decompressed, except that it may take slightly longer to load than usual.

> *Note:* Programs that improve system performance typically trade speed for space; that is, if the utility improves speed, you usually have to give up memory space for this improvement. On the other hand, if the utility improves space use, this benefit usually costs operating speed.

You can also run Squish for especially large existing files stored on your disk. You probably have many hundreds of files currently on your disk. It may not be worth your time to compress all those files; you may want to compress only the largest of them. Squish works equally well with a disk containing only some, and not all, files in compressed, Squish format. When memory-resident, Squish can tell the difference between a squished and an unsquished file.

Squish is available from

SunDog Software Corporation
264 Court Street
Brooklyn, New York 11231
(718) 855-9141

ENHANCING YOUR CONSOLE'S POWER

Your console is the most important part of your computer system in that it is the means by which you control the system and by which the system responds to you. Should the keyboard not "feel" right to you, or should you be uncomfortable with its setup or behavior (mushy keys, poor key layout, and so on), this will influence the way you use your system and the amount of time you work with it. Therefore, it is important that you feel comfortable with the keyboard and display.

There are many ways to customize the keyboard and make it much more powerful. You can redefine the keys so that you can do more from the keyboard. For example, by using the Keyworks program, you can redefine any key on your keyboard to actually type a different character, word, command, sentence, or paragraph.

Another utility acts on your display. Scroll & Recall gives you the ability to take a second look at any data that has been displayed for you in a line-by-line manner but has since scrolled off the screen. How many times have you wanted to move backward to see something that scrolled quickly off the screen? Or how often have you run a long program that produced results that you didn't write down, and that you'd like to see again?

Extending Keyboard Power with Keyworks

Many application programs use long sequences of keystrokes to accomplish tasks. For instance, many commercial database services require you to connect your computer to theirs through a dial-up telephone connection. You may have to sign on to the service's computer, enter a password, and then pass through five levels of menus just to read some news. The keystrokes might be

LOGON JUDD 123456 3 2 1 4 5 READ #1

Typing this entire sequence every time you access the database is a chore.

Keyworks simplifies such tasks, enhancing the keyboard by letting you substitute key combinations such as Alt-F, which normally don't do anything, for a string of keystrokes. When you redefine a key as some sort of an instruction set—for instance, when you redefine the F3 key to type DIR A: and press Return—you have created your own keyboard macro. A macro is a series of instructions that are called up by a single command or keystroke combination and executed at once, whether the instructions are stored in memory or in a file on the disk. By using Keyworks to create a keyboard macro you can even represent a whole paragraph with one key; then whenever you press that key, the paragraph will appear. If you use WordStar or any other program that requires a series of keystrokes to implement certain features, this program is for you.

As was pointed out in Chapter 10, you can use the PROMPT command to redefine your function keys in specific, limited ways. Keyworks is menu driven, so it is easier to use than the DOS PROMPT command. Keyworks is also significantly more powerful in both the scope of its commands for key redefinition and the ease with which you can define extremely powerful sequences of keystrokes. You can also prepare entirely different sets of key reassignments with Keyworks and install them dynamically at your convenience. Since Keyworks is memory resident, you can change this set of key definitions either from the DOS prompt or from within an executing application program.

Keyworks is a keyboard macro program with extraordinary versatility. It actually includes a complete programming language. One of the many features of this memory-resident program is that you can directly edit the macros you have defined. When you select this option, Keyworks implements full-screen mode, similar to many word processors, allowing you to edit the macros directly. Cut-and-paste capabilities allow you to create new, complex macros from old ones.

Several other useful capabilities come with Keyworks, such as a way to encrypt confidential disk files for security purposes. Most essential DOS features are implemented as well, enabling you to reproduce DOS commands in a *pop-up* display while other programs are running. (In a pop-up display, all of the screen's contents appear instantaneously, instead of appearing line by line as they are written to the screen.) All of Keywork's features are available from a pop-up system of menus.

Keyworks's menu system is very accessible. You can also use Keyworks to set up your own system of menus and help screens. Although it requires more work than using the PreCursor utility described earlier, Keyworks has more potential power because of its macro language, which is as powerful as many high-level programming languages and allows decision making, looping, and flow-of-control commands.

Keyworks is available from

The Alpha Software Corporation
30 B Street
Burlington, Massachusetts 01803
(617) 229-2924

Terminal Emulators

Many people use their computers to connect to a mainframe. Whether it be the mainframe at school or the one at work, chances are it does not quite understand the communications codes used by the IBM PC. However, chances are also that it does understand other terminal types, such as Digital Equipment Corp's VT100 series.

To be able to use the other computer effectively, you need a way to translate the codes the mainframe sends out to a VT100 to your IBM PC's own set of codes (much like code pages). There are programs to do this, and often they are included in communications packages. Smartcom II and III, Crosstalk, and others all contain *terminal emulators*, or programs that make the PC think it is talking to another PC, and the mainframe think it is talking to a VT100.

Most mainframes have extensive graphics capability. The IBM PC also has this capability, but most terminal emulators do not. To get this capability, you need to buy software designed to emulate a terminal that can handle the mainframe's graphics. These emulators are usually sold independently and can be costly. Thus, when you buy a modem and communications package and you know what mainframe you will be connecting to, look into what terminals the mainframe supports and what terminals your communications software can emulate. Make sure that if you need graphics, your software can handle this capability.

Enhancing Your Communications Capabilities with FREEWAY

Communications has always been a popular DOS application area. A communications program such as FREEWAY allows your DOS computer to connect to other DOS computers, to mainframe computers, to interesting and helpful computerized bulletin boards, and to automated information services such as CompuServe.

Figure 20.10 depicts how DOS microcomputers typically establish connections to other computer systems. In each case, a modem must be connected to one of the DOS serial ports, and all necessary communications parameters must be set up. At the very least, connection involves using the MODE command (see Chapter 12) to establish data transmission parameters. Then you must send your data to the modem along with the requisite control codes to manage the modem's functions.

Communications software such as FREEWAY performs all setup and transmission tasks, which require a complex sequence of steps, for you. As you can see in Figure 20.11, FREEWAY has a very simple appearance that belies the power of the software.

FREEWAY has several built-in terminal capabilities, including a simple TTY and a variety of sophisticated emulation capabilities. Like many communications software packages, it relieves you of the burden of initializing your ports and your modem. Through the increasingly common feature of prepared scripts, you can completely automate your computer's communications setup as well as the required log-on sequence for connecting to the remote computer.

Figure 20.10 also suggests that it is possible to log on to mainframe or minicomputers; other DOS microcomputers; or a variety of information services, such as CompuServe, Dialog, or a neighborhood bulletin board service. You need only establish the setup, transmission parameters, and terminal emulation differently for each of these possibilities. FREEWAY does all of this for you.

Although FREEWAY has many competitors, this package is well designed and easy to use. Regardless of your communications objective, you should definitely buy one of the software packages in this class if you intend to connect your computer to other computers.

FREEWAY is available from

Kortek, Inc.
505 Hamilton Ave.
Palo Alto, CA 94301
(415) 327-4555

Reissuing Previous DOS Commands with ReComm

Many commands you issue in DOS are repetitions of commands you issued earlier in the same session. Sometimes you issue the same command several

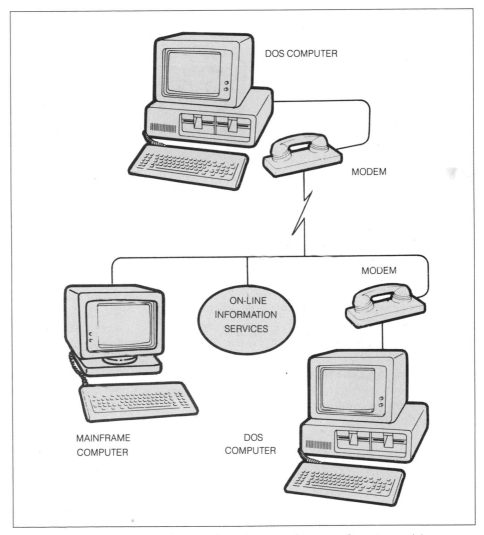

FIGURE 20.10: Communications software performs the required setup, configuration, and data transmission steps to facilitate computer connections. A DOS computer uses one of its serial ports to connect, through a modem and telecommunications channel, to another DOS computer, a mainframe or minicomputer, or an on-line information service.

times; at other times, you issue a similar command with only minor variations. ReComm is a utility that can instantaneously call back to the DOS prompt any command issued previously. It even saves and recalls command and text sequences from within many application programs.

ReComm has a built-in line editor, so you can use the cursor keys to make any desired edits to the recalled command before reissuing it. This means that you

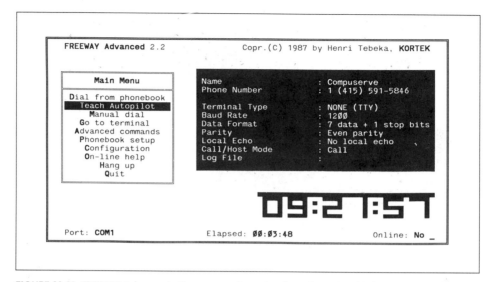

FREEWAY Advanced 2.2   Copr.(C) 1987 by Henri Tebeka, **KORTEK**

Main Menu

Dial from phonebook
Teach Autopilot
Manual dial
Go to terminal
Advanced commands
Phonebook setup
Configuration
On-line help
Hang up
Quit

Name   : Compuserve
Phone Number   : 1 (415) 591-5846

Terminal Type   : NONE (TTY)
Baud Rate   : 1200
Data Format   : 7 data + 1 stop bits
Parity   : Even parity
Local Echo   : No local echo
Call/Host Mode   : Call
Log File   :

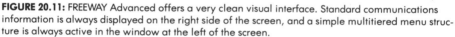

Port: **COM1**   Elapsed: **00:03:48**   Online: **No** _

FIGURE 20.11: FREEWAY Advanced offers a very clean visual interface. Standard communications information is always displayed on the right side of the screen, and a simple multitiered menu structure is always active in the window at the left of the screen.

can easily correct errors in the last-issued DOS command as well. (You merely press Return to reissue the command.)

All of ReComm's activities occur at the bottom of the screen when you call it up with a redefinable hot key. Help is also available, as usual, at the touch of the F1 key (see Figure 20.12). Active screens are saved and restored after ReComm has completed its operations.

ReComm is available from

Computer Options
198 Amherst Avenue
Berkeley, California 94708
(415) 525-5033

CONVERTING FILE AND DISK FORMATS

There are many programs available that perform the same task, but usually you cannot use the files of one program in another. For example, there are many word processing programs, but you cannot move a file from one word processor directly into another word processor, because most word processors make extensive use of special control codes to perform their text formatting. The file must first be converted to a format that the new word processor can understand. Many conversion programs perform this function, although each one can convert to or from only a very few programs.

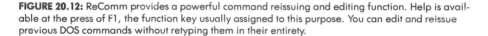

```
╔══════════════════════ ReComm Commands ══════════════════════╗
║          Cursor Movement              │           Delete          ║
╟───────────────────────────────────────┼───────────────────────────╢
║  Left arrow        = Left one char    │ Del       = Character under cursor ║
║  Right arrow       = Right one char   │ Bksp      = Character left of cursor ║
║  Ctrl-left arrow   = Left one word    │ Ctrl-Home = To beginning of command ║
║  Ctrl-right arrow  = Right one word   │ Ctrl-End  = To end of command ║
║  Home              = Start of command │                           ║
║  End               = End of command   │                           ║
╟───────────────────────────────────────┼───────────────────────────╢
║          Buffer Control               │           Other           ║
╟───────────────────────────────────────┼───────────────────────────╢
║  PgUp       = Display previous command│ Enter = Execute displayed command ║
║  PgDn       = Display next command    │ Esc   = Cancel, return to program ║
║  Ctrl-PgUp  = Delete displayed command│ Ins   = Turn insert mode on/off ║
║  Ctrl-PgDn  = Delete all buffer cmds  │ F1    = Turn Help on/off   ║
╟───────────────────────────────────────┴───────────────────────────╢
║          Alt-=    Enables/disables command capture                 ║
╚════════════════════════════════════════════════════════════════════╝
╔════════════════════════════════════════════════════════════════════╗
║  ReComm Version 1.Ø        Computer Options        Press F1 for Help ║
╟────────────────────────────────────────────────────────────────────╢
║  CHKDSK A: /F                                                        ║
╚════════════════════════════════════════════════════════════════════╝
```

FIGURE 20.12: ReComm provides a powerful command reissuing and editing function. Help is available at the press of F1, the function key usually assigned to this purpose. You can edit and reissue previous DOS commands without retyping them in their entirety.

Like word processors, some computer systems are not compatible. To load a disk from one operating system into another (from CP/M to DOS, for example, or from DOS to UNIX), you must convert the entire contents of the disk to a format acceptable to the other system. Each operating system writes its files in a certain way at certain places on a disk; in addition, different operating systems use different storage and formatting schemes.

For example, even though you use 5¼-inch diskettes for all your operating systems, the systems' different layouts nevertheless inhibit compatibility. Even if you use a single operating system (such as DOS) but switch to a different machine (from an IBM PC-AT to an IBM Personal System/2, for example), you may encounter compatibility problems. One machine might use 3½-inch diskettes, and the other machine might use 5¼-inch diskettes; both can use the same application programs and the same version of DOS, but the data must be converted from one diskette format to another. The following programs offer this kind of service.

Changing Disk Sizes with Brooklyn Bridge

The Brooklyn Bridge utility package offers two separate programs. One program runs on a computer with 3½-inch diskettes, and the other program runs on a computer with 5¼-inch diskettes. This utility package is similar to a communications program, but its purpose is more focused: It allows you to specify file names to be transferred between two different disk drives.

Brooklyn Bridge transfers the specified files between machines by means of cables connecting serial ports on each machine—an inexpensive and creative solution to the problem of hardware incompatibility.

Brooklyn Bridge is available from

White Crane Systems
6889 Peachtree Ind. Blvd.
Norcross, Georgia 30092
(404) 454-7911

Reading Different Machine Formats with XenoCopy-PC

XenoCopy-PC converts the diskette formats of files from various operating system formats. It is no longer as necessary for DOS users as it once was, since fewer and fewer offices have multiple machines with incompatible operating systems. However, if your office still has an old TeleVideo running a CP/M word processor, for example, and various newer IBM PCs and compatibles running a version of the same word processor, XenoCopy-PC is the right package to own.

XenoCopy-PC pays for itself every time someone working with a DOS-formatted diskette on an IBM computer must use a file written on a CP/M-based machine. XenoCopy-PC is very easy to use, offering a simple menu-selection procedure to specify each of the two incompatible diskette formats.

XenoCopy-PC is available from

XenoSoft
1454 Sixth Street
Berkeley, California 94710
(415) 525-3113

Rewriting Word Processing Formats with R-Doc/X

R-Doc/X is a very handy program to have when one or more people are using two or more word processors. It converts word processing files to different formats for use by other word processors. If your office has several people using different word processors, you don't necessarily have to force everyone to use the same program for consistency. You and your staff also don't have to spend time and effort learning a new word processing system if everyone is already comfortable with his or her current one. Instead, users can just convert their word processed documents to other formats as necessary; they then will be able to work on each other's files.

R-Doc/X does a good job of converting files, but there are some commands it cannot understand and hence does not convert properly. For instance, R-Doc/X cannot understand headers and footers, multicolumn documents, and specific types of tab stops. Therefore, if one of your word processors uses these features, you should make sure the conversion will be sufficient before you select this program.

R-Doc/X is available from

Advanced Computer Innovations
1227 Goler House
Rochester, New York 14620
(716) 454-3188

ORGANIZING YOUR WORK

Many of the minor organizational tasks you perform manually while working with your computer can be handled much more efficiently or eliminated altogether by the computer: keeping manual records (such as a date book or a phone directory), turning around to check a wall clock, rifling through drawers or under papers for a calculator, or scrawling and deciphering notes to yourself, for example. Two programs, Sidekick and Metro, offer features such as record-keeping, a clock display, a calculator, and a simple word processor adequate for quick notes. They should make your life quite a bit easier.

Organizing Your Desktop with Sidekick

Sidekick is a desktop organizer. Its name derives from the sidekicks of the old West, who were trusty companions. You can call up Sidekick at any time by pressing its hot key, since it is a memory-resident program.

Sidekick incorporates many features. It main menu, shown in Figure 20.13, outlines everything Sidekick can do. For example, you can move the menu bar or type a letter. If you type the letter *N* or press F2, you will find yourself in the NotePad section of Sidekick, which allows you to type and save notes for yourself or for later inclusion in a file. It is actually a miniversion of a word processor, using a set of control codes similar to that found in WordStar. The NotePad feature is useful as a rapid editor for small database programs, as well as for small batch files in DOS.

You can also access an on-screen calculator, a calendar, and an automatic phone dialer, should you have a modem connected. Sidekick also includes a phone directory that works with the autodialer, and a datebook that can keep track of your appointments.

Sidekick is available from

Borland International
4585 Scotts Valley Drive
Scotts Valley, California 95066

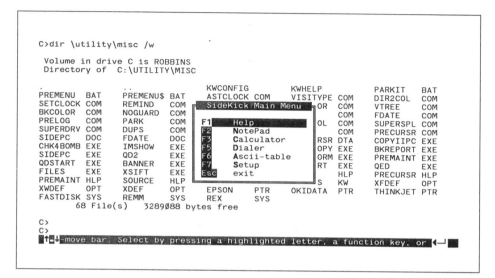

FIGURE 20.13: Sidekick's main menu is a pop-up display of the function-key assignments used to obtain Sidekick's various services. Simple cursor selection and a Return keypress allows entry into a Help function, the word processor (NotePad), the calculator, the telephone dialer, the ASCII table display, and the setup of Sidekick itself.

Managing Your Desktop with Metro

Metro simplifies the task of managing memory and memory-resident (TSR) software. It does this by combining all of the major functions in a TSR into one program. An advantage of this concept is that all of the separate modules of the program work together and can even share data, but do not get in each other's way. That is, one will not overwrite or destroy another or cause unpredictable system errors. The price paid for all of this convenience is memory. Metro requires, at minimum, 80K to 100K of memory.

Metro comes with the following modules: Appointment Book, Calculator, Clipboard, Editor, Filer, Kaleidoscope, List Manager, Macros, Notepad, Phonebook, Special Characters, and Watch. These modules function as their names imply. You can use the simple editor in place of DOS's EDLIN. The list manager is a simple, one-column DBMS. You can enter several different lists and sort the rows in each list however you want. Macros is a standard keyboard macro definition program; it has the capability of learning macros and editing all of your macros directly. Notepad is a simple, eight-page word processing notebook. This feature is probably the handiest next to Macros, and is very easy to use.

Phonebook provides a database organized into distinct screens resembling Rolodex cards in function. There is even a built-in autodialer. Special Characters is simply a list of the available ASCII codes. Watch can simultaneously time 100 events, via 100 stop watches. You can also change the system date and time using this module.

Clipboard ties all of the modules together. If you delete something from the module you are using, it is pasted to the clipboard. If you delete something else or specifically move other data to the clipboard, the previous contents of the clipboard are deleted. However, if you send something to the clipboard and then enter another module, you can retrieve the clipboard's contents in the new module, a convenient cut and paste feature.

All of the modules automatically save any changes that you have made. Thus, if you enter a new page into the notebook and quit it, you can turn the computer off and return to it later. Metro also offers the very useful feature of being able to disappear for a short time. That is, if the Metro window is obscuring something on your screen, you can hold down both Shift keys and the window will disappear until you release the keys, at which time it will reappear.

Metro is available from

Lotus Development Corporation
90 Annex
Atlanta, Georgia 30390-0370
(800) 345-1043

PUBLIC-DOMAIN SOFTWARE

The programs we've discussed so far in this chapter (like DOS itself and your application programs) have all been copyrighted. That means the author or publisher claims—and the law recognizes—certain rights with respect to the copyrighted work. The most important of these for software are the rights to reproduce the work and to distribute it to the public. The copyright holder also has the right to authorize others to reproduce and distribute the work. He or she may or may not choose to distribute the work or to charge money for copies of it, but no one who is not authorized has the right to do so.

If no copyright claim is asserted—that is, if no copyright notice is included in the work—the work is said to be in the *public domain*. This means that anyone may reproduce and distribute it. As a result, it is unlikely that anyone will be able to sell it for a profit, since nobody's right to it is exclusive. In describing software, the term *public domain* is often used somewhat loosely to refer to any software that is not sold commercially, even if a copyright is claimed. Sometimes, because of the high cost of marketing a program or for some other reason, a programmer may choose to either give a program away or "sell" it by requesting donations on the honor system.

Free Access

If an author gives up all rights to a program and distributes the program freely to anyone who wants it, the program legally becomes part of the public domain. It can be freely copied by anyone and distributed at will to anybody.

Shareware

Shareware is software that is not sold commercially, but for which the author maintains a copyright. This kind of software usually has a small message printed on the screen asking for donations to the author to help defray the cost of producing the program. Some programs even tell you to pass the copy along to a friend if you do not want the program. In this case, you need not pay anything for it.

Limitware

Limitware describes software that is copyrighted by the author and distributed in a limited form free of charge. Limitware programs usually are complete working versions of a program, with some critical aspect missing, such as the ability to save files or the ability to process more than a few records. These programs are distributed with the express purpose of allowing you to see what they do and how they work. If you like them, then you can send payment to the author, who will provide a complete working version. Additionally, payment often brings added value, such as documentation and sometimes phone support.

Registration Fees

Some public-domain (or quasi–public-domain) software requires or requests you to send a payment to the author. In these instances, the author usually holds the copyright on the program. This means that even if you acquire this program from a public-domain diskette service and then make a copy for someone else, you may still be in violation of copyright laws, just as if you had copied a commercial program. Thus, before you hand out or use free software, be sure you know what limitations have been placed on that software.

Software Pranksters

Pranksters exist in the realm of public domain software; some are more dangerous and insidious than others. One type of public domain prank is to release a program that looks useful but actually erases your hard disk or, more surreptitiously, destroys only portions of files. Nobody except the pranksters know the reasons for such programs.

You will rarely come across one of these programs from a major public-domain distribution company, since these companies check the programs they distribute before they are released. Be wary, however, of programs you download from computerized bulletin board systems (BBS); other people have just as easy access to the system as you do, and any one of them could easily load a prank program onto the BBS for you to download and run.

Where to Get Public-Domain Software

You can get public domain software almost anywhere. Perhaps the easiest way to get such programs is through friends who have already acquired the software you want. You can also ask the salesperson at your local computer store; sometimes salespeople have libraries of public domain programs that they'll let you copy, or they may know a person or a company that distributes the type of software you want.

You can also order public-domain software through various companies, such as The Public (Software) Library, that specialize in public-domain software. These companies send out semiregular newsletters or catalogs of their current stock and some reviews of available programs. These companies may require a nominal membership fee, mostly to pay for overhead, the cost of the disk itself, and the cost of printing the catalog. They supply from one to many programs on a disk. Disks average between 5 and 10 dollars each.

Public-domain software is available from many sources, including

The Public (Software) Library
P.O.Box 35705
Houston, Texas 77235-5705
(713) 721-5205

and

Public Brand Software
P. O. Box 51315
Indianapolis, Indiana 46251
(800) 426-3475

SUMMARY

DOS is clearly not the end-all for your computing needs. There are thousands of additional utilities, from hundreds of utility vendors, that can extend the power and capabilities of your disk operating system dramatically. This chapter has mentioned only a few of the many excellent products available.

For additional information about the sector and track structure of DOS disks, see

- Chapter 1, "DOS and the Computer System: An Overview"

For additional information about using the ECHO command and redirection to send control codes to the communications ports, see

- Chapter 8, "Batch-File Subcommands"
- Chapter 17, "Pipes, Filters, and Redirection"

For additional information about using batch files to set up menu systems, see

- Chapter 9, "Complete Batch-File Examples"

For additional information about redefining the function keys and the PROMPT command, see

- Chapter 10, "Configuration Possibilities"

For additional information about backing up files and disks with the DOS BACKUP command, see

- Chapter 18, "Backups and Restorations"

For additional information about disk clusters and DOS disk management methods and about disk structures and layouts, see

- Chapter 21, "A Closer Look behind the Scenes of DOS"

You've now learned all of the command capabilities in DOS and some of the ways you can expand those capabilities with utility software. The next chapter will take you behind the scenes of DOS. You will learn how DOS actually sets up its file system and its directory structure.

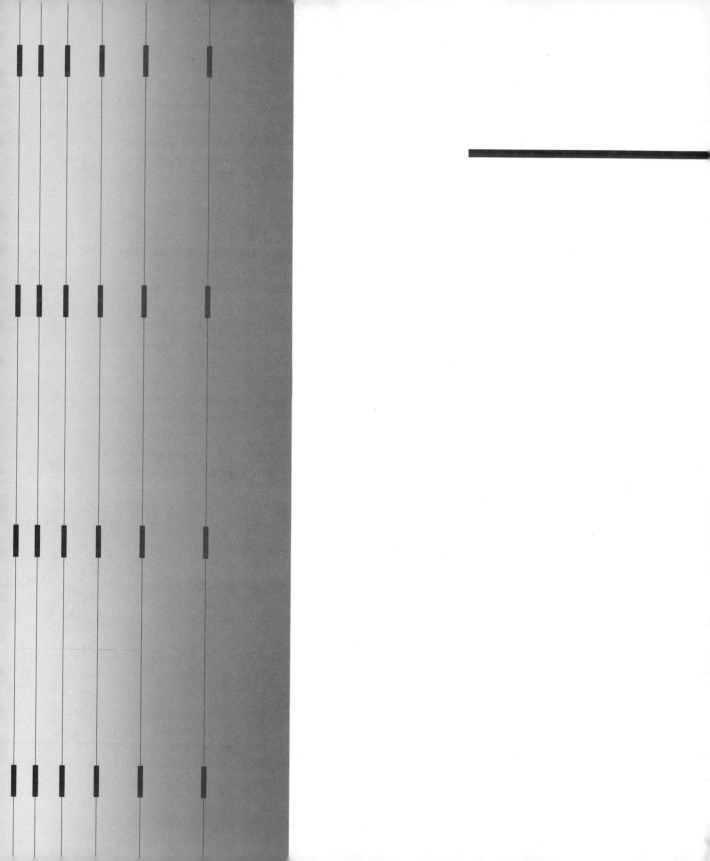

A Closer Look
at the Disk System

A CLOSER LOOK
AT THE DISK SYSTEM

The previous chapters of this book have presented all the information about the way DOS stores information on disk that you will usually need to make effective use of your computer system. Nonetheless, there may be times when you find it helpful (or simply interesting) to look behind the scenes and see how DOS handles the disk-related tasks it conceals from you so successfully.

This chapter takes a closer look at some of the disk-storage issues that were briefly introduced in the first part of this book, including the file-allocation table (FAT), tracks and sectors on both floppy and hard disks, and the history and evolution of storage devices. You'll also learn more about file management, bootstrapping, and the hidden DOS files. The chapter concludes with some practical suggestions for using the CHKDSK command, first discussed in Chapter 2, to help solve the disk problems you may encounter.

THE EVOLUTION OF STORAGE MEDIA

A brief history of the primary storage devices DOS and other systems have used may prove enlightening as a background to this discussion. Many different devices have been developed to store data.

Punched Cards

One of the first storage media was *punched cards*. Each card contained a pattern of small holes that could be interpreted as information when the cards were fed into a *card reader*, one at a time. The card reader physically scanned the holes in the card to retrieve information. Each hole (or rather, the spot where a hole could be punched) represented a bit; its punched/not-punched status was interpreted as a binary value. Often, huge stacks of these cards were required for even the simplest programs, and the reading process itself could proceed very slowly. Many mainframe installations still use punched cards today.

Cassette Tapes

When personal computers were introduced in the late 1970s, the first storage devices were inexpensive cassette tapes, which recorded a mechanical waveform of varying frequencies on the tape to represent the data. These cassette storage mechanisms were often unreliable, particularly because of wear and stretching of the tape medium itself. The tapes were also very slow; even inexpensive home computers soon switched from tape storage to disk storage.

Floppy Disks

Disk storage in the 1980s has been dominated by floppy disks. These are actually small disks made of the same material as cassette tapes. The advantage of disks lies in the speed of the rotating disk as opposed to the streaming tape and the ability of the read/write head to move radially across the disk to other tracks, instead of having to move an entire cassette tape sequentially past it to access any particular piece of information. Floppy disks are easy to store but require more careful handling than cassette tapes.

Hard Disks

To increase the speed of access, durability of the medium, and volume capacity of floppy disks, hard disks are beginning to dominate the commercial market in the late 1980s. Able to store much more data than a floppy disk, hard disks also access data much more quickly and because they are sealed, they are more durable as well. Hard disks are less subject to mechanical failure than floppy disks, but since they hold more data, they require more time to periodically back up their large volumes of data.

Microfloppy Diskettes

An interesting compromise solution to the question of disk storage is evolving in the microcomputer world. Diskettes are becoming more available, although at slightly higher cost, that store much more than a standard double-sided, double-density, 360K diskette. First the 1.2MB, high-capacity floppy became available and was the disk drive of choice on new IBM PC-AT and compatible machines. Then 3½-inch 720K microfloppy disks became standard on several microcomputers and on most laptop portables that contained disk drives of any sort.

Now 3½-inch, 1.44MB microfloppy disks are becoming the disk of choice in the newest computers. They are standard on the IBM PS/2 line of computers, and they are becoming both available and necessary on a range of laptop portables. They are essential to those computers that run IBM OS/2 or MS OS/2.

These latest successors to DOS require a large-volume floppy disk drive for program execution.

Future Developments

Still being developed, optical disks represent a way to store even greater amounts of information than currently available media. These disks work in essentially the same way as the compact laser disks that have become so popular in the audio field. They are less prone to damage because of their few moving parts. Because the information on the disk is read optically, by a laser beam, no mechanical part of the reading device comes in contact with the disk, and so it does not wear out. Optical disks are much more durable, although certain forms are subject to magnetic effects. Optical disks are still in the final development stage, and it may be a while before they are available to the average computer user.

With the increasing capacity of memory chips, it may also be possible in the future to store vast amounts of data on chips. These would be as indestructable as today's chips, but they would be subject to electrical problems. Today's chips require a constant electrical current to remain active. If that current fluctuates or stops, data can be lost. What is needed are chips that retain large amounts of data without constant application of power. In the short term, however, it is more likely that the power requirements for the newest high-density memory chips will be much lower. This may set the stage for self-contained batteries to be used to maintain a constant source of power during power loss or reduction.

A CLOSER LOOK AT FLOPPY DISKS

The most common storage medium currently is the small, floppy disk. The mid 1980s saw the 5¹/₄-inch diskette (the microcomputer version of the larger 8-inch diskette used on mainframes and minicomputers in the 1970s) popularized on IBM microcomputers and compatibles. In the late 1980s, the 3¹/₂-inch hard-shell microfloppy stepped to the fore as the floppy medium of choice on the IBM PS/2 series of computers and all the latest compatibles. Figure 21.1 presents an example of a 5¹/₄-inch floppy disk.

DOS Tracks, Sectors, and Clusters

Diskettes are coated with a magnetically sensitive material. Data is written to a disk by changing the magnetic orientations of the particles on the disk into patterns of on/off voltage states equivalent to binary values. The same disk heads that wrote this information onto the disk can later read the electromagnetic state of these same particles. This read/write disk head can translate those on/off particle (voltage) states back into digital 1's and 0's, thereby reconstructing the stored data values. Since the diskette surface itself rotates about the center hub, the data is written in circular *tracks* around the disk. Data is written onto these tracks in groups of 512 bytes (8 bits per byte) called *sectors*. These are illustrated in Figure 21.2.

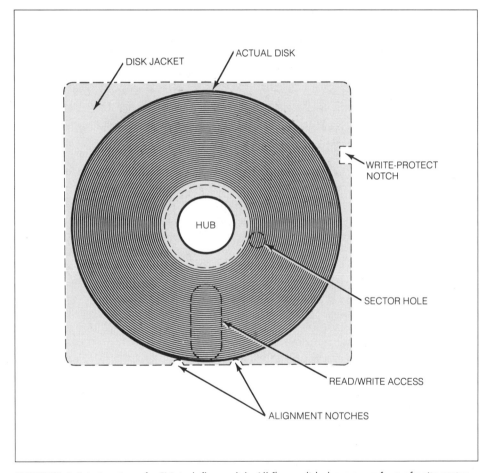

FIGURE 21.1: Exterior view of a 5¼-inch floppy disk. All floppy disks have some form of write protection capability; covering the notch at the upper right of this diskette disables the writing mechanism of the drive. Access to the magnetic surface for reading and writing is through the large oval at the bottom center of the disk. The circular hub of the diskette usually has a reinforced edge where the drive mechanism grabs hold of the diskette. Alignment is assured via the two notches at the bottom of the diskette.

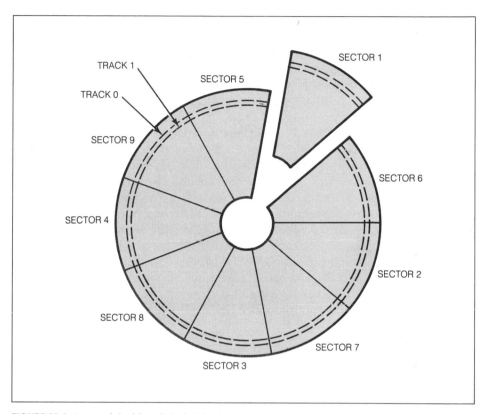

FIGURE 21.2: A typical double-sided, double-density, 360K diskette has nine sectors per track and 40 tracks (numbered 0 to 39). Notice the *interleaving;* each successive sector is not physically adjacent to the previous one, but is alternated (or interleaved). This technique improves disk performance during alternate reading and writing sequences.

Although the data is physically stored on the disk in 512-byte groups called sectors, it is actually written or read by DOS in larger groups called *clusters*. Each cluster consists of one or more sectors of data and represents a tradeoff between speed of access and overhead to manage these separate storage units. You'll learn more about clusters later in this chapter. For now, you should keep in mind that the default number of sectors per cluster varies from one (on a 1.2MB floppy disk) to two (on a typical 360K floppy disk) to four (on a 10MB IBM PC-XT), and back to two again (on a 20MB IBM PC-AT).

DOS 1.X formatted 5¼-inch diskettes with only 8 sectors on each track. In later versions starting with 2.00, DOS wrote 9 sectors on standard double-density diskettes; with version 3.0, this number increased to 15 sectors per track of a high-capacity 5¼-inch diskette and as many as 18 sectors on the tracks of a high-density 3½-inch microfloppy diskette. Each disk consists of either 40 or 80 tracks, numbered from 0 and to 39 or 79, working inward.

Double-Sided Disks and Cylinders

Double-sided disks represented a first solution to the problem of limited storage. On a single-sided disk, there was only one read/write head. This electromagnetic device is the part of the disk drive that actually comes into contact with the diskette and changes (or reads back) the magnetic orientations of the surface particles. A simple way to increase the storage capacity and apparent speed of a floppy disk is to add a second read/write head.

In a double-sided disk drive, each side of a diskette is read or written using one of the two heads. Mounting these heads on a U-shaped bracket doubles the effective storage capacity of a diskette. What had been the original side is now called *side 0*, with the new side is called *side 1*. The BIOS actually locates data on a disk by specifying its side number, as well as the track number, beginning with track 0 at the outer ring of a diskette and ending with the highest track number possible for that diskette (for example, 39 for a double-sided, double-density, 360KB disk, or 79 for a high-capacity, 1.2MB disk).

Figure 21.3 illustrates this three-dimensional view of the data on a diskette. The tracks on either side of a diskette, at the same radial position, are together known as a *cylinder*, since when viewed three-dimensionally, they have a cylindrical form.

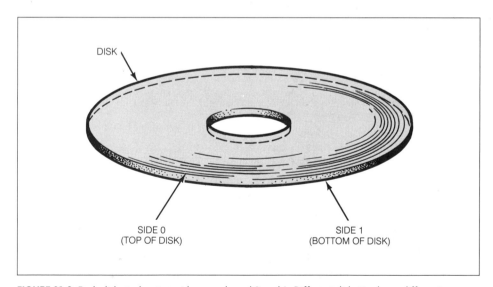

DISK

SIDE 0
(TOP OF DISK)

SIDE 1
(BOTTOM OF DISK)

FIGURE 21.3: Each diskette has two sides, numbered 0 and 1. Different diskettes have different numbers of cylindrical tracks: for example, DSDD 360K 5¼-inch diskettes have 40 tracks, and 3¼-inch diskettes contain 80 tracks. A cylinder consists of the data on both sides of a diskette at each track location.

Disk Organization

All disks are formatted into four logical areas. A *logical* area, as opposed to a *physical* area, is an abstract construct, as opposed to a physical construct. For example, the borders between states are not physical borders (for the most part) but have been agreed upon by the governing bodies in those states, so states can be said to be *logically* defined. Continents, however, are, to a greater degree, physically defined.

The four logical areas on a disk each store different types of data. DOS must make sure it does not exceed the capacity of any of those areas. The four logical areas are the *boot record*, the *data* area, the *file-allocation table*, and the *root directory*.

The *boot record* is put on every diskette, system or otherwise, because of the value of the data it contains. This area contains the basic instructions the computer needs to start, or *bootstrap*, itself.

The *data area* is the largest area on the disk. It contains the subdirectory structures and all user-created data on the disk. The next two sections discuss the file-allocation table and the root directory.

Keeping Track of Files: The File-Allocation Table

When you store data on a disk drive, how does DOS keep track of files? For instance, suppose you write a 2500-byte file to a newly formatted double-sided, double-density (DSDD) floppy disk. As you'll read about in more depth later in the section on hard disks, DOS actually reads or writes data to or from disks in groups of sectors called *clusters*. The cluster concept allows the DOS file mechanism to be treated consistently, regardless of whether a cluster contains only 1 sector or 16 sectors. A DSDD diskette has two sectors per cluster.

Assume your 2500-byte file is named FILEA. Since each cluster written by DOS contains two sectors, or 1024 bytes, the entire file requires two complete clusters and one partial cluster. Figure 21.4 depicts this allocation approach. The partial last cluster requires only 452 bytes to complete the total 2500-byte file size, leaving 572 bytes unused and therefore wasted at the end of this cluster. This space is called *slack*, and it is the primary cost of the cluster mechanism.

Nearly every file on a disk has some space wasted at the end of the last cluster. However, read and write operations are faster overall if multiple sectors can be read or written at the same time. The accepted cost for this speed is a variable amount of space lost to you at the end of each file. The smaller your files, the more clusters you will have that exhibit slack; the larger your files, the less overall slack your disks will contain.

DOS applies the cluster concept applies to viewing all the sectors on a disk. DOS treats all sectors as a one-dimensional series of numbers, beginning after the reserved *system area*. This system area consists of the first several sectors

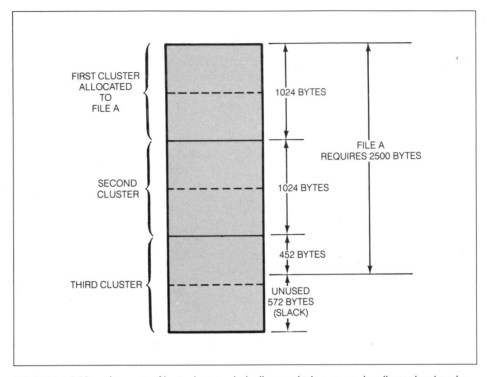

FIGURE 21.4: DOS reads or writes files in clusters, which allows multiple sectors to be allocated and read or written at one time. On a DSDD diskette, a cluster consists of two sectors. Writing the 2500-byte FILEA file requires two complete clusters and a partial third cluster. Only 452 bytes of the third cluster are really required, leaving 572 bytes of this allocated cluster unused. This wasted space is called *slack*.

located on cylinder 0 of your disk. As shown in Figure 21.5, these sectors are reserved for the boot record, two copies of the file-allocation table (discussed later), and the directory table. This area contains system information necessary for proper identification and location of all files stored on the disk.

DOS actually views the beginning of the file data area as starting with cluster 2. FILEA consumes three complete clusters (clusters 2, 3, and 4). The BIOS must see the disk from a hardware point of view; the simple, one-dimensional cluster numbering approach taken by DOS must be translated into a real, three-dimensional coordinate value that specifies the track, side, and sector location to be read or written.

In the case of FILEA, the BIOS notes that this file is written to cylinder or track 0, side 1, sectors 4 to 9. Tracks are filled sector by sector, side by side. When a track is full, the next track on that cylinder is used. When a cylinder is full, the next cylinder radially inward is used.

This method minimizes the time-consuming movement of the disk heads in and out and across different tracks during the initial writing of data. Once the

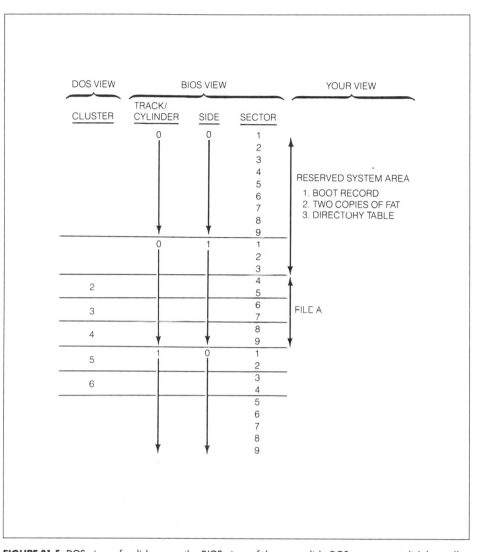

FIGURE 21.5: DOS view of a disk versus the BIOS view of the same disk. DOS manages a disk logically, viewing groups of sectors as a one dimensional column of cluster numbers. The BIOS translates these numbers into the three-dimensional coordinates necessary to identify the precise track, side, and sector at which the data is to be written or read. This figure also shows the user's view of the disk organization of the space after the system reserved area. This system area occupies a variable number of sectors at the beginning of each disk; the precise number of sectors depends on the size of the disk or partition and the cluster size in use for the disk. In this example of a double-sided, double-density diskette, 12 sectors are reserved for the boot record, the two copies of the FAT, and the directory table. FILEA is allocated three clusters (numbered by DOS as 2, 3, and 4) beginning with sector 4 on side 1 of track 0 (as seen by the BIOS).

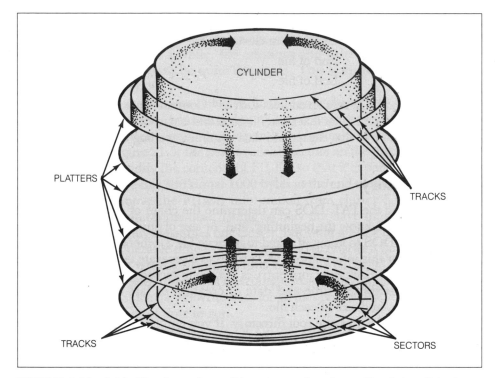

FIGURE 21.6: A hard disk differs from a floppy diskette in a number of ways. The obvious distinction, seen here, is that a diskette has only one physical magnetic platter, whereas hard disks have multiple platters, each with two addressable sides, and each using the same track and sector format as a single diskette. The heavy black vertical lines visually highlight the skeletal cylinder formed by multiple concentric tracks on several parallel platters.

must be positioned *against* the disk surface and must stay precisely *at* the surface all the time. The distance of the head from the disk surface must not vary, since the strength of the signal being written to the disk decreases drastically over short distances. The power output cannot be varied fast enough to accommodate distance changes, so the head must stay the same distance away from the surface to ensure that all data is written at the same strength. Since the head is in actual contact with the disk surface, there is much wear on the head and the disk, giving floppy disks a lifetime of about 40 hours of use and their drives a few years, under normal conditions.

In hard disks, on the other hand, the read/write head *hovers above* the disk platter by a very slight amount, an amount smaller than the height of a fingerprint, thus eliminating disk wear caused by friction. To achieve this, however, a hard disk spins at a high speed (3600 rpm); the air turbulence over the top of the disk is enough to cause a small breeze, which pushes the head very slightly away from the disk. However, if this breeze is interrupted, by a particle of dirt or smoke, for instance, the head will hit the disk surface, destroying data wherever it strikes. This failure is known as a *head crash*, and it can completely destroy a hard disk.

To make hard disks less vulnerable to their environment, they are sealed and the air in them is microfiltered to purify it. Hard disks thus are much more durable than floppy disks. In fact, unless they are sharply shaken or hit while running, hard disks are difficult to damage.

Hard disks also can store vastly more data than floppy disks, a benefit that entails a more complex file-management system.

Tracks, Sectors, and Clusters on Hard Disks

The next example assumes a hard disk with two platters. Hard disks contain more than 600 tracks per inch and, currently, 17 to 25 sectors per track. A two-platter disk holds well over 20 megabytes of data.

The cluster size of a hard disk is part of the information laid down in its boot record by the FORMAT command. Just as the cluster size of a floppy disk is determined according to its size and density, the cluster size of a hard disk is determined by its capacity. If a hard disk has multiple partitions, the cluster size of a given partition is determined by its size.

For DOS versions 3.X, the cluster size (for hard disks larger than 10 megabytes) is 2K (2,048 bytes), or 4 sectors. For earlier versions of DOS, this cluster size may be 8 or 16 sectors. The larger the cluster size, the greater potential for wasted space on your disk, since even the smallest file is allocated at least one entire cluster of space. In other words, a 250-byte file is assigned an entire cluster for storage, even if the cluster is 8 sectors, or 4096 bytes. As discussed in the section on floppy diskettes, files almost always have wasted space in the last cluster assigned to them, even if only one cluster is assigned to a small file. The other side of this coin is that access speed to files (actually, to the disk location containing the beginning of the file) is very fast. During the formatting process for any disk, DOS decides how many sectors to include in a disk's cluster. In this way, DOS strikes a balance between access speed and storage space slack.

DETERMINING YOUR CLUSTER SIZE

You can determine your hard disk's current cluster size by typing DIR from any directory, jotting down the number of bytes available, and then typing

    COPY CON: TESTFILE
    Sample data line
    ^ Z <Return>

This command creates a small file and stores it in your current directory. Now type DIR again and note the available memory. Subtract this amount from your previous amount. The resulting value is the number of bytes in each cluster on your disk. Divide by 512 to determine how many sectors are in each cluster. This method of calculation works because DOS must allocate an entire cluster to your minimal file, since a cluster is the smallest unit of space DOS recognizes. An example follows.

You can always enter DIR to obtain a current directory listing. The last line of that listing indicates how much total disk space remains free for additional files. For instance, you enter

DIR

to obtain a directory listing whose last line is

17 File(s) 3325952 bytes free

You can then create a small test file at the command line by using the COPY command. Enter

COPY CON: TESTFILE
Simple Sample Stuff ^ Z < Return >

DOS will respond with

1 File(s) copied

If you then enter a request for an updated directory listing, such as

DIR

DOS will display information about all the files in the directory. This will include all the file information discussed so far as well as information about the new file you just created. The last two lines of this listing will display the information about this new file and about the available disk space:

TESTFILE 19 8-14-88 11:02a
18 File(s) 3323904 bytes free

At this point, you can delete the test file by entering

ERASE TESTFILE

and then perform some calculations to determine your disk's cluster size. To find the number of bytes per cluster, perform the following calculation:

$$
\begin{array}{r}
3{,}325{,}952 \\
-\ 3{,}323{,}904 \\
\hline
2{,}048 \text{ bytes per cluster}
\end{array}
$$

To find the number of sectors per cluster, calculate

$2{,}048/512 = 4$ sectors per cluster

DISK OPERATIONS

Now that you've seen how space is maintained on a disk, take a closer look at how DOS manages this space and the files stored on it. In this section, you'll explore the basic input/output system (BIOS) of the computer, the bootstrapping procedure, and the hidden DOS files that manage your system.

File Management

Each entry in the FAT can contain one of four values. Remember that the FAT is indexed by clusters. These four values correspond to whether the given cluster is available, in use (in this case, the value points to next cluster), bad, or the last cluster in a file.

Like the FAT, the first byte of a file name stored in the directory can have four different values, as shown in Table 21.1. As you can see, for instance, the first byte of the name of a deleted file is the Greek symbol sigma (ASCII 229 decimal); when you delete a file, a sigma replaces the first byte of the file name in the directory, and the FAT entries are marked "available." However, the actual data is still on the disk. Thus, when you invoke a deletion recovery program (see the Norton Utilities in Chapter 20), that recovery program can search the disk directory cluster by cluster for files whose names begin with sigma, and then use the FAT to reconstruct the file chain and the file.

FIRST BYTE	DESCRIPTION
Letter	First letter of file name
0	Empty directory entry
.	Hierarchical structure entry for DOS
ς	Deleted file

TABLE 21.1: Values for First Byte of File Names Stored in the Directory

Basic Input/Output System

The computer works on many different levels. The level you work with, the DOS command level, is the highest of these. The next level is the interpretation level, followed by the translation level, the actuation level, and, finally, the physical level. These levels are diagrammed in Figure 21.7 and explained here.

The *DOS command level* is the most recognizable level. It is the interface between the operating system and the user. This is the level at which you issue commands and the computer outputs the results of computer- or user-initiated operations.

The *interpretation level* is the first internal level. This is the level at which DOS examines your commands to make sure they are valid. If a command is invalid, for instance, if you specify an invalid file name, DOS returns an error message.

The interpretation level passes the command on to the *translation level*. Here the command is put into the binary format that the computer can handle.

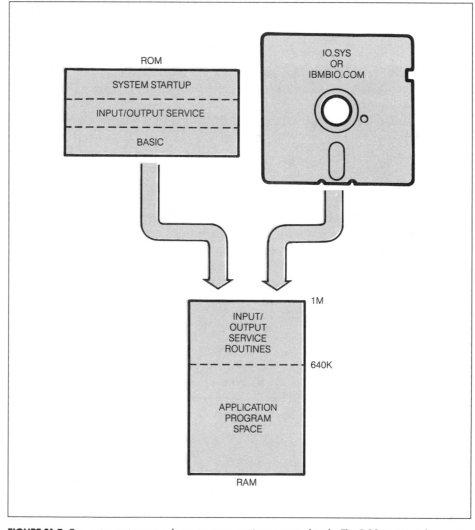

FIGURE 21.7: Computer systems can be seen as operating at many levels. The DOS command prompt is the primary level that users see. One level down is the DOS code itself that interprets your command requests, ensuring that they are correctly constructed. Next, valid requests are translated into binary machine commands. These machine requests are then executed to activate the required system tasks. These tasks are actually implemented at the physical level of voltages and electronic circuits.

The *actuation level* is the level at which translated commands are examined and executed.

The *physical level* is where commands actually work. This is the level where voltages actually course through the electronic circuits on their way to fulfilling their tasks.

Thus, the computer works on several levels at once, and each level interacts with those above and below it. DOS inhabits the command, interpretation, and translation levels. The *basic input/output system (BIOS)* inhabits the physical level.

The BIOS (pronounced *bye-oss*) is encoded on read-only, permanently programmed chips; you cannot change this programming. These chips are formally referred to as read-only memory, or ROM, as opposed to random-access memory, where stored information can be rewritten any number of times. Also note that not all of the basic input/output functions of DOS are resident in this hardware BIOS, which varies from computer manufacturer to computer manufacturer. The DOS system file IO.SYS (in MS-DOS systems) or IBMBIO.COM (in PC DOS systems) is also responsible for some of the generalized tasks of peripheral input and output control.

The BIOS is *hardware bound*, meaning that it is programmed with a certain system configuration in mind. BIOS is hardware bound because it uses routines that have been programmed into the specific chips and stored in certain areas of those chips. For example, your computer's BIOS might use a routine, programmed a certain way to control screen output. On another computer, this routine may be located at a different physical address, so your computer's BIOS would not work in this machine.

The BIOS controls the most fundamental input and output procedures in a computer. It contains a series of specific I/O routines unique to each system configuration. Together with the routines in IO.SYS or IBMBIO.COM, DOS builds the RAM-resident code for managing system I/O operations. Figure 21.8 shows how this merger takes place during bootstrapping to create actual code for use in DOS operations. This code is placed in the reserved area above the 640K program maximum and below the 1MB maximum DOS addressibility.

DOS is a manager much as BIOS is. However, DOS is not as hardware-specific as BIOS. DOS can work on many computers, each using a different BIOS as the interface between DOS and the physical machine. DOS is therefore the interface between the user and BIOS. How a BIOS actually performs or controls a physical function in the computer is what makes BIOS hardware specific. But the chores each BIOS performs are common across machines.

You use DOS instead of directly accessing your computer's BIOS because doing so allows you to move your applications from computer to computer; each machine's BIOS handles the basic hardware functions specific to the computer.

Part of your computer's memory-resident BIOS is sometimes referred to as ROM BIOS. If a computer has some device attached, such as an enhanced graphics adaptor, the adaptor's own ROM BIOS will supplement, or sometimes

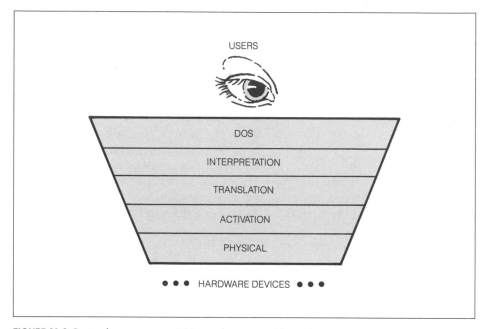

FIGURE 21.8: During bootstrapping, DOS uses the ROM-resident startup routines to merge input/output logic from ROM locations with additional input/output routines in the IO.SYS (for MS-DOS) or IBM-BIO.COM (for PC-DOS) files. The actual code that will control hardware input/output is placed into RAM at reserved locations above 640KB (the maximum program space) and below 1MB (the maximum DOS address).

even supplant (depending on the board), the individual machine's ROM BIOS.

The BIOS can be accessed directly by an applications programmer, which provides great flexibility and speed in the execution of programs, since the DOS intermediary is removed. Compatibility problems occur, however, when you try to run a program that does not send its requests through DOS, but rather goes directly to the BIOS, on different machines.

Bootstrapping the Computer

The ROM BIOS of your computer maintains a special set of permanent (ROM) instructions. After you successfully start the computer, it follows its pre-programmed instructions and goes to the first sector of the disk, where a short routine called the *boot record* is located. This routine provides the instructions for the computer to start—in effect, to pull itself up by its bootstraps.

When the boot record is loaded into memory, the instructions in this record assume control of the computer. The bootstrap code next loads and activates the

BIOS software (IO.SYS or IBMBIO.COM) and the file manager (MSDOS-.SYS or IBMDOS.COM). The bootstrap code then runs and transfers full system control to the COMMAND.COM file, which is the command interface between you and the computer.

The computer is booted using a cold start or a warm start. A cold start occurs when the computer is first turned on, or turned off and then on, and must go through a complete systems check. The term *cold* is used because the computer must warm up to work. A warm start occurs when the computer is rebooted while it is on—for instance, when a program reboots the computer, or when you press Ctrl-Alt-Del simultaneously. The term *warm* is used because the computer is already warmed up and does not have to perform a complete systems check before it starts work. Specifically, a warm boot bypasses the time-consuming memory tests.

Hidden Files: Working behind the Scenes

DOS contains several *hidden files*, files invisible to directory-oriented commands, that influence and control the system. These files are essential to DOS. They are hidden because you should not need to see or work with them, and they are too critical to open them to the risk of damage. You can see how many hidden files there are on your disk and how much space they consume by executing a CHKDSK command. At a minimum, DOS has two hidden files: IBMBIO.COM (or IO.SYS) and IBMDOS.COM (or MSDOS.SYS).

THE HIDDEN BIOS SOFTWARE

Part of the BIOS software is usually contained in a hidden file named IBM-BIO.COM (in PC-DOS) or IO.SYS (in MS-DOS). This program translates between DOS and the physical system. If a ROM BIOS is present, then this file supplants it and is the control program between DOS and the drive's BIOS system. This file contains the drivers necessary to manage all physical devices, such as the ones connected to the various ports (see Chapter 13).

THE DOS KERNEL

Another hidden file, IBMDOS.COM (in PC-DOS) or MSDOS.SYS (in MS-DOS), contains the program that actually sets up DOS's buffers and other file-management utilities. This file contains the procedures for executing other MS-DOS commands as well. This file also contains the DOS *kernel*, which is the part of DOS that handles functions needed by applications programs. The kernel performs the actual work of file, record, and memory management and character input and output; it also accesses the real-time clock.

THE COMMAND PROCESSOR

The command processor manages your work at the keyboard. It translates between you and DOS. The file COMMAND.COM, which is *not* a hidden file, contains the command processor. This file includes procedures for accomplishing tasks, and indicates where in MSDOS.SYS (or IBMDOS.COM) these procedures are executed. This file contains the procedures for resident commands, such as COPY, DELETE, RENAME, and TYPE.

You can, if you must, change the names of the commands in the COMMAND.COM file. For example, using the DEBUG program, you can change the name of the TYPE command to TAPE. Now when you execute TYPE, you will get an error message; you must enter TAPE instead. COMMAND.COM contains a table indicating the name and syntax of each command and the command procedure, or where to go to get the command procedure. If you change the name of a command in this table, DOS uses that new name. Thus, you can, for example, remove the name DELETE from DOS's vocabulary or rename the currently allowable commands to provide some protection against their misuse or abuse.

COMMAND.COM is composed of three parts: a resident part, an initialization part, and a transient part. The resident part of COMMAND.COM is loaded into memory after the DOS kernel and all of its memory allocations. It processes Ctrl-Break keystrokes and Ctrl-C errors and manages the memory assignments for transient programs. The resident part of COMMAND.COM is the culprit responsible for the familiar "Abort, Retry, Ignore?" message. It is also responsible for reloading the transient part of COMMAND.COM.

System startup brings the initialization part of COMMAND.COM into memory. This part has the single purpose of activating and executing the commands in your AUTOEXEC.BAT file.

The transient part of COMMAND.COM, which can be overwritten by other programs since it resides in high memory, is responsible for the command prompt and for reading and executing user commands. Sometimes when you finish working with a program you will see the drive light come on before you see the prompt. This occurs because part of the program you were using overwrote the memory where the transient part of COMMAND.COM resided. The resident part saw this and reloaded the transient part so that you could again use your complete DOS system.

How COMMAND.COM Works

COMMAND.COM processes the commands that you give the system. Some of them can be handled simply, and others require much complex logic for processing. The more complex commands are included as separate command procedures executed as .COM or .EXE files (these are the *external commands*), and the simpler commands are included in the logic of the COMMAND.COM program itself (these are the *internal commands*). COMMAND.COM also processes batch files (see Chapters 7 through 9). To execute a command, whether it be internal (defined in COMMAND.COM) or external (defined in a separate command procedure file), COMMAND.COM must follow a standard search routine.

First COMMAND.COM must determine whether the command is internal. If the command is not internal, COMMAND.COM looks at external disk-resident files. If the command still cannot be located, DOS generates an error message. The search starts in the current directory and works its way along the path. COMMAND.COM tests files by matching the eight-character file name first with .COM files, then with .EXE files, and finally with .BAT files. The error generated will read

Bad command or file name

When COMMAND.COM finds the requested .COM or .EXE file, it calls up the EXEC command to execute the instructions in the .COM or .EXE file. Memory space above the resident part of DOS is used to load the new command procedure (program or command), and control is transferred to the new procedure. When the procedure has finished executing, control is transferred back to the program that called it in the first place—namely, COMMAND.COM. The resident part then checks whether the transient part of COMMAND.COM was overwritten by the new program; if it was, the resident part will reload the transient part, if necessary.

SOLVING DISK PROBLEMS

As you've seen throughout this chapter, the system DOS uses for storing information on disk is logically complex and physically dependent on delicate electronic devices. Although the system works remarkably well, almost every DOS user eventually encounters a disk error message. As discussed under the individual messages in Appendix B, when you see one of these messages, you can either turn to one of the utility packages described in Chapter 20, such as The Norton Utilities, or use the limited correction facilities that DOS provides through the CHKDSK command.

Finding and Correcting Problems with CHKDSK

CHKDSK was introduced in Chapter 2. Briefly, it provides various information about disk and internal memory use and can, with its /F switch, fix some of the disk problems it discovers. In the context of this chapter, it's worth considering how you can use CHKDSK both in diagnosing and in correcting disk errors.

Diagnosing Disk Errors

Three items that may appear on the CHKDSK display are potentially helpful in pinpointing disk errors. Whenever CHKDSK finds sectors that have been blocked off from use because of some defect detected by the computer, it reports the number of bytes in bad sectors. When you enter CHKDSK with a wildcard parameter:

CHKDSK *.*

asking DOS to check all the files on the disk, the screen will report any FAT errors discovered, as well as the number of noncontiguous blocks.

To correct file-allocation errors, you can use the CHKDSK /F command, as discussed in the following section; and to optimize file storage on a badly fragmented disk (that is, one with many noncontiguous clusters), you can use a utility program such as VOPT, discussed in Chapter 20. Moreover, the Norton Utilities contains a Disk Test program, DT.EXE, which identifies and marks bad disk sectors to ensure that no future sector allocation will make those bad sectors available to a requesting program.

Correcting Disk Errors

If cluster chains in the FAT somehow become disrupted, causing lost files, and /F was specified, CHKDSK will recall these files and rename them in the form FILE*nnnn*.CHK, where *nnnn* is a sequential numbering of the recovered files. These recovered file fragments will be placed in the root directory; you must examine each of them to determine which files they were. Frequently, lost files are the result of running a program that keeps a file open during execution and then turning off the computer without properly exiting the program. Usually, you can't do much with these files other than delete them, thereby recapturing the disk space they consume. CHKDSK will tell you the total number of lost clusters it finds and the total space recovered. Occasionally, you can use your word processor with a recovered file and save reentering all of the data you otherwise would lose.

The CHKDSK /F approach merely reclaims space on your disk and occasionally allows you to reclaim some ASCII file information. You can do this by using your word processor to edit the specially created *FILEnnnn* files. At other times, CHKDSK's /F option will not recover files. Your only remaining DOS option is the RECOVER command, discussed in Chapter 19.

Recovering Deleted Files with the Norton Utilities

A more powerful, though more difficult to use, recovery procedure is available through another of the Norton Utilities, the NU.EXE program.

You can run the NU program by selecting its name from the Norton Integrator menu. Highlighting NU on the menu results in the display shown at the right side of Figure 21.9.

```
                    ┌─ The Norton Integrator ─┐
 ASK
 BEEP
 DS  Directory Sort    Norton Utility        NU [filespec][switches]
 DT  Disk Test           View and edit any disk area, use powerful data-
 FA  File Attributes     recovery tools to UnErase deleted files,
 FF  File Find           recover lost data, and repair damaged disks.
 FI  File Info
 FR  Format Recover    NU exam.me
 FS  File Size           Run NU, with "exam.me" opened for editing.
 LD  List Directories
 LP  Line Print        Switches
 NCD Norton CD           /D0   Default screen driver, for 100% compatibles
 NU  Norton Utility      /D1   Screen driver for BIOS-compatible machines
 QU  Quick UnErase       /D2   Ansi.sys screen driver for non-compatibles
 SA  Screen Attributes   /Bn   Set Background color; n=0 to 15
 SD  Speed Disk          /Fn   Set foreground color; n=0 to 15
 SI  System Information  /BW   Use with monochome monitor on a CGA card
 TM  Time Mark           /EBCDIC Use EBCDIC character encoding
 TS  Text Search         /EXT  Display EXTended characters (above 127)
 UD  UnRemove Directory  /TV   For TopView, Windows and other environments
              more...    /M    Maintenance--bypasses logical sectors (AE)
                         /P    Display printables only; suppress graphics
 NU
                                              Press F1 for Help
```

FIGURE 21.9: Using the Norton Integrator menu is the easiest way to select any of the powerful utilities in this package. The most powerful utility is NU, which lets you restore deleted files and recover all or most of the data within the files, even if portions of the sector storage space have already been reused by DOS. In maintenance mode (/M), you can even modify physical disk sectors without passing through DOS's file management logic.

You can then enter the exact form of the command you want to use, or simply press Return, which results in the main NU menu screen shown in Figure 21.10. Through this menu, you can explore various aspects of your disks or go directly into unerase mode.

Selecting UnErase on the main NU menu lets you select the drive or directory containing the erased file and then actually select which file to reconstruct. This screen appears in Figure 21.11.

```
┌─────────────────────────────────────────────────────────────────────┐
│  │
│  ┌──────────────────────────────────────────────────────────────┐  │
│  │   The Norton Utilities  Advanced Edition  (C) Copr 1987, Peter Norton │
│  │         10:04 am, Sunday, March 6, 1988                       │  │
│  │ ┌────────────────────────────────────────────────────────┐   │  │
│  │ │                    ▒▒Main menu▒▒                        │   │  │
│  │ │                                                         │   │  │
│  │ │                  Explore disk                           │   │  │
│  │ │                 ▒▒UnErase▒▒▒▒▒▒▒▒▒▒▒▒▒▒▒▒               │   │  │
│  │ │                  Disk information                       │   │  │
│  │ │                  Quit the Norton Utilities              │   │  │
│  │ │                                                         │   │  │
│  │ │              UnErase a deleted or erased file           │   │  │
│  │ └────────────────────────────────────────────────────────┘   │  │
│  │ ┌─────────┬──────┬──────────────────────────┬────────────┐   │  │
│  │ │Item type│Drive │Directory name            │File name   │   │  │
│  │ │Directory│ D:   │\UTILITY\NORTADV          │Dir area    │   │  │
│  │ └─────────┴──────┴──────────────────────────┴────────────┘   │  │
│  └──────────────────────────────────────────────────────────────┘  │
└─────────────────────────────────────────────────────────────────────┘
```

FIGURE 21.10: NU displays its main menu screen. Although you can explore information about any of your system's disk drives, the unerase mode is popular for recovering files that have been erased and that may have some of their sectors reused by the operating system.

```
┌─────────────────────────────────────────────────────────────────────┐
│  │
│  ┌──────────────────────────────────────────────────────────────┐  │
│  │ Menu 2.1                                                       │  │
│  │              ▒▒Change drive or directory▒▒                     │  │
│  │                                                                │  │
│  │                                                                │  │
│  │                Change drive                                    │  │
│  │               ▒▒change Directory▒▒▒▒▒▒▒▒                       │  │
│  │                Return to Recover erased file                   │  │
│  │                                                                │  │
│  │              Change current directory                          │  │
│  │                                                                │  │
│  │                                                                │  │
│  │ ┌─────────┬──────┬──────────────────────────┬────────────┐   │  │
│  │ │Item type│Drive │Directory name            │File name   │   │  │
│  │ │Directory│ D:   │\UTILITY\NORTADV          │Dir area    │   │  │
│  │ └─────────┴──────┴──────────────────────────┴────────────┘   │  │
│  └──────────────────────────────────────────────────────────────┘  │
└─────────────────────────────────────────────────────────────────────┘
```

FIGURE 21.11: The menu screen used by Norton's NU program to change the specified drive or directory containing the proposed file to be restored. After specifying the drive or directory name, you can specify a list of possible file names to unerase by selecting the last choice on the menu.

Requesting the Change Directory choice displays a visual directory map, as shown in Figure 21.12. You merely need to use the cursor keys to select one of the directories displayed and even to scroll beyond the display to see and select other directories on the disk. In this example, the PALANTIR directory is selected; it is located on drive D, in the \PROGRAMS\WORDPROC directory.

You then select a file name to be recovered from the subsequent listing, shown in Figure 21.13. This directory contains only one file that has been deleted and therefore is a candidate for restoration.

The first question asked by NU after a file is selected for unerasure is the character to be used in place of the question mark (?) displayed to indicate a deleted file name. Entering the letter *j*, for example, displays the next screen in this recovery process, shown in Figure 21.14.

This recovery menu displays all of the principal choices you now have for reconstructing your file. You can leave recovery processing to Norton's automatic algorithm, or you can look at individual sectors and clusters in order to select the data for your reconstructed file. You can even ask NU to search the entire disk for uniquely specified character strings as an aid to locating the sectors to be included in the reconstructed file.

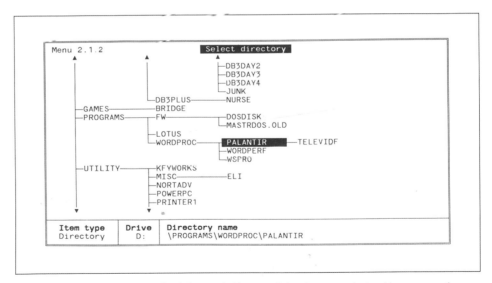

FIGURE 21.12: The visual map of a disk provided by NU's Select Directory choice. You may use the cursor keys to scroll around the map and to select the target directory that is to contain the files to be restored.

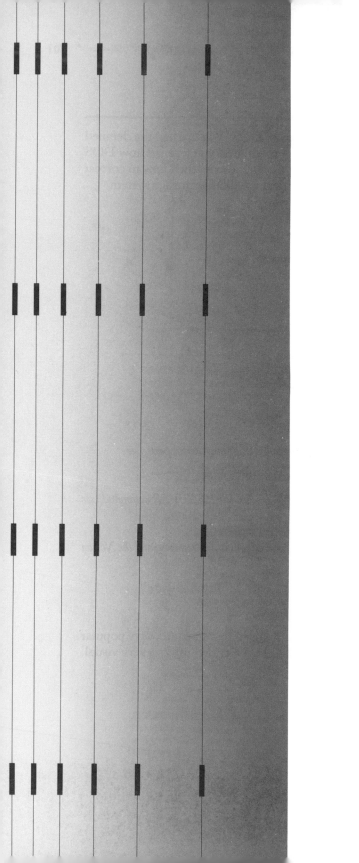

WINDOWS AND DOS

WINDOWS AND DOS

Microsoft Windows offers a graphics- or object-oriented interface to a multitasking DOS operating environment on IBM and compatible personal computers. The Windows operating environment provides an additional layer of control between DOS and applications software to allow you to use your computer's capacity more fully.

Although Windows may appear to be primarily a graphics-interface extension of DOS, it is in fact an enhanced operating environment that permits multitasking and data transfer operations that are difficult to perform under DOS alone.

INTRODUCTION TO WINDOWS

This chapter describes the operation of Windows and some of its utility programs. These programs are all designed specifically to operate under and interface with the Windows environment; they cannot run without Windows. As the number of personal computer systems running Windows grows, more commercial software packages are being introduced, redesigned, or upgraded to operate under or interface with this environment.

Two principal characteristics distinguish the Windows operating environment from the more recognizable command-line orientation of DOS. First, it is a completely new visual interface for users. Your connection to the computer and its operations no longer requires carefully constructed command requests. Instead, the interface consists of full screen displays controlled by a pointing device, typically a mouse. The mouse controls the location of the screen cursor, and therefore the selection of various operations, applications, and DOS commands. All programs and commands are selectable by the mouse, so you are no longer forced to learn and remember the commands. When a selection requires more information, such as additional parameters on a DOS command, Windows prompts you for the additional information in what is called a dialog box (a small screen window).

The second distinguishing feature of the Windows environment is *multitasking*. In DOS, you can only run one program at a time. In Windows, multiple programs can run simultaneously. Windows can manage the sharing of the CPU time cycles in a manner similar to the way DOS can enable print spooling to proceed concurrently with a main foreground program. All programs installed under Windows are able to proceed, sharing the CPU under the supervision of the main Windows software.

In fact, Windows itself is simply a program that runs under DOS. Its role, then, is to present a user interface that is easier both to use and to understand, as well as to manage the concurrent running of several programs designed to run under the Windows environment. Unlike a true multitasking environment such as OS/2, which provides its multiprocessing features to all programs running on your computer, Windows provides multitasking ability only to those programs installed within it.

Furthermore, Windows is limited by the standard DOS restrictions (like 640KB of memory), and so must multitask its programs within that restrictive memory span. A true multitasking operating system like OS/2 can directly use and allocate much more memory (up to 16MB) to the various programs sharing both the CPU and the available memory.

> *Note:* This chapter discusses the features of Windows version 2 and does not attempt to describe all the differences between versions 1 and 2. If you have the option of purchasing one version or the other, you will probably find the later version easier to use.

Windows and DOS

Most software packages currently available are designed to run under DOS as stand-alone applications. Most such applications can run under the Windows operating environment, but they generally can make no use of the graphics interface or multitasking capacities of Windows. The primary benefit to be derived from running standard DOS applications under Windows is that you can load and run several of these applications at the same time. Once multiple applications are loaded, you can switch from one to another without first exiting the current application. In addition to reducing the amount of time required to load individual software packages, Windows lets you transfer data between various applications.

Running DOS Programs under Windows

Although you can load and run several programs simultaneously under the Windows environment, you can directly access only one of these programs, the *active* program or window, at any one time. The program in the active window operates in much the same way as any program running under standard DOS. Programs designed to run under Windows continue to run even when they are not in the active window. Standard DOS programs, on the other hand, run only when they are in the active window. When another window is active, these programs suspend execution.

There are two principal ways to switch between different windows, using the keyboard or the mouse. You may press the Alt-Esc key combination one or more times; pressing Alt-Esc switches windows successively. Depending upon how many windows you have, you will activate one after the other, stopping when you have reached the desired one. Alternatively, if your system has a mouse, you can simply move the cursor to any point within the desired window, then click the mouse.

If the desired window is currently represented as a small symbol at the bottom of your screen (an *icon*—see below), you may select it with the mouse, then select either the Restore or Maximize options from the pop-up dialog box that will appear. Windows will then either restore the window to its original size or enlarge it to fill the screen.

Multitasking under Windows

Windows allows software increased hardware independence and provides users an intuitive graphic interface to DOS. Windows also lets both users and programs more fully utilize the processing capacity of personal computers. The original concept of personal computers—"One user, one machine, one program"—gradually evolved to "One user, one machine, several RAM-resident utilities, one main program." Windows extends this concept the next logical step: to "One user, one machine, many programs."

As noted above, multitasking works by sharing the CPU among various programs. It is a form of time sharing. Since the CPU performs its tasks much faster than most peripheral devices (like printers) and certainly much faster than most users can type, there is always time to spare from the processing chip's point of view.

These spare time cycles can be used by other programs, rather than have everything grind to a halt while one program waits for a user to press Return, or a printer to complete a slow I/O operation. This rapid switching from one program to another creates the *appearance* of multiple programs actually running simultaneously. This is not the real case, since there is only one CPU, and it can at any given moment service only one program. But the rapid context switching creates what is commonly called a multitasking or multiprocessing environment.

Hardware Requirements of Windows

Version 1.0 of Windows runs on any IBM PC, XT, AT, 386, PS/2, or compatible computer equipped with at least 320KB of RAM, two 360KB disk drives, and a CGA graphics display. Version 2.0 requires at least one 1.2MB disk drive.

Running Windows on just these minimal configurations, however, is only minimally productive as the environment requires considerable disk activity and CPU processing. In part because of this overhead, a realistic minimum configuration is a PC-AT or compatible computer with 640KB of RAM, a 20MB hard disk, an EGA graphics display, and a mouse pointing device. Windows can also use extended memory (see Appendix G) to increase operating speed.

INSTALLING WINDOWS

The Windows operating environment and its associated utilities and programs require a significant amount of disk storage space. Version 2.0 is delivered on nine 360KB disks. Before you can run Windows on your personal computer, you must install it for your specific hardware configuration.

Installing Windows on your computer is extremely easy. However, be sure *not* to use the DOS command APPEND prior to running the Windows setup procedure; you should temporarily remove this command from use before taking the steps described here.

Regardless of whether you are installing Windows on a dual-diskette or a hard disk system, the simple instructions begin the same way. Place the Setup diskette into drive A and enter

A:
SETUP

Microsoft's initialization program takes over, as Figure 22.1 shows, and prompts you for information regarding your particular hardware configuration. This first screen illustrates the type of information you must have to continue with the Windows installation. You must, for example, know enough about your system to tell Setup what kind of mouse, monitor, and printer you are using, and the port to which your printer is connected.

You can run Windows from floppy diskettes, although the program works very slowly under such a setup. The following example of an installation sequence assumes that you are using a hard disk, choice H in Figure 22.2. Choice H is the default selection.

A typical Windows installation creates a directory for the Windows files. As Figure 22.3 shows, the default directory is called WINDOWS, although you can change this name before Windows actually creates and uses that directory on your system.

Although the Windows SETUP program supports primarily IBM, AT&T, and Tandy computers (see Figure 22.4), in fact, it supports literally hundreds of compatibles as well. You need only select which class of computer you are using.

```
SETUP PROGRAM for Microsoft Windows Version 2

Setup prepares Windows to run on your computer.

To run Setup you need to know the following:

    *  what kind of pointing device (mouse) you have, if any
    *  what kind of graphics adapter (display) you have
    *  what kind of printer(s) you have, if any
    *  which port your printer is connected to

To set up Windows properly, you should complete the Setup program.
You can leave the Setup process by pressing CONTROL+X (press and hold
the CONTROL key, and press the X key). Please keep in mind that Setup will
not be completed and Windows will not be installed on your computer.

     ┌──────────────────────────────────────────────────────┐
     │ WHEN YOU'RE READY TO                           PRESS  │
     ├──────────────────────────────────────────────────────┤
     │ Continue Setup                                 ENTER  │
     │ Exit without completing Setup              CONTROL+X  │
     └──────────────────────────────────────────────────────┘
```

FIGURE 22.1: Initial Windows Setup screen. You are prompted for information regarding your individual hardware configuration. You must answer the questions displayed here during your actual installation of Windows. Press Ctrl-X to exit from the setup process to determine the answers before continuing, or press Return to continue setting up your system.

```
You can set up Windows to run from floppy disks or from your hard disk.
Please indicate what kind of disks you want.

     ┌──────────────────────────────────────────────────────┐
     │ WHEN YOU'RE READY TO                           PRESS  │
     ├──────────────────────────────────────────────────────┤
     │ Install on 1 high capacity disk (1.2MB or more)   1  │
     │ Install on 2 5.25" disks (360KB)                  2  │
     │ Install on 2 3.5" disks (720KB)                   3  │
     │ Install on a hard disk                          [H]  │
     ├──────────────────────────────────────────────────────┤
     │ Exit without completing Setup              CONTROL+X  │
     └──────────────────────────────────────────────────────┘
```

FIGURE 22.2: Windows disk installation choices. You can install and run the Windows environment from any of the three diskette combinations listed here or from a hard disk. The hard disk option, H, is highlighted as the default choice.

```
Windows will now be set up on your hard disk in the directory shown
below.

  - If you want to use a different directory and/or drive, use the
    BACKSPACE key to delete the name shown, then type the correct name.

C:\WINDOWS
```

```
WHEN YOU'RE READY TO                              PRESS

Continue Setup                                    ENTER
Exit without completing Setup                     CONTROL+X
```

FIGURE 22.3: Windows creates a directory to store all of its support files. Although most systems accept the default name, WINDOWS, you can change that name here before Windows actually makes the directory and copies the files from your Windows diskettes into it.

```
Below is a list of computers on which you may set up Windows.

  - Use the DIRECTION (↑,↓) keys to move the highlight to your selection.

IBM PC, XT, AT (or 100% compatible)
IBM Personal System/2 Model 25 or 30
IBM Personal System/2 Model 50, 60, or 80
AT&T Personal Computer
Tandy 1000
```

```
WHEN YOU'RE READY TO                              PRESS

Confirm your choice                               ENTER
Exit without completing Setup                     CONTROL+X
```

FIGURE 22.4: Computers supported by Windows. Select your computer's class and then press the Return key. If your computer is not one of the listed IBM, AT&T, or Tandy computers, the compatibility of your system will now be tested.

Once you have identified the general class of your computer, you must specify which of many different display adapters your system uses. Windows supports all of the standard CGA, EGA, and VGA adapters, as well as a host of other popular alternatives, as shown in Figure 22.5.

DOS recognizes many different international keyboards. Chapter 11 discussed the steps required to prepare your DOS for using a different keyboard. You must tell Windows which keyboard layout your system uses. Figure 22.6 lists the choices currently available from Windows.

Although you can operate Windows without a pointing device, you really shouldn't. The program is designed for use with a mouse, or at least with some form of pointing device such as a trackball or joystick. Figure 22.7 shows the choices available to you during Windows installation.

After you have responded to the various setup screens (Figures 22.1 to 22.7), Setup displays a summary of the key information it gathered from you (see Figure 22.8) and prompts you for confirmation. Press Return if the information is accurate or select any of the answers for correction; Windows will return to the appropriate screen to let you modify your earlier answer.

When you have confirmed your answers, Setup loads several programs (KERNEL.EXE, USER.EXE, MSDOS.EXE, and MSDOSD.EXE). Setup also copies from the Setup diskette to your hard disk a number of necessary files and then prompts you to insert your other Windows diskettes in succession. Figure 22.9 shows the first of several prompt screens.

```
  Please select your display adapter from the following list.

   - Use the DIRECTION (↑,↓) keys to move the highlight to your selection.

  IBM (or 100% compatible) EGA (> 64K) with Enhanced Color Display
  IBM (or 100% compatible) CGA (Color/Graphics Adapter)
  IBM EGA with High-Resolution Monochrome Display
  IBM EGA with Enhanced Color Display (black and white)
  IBM EGA with Enhanced Color Display or PC Color Display (color)
  IBM MCGA (Multi-Color Graphics Array)
  IBM (or 100% compatible) VGA (Video Graphics Array)
  Hercules Adapter with High-Resolution Monochrome Display
  AT&T Color DEB (Display Enhancement Board)
  AT&T Monochrome (Indigenous Display Board)
  Compaq Portable Plasma
  Tandy 1000 Color
  Other (requires disk provided by a hardware manufacturer)


        ┌──────────────────────────────────────────────────────┐
        │ WHEN YOU'RE READY TO                          PRESS   │
        ├──────────────────────────────────────────────────────┤
        │ Confirm your choice                           ENTER  │
        │ Exit without completing Setup             CONTROL+X  │
        └──────────────────────────────────────────────────────┘
```

FIGURE 22.5: Windows display adapter options. Use the cursor keys to highlight the display adapter installed on your computer and then press Return. As is true during the entire setup operation, you can abort the process by typing Ctrl-X.

```
Please select your keyboard from the following list.

  - Use the DIRECTION (↑,↓) keys to move the highlight to your selection.

US keyboard
AT&T keyboard
Tandy 1000 keyboard
British keyboard
Dutch keyboard
French keyboard
German keyboard
Italian keyboard
Spanish National keyboard
Swedish/Finnish keyboard
Other (requires disk provided by a hardware manufacturer)



      ┌──────────────────────────────────────────────────────┐
      │ WHEN YOU'RE READY TO                           PRESS  │
      ├──────────────────────────────────────────────────────┤
      │ Confirm your choice                            ENTER  │
      │ Exit without completing Setup              CONTROL+X  │
      └──────────────────────────────────────────────────────┘
```

FIGURE 22.6: Keyboard layouts known to Windows. The default U.S. keyboard is highlighted, but you can use the cursor keys to select one of the other layouts.

```
Please select your pointing device from the following list.

  - Use the DIRECTION (↑,↓) keys to move the highlight to your selection.

Microsoft Mouse (Bus or Serial)
No mouse or other pointing device
Microsoft Mouse connected to PS/2 Mouse Port
IBM Personal System/2 Mouse
Mouse Systems Mouse connected to COM1:
Mouse Systems Mouse connected to COM2:
VisiOn Mouse connected to COM1:
VisiOn Mouse connected to COM2:
Logitech Mouse
AT&T Keyboard Mouse
Other (requires disk provided by a hardware manufacturer)



      ┌──────────────────────────────────────────────────────┐
      │ WHEN YOU'RE READY TO                           PRESS  │
      ├──────────────────────────────────────────────────────┤
      │ Confirm your choice                            ENTER  │
      │ Exit without completing Setup              CONTROL+X  │
      └──────────────────────────────────────────────────────┘
```

FIGURE 22.7: Selection screen listing the most popular pointing devices for Windows use. Using one of these common pointing devices facilitates your use of Windows, since software support for them is included in the Windows package.

```
Below is a list of the items you've selected.

   - If these items are correct, press the ENTER key.
   - If you want to change an item, use the DIRECTION (↑,↓) keys to move the
     highlight to the item, then press the ENTER key.
╔═══════════╗
║No Change  ║
╚═══════════╝
IBM (or 100% compatible) CGA (Color/Graphics Adapter)
US keyboard
Mouse Systems Mouse connected to COM1:




         ┌─────────────────────────────────────────────────────┐
         │ WHEN YOU'RE READY TO                        PRESS    │
         ├─────────────────────────────────────────────────────┤
         │ Confirm your choice                         ENTER    │
         │ Exit without completing Setup               CONTROL+X│
         └─────────────────────────────────────────────────────┘
```

FIGURE 22.8: Setup confirmation screen. Earlier answers are summarized, and you have a last chance to confirm or correct them. Pressing Return accepts the displayed choices; selecting any one of them with the cursor keys recalls the appropriate earlier screen display so you can change your answers.

```
                    ┌───────────────────┐
                    │   ──┤■├──          │
                    └───────────────────┘

Insert the Build Disk in the following drive:
╔════════════════════════════════════════════════════╗
║A:                                                    ║
╚════════════════════════════════════════════════════╝
   - If you want to use a different directory and/or drive, use the
     BACKSPACE key to delete the name shown, then type the correct name.




         ┌─────────────────────────────────────────────────────┐
         │ WHEN YOU'RE READY TO                        PRESS    │
         ├─────────────────────────────────────────────────────┤
         │ Continue Setup                              ENTER    │
         │ Exit without completing Setup               CONTROL+X│
         └─────────────────────────────────────────────────────┘
```

FIGURE 22.9: SETUP requires the Build diskette first. This step loads the main Windows file and overlay instructions. Among other, smaller files, the Windows drivers for your earlier choices are loaded at this time (for the mouse, the keyboard, and so on).

Next, you'll need to install one or more printers or plotters in your Windows configuration. The screen shown in Figure 22.10 prompts you for this step, allowing you to select choice I repeatedly until you have installed all printer and plotter devices. You can then continue with the rest of the installation.

Selecting I produces a multiscreen list of output device choices, part of which is shown in Figure 22.11. Use the up and down cursor keys to scroll through the many printer and plotter choices.

Windows must know the port to which each device used for output is connected. Even though DOS can support more than two serial communications ports, Windows offers only COM1 and COM2 serial support. Figure 22.12 lists the output port selections available.

After you specify a port, the screen shown in Figure 22.10 will be redisplayed. If you have more than one printer or plotter installed, you can specify it now by selecting I once again and then specifying the port to which the device is connected. When you are done specifying devices, you can continue with the rest of the Windows setup.

Continuing the Windows setup displays the screen shown in Figure 22.13, which allows you to specify the country for your Windows operation. Just as for DOS (see Chapter 11), this specification determines the currency symbol, separator symbols for the date and time, and other country-specific features used by Windows.

```
Setup will allow you to install a printer or plotter.


   ┌─────────────────────────────────────────────────────┐
   │ WHEN YOU'RE READY TO                          PRESS  │
   ├─────────────────────────────────────────────────────┤
   │ Install a printer or plotter                   I     │
   │ Continue Setup                                 C     │
   ├─────────────────────────────────────────────────────┤
   │ Exit without completing Setup              CONTROL+X │
   └─────────────────────────────────────────────────────┘
```

FIGURE 22.10: Output device configuration. You can continue with the installation, or you can specify one or more output devices at this point. Choosing I on this screen displays the screen shown in Figure 22.11, which presents a series of output device choices.

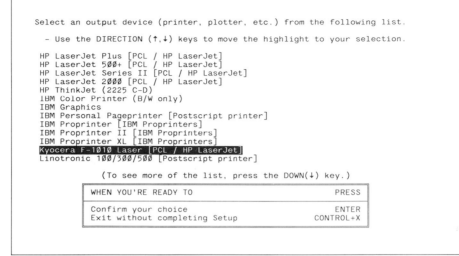

Select an output device (printer, plotter, etc.) from the following list.

  - Use the DIRECTION (↑,↓) keys to move the highlight to your selection.

HP LaserJet Plus [PCL / HP LaserJet]
HP LaserJet 500+ [PCL / HP LaserJet]
HP LaserJet Series II [PCL / HP LaserJet]
HP LaserJet 2000 [PCL / HP LaserJet]
HP ThinkJet (2225 C-D)
IBM Color Printer (B/W only)
IBM Graphics
IBM Personal Pageprinter [Postscript printer]
IBM Proprinter [IBM Proprinters]
IBM Proprinter II [IBM Proprinters]
IBM Proprinter XL [IBM Proprinters]
Kyocera F-1010 Laser [PCL / HP LaserJet]
Linotronic 100/300/500 [Postscript printer]

          (To see more of the list, press the DOWN(↓) key.)

WHEN YOU'RE READY TO	PRESS
Confirm your choice	ENTER
Exit without completing Setup	CONTROL+X

FIGURE 22.11: One of several screens displaying output devices compatible with Windows. Use the cursor-control keys to select the desired device; then press Return. You will then be asked to indicate the port being used for the specified device.

Select the port your printer/plotter is attached to from the following list.

  - Use the DIRECTION (↑,↓) keys to move the highlight to your selection.

LPT1:
LPT2:
LPT3:
COM1:
COM2:
EPT:
None

WHEN YOU'RE READY TO	PRESS
Confirm your choice	ENTER
Exit without completing Setup	CONTROL+X

FIGURE 22.12: Output port selections. You must select one of these ports for each printer or plotter you specify during the Windows setup.

was changed after the manuals and documentation were complete. The special files containing this last-minute information are disk resident. Setup tries to make sure that you read this information by including this screen in the installation process.

When you are done viewing the text information, your current directory will be \WINDOWS, and you can begin operating the WINDOWS program by typing WIN. You can later modify the path (perhaps set from AUTOEXEC-.BAT) to include \WINDOWS; this will allow you to initiate Windows at any time, regardless of current drive or directory.

Do not skip the final steps of reading the README files during the setup process. The advice and information contained in those text files may be relevant and even critical to your system. For instance, information about many popular laser printers, and the use of soft fonts on those printers, is contained only in the README files. Additional information about Windows performance and advice regarding system modification for performance and convenience also appears on these important text screens.

The Windows operating environment that results from the initial installation procedure is more than sufficient for a beginning user. From this environment, you can use utility programs and follow printed instructions to modify Windows to accept changes in system hardware and in the use of current hardware.

You can also have Windows automatically load one or more software applications whenever you load Windows into the computer. Although this may significantly increase the amount of time required to start Windows, you will have all the applications opened in this manner available at the beginning of the Windows session instead of having to load them one by one later.

Because of the way Windows manages memory, especially for true multitasking operations and programs with large memory requirements, it is often necessary to load programs into the Windows environment by order of decreasing memory requirements (that is, starting with the program with the largest memory requirement first). Although this sequential loading of programs can be performed manually, allowing Windows to do it for you is obviously easier.

Using Windows

You usually load Windows by entering WIN at the DOS prompt. You can write a simple batch file to set the default drive and directory and to enter the request to DOS to run WIN. When installed on a hard disk, Windows is usually stored in the \WINDOWS subdirectory, so you must either change to that directory (using the DOS CD command) or ensure that \WINDOWS is on the path.

Once you have entered the WIN command, by whatever means, Windows displays the Microsoft logo and begins operation. The time required for Windows to become functional depends on the speed of your computer and disk drives and on the number of applications that Windows has been configured to start automatically. When the Windows operating environment is completely set up, a full-screen window similar to the one in Figure 22.16 appears.

The window in Figure 22.16 is for the Windows MS-DOS Executive application program in version 2. MS-DOS Executive is always available during a Windows session and is used to initiate other applications and perform some DOS disk operations. The use of the MS-DOS Executive will be discussed shortly, but first take a brief look at the areas of the window and the icons on it.

The Components of a Windows Screen

The standard window in a Windows application has three primary and two secondary (optional) components. The first primary area consists of the top two lines of the window: the title bar and the Command menu. The title bar contains the name of the application and (in versions 2.X) three icons, one on the left and two on the right. The Command menu displays the names of the commands associated with a particular application (File, View, and Special, in Figure 22.16). The second primary area is the work area, or working window. The third primary area, which appears as a dark or inverse stripe across the bottom of the screen, is the icon display area. Applications that are loaded but not shown in the work area as full or partial windows are displayed here as icons.

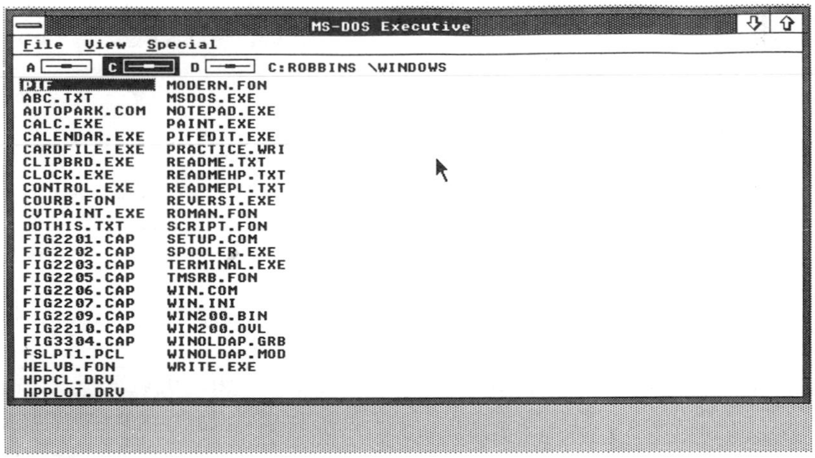

```
┌──────────────────────────────────────────────────────────────┐
│ ▬                        MS-DOS Executive                ⇩  ⇧ │
│ File  View   Special                                          │
│ A ▭═╸ C ▭═╸ D ▭═╸ C:ROBBINS \WINDOWS                          │
│ PIF          MODERN.FON                                       │
│ ABC.TXT       MSDOS.EXE                                       │
│ AUTOPARK.COM  NOTEPAD.EXE                                     │
│ CALC.EXE      PAINT.EXE                                       │
│ CALENDAR.EXE  PIFEDIT.EXE                                     │
│ CARDFILE.EXE  PRACTICE.WRI                                    │
│ CLIPBRD.EXE   README.TXT                                      │
│ CLOCK.EXE     READMEHP.TXT        �k                           │
│ CONTROL.EXE   READMEPL.TXT                                    │
│ COURB.FON     REVERSI.EXE                                     │
│ CUTPAINT.EXE  ROMAN.FON                                       │
│ DOTHIS.TXT    SCRIPT.FON                                      │
│ FIG2201.CAP   SETUP.COM                                       │
│ FIG2202.CAP   SPOOLER.EXE                                     │
│ FIG2203.CAP   TERMINAL.EXE                                    │
│ FIG2205.CAP   TMSRB.FON                                       │
│ FIG2206.CAP   WIN.COM                                         │
│ FIG2207.CAP   WIN.INI                                         │
│ FIG2209.CAP   WIN200.BIN                                      │
│ FIG2210.CAP   WIN200.OVL                                      │
│ FIG3304.CAP   WINOLDAP.GRB                                    │
│ FSLPT1.PCL    WINOLDAP.MOD                                    │
│ HELVB.FON     WRITE.EXE                                       │
│ HPPCL.DRV                                                     │
│ HPPLOT.DRV                                                    │
└──────────────────────────────────────────────────────────────┘
```

FIGURE 22.16: Initial Windows version 2.03 screen display. Files in the current directory (\Windows) of the current drive (C) are displayed. The default drive is represented by a highlighted icon; the first entry in the directory also is highlighted. Available options include the three main pull-down menu choices: File, View, and Special.

Depending on the application, two other components, vertical and horizontal scroll bars, may appear in the window. If present, the vertical scroll bar appears at the right side of the work area, and the horizontal scroll bar appears immediately above the icon display area. When displayed, the scroll bars can be used to scroll the work area to display any information that exceeds the number of lines, or the number of characters in a line, of the work area. The scroll bars are used as they are in word processing or spreadsheet programs that display only a portion of a document or spreadsheet at a time. The use of scroll bars is described later in this chapter.

The title bar in Figure 22.16 displays three icons. The two icons on the right side of the title bar, a down arrow and an up arrow, control the display of the associated window. The down arrow, or minimize box, changes the window into an icon. The up arrow, or maximize box, expands the window to a full-screen display. When a window has been maximized to a full-screen display, the up arrow changes to a double up arrow, or window restore box. This box restores the window to its previous display size.

The third icon, on the left side of the title bar, is the Control menu box. This box provides access to the Control menu, which is common to all Windows applications. Choices on this menu control the size, location, display status, and termination of an application and its associated window. They are outlined in the section "Using the Control Menu."

The components of the title bar just described are included in version 2 only; the title bar in version 1 simply displays the name of the application program. Similar features are available in version 1, but they are generally less convenient to use.

RUNNING WINDOWS

Windows provides a graphics-oriented interface that allows a user to perform various operations by selecting the appropriate commands from pull-down menus. Displaying a pull-down menu and selecting commands can be accomplished by using a pointing device, such as a mouse, or by entering a series of multikey keyboard commands (entered as Alt plus the selected key). The keyboard commands are inconvenient at best and confusing at worst; using a mouse is strongly recommended for users of Windows. The examples in the remainder of this chapter assume the use of a mouse pointing device.

If your cursor is not positioned on one of the Windows icons or on a text choice, it will appear as a small arrow on your screen. This arrow is the mouse pointer. To select an icon on a window, you position the pointer by moving the mouse so that the pointer tip is on the icon. After you have correctly positioned the pointer, you activate the icon by pressing the mouse button. On mouse devices that have two or more buttons, this is usually the left button. When you press the button, either the icon will change color, indicating that it can be moved to another location on the screen, or a pull-down menu will appear.

In Figure 22.17, the Control menu box has been selected, and its menu is displayed because the mouse button has been pushed. If the mouse button is released while the pointer is still inside the icon, the menu will remain on screen. If the mouse button is clicked with the pointer on some empty area of the screen, the menu will disappear. However, if you move the pointer to the Command menu with the mouse button still pressed, the menu command touched by the pointer will change its display characteristics (usually to white letters on a colored background) to indicate it has been selected. If you move the pointer off the command, the command will revert to its original display and will not be selected. To execute a command on a menu, select it with the pointer and release the mouse button. If you don't want to execute any of the commands on a menu, move the pointer back to the menu icon or to an empty area of the screen before releasing the mouse button.

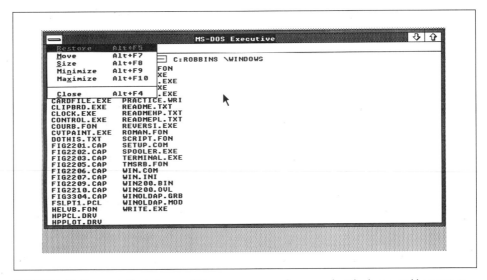

FIGURE 22.17: The main Control menu. This menu appears after you select the horizontal box icon in the upper-left corner of any window. The six controls displayed are available to you for managing any window. From the menu, you can move a window around the screen and adjust its size any way you like. You can replace the entire window with an icon only, expand the window to fill the screen, restore the window to its original size, or close the window.

Note: Frequently one or more of the commands in a pull-down menu will be disabled because they are invalid or meaningless at the time. When a command has been disabled, it is displayed in a different color, shade, or font than valid commands. For example, the Print choice in Figure 22.47, later in this chapter, appears dimmer than the other options. This indicates that it is not a valid choice for the currently selected file. When the pointer touches a disabled command, the display characteristics do not change. If you release the mouse button while it is touching a disabled command, the menu will disappear.

USING THE CONTROL MENU

The Control menu, shown in Figure 22.17, is available in every application designed to operate in the Windows environment. It controls the display of an application window and closes (terminates) an application program. The commands on this menu are as follows:

Restore:	Restores window appearance and size to original values. Also accessible as Alt-F5 key combination.
Move:	Moves the window to another location on a multiple window display. Also accessible as Alt-F7 key combination.
Size:	Adjusts the size of the window in a multiple-window display. Also accessible as Alt-F8 key combination.
Minimize:	Closes the active window, reducing it to an icon in the icon display area at the bottom of the screen. Also accessible as Alt-F9 key combination.
Maximize:	Expands a window or an icon to the largest possible screen size. Also accessible as Alt-F10 key combination.
Close:	Closes a window, terminating the current application program and removing it from the Windows environment. Also accessible as Alt-F4 key combination.

As you can see, each of these commands also can be activated by an Alt-keystroke combination. You can use keystroke commands regardless of whether a pointing device (a mouse) is installed, but pointing is usually easier.

USING MS-DOS EXECUTIVE

MS-DOS Executive is the primary control application in the Windows environment. It is initiated automatically when Windows is loaded into the computer system, and it must remain active as long as Windows is running. MS-DOS Executive performs the following three primary functions:

1. It loads and runs other application programs in Windows.
2. It displays the current disk directory listing.
3. It provides access to DOS disk-control operations such as file COPY, DELETE, and RENAME; disk FORMAT; and subdirectory creation and alteration.

When Windows is first loaded, MS-DOS Executive is the only application window open. If additional applications have been open, they will appear as icons in the icon display area at the bottom of the screen.

Figure 22.16, presented earlier, shows a sample MS-DOS Executive window. The actual directory list and disk drive icons vary between computer systems. At the top of the work area, a disk drive icon is displayed for each disk drive on the computer system. The icon for the current default disk drive is displayed in inverse video. To the right of the disk icons, the default drive letter, volume label, and current subdirectory path is displayed. Below the disk icons is a directory listing of the files in the current subdirectory. Generally, the first file in the directory listing is displayed in inverse video to mark it as the default selection.

Changing the Default Disk Drive

You can change the default disk drive by positioning the pointer inside the icon for the disk drive that is to become the new default drive and then clicking the mouse button once. The icon for the original default disk drive will revert to normal video display, and the new default drive icon will change to inverse-video display. The default drive letter, volume label, and subdirectory path of the new default drive will then be displayed, as will a directory listing of the files in that subdirectory.

Selecting a File from the Directory List

To change the selected file in the directory list, move the pointer onto the file name and click the mouse button once. The previously selected file name will be restored to normal display, and the new file name will display in inverse video.

Using the MS-DOS Executive Command Menu

MS-DOS Executive provides three pull-down menu commands (File, View, and Special) in the Command menu at the top of the window. The functions of the commands available under these three menus are described in the following sections. Position the pointer on a Command menu command and hold down the mouse button; the pull-down menu for that command will be displayed.

With the mouse button still pressed, move the pointer down through the pull-down menu. As the pointer passes over a command, the command is selected and displayed in inverse video. If you release the mouse button, the selected command will be performed on the selected file or files in the work area. If additional information or verification is required to complete a command, one or more pop-up windows will appear.

CONTROLLING DOS FILES

Figure 22.18 shows the File command pull-down menu. The command functions available here are performed on the currently selected file shown in the work area. The command functions are as follows:

RUN: Brings an application .COM, .EXE, or .BAT file into the Windows environment and executes it. If a Windows application is being run, a window will be open for it on the screen. If a standard DOS application is being run, the display screen will revert to normal DOS mode, and the application will run as it normally does under DOS.

LOAD: Loads and executes Windows and standard DOS applications in the Windows environment, but with the applications displayed as icons in the icon display area. No window will be open for the application.

COPY: Copies one or more selected files to another disk or directory. You can copy more than one file at a time by selecting multiple files from the work area directory list. To select more than one file, press and hold the Shift key on the keyboard while pointing to and selecting the files with the mouse.

GET INFO: Displays full directory information for the selected file.

DELETE: Deletes the selected files.

PRINT: Sends one or more ASCII text files to the Windows print spooler.

RENAME: Renames the selected file.

VIEWING DOS DIRECTORY CONTENTS

Figure 22.19 shows the View command pull-down menu. The command functions available here determine how the file list appears in the work area. Normally, the file name and extension of all files in the current subdirectory are displayed in alphabetical order by file name. By selecting different options, you can organize the file list by date, time, size, or extension. Only program files or files matching a specified naming convention are displayed. The \WINDOWS directory files listed behind the pull-down View window appear in the default short format.

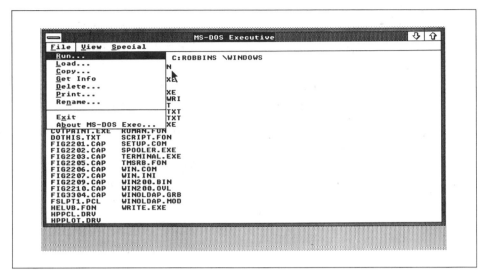

FIGURE 22.18: The File command pull-down menu. This menu lets you perform DOS operations on the files in the displayed directory. You can run a program or batch file, load a program or batch file for later execution, or obtain the equivalent of the DOS commands COPY, ERASE, RENAME, and DIR. If the highlighted file is printable, the PRINT command option is also available.

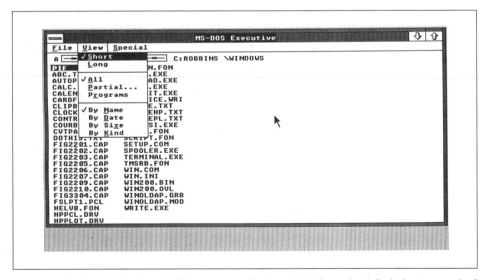

FIGURE 22.19: The standard View pull-down menu. Check marks indicate the default choice in each of the three categories of this menu. By default, all files appear in name order using the short format, which displays showing only the base name and extension of each file.

Moving the mouse down the menu to select the long format results in a display similar to Figure 22.20. Notice that a vertical scroll bar appears on the right side of your screen since there are more files in this directory than can be displayed on one screen. You can move the mouse to the scroll bar and select a different portion of the directory list for display, by clicking the mouse button on different portions of the scroll bar. The long file-name format will remain in effect until you again select the short format.

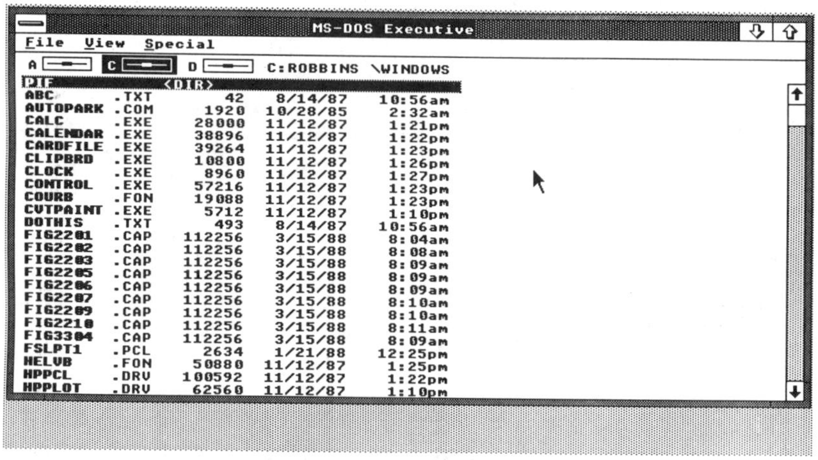

FIGURE 22.20: The long format of a Windows directory. The date, time, size, and complete file name are displayed. Notice the vertical scroll bar on the right of the Windows screen, denoting that there is more information to view. In this case, there are more files in this directory than can be displayed on one screen.

USING SPECIALIZED DOS COMMANDS

Figure 22.21 shows the Special command pull-down menu. The command functions available from this menu provide access to common DOS operations associated with hard disk use on a personal computer (formatting new disks, changing or assigning a disk volume label, creating new disk subdirectories, or changing the current subdirectory on a disk drive).

The Special menu also includes the command to terminate a Windows session (End Session). If you select End Session, a pop-up window appears requesting verification (see Figure 22.22). If you select the OK icon, Windows closes any open windows. If an open window or loaded application contains new or modified data that has not been saved to disk, a pop-up window allows you to save or discard that data.

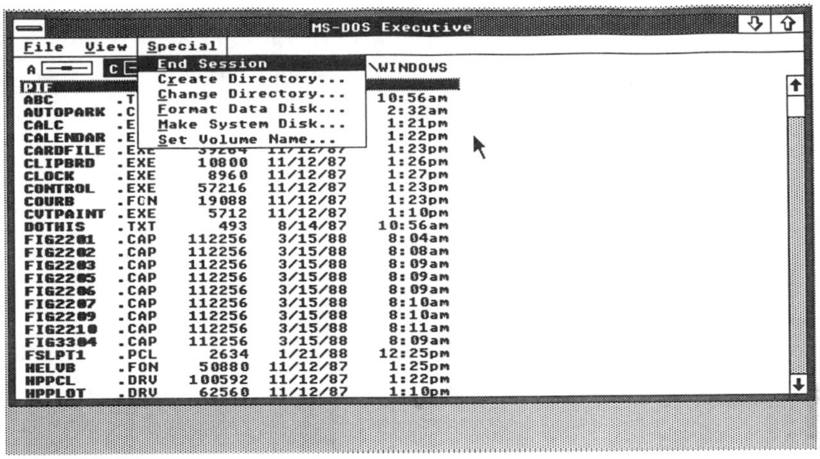

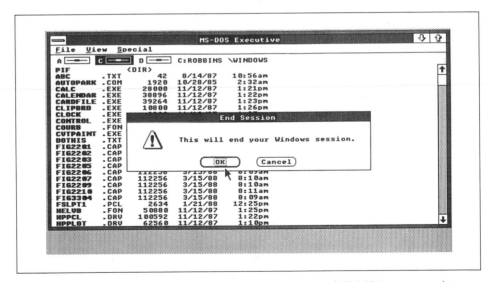

FIGURE 22.21: The Special pull-down menu. Miscellaneous but important DOS command capabilities are available from this menu. The choices here are equivalent to the DOS MD, CD, FORMAT, FORMAT/S, and LABEL commands. The Windows command for ending the Windows session is also available from this menu.

FIGURE 22.22: Selecting End Session on the Special pull-down menu of MS-DOS Executive results in this simple pop-up confirmation panel. You use the mouse or cursor-control keys to select whether to terminate your entire Windows session or to cancel the request and return to your Windows session.

Saving Time and Energy with Windows Applications

The Windows directory contains several built-in .EXE files. Most of these (shown in Figure 22.23) are unique application programs included with your Windows software. In this section, you'll explore these useful tools. You can then decide which ones best serve your own needs.

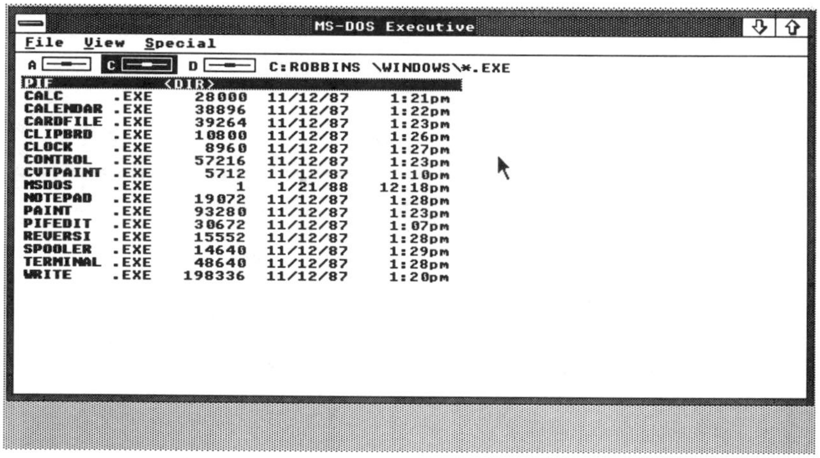

FIGURE 22.23: .EXE programs included with Windows. This display appears when you select the Programs choice on the View pull-down menu. Running any one of these programs requires only that you highlight its name (either by selecting it with the mouse or the cursor-control keys) and then press Return.

Performing On-Screen Calculations

The Calculator application, shown in Figure 22.24, functions as a standard 10-key calculator. When this application is active, you can use it to perform calculator operations by positioning the pointer over the appropriate key and clicking the mouse button or by typing the appropriate keys on the keyboard. This application also can transfer and receive information from other applications.

The on-screen calculator resembles a common pocket calculator. It includes the standard number keys, arithmetic functions, and single-value memory location. The only additional feature of the Windows calculator is a square-root button located above the percent key.

The screen cursor (normally an arrow elsewhere on the screen) appears as a small octagonal symbol. You can move this symbol directly over any of the calculator keys with your mouse. Pressing the mouse button is then equivalent to

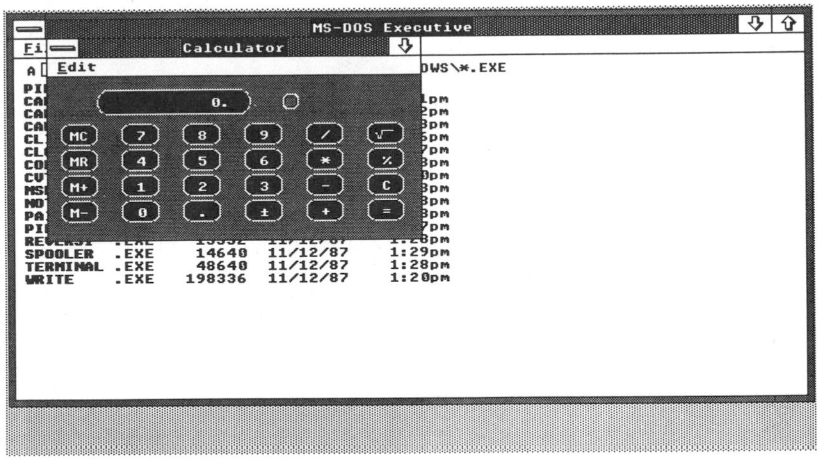

FIGURE 22.24: The automated screen version of your personal calculator. This visual calculation function is one of the many application programs included in the Windows environment.

pressing that key on the keyboard. Calculations proceed as they would on any portable calculator, with intermediate and final numeric results shown in the calculator display window. In Figure 22.24, this window shows a value of 0. The push-button cursor is located just to the right of the calculation window.

Maintaining Your Appointment Calendar

Various desktop software packages offer a date and time appointment calendar. Windows offers CALENDAR.EXE, which runs in a window on the desktop. Figure 22.25 shows the initial view of this software facility. Optional settings dictate the size, shape, and contents of each window application when it first appears on the desktop. In this case, the appointment calendar is set to November 15, 1988 (today's date), beginning with 8:00 A.M. and showing one-hour intervals.

As you can see in Figure 22.25, the previously active Calculator function is still available. Its window has simply been shrunk (minimized) to a small icon. Windows places this icon at the bottom of the screen to remind you of the program's availability. MS-DOS Executive is still available and can be partially seen on the screen. It is said to be in the *background*, since the primary window is running the Calendar program.

In Figure 22.26, two steps have been taken. First, MS-DOS Executive has been minimized to reduce the visual clutter on the screen. This leaves only the

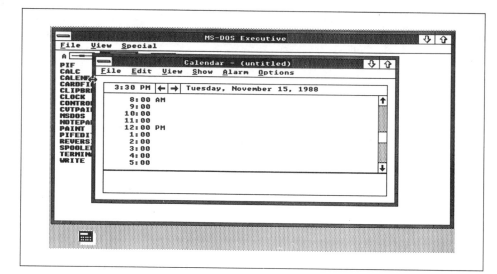

FIGURE 22.25: Initial window display of the Calendar feature. Current time and date is displayed, as are the entries for this date, beginning at 8:00 A.M. No appointments have yet been entered on this system for this date. Notice the small icon at the bottom of the screen. It represents the active and available Calculator program, whose desktop window has been minimized by a Control menu choice.

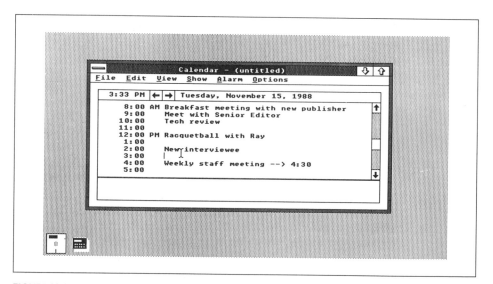

FIGURE 22.26: Only the Calendar window is being displayed at full size. Other active programs are MS-DOS Executive and the Calculator. Both of these programs appear as small icons at the bottom of the screen. The disk represents MS-DOS Executive; the miniature calculator represents the Calculator program.

window containing the Calendar on the screen, plus the two icons now visible in the display area at the bottom of the screen.

You can make entries for different times on the visible schedule. In Figure 22.26, appointments have been made for 8:00, 9:00, 10:00, 12:00, 2:00, and 4:00. The cursor for the next entry is on the 3:00 line. This calendar is completely new and has not yet been named; thus, the file name *untitled* appears on the top title bar.

The Calendar program has six pull-down menus: File, Edit, View, Show, Alarm, and Options. Figure 22.27 displays the pull-down contents of the File menu. This File choice is common across the desktop applications, as are most of the features listed here.

As you can see, you can create new entries or files (New), open existing entries or files (Open), save your current work to a new or existing file (Save), back up your current work to a uniquely specified file (Save As), print your schedule (Print), or delete files (Remove). You can also always close an application window (Exit) or display information about the application (About ...).

To save a copy of your appointments schedule under a different name, you select the Save As choice, which displays the screen shown in Figure 22.28. The dialog box shows the current name as the default name and permits you to type over that name with another one.

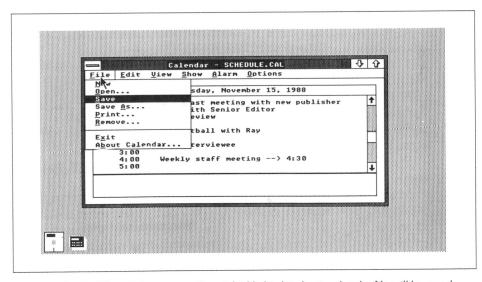

FIGURE 22.27: The File pull-down menu. Save is highlighted, indicating that the file will be saved under its current name—in this case, SCHEDULE.CAL (shown in the title line at the top of the window).

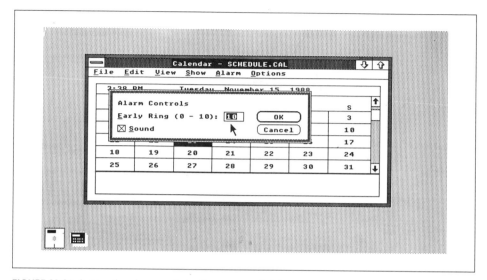

FIGURE 22.31: Setting the alarm controls. You can specify how many minutes (up to 10 minutes) in advance of an appointment the alarm is to go off. You can also specify whether the alarm is to be audible (by clicking the sound box and displaying an X) or visible only.

also set the alarm to go off up to 10 minutes in advance of an appointment time. At the specified time, a dialog box will appear or an icon will flash. Figure 22.31 shows the screen when you select the Alarm pull-down menu. In this dialog box, you set the time precedence value and indicate whether you want your alarm to be audible as well as visible.

Up to this point, the screen displays have all shown 1-hour intervals using a 12-hour clock and beginning at 8:00 A.M. These settings all are adjustable from the Day Settings choice of the Options pull down menu. Figure 22.32 shows the day settings available to you.

If you prefer your appointment calendar based on 15-minute intervals rather than 60-minute intervals, you choose this option to change the specification. Naturally, if you use 15-minute intervals, any single screen will display less total time.

When an alarm has been set for a particular appointment, the visual indicator appears as a small bell icon to the left of the appointment time, as seen next to the 3:00 slot in Figure 22.33.

Scrolling on a particular date is easily accomplished using the cursor keys (up and down arrows) or the vertical scroll bar and the mouse. Figure 22.34 shows the result of scrolling down the day from the range 8:00 A.M. to 5:00 P.M. to the range 2:00 P.M. to 11:00 P.M.

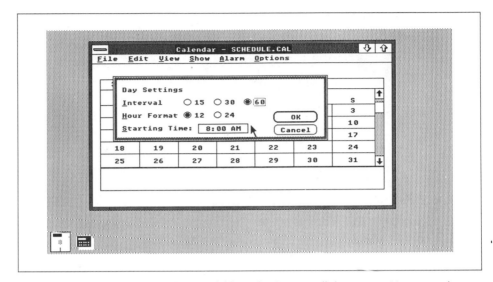

FIGURE 22.32: Day Settings dialog box, available on the Options pull-down menu. You can set the appointment interval to 15, 30, or 60 minutes by selecting the number with your mouse. Similarly, you can switch between a standard 12-hour clock or a 24-hour format. You can directly enter the starting time for your display in the starting time box.

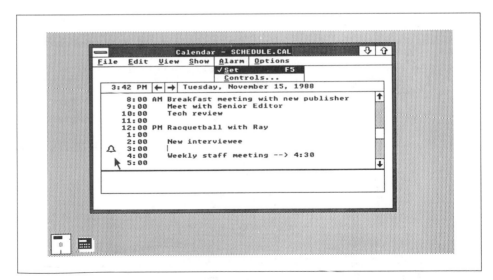

FIGURE 22.33: An alarm has been set for 3:00 on Tuesday, November 15, so the bell icon appears next to that line on the display. You set alarms by using the Set choice on the Alarm pull-down menu. The Controls choice produces the dialog box shown in Figure 22.31.

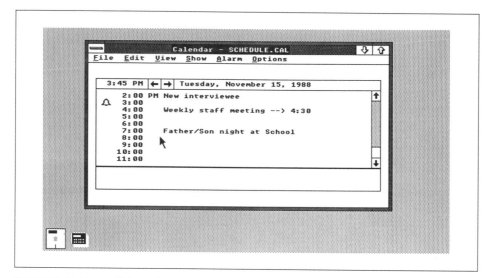

FIGURE 22.34: You scroll down the time intervals of a day using either the scroll bar at the right of the screen or the up and down arrow keys. Position the mouse at the desired time, then press the button once to enter new information for that time.

Building Your Own Simple Data Base

Complex data-base management systems provide powerful capabilities for managing large amounts of data. The commands and tools available in these DBMS program are often much more than is necessary for many simple files of information. The concept behind the Windows card file program is that much information is easily stored on the equivalent of a 3 × 5-inch card. Thus, with the Cardfile, you create visual cards on your computer screen. When you run the Cardfile program from MS-DOS Executive, the screen shown in Figure 22.35 appears.

As the figure shows, the Cardfile offers five pull-down menus. The first three menus perform functions similar to those they perform in the Calendar program. The Card and Search menus are unique to the Cardfile program. Notice in the figure that the MS-DOS Executive window has been maximized and no longer appears as an icon. However, the Calendar program has been minimized and now appears only as an icon at the bottom of the screen.

When setting up a card file, the first step to take is to give your card a title, or index line. Select Index on the Edit menu, shown in Figure 22.36, to obtain the proper dialog box.

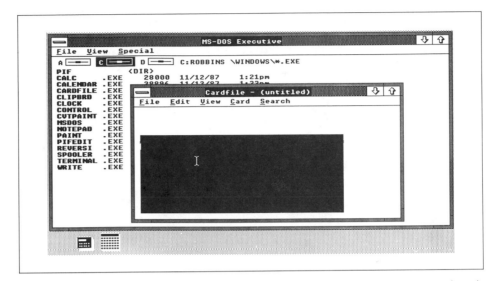

FIGURE 22.35: First appearance of the Cardfile window. As with the Calendar, you can give each card file a unique file name. Card files are untitled until you enter a name. The first blank is displayed for your information entry.

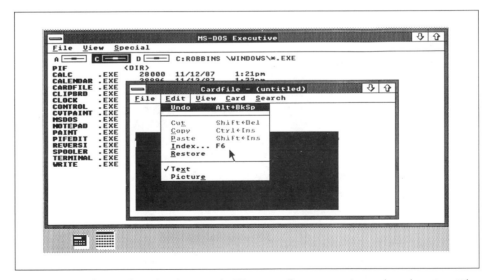

FIGURE 22.36: Selecting the Index choice on the Edit menu allows you to give each card a unique title, or index line. The name refers to the method Windows uses internally to store and retrieve individual file cards (via an index into the file).

The resulting dialog box, shown in Figure 22.37, allows you to enter a brief title for the card. This *index line* appears at the top of each card on the computer screen. The Cardfile also uses the characters in these index lines to arrange the cards for display. The default arrangement of the cards on your monitor is standard alphabetic order.

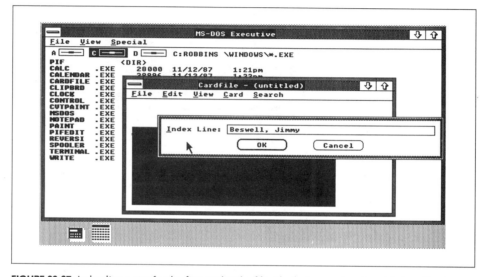

FIGURE 22.37: Index line entry for the first card in the file. The last name is entered first, so that later automatic alphabetizing by the Cardfile program will sort the cards into a logical order.

After you enter the index line, the dialog box disappears, and the card is redisplayed with the index line entry appearing as the first line on the card. You can then begin typing any information you would like to appear and be stored on this card. Figure 22.38 shows a completed card entry for Jimmy Beswell, a racquetball opponent of the person keeping this example card file.

To add additional cards to this simple card file select the Card pull-down menu. As Figure 22.39 shows, you then choose Add (or alternatively have pressed F7) to create a new blank card on your screen.

Adding a new card to your file causes the Cardfile program to ask you for the title of the card. Figure 22.40 shows the dialog box that appears.

The resulting display shows a new card that is blank except for the index line at the top of the card (see Figure 22.41). The former card is obscured except for the index line (Beswell, Jimmy). The new current card is now ready for information entry.

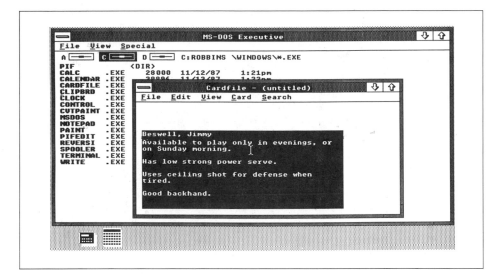

FIGURE 22.38: First card entry for a card file of racquetball opponents. The individual's name is used as the index line, for easy alphabetizing. Notes about each individual's game skills are kept for later reference.

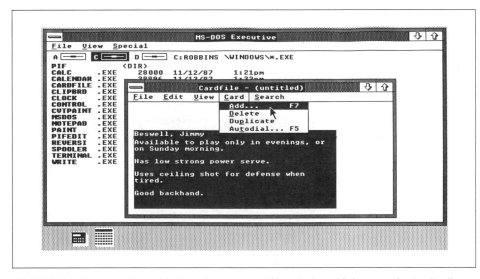

FIGURE 22.39: You can add new blank cards to your card file with the Add choice on the Card pull-down menu. You will be asked to give the card a title (index line) before you enter new information on that card.

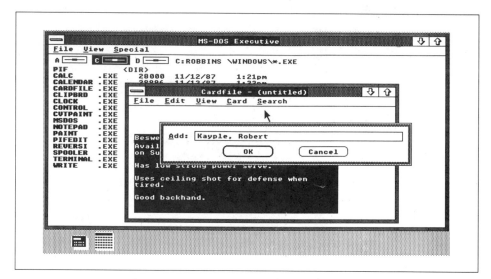

FIGURE 22.40: A new card added after your first one (Beswell, Jimmy) must first be given a title line. This second card is given the index line Kayple, Robert. This card, like all cards, will later be quickly accessible via the Search menu simply by entering the first letters of the index line (in this case, the person's name).

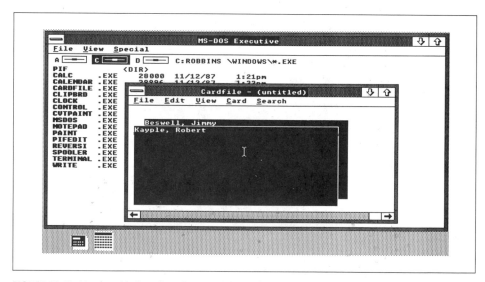

FIGURE 22.41: Newly added cards at the top of the deck, or file. This facilitates the expected entry of information onto the card. Once this display appears, you can begin typing, and the text will appear on the card.

Figure 22.42 shows the completed second card. All notes about Robert Kayple have been entered onto his card and are visible on the screen.

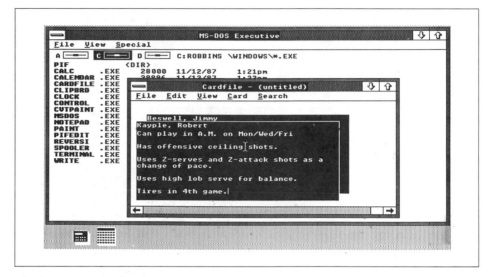

FIGURE 22.42: A second card, entered in the card file under the index line Kayple, Robert. The card file program displays the top index line for several cards at a time, so that you can easily select cards with your mouse. Selecting an index line moves its card to the top of the deck, where you can read the card's contents.

You can add other cards by selecting Card/Add. Figure 22.43 shows a deck containing a third racquetball opponent's card. Since all three cards fit on one screen, Windows does not yet need to display a scroll bar.

A useful tool when your card deck becomes much larger is the Search pull-down menu. As you can see in Figure 22.44, you only need to enter the first several characters of the index line to enable the Cardfile program to quickly find a particular card.

At any time you can change the appearance of your card file from its default view of complete cards, as shown so far, to an alternative view displaying only the index lines for the card entries. These two choices appear on the pull-down View menu, shown on Figure 22.45.

Figure 22.46 displays the card file as a list of index lines, or titles, for easy reference. Naturally, more card titles can appear on one screen display in this format than in the alternative format displaying complete cards.

When you're done working on your card file, you will most likely want to save it to a disk file. In fact, you should probably save it to a disk earlier than that to ensure that a power failure doesn't cost you a great deal of work. Once you've saved your work, your data will be protected.

Figure 22.47 displays the File menu, including the standard choices for creating, opening, and saving files. It also contains useful choices for printing individual cards (one to a page) and for printing your entire card file (multiple cards per printed page).

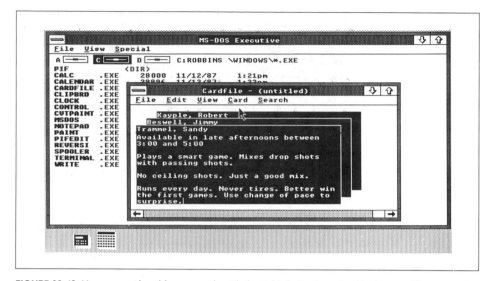

FIGURE 22.43: You can easily add more cards with the Add choice from the Card menu. If more cards were created than fit on one screen, a horizontal scroll bar would appear, allowing you to scroll through the deck from front to back (left to right on the scroll bar).

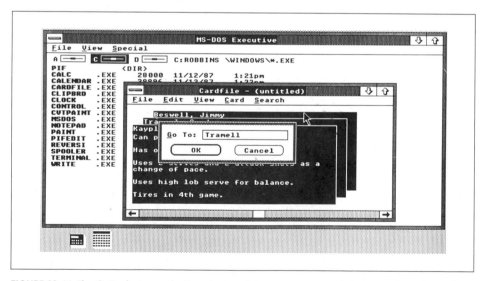

FIGURE 22.44: The GoTo choice on the Search menu lets you enter several characters from the card's title, or index line. The program quickly finds the specified card and makes it the topmost card on the deck, as the next figure shows.

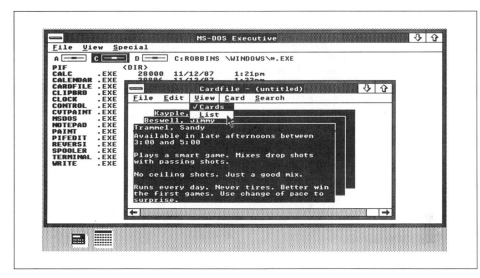

FIGURE 22.45: You can view your card file in two ways: either as a deck of titled cards (the Cards option), or as a list of card titles (the List option). Selecting List displays the screen in Figure 22.46.

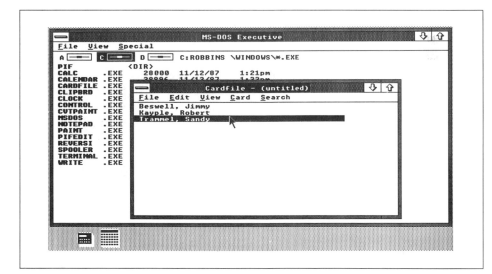

FIGURE 22.46: Your card file as a list of titles, or index lines. In this format, you can see more entries on a single screen and thus can easily and quickly select the next card you want to see or modify.

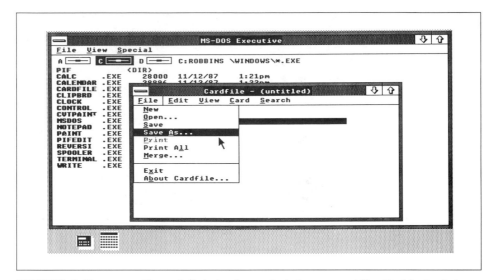

FIGURE 22.47: File menu, with standard choices for manipulating your card files. Useful print choices appear here to print individual cards, one to a page, and to print several cards on a single page.

All cards are printed with a solid border for easy visual separation. Figure 22.48 shows a printout of the three cards created in this card file session.

One last feature of the Cardfile program is its ability to dial a telephone number. This feature is included in case your cards represent a person or business that you want to call. Selecting the Autodial choice from the Card menu displays the screen in Figure 22.49.

In the Phone Settings dialog box, you can set the baud rate to 300 or 1200, the port to COM1 or COM2, and the dialing to pulse or tone (touch tone). The card file program will automatically enter the first phone number it finds on the topmost card displayed on your screen, or you can enter another number. Once you are ready, selecting OK causes the card file program to send the appropriate signals to your modem to dial the phone.

Suppose at this time that you have correctly saved your card file as RACQUET. As you can see in Figure 22.49, the formerly untitled card file is now called RACQUET.CRD. The default .CRD extension was added when the file was saved as RACQUET from the File menu.

You can now maximize the MS-DOS Executive window to select the Special menu and end the Windows session. Windows will check to verify that other sessions have had their data updates properly saved. In Figure 22.50, Windows discovered that your calendar entries have not been updated in the file named SCHEDULE.CAL.

```
Beswell, Jimmy
Available to play only in evenings, or
on Sunday morning.

Has low strong power serve.

Uses ceiling shot for defense when
tired.

Good backhand.
```

```
Kayple, Robert
Can play in A.M. on Mon/Wed/Fri

Has offensive ceiling shots.

Uses Z-serves and Z-attack shots as a
change of pace.

Uses high lob serve for balance.

Tires in 4th game.
```

```
Trammel, Sandy
Available in late afternoons between
3:00 and 5:00

Plays a smart game. Mixes drop shots
with passing shots.

No ceiling shots. Just a good mix.

Runs every day. Never tires. Better win
the first games. Use change of pace to
surprise.
```

FIGURE 22.48: Results of selecting Print All from the File menu. All three cards appear on one page; each card is printed with a solid border for easy identification and perhaps cutting.

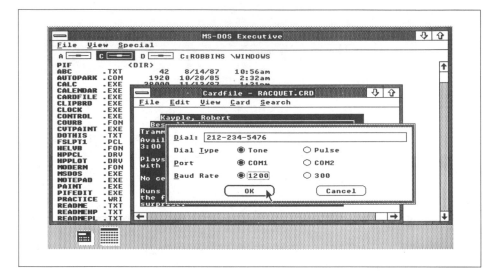

FIGURE 22.49: Autodial option on the Card menu. You can enter a phone number in the Dial text box (for example, 212-234-5476), or you can allow the program to automatically find the phone number on the topmost card in your file. The first phone number, if any, on the topmost card is placed in the Dial text box. That number is then dialed through your connected modem as soon as you select OK.

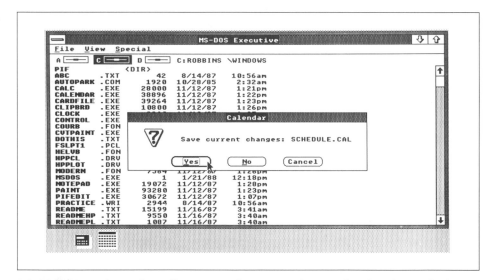

FIGURE 22.50: Windows will not allow you to end a session with outstanding data changes that have not been saved to a disk. In this example, you tried to end the session after saving your card file work. Windows discovers that the SCHEDULE.CAL file had not been updated and so provides you the opportunity to correct this possible oversight before you lose your work.

Spooling Your Output Information

Spooling (see Chapter 16) is even more powerful under Windows than under DOS alone. You can configure Windows to understand several pieces of output hardware (during the Setup procedure) at one time, and because of the multi-tasking capabilities of Windows, you can just as easily have different output spools, or streams, actively working at the same time.

Each separate output device in your system can print files from a different queue of file names. Different programs in your system can be responsible for sending output to each of the output ports and the different devices connected to those ports. Using MS-DOS Executive to run SPOOLER.EXE, you can view and manipulate all of this simultaneous output. The example system in Figure 22.51 has been configured to expect output to LPT1 to actually be connected to an HP LaserJet printer. Also, output to LPT2 will be directed to an HP plotter.

Since you can have multiple output streams executing simultaneously, Windows provides the Priority pull-down menu (see Figure 22.52) to let you influence which queue(s) achieves better response. No matter how many queues exist, you can specify whether each queue is to receive low or high priority service. Since Windows intercepts CPU timer interrupts and then allocates

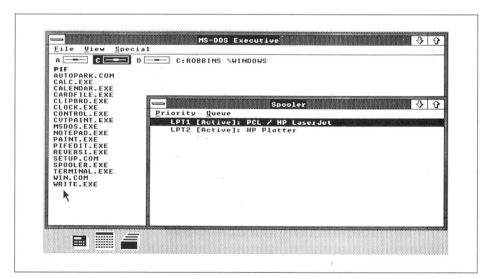

FIGURE 22.51: Results of executing the SPOOLER.EXE program. The initial window displays all configured output devices, the ports associated with them, and two pull-down menus: Priority and Queue. This display also indicates whether each queue is actively open for accepting and processing output data (Active), or is paused and temporarily closed to output processing. Notice that MS-DOS Executive is being displayed in a background window, and that the recently used Cardfile program has been minimized and is visible as a new icon at the bottom of the screen.

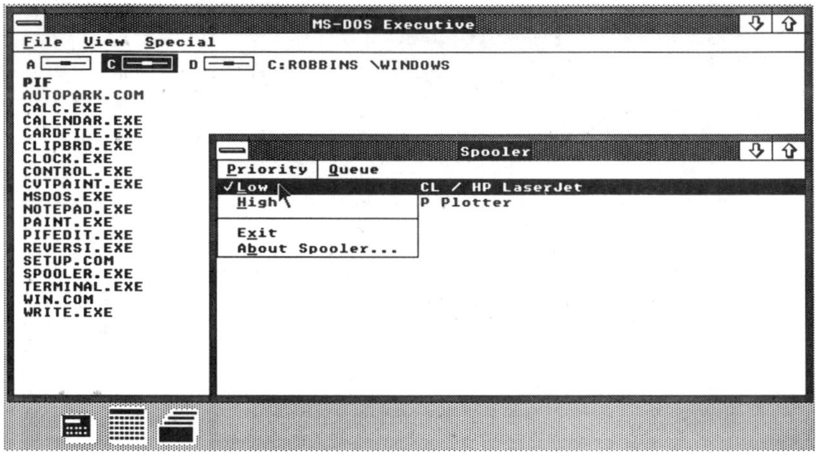

FIGURE 22.52: The Priority pull-down menu of the SPOOLER.EXE program. You can set the processing priority of each spool to one of two relative values: high or low. This lets you specify which of multiple output streams should achieve faster performance results.

time to each of the programs running under it (including the spools), a high-priority spool will achieve better output processing performance than will a low-priority spool.

When the Spooler program begins, after Windows itself begins, all configured output devices have separate spools that are open and actively queueing output information. Each of the possible file names queued for printing on a particular device is listed in the main SPOOLER window, just below the port and device line shown earlier in Figure 22.51. You can control whether any of these individually queued up file names are to be temporarily paused or canceled completely.

Figure 22.53 shows the Queue pull-down menu. Notice that the Terminate option is dimmed, since there is currently no file name in the highlighted queue (HP LaserJet) available for cancellation.

Making Notes and Performing Other Simple File Editing

Windows lets you manipulate text in several ways. The easiest and simplest mechanism for text manipulation is the Notepad program, shown in Figure 22.54. Notice that before Notepad was run, the Spooler window was minimized; it now appears as a new icon at the bottom of the screen.

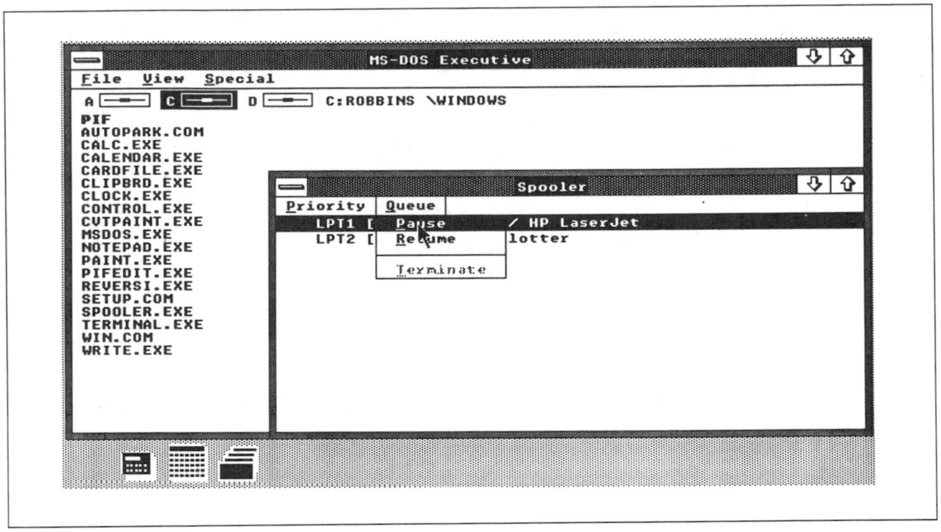

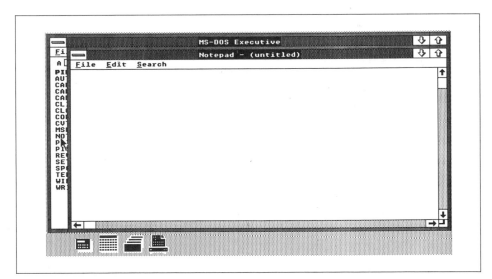

FIGURE 22.53: The Queue pull-down menu. Each queued file can be paused, or halted from printing. When you are ready to continue printing, you must return to this menu and select Resume. Although the Terminate option is not currently available, you can normally use this choice to completely remove (cancel) a print job from a queue.

FIGURE 22.54: The initial Notepad program window. Only three pull-down menus are provided: File, Edit, and Search. Use File to manipulate all the data on the notepad at once, Edit to manipulate individual characters and strings in the file, and Search to locate specific text strings on the Notepad.

When the Notepad program begins, the cursor appears as a blinking vertical bar, as it did in the Cardfile program. You can simply begin typing text onto the Notepad; in fact, you are entering information into the memory-resident portion of what will later become a disk file. Figure 22.55 shows a typical entry sequence.

Although it's not apparent until you enter some text, the default status of the Notepad is line mode. All text stays on a single line until you press the Return key. If you enter more text than can be seen on the screen, the Notepad scrolls the viewing window to the right so you can see your most recently entered characters.

This wide scrolling mode is not the typical way in which the Notepad was designed to work. It is more likely that your text entries will be short notes, and the Notepad will perform the function anticipated by its name of simply storing brief remarks or notes. Programmers can take advantage of the Notepad's simplicity and use it as a convenient programming editor. Computer languages typically work on a line-by-line command basis.

The File menu visible in Figure 22.56 works like other file menus discussed so far. Note the vertical scroll bar on the right side of the screen. Windows expects note files to exceed the size of the on-screen window; you can use the vertical scroll bar to move up and down through the file's contents.

Selecting the Edit menu displays the screen in Figure 22.57. Word wrap has been turned on in this figure to allow the Notepad to be used as a simple letter

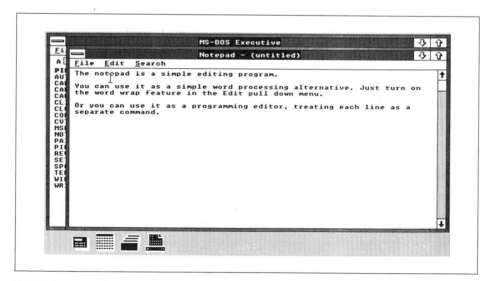

FIGURE 22.55: First data entry in the Notepad. Typically used for jotting down short and simple notes, the Notepad can be used as a handy programming editor or as a simple, word-wrapping text processor. Note that word wrap is an option, not a default feature.

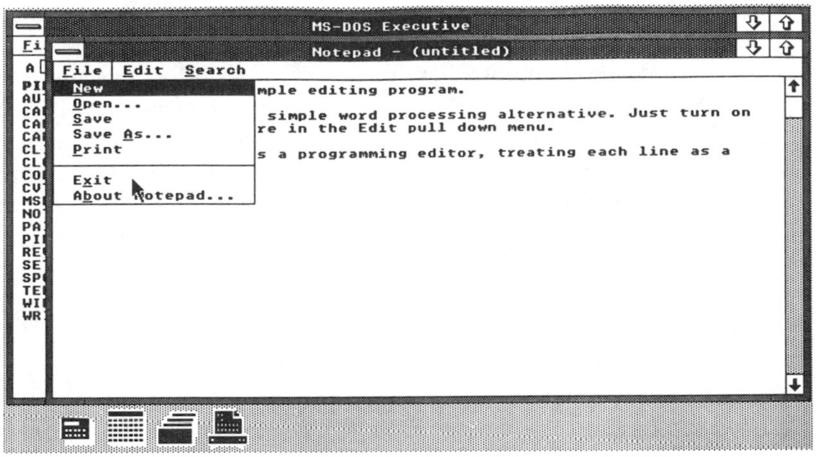

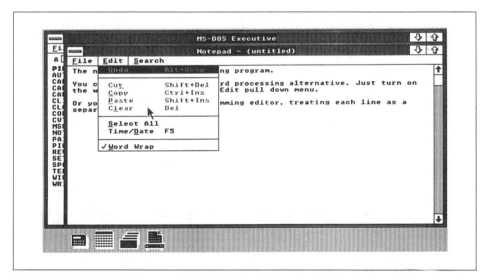

FIGURE 22.56: The File pull-down menu on the Notepad. You can create a new file to store the Notepad's contents, open an old file and display its contents on the Notepad, save the current Notepad contents to disk, save the current Notepad contents in a specifically named alternate file, and send the Notepad's contents to a queue for printing.

FIGURE 22.57: The Edit pull-down menu of the Notepad. Word wrap has been turned on as a feature of text entry. None of the text-manipulation commands (Cut, Paste, Undo, and so on) are available, because no text has been highlighted or just recently deleted.

writer; paragraphs flow more easily when word wrap is used. However, note that you cannot yet use the text-manipulation commands since you have not selected any text for them to operate on.

Built into the Windows environment is both a concept and a program called the Clipboard (CLIPBRD.EXE). Whenever character data is deleted, copied, or moved around in the Windows environment, a copy of that data is stored in a memory buffer. This buffer is analogous to a clipboard and paper. Unless the paper on the clipboard is actually thrown away, you can retrieve it and restore the data placed on it to its former location, and you can just as easily insert a copy of that data at any other location as well.

In Windows, data that has been highlighted (selected) by cursor and mouse manipulation can be operated on by the Edit menu commands. The data usually is moved temporarily onto the internal Clipboard until you decide what its final disposition will be. In Figure 22.58, the second paragraph on the Notepad has been selected by the mouse. It appears in reverse video behind the Edit pull-down menu. Since a text string has been selected and can be acted upon, the formerly italicized Cut, Copy, and Clear options are now available.

Suppose, for instance, that you had selected Cut in Figure 22.58. The entire second paragraph would have been removed (cut) from its existing location. Since there is now information on the Clipboard, the next time you call up the

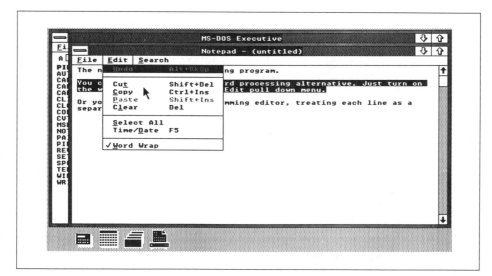

FIGURE 22.58: The Edit menu shows Cut, Copy, and Clear newly available. This is because a text string has been selected on the Notepad for manipulation in some way. Cut removes the string from its current location, saving a copy of the string on the Clipboard for later use. Copy leaves the string as it is and where it is, but deposits a copy of it on the Clipboard for later access. Clear erases the text completely; you will be unable to transfer it to another application, although you can use the Undo command to restore the deleted text in this application.

Edit menu, the Undo and Paste choices will be displayed in normal letters, indicating that they are available as choices.

Figure 22.59 shows the screen after the second paragraph was first cut, the cursor was moved to the end of the notes, and Paste was selected. The paragraph was reinserted (pasted) into the Notepad at the location of the cursor. The net effect in this case was to move the second paragraph from the middle of the document to the end. You could now select Undo to reverse the editing steps. You can use Undo to undo any editing step, whether a cut-and-paste or a simple deletion (clear).

When your notes become more voluminous, you may need the help offered on the Search pull-down menu. As shown in Figure 22.60, you can find any specified character string. When you select Find, a dialog box appears where you can enter the string for which you want the Notepad program to search.

After each occurrence of the specified string is found, you can press the F3 function key or select Find Next from the Search menu to ask the Notepad program to find the next occurrence of the same string. It's important to realize that the searching begins at the point where the cursor is located and proceeds until the end of the notes is reached. Therefore, you should move the cursor to the top of the file before you issue a search request. When the program can find no more occurrences of the string a dialog box appears (see Figure 22.61).

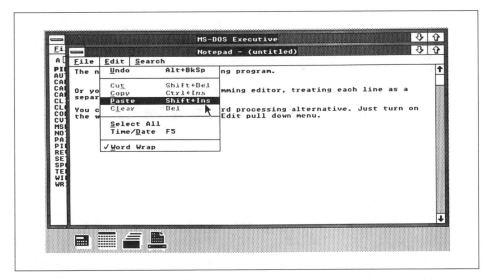

FIGURE 22.59: First the middle paragraph was cut, then the cursor was moved to the end of the Notepad text, and finally the paragraph was pasted back into the Notepad at the new location.

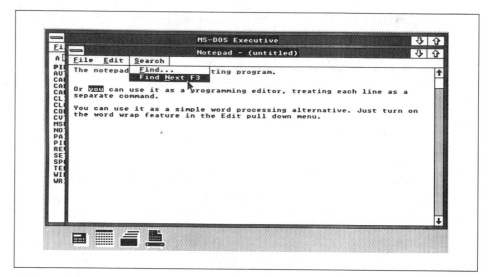

FIGURE 22.60: Find was selected to locate occurrences of the string *you* in the document. The first occurrence is displayed in reverse video. You can select Find Next on the Search menu to locate the next occurrence of the string in the text. Case is ignored in the search, so the *You* at the beginning of the next paragraph would be highlighted next.

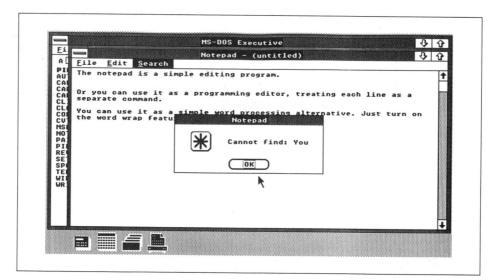

FIGURE 22.61: After finding all occurrences of the specified string in the Notepad, the program displays a pop-up window, indicating that no more occurrences can be found. In this case, the string *you* was found twice before this dialog box appeared. The same type of box would appear immediately if no occurrences at all could be found.

Controlling Your Windows Configuration

When your Windows environment is initially configured, the Setup program asks you to enter a number of important items of information. You can change some of these values at any time by invoking the CONTROL.EXE program (see Figure 22.62).

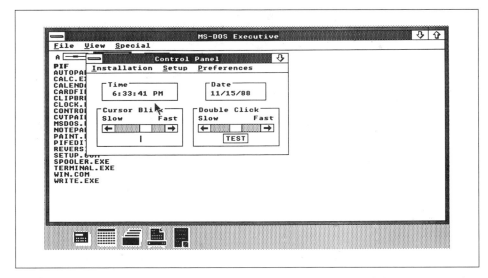

FIGURE 22.62: The Control Panel as it first appears. Three pull-down menus (Installation, Setup, and Preferences) are provided, and the initial display contains the system date and time and a sliding-scale control of the cursor blink rate and the mouse double-click time separation. All of these values can be changed from this window.

You can directly change the system date and time from this window, known as the Control Panel, achieving the same results as when you use the DATE and TIME commands at the DOS prompt. The other features unique to the Control Panel are the cursor blink rate and the time interval between double clicks from your mouse. Notice the word TEST underneath the double-click box.

Some applications require that you double-click the mouse button. To distinguish between a double-click and two successive yet separate clicks, Windows tests the amount of time that elapses between the clicks. The scroll bar in the Double Click box allows you to adjust this interval. You can then move the cursor into the TEST box and try to double-click the mouse. If Windows recognizes the two clicks as a double click, based on your interval setting, then the word TEST will invert (white on black to black on white, or vice versa).

The Control Panel also lets you install or remove printer and font information. Figure 22.63 shows the options available under the Installation pull-down menu.

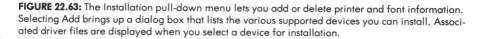

FIGURE 22.63: The Installation pull-down menu lets you add or delete printer and font information. Selecting Add brings up a dialog box that lists the various supported devices you can install. Associated driver files are displayed when you select a device for installation.

The printer driver files used during this control function are obtained from the Utilities disk files on your original disks or from the \WINDOWS directory on your installed hard disk. You can also add or remove output fonts to your Windows installation with this menu. Although the minimum required fonts are automatically loaded during setup, you can override the initial settings and add or delete specific font files available to you.

You can review the current output device and port connections by selecting the Printer choice on the Setup pull-down menu, shown in Figure 22.64.

The Printer choice lets you specify which printer is to be used as the default printer for output from applications designed and configured for Windows operation. Simply move the cursor to the name of the desired printer and click OK. After selecting the default printer, you can enter the printer timeout information in the new dialog box that appears (already visible in Figure 22.64).

A second option on the Setup pull-down menu is Connections. Selecting this option results in the display in Figure 22.65, which lists currently configured printers and plotters and the port to which each is connected.

Miscellaneous Windows system values can be set from the Preferences menu, shown in Figure 22.66.

A dialog box is displayed when you select any of the choices on the Preferences menu, further information clarifying your requirements is solicited by Windows. For example, Figure 22.67 shows the result of selecting Screen Colors from the Preferences pull-down menu.

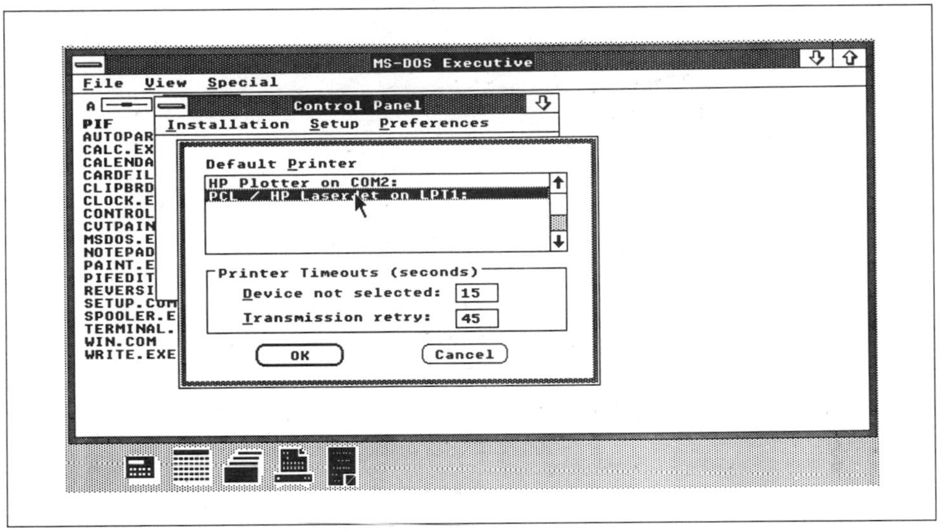

FIGURE 22.64: The Printer selection on the Setup pull-down menu. Currently configured printers and plotters are displayed. You can specify the system default printer and adjust its timeout values (in seconds) on this screen. This example shows a maximum 15 seconds wait before Windows will notify you of an offline condition. Also, Windows will wait for 45 seconds for an online printer to print successfully before notifying you of an error.

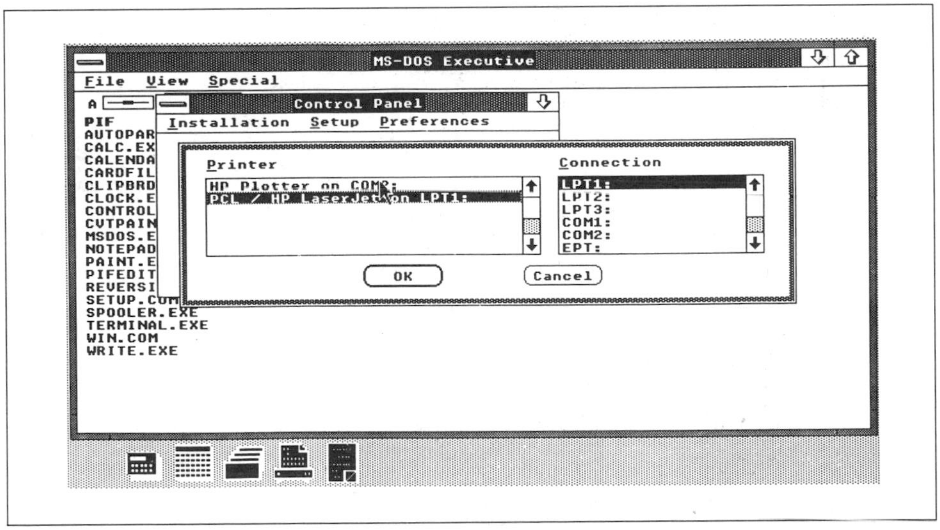

FIGURE 22.65: The Connections choice on the Setup menu. All configured printers and plotters are listed. As you select each one (with the mouse or cursor keys), the port to which that device is connected is highlighted on the right. You can change the port connection by selecting a different port name in the Connection box.

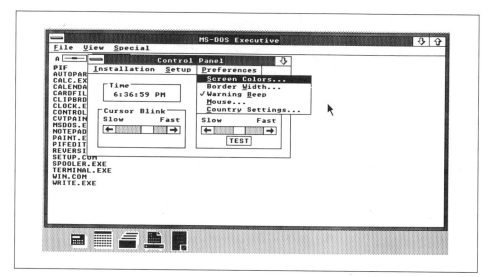

FIGURE 22.66: The Preferences pull-down menu. Miscellaneous Windows settings are accessible here: country settings, mouse speed and click settings, system beep status, window borders thickness, and color intensity and hues for color monitors.

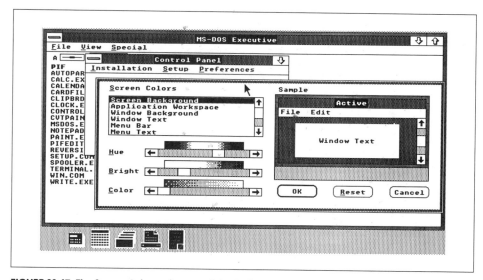

FIGURE 22.67: The Screen Colors submenu of the Preferences pull-down menu. You can now determine, on a sliding scale, values to be used for the hue, brightness, and color saturation of all items displayed by Windows. First, you must select which item is to be influenced (such as the menu bar or the screen background). Then you use your mouse to point to different places on the graduated bars for hue, brightness, and color. The Sample window on the right changes appearance to reflect your choices.

All aspects of a Windows display, including the backgrounds of the different portions and the contents of those portions of the screen, can be controlled from this Preferences menu. Generally, moving the brightness and color bars to extreme rightmost and leftmost values produces the sharpest contrast between background and foreground. However, this also reduces the intensity of color on color monitors.

Playing Reversi: Having Some Fun

Microsoft includes a game called Reversi in the Windows desktop applications package. As Figure 22.68 shows, this game looks similar to the more sophisticated game, go; Reversi follows similar rules for moves to capture territory owned by your opponent's pieces (circles).

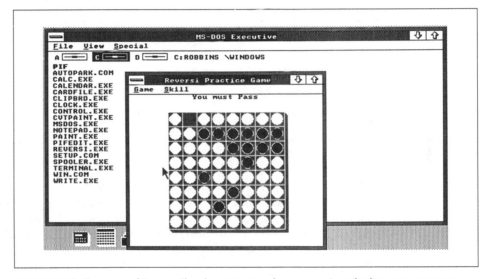

FIGURE 22.68: The game of Reversi. The object is to trap the opponent's circles between your own, thereby turning an opponent's white circles to black, enlarging the territory on the board owned by circles of your color.

At the end of the game, the player owning the most territory is the winner. The game goes quickly (very quickly, if you play against the computer), and it's both intellectually challenging and fun. It can be more fun if you pull down the Game menu before each of your moves to select the Hint choice. The computer then places the cursor in the best location for your next move. Naturally, do this only for the first game or two to quickly learn how to play the game successfully.

Producing Analog Clock Displays

Computers typically display time in digital format. Windows has a program called CLOCK.EXE, however, that displays the time of day in analog format (see Figure 22.69).

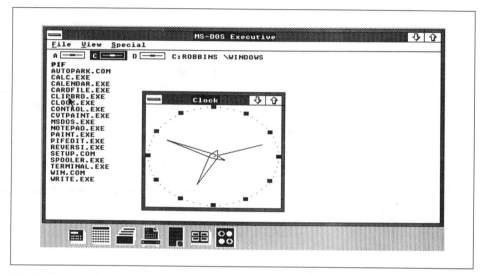

FIGURE 22.69: A colorful way to tell time when in Windows. This analog display shows standard hour and minute hands and a moving second hand. Notice that the control panel and the Reversi game have both been minimized to icons at the bottom of the screen.

This analog clock keeps and displays accurate time, regardless of where you move it on your screen. You can use the control box menu (in the upper-left corner of the clock display) to move the clock or to change the size of the clock. In fact, as Figure 22.70 (presented later) shows, even if you minimize the clock to an icon, it continues to keep and display the correct time. Of course, this is because Windows is a multitasking environment, and the Clock program continues to run, even though its visual output appears only in the minimized icon.

Accessing the Clipboard Directly

When you learned about the Notepad earlier in this chapter, you learned that any text that is deleted or cut is actually temporarily stored in a memory-resident buffer called the Clipboard. During normal use of the other application programs, you never actually see or manipulate the temporary data stored in this Clipboard.

You can run the program CLIPBRD.EXE under Windows to display the current contents of the Clipboard. As Figure 22.70 shows, the Clipboard contains the character string last cut from the Notepad, in Figure 22.58. This cutting could have been undone in the Notepad by selecting Undo from the Edit menu, or this data acquired from the Notepad and now available on the Clipboard could be placed in another application. For example, if you activate the Cardfile application and select the Paste function, the current contents of the Clipboard (the two sentences in Figure 22.70) will be inserted on the top card in the Cardfile.

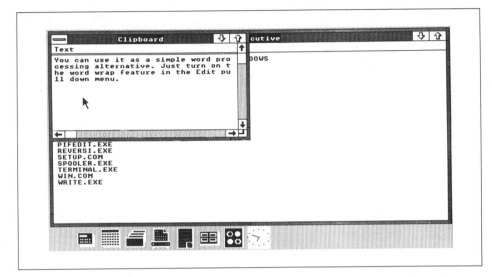

FIGURE 22.70: Initial display of the Clipboard (CLIPBRD.EXE), showing its current contents. In this session, the contents of the Clipboard were deposited by the Cut command last used from the Notepad application and shown in Figure 22.58.

Suppose, for example, that you minimized the Clipboard and MS-DOS Executive and then restored the Cardfile. Figure 22.71 displays the new screen display. The Clipboard icon appears at the bottom of the screen, and MS-DOS Executive returns to the leftmost position at the bottom of the screen. The Cardfile icon is removed in favor of the real Cardfile display.

If you select all the text information on Jimmy Beswell's card and then pull down the Edit menu, you can then copy that data. This choice leaves the card untouched, but deposits a copy of all the text on the Clipboard, wherever the icon or window representing it happens to be located. However, whatever used to be on the Clipboard is now gone forever.

Figure 22.72 shows the information most recently acquired from the Cardfile now available on the Clipboard (whose window size has been adjusted using the Size choice on the Control menu).

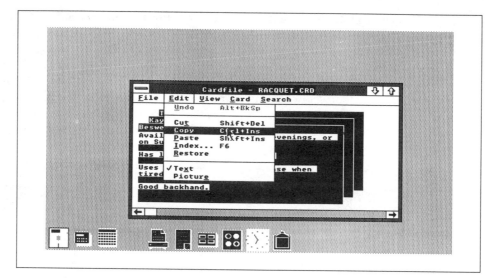

FIGURE 22.71: Minimizing the Clipboard and MS-DOS Executive windows and restoring the Cardfile window. Text on one card is selected followed by the Copy function on the Edit menu. This text is immediately available for pasting into another application because all it is now on the Clipboard.

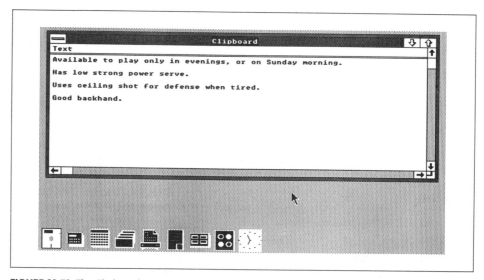

FIGURE 22.72: The Clipboard contains only the most recent information deposited in it, usually by Delete, Cut, or Copy commands. The Clipboard immediately reflects the copy operation most recently performed in the Cardfile program (see Figure 22.71). When this occurs, the former contents, shown in Figure 22.70, are discarded.

Once again, remember that you should save your work at regular intervals. In a complex Windows environment containing many simultaneous applications, such as the example you've worked with here, it is easy to forget what data has been saved and what has not. Windows will not allow you to end a session (by selecting End Session on the MS-DOS Executive Special menu) without prompting you to save any new data. Figure 22.73 displays one of the prompt boxes displayed by Windows if you forget to save recent updates.

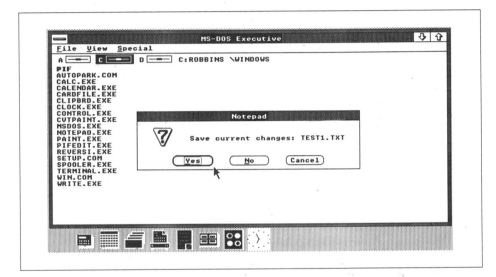

FIGURE 22.73: Windows reminds you to save your work if you try to end a session without doing so. In this case, the Notepad data had previously been saved to a file called TEST1.TXT, but further adjustments during the session have not been saved. Selecting Yes now correctly updates the disk file to reflect these changes. A similar box appears for each application with changes or updates that have not been saved.

SUMMARY

You have learned about the Windows multitasking operating environment in this chapter. You have seen how to run multiple DOS programs simultaneously and how to relate DOS commands to Windows' more intuitive, graphic, mouse-based user interface. You have learned the steps necessary to install and configure Windows, and you have seen the wide range of applications that are part of the Windows package.

For additional information about international country and keyboard support, see

- Chapter 11, "International Setup"

For additional information about computer communications, see

- Chapter 12, "Computer Communications"

For additional information about printers and other hardware connected to DOS through serial ports, see

- Chapter 13, "Software Ports and Hardware Devices"

For additional information about spooling techniques, see

- Chapter 16, "Advanced Printing Techniques"

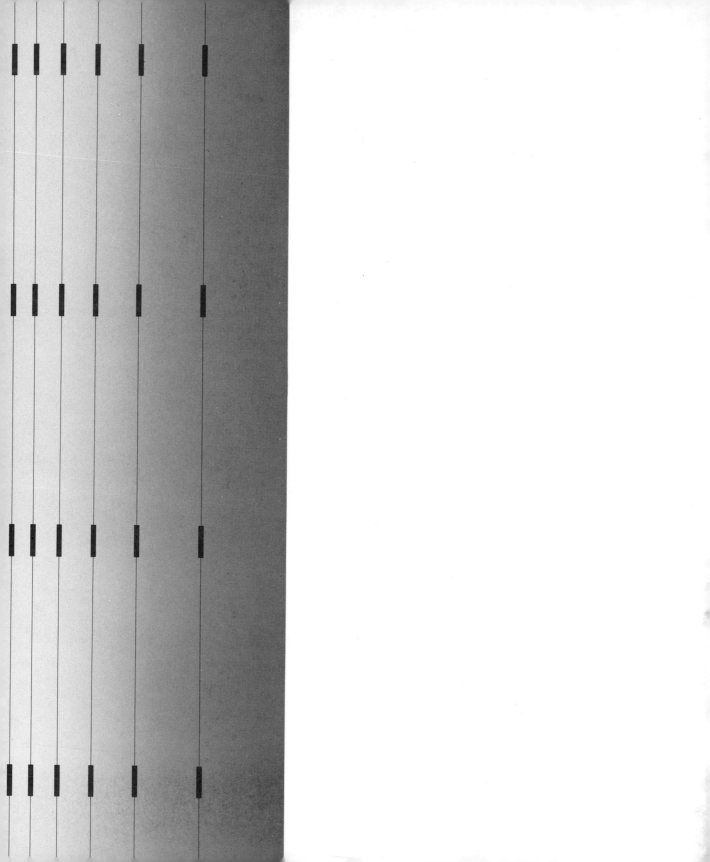

GLOSSARY

This appendix defines all of the important DOS-related terms used in this book. Although these terms are defined in the text when they are introduced, the glossary presented here offers concise definitions that will refresh your memory when you read a chapter later in the book, or when you simply can't remember the meaning of a particular term.

acoustic coupler   An early type of modem, still in fairly common use, that connects to the telephone lines indirectly, using a handset and small speakers. *Compare with* **direct-connect modem**.

active partition   The section of a hard disk containing the operating system to be used when the hardware powers up.

alphanumeric   Belonging to that part of a character set that includes the letters, numerals, and certain commonly used symbols, such as punctuation marks.

analog   Involving the representation of numerical values (often quantifiable physical phenomena such as temperature or frequency) using continuously variable physical properties, such as voltage. *Compare with* **digital**.

analog-to-digital converter   A device used to convert analog electrical signals to digital signals. *Compare with* **digital-to-analog converter**.

ANSI (American National Standards Institute)   An organization that recommends standards in various fields, including electronics. The standard partly encoded in the ANSI.SYS file defines how certain console control sequences are treated.

ANSI driver   A device driver, contained in the ANSI.SYS file, that loads additional support for advanced console features.

application software   Programs whose purpose is to carry out some real-world operation that the user would otherwise have to perform manually. Word processors and spreadsheet packages are examples of application software. Systems software, by contrast, is designed to perform the internal, "housekeeping" operations that enable a computer to run application software.

archive bit   A bit in a file specification that indicates whether the file in question needs to be backed up.

ASCII (American Standard Code for Information Interchange)   The coding scheme whereby every character the computer can access is assigned an integer code. *Standard* ASCII codes range from 0 to 127 and are consistent from machine to machine and from software package to software package. *Extended* ASCII codes range from 128 to 255 and vary considerably, sometimes including foreign-language characters and sometimes including graphic characters. *See also* **code page**.

assembly language   A symbolic form of computer language used to program computers at a fundamental level. *Compare with* **high-level language**, **machine language**.

asynchronous communications   *See* **serial communications**.

AUTOEXEC.BAT   A batch file executed automatically whenever the computer is booted. It usually includes commands to set the prompt and path, to set initial values for environmental variables, and to invoke appropriate memory-resident (TSR) programs.

background task   A second program running on your computer; usually, a printing operation that shares the CPU with your main task. Background tasks are distinguished by the fact that they do not accept keyboard input or produce screen output; once initiated, they run independently. *Compare with* **foreground task**.

bar code   A code in which letters and numbers are represented by black bars of varying width. The code can be "read" electronically and entered into a computer as digital data.

base name   The portion of a file name to the left of the period separator; it can be up to eight characters long.

baseband network   A network that transmits information via pulses rather than a carrier signal. *Compare with* **broadband network**.

BASIC (Beginners All-purpose Symbolic Instruction Code)   A high-level computer language using simple logical structures and a vocabulary similar to English. Some version of BASIC is supplied with most personal computers sold today.

batch file   An ASCII file containing a sequence of DOS commands that, when invoked, assume control of the computer, executing the commands as if they were entered successively by a computer user.

baud rate   The speed of data transmission. *Baud* is usually used to mean the number of bits per second.

binary   A numbering system that uses powers of 2 to generate all other numbers. The two binary digits, 1 and 0, correspond to the off/on voltage states of the electronic components of a computer. Thus, these voltages can be used to represent information. *Compare with* **decimal**, **hexadecimal**.

BIOS (Basic Input/Output System)   The fundamental level of operating system code used to control all interrupts and peripheral-device transmissions.

bit   One-eighth of a byte. A bit is a binary digit, either 0 or 1. *See also* **byte**.

bit forcing   Condition in which the parity bit in a serial data stream is always set to 1 and used as the eighth bit. Also known as mark parity. *Compare with* **bit trimming**.

bit mapping   The way a graphics screen is represented in the computer. The status of each point on the screen is stored in memory. Bit mapping usually signifies point-to-point graphics.

bit trimming   Condition in which the parity bit in a serial data stream is always set to 0 and used as the eighth bit. Also known as space parity. *Compare with* **bit forcing**.

booting up   *See* **bootstrapping**.

boot record   The section on a disk that contains the minimum information DOS needs to start the system. The boot record contains the system ID, the number of bytes per sector, and the number of sectors per cluster. It also contains the number of system-reserved sectors, the number of FAT copies, the maximum number of root directory entries, and the total number of sectors on your hard disk. Last, it contains a format ID, the number of sectors per FAT and per track, and the number of disk heads.

bootstrapping   The process by which a computer starts operating when it is first turned on or restarted with Ctrl-Alt-Del. DOS contains the instructions a computer needs to carry out its startup operations, and nearly all of DOS is stored on disk. The computer's ROM contains a small set of instructions—the bootstrap routine—the system needs to locate the DOS routines and thus "pull itself up by its bootstraps." Computer users also speak of *booting* a disk or program; this simply means loading a program into memory and starting it. *See also* **cold booting**, **warm booting**.

branching   The transfer of control or execution to another statement in a program or batch file. *See also* **decision making**.

break key   The control-key combination that interrupts an executing program or command; activated by pressing the ScrollLock key while holding down the Ctrl key.

bridge   The interface between more than one similar network.

broadband network   A network that uses signals that modify a carrier wave, rather than pulses, to transmit data. *Compare with* **baseband network;** *see also* **carrier wave.**

broadcasting   Sending a message to all or some workstations on a network.

buffer   An area in memory set aside to speed up the transfer of data, allowing blocks of data to be transferred at once.

bus network   A network configuration in which the server sends a signal that passes through all of the nodes on the network, though only the intended receiver node intercepts the signal. *Compare with* **ring network, star network**.

byte   The main unit of memory in a computer. A byte is an eight-bit binary number. One character usually takes up one byte. *See also* **bit.**

C   A computer language popular in microcomputer applications, featuring access to low-level functions and terse syntax.

cache   A portion of memory reserved for the contents of recently referenced disk sectors. Facilitates faster reaccess of the same sectors.

carrier-sense multiple access (CSMA)   A network protocol in which each node sends data only if the network is not busy. If it is, the node waits.

carrier wave   A constant signal whose properties are modified to represent transmitted data. For example, a constant tone that is changed to high to represent one value, such as binary 1, or to low to represent something else, such as binary 0.

case sensitivity   Distinguishing between capital letters and lowercase letters. ASCII assigns different values to the capital and lowercase forms of a letter. Thus, most operations involving text are case sensitive unless, for the sake of user friendliness, a program has been written to ignore case.

CD ROM   Optical storage technique in which data is written to and read from a compact disk with lasers. The data cannnot be rewritten or changed because the writing process physically changes the disk.

chaining   Passing execution control from one batch file to another. Chaining represents an unconditional transfer of control.

channel   A data path.

character set   In DOS, a complete group of 256 characters that can be used by programs or system devices; consists of letters, numbers, control codes, and special graphics or international symbols. *See also* **ASCII**, **code page**, **extended ASCII codes**.

circuit   In networking, the interconnection of several computers via electrical channels.

cluster   A group of contiguous sectors on a disk; the smallest unit of disk storage that DOS can manipulate.

coaxial cable   A type of cable made of insulated wire enclosed in conductive shielding. *Compare with* **twisted pair**.

COBOL   A high-level programming language; usually used for business applications.

code page   A character set that redefines the country and keyboard information for non-U.S. keyboards and systems.

cold booting   The type of bootstrapping that occurs when the computer's power is first turned on and DOS starts the computer operating. Cold booting involves more extensive internal testing than warm booting, which occurs after the computer is reset with Ctrl-Alt-Del. *See also* **bootstrapping**, **warm booting**.

collision   Loss of data occurring when two network nodes transmit at the same time.

collision avoidance   Condition in which data is transmitted on a network without taking the extra time and effort to detect a possible collision. In the event of an actual collision, transmission continues with garbled information. The transmitting stations will know later that a collision has occured when the expected response from the receiving station is not received. *Compare with* **collision detection**.

collision detection   Condition in which transmission is stopped, with both transmitters retransmitting after a random amount of time. *Compare with* **collision avoidance**.

COMMAND.COM   The command processor supplied with DOS.

command line   The line on which a command is entered. This line contains the command and all of its associated parameters and switches. In spite of the name, it may actually consume more than one screen line, since it is terminated by a carriage return.

command processor   The program that translates and acts on commands.

comment   A note written into the text (source code) of a computer program (such as a DOS batch-file program) to explain some aspect of the program's operation to the user. A command word (often REM) or special symbol precedes the comment and instructs the computer to ignore it. Also called a remark.

composite monitor   A type of monitor that receives a single signal for all colors at once. *Compare with* **monochrome monitor**, **RGB monitor**. *See also* **CRT**.

compressed print   Printing that allows more than 80 characters on a line of output (usually 132 characters, but newer printers allow up to 255 characters per line).

computer-aided design (CAD) program   A sophisticated software package containing advanced graphics and drawing features; used by engineers, architects, and designers for drawing and design applications.

COMSPEC   The environment variable that contains the path leading to the resident command processor.

concatenation   The placing of two text files together in a series.

conditional statement   A statement in a batch file that controls the next step to be executed in the batch file, based on the value of a logical test.

CONFIG.SYS   An ASCII text file containing system configuration commands.

configuration   An initial set of system values, such as the number of buffers DOS will use, the number of simultaneously open files DOS will allow, and the specific devices that the system will support.

console   The combination of your system's monitor and keyboard.

contiguous sectors   Physically adjacent disk clusters used by a file.

control codes   ASCII codes that do not display a character but perform a function, such as ringing a bell or deleting a character.

conventional memory   The RAM from 0 to 640K that DOS ordinarily is designed to use. *See also* **expanded memory**, **extended memory**, **RAM**.

copy protection   Mechanism contained in diskettes that inhibits diskette copying using conventional commands.

country code   A configuration feature specifying the country for which you want to use a copy of DOS. This code internally sets up the date and time formats, the collating sequence, the capitalization style, the currency symbol, and the decimal separators to be used.

CPU (Central Processing Unit)   The main chip that executes all individual computer instructions.

CRT (Cathode Ray Tube)   The type of vacuum tube used in televisions and computer monitors; produces an image by shooting electrons against a photosensitive screen. Composite, monochrome, and RGB monitors all use CRTs. *Compare with* **LCD, plasma display**.

Ctrl-Z   The end-of-file marker.

cursor   The blinking line or highlighting box that indicates where the next keystroke will be displayed or what data the next control code entered will affect.

cutting and pasting   Selecting text from one part of a document or visual display and moving it to another location.

cylinder   Two tracks at the same radius on different sides of a double-sided disk; may be extended to include multiple platters on a hard disk. For example, side 0, track 30; side 1, track 30; side 2, track 30; and side 3 track 30 form a cylinder.

daisy-wheel printer   A printer that uses a disk with fully-formed characters on arms radiating from its center. Characters are printed by rotating the disk and striking an arm with a hammer. *Compare with* **dot-matrix printer, ink-jet printer, laser printer, thermal printer**.

data area   The tracks on a disk that contain user data.

database   A collection of data organized into various categories. For example, a phone book is a database.

database management system   A program that allows the creation of specially organized files, as well as data entry, manipulation, removal, and reporting for those files.

data bits   The binary digits that represent data when the computer is communicating. *Compare with* **start bit, stop bit, parity bit.**

data disk   A disk that has been formatted without the /S switch. The disk can contain only data; it cannot contain system files.

data stream   The data transmitted between two computers or computer components.

dead key   A reserved key combination on international keyboards that outputs nothing itself but allows the next keystroke to produce an accent mark above or below the keystroke's usual character.

debugging   The process of discovering what is wrong with a program, where the problem is located, and how to solve the problem.

decimal   A numbering system in base 10. *Compare with* **binary**, **hexadecimal**.

decision making   A point in a program (for example, a batch file) at which execution can continue along at least two different paths, depending on the results of a program test. Also known as logical testing. *See also* **branching**.

default value   The standard value of a variable or system parameter.

deferred execution   The mode of execution used in a program or batch file, in which commands are not carried out until values for command parameters are entered or computed. By contrast, when DOS is used interactively, commands are entered with their parameter values and carried out immediately.

delimiter   A special character, such as a comma or space, used to separate values or data entries.

destination   The targeted location for data, files, or other information generated or moved by a DOS command. *Compare with* **source**.

device   Any internal or external peripheral hardware.

device driver   A special program that must be loaded before a device can be used; the part of DOS that first intercepts an interrupt. Also known as an interrupt handler.

device name   Logical name that DOS uses to refer to a device.

digital   A representation of numeric values based on a collection of individual digits, such as 0's and 1's in the binary number system. *Compare with* **analog**.

digital-to-analog converter   A device used to convert digital information into an analog voltage whose strength is proportional to the numeric value of the digital signal. *Compare with* **analog-to-digital converter**.

digitizer   A device with a movable arm that is used to trace the lines in an image or drawing. The X-Y coordinate values representing the lines are read into the computer as numeric values, allowing the computer and its software to reconstruct and work with an internal (digitized) version of the image. *Compare with* **optical scanner**.

direct-connect modem   A type of modem that connects to the phone directly through the wiring, not through the handset. Direct-connect modems typically can answer and dial the phone themselves. They are less error prone because outside phone noise is eliminated. *Compare with* **acoustic coupler**.

directory   A grouping of files on a disk. These files are displayed together and may include references to other directories (subdirectories).

directory tree   The treelike structure created when a root directory has several subdirectories, each subdirectory has subdirectories, and so on.

disk drive   A hardware device that accesses the data stored on a disk.

diskette   A flexible, removable oxide-coated disk used to store data. Also called a floppy disk. *Compare with* **hard disk**.

disk optimizer   A program that rearranges the location of files stored on a disk in order to make the data in those files more quickly retrievable.

DOS (Disk Operating System)   A disk manager and the program that allows computer-user interaction.

DOS environment   A part of memory set aside to hold certain default values, such as COMSPEC, PATH, LASTDRIVE, and so on, needed in the current environment.

DOS prompt   The visual indication that DOS is waiting for a command or prompting you for input; usually C> or A>.

dot-matrix printer   A printer that represents characters by means of a grid of tiny dots. *Compare with* **daisy-wheel printer**, **ink-jet printer**, **laser printer**, **thermal printer**.

double-density diskette   A diskette on which magnetic storage material is arranged twice as densely as on diskettes commonly in use in the early days of IBM PCs, allowing the storage of twice the earlier amount of data. Usually refers to a 360K, 5¼-inch diskette. *Compare with* **high-capacity diskette, single-density diskette**.

drive identifier   A single letter representing a disk drive; for example, drive A or drive B. In commands, usually requires a colon after it; for example, A:.

DRIVER.SYS   A file containing a device driver for an extra external disk drive. Used in the CONFIG.SYS file.

dual tasking   Condition in which two tasks or programming events occur simultaneously.

duplicity   In serial communications, the indication of whether data is sent to the receiving computer, sent back, and displayed or is sent without verification. *See also* **full duplex**, **half duplex**.

echoing   The condition in which the video monitor displays the keystrokes you enter.

EDLIN   The DOS line editor.

EMS (Expanded Memory Specification)   *See* **LIM EMS**.

end-of-file marker   A Ctrl-Z code that marks the logical end of a file.

environment   *See* **DOS environment**.

error level   A code, set by programs as they conclude processing, that tells DOS whether an error occurred and, if so, the severity of that error.

even parity   *Parity* is a method of verifying the accuracy of information exchanged between computers. The sending computer adds an extra bit to the end of each data byte transmitted. If even parity has been specified, the sum of all the 1 bits in the byte plus this parity bit must be an even number. That is, if the number of 1 bits is already even, the parity bit must be 0. If it is odd, the parity bit must be 1. The receiving computer tests the parity of each byte as it comes in. If it finds a mismatch, the receiver knows there has been an error in transmission. *Compare with* **odd parity**.

expanded memory   In IBM PC, XT, AT, and compatible computers based on the Intel 8088 CPU chip, RAM ranging from 640K to 8MB. This memory is purchased in the form of expansion cards, which are supplied with their own device-driver software and must conform to an industry standard known as the LIM specification. *Compare with* **extended memory**. *See also* **conventional memory, LIM EMS, RAM**.

expansion cards   Add-on circuit boards through which hardware can increase the power of the system, such as adding extra memory or a modem.

expansion slots   Connectors inside the computer in which expansion cards are placed so that they tie in directly to the system.

extended ASCII codes   ASCII codes between 128 and 255, which usually differ from computer to computer.

extended DOS partition   A hard-disk partition used to exceed the 32Mb, single-disk barrier; it can be divided into logical disk drives. *Compare with* **primary DOS partition**.

extended memory   In IBM PC AT and compatible computers based on the Intel 80286 microprocessor chip, built-in RAM ranging from 1 to 16MB. The /E switch to the VDISK.SYS device driver, when it is included in your CONFIG.SYS file, makes this space accessible to DOS in the form of a RAM disk. *Compare with* **expanded memory**. *See also* **conventional memory, LIM EMS, RAM, RAM disk**.

external buffer   A device, connected to the computer and another device, that can store data until the device is ready to accept it.

external command   To the user, each command in DOS or a high-level language such as BASIC is a single instruction. To the computer, however, a single command is actually a series of the much more detailed machine-language instructions it needs. In effect, each command is actually a small program or routine, stored as a file. In DOS, these command files are either loaded into the computer's active memory along with the rest of DOS when the computer is turned on or stored on disk until needed. External, or nonresident, commands are those that are stored on disk until needed. To use an external command, you must make sure it is accessible to DOS. That is, either the command file must be located in the current default directory, or you must define a path to the directory where it is located. *Compare with* **internal command**.

file   A collection of bytes, representing a program or data, stored as a named group on a disk.

file-allocation table (FAT)   A table of clusters stored on a disk that tells DOS whether a given cluster is good, bad, continued, or the end of a chain of clusters.

file-control block   An obsolete data structure used by some older programs to keep track of files in memory.

file locking   A way to prevent a network user from accessing a file that is already in use by another user.

file name   The name of a file on a disk. Usually refers to the base name, but can include the extension as well.

file-name extension   The one to three characters after the period following the base name in a file specification. Used to specify the type of information in a file.

filter   A program that accepts data as input, processes it in some manner, and then outputs the data in a different form.

fixed disk   IBM term for a hard disk.

floppy disk   *See* **diskette**.

flow of control   The order of execution of commands, as in batch files; how the control passes from one command to another, even when the next command to be executed is not located sequentially in the file.

foreground task   The main program running on your computer, as opposed to the less visible background task (usually a printing job). The foreground task controls the computer's acceptance of keyboard input and transmission of output to the screen. *Compare with* **background task**.

formatting   Low-level formatting places timing marks on a disk to arrange the tracks and sectors for subsequent reading and writing; such formatting normally is done by a disk manufacturer. High-level formatting, done by you with the DOS FORMAT command, creates a root directory, a boot record, and a file-allocation table.

fragmentation   A condition in which many different files have been stored in noncontiguous clusters on a disk.

full duplex   In serial communications, sending data to the receiving computer, having that computer send back a copy of the received data, and then displaying the returned copy on the sender's screen. This method is used to verify the accuracy of transmission. *Compare with* **half-duplex**.

function keys   Special-purpose keys on a keyboard, which can be assigned unique tasks by DOS or by application programs.

gateway   The interface between two networks.

global characters   *See* **wildcards**.

graphics mode   The mode in which all screen pixels on a monitor are addressable and can be used to generate detailed images. *Compare with* **text mode**.

half duplex   In serial communications, sending data to a receiving computer and then displaying only the data that was sent (as opposed to the copy of the data returned from the receiving computer). This method is used for transmissions in which verification is not required. *Compare with* **full duplex**.

handshaking   The exchange of signals by which two communicating computational devices synchronize their operation. For example, since a printer can never print as fast as a computer can transmit, it must periodically signal the computer to stop sending data until the printer can accept more.

hard disk   A rigid platter that stores data at a higher density than a floppy diskette and allows faster access. It is sealed in an airtight compartment to avoid contaminants that could damage or destroy the disk. *Compare with* **diskette**.

hardware   The physical components of a computer system (for instance, printers, adapter cards, cables). *Compare with* **software**.

hardware dependency   The design of software in such a way that it requires specific hardware or a specific computer system to run properly.

hardware interrupt   A signal from a device to the CPU, indicating that an event has taken place.

head crash   A collision between the read/write head and the disk platter of a hard disk, which physically damages the disk and the data on it.

help file   A file of textual information containing explanations of commands and modes along with other on-screen tutorial information.

hexadecimal   A numbering system in base 16. A single eight-bit byte can be fully represented as two hexadecimal digits. *Compare with* **binary**, **decimal**.

hidden files   Files whose names do not appear in a directory listing. Usually refers to DOS's internal system files, IBMBIO.COM (or IO.SYS) and IBMDOS.COM (or MSDOS.SYS), but can also refer to certain files used in copy-protection schemes.

high-capacity diskette   A 1.2MB, 5¼-inch floppy diskette. *Compare with* **double-density diskette**, **single-density diskette**.

high-level language   Programming language containing a set of English-like instructions for directing the computer's operations.

high-resolution mode   The mode on a video monitor in which all available pixels are used to provide the most detailed screen image possible. On a color monitor, this mode reduces the possible range of colors that can be used. *Compare with* **medium-resolution mode**.

host computer   Central computer in a computer network. The host computer often holds the primary network operating code, as well as network device drivers. It also controls setup of workstations and communcations parameters for other computers located on the network and for gateway communications to other networks.

hot key   A key combination used to signal a memory-resident program to begin operation. *See also* **TSR program**.

housekeeping   For directories and files, making sure the directory stays intact and well organized and that unnecessary files are deleted. Broadly, any activity, by the user or the machine itself, directed toward maintaining the system rather than running application software to produce results.

hub   The center hole of a diskette.

ink-jet printer   A printer that forms characters by spraying ink in a dot pattern. *Compare with* **daisy-wheel printer**, **dot-matrix printer**, **laser printer**, **thermal printer**.

interface   The boundary between two things, such as a computer and a peripheral device. Also, the connection between a computer program and a user, consisting of an input device (usually a keyboard) and an output visual device (usually a video monitor).

internal command   To the user, each command in DOS or a high-level language such as BASIC is a single instruction. To the computer, however, a single command is actually a series of the much more detailed machine-language instructions it needs. In effect, each command is actually a small program or routine, stored as a file. In DOS, these command files are either loaded into the computer's active memory along with the rest of DOS when the computer is turned on or stored on disk until needed. Internal, or resident, commands are those that are loaded into memory along with the rest of DOS. *Compare with* **external command**.

interrupt   A signal sent to the CPU by a device (hardware interrupt) or a process (software interrupt), indicating a request for service or support from the system. *Compare with* **software interrupt**.

interrupt handler   *See* **device driver**.

I/O (input/output)   Information accepted by the CPU (*input*) or sent by the CPU to a peripheral device (*output*).

insert mode   Mode in which all typed characters are inserted in the line and before the cursor. Existing characters on the line are moved to the right to make room for the new characters. *Compare with* **typeover mode**.

kernel   The part of DOS that performs high-level file management. Contained in the hidden file MSDOS.SYS on MS-DOS systems, or in IBMDOS.COM in PC-DOS systems.

keyboard driver   The routine that responds to a keyboard interrupt, produced by pressing a key. This routine translates the scan code received from the keyboard hardware (indicating which key was pressed) into an ASCII code. It also handles unique key combinations, such as Ctrl-C.

keyboard translation table   An internal table, contained in the keyboard driver, that converts hardware signals from the keyboard into the correct ASCII codes.

key combination   When two or more keys are pressed simultaneously, as in Ctrl-ScrollLock or Ctrl-Alt-Del.

key redefinition   Assigning a nonstandard value to a key.

kilobyte (K)   1024 bytes.

LAN   *See* **local-area network**.

landscape mode   Printer output not in the usual format, but rather with the wider part of the paper positioned horizontally, as in a landscape picture. *Compare with* **portrait mode**.

laser printer   A printer that produces images (pictures or text) by shining a laser on a photostatic drum that picks up toner and then transfers the image to paper. It offers the highest resolution (that is, the sharpest image) of any standard computer printer. *Compare with* **daisy-wheel printer**, **dot-matrix printer**, **ink-jet printer**, **thermal printer**. *See also* **letter-quality printer**.

LCD (Liquid Crystal Display)   A method of producing an image using electrically sensitive crystals suspended in a liquid medium.

letter-quality printer   A printer that forms characters comparable to those of a typewriter. Uses a daisy-wheel or thimble mechanism, each of which contains fully-formed character images. A hammer strikes the correct character, which strikes a ribbon and leaves an image on the paper.

LIM EMS (Lotus-Intel-Microsoft expanded memory specification)   An industry standard that enables the use of memory beyond the 640K DOS program limit. Through the use of a consistent software driver interface, the expanded memory manager (EMM.SYS), programs can be written or rewritten under DOS to address large amounts of memory (up to 8MB under the LIM 3.2 standard, and up to 32MB under the 1987 LIM 4.0). The expanded memory is treated as separate 16K pages that are accessed through a low-memory windowing technique managed by EMM.SYS.

line editor   A program that can make textual changes to an ASCII file, but that can change only one line of the file at a time.

line feed   When the cursor on a screen moves to the next line, or when the print head on a printer moves down the paper to the next line. Caused by transmission of a control code (ASCII 10 or Ctrl-J) to the print or display device.

literal   Data, such as a command parameter, that is accepted exactly as it was submitted and not interpreted as, say, a control code.

local task   Any task that can be performed at a workstation independent of a remotely located process or peripheral device.

local-area network (LAN)   A way of linking several personal computers to one main personal computer so that all computers can communicate directly and have access to the same files and peripheral devices. *Compare with* **wide-area network**. *See also* **network**.

lockup   A state in which the computer will not accept any input and may have stopped processing. The computer must be rebooted to resume operation.

log file   A separate file, created with the DOS BACKUP command, that keeps track of the names of all files written to the backup diskettes.

logging on   Signing onto a remote system, such as a mainframe or tele-communications service.

logical   Defined based on a decision, not by physical properties.

logical drives   Disk drives, created in an extended DOS partition, that do not exist as separate disk drives, although DOS treats them as if they do. A means for DOS to access a physical disk that has more than 32MB available.

logical testing   *See* **decision making**.

machine language   The most fundamental format in which to program a computer, using instructions made up entirely of strings of 0's and 1's. *Compare with* **assembly language**, **high-level language**.

macro   A set of commands, often memory resident, that are activated by a single command or keystroke. When executed, they appear to the program executing them as if they were being entered by the user.

mark parity   *See* **bit forcing**.

media   The cables or phone wires used for channels in a network (transmission media). The disks or tapes used to store data files on a computer (storage media).

medium-resolution mode   The mode on a Color Graphics Adapter in which only 320 × 200 pixels of resolution are allowed. *Compare with* **high-resolution mode**.

megabyte (MB)   1024 kilobytes.

memory   The circuitry in a computer that stores information. *See also* **RAM**, **ROM**.

memory resident   Available in physical memory for immediate execution, as opposed to having to be loaded from a disk file.

menu   A set of choices displayed in tabular format.

metasymbols   Special single-character codes used by the DOS PROMPT command to represent complex actions or sequences to be included in the DOS prompt.

microfloppy diskette   A 3½-inch diskette format used in the new IBM Personal System/2 and many other computers.

modem   *Mo*dulator/*dem*odulator; a device that allows computers to communicate over telephone lines. The telephone system is designed to carry signals in the audible frequency range, but a computer's output is outside this range. A modem generates an audible tone and superimposes the digital information upon it.

monitor   The device used to display images; a display screen. *See also* **composite monitor**, **CRT**, **monochrome monitor**, **RGB monitor**.

monochrome monitor   A video display using two colors only: a background and a foreground color. *Compare with* **composite monitor**, **RGB monitor**.

mouse   A device that moves the screen cursor by means of a hand-held apparatus moved along a surface such as a desk. The computer can tell how far and in which direction the mouse is being moved.

multitasking   Two or more computing applications executing simultaneously.

national language-support operations   The DOS 3.3 feature that supports displays and printers, using a new range of code and character groupings.

NETBIOS   The base-level programming that controls data transfer between workstations and servers in a network.

network   Several computers, connected together, that can share common data files and peripheral devices. *See also* **bus network**, **local-area network**, **ring network**, **star network**.

network software   The layers of software that govern and facilitate the transfer of data within a network.

nibble   Four bits, or half a byte.

NLSFUNC (national language-support function)   Function that loads in the routines necessary to maintain code pages and the CHCP command.

node   The point where several channels meet in a network. Also, the endpoint of a channel (that is, a workstation).

octal   A numbering system in base 8.

odd parity   *Parity* is a method of verifying the accuracy of information exchanged between computers. The sending computer adds an extra bit to the end of each data byte transmitted. If odd parity has been specified, the sum of all the 1 bits in the byte plus this parity bit must be an odd number. That is, if the sum of the bits is already odd, the parity bit must be 0. If it is even, the parity bit must be 1. The receiving computer tests the parity of each bit as it comes in. If it finds a mismatch, the receiver knows there has been an error in transmission. *Compare with* **even parity**.

operating system   A comprehensive software package that acts as an intermediary between users and applications on the one hand, and the machine with its disk drives and other hardware devices on the other. *See also* **DOS**.

optical character reader (OCR)   A device that reads text into a computer. OCRs are designed to recognize a more-or-less narrow range of typefaces, translating the graphic image of a letter into its ASCII value for processing by the computer. *Compare with* **digitizer**.

optical scanner   A device that enters images into a computer.

optical storage   A way of storing data on compact disks; the small depressions on the disk are read by a scanning laser beam and translated into digital form.

overlay files   Files containing additional command and control information for sophisticated and complex programs. Large and seldom-used parts of programs can be placed in overlay files and loaded only as needed. This technique can reduce the overall memory requirements of an application program.

overwrite mode   *See* **typeover mode**.

overwriting   Typing new data over what is already there.

parallel communications   Data transmission in which several bits are transferred or processed at one time.

parameter   An extra item of information, specified with a command, that determines how the command executes. With most DOS commands, the parameters are the names of files upon which the command is to operate. *See also* **literal**, **variable parameter**.

parity   A method of verifying the accuracy of information exchanged between computers. The sending computer adds an extra bit to the end of each data byte transmitted. Depending on the type of parity (even or odd) agreed upon, the sum of all the 1 bits in the data byte plus this parity bit must be either even or odd. If the sum of the bits is an odd number, the parity bit must be 1 to achieve even parity and 0 for odd parity. The receiving computer tests the parity of each byte as it comes in. If it finds a mismatch, the receiver knows there has been an error in transmission.

parity bit   The bit, added to the end of a stream of data bits, that makes the total of the data bits and the parity bits odd or even. *See also* **parity**.

parity error   An error generated when one type of parity is specified (even or odd) and the parity bit sets the opposite parity (odd or even). *See also* **parity**.

partition   The section of a hard disk that contains an operating system. One hard disk can have up to four partitions.

Pascal   A high-level language used mainly to teach the principles of computer programming. Extended versions, with more powerful and easier-to-use features than the original definition of the language, have become popular in programming personal computers.

range A contiguous series of values (minimum to maximum, first to last, *n* to *xn*, and so on).

read-after-write verification An extra level of validity checking, invoked with the VERIFY command or the /V switch. In this method, DOS rereads data after writing it to a disk, comparing the written data to the original information.

read-only status Indicates that a file cannot be updated but can only be read.

read/write bit The bit in a file specification that indicates whether a file can accept changes or deletions or can only be accessed for reading.

read/write head A disk-drive mechanism that reads data from and writes data to a disk.

record lock A means of preventing a network user from accessing a record that is already in use by another user.

redirection Causing a program to receive input from a file or device other than the keyboard or to send its output to a file or device other than the screen. *See also* **piping**.

redirector The layer in a network software that determines whether data should be allowed to cross from the network to the workstation or vice-versa.

remark *See* **comment**.

reserved names Words in a programming language or operating system that should be used only in a particular context.

resident command *See* **internal command**.

resource allocation   Making system facilities available to individual users or programs.

reverse video   Black letters on an illuminated background.

RGB monitor   A type of monitor in which the color signal for each color is sent independently. *RGB* stands for red, green, blue, the primary monitor colors. *Compare with* **composite monitor**, **monochrome monitor**. *See also* **CRT**.

ribbon cable   Type of cable used to connect two devices that need many different connections; a flat cable of up to 25 wires.

ring network   A network configuration in which a cable connects all workstations and servers in a circular pattern. *Compare with* **bus network**, **star netowrk**. *See also* **token ring network**.

ROM (read-only memory)   The section of memory that you can only read. ROM contains the basic computer operating system and system routines.

root directory   The first directory on any disk.

scan code   The hardware code representing a key pressed on a keyboard. Converted by a keyboard driver into an ASCII code for use by DOS and application programs.

scrolling   The up or down panning of your screen's display, as a window into a file (vertical scrolling). Also, the right or left panning of your screen's display, as a window into a file (horizontal scrolling). Also, the action of a DOS screen when all twenty-five lines roll up one by one when a screen is full and a new line is displayed or entered.

secondary command processor   A second copy of the COMMAND.COM file, invoked either to run a batch file or to provide a new context for subsequent DOS commands.

subcommands   A special type of command used by DOS primarily in batch files.

subdirectory   A directory contained in another directory or subdirectory. Technically, all directories other than the root directory are subdirectories. *See also* **directory tree**.

switch   A parameter included in a DOS command, usually preceded by the slash (/) symbol, that clarifies or modifies the action of the command.

synchronization   The coordination of a sending and a receiving device, so that both send and receive data at the same rate.

synchronous communication   Communication in which the space between characters sent over a line is uniform, and start and stop bits are unnecessary.

syntax   The form and sequence in which you enter a command; includes spelling, parameter locations, and so on.

system disk   A disk containing the DOS files necessary to boot the system.

text mode   The mode in which standard ASCII characters can be displayed on a monitor. *Compare with* **graphics mode**.

thermal printer   Type of printer that forms characters using a heating process and heat-sensitive paper. Compact and inexpensive but producing relatively poor-quality print, thermal printers are commonly used in portable and laptop computers and in desktop calculators. *Compare with* **daisy-wheel printer**, **dot-matrix printer**, **ink-jet printer**, **laser printer**.

time slice   The smallest unit of time managed and assigned by the operating system to programs and other processing activities.

timeout   A specified amount of time after which an error is generated if an expected occurrence does not take place.

toggle   A hardware switch or software command that changes a setting from one of its two possible states to the other.

token   A bit pattern passed from station to station in a network allowing the station that has it to transmit data over the network.

token ring   A ring network that uses token passing as its protocol. *See also* **ring**.

topology   The configuration of a network. *See also* **bus network**, **ring network**, and **star network**.

touch screen   A screen that is ringed by light beams. When you touch the screen and the beams are interrupted, the computer can tell where you are pointing.

track   A circular stream of data on the disk. Similar to a track on a record, except that tracks on computer disks are not spiral.

transient command   A command whose procedures are read from the disk into memory, executed from memory, and then erased from memory when finished. Also called external command.

TSR program   A program that, when executed, carves out a piece of memory for itself and stays there. When you are done with the TSR program, it allows you to continue what you were previously doing. The term *TSR* is short for terminate and stay resident. Also called a RAM-resident program. *See also* **hot key**.

twisted pair   A type of cable, such as telephone cable, that consists of two wires, one wrapped around the other. Twisted pair is easier to work with than coaxial cable, but it cannot handle as high a transmission rate. *Compare with* **coaxial cable**.

typeover mode   Mode in which each character typed replaces the current character at the cursor location. *Compare with* **insert mode**.

uninterruptable power supply (**UPS**)   A continually charging battery that powers your computer should the main source of power fail.

utility program   A supplemental routine or program designed to perform a specific operation, usually to modify the system environment or perform housekeeping tasks.

variable parameter   A named element, following a command, that acts as a placeholder; when you issue the command, you replace the variable parameter with the actual value you want to use. *Compare with* **literal**.

VDISK.SYS   Device driver used to create a RAM disk.

verbose listing   A listing of all files and subdirectories contained on the disk and path specified in the command. Activated by the CHKDSK command with the /V switch.

virtual disk   *See* **RAM disk**.

voice recognition   The ability of a computer to recognize and respond to spoken words.

volume label   A name, consisting of up to 11 characters, that can be assigned to any disk during a DOS FORMAT operation or after formatting with the LABEL command.

WAN   *See* **wide-area network**.

warm booting   Resetting the computer using the Ctrl-Alt-Del key combination. *See also* **bootstrapping**, **cold booting**.

wide-area network (WAN)   A network that has terminals wired in from outside the building that houses the central processing computer and main storage devices. *Compare with* **local-area network**. *See also* **network**.

wide directory listing   An alternate output format that lists file names in five columns.

wildcards   Characters used to represent other characters. In DOS, * and ? are the only wildcard symbols. The question mark represents a single character, and the asterisk represents zero or more characters.

word   A unit of computer storage, typically two bytes in PC usage.

word processor   An application program that allows the creation, correction and reformatting of documents before they are printed. Most of the common word processing programs work with DOS. Occasionally, a computer system is designed to be used exclusively for word processing. Such systems do not use DOS.

WORM drive   A type of optical storage device in which data can be stored once and accessed as often as needed, but cannot be erased or changed. The term *WORM* is short for write once, read many times.

write-protection   Technique that gives a disk read-only status by covering the write-protect notch. Also, a feature of the ATTRIB command which, when set, allows files to be read from, but not written to.

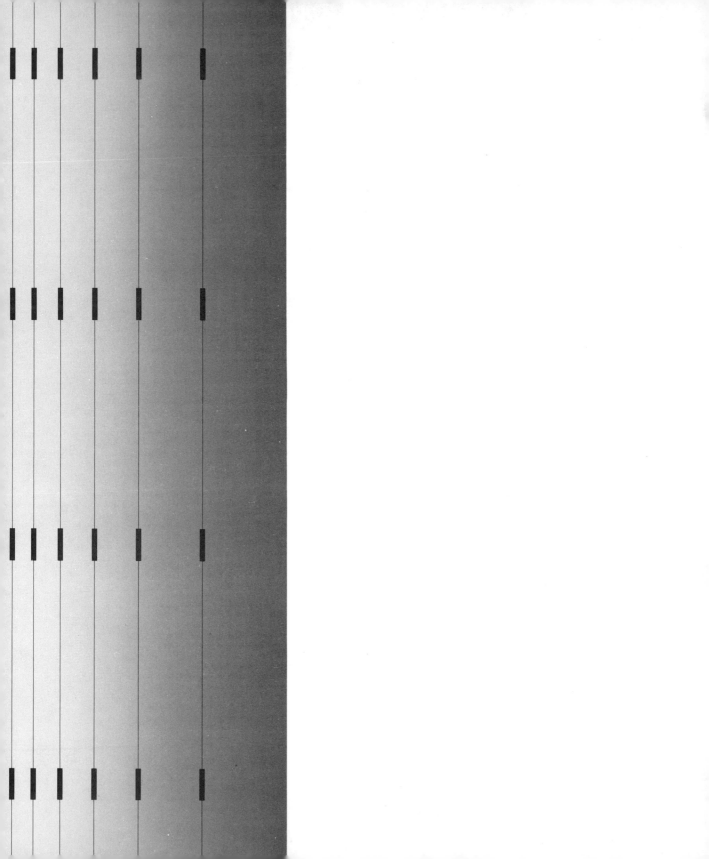

DOS ERROR AND
INFORMATION MESSAGES

DOS can do many things, but it must be given clear instructions by you. If your command contains incorrect syntax or illogical requests, DOS often can recognize and alert you to the problem. It lets you know this by displaying an *error message*. DOS also presents messages to request information from you or simply to let you know what it is doing. This appendix lists these messages alphabetically and discusses the potential causes of each message, and (if there is a problem) some possible solutions.

There are several types of messages. *Device errors* occur when something happens during a read or write operation to the disk or any other device. A device error causes DOS to display an error message and then prompt you for further directions. A typical prompt looks like this:

Abort, Retry, Ignore, Fail? _

If you select Abort, DOS terminates the program that requested the read/ write operation. Selecting Retry directs DOS to attempt again to read or write the information. This option usually offers the best solution, since the most common reason for a device error is that the specified device is not ready. Choosing Ignore asks DOS to continue running the current program from the point of the error message. Fail is similar to Ignore, but it asks DOS to continue running the program from the point just after the system call just requested. Both of these last two choices may lead to data loss or file corruption; do not select them unless you know precisely what the results will be.

You will need to take steps to alleviate the problem and *then* press the first letter of the choice you want. For example, if you left the drive door open and asked for a directory listing, DOS would display a device error message. Close the door and type "R" for Retry, and your directory should be redisplayed, unless something else also goes wrong.

Hardware errors involve problems with the computer equipment outside of read/ write operations.

The next class of error message, *execution errors*, includes errors generated during the execution of a command or program. They may have nothing to do with the physical characteristics or setup of the computer, but rather with how the command was entered, or what the program was supposed to do.

The third class of errors consists of *data corruption* errors. These errors occur when information has gone bad on a disk or in memory and needs to be corrected.

The fourth class of message are those displayed for *information* only (such as a code-page status message). These do not require any input or corrective action.

The fifth class of message consists of *requests*. Request messages occur when DOS needs more information from you or requires you to do something, such as swap disks. Requests can come from either devices or programs and are not necessarily the result of errors.

Startup errors are those occuring only when DOS performs its internal diagnostic tests after the machine is turned on. These errors may involve incorrect specification of some item in the CONFIG.SYS file.

DOS informs you of *disk problems* when the FORMAT command finds that a disk, or part of a disk, cannot be formatted.

Operator errors occur when you insert a disk incorrectly, or at the wrong time.

DOS also presents messages to alert you to any errors it encounters in programs you write. Most of these involve assembly-language programming, a topic that is beyond the scope of this book. Assembly-language programming errors are not listed in this appendix. Other programming errors, however, involve incorrect use of the DOS batch-file programming language discussed in Part III. These are listed here as *batch-file programming errors*.

Keep in mind that these categories are purely informal and are included simply as descriptions. Some of them may overlap. More important are the causes of individual messages and your responses.

This appendix lists all DOS messages in alphabetical order along with their type, the source that generated the message, the cause of the error or message, and solutions or actions to take to rectify the error or satisfy the message, if any exist. When the source of an error is a command internal to DOS itself, that internal command will be cited for more precision.

Abort edit (Y/N)?

Type: Request message
Source: EDLIN
Cause: You attempted to quit EDLIN.
Response: Type Y to quit or N to go back to the * prompt.

Access denied

Type: Execution error
Source: I/O commands

Cause: You tried to access a file incorrectly (for example, you tried to write to a read-only file).

Response: Use another file or change the attributes of the file you tried to access; then try the operation again.

Active code page: **xxx**

Type: Information message

Source: CHCP

Cause: This message appears when you run the CHCP command asking DOS to display the number of the code page it is currently using.

Response: No response required.

Active code page for device **ddd** *is* **nnn**

Type: Information message

Source: MODE CODEPAGE

Cause: MODE generates this message to notify you of the current code page status.

Response: No response required.

Active code page not available from CON device

Type: Information message

Source: KEYB

Cause: DOS could not determine the CON code page when the KEYB status request was issued.

Response: Install the driver for code-page switching on the CON: device.

Add **d:\path\filename?**

Type: Request message

Source: REPLACE

Cause: When you executed REPLACE, you asked to be prompted. This message asks whether you want the file added to the target disk.

Response: Reply Y or N, and then press Enter.

Adding d:\path\filename

> **Type:** Information message
> **Source:** REPLACE
> **Cause:** REPLACE is adding the specified file to the target.
> **Response:** No response required.

All files canceled by operator

> **Type:** Information message
> **Source:** PRINT/T
> **Cause:** You canceled the printing of all of the files in the print queue.
> **Response:** No response required. This message will also appear on the printer.

All logical drives deleted in the Extended DOS partition

> **Type:** Information message
> **Source:** FDISK
> **Cause:** You deleted all of the defined drives in the extended DOS partition on your hard disk.
> **Response:** No response required. You can now delete the extended DOS partition, if you wish.

All specified file(s) are contiguous

> **Type:** Information message
> **Source:** CHKDSK
> **Cause:** None of the files on the specified disk are fragmented.
> **Response:** No response required.

Allocation error, size adjusted

> **Type:** Information message
> **Source:** CHKDSK or CHKDSK/F
> **Cause:** An incorrect cluster number appears in the file-allocation table.
> **Response:** If you entered CHKDSK, type CHKDSK/F to correct the file size.

APPEND already installed

Type: Execution error; information message

Source: APPEND

Cause: You tried to execute APPEND from a disk when it was already loaded into memory.

Response: Execute APPEND from memory by not preceding it with a drive or path specification.

APPEND / ASSIGN conflict

Type: Execution error

Source: APPEND

Cause: You tried to load APPEND after ASSIGN had been executed.

Response: Load APPEND first and then ASSIGN.

APPEND / TopView conflict

Type: Execution error

Source: APPEND

Cause: You tried executing APPEND after entering TopView.

Response: Exit TopView, execute APPEND, and then return to TopView.

Attempted write-protect violation

Type: Execution error

Source: FORMAT

Cause: You tried to format a write-protected diskette.

Response: Insert a new diskette or remove the write-protect label on the current diskette.

*** *Backing up files to drive* x *** *Diskette Number:* x

Type: Information message

Source: BACKUP

Cause: BACKUP is displaying the names of the files it is currently processing.

Response: No response required.

Backup file sequence error

Type: Execution error

Source: RESTORE

Cause: You inserted a diskette out of sequence for a file that is backed up on several diskettes.

Response: Restart RESTORE and use the correct diskette order.

Bad call format

Type: Device error

Source: Device driver

Cause: You sent an incorrect header length request to the driver.

Response: If you are using a canned program, contact your dealer.

Bad command

Type: Device error

Source: Device driver

Cause: A driver sent a bad command to its device.

Response: Check your device specifications and interfacing protocols. Review your program for possible mistakes.

Bad command or file name

Type: Execution error

Source: DOS

Cause: You entered an invalid command or misspelled a file name.

Response: Check your spelling. If you are trying to execute a batch file, check the path and your current directory.

Bad or missing Command interpreter

Type: Execution error

Source: DOS

Cause: One of the following errors occurred: The disk you are trying to boot does not have a COMMAND.COM file; at bootup, an error occurred during COMMAND.COM loading; you moved COMMAND.COM to a different directory after you started the computer, and DOS is lost; the COMSPEC = environment variable led to a directory not containing COMMAND.COM; while reloading COMMAND.COM, you set the environment space to a size not between 160 and 32768; the SHELL specification in CONFIG.SYS is incorrect.

Response: Perform a warm boot or fix any of the mistakes listed here and reboot. If you cannot load the system, boot from another diskette containing COMMAND.COM; then copy COMMAND.COM to the problem diskette's root directory.

Bad or missing filename

Type: Startup error

Source: DOS

Cause: One of the following errors occurred: DOS could not find the file specified in a DEVICE =*filename* statement in the CONFIG.SYS file; a break address exceeded machine size; an error occurred during a driver load operation.

Response: Check your spelling in CONFIG.SYS; correct the coding in an incorrect device driver; or contact your dealer.

Bad or missing Keyboard Definition File

Type: Execution error

Source: KEYB

Cause: DOS could not find the KEYBOARD.SYS file, or the file was invalid.

Response: Place the KEYBOARD.SYS file where DOS can find it (such as with the APPEND specification). If the KEYBOARD.SYS file is readily accessible to DOS, make a new copy of it from the DOS Startup/Operating diskette.

Bad Partition Table

Type: Execution error

Source: FORMAT

Cause: The fixed disk does not have a DOS partition, or the partition is invalid.

Cannot create extended DOS partition
without primary DOS partition on disk 1

> **Type:** Execution error
>
> **Source:** FDISK
>
> **Cause:** You must have a primary DOS partition on the first fixed disk drive.
>
> **Response:** Create a primary DOS partition on the disk using FDISK and then create an extended partition.

Cannot create a zero cylinder partition

> **Type:** Execution error
>
> **Source:** FDISK
>
> **Cause:** You tried to create a partition with no size (0 cylinders).
>
> **Response:** When you create a partition, specify a size of at least 1 cylinder.

Cannot delete extended DOS partition
while logical drives exist

> **Type:** Execution error
>
> **Source:** FDISK
>
> **Cause:** You tried to remove an extended DOS partition that still had logical drives defined for it.
>
> **Response:** Using FDISK, remove all of the logical drives from the extended partition; then delete the extended partition.

Cannot DISKCOMP to or from a network drive

> **Type:** Execution error
>
> **Source:** DISKCOMP
>
> **Cause:** DISKCOMP does not work on shared network drives.
>
> **Response:** In nonshared situations, enter
>
> **COMP *.***
>
> In shared situations, pause the server, execute a DISK-COMP command, and then continue server operation.

Cannot DISKCOPY to or from a network drive

Type: Execution error

Source: DISKCOPY

Cause: DISKCOPY does not work on network or shared drives.

Response: In nonshared situations, enter

COPY *.*

In shared situations, pause the server, execute a DISKCOPY command, and then continue server operation.

Cannot do binary reads from a device

Type: Execution error

Source: COPY

Cause: You cannot copy from a device using the /B parameter because COPY needs to be able to detect the end-of-file marker.

Response: Do not use /B, or use /A after the device name in the COPY command line.

Cannot edit .BAK file—rename file

Type: Execution error

Source: EDLIN

Cause: EDLIN will not load a .BAK file, as it assumes that the file is a backup version and that a more recent copy is available for editing.

Response: Rename the file with a different extension or copy the file with another name and extension.

Cannot Exec BASICA.COM

Type: Execution error

Source: BASIC

Cause: You typed BASIC, but BASICA cannot be found.

Response: Make sure BASICA is in the current directory.

Cannot execute FORMAT

> **Type:** Execution error
>
> **Source:** BACKUP
>
> **Cause:** You tried to make a backup copy on an unformatted floppy disk. BACKUP therefore needs to format the disk, but it cannot find FORMAT in the current directory or along the path.
>
> **Response:** Replace the unformatted diskette with a formatted diskette and press a key, or restart BACKUP making sure the FORMAT command is available.

Cannot FDISK with network loaded

> **Type:** Execution error
>
> **Source:** FDISK
>
> **Cause:** You tried to use FDISK on a networked hard disk.
>
> **Response:** Restart the system and execute FDISK before loading the network software.

Cannot find System Files

> **Type:** Execution error
>
> **Source:** FORMAT
>
> **Cause:** FORMAT could not find the hidden system files.
>
> **Response:** Change to a drive with the system files on it.

Cannot FORMAT a network drive

> **Type:** Execution error
>
> **Source:** FORMAT
>
> **Cause:** You cannot use FORMAT with a network or shared drive.
>
> **Response:** In sharing situations, pause the server, execute FORMAT, and then continue server operation.

Cannot format a ASSIGNed or SUBSTed drive

> **Type:** Execution error
>
> **Source:** FORMAT

Cause: You tried to format a disk with an ASSIGN or SUBST command in effect.

Response: Type ASSIGN to remove the assignments and then format the disk.

Cannot FORMAT nonremovable drive x

Type: Execution error

Source: BACKUP

Cause: When you executed BACKUP, you used the /F option. You can use this option only on diskettes and nonnetwork drives.

Response: Terminate the BACKUP operation and prepare the hard disk with FORMAT; then reexecute the BACKUP command.

Cannot JOIN a network drive

Type: Execution error

Source: JOIN

Cause: You tried to use JOIN with a network drive.

Response: No response required.

Cannot LABEL a network drive

Type: Execution error

Source: LABEL

Cause: You tried to change the volume label on a block device that has been redirected.

Response: No response required.

Cannot load COMMAND, system halted

Type: Execution error

Source: DOS

Cause: The COMMAND.COM file was not on the specified COM-SPEC path; the RAM where DOS tracked available memory went bad.

Response: Cold boot DOS.

Cannot perform a cyclic copy

> **Type:** Execution error
>
> **Source:** XCOPY
>
> **Cause:** You incorrectly specified the /S parameter in a copy operation so that the destination was included as part of the source. The source is a directory that contains the destination directory.
>
> **Response:** Change source and target directories as needed, and reissue the XCOPY command.

Cannot recover entry, processing continued

> **Type:** Information message, data corruption error
>
> **Source:** CHKDSK
>
> **Cause:** A serious FAT chaining error has occurred: the FAT chain of clusters is corrupted.
>
> **Response:** Replace diskette or reformat hard disk and attempt to restore data from alternate sources; use a file-recovery program to recover as many clusters as possible.

Cannot RECOVER a network drive

> **Type:** Execution error
>
> **Source:** RECOVER
>
> **Cause:** RECOVER cannot be used on a shared network drive.
>
> **Response:** In a sharing situation, pause the server, execute RECOVER, then continue server operation.

Cannot start COMMAND, exiting

> **Type:** Execution error
>
> **Source:** DOS
>
> **Cause:** COMMAND.COM could not be loaded because there is not enough memory available or the FILES = value in CONFIG.SYS is too small.
>
> **Response:** Increase the FILES = value or restart DOS.

Cannot use FASTOPEN for drive x

Type: Execution error

Source: FASTOPEN

Cause: You attempted to use FASTOPEN on a joined, assigned, substituted, or floppy drive.

Response: Undo any drive or directory reassignments.

Cannot use PRINT—use NET PRINT

Type: Execution error

Source: PRINT

Cause: You attempted to use PRINT on a networked computer.

Response: Use NET PRINT instead of PRINT.

Cannot SUBST a network drive

Type: Execution error

Source: SUBST

Cause: You tried to use SUBST with a network drive or path.

Response: Use PAUSE if you must establish the substitution.

Cannot SYS a network drive

Type: Execution error

Source: SYS

Cause: You tried to use SYS to transfer DOS files to a shared network drive.

Response: For a shared drive, use PAUSE and CONTINUE.

Cannot XCOPY from a reserved device

Type: Execution error

Source: XCOPY

Cause: You tried to execute XCOPY from a character device (a printer or communication port).

Response: Copy the data you need into a file and then use that file as the source for your XCOPY command.

Cannot XCOPY to a reserved device

Type: Execution error

Source: XCOPY

Cause: You tried to execute XCOPY to a character device (printer, communication port, or NULL). As a reserved device name in DOS, NULL is equivalent to a waste basket: DOS discards any information sent to that device.

Response: Specify a block or file device instead of a character device and reexecute XCOPY.

CHDIR..failed, trying alternate method

Type: Execution error

Source: CHKDSK

Cause: Unknown

Response: Reboot and execute CHKDSK again.

Code page not prepared

Type: Execution error

Source: MODE SELECT

Cause: The specified code page was not defined to the device, or the prepared code page does not have the correct font for the current video mode.

Response: First execute MODE PREPARE to define the code page to the device and then reenter MODE SELECT. If necessary, change the number of subfonts in the DEVICE = DISPLAY statement in the CONFIG.SYS file and reboot.

Code page xxx not prepared for all devices

Type: Execution error

Source: CHCP

Cause: Either the device was not prepared properly for this code page, or the device has failed or is busy.

Response: Use MODE to prepare all devices. Make sure the printer is on line and not busy and then reexecute CHCP.

Code page xxx not prepared for system

Type: Execution error

Source: CHCP

Cause: CHCP cannot select a code page if NLSFUNC has not been loaded, if you have mismatched country and code pages, or if you have not prepared any devices.

Response: Make sure NLSFUNC has been loaded and prepare the device using MODE.

Code page operation not supported on this device

Type: Execution error

Source: MODE

Cause: The specified device is not really a device, or it cannot support code pages. The specified device may not have been properly loaded in the CONFIG.SYS file.

Response: Make sure you spelled the device name correctly; then update the CONFIG.SYS files and reboot, repeating the command.

Code page yyy is not valid for given keyboard code

Type: Execution error

Source: KEYB

Cause: The specified code page cannot be used with your keyboard.

Response: Use the MODE command to respecify a correct code page or use a KEYB command parameter.

Code page specified has not been prepared

Type: Execution error

Source: KEYB

Cause: The specified code page has not been prepared for CON, which is the current device.

Response: Prepare CON using the MODE command.

Code page specified is inconsistent with invoked code page

Type: Information message

Source: KEYB

Cause: The specified code page is not currently active but will become the active code page. The CON code page will remain the same, leading to the possibility that your keyboard and printer could be using different code pages.

Response: Use MODE to load a CON code page that matches the keyboard code page.

Code page specified is inconsistent with the selected code page

Type: Information message

Source: KEYB

Cause: Your specified code page has been prepared but is not active for CON. The code page is active for the keyboard, however. The CON and keyboard devices thus have mismatched code pages.

Response: Use MODE to reselect the code page.

Code page xxx

Type: Information message

Source: MODE

Cause: This message is the response to the MODE STATUS command.

Response: No response required.

Code pages cannot be prepared

Type: Execution error

Source: MODE

Cause: There are duplicate code pages on the device, or too many code pages have been specified for the device. Note that for the IBM Quietwriter III Model 5202 printer, you cannot duplicate the hardware code page used in the CONFIG.SYS file's DEVICE = command.

Response: Use MODE or STATUS to determine the number of code pages allowed for a particular device; then respecify the MODE command.

Compare error(s) on Track **xx**, *side* **yy**

Type: Information message

Source: DISKCOMP

Cause: This message indicates the location of inconsistent data between two diskettes.

Response: Retry DISKCOPY (or some other disk copying program), or compare the directory listings for both disks to determine which files were not successfully copied.

Command format: **DISKCOPY d: d: [/1] [/8]**

Type: Execution error

Source: DISKCOPY

Cause: An incorrect parameter or filename was specified.

Response: Reenter the command correctly.

*COM**n**:bbbb,p,d,s,t, * initialized*

Type: Information message

Source: MODE

Cause: The asynchronous communications adapter has been initialized with the following: adapter number n, baud rate *bbbb*, parity p (even e, odd o, none n), data bits d, stop bits s, device type t, * (serial printer p, other device −).

Response: No response required.

Compare error at **OFFSET** **xxxxxxxx**

Type: Information message

Source: COMP

Cause: This message displays in hexadecimal notation the offset location where the two files to be compared differ.

Response: No response required.

Compare another diskette (Y/N)?

Type: Request message

Source: DISKCOMP

Cause: This message asks whether you want to compare more diskettes after one DISKCOMP operation is complete.

Response: Enter Y to compare more diskettes or N to exit DISKCOMP.

Compare more files (Y/N)?

Type: Request message

Source: COMP

Cause: This message asks whether you want to compare more diskettes after one COMP operation is complete.

Response: Enter Y to compare more files or N to exit COMP.

Compare process ended

Type: Information message

Source: DISKCOMP

Cause: This message indicates that the DISKCOMP operation is complete.

Response: No response required.

Comparing x sectors per track, n side(s)

Type: Information message

Source: DISKCOMP

Cause: This message indicates that DISKCOMP is comparing the diskettes.

Response: No response required.

Configuration too large for memory

Type: Execution error

Source: DOS

Cause: This message appears when the FILES and BUFFERS commands in the CONFIG.SYS file, or the resetting of the environment space, do not leave enough memory for COM-MAND.COM to be reloaded.

Response: Reboot with a different disk and then change the values to leave enough memory for COMMAND.COM.

Contains xxx *non-contiguous blocks*

Type: Information message

Source: CHKDSK

Cause: This message indicates the number of pieces into which a file is fragmented.

Response: No response required. However, the existence of many fragmented files slows down disk operations. Copying files to another disk will combine the fragments and speed up future file access operations.

Convert directory to file (Y/N)?

Type: Request message

Source: CHKDSK

Cause: The displayed directory has much bad information and cannot effectively be used as a directory.

Response: Type Y to convert the directory to a file so that you can check it; type N if you do not want to convert the directory to a file.

xxx *lost clusters found in* yyy *chains.*
Convert lost chains to files (Y/N)?

Type: Information message; request message

Source: CHKDSK

Cause: While another program was accessing the disk, the system was turned off or Ctrl-Break was pressed, scrambling the file being accessed. CHKDSK asks you if you wish it to clean up this scrambling.

Response: Type Y, so long as the F parameter is in effect, to clean up the disk and allow the scrambled blocks to be used by other files. If F was not invoked, then CHKDSK will display information messages only, doing nothing to the disk. If /F was not specified, you can answer N and then reissue the CHKDSK /F command.

Copy another diskette (Y/N)?

Type: Request message

Source: DISKCOPY

Cause: DISKCOPY is asking you whether it should make another disk copy.

Response: Enter Y to make another copy or N to exit DISKCOPY.

Copy process ended

Type: Information message

Source: DISKCOPY

Cause: The copy operation has been completed.

Response: No response required.

Copying xxx tracks
x Sectors/track, n Side(s)

Type: Information message

Source: DISKCOPY

Cause: The DISKCOPY operation is in progress.

Response: No response required.

Current code page settings

Type: Information message

Source: MODE

Cause: This message displays a list of the active and system global code pages requested with the MODE GET GLOBAL command.

Response: No response required.

Current drive is no longer valid

Type: Execution error

Source: COMMAND

Cause: You deleted the network drive, and the prompt setting needs to determine what drive you are using.

Response: Move to a valid drive.

Current keyboard code: **xx** *code page:* **yy**
Current CON code page: **zzz**

Type: Information message

Source: KEYB

Cause: This message displays the current keyboard code, code page, and CON code page.

Response: No response required.

Current keyboard does not support this code page

Type: Execution error

Source: MODE

Cause: A mismatch was found between the keyboard code and the specified code page.

Response: Change the KEYB command line to the desired code page and reexecute the MODE PREPARE command.

d:*drive deleted*

Type: Information message

Source: FDISK

Cause: This message appears during deletion of a logical drive in an extended DOS partition.

Response: No response required.

Delete current volume label (Y/N)?

Type: Request message

Source: LABEL

Cause: You attempted to enter a new volume label when one already exists.

Response: Enter Y to delete the current volume label or N not to delete it.

Device error during Status
Device error during Prepare
Device error during Select
Device error during write of font file to device

> **Type:** Execution error
>
> **Source:** MODE
>
> **Cause:** The device reported an error when the specified MODE function was performed. These errors are caused by the absence of a DEVICE = statement in the CONFIG.SYS file or a device's inability to accept all of the code page information to support code pages.
>
> **Response:** Check your specification of DEVICE = and the configuration of the device; then reboot.

Device or code page missing from font file

> **Type:** Execution error
>
> **Source:** MODE
>
> **Cause:** When MODE sent the indicated font to the device using PREPARE, DOS sent the error indicating that the font file does not have a definition for the specified code page and device. Also, if you are using the Quietwriter III printer model 5202, you may get this error while trying to use a hardware code page if this page is not defined in the font file.
>
> **Response:** Use a supported code page. If you are using the Quietwriter III, change the DEVICE = command in the CONFIG.SYS file and reboot.

Device ddd *not prepared*

> **Type:** Information message
>
> **Source:** MODE
>
> **Cause:** This message is the response to the MODE or STATUS command when no code pages have been prepared.
>
> **Response:** No response required.

Dir path listing for volume xxxxxxx

> **Type:** Information message
>
> **Source:** TREE

Cause: This message displays the volume label of the disk.

Response: No response required.

Directory entries adjusted

> **Type:** Information message
>
> **Source:** VDISK
>
> **Cause:** VDISK changed the number of directory entries in the DE-VICE = VDISK.SYS statement in the CONFIG.SYS file.

Response: No response required.

Directory is joined, tree past this point not processed

> **Type:** Information message
>
> **Source:** CHKDSK
>
> **Cause:** CHKDSK did not check a directory that is actually a joined drive.

Response: No response required.

Directory is totally empty, no . or .., tree past this point not processed

> **Type:** Information message
>
> **Source:** DOS
>
> **Cause:** DOS found a directory that does not contain the two files "." and "..". These files may have been left out (by DOS) during an updating operation that was interrupted.

Response: Use RECOVER to try to restore the damaged files.

Disk Boot failure

> **Type:** Execution error
>
> **Source:** DOS
>
> **Cause:** An error occurred while DOS was being loaded into memory.

Response: Reboot. If the error still appears, try booting with a different disk and then use CHKDSK or other utilities to examine and fix the defective disk.

Do you see the rightmost

    Type: Req

    Source: MC

    Cause: Thi

  Response: An
      scr

Do you wish to use the
partition active (Y/N)

    Type: R

    Source: F.

    Cause: T
      C

  Response: /
      1
      {

Does pathname spe
on the target (F =

    Type:

    Source:

    Cause:

  Response

DOS partition a

    Typ

    Sourc

    Caus

  Respon

Drive d: *alreac*

    Ty

    Sou

    Cause: The file to be renamed could not be found, the file name you specified for renaming already exists as another file, or you are renaming a file with the same name.

  Response: Check your spelling and verify the names you are using; then retry the command.

Enter current Volume Label for Drive d (Press ENTER for none):

    Type: Request message

    Source: FORMAT

    Cause: You have tried to format your hard disk, which would mean losing any information—data and programs—stored on it. To prevent you from doing this accidentally, FORMAT requires you to enter the hard disk's volume label.

  Response: Enter the hard disk's volume label if you wish to format the hard disk.

Enter partition size............: [dddd]

    Type: Request message

    Source: FDISK

    Cause: You need to specify the size of the partition you wish to create.

  Response: Press Enter to make the number shown in brackets the partition size. To specify a different size, enter a new number.

Enter primary file name

    Type: Request message

    Source: COMP

    Cause: You need to enter a primary file name.

  Response: Specify the filespec of one of the two files to be compared.

Enter 2nd file name or drive id

    Type: Request message

    Source: COMP

    Cause: You need to specify the second of the two files to be compared.

Response: Specify the filespec of the second file to be compared.

Enter starting cylinder number..: [dddd]

Type: Request message

Source: FDISK

Cause: You are using the "Create DOS Partition" option and need to specify the starting cylinder for the DOS partition.

Response: Press Enter to use the value in the brackets; otherwise, specify your own starting point.

Enter the number of the partition you want to make active.........: []

Type: Request message

Source: FDISK

Cause: You are using the "Change Active Partition" option and need to specify the partition to be activated.

Response: Enter the number of the partition to be activated.

Entry error

Type: Execution error

Source: EDLIN

Cause: EDLIN found a syntax error.

Response: Correct the error and reissue the command.

Entry has a bad attribute (or size or link)

Type: Data corruption error

Source: CHKDSK

Cause: A directory entry contains an error. If the message is preceded by a period, then the current directory contains the error. If the message is preceded by two periods, then the parent directory contains the error.

Response: Run CHKDSK using the /F parameter to change the damaged directory.

Eof mark not found

> **Type:** Information message
> **Source:** COMP
> **Cause:** While comparing nontext files, COMP could not find the end-of-file marker in a file.
> **Response:** No response required.

Error during read of font file

> **Type:** Data corruption error
> **Source:** MODE
> **Cause:** While reading from a font file, MODE found an I/O error.
> **Response:** Use another copy of the font file and reexecute processing.

Error found, F parameter not specified
Corrections will not be written to disk

> **Type:** Information message
> **Source:** CHKDSK
> **Cause:** An error was detected somewhere on the disk. Since you did not specify the /F parameter when you invoked CHKDSK, CHKDSK will perform the error analysis and simulate a solution, but will not change anything on the disk.
> **Response:** To correct the problem, reexecute the command using the /F parameter.

Error in COUNTRY command

> **Type:** Execution error
> **Source:** DOS
> **Cause:** When you used the COUNTRY command, you did not specify a code page and did not request the default setting; or the country information file is invalid or contains a formatting error.
> **Response:** Check the country information and the COUNTRY = statement in the CONFIG.SYS file and reboot.

Error in EXE file

Type: Execution error

Source: DOS

Cause: An error occurred in the relocation information generated by LINK, possibly due to a change in the file.

Response: Use the backup copy of a store-bought program. If the error reappears, contact your dealer. If you wrote the program, relink it.

Error loading operating system

Type: Execution error

Source: DOS

Cause: An error appeared when you attempted to load the operating system from your hard disk.

Response: Reboot. If the error still occurs, recopy the system to your hard disk and reexecute processing.

Error opening log file

Type: Execution error

Source: BACKUP

Cause: An error occurred during the requested opening or creation of a backup log file. The error may result from an invalid drive or path specification, a file-sharing conflict, or a lack of appropriate directory entries in the root directory.

Response: Check your log-file specification. Be sure that you are not attempting to create the log file on the destination disk.

Error reading fixed disk

Type: Data corruption error

Source: FDISK

Cause: After trying five times, FDISK still could not read the startup record of the hard disk.

Response: Retry FDISK several times. If the error is regenerated every time, consult you computer's user's manual or contact your local dealer for assistance.

Error reading partition table

Type: Data corruption error; device error

Source: FORMAT

Cause: An error occurred during a partition table read operation.

Response: Rerun FDISK.

Error writing fixed disk

Type: Data corruption error

Source: FDISK

Cause: After trying five times, FDISK still could not write the startup record of the hard disk.

Cause: Retry FDISK several times. If the error is regenerated every time, consult your computer's user manual or contact your dealer.

Error writing partition table

Type: Data corruption error; Device error

Source: FORMAT

Cause: An error occurred during a partition table write operation.

Response: Rerun FDISK.

Error writing to device

Type: Information message

Source: DOS, various commands

Cause: An I/O error occurred when data was sent to a device, most likely because the device cannot handle the amount of information being sent. This message also appears if the device is off line or is not powered up.

Response: Reduce the amount of data being transmitted at one time and reexecute processing.

Errors on list device indicate that it may be off-line. Please check it.

Type: Hardware error

Source: PRINT

Cause: The background-printing device is off line.

Response: Check the connections and make sure the background-printing device is turned on.

EXEC failure

Type: Execution error

Source: DOS, various commands

Cause: An error occurred when DOS tried to read a command from the disk because the FILE = statement in the CONFIG.SYS file was not set to a sufficiently large value.

Response: Change the FILES = value and reboot. If the problem persists, the disk itself may contain a hardware error.

Extended DOS partition already exists

Type: Information message

Source: FDISK

Cause: There can only be one extended DOS partition per hard disk.

Response: No response required. Use the Display Partition Information option on the FDISK main menu to see what partitions have been set up.

Extended DOS partition deleted

Type: Information message

Source: FDISK

Cause: This message confirms the deletion of the extended DOS partition and everything in it.

Response: No response required.

Extender card switches do not match the system memory size

Type: Hardware error

Source: VDISK

Cause: The settings on your memory extended card do not match the total system memory value. VDISK does not use memory that is in an expansion unit.

Response: Verify your extended card switch settings.

Failure to access Code page Font File

      Type: Execution error

    Source: MODE

     Cause: MODE could not gain access to the specified code page font file.

  Response: Check the spelling of your command specification and be sure the specified font file exists; then reexecute processing.

Failure to access COUNTRY.SYS

      Type: Execution error

    Source: SELECT

     Cause: Access to the COUNTRY.SYS file failed when SELECT could not verify the three-digit country code.

  Response: Make sure the COUNTRY.SYS file is on the indicated drive and retry the command.

Failure to access device: **xxx**

      Type: Execution error

    Source: CODE PAGE operations

     Cause: The specified DEVICE in a code page operation could not be opened.

  Response: Check the spelling of your specification. Make sure the indicated device is loaded using the DEVICE = command in the CONFIG.SYS file. If the device is not specified correctly, modify your CONFIG.SYS file appropriately and then reboot.

Failure to access KEYBOARD.SYS

      Type: Execution error

    Source: SELECT

     Cause: The source diskette does not contain the KEYBOARD.SYS file.

  Response: Verify that the source disk has a copy of the KEYBOARD.SYS file.

FASTOPEN already installed

Type: Information message

Source: FASTOPEN

Cause: You tried to load FASTOPEN again.

Response: To reload FASTOPEN, you must reboot.

FASTOPEN installed

Type: Information message

Source: FASTOPEN

Cause: FASTOPEN was successfully loaded and executed.

Response: No response required.

FCB unavailable

Type: Device error

Source: DOS

Cause: The FCBS command, while file sharing was loaded, did not specify enough FCBs to be open.

Response: Redefine the FCBS command in the CONFIG.SYS file and reboot.

File allocation table bad, drive x
Abort, Retry, Ignore, Fail?

Type: Device error

Source: DOS

Cause: You are attempting to read absolute sectors on a network drive.

Response: Use the Loader Write **filespec** option of the DEBUG command.

File AND File

Type: Information message

Source: COMP

Cause: This message lists the paths and file names of the files being compared.

Response: No response required.

File xxx *canceled by operator*

> **Type:** Information message
> **Source:** PRINT
> **Cause:** This message is output to the printer when you cancel printing to remind whoever reads the printout that the output was interrupted and that the printout may be incomplete.
> **Response:** No response required.

File cannot be copied onto itself

> **Type:** Execution error
> **Source:** COPY, XCOPY
> **Cause:** You attempted to copy a file onto itself.
> **Response:** Modify the destination file specification so that it contains a different directory and name.

File creation error

> **Type:** Execution error
> **Source:** DOS, various commands
> **Cause:** A file could not be created or renamed.
> **Response:** Check the attributes of the file to make sure you are not renaming or changing a read-only file. Use CHKDSK to determine whether the directory is full or whether something else is wrong.

File is cross-linked
on cluster xxx

> **Type:** Data corruption error; hardware error
> **Source:** CHKDSK
> **Cause:** A cluster is cross-linked with two or more files.
> **Response:** Make new copies of each of the filenames, delete the original files, and then check the new files for problems and change them if necessary.

filename *is currently being printed*
filename *is in queue*

> **Type:** Information message
> **Source:** PRINT
> **Cause:** This status message appears when you queue a file for printing.
> **Response:** No response required.

File is READ-ONLY

> **Type:** Execution error
> **Source:** EDLIN
> **Cause:** You tried to edit a read-only file.
> **Response:** Use ATTRIB or another utility to change the read-only attribute bit of the file to read/write.

File name must be specified

> **Type:** Execution error
> **Source:** EDLIN
> **Cause:** You did not specify a file name when you invoked EDLIN.
> **Response:** Rerun EDLIN using a file name.

File not found

> **Type:** Execution error
> **Source:** DOS, various commands
> **Cause:** DOS or a particular command could not find a specified file.
> **Response:** Check the spelling of your specification. Make sure the indicated file is where it is supposed to be. If it is not, move it.

File not in PRINT queue

> **Type:** Execution error
> **Source:** PRINT
> **Cause:** You tried to cancel a file in the print queue that is not actually in the print queue.

Response: Check the spelling of your specification and reexecute processing.

File sharing conflict

Type: Execution error

Source: COMP

Cause: You tried to compare two files while one of the files was being used (and hence locked) by another process.

Response: Reissue COMP later, when the file is available.

Files compare OK

Type: Information message

Source: COMP

Cause: This message appears after a successful comparison of two files.

Response: No response required.

* * * Files were backed up xx/xx/xxxx * * *

Type: Information message

Source: RESTORE

Cause: This message displays the date the files on the backup diskettes were backed up.

Response: No response required.

First cluster number is invalid, entry truncated

Type: Information message

Source: CHKDSK

Cause: The indicated file has an invalid data area pointer.

Response: Use the /F parameter to truncate the file to zero length.

Fixed backup device d: is full

Type: Execution error

Source: BACKUP

        Cause: The hard disk you are attempting to back up files onto is full.

Response: Make space on the hard disk or back up onto another disk.

Font file contents invalid

         Type: Execution error; Data corruption error

     Source: MODE

      Cause: The specified file is not a font file, you misspelled the file name, or the file has been changed or damaged so that it now has an unacceptable format.

Response: Check the font-file name specification and reexecute processing. If the error reoccurs, recopy the master copy and execute processing again. **Note:** When this error occurs, all specified code pages become undefined and must be redefined.

FOR cannot be nested

         Type: Batch-file programming error

     Source: DOS

      Cause: You used two or more FOR commands on one line in a batch file.

Response: Redo your FOR commands and reexecute processing.

Format failure

         Type: Disk problems

     Source: FORMAT

      Cause: The disk to be formatted is unusable.

Response: Use another disk.

FORMAT not supported on drive d

         Type: Execution error

     Source: FORMAT

      Cause: The disk device driver (probably a RAM disk) does not support or require formatting.

Response: Select another disk drive identifier, and resubmit the FORMAT request.

844 — DOS ERROR AND INFORMATION MESSAGES

Formatting while copying

> **Type:** Information message
> **Source:** DISKCOPY
> **Cause:** During a DISKCOPY operation, the destination diskette was found to contain unformatted tracks. These will be formatted by DISKCOPY during the copy process.
> **Response:** No response required.

General Failure

> **Type:** Device error; operator error
> **Source:** DOS
> **Cause:** An undocumented error occurred. Typical causes are mismatched diskette and drive types, improper insertion of the diskette, and improper formatting of the diskette.
> **Response:** Retry processing several times. If the error recurs, abort processing and try to find the error cause. Contact your dealer if the error is in store-bought software.

Hardware code pages:
Prepared code pages:

> **Type:** Information message
> **Source:** MODE
> **Cause:** This message is the response to the MODE status request.
> **Response:** No response required.

Has invalid cluster, file truncated

> **Type:** Information message
> **Source:** CHKDSK
> **Cause:** The specified file contains an invalid data-area pointer.
> **Response:** Use the /F parameter to truncate the file at the last valid data block.

Illegal device name

> **Type:** Execution error
> **Source:** MODE

Cause: You specified the wrong device name for a particular type of device, possibly by a simple misspelling.

Response: Reisssue the command using the correct device name.

Incompatible system size

Type: Execution error

Source: SYS

Cause: You are copying DOS to a diskette that does not have enough space set aside for your version of DOS.

Response: Enter FORMAT/S for a new diskette and then copy your files to the new diskette from the old diskette.

Incorrect APPEND version

Type: Information message; Execution error

Source: APPEND

Cause: You initially loaded a version of APPEND that is different than the one you are trying to use now.

Response: Verify your path setting or determine why you are calling a different APPEND version and rectify the problem. You may have started with the network APPEND command and are now using a local version.

Incorrect DOS version

Type: Execution error

Source: DOS

Cause: You are currently running a version of DOS that does not support the command (or the version of the command) that you wish to use.

Response: Make sure you are using commands for the specific version of DOS that you are using. If you are on a network, then reset the path to access a local version of DOS that has the correct version for the command you wish to use.

Incorrect number of parameters

Type: Execution error

Source: Various commands

Cause: You specified the wrong number of parameters on the command line.

Response: Reenter the command line with the correct number of parameters.

Incorrect parameter

Type: Execution error

Source: SHARE

Cause: You specified an invalid parameter on the SHARE command line, possibly by a simple misspelling.

Response: Reissue the command with the correct parameter.

Incorrect parameter

Type: Execution error

Source: GRAFTABL

Cause: You specified an invalid parameter, possibly by a simple misspelling. Any code pages currently loaded are not changed.

Response: Reissue the command with the correct parameter.

Infinite retry on parallel printer time-out

Type: Information message

Source: MODE

Cause: You specified P for the first option.

Response: No response required.

Infinite retry not supported on Network printer

Type: Execution error

Source: MODE

Cause: You requested infinite retry, but printer errors cannot be detected using the network interface.

Response: Do not request infinite retry, or use a nonredirected printer.

Insert backup diskette **xx** *in drive* **x:**
Strike any key when ready

Type: Request message

Source: RESTORE

Cause: You need to insert the specified diskette to continue restoring your data.

Response: Insert the specified diskette and press a key to continue.

Insert backup source diskette in drive x
Strike any key when ready

Type: Request message

Source: BACKUP

Cause: You need to insert the specified diskette to continue backing up your files.

Response: Insert the specified diskette and press a key to continue.

Insert backup target diskette y *in drive* x
Strike any key when ready

Type: Request message

Source: BACKUP

Cause: You need to insert the next diskette so that the backup operation can continue.

Response: Insert the specified diskette and press a key to continue.

Insert disk with batch file
and strike any key when ready

Type: Request message

Source: DOS

Cause: The batch processor cannot find the next batch command to execute because the diskette containing the batch file was removed or replaced.

Response: Reinsert the diskette with the batch file on it and press a key to continue. Press Ctrl-Break to end batch processing.

Insert disk with \ *COMMAND.COM in drive* x
and strike any key when ready

Type: Request message

Source: DOS

Cause: The disk containing the COMMAND.COM file has been removed or replaced.

Response: Reinsert a DOS diskette and press a key to continue.

Insert diskette for drive x *and strike any key when ready*

      Type: Request message

    Source: DOS

     Cause: DOS needs to access a physical disk drive and hence needs the diskette that was in that drive.

 Response: Insert the specified diskette (if it is not already inserted) and press a key to continue.

Insert DOS disk in drive x
and strike ENTER when ready

      Type: Request message

    Source: FORMAT

     Cause: FORMAT requires a DOS system diskette.

 Response: Insert a DOS system diskette in the specified drive and press a key to continue.

Insert DOS diskette in drive A:
Press any key when ready ...

      Type: Request message

    Source: FDISK

     Cause: A DOS partition was successfully created on the current hard disk.

 Response: Insert the requested disk and press a key to reboot the system. You can now format the partition.

Insert first diskette in drive x
Insert second diskette in drive x

      Type: Request message

    Source: DISKCOMP

     Cause: These DISKCOPY prompts tell you where to put the two diskettes to be copied.

 Response: Insert the diskettes in the proper drives and press a key to continue.

Insert last backup diskette in drive x

> **Type:** Request message
>
> **Source:** BACKUP
>
> **Cause:** You specified the /A parameter.
>
> **Response:** Insert the last backup target diskette used in the last backup operation and press a key to continue.

Insert new diskette for drive x
and press ENTER when ready

> **Type:** Request message
>
> **Source:** FORMAT
>
> **Cause:** You need to insert the disk you wish to have formatted in the specified drive.
>
> **Response:** Insert the specified diskette in drive *x* and press a key to continue formatting.

Insert restore target xx *in drive* yy
Strike any key when ready

> **Type:** Request message
>
> **Source:** RESTORE
>
> **Cause:** This prompt asks you to insert the diskette to be restored in a drive.
>
> **Response:** Insert the specified disk in the specified drive and press a key to continue.

Insert source diskette in drive x
Insert target diskette in drive x

> **Type:** Request message
>
> **Source:** DISKCOPY
>
> **Cause:** You need to insert the source and target diskettes for DISK-COPY to begin operation.
>
> **Response:** Insert the specified disks in the specified drives and press a key to initiate the copy operation.

Insert system disk in x
and strike any key when ready

        Type: Request message

     Source: SYS

      Cause: SYS cannot load the DOS files because the disk containing them is not in the specified drive.

  Response: Insert the specified disks into the specified drive and press a key to continue.

Insert target diskette in drive B:
Strike any key when ready

        Type: Request message

     Source: SELECT

      Cause: You specified the B drive as the target drive for the SELECT operation.

  Response: Insert the target diskette into drive B and press a key to continue.

Insufficient disk space

        Type: Information message

     Source: DOS, various commands

      Cause: The disk does not have enough free space to store your file.

  Response: Run CHKDSK to make sure this message is valid. If it is, use another diskette, or delete files on the current diskette to make more room.

Insufficient memory

        Type: Information message

     Source: Various commands

      Cause: Not enough memory is available to process your command.

  Response: Change the BUFFERS = command in the CONFIG.SYS file to a lower value. If the message reappears, you need to obtain more memory. Be aware that TSR programs consume memory; removing one or more of these programs from memory may solve the problem.

Insufficient memory for system transfer

      Type: Information message

    Source: FORMAT, SYS

     Cause: Not enough memory is available to allow the transfer of the system files.

 Response: See the message *Insufficient memory*.

Insufficient room in root directory
Erase files from root and repeat CHKDSK

      Type: Execution error

    Source: CHKDSK

     Cause: CHKDSK could not recover all of the lost chains into files because not enough space was available in the root directory.

 Response: Review the recovered files, deleting or relocating the ones you can, and rerun CHKDSK to recover the remaining chains.

Intermediate file error during pipe

      Type: Execution error

    Source: DOS

     Cause: Either or both of the intermediate pipe files could not be created, for one of the following reasons: a full root directory, the inability of DOS to find the piping files, or the lack of enough disk space to hold the piped data.

 Response: Make room in the default drive root directory by erasing some files; then reissue the command.

Internal stack overflow
System halted

      Type: Information message

    Source: DOS

     Cause: The memory resources available to the stack have all been used, usually due to a series of recursive hardware interrupts.

 Response: Add a STACKS command to the CONFIG.SYS file to increase the available stack resources.

Invalid baud rate specified

> **Type:** Information message
>
> **Source:** MODE
>
> **Cause:** A parameter contains an error.
>
> **Response:** You can use only the following baud rates: 100, 150, 300, 600, 1200, 2400, 4800, 9600, or 19,200 (you need to type only the first two digits of any number).

Invalid characters in volume label

> **Type:** Execution error
>
> **Source:** FORMAT
>
> **Cause:** You entered characters for the volume label that are not valid file name characters. The name you entered may contain a period (.). The length of the name must be between 1 and 11 characters.
>
> **Response:** Reissue the command using valid file name characters and a name of the right length.

Invalid code page specified

> **Type:** Execution error
>
> **Source:** KEYB
>
> **Cause:** You cannot use the specified code page with the specified language.
>
> **Response:** Correct and reissue your command.

Invalid COMMAND.COM in drive n

> **Type:** Information message
>
> **Source:** DOS
>
> **Cause:** You have switched disks or inadvertently copied a different version of COMMAND.COM onto your disk.
>
> **Response:** Insert a diskette with the correct version of DOS on it and press a key to continue.

Invalid country code or code page

> **Type:** Execution error
>
> **Source:** COUNTRY
>
> **Cause:** The COUNTRY = statement in the CONFIG.SYS file is invalid.
>
> **Response:** Change the COUNTRY = value to one that is valid and reboot.

Invalid country code

> **Type:** Execution error
>
> **Source:** SELECT
>
> **Cause:** You specified an invalid three-digit country code, or the code you specified is not defined in the COUNTRY.SYS file.
>
> **Response:** Enter a valid three-digit code.

Invalid current directory

> **Type:** Data corruption error
>
> **Source:** CHKDSK
>
> **Cause:** An unrecoverable disk error occurred during a read operation for the current directory.
>
> **Response:** Use a disk utilities package to ascertain the exact nature of the problem and a possible remedy for it.

Invalid date

> **Type:** Execution error
>
> **Source:** DOS, various commands
>
> **Cause:** When specifying the date, you did not use a hyphen or slash as a delimiter, or you specified an invalid date.
>
> **Response:** Enter the date in a valid format.

Invalid device

> **Type:** Execution error
>
> **Source:** CTTY

Cause: You entered an invalid device name

Response: Reissue the command with a valid device name.

Invalid device parameters from device driver

Type: Data corruption error

Source: FORMAT

Cause: The number of hidden sectors is not an exact multiple of the number of sectors per track, or the DOS partition appears not to start on a track boundary.

Response: Use FDISK to create a new partition and then reexecute FORMAT.

Invalid directory

Type: Execution error

Source: DOS, various commands

Cause: You named a nonexistent directory in the path specification, possibly by a simple misspelling.

Response: Respecify the path.

Invalid disk change

Type: Operator error

Source: DOS

Cause: You switched diskettes while files were still open.

Response: Reinsert the diskette that was being used.

Invalid drive in search path

Type: Execution error

Source: DOS

Cause: You named an invalid drive identifier in the path specification, possibly by a simple misspelling.

Response: Respecify the path using a valid drive identifier.

Invalid drive or file name

Type: Execution error

Source: DOS, various commands

Cause: You specified an invalid drive or file name.

Response: Reissue the command with valid specifications.

Invalid drive specification

Type: Execution error

Source: Various commands

Cause: You entered an invalid drive identifier, or the source and target drive specifications in a command are the same.

Response: Enter the correct identifiers.

Invalid drive specification
Source and target drives are the same

Type: Execution error

Source: BACKUP, RESTORE

Cause: You entered the same drive identifier for both the source and target drives.

Response: Reissue the command using different identifiers for the source and target drives.

Invalid drive specification
Specified drive does not exist, or is non-removable

Type: Execution error

Source: DOS, various commands

Cause: You entered an invalid drive identifier in the command line, possibly by a simple misspelling.

Response: Reissue the command with a valid drive identifier.

Invalid environment size specified

Type: Execution error

Source: DOS

Cause: You specified the environment size using nonnumeric characters, or you specified a size not in the acceptable range.

Response: Use the correct parameters and stay within the acceptable range when you reissue the command.

Invalid file name or file not found

Type: Information message; Execution error

Source: RENAME, TYPE

Cause: You used an invalid or nonexistent file name, possibly by a simple misspelling, or you used global characters in a TYPE command.

Response: Reissue the command correctly, adding paths if necessary.

Invalid keyboard code

Type: Execution error

Source: SELECT

Cause: The two-character keyboard code you issued was invalid or could not be found in the KEYBOARD.SYS file (the file may have been altered). You may have simply misspelled the code.

Response: Verify that the KEYBOARD.SYS file was not altered. Enter the correct code.

Invalid keyboard code specified

Type: Execution error

Source: KEYB

Cause: You specified an invalid keyboard code, possibly by a simple misspelling.

Response: Correct the mistake and reissue the command.

Invalid media or Track 0 bad—disk unusable

Type: Disk problem

Source: FORMAT

Cause: Track 0 could not be formatted, indicating a bad disk, or the disk and drive types are mismatched.

Response: If track 0 is the problem, use another disk. Otherwise, place a correct disk in the drive.

Invalid number of parameters

Type: Execution error

Source: Various commands

Cause: You specified the wrong number of parameters on the command line.

Response: Reissue the command with the correct number of parameters.

Invalid parameter

Type: Execution error

Source: DOS, various commands

Cause: You incorrectly entered a parameter on the command line, possibly by a simple misspelling.

Response: Reissue the command with the correct parameters.

Invalid parameters

Type: Execution error

Source: DOS, various commands

Cause: You entered invalid or out-of-order parameters.

Response: Reissue the command correctly.

Invalid partition table

Type: Disk or data corruption error

Source: Startup procedures

Cause: During startup, DOS found invalid information in the partition information area.

Response: Reboot DOS from diskette and use FDISK to fix any errors in the partition definitions.

Invalid path

Type: Execution error

Source: Various commands

Cause: You entered a path with invalid characters, an invalid file name, or more than 63 characters.

Response: Check your spelling and reissue the command in the correct format with the correct information.

Invalid path, not directory
or directory not empty

Type: Execution error

Source: RMDIR

Cause: You did not specify a valid directory name in the path; the directory to be removed still contains entries for other files and subdirectories, or you are trying to remove the current directory.

Response: Check your spelling and enter a valid directory name, empty the directory you wish removed, or change to a different directory and reexecute processing.

Invalid path or file not found

Type: Execution error

Source: ATTRIB, COPY

Cause: You specified a nonexistent file or directory, possibly by a simple misspelling.

Response: Check your spelling, the file name, and the availability of files before reissuing the command.

Invalid path or parameter

Type: Execution error

Source: APPEND

Cause: You specified a path and both the /X and /E parameters; these can be specified only the first time you invoke APPEND.

Response: To respecify APPEND with the /X and /E parameters, reboot and reexecute processing.

Invalid signature in COUNTRY.SYS file

Type: Disk or data corruption error

Source: SELECT

Cause: The COUNTRY.SYS file does not contain the correct header.

Response: Determine whether the COUNTRY.SYS file has been altered or overwritten. If it has been, reload a copy from your backup disks.

Invalid signature in KEYBOARD.SYS file

Type: Disk or data corruption error

Source: SELECT

Cause: The KEYBOARD.SYS file does not contain the correct header.

Response: Determine whether the KEYBOARD.SYS file has been altered or overwritten. If it has been, reload a copy from your backup disks.

Invalid STACK parameters

Type: Execution error

Source: STACKS = in CONFIG.SYS

Cause: You specified an invalid number of stacks or an invalid stack size.

Response: Specify a valid number of stacks and a valid size and reboot.

Invalid subdirectory entry

Type: Disk or data corruption error

Source: CHKDSK

Cause: CHKDSK found invalid data in the specified subdirectory.

Response: Use the /F or /V parameters when invoking CHKDSK.

Invalid switch character

Type: Execution error

Source: VDISK

Cause: There was a forward slash in the DEVICE = VDISK.SYS statement in the CONFIG.SYS file, but the next character was not an E. Therefore, VDISK will be installed in conventional (low) memory.

Response: Reenter the DEVICE command using the correct syntax.

Cause: While you were backing up to a hard disk, the hard disk became full, and the most recently backed-up file was not saved on the hard disk. This message also indicates a possible file-sharing error.

Response: Delete files on the target disk and rerun the BACKUP command.

Line too long

Type: Execution error

Source: EDLIN

Cause: You executed a REPLACE command in EDLIN, but the replacement line exceeded the 253 character limit allowed on one EDLIN line.

Response: Break up lines exceeding 253 characters and reexecute processing.

List output is not assigned to a device

Type: Execution error

Source: PRINT

Cause: You specified an invalid printing device.

Response: Reissue the command specifying a valid device.

Lock Violation

Type: Information message

Source: XCOPY

Cause: While trying to read files, XCOPY encountered one or more files that were locked against reading.

Response: Wait a few moments and reexecute the command. Continue this procedure until you gain access to the file or decide to do without the locked file.

Logging to file x

Type: Information message

Source: BACKUP

Cause: This message occurs when you specify the /L parameter. File **x** is the log file to which information about the backup is being written.

Response: No response required.

Logical DOS drive created, drive letters changed or added

Type: Information message

Source: FDISK

Cause: You created a logical DOS drive, and it was assigned a drive identifier.

Response: No response required. Before you use the drive, however, you must format it.

LPT#: not rerouted

Type: Information message

Source: MODE

Cause: This message indicates that all data sent to this port will go to this port and will not be rerouted.

Response: No response required.

LPT#: rerouted to COMn:

Type: Information message

Source: MODE

Cause: This message displays the current rerouting of the parallel port.

Response: No response required.

LPT# set for 80

Type: Information message

Source: MODE

Cause: This message appears when you use MODE to set the printer line length to 80 characters per line.

Response: No response required.

LPT# set for 132

> **Type:** Information message
> **Source:** MODE
> **Cause:** This message appears when you use MODE to set the printer line length to 132 characters per line.
> **Response:** No response required.

Make sure a diskette is inserted into
the drive and the door is closed

> **Type:** Request message
> **Source:** DISKCOMP, DISKCOPY
> **Cause:** There is no disk in the drive, or the door is open.
> **Response:** Place a disk in the drive or close the drive door.

Maximum available space for partition is **xxxx** *cylinders*

> **Type:** Information message
> **Source:** FDISK
> **Cause:** This message tells you how much space is available for a partition when you choose the Create DOS Partition option.
> **Response:** No response required.

Maximum number of logical DOS drives installed

> **Type:** Information message
> **Source:** DOS
> **Cause:** All available drive letters have been assigned.
> **Response:** To create a new drive, delete a current drive to free a letter.

Memory allocation error
Cannot load COMMAND, system halted

> **Type:** Information message
> **Source:** DOS
> **Cause:** An executing program overwrote the portion of physical

memory that contains DOS's list of programs and memory assignments.

Response: Reboot.

Missing from the file is either the device ID or the code page

Type: Execution error; Spelling or specification error

Source: MODE

Cause: You entered an invalid code page, or the attached printer is not supported by the .CPI file.

Response: Prepare the code pages again, specify a valid code page, or match the code page to the printer you have.

Missing operating system

Type: Information message; execution error

Source: Startup routines

Cause: The boot area of your fixed disk, when started, does not contain a valid DOS boot record.

Response: Reboot using a diskette. Use FORMAT/S to install DOS on the hard disk, or use SYS. If you use FORMAT, back up your files first, as they will be erased.

MODE fff Code page function completed

Type: Information message

Source: MODE

Cause: This status message indicates the end of a function.

Response: No response required.

– More –

Type: Information message; request message

Source: MORE

Cause: Message indicating the current screen is filled and there is more data to be shown.

Response: Press any key to display the next screen.

Must specify COM1, COM2, COM3, or COM4

Type: Spelling or specification error

Source: MODE

Cause: Invalid or nonexistent serial port specified.

Response: Specify a correct serial port and reexecute processing.

Must specify destination line number

Type: Execution error

Source: EDLIN

Cause: You issued a Move or Copy command without a valid destination.

Response: Respecify the command, using a valid destination line number.

Must specify ON or OFF

Type: Execution error

Source: BREAK

Cause: When issuing the BREAK command, you did not specify ON or OFF (or you specified something else).

Response: Respecify BREAK using either ON or OFF.

Name of list device [PRN]:

Type: Request message

Source: PRINT

Cause: This message appears the first time you invoke PRINT after booting DOS.

Response: Enter the name of a device to receive PRINT's output or press Enter for PRN to accept the default setting.

NLSFUNC already installed

Type: Information message

Source: NLSFUNC

Cause: You have already loaded resident NLSFUNC once and cannot load it again.

Response: No response required.

No Append

Type: Information message

Source: APPEND

Cause: APPEND has no directories specified.

Response: No response required.

No code page has been SELECTED

Type: Information message

Source: MODE

Cause: No code page was selected for the specified device in your MODE STATUS request.

Response: No response required.

No Extended DOS partition to delete

Type: Spelling or specification error

Source: FDISK

Cause: FDISK cannot delete the extended DOS partition because it does not exist.

Response: No response required.

No files added

Type: Information message

Source: REPLACE

Cause: You invoked REPLACE with the /A parameter, but all of the source files already exist in the target directory.

Response: No response required.

No files found

Type: Information message

Source: REPLACE

Cause: REPLACE could find no source files in the specified directory or along the specified path.

Response: No response required.

No fixed disks present

Type: Hardware error; operator error; information message

Source: FDISK

Cause: FDISK could find no hard disk drive attached to the computer. This could be because of improper installation, because you did not turn on your expansion unit, or because you do not have a hard disk.

Response: Make sure the expansion unit is turned on; then determine the cause of the problem and correct it.

No free file handles
Cannot start COMMAND, exiting

Type: Execution error

Source: DOS

Cause: Too many files are currently open to allow the loading of a secondary command processor.

Response: Close some files in one of your running application programs or increase the value of the FILES = command in the CONFIG.SYS file and reboot.

No logical drives defined

Type: Information message

Source: FDISK

Cause: You have not defined any logical drives in the extended partition.

Response: Use FDISK to create the logical drives and then use FORMAT to format them.

No paper

Type: Hardware error

Source: Printer

Cause: The printer you are using is not turned on or has run out of paper.

Response: Turn the printer on or feed it some paper.

No partitions defined

Type: Information message

Source: FDISK

Cause: You have not defined any partitions on the hard disk.

Response: Use FDISK to set up some partitions and divide them into logical drives, then use FORMAT to format them.

No partitions to delete

Type: Information message

Source: FDISK

Cause: You tried to delete partitions, but none have been defined.

Response: No response required.

No partitions to make active

Type: Information message

Source: FDISK

Cause: You cannot change the active partition because no partitions have been defined.

Response: Define one or more partitions and make one active.

No Path

Type: Information message

Source: PATH

Cause: You have not specified a path.

Response: No response required.

No Primary DOS partition to delete

Type: Execution error

Source: FDISK

Cause: You tried to delete a nonexistent partition.

Response: Reenter the deletion request, specifying a valid partition.

No retry on parallel printer time-out

> **Type:** Information message
> **Source:** MODE
> **Cause:** You did not specify retry for time-out errors (by using the P parameter).
> **Response:** No response required.

No room for system on destination disk

> **Type:** Execution error
> **Source:** SYS
> **Cause:** The system files cannot be transferred to the destination disk because of a lack of space at the beginning of the diskette.
> **Response:** Enter FORMAT/S for a blank diskette and then copy your files to it.

No room in directory for file

> **Type:** Execution error
> **Source:** EDLIN
> **Cause:** The disk directory is full. When you attempted to save your data from EDLIN, it was not saved, but lost.
> **Response:** Run EDLIN again after you have freed some directory space.

No room in root directory

> **Type:** Execution error
> **Source:** LABEL
> **Cause:** The specified partition size exceeds remaining disk space, or exceeds the maximum allowable partition size.
> **Response:** If you specified the label correctly, delete a file from the root directory and reexecute processing.

No source drive specified

> **Type:** Execution error

Source: BACKUP

Cause: You did not specify a source drive parameter.

Response: Specify drives for both the source and the destination, and reexecute processing.

No space for a xxxx cylinder partition

Type: Execution error

Source: FDISK

Cause: The specified partition size is larger than the remaining disk space can accommodate.

Response: Specify a smaller size.

No space to create a DOS partition

Type: Information message

Source: FDISK

Cause: You tried to create a DOS partition, but there is no room left on the current disk to create another partition.

Response: Reduce the size of the existing partitions.

No space to create logical drive

Type: Information message

Source: FDISK

Cause: No more space is available in the partition to create another logical drive.

Response: Reduce the size of existing logical drives by deleting and then recreating them.

No subdirectories exist

Type: Information message

Source: TREE

Cause: The drive you wish to examine does not contain directories other than the root directory.

Response: No response required.

No system on default drive

    Type: Information message

    Source: SYS

    Cause: The disk from which you are trying to copy the system does not contain the operating system files.

    Response: Use a source disk that contains the system files.

No target drive specified

    Type: Execution error

    Source: Various commands

    Cause: When invoking a command, you did not specify the target drive.

    Response: Reissue the command with the correct parameters.

No version of Graphic Character Set Table is already loaded

    Type: Information message

    Source: GRAFTABL

    Cause: No character tables have been loaded using GRAFTABL since DOS was started.

    Response: No response required. DOS will automatically load the default graphic character set table.

Non-DOS disk

    Type: Device, disk, or data corruption error

    Source: DOS, CHKDSK, various commands

    Cause: The file-allocation table is bad, or you tried to read from a diskette that is not DOS compatible or has not yet been formatted.

    Response: Run CHKDSK to see if the FAT can be fixed; otherwise, reformat the disk and retry the command.

Non-Standard version of Graphic Character Set Table is already loaded

    Type: Information message

    Source: GRAFTABL

Cause: This message indicates that a character table was loaded but then changed, so that it is now different from any table previously defined. Loading a new table will overwrite this table.

Response: No response required.

Non-System disk or disk error
Replace and strike any key when ready

Type: Disk or data corruption error

Source: Startup routines

Cause: The hidden files IBMBIO.COM and IBMDOS.COM could not be located on the disk that you used to boot the system, or an error occurred while the system tried to read information from the disk during booting.

Response: Use a different DOS diskette for booting.

* * * Not able to back up file * * *

Type: Execution error

Source: BACKUP

Cause: A file-sharing conflict occurred during backup processing.

Response: Reissue the command after a few moments, using the /M parameter.

* * * * Not able to restore file * * *

Type: Execution error

Source: RESTORE

Cause: A file-sharing conflict occurred during the restore process.

Response: Reissue the command after a few moments.

Not enough memory

Type: Information message

Source: SHARE, REDIR.

Cause: Not enough memory is available to start SHARE and REDIR.

Response: No response required.

Not enough room to merge the entire file

        Type: Information message

     Source: EDLIN

      Cause: The Transfer command could not completely merge a file due to a memory shortage.

  Response: Install more memory or use smaller files for merge operations.

Not found

        Type: Information message; execution error

     Source: EDLIN

      Cause: The specified string was not found by the Replace or Search command.

  Response: Verify the spelling and capitalization of the string and re-execute processing.

Not ready

        Type: Device error

     Source: DOS

      Cause: The device being accessed is not set up correctly.

  Response: Check the device that you are attempting to use to make sure the setup is correct (for example, make sure the drive doors are closed, the printer is on line, the device is plugged in, and all cables are firmly attached).

One or more CON code pages invalid for given language

        Type: Information message

     Source: KEYB

      Cause: The keyboard translation tables could not be created because one or more of the specified code pages did not correctly match the specified language.

  Response: Reenter the KEYB command with a valid combination of keyboard code and code page number.

Only non-bootable partitions exist

Type: Information message

Source: FDISK

Cause: While defining partitions on your hard disk, you did not define an active partition containing the system files and boot information.

Response: Repartition the disk with a primary DOS partition.

Only partitions on Drive 1 can be made active

Type: Information message

Source: FDISK

Cause: Since the system can be booted only from the first hard disk, you do not need to specify any active partitions on other drives.

Response: No response required.

Parameters not compatible

Type: Spelling or specification error

Source: Various commands

Cause: When invoking a command, you specified at least two incompatible parameters on the command line.

Response: Reissue the command with correct parameters.

Parameters not compatible with fixed disk

Type: Execution error

Source: FORMAT

Cause: You tried to format a hard disk using the /1 or /8 parameter.

Response: Reissue the command correctly.

Parity error or nonexistent memory error detected

Type: Device error

Source: DEBUG

Cause: The hardware failed.

Response: Reboot or run a diagnostic test.

Partition selected (#) is not bootable, active partition not changed

Type: Execution error

Source: FDISK

Cause: You attempted to activate a partition that cannot be booted.

Response: Reissue the command specifying a bootable partition.

Partition 1 is already active

Type: Information message

Source: FDISK

Cause: Only one partition is defined, and it is marked active.

Response: No response required.

Partition xx made active

Type: Information message

Source: FDISK

Cause: You have successfully made partition *xx* the active partition.

Response: No response required.

Path not found

Type: Spelling or specification error

Source: DOS, various commands

Cause: You specified an invalid path or directory.

Response: Use the correct information and reissue your command.

Path too long

Type: Spelling or specification error

Source: Various commands

Cause: You specified a path on the command line that exceeded the maximum length of 63 characters.

Response: Reissue the command with a path of the right length.

Press any key to begin adding file(s)

Type: Request message

Source: REPLACE

Cause: REPLACE is giving you time to insert the correct disk or to change your mind and abort the process.

Response: Press a key when you are ready to continue.

Press any key to begin copying file(s)

Type: Request message

Source: XCOPY

Cause: XCOPY is giving you time to insert the correct disk or to decide to cancel the XCOPY request.

Response: Press a key to continue.

Press any key to begin recovery of the file(s) on drive x

Type: Request message

Source: RECOVER

Cause: RECOVER is giving you time to insert the correct disk or to decide to cancel the recovery request.

Response: Insert the specified disk and press a key to continue.

Press any key to begin replacing file(s)

Type: Request message

Source: REPLACE

Cause: REPLACE is giving you time to insert the correct disk or to decide to cancel the recovery request.

Response: Insert the correct diskettes, as needed, and then press any key to continue.

Previously prepared code page replaced

Type: Information message

Source: MODE

Cause: A code page is currently using the space saved for new fonts, so an old font was replaced.

Response: No response required. Use MODE or STATUS to determine the available code pages.

Primary DOS partition already exists

Type: Information message

Source: FDISK

Cause: You have already defined a primary DOS partition on the current hard disk.

Response: No response required.

Primary DOS partition created

Type: Information message

Source: FDISK

Cause: The primary DOS partition has been created and assigned a drive letter.

Response: You must now format the partition.

Primary DOS partition deleted

Type: Information message

Source: FDISK

Cause: You have successfully deleted the primary DOS partition and its contents from the disk.

Response: No response required.

Print queue is empty

Type: Information message

Source: PRINT

Cause: PRINT is not printing any files.

Response: No response required.

Print queue is full

> **Type:** Execution error
> **Source:** PRINT
> **Cause:** You sent a file to the print queue, but exceeded the limit on the number of files that the queue can hold.
> **Response:** Wait for one of the files in the queue to be printed; then retransmit your file.

Printer error

> **Type:** Execution error
> **Source:** MODE
> **Cause:** MODE could not set the printer because DOS detected an I/O error, the printer ran out of paper, the printer is switched off, or the printer is off line.
> **Response:** Correct the problem and reexecute processing.

Printer lines per inch set

> **Type:** Information message
> **Source:** MODE
> **Cause:** You attempted to reset the lines per inch setting on the printer.
> **Response:** No response required.

Probable non-DOS disk
Continue (Y/N)?

> **Type:** Disk or data corruption error
> **Source:** CHKDSK
> **Cause:** The file-allocation table is bad, or the disk was not formatted.
> **Response:** Use the /F parameter to correct to problem, or reformat the disk.

Processing cannot continue
(error cause)

> **Type:** Information message
> **Source:** CHKDSK

Cause: The message indicates the reason for the problem.

Response: No response required.

Program too big to fit in memory

Type: Execution error

Source: DOS

Cause: Not enough free memory is available to load the program.

Response: Free memory by using fewer buffers in the BUFFERS = command in the CONFIG.SYS files. If you do this and the message is repeated, the system does not contain enough memory to run your application. Remove some memory-resident programs or rewrite your application using overlay or modular techniques.

Read error, COUNTRY.SYS

Type: Disk or data corruption error

Source: SELECT

Cause: Your diskette may be damaged; hence, SELECT cannot find the three-digit country code in the COUNTRY.SYS file.

Response: Use another diskette and reexecute processing.

Read error, KEYBOARD.SYS

Type: Disk or data corruption error

Source: SELECT

Cause: Your diskette may be damaged; hence, SELECT cannot find the three-digit country code in the KEYBOARD.SYS file.

Response: Use another diskette and reexecute processing.

Read error in: x:\level1\level2

Type: Disk or data corruption error

Source: EDLIN

Cause: EDLIN could not read the file *x:\xxxx\xxxx*.

Response: Move the file or a backup copy to another disk and reexecute processing.

Read fault

> **Type:** Device error
> **Source:** DOS
> **Cause:** DOS could not read anything from the specified device.
> **Response:** Reinsert the diskette. If the error is repeated, abort the command and then retry it with a different diskette.

Reinsert diskette for drive x
and strike Enter when ready

> **Type:** Request message
> **Source:** FORMAT
> **Cause:** If you specified the /S option, FORMAT needs to load the rest of the system files.
> **Response:** Insert the diskette and press Enter.

Replace <d:path\filename> *(Y/N)?*

> **Type:** Request message
> **Source:** REPLACE
> **Cause:** You need to confirm a replacement.
> **Response:** Enter Y to replace the file; enter N not to replace the file.

Replacing <d:path\filename>

> **Type:** Information message
> **Source:** REPLACE
> **Cause:** This message indicates which file is being replaced.
> **Response:** No response required.

Requested logical drive size exceeds
the maximum available space

> **Type:** Spelling or specification error
> **Source:** FDISK
> **Cause:** You specified a drive size larger than the space left in the extended DOS partition.
> **Response:** Specify a new, smaller drive size.

Requested partition size exceeds the maximum available space

Type: Spelling or specification error

Source: FDISK

Cause: You specified a partition size larger than the space left on the disk.

Response: Specify a new, smaller partition size.

Resident part of PRINT installed

Type: Information message

Source: PRINT

Cause: PRINT has been successfully installed.

Response: No response required.

Resident portion of MODE loaded

Type: Information message

Source: MODE

Cause: Part of MODE has been loaded into memory to execute a command.

Response: No response required.

Resident portion of NLSFUNC loaded

Type: Information message

Source: NLSFUNC

Cause: Code page switching is now available.

Response: No response required.

Restore file sequence error

Type: Information message; execution error

Source: RESTORE

Cause: You did not insert the diskettes in the right order, so files were not restored.

Response: Reissue the RESTORE command, this time inserting the disks in the correct order.

*** *Restoring files from drive* xx ***

Type: Information message

Source: RESTORE

Cause: This message lists the files that were restored.

Response: No response required.

*** *Restoring files from drive* y ***
Source x

Type: Information message

Source: RESTORE

Cause: Source files are being restored.

Response: No response required.

Same drive specified more than once

Type: Spelling or specification error

Source: FASTOPEN

Cause: You specified the same drive identifier twice on the FAST-OPEN command line.

Response: Reissue the FASTOPEN command using each drive identifier only once.

Sector not found

Type: Device error

Source: DOS

Cause: A data sector on the disk could not be found.

Response: Reenter the command. If the error recurs, abort the command and use a different diskette.

Sector size adjusted

Type: Information message

Source: VDISK

Cause: VDISK changed the sector-size specification in the DE-VICE = VDISK.SYS line in the CONFIG.SYS file.

Response: No response required.

Sector size too large in file **filename**

Type: Execution error

Source: Startup files

Cause: You specified a device driver that uses a sector size larger than the size defined for DOS.

Response: Change the sector size so that it matches that of DOS. If the program is purchased software, return it to the dealer.

Seek

Type: Device error

Source: DOS

Cause: DOS could not find a track on the disk.

Response: Reinsert the diskette, use another drive, or run CHKDSK.

SHARE already installed

Type: Information message

Source: SHARE

Cause: You have already loaded SHARE and cannot do so again.

Response: No response required.

Sharing Violation

Type: Device error; execution error

Source: SHARE, XCOPY

Cause: One of two things has happened: you may have used an invalid sharing mode while trying to access a file; this error usually occurs when someone else is waiting to access the same file in compatibility mode or in sharing mode and so prevents you from using the file concurrently. Or, a file that XCOPY is trying to access is currently locked by another user.

Response: Reexecute processing or abort the SHARE command and enter it again later; wait until the file is available (after a few moments, typically) and reexecute XCOPY.

Source diskette bad or incompatible

Type: Disk or data corruption error
Source: DISKCOPY
Cause: A source diskette error occurred, or the source diskette is not compatible with the source drive.
Response: Check your disk and drive configuration.

Source does not contain backup files

Type: Information message
Source: RESTORE
Cause: The source disk does not contain any backup files to be restored.
Response: No response required.

Source path required

Type: Execution error
Sourcc: REPLACE
Cause: You did not specify a path to the source of the replacement files.
Response: Reinvoke REPLACE specifying a source path.

Specified COMMAND search directory bad

Type: Execution error
Source: Various commands
Cause: You specified an invalid path.
Response: Reissue the command with a valid path.

Specified drive does not exist, or is non-removable

Type: Spelling or specification error
Source: DISKCOPY, DISKCOMP

Cause: You specified a fixed disk drive or an undefined drive.

Response: Reissue the command with the correct drive identifier.

Syntax error

Type: Execution error

Source: DOS

Cause: You entered the command incorrectly.

Response: Reissue the command with the correct format and spelling.

System files restored
The target disk may not be bootable

Type: Information message

Source: RESTORE

Cause: During the restore process, the files IBMBIO.COM and IBMDOS.COM were restored. If these files are from a previous version of DOS, your disk may not be bootable.

Response: Use SYS to transfer the correct version of the files to the disk from your master copy. You can use VER to help determine the DOS version numbers involved.

System transferred

Type: Information message

Source: FORMAT

Cause: The two hidden system files have been transferred to the newly formatted disk, an operation that occurs when you specify the /S parameter.

Response: No response required.

System will now restart
Insert DOS diskette in drive A:
Press any key when ready

Type: Information message

Source: FDISK

Cause: To install the new partition information, the system must be rebooted.

Response: Insert a DOS diskette in drive A and reboot the system.

Target cannot be used for backup

Type: Execution error

Source: BACKUP

Cause: An error occurred during writing to the destination disk.

Response: Use another disk. If the error recurs, restart the system or use another device as the backup operation target.

Target diskette may be unusable

Type: Disk or data corruption error

Source: DISKCOPY

Cause: This message appears when DISKCOPY encounters an unrecoverable read, write, or verify message.

Response: The error will correspond to the source or target diskette. Either repeat the operation using a different target disk (if the target disk was at fault) or make a new source disk by copying all of the source files to another diskette first; then reissue the DISKCOPY command.

Target diskette unusable

Type: Disk or data corruption error

Source: DISKCOPY

Cause: The target diskette is dirty, damaged, or of too poor quality to be used, or the drive is malfunctioning.

Response: Use another drive or diskette and reexecute processing.

Target diskette is write protected
Correct, then strike any key

Type: Execution error

Source: DISKCOPY

Cause: Your target disk is write protected.

Response: Remove the write-protect label and press a key.

Target is full

Type: Execution error

Source: RESTORE

Cause: Your destination disk has no more space available.

Response: Make room on the disk by deleting any unneeded files, or use a different target disk.

10 Mismatches—ending compare

Type: Information message

Source: COMP

Cause: The files being compared contained 10 mismatched locations. COMP assumes that any further comparison will yield more mismatches, and, hence, that the files are not the same; COMP will stop.

Response: No response required.

Terminate batch job (Y/N)?

Type: Request message

Source: DOS

Cause: You interrupted the execution of a batch file.

Response: Enter Y to halt batch-file execution or N to continue execution.

Current keyboard code: xx
Code page: yyy
Current CON code page: zzz

Type: Information message

Source: KEYB

Cause: You used the KEYB query function.

Response: No response required.

The current active partition is x

Type: Information message

Source: FDISK

Cause: You chose the Change Active Partition option.

Response: No response required.

The last file was not restored

Type: Execution error

Source: RESTORE

Cause: You interrupted the restore process in the middle of the last restoration; or the target disk ran out of room, and the last file, which was partially restored, was deleted.

Response: If you ran out of room, make room on the disk and continue the restore process from where you left off. If you stopped the process, reissue RESTORE for the files that have not been restored yet.

The only bootable partition on Drive 1 is already marked active

Type: Information message

Source: FDISK

Cause: You have only one partition on the drive, and it is the active, boot partition.

Response: No response required.

Too many Block Devices

Type: Execution error

Source: DOS

Cause: You tried to use more than the maximum 26 block device units.

Response: Modify the DEVICE = command line in the CONFIG.SYS file to use only 26 block device units (including those used by DOS).

Too many drive entries

Type: Execution error

Source: FASTOPEN

Cause: You specified too many drive identifiers on the command line.

Response: Reissue the command with fewer drive identifiers.

Too many files open

Type: Execution error

Source: EDLIN

Cause: EDLIN could not open the specified file.

Response: Reduce the number of open files or reconfigure your system to allow more files (using FILES = in CONFIG.SYS).

Too many name entries

Type: Execution error

Source: FASTOPEN

Cause: The requested number of entries for files and subdirectory names on all drives exceeded 999.

Response: Reduce the number of entries to fewer than 999.

Too many open files

Type: Execution error

Source: XCOPY

Cause: Insufficient file handles are available for use.

Response: Increase the FILES = command line in the CONFIG.SYS file to at least 20.

Top level process aborted, cannot continue

Type: Execution error

Source: Bootup

Cause: A disk error occurred and command was forced to halt during bootup.

Response: Use another DOS disk.

Total disk space is xxxx cylinders

Type: Information message

Source: FDISK

Cause: This message displays the total available space on the hard disk.

Response: No response required.

Transfer size adjusted

Type: Execution error

Source: VDISK

Cause: Number of sectors exceeded 8.

Response: No response required (8 is used).

Tree past this point not processed

>**Type:** Information message
>
>**Source:** CHKDSK
>
>**Cause:** This message follows another error message indicating why CHKDSK was not able to continue.
>
>**Response:** No response required.

Unable to create directory

>**Type:** Execution error
>
>**Source:** DOS, various commands
>
>**Cause:** One of the following errors occurred: the directory you are trying to create already exists; you specified an invalid directory on the path; the root directory is full; a file in the specified parent directory already exists by the name you want to use; you specified an invalid directory name.
>
>**Response:** Verify that you entered a valid directory name and path and that no file already exists with the name you wish to use.

Unable to create KEYB table in resident memory

>**Type:** Execution error
>
>**Source:** KEYB
>
>**Cause:** The KEYB command has already been installed. Your request exceeds the amount of memory that has already been allocated to it.
>
>**Response:** Reboot and then reinstall KEYB with your new configuration.

Unable to shift screen left

>**Type:** Execution error
>
>**Source:** MODE
>
>**Cause:** The screen cannot be further shifted to the left without exceeding the allowable limit.
>
>**Response:** No response required.

Unable to shift screen right

Type: Execution error
Source: MODE
Cause: The screen cannot be further shifted to the right without exceeding the allowable limit.
Response: No response required.

Unable to write BOOT

Type: Disk or data corruption error
Source: FORMAT
Cause: The boot record could not be written on the disk, because of a defective first track.
Response: Use another diskette and reexecute processing.

Unrecognized command in CONFIG.SYS

Type: Execution error
Source: Startup
Cause: You specified an invalid command in the CONFIG.SYS file.
Response: Specify a valid command and reboot.

Unrecoverable error in directory

Type: Disk or data corruption error
Source: CHKDSK
Cause: CHKDSK found an error while examining a directory.
Response: Attempt to recreate the data from alternative sources.

Unrecoverable file sharing error

Type: Execution error
Source: Various commands
Cause: A file-sharing conflict has arisen. Your files cannot be restored.
Response: Attempt to recreate the data from alternative sources.

Unrecoverable read error on drive x
Track xx, *side* x

> **Type:** Disk or data corruption error
>
> **Source:** DISKCOMP
>
> **Cause:** DISKCOMP tried four times to read the data on the disk in the specified drive, but could not.
>
> **Response:** Reexecute DISKCOPY (to recreate the target disk) or DISKCOMP with different target disks, or copy all of the readable files to another disk.

Unrecoverable read error on source
Track xx, *side* x

> **Type:** Media or data corruption error
>
> **Source:** DISKCOPY
>
> **Cause:** After four attempts at reading the source diskette, DISK-COPY moved on to the next batch of data. The target disk may now contain an incomplete copy.
>
> **Response:** Use COPY *.* to copy files from the source diskette. Reformat or discard the bad disk.

Unrecoverable write error on target
Track xx, *side* x

> **Type:** Media or data corruption error
>
> **Source:** DISKCOPY
>
> **Cause:** DISKCOPY was unable to write data to the target diskette.
>
> **Response:** Reissue the DISKCOPY command with a different diskette.

VDISK not installed—insufficient memory

> **Type:** Execution error
>
> **Source:** VDISK
>
> **Cause:** There is not enough available memory in the system.
>
> **Response:** Reduce the requested size of the RAM disk.

VDISK Version 3.30 Virtual Disk x

Type: Information message
Source: VDISK
Cause: VDISK is being installed with drive letter *x*.
Response: No response required.

VERIFY is on ¦ off

Type: Information message
Source: VERIFY
Cause: This message displays the current status of VERIFY.
Response: No response required.

Volume label (11 characters, ENTER for none)?

Type: Request message
Source: FORMAT
Cause: FORMAT asks you to enter a one- to eleven-character volume label for the current disk.
Response: Enter a label; then press Enter.

WARNING! ALL DATA ON NON-REMOVABLE DISK DRIVE X WILL BE LOST
Proceed with Format (Y/N)?

Type: Information message; request message
Source: FORMAT
Cause: FORMAT requests confirmation that you wish to format the specified hard disk.
Response: Type Y to format or N not to format the hard disk.

Warning! Data in the extended DOS partition could be DESTROYED. Do you wish to continue........? [n]

Type: Information message; request message
Source: FDISK

Cause: You chose the Delete Extended Partition option, and this is the ensuing warning message.

Response: Type Y and press Enter to delete the extended partition; type N to abort this operation.

Warning! Data in the Primary DOS partition
could be DESTROYED. Do you wish to
continue...........?[n]

Type: Information message; request message

Source: FDISK

Cause: You chose the Delete Primary Partition option, and this is the ensuing warning message.

Response: Type Y and press Enter to delete the primary partition; type N to abort this operation.

Warning—directory full
xxx *file(s) recovered*

Type: Execution error

Source: RECOVER

Cause: There is not enough space left on the disk to recover more files.

Response: Free sufficient space and rerun RECOVER.

Warning! Diskette is out of sequence
Replace the diskette or continue if okay
Strike any key when ready

Type: Execution error

Source: RESTORE

Cause: You inserted the wrong disk for restoration.

Response: Use the correct diskette.

Warning! File **xx** *is a read-only file*
Replace the file (Y/N)?

Type: Information message; request message

Source: RESTORE

Cause:	The file indicated is a read-only file, and hence cannot be automatically overwritten.
Response:	Enter Y to overwrite the file or N not to overwrite the file.

Warning! File xx
was changed after it was backed up
Replace the file (Y/N)?

Type:	Information message; request message
Source:	The file to be restored is an earlier version of one that already exists on the disk.
Response:	Enter Y to replace the latest version with the earlier version or N to abort the replacement operation.

Warning! Files in the target drive
d:\BACKUP directory will be erased
Strike any key when ready

Type:	Information message
Source:	BACKUP
Cause:	This warning appears when you issue the BACKUP command using a subdirectory as the target.
Response:	Press Ctrl-Break to halt execution if you do not wish to continue; press any key to continue.

Warning! Files in the target drive
d:\root directory will be erased
Strike any key when ready

Type:	Information message
Source:	BACKUP
Cause:	This warning appears when you issue the BACKUP command using a diskette drive as the target.
Response:	Press Ctrl-Break to halt execution if you do not wish to continue; press any key to continue.

Warning! No files were found to back up

Type:	Information message
Source:	BACKUP

Cause: DOS found no files to back up.

Response: No response required.

Warning! No files were found to restore

Type: Information message

Source: RESTORE

Cause: DOS found no files to restore.

Response: Make sure you specified the desired file names correctly.

Warning! Target is full

Type: Information message

Source: RESTORE

Cause: The target diskette is full. No more files will be restored.

Response: No response required.

Warning! The partition marked active is not bootable

Type: Information message

Source: FDISK

Cause: You have marked an unbootable partition as active.

Response: Change the active partition to one that is bootable.

Write fault

Type: Device error

Source: DOS

Cause: Dos could not write anything to the disk.

Response: Reinsert the disk and reexecute the command. If the error recurs, abort the operation and retry the command with another disk.

Write protect

Type: Device error

Source: DOS

Cause: The disk is write protected and hence cannot be written to.

Response: Make sure you wish to write on the diskette; then remove the write protection (peel off the label covering the write-protect notch).

xxxxxxxxxxxx *bytes disk space freed*

Type: Information message

Source: CHKDSK

Cause: This message indicates the amount of memory freed using the /F parameter.

Response: No response required.

xxxxxxxxxx *code page driver cannot be initialized*

Type: Execution error

Source: PRINTER.SYS, DISPLAY.SYS

Cause: You used incorrect parameters in a DEVICE = command in the CONFIG.SYS file.

Response: Correct the mistakes and reboot.

xxxxxxxxx *device driver cannot be initialized*

Type: Execution error

Source: DOS

Cause: The parameters for a DEVICE = command were invalid.

Response: Correct the mistakes and reboot.

xxxx *error on file* yyyy

Type: Execution error

Source: PRINT

Cause: A disk error occurred during printing. Printing is stopped.

Response: Check the disk drive and reexecute processing.

xxx *files added*

Type: Information message

Source: REPLACE

Cause: This status message indicates the number of files added to the target directory.

Response: No response required.

x *is not a choice. Enter a choice*

Type: Execution error

Source: FDISK

Cause: You entered an invalid option.

Response: Reenter a valid option number.

x *is not a choice. Enter Y or N*

Type: Execution error

Source: FDISK

Cause: You entered an invalid option.

Response: Enter Y or N.

x *is not a choice. Please enter* y-z

Type: Execution error

Source: Various commands

Cause: You entered an invalid option.

Response: Enter a valid option in the range y to z.

xxx *lost clusters found in* yy *chains*
Convert lost chains to files (Y/N)?

Type: Request message

Source: CHKDSK

Cause: The disk contains unconnected data (due to an interrupted I/O operation).

Response: Enter Y (assuming you used the /F parameter) to convert the lost data into usable data.

xxxxxx *of* xxxxxx *bytes recovered*

Type: Information message

Source: RECOVER

Cause: This status message appears when RECOVER completes its recovery process.

Response: No response required.

nnn *version of Graphic Character Set Table is already loaded*

Type: Information message

Source: GRAFTABL

Cause: You are trying to load a table that is already loaded.

Response: No response required.

nnn *version of Graphic Character Set Table is now loaded*

Type: Information message

Source: GRAFTABL

Cause: You have loaded a table.

Response: No response required.

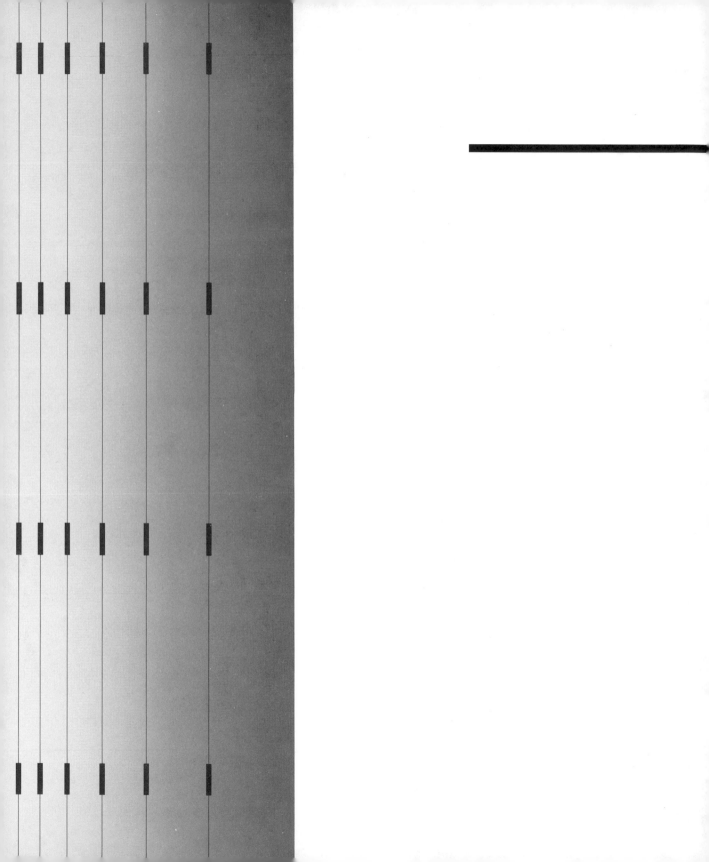

ASCII Codes, Code Pages, Character Sets, and Numbering Systems

ASCII CODES,
CODE PAGES, CHARACTER SETS,
AND NUMBERING SYSTEMS

Throughout this book, you've seen references to ASCII, the computer industry standard that enables computers to work with text data by assigning a numerical value to each character. Chapter 11 discusses the provisions DOS offers for using the special characters (such as currency symbols and accented letters) that some foreign languages require. As you saw there, DOS makes these characters available through the use of *code pages* for different nations and languages. This appendix explores the relationship between ASCII codes, DOS code pages, character sets, and numbering systems.

What Is a Character Set?

Broadly speaking, a *character set* is simply any set of characters grouped together for a common purpose. Thus, the versions of the Latin alphabet (along with numerals, punctuation marks, and other symbols) used by different nations and language communities can each be considered separate character sets. In the context of computers, a character set is the set of characters available on a given machine. All versions of DOS can maintain in the computer's memory at least one character set, comprising all of the capital and lowercase letters of the English language, numerals, punctuation, and other symbols, as well as some foreign letters (such as accented vowels). This set is known as ASCII (pronounced "ask-ee"), the American Standard Code for Information Interchange, discussed in the following paragraphs. Beginning with version 3.0, DOS can maintain in memory, at any given time, one of at least five different versions of the ASCII set—in effect, five different character sets, known as code pages. DOS version 3.3 makes available 21 different code pages. The most commonly used is the standard U.S. code page (see Table C.1); the next most common is the multilingual code page (see Table C.2). Three other code page tables available in DOS 3.3 are shown in Tables C.3, C.4, and C.5.

Hex Digits 1st → 2nd ↓	0-	1-	2-	3-	4-	5-	6-	7-	8-	9-	A-	B-	C-	D-	E-	F-
-0		►		0	@	P	`	p	Ç	É	á	▓	└	⊥	α	≡
-1	☺	◄	!	1	A	Q	a	q	ü	æ	í	▒	┴	╤	β	±
-2	☻	↕	"	2	B	R	b	r	é	Æ	ó	▓	┬	╥	Γ	≥
-3	♥	‼	#	3	C	S	c	s	â	ô	ú	│	├	╙	π	≤
-4	♦	¶	$	4	D	T	d	t	ä	ö	ñ	┤	─	╘	Σ	⌠
-5	♣	§	%	5	E	U	e	u	à	ò	Ñ	╡	┼	╒	σ	⌡
-6	♠	▬	&	6	F	V	f	v	å	û	ª	╢	╞	╓	µ	÷
-7	•	↨	'	7	G	W	g	w	ç	ù	º	╖	╟	╫	τ	≈
-8	◘	↑	(	8	H	X	h	x	ê	ÿ	¿	╕	╚	╪	Φ	°
-9	○	↓	)	9	I	Y	i	y	ë	Ö	⌐	╣	╔	┘	Θ	∙
-A	◙	→	*	:	J	Z	j	z	è	Ü	¬	║	╩	┌	Ω	·
-B	♂	←	+	;	K	[	k	{	ï	¢	½	╗	╦	█	δ	√
-C	♀	∟	,	<	L	\	l	|	î	£	¼	╝	╠	▄	∞	ⁿ
-D	♪	↔	-	=	M	]	m	}	ì	¥	¡	╜	═	█	ø	²
-E	♫	▲	.	>	N	^	n	~	Ä	₧	«	╛	╬	█	ε	■
-F	☼	▼	/	?	O	_	o	⌂	Å	ƒ	»	┐	╧	▀	∩	

TABLE C.1: U.S. ASCII Table (Code Page 437 in DOS 3.3)

ASCII

As you've just seen, the name ASCII is misleading on two counts: the use of this code is not confined to North America, and the code is only partly standardized. Nonetheless, in spite of the national variations embodied in the DOS code pages, the versions of ASCII have more similarities than differences.

As originally defined, ASCII is based on the use of seven bits to represent a character: these seven bits can be combined into 128 (2^7) different values. Adding an eighth bit, as in the DOS code pages, allows 256 (2^8) characters. This number may seem more than adequate for representing all of the characters anyone might need to use, but, as the presence in DOS 3.X of the foreign code pages testifies, it is not. The alphanumeric characters represent a relatively small proportion of the ASCII set; with all of the control codes and graphics characters, including every variant accented letter in the Latin alphabet would easily exceed the available number of codes. But since each language requires only a few variant letters and symbols, it makes sense for the programmers who wrote DOS to

Hex Digits 1st → 2nd ↓	0-	1-	2-	3-	4-	5-	6-	7-	8-	9-	A-	B-	C-	D-	E-	F-
-0		►		0	@	P	`	p	Ç	É	á	▒	└	ð	Ó	-
-1	☺	◄	!	1	A	Q	a	q	ü	æ	í	▓	┴	Ð	ß	±
-2	☻	↕	"	2	B	R	b	r	é	Æ	ó	▓	┬	Ê	Ô	=
-3	♥	‼	#	3	C	S	c	s	â	ô	ú	│	├	Ë	Ò	¾
-4	♦	¶	$	4	D	T	d	t	ä	ö	ñ	┤	─	È	õ	¶
-5	♣	§	%	5	E	U	e	u	à	ò	Ñ	Á	┼	ı	Õ	§
-6	♠	▬	&	6	F	V	f	v	å	û	ª	Â	ã	Í	µ	÷
-7	•	↨	'	7	G	W	g	w	ç	ù	º	À	Ã	Î	þ	¸
-8	◘	↑	(	8	H	X	h	x	ê	ÿ	¿	©	└	Ï	Þ	°
-9	○	↓	)	9	I	Y	i	y	ë	Ö	®	╣	╔	┘	Ú	¨
-A	◎	→	*	:	J	Z	j	z	è	Ü	¬	║	╩	┌	Û	·
-B	♂	←	+	;	K	[	k	{	ï	ø	½	╗	╦	█	Ù	¹
-C	♀	∟	,	<	L	\	l	|	î	£	¼	╝	╠	▄	ý	³
-D	♪	↔	-	=	M	]	m	}	ì	Ø	¡	¢	═	¦	Ý	²
-E	♫	▲	.	>	N	^	n	~	Ä	×	«	¥	╬	Ì	¯	■
-F	☼	▼	/	?	O	_	o	△	Å	ƒ	»	┐	¤	▀	´	

TABLE C.2: Multilingual ASCII Table (Code Page 850 in DOS 3.3)

group them into separate character sets that differ only slightly. These variations occur in the second half of an ASCII set (codes 128 to 255); the ASCII codes from 0 to 127 are genuinely standard.

Control Characters

Codes 0 through 31 are known as *control characters*, or nonprinting characters. Instead of displaying a symbol on an output device, invoking one of these codes instructs the computer to perform some hardware operation. For example, code 7 sounds the computer's bell or beeper, and code 13 causes a carriage return. Because these codes are really unique, one-byte values in the character set, they are considered "characters."

Hex Digits 1st → 2nd ↓	0-	1-	2-	3-	4-	5-	6-	7-	8-	9-	A-	B-	C-	D-	E-	F-
-0		►		0	@	P	`	p	Ç	É	á	▓	└	╨	α	≡
-1	☺	◄	!	1	A	Q	a	q	ü	À	í	▒	┴	╤	β	±
-2	☻	↕	"	2	B	R	b	r	é	È	ó	▓	┬	╥	Γ	≥
-3	♥	‼	#	3	C	S	c	s	â	ô	ú	│	├	╙	π	≤
-4	♦	¶	$	4	D	T	d	t	ã	õ	ñ	┤	─	╘	Σ	⌠
-5	♣	§	%	5	E	U	e	u	à	ò	Ñ	╡	┼	╒	σ	⌡
-6	♠	▬	&	6	F	V	f	v	Á	Ú	ª	╢	╞	╓	µ	÷
-7	•	↨	'	7	G	W	g	w	ç	ù	º	╖	╟	╫	τ	≈
-8	▫	↑	(	8	H	X	h	x	ê	Ì	¿	╕	╚	╪	Φ	°
-9	○	↓	)	9	I	Y	i	y	Ê	Õ	Ò	╣	╔	┘	Θ	∙
-A	◎	→	*	:	J	Z	j	z	è	Ü	¬	║	╩	┌	Ω	·
-B	♂	←	+	;	K	[	k	{	Ì	¢	½	╗	╦	█	δ	√
-C	♀	∟	,	<	L	\	l	|	Ô	£	¼	╝	╠	▄	∞	ⁿ
-D	♪	↔	-	=	M	]	m	}	ì	Ù	¡	╜	═	█	φ	²
-E	♫	▲	.	>	N	^	n	~	Ã	Pt	«	╛	╬	█	ε	■
-F	☼	▼	/	?	O	_	o	⌂	Â	Ó	»	┐	╧	▀	∩	

TABLE C.3: Portuguese ASCII Table (Code Page 860 in DOS 3.3)

Alphanumeric Characters

Codes 32 through 127 represent numbers, letters, punctuation marks, and some of the commonly used mathematical symbols and Greek letters. For example, code 65 represents the capital letter *A*, and code 97 represents the lowercase *a*. If you look at the code pages in Figures C.1 through C.5, you'll see that this part of ASCII does not vary from version to version. (Keep in mind, however, that different keyboard layouts assign individual codes to different keys; this mediation relies on keyboard scan codes and is discussed in Chapter 11.)

Extended ASCII Characters

Codes 128 through 255 are known as *extended* ASCII characters. This part of the character set varies from computer to computer and, within DOS 3.X, from code page to code page. (The availability of particular characters within this range also varies from printer to printer; consult your printer's documentation for a list of the characters it can generate.) These characters are usually foreign

Hex Digits 1st→ 2nd↓	0-	1-	2-	3-	4-	5-	6-	7-	8-	9-	A-	B-	C-	D-	E-	F-
-0		►		0	@	P	`	p	Ç	É	¦	▓	└	⊥	α	≡
-1	☺	◄	!	1	A	Q	a	q	ü	È	´	▓	┴	╦	β	±
-2	☻	↕	"	2	B	R	b	r	é	Ê	ó	▓	┬	╥	Γ	≥
-3	♥	‼	#	3	C	S	c	s	â	ô	ú	│	├	⊥	π	≤
-4	♦	¶	$	4	D	T	d	t	Â	Ë	¨	┤	─	╘	Σ	⌠
-5	♣	§	%	5	E	U	e	u	à	Ï	˛	╡	┼	╞	σ	⌡
-6	♠	▬	&	6	F	V	f	v	¶	û	³	╢	┌	╟	μ	÷
-7	•	↨	'	7	G	W	g	w	ç	ú	¯	╖	╟	╫	τ	≈
-8	◘	↑	(	8	H	X	h	x	ê	¤	Î	╕	└	╪	Φ	°
-9	○	↓	)	9	I	Y	i	y	ë	Ô	⌐	╣	╔	┘	Θ	•
-A	◎	→	*	:	J	Z	j	z	è	Ü	¬	║	╩	┌	Ω	·
-B	♂	←	+	;	K	[	k	{	ï	¢	½	╗	╦	█	δ	√
-C	♀	∟	,	<	L	\	l	¦	î	£	¼	╝	╠	▄	∞	ⁿ
-D	♪	↔	-	=	M	]	m	}	=	Ù	¾	╜	═	█	ø	²
-E	♫	▲	.	>	N	^	n	~	À	Û	«	╛	╬	█	ε	■
-F	☼	▼	/	?	O	_	o	△	§	ƒ	»	┐	┴	▀	∩	

TABLE C.4: Canadian-French ASCII Table (Code Page 863 in DOS 3.3)

letters, more Greek and mathematical symbols, and graphics characters (straight lines, corners, and dot patterns that can be combined to create pictorial effects).

MAPPING ONE CHARACTER SET ONTO ANOTHER

When a computer is operating in *text mode* (as opposed to *graphics mode*), it sends output through its communications ports in the form of ASCII values. The output device must have its own way of translating the character value into instructions that tell it exactly how to form the character. For a video monitor, these instructions will specify which pixels on the screen to illuminate; for a daisy-wheel printer, they will say how far to rotate the print wheel to bring the correct letter into position, when to strike the hammer, and so on. These instructions are produced by microprocessor chips, located within adaptors (for video monitors) or within the peripheral device itself (for printers).

The process of matching ASCII codes against characters in a character set is called *mapping*. For the sake of consistency, computers, printers and displays all

Hex Digits 1st → 2nd ↓	0-	1-	2-	3-	4-	5-	6-	7-	8-	9-	A-	B-	C-	D-	E-	F-
-0		►		0	@	P	`	p	Ç	É	á	░	└	╨	α	≡
-1	☺	◄	!	1	A	Q	a	q	ü	æ	í	▒	┴	╤	β	±
-2	☻	↕	"	2	B	R	b	r	é	Æ	ó	▓	┬	╥	Γ	≥
-3	♥	‼	#	3	C	S	c	s	â	ô	ú	│	├	╙	π	≤
-4	♦	¶	$	4	D	T	d	t	ä	ö	ñ	┤	─	╘	Σ	⌠
-5	♣	§	%	5	E	U	e	u	à	ò	Ñ	╡	┼	╒	σ	⌡
-6	♠	▬	&	6	F	V	f	v	å	û	ª	╢	╞	╓	µ	÷
-7	•	↨	'	7	G	W	g	w	ç	ú	º	╖	╟	╫	τ	≈
-8	◘	↑	(	8	H	X	h	x	ê	ÿ	¿	╕	╚	╪	Φ	°
-9	○	↓	)	9	I	Y	i	y	ë	Ö	⌐	╣	╔	┘	Θ	∙
-A	◙	→	*	:	J	Z	j	z	è	Ü	¬	║	╩	┌	Ω	·
-B	♂	←	+	;	K	[	k	{	ï	ø	½	╗	╦	█	δ	√
-C	♀	∟	,	<	L	\	l	|	î	£	¼	╝	╠	▄	∞	ⁿ
-D	♪	↔	-	=	M	]	m	}	ì	Ø	¡	╜	═	▌	φ	²
-E	♫	▲	.	>	N	^	n	~	Ä	Pt	«	╛	╬	▐	ε	■
-F	☼	▼	/	?	O	_	o	△	Å	ƒ	¤	┐	╧	▀	∩	

TABLE C.5: Norwegian ASCII Table (Code Page 865 in DOS 3.3)

use the same character sets and coding system for ASCII codes 32 through 127. This ensures that when you press a key, the desired character will be displayed, and the same character will be printed by your printer. To display or print characters represented by ASCII codes 128 through 255, you must know which code page contains the character. Standard U.S. code page (437) characters can be generated by most video monitors and printers, but only some monitors and printers can accurately reproduce the specialized characters found in the other code pages. See Chapter 11 for more information about the preparatory steps required for using these other devices.

Numbering Systems

Computers use a variety of numbering systems. The most basic numbering system is the binary system, in which there are only two digits: 0 and 1. The digital circuitry used in computers operates by using small voltages that turn magnetic bits on or off. Therefore, 0 and 1 are used to represent the two states off and on, respectively.

Counting in binary is not difficult, but it does differ significantly from the standard decimal-numbering scheme. The progression of numbers and their matching decimal conversions are shown in Table C.6.

Chapter 12 contains a detailed explanation of the binary numbering system. The general rule for converting numbers from binary to decimal is to multiply the number in every binary number column by 2 raised to the column-number power. You count column numbers from the right, starting with 0. To convert the binary number 1101, for example, you perform this calculation:

$$(1 \times 2^0) + (0 \times 2^1) + (1 \times 2^2) + (1 \times 2^3)$$
$$= 1 + 0 + 4 + 8$$
$$= 13$$

In this calculation, any number to the 0 power (2^0 in this case) is defined as equal to 1. This is called *counting in base 2*.

The *decimal* system counts in base 10. Using the same method of converting binary numbers, breaking down the decimal number 2014 into its component parts works like this:

$$(4 \times 10^0) + (1 \times 10^1) + (0 \times 10^2) + (2 \times 10^3)$$
$$= 4 + 10 + 0 + 2000$$
$$= 2014$$

BINARY	DECIMAL
0	0
1	1
10	2
11	3
100	4
101	5
110	6
111	7
1000	8
1001	9
1010	10

TABLE C.6: Binary-to-Decimal Conversion

The last major numbering system computers use is the *hexadecimal* system, which counts in base 16. This system uses 16 digits—0–9 and A–F—which form the counting sequence 0123456789ABCDEF. To count in this system, you use the same method you use for other numbering systems. The hexadecimal number BA7 translates to decimal form as

$$(7 \times 16^0) + (A \times 16^1) + (B \times 16^2)$$

which is equal to

$$7 + (10 \times 16^1) + (11 \times 16^2)$$

which is also equal to

$$7 + 160 + 2816$$
$$= 2983$$

Table C.7 demonstrates how to count in hexadecimal format.

Hexadecimal notation is convenient for byte values because a hexadecimal digit is equivalent to 4 ($2^4 = 16$) binary digits (called a *nibble*) and there are 8 bits ($2^8 = 256$-character set) in a byte. A byte can therefore be represented by two hexadecimal digits.

HEXADECIMAL	DECIMAL
0	0
1	1
.	.
.	.
9	9
A	10
B	11
.	.
.	.
F	15
10	16
.	.
.	.
1A	26

TABLE C.7: Hexadecimal-to-Decimal Conversion

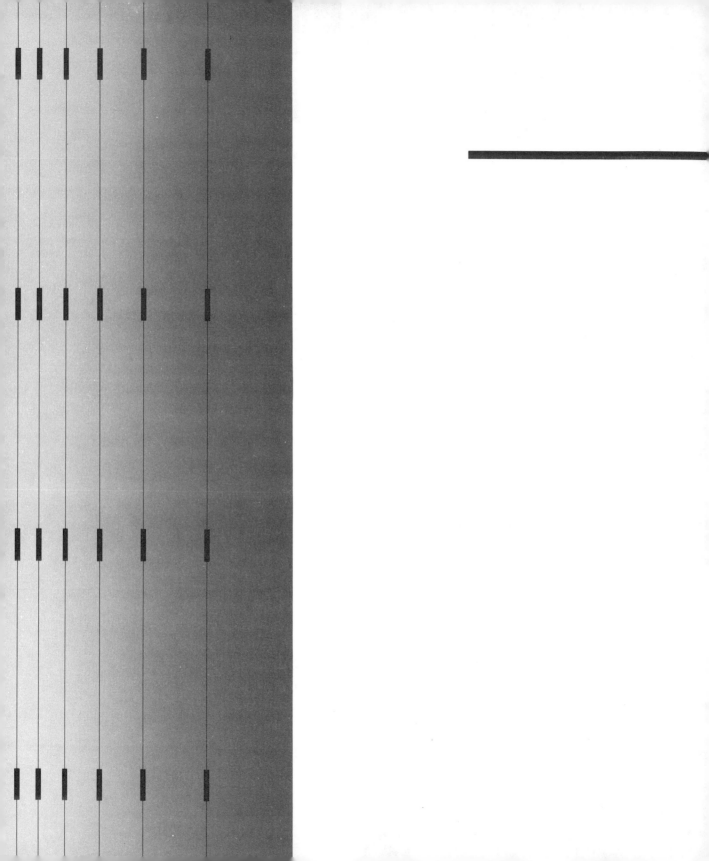

DOS REVISION HISTORY

DOS Revision History

When DOS was introduced with the first IBM personal computers, it was not nearly as powerful as it is today. For instance, in versions 1.X, hierarchical directories did not exist; they were included in versions 2.X and beyond. Hierarchical directories are only one example of the evolutionary growth in the power of DOS. Many of the commands have been borrowed from other operating systems, such as AT&T's UNIX. For example, piping (using the ¦ character) had been available on UNIX systems for a long time, but it was implemented in DOS only starting with revision 2.0. So what may seem to you to be many new and exciting features have actually been around for quite some time.

This appendix traces the major features of DOS, starting with version 1.0, and brings you up to the latest version, DOS 3.31. If you are upgrading, or considering upgrading, to 3.X, this appendix will show you precisely the value of a later version than your current one.

Version 1.00 (Introduced 1981)

When version 1.0 was released, DOS could do very little by comparison to version 3.3. This appendix assumes version 1.0 as a relative base and presents the improvements and enhancements from that point on.

The first enhancements to DOS appeared in version 1.10.

New Commands in Version 1.10

EXE2BIN   Converts .EXE files to .COM files

Enhanced Commands in Version 1.10

COPY	Concatenates files, verifies the copy, and works with binary files
DATE	Is resident
MODE	Redefines COM: port protocols and can reassign the parallel port to the serial port
TIME	Is resident; appears in directory listings

New Features in Version 1.10

Version 1.10 supports double-sided drives.

VERSIONS 2.0, 2.1 (INTRODUCED 1983)

Versions 2.X introduced many new features that became fundamental to all future DOS releases. Most notable among these features are hierarchical directories, piping, and redirection of input and output. If you have not used directories and you have a hard disk, you are in for quite a surprise, as directories provide an easy and effective way of organizing your hard disk. Version 2.1 is a version of 2.0 that supports international symbols and additionally can run the IBM PCjr computer; it has all of the same commands. Version 2.1 of PC-DOS is equivalent to version 2.01 of MS-DOS. MS-DOS actually released separate upgrades numbered 2.11 and 2.25 that corrected some bugs and offered additional support for extended characters 128 to 255.

New Commands in Versions 2.00 and 2.10

ASSIGN	Assigns new drive call letters
BACKUP	Copies files in backup format to a diskette
BREAK	Allows the use of Ctrl-Break in programs
CHDIR	Changes the current directory
CLS	Clears the screen
CTTY	Changes the current console
ECHO	Allows commands to be executed but not seen
FDISK	Partitions the hard disk
FOR	Provides looping statement in batch files
GOTO	Provides branching statement in batch files
GRAPHICS	Allows Shift-PrtSc to print graphics screens
IF	Provides conditional statement in batch files
MKDIR	Creates a directory
PATH	Specifies other directories for DOS to check
PRINT	Queues files sent to the printer
PROMPT	Changes the system prompt
RECOVER	Allows restoration of sector-flawed files
RESTORE	Reads in BACKUP files

RMDIR	Deletes a directory
SET	Defines DOS environment strings
SHIFT	Adds new variables in batch files
TREE	Displays the directory structure
VER	Displays the number of the DOS version you are using
VERIFY	Causes DOS to check what it saves to disk
VOL	Displays the label of the disk you specify

Enhanced Commands in Versions 2.00 and 2.10

CHKDSK	Works with fixed disks; optionally recovers lost files
COMP	Compares several files
DEBUG	Permits assembler commands to be entered directly into memory
DIR	Displays volume label, amount of space remaining, and directories
DISKCOPY	Works on 9-sector disks
DISKCOMP	Works on 9-sector disks
EDLIN	Has four new commands: C, M, T, and P
ERASE	You must press Return at the prompt
FORMAT	Formats 9 sectors or track, defines labels, and formats hard disks

New Device Names in Versions 2.00 and 2.10

LPT2:	Second parallel port
LPT3:	Third parallel port
COM2:	Second serial communications port

New Features in Versions 2.00 and 2.10

Version 2.X introduces meanings for certain characters. Piping is implemented with the ¦ symbol; redirection is implemented with the <, >, and >> symbols; and directories are implemented, with the \ symbol specifying the root directory.

The new CONFIG.SYS file is read at system startup and will specify certain parameters that the system needs to configure itself, such as device drivers and the number of buffers to use.

Version 1.X did not support hard disks. Not only does version 2.X support hard disks, but you can now divide the hard disk into different sections (partitions), each of which can be used by a different operating system, such as UNIX or XENIX. You may now also boot the system from the fixed disk, thus eliminating any need for floppy disks except for transporting programs and making backup copies. Also included with versions 2.X are the utility commands BACKUP and RESTORE (to save and reload your disk data).

In version 2.X, diskette capacity was increased by 20K per side, thanks to a higher sector density (9 sectors per track, as opposed to 8). If you have many diskettes formatted under versions 1.X, you will *not* need to reformat them, as versions 2.X can read them without trouble.

In the CONFIG.SYS file, you can also specify the number of disk buffers to be set up and used internally by DOS. A disk buffer is an area of memory set aside to facilitate data transfer between the disk drive and the computer. More disk buffers—up to a point—can increase the speed of disk operations dramatically.

Hierarchical directories, a feature new in version 2.00, are logical divisions on one disk that allow you to group files, an operation very much like putting papers into file folders in a file cabinet. Files can be moved between directories, and directories can be created or removed. The term *hierarchical* is derived from the structure of the directories. There is one directory at the top (like a master file) that can contain files and other *sub*directories (file folders). These subdirectories contain more files and other subdirectories (smaller folders), and so on. This structure is also called a *tree structure* because if you diagram it, it looks like an upside-down tree. Because of this, the top-level directory (\) is termed the *root directory*.

After a disk has been formatted, you can specify an 11-character name for the entire disk, such as PROGRAMS or DRIVE C or whatever you like. This naming feature is available with the FORMAT command in version 2.00.

Version 2.00 can also (via the PROMPT command) redefine the keyboard and can issue certain commands from within a program to influence the cursor and screen colors.

Version 3.00 (Introduced 1984)

DOS 3.00 incorporates the next major set of changes to DOS. Each of the secondary revisions (3.1, 3.2, 3.3) added specific additional features.

DOS 3.3 is the last official DOS X.Y released for the PC family of computers. DOS 3.3 brings a few new features to DOS, some of which (such as FAST-OPEN) duplicate commands and features previously found only in add-on or add-in utility software.

New Commands in Version 3.00

ATTRIB	Allows you to modify the read-only attribute
GRAFTABL	Specifies parameters for CGA
KEYB*XX*	Changes the keyboard to that of another country;
LABEL	Allows you to change the label without FORMAT
SELECT	Specifies different punctuation conventions
SHARE	Implements file sharing on networks

New Commands in Version 3.10

JOIN	Allows a drive to act as a subdirectory
SUBST	Allows a directory to act as a drive

New Commands in Version 3.20

REPLACE	Allows files to be copied selectively
XCOPY	Copies files selectively or in groups; copies complete subdirectories

Enhanced Commands in Version 3.20

ATTRIB	Changes the archive bit
COMMAND	Specifies the environment size
DISKCOMP	Supports 720K diskettes
DISKCOPY	Supports 720K diskettes
FORMAT	You must enter the default drive letter and (optionally) the volume label
SHELL	Specifies the environment size and executes AUTOEXEC.BAT
SELECT	Selects a keyboard template, formats the fixed disk, and copies DOS files to the fixed disk

New Features in Version 3.20

DRIVER.SYS allows you to copy files from one diskette to another with a different capacity while using the same drive.

New Commands in Version 3.30

APPEND	Supplies path-like support for files other than .EXE, .COM, and .BAT files
FASTOPEN	Speeds up disk access
NLSFUNC	Loads National Language Support routines
CHCP	Changes the current code page

Enhanced Commands in Version 3.30

ATTRIB	Allows multiple files to be modified
BACKUP	Formats diskettes, makes a log file, is faster, can use a time-stamp parameter
DATE	Sets the permanent clock date
FDISK	Divides the hard disk into logical drives
GRAFTABL	Loads multiple code pages into memory
KEYB	Replaces KEYBXX, allows additional templates
MODE	Selects code pages and more communications devices
RESTORE	Can use a time and date stamp; will RESTORE non-existing files
TIME	Sets the permanent clock

New Features in Version 3.30

DISPLAY.SYS	Specifies code-page switching on display devices
PRINTER.SYS	Specifies code page switching on certain printers
KEYBOARD.SYS	Supplies information for the KEYB command

New Features in Version 3.31

The major improvement in this minor upgrade is in the new ability of the FDISK command to create new disk partitions exceeding 32MB.

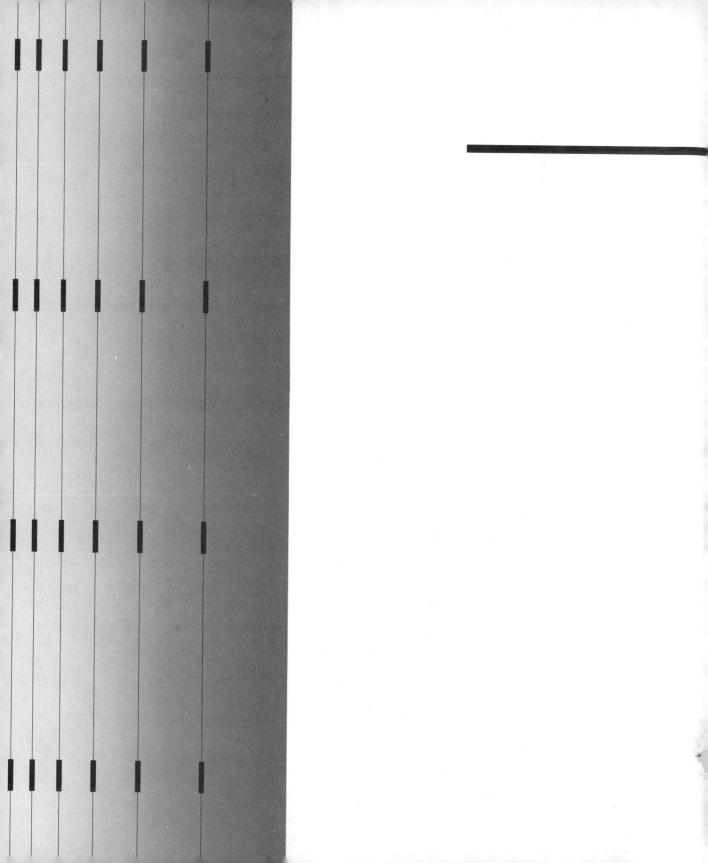

Typical System Problems and Their Cures

TYPICAL SYSTEM PROBLEMS
AND THEIR CURES

T his appendix describes some common problems you might confront while using your computer system and suggests some possible courses of action to remedy these problems. This appendix does not list individual errors for which DOS provides messages (see Appendix B for that information), but rather describes general types of problems and their causes and solutions. The intention is to give you an intuitive feel for the probable cause of different classes of problems. You should then be able to identify more rapidly the nature of a problem and to solve the problem more rapidly as well.

SAVING TIME AND MONEY BY SOLVING SIMPLE PROBLEMS

When an error occurs in your system, (the display is scrambled, the printer prints documents other than the one you requested, the printer prints the wrong document in the wrong language), your system may have serious problems—or it may have a minor problem that you can quickly solve with a little effort. Naturally, you can always take your entire system to your dealer, foregoing its use for a period of time along with a fair sum of money. In the end, you may get it repaired, but you may discover that nothing major was wrong; you may spend as much to diagnose the problem as to fix it.

By performing some simple tests, you can easily narrow down the possibilities of what might be wrong. This might be enough to save a technician some time or to rectify the problem yourself. At the very least, you'll learn a lot more about your system. The fundamental goal in these diagnostic techniques is to eliminate possible causes and to identify probable causes. Treating the possibilities one at a time is the most successful approach.

Consider an example. Suppose you are printing a document, and the printer stops printing spaces and begins adding strange symbols. Suppose it also replaces every occurrence of the letter *E* with a block symbol. You might be tempted to take the whole unit in for repair, but with a little patience you can solve the problem.

First, start with the easiest part of the system to test: the software. Try printing a different document to see if the same problems occur. If they do, try printing your program disk on a different computer, if you can. If it prints fine on that computer, then you can assume that the software is working properly. Now, if the software works, the problem must be in the computer itself, in your system's printer driver, in the printer card, in the printer itself, or in the connection between the printer and computer. The next-easiest elements to test are the printer and cable.

Connect your printer, if possible, to another computer (the one with which you just successfully tested your software). Connect your printer to that computer using the cable on the other computer. Does this combination work correctly? If so, then you can assume that your printer works fine. You've further narrowed the culprit list down to the cable, the printer card, the driver, or the computer itself. Now replace the printer cable connecting your printer to the other computer with the cable that connected your computer to your printer. Run the printing test once more. If the printing problems recur, then you've successfully identified the problem as a faulty cable. Cables can be replaced easily, so go to the store and buy a new cable. This whole process can take a very small amount of time on your part, save you a lot of money in diagnostic costs, and provide you with immeasurable satisfaction.

A few standard rules emerge from this example:

- First, the computer is just a machine, and by working with it a little, you often can fix it quite easily.
- Second, if something does go wrong, start with the easiest element to replace (swap) and then proceed to the more difficult elements.
- Third, be patient. Spending a little time trying to figure out the problem may save you much more time and effort later.

If this process seems complicated, consider this: If your television picture became scrambled, the first thing you would do is change the channel. If all of the channels were scrambled, you could reason that the problem was with your antenna or your television. You might then check the antenna, the dial, and then maybe the outlet for any problems. You might connect your televison to a different antenna, if you happen to have one. Does the problem go away? If it does, you buy a new antenna. If it doesn't, you take the set to the repair shop and get it fixed.

A computer, when problems like those just described occur, can be diagnosed the same way. All you need is a basic understanding of how the system works and the components that make it work. You can easily diagnose and even fix many problems yourself.

Should you have problems with your computer and not know where to start, even with all the ideas from this appendix, call your dealer. He or she will often be willing to suggest a few procedures for you to try. Your dealer will have a more satisfied customer if you save money by solving the problem yourself, and if you can't solve the problem, your dealer will be able to fix the problem more quickly if you've already taken some of the steps necessary to diagnose the problem.

SOLVING GENERAL CATEGORIES OF COMPUTER PROBLEMS

Many problems can arise during the operation of your computer system. Appendix B is testimony to that fact. This section describes three of the more common problems that occur in DOS environments. Difficulties in running memory-resident software are frustrating to nearly everyone wishing to benefit from these programs' features. Problems in setting up and configuring various peripheral devices annoy even experts. Computer systems that overheat are often a direct result of adding one too many special function boards to your system box.

Problem Type 1: Program conflicts with memory-resident software.

Cure: Remove memory-resident programs one by one until the system works properly again to identify the problem program. Do this by successively rebooting the system and loading all but one of the formerly loaded programs. Then reexecute the command or program that didn't work before to see if it works with the remaining TSRs.

Problem Type 2: Peripheral devices don't work with your software.

Cure: Check the user's manual for the device and verify that the configuration of your program is appropriate for your peripheral hardware. Especially check the screen and printer device drivers and types.

Problem Type 3: Computer is overheating.

Cure: Verify that the fan is working. Verify that the ventilation holes, both for air intake and expulsion, are unobstructed. Feel the back of the unit to see if it is excessively warm; you may need a more powerful fan or power supply. If you cannot remedy the problem yourself, see your dealer or maintenance department.

DOS COMMAND AND PROGRAM EXECUTION FAILURES

System failures are not always due to hardware problems or software conflicts. Sometimes they are the result of a user input error—your error. This section discusses the possible errors that you might make in command or parameter entry.

Problem: Command works overall, but the files affected were not the intended files, or the selected files were not processed in the expected way.

Cause: Wildcards were used improperly.

Cure: If anything past the * is ignored, use the ? wildcard.

Cause: You are in the wrong directory and have executed a file with the same name as the file you want, but configured differently.

Cure: Change to the correct directory.

Cause: You improperly sequenced the specifications in your PATH or APPEND command.

Cure: Check the order of directories and respecify the command.

Cause: You forgot to include a parameter.

Cure: Reenter the command, including the missing parameter.

Cause: You included an extra parameter.

Cure: Reenter the command, eliminating the extra parameter.

Problem: *The command executed in an unexpected manner.*

Cause: Another file of the same name but with a different extension was executed; for instance, you may have tried to execute TEST.BAT by typing TEST, but executed TEST.EXE instead. This problem can occur among .COM, .BAT, and .EXE files, since they can all be executed without specifying their extensions.

Cure: Specify the file extension in the command or check and revise the current and PATH directories.

Cause: Another file of the same name with or without the same extension was executed due to the sequence of the PATH or APPEND specification.

Cure: Resequence the PATH or APPEND setting so that the directory containing the desired file comes before the directory containing the file you do *not* want executed. Remember that the directories specified by PATH and APPEND are searched sequentially from beginning to end.

Cause: You typed the wrong command name, such as DISKCOMP instead of DISKCOPY or instead of COMP.

Cure: Type the correct command name.

Problem: A command scrambles the display, locks the system, or generates a parity error.

Cause: The command is incompatible with memory-resident programs.
Cure: See General Problem Type 1.

Cause: The command file became scrambled.
Cure: Sometimes, data saved on the disk can become scrambled. Recopy or reenter the program and reexecute processing.

Cause: The disk is bad.
Cure: The disk surface may be damaged. Use CHKDSK to determine whether a media problem exists. If there is a problem, recopy the data onto another diskette, or have your hard disk serviced if you cannot rectify the problem using available software.

Cause: The program is configured for a different screen.
Cure: See General Problem Type 2.

DISK ACCESS PROBLEMS

Disks are central to much of your computer use. You store your files on them, you obtain new software on them, you back up data to them, you access them constantly over the course of a typical computer session. You can significantly reduce frustration by learning how to handle the range of possible disk problems discussed in this section.

Problem: When you try to access the disk, it does not stop, you cannot hear or feel any head movement, and the display is not being updated to tell you that the computer is actually accomplishing anything.

Cause: There is not a diskette in the drive, or the drive door is open.
Cure: Insert a diskette in the drive or close the drive door.

Cause: The disk is unformatted.
Cure: Format the disk.

Cause: The specified path contains numerous directories or the amount of data being loaded is very large.

Cure: If a blinking message telling you to wait appears, processing is underway. However, unless the current program explicitly asks you to wait, you should not need to wait more than a minute or so for something to happen without an indicator appearing on the screen.

Problem: *Inconsistent disk failures occur: the screen displays many error messages, which may not always be the same, your programs don't work, or the system locks.*

Cause: Poor ventilation and extra circuit cards inside of the computer can combine to make the interior of the system unit excessively warm. Heat causes chips and circuitry to malfunction.

Cure: See General Problem Type 3.

Cause: Media problems occur: the disk may be storing information on parts of the disk that the computer does not know are bad, and hence the data is subject to error.

Cure: Recopy your programs or data to another area of the disk and use that file. Leave the bad data on the disk so that the computer will not again use that area of the disk. If you have any diagnostic programs, use these to test for errors. The Disk Test utility in the Norton Utilities will not only check for disk problems, but will mark bad clusters so they won't be reused for later file storage. Also, use CHKDSK to see if it can find any errors.

Cause: You are on a network and lockup-prevention software is not available or not working correctly.

Cure: If you do not have lockup-prevention software, contact your network dealer. If you do and it is not working correctly, make a new copy of your NETBIOS or other support programs. If the problem recurs, consult your dealer.

Problem: *The wrong directory is displayed or the wrong disk is accessed.*

Cause: You are running a program in another directory by using PATH and APPEND.

Cure: If directory paths are not supported by the program, you must exit the program and execute it from the directory containing the desired program. If directory paths are supported, consult your application software user's manuals to determine how to specify which directory should be displayed.

Cause: You did not specify the drive you wanted.
Cure: Specify the correct drive.

Cause: You did not *correctly* specify the drive you wanted.
Cure: Specify the drive correctly.

Cause: You are not in the directory you think you are in.
Cure: Check the directory name to determine the current directory.

Problem: Much abnormal noise and/or use of the drive. The drive takes a long time to access data.

Cause: A media problem exists.
Cure: Copy as much of your disk as you can onto a new diskette and use that instead.

Cause: Your program is very fragmented. If you have a hard disk, programs and data may not be stored sequentially on the disk, resulting in much head movement, which causes noise.
Cure: Buy a disk optimization program, such as VOPT or the Norton Utilities, to eliminate file fragmentation.

Problem: The disk is not activated when it is being accessed, and the operation fails or the computer locks.

Cause: Your system has heat-dissipation problems.
Cure: See General Problem Type 3.

Cause: Your disk controller has problems.
Cure: Run CHKDSK along with any other diagnostic programs you have. Turn off the computer and reboot. If the problem recurs, contact your dealer.

Cause: Resident program interaction problems exists.
Cure: See General Problem Type 1.

SCREEN PROBLEMS

Your most obvious connection with your computer is your console. The video monitor is DOS's primary output display device. It also displays the keystrokes you enter. Difficulties in viewing these types of information can prevent you from effectively using your system. This section discusses the most common problems affecting computer screens.

Problem: The display is snowy.

Cause: The program is configured for a different screen.

Cure: Check the application software user's manual and verify that the configuration of your program is appropriate for your hardware. Especially check the screen drivers and display types. Also check the application software user's manual to learn if a CGA snow-suppression mode is available.

Problem: The display moves horizontally or vertically.

Cause: The screen controls are not set correctly. Like television sets, most computer monitors have knobs to adjust screen movement.

Cure: Adjust the controls. This task is easy if the controls are external, or can be reached with a screwdriver from the outside. On many machines, however, you must remove the computer case. If this seems too daring, take your computer to a dealer for adjustment.

Problem: The display is jittery.

Cause: The printer may be too near your computer. During printing, this problem occurs with some portables that have a printer sitting directly on top of them or built into them.

Cure: Raise the printer above the top of the computer by at least six inches, experiment with placing different thicknesses of metal or wood between the computer and printer, or remove the printer from the top of the computer.

Cause: The video controller card or the power supply is malfunctioning.

Cure: Have your unit serviced.

Problem: No image appears on the screen.

Cause: The program is configured for a different screen.

Cure: Check the application software user's manual and verify that the configuration of your program is appropriate for your hardware. Especially check the screen drivers and display types.

Cause: Your system is frozen.

Cure: Check whether the disk is being accessed; there may be a resident-program conflict. Follow the guidelines for General Problem Type 1.

Problem: *The display is frozen, and the keyboard has no effect.*

Cause: There is a resident-program conflict.

Cure: See General Problem Type 1.

Cause: Your system is poorly ventilated.

Cure: See General Problem Type 3.

Problem: *Incoherent data appears on the screen.*

Cause: The device drivers are mismatched.

Cure: See General Problem Type 2.

Cause: The cables are malfunctioning.

Cure: Have the cables checked by a dealer or borrow a friend's cables and try them on your machine.

KEYBOARD PROBLEMS

Since you issue most command requests from a keyboard, you are helpless without a working keyboard. Sometimes the problem really is a broken keyboard; often, however, the keyboard may only appear to be broken. This section discusses the keyboard problems you may encounter during system use.

Problem: *When you press a key, nothing happens.*

Cause: A program is still executing and does not require input.

Cure: Wait until processing ends.

Cause: The keyboard-computer link is broken.

Cure: Check the cable connection. Turn the power off before connecting a keyboard cable.

Cause: Dust or dirt on the keyboard's circuits could be shorting out all or part of the keyboard.

Cure: Turn the system off. Get some circuit-cleaning spray from a local electronics shop and spray the keyboard, or call the manufacturer or alternatively your dealer.

Cause: Scroll-Lock or Num-Lock is set inappropriately for the software application.

Cure: Press the Scroll-Lock Key once and then retry the application. Try the Num-Lock Key next, if the problem continues.

Problem: **When you press a key, more than one character appears (this is called key bounce).**

Cause: Dust on the keyboard is causing the key to send multiple signals.

Cure: Clean the keyboard circuitry.

Cause: You are typing too lightly.

Cure: Press keys harder.

Cause: The computer is an older or cheaper model and the contacts under the keys on the keyboard are worn.

Cure: Consider buying a replacement keyboard.

Problem: **The keyboard prints only in uppercase.**

Cause: The Cap-Lock button is engaged.

Cure: Press the Cap-Lock key.

Problem: **Numeric keypad isn't working properly.**

Cause: The Num-Lock key is engaged.

Cure: Press the Num-Lock key.

PRINTER PROBLEMS

You can continue processing without a printer. You can produce results and handwrite them onto a piece of paper. However, since printed output is the most obvious result of nearly all computer programs, you're going to be unhappy if your printer is not working. This section discusses the most frequent causes of printing difficulties.

Problem: **The printer does not print.**

Cause: The cables are not attached.

Cure: Attach cables, preferably with the computer turned off.

Cause: The printer is connected to a different port than the one to which the computer is trying to write.

Cure: Follow the MODE command rule for changing and configuring the output ports.

Cause: The printer is not turned on.

Cure: Turn on the printer.

Cause: The device and driver are incompatible.

Cure: See General Problem Type 2.

Cause: The printer is not set to the correct baud rate.

Cure: See the MODE command.

Cause: The printer switches are not set correctly.

Cure: Consult your printer manual for the proper switch settings.

Cause: The cable is not working.

Cure: Try another cable.

Cause: The printer card is damaged.

Cure: Try your printer and cable on another computer. Consult your dealer.

Cause: The software is malfunctioning.

Cure: Try performing the same operation with your software on another computer.

Cause: The printer is out of paper.

Cure: Add paper.

Problem: *The printer prints garbled information.*

Cause: The device and driver are incompatible.

Cure: See General Problem Type 2.

Cause: The printer port is not configured properly.

Cure: See the MODE command.

Cause: The cable is damaged, or you bought the wrong cable.

Cure: Use the cable on another system to see if it works.

Cause: The printer is not configured properly.

Cure: Consult your printer manual regarding the proper setting of both its DIP switches and those on the computer to ensure compatibility between your system and your printer.

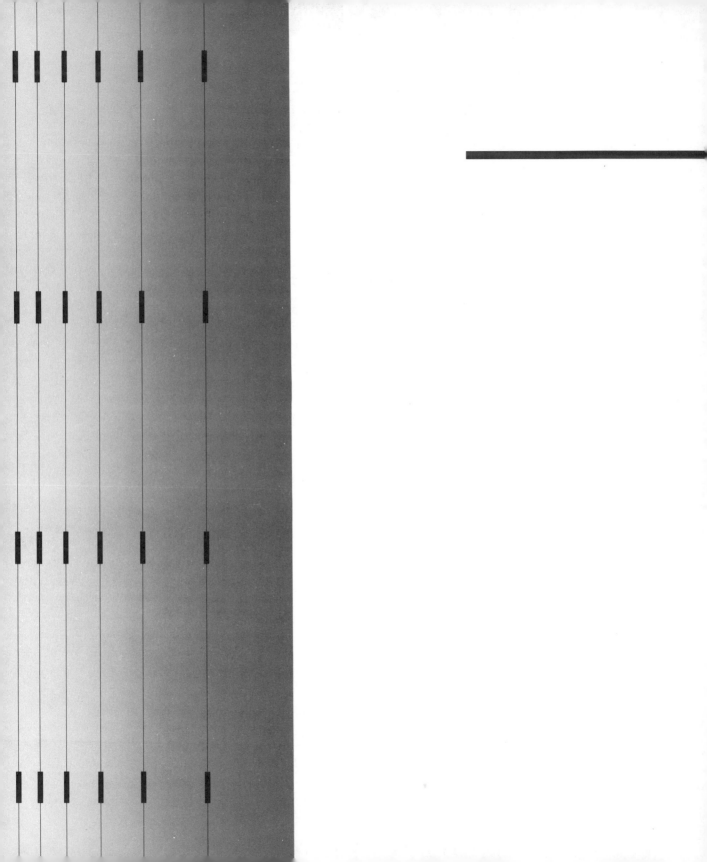

BREAKING THROUGH THE 640KB MEMORY LIMIT

Breaking through
the 640KB Memory Limit

Twenty years ago, sophisticated programs could be (and were) written using computers with as little as 4KB of memory. In the early 1980s, users and developers alike marveled at the DOS facility for addressable program space of up to 640KB. Times change.

And they continue to change. Within a few years, applications were being written that consumed all of that 640KB—and begged for more. Spreadsheets frequently displayed a "memory full" message as the range of cells and formulas quickly exceeded available space. Integrated packages discovered scarce file space left in memory after all the requisite code to support the multiple applications was loaded.

Users discovered that DOS and their individual application programs didn't always do everything they wanted. Consequently, memory-resident software surged in popularity in the mid eighties. These packages consumed portions of the 640KB memory limit.

Users also wanted easier access to multiple programs. This led to various programming solutions, from common data-file formats to conversion programs to simultaneous program execution. Programs such as Desqview and Windows approach this requirement for simultaneity in different ways (see the discussion that follows), but the performance of both still suffers when available memory is limited.

Early Solutions to Memory Restrictions

Limitations on memory affect programs in two primary ways. In the first case, the program must reference data files that are larger than can fit into what little memory remains after the program itself is loaded. This limitation affects word processors such as WordPerfect and WordStar. In the second case, the program itself requires more memory for its own code routines and logic than is available. This limitation affects more recent and sophisticated DOS programs such as dBASE IV and Framework II. Some programs struggle with both limitations and meet those constraints with the two solutions presented in this section.

Referencing Large Data Files

Data bases are often quite large, easily exceeding 640KB. In fact, the most common data base applications on microcomputers are inventory files and customer or client mailing lists. These files often exceed one megabyte in size. Data base programs and word processors don't even fight the constraint; these packages simply spill excess memory requirements right over into disk space.

In essence, then, a large file is maintained on disk; the application program brings into memory only a piece of the file at a time. The program uses this piece and then updates the disk file. Then the program brings another piece of the data file into the memory buffer area to be used by the application program. Most word processors and data base managers use this technique (see Figure F.1).

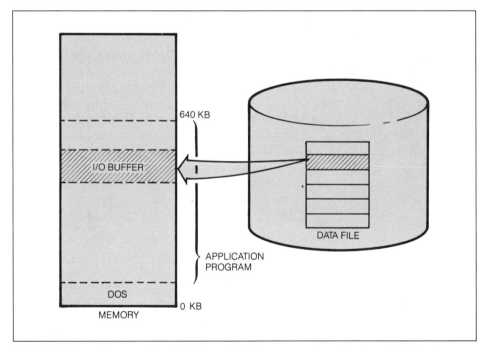

FIGURE F.1: The solution seen here is implemented when a program must access a data file whose size exceeds available physical memory. A portion of memory (a buffer) within the application program's addressable space is designated to hold the desired portion of the data file. Whichever portion of the data file is being referenced determines at each moment the contents of the memory-resident buffer. The program itself reserves a small data area within the application's address space and designates it as an input/output buffer. Depending on what portion of the disk-based data file you reference, the program fills the buffer with the portion of the file containing the desired data.

Loading Large, Sophisticated Programs

Most popular application software packages contain more instructions and coding sequences than can fit at once into conventional DOS memory. Remember that this conventional memory is constrained to 640KB, as shown in Figure F.2.

The actual limit of 1MB is a constraint of the 8086 and 8088 chips from Intel, which construct their memory addresses using 20 bits (2^{20} = 1MB). IBM PC and PC-XT computers and compatibles are absolutely restricted by the hardware in this way. This is also true for machines using the newer 80286 chip in real mode; the IBM PC-AT and compatibles fall into this category.

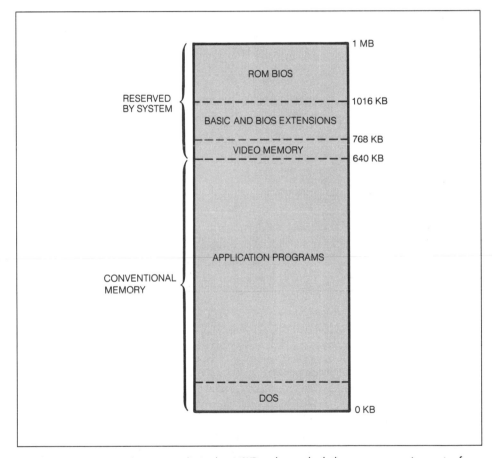

FIGURE F.2: Conventional memory is limited to 640KB and spans both the memory requirements of your DOS version and the needs of your individual application program. Upper memory is accessible to the Intel chips that run DOS, but is used only for special purposes: 128KB is reserved for video memory, and the remaining 256KB is reserved for read-only memory tasks, primarily the built-in BIOS.

Many users do not avail themselves of all the capabilities of programs that offer many advanced features. Recognizing this reality is fundamental to this next solution to memory limitation. Figure F.3 illustrates how *overlays*, or submodules, provide a solution to the memory-limitation problem.

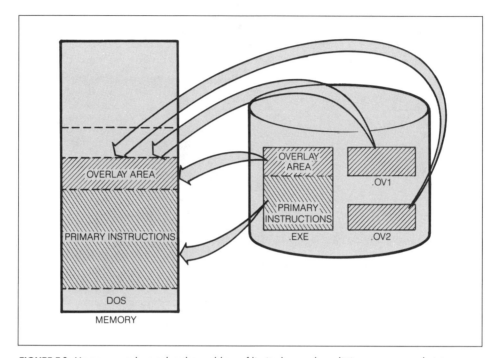

FIGURE F.3: Memory overlays solve the problem of limited space by splitting program code into a main module and one or more submodules. If the main code, loaded at program startup, does not contain the needed instruction sequence, then the appropriate overlay module containing the required code is loaded into memory. This code overwrites a clearly designated portion of memory, called the overlay area.

When designing an application, the program designer can specify certain routines as always resident. These should be the most common routines, the ones the user will probably want to use frequently. The designer can place less frequently needed routines in an auxiliary load module, known as an *overlay file*. Some extremely feature-rich software packages, such as CAD (computer aided design) programs, often have two or three overlay files.

When the program runs, it determines which feature the user is calling, either via a command prompt or through a menu mechanism. If that particular feature is not supported by the instructions in the portion of the package currently in memory, then the overlay file containing the proper instructional routines is loaded into memory. Typically, a designated portion of memory, called the *overlay area*, is used as the temporary home for these overlay routines.

In this way, an application can contain an unlimited number of features. If loaded at the same time, these features could easily consume hundreds of kilobytes more than can fit into conventional memory. The overlay mechanism ensures that conventional memory is never exceeded, and that when a particular feature is activated, the code to support the feature is loaded.

Overlays are a form of demand loading that works quite successfully for many programs. The primary disadvantage of this technique is the extra processing overhead required to load a disk-based module to obtain access to specific code when requested. An additional problem of the overlay technique is the designer effort and knowledge necessary to split the support routines into separate modules and properly prepare the overlay files.

Overlays were a good first solution to the memory limitation problem. Faster and easier methods have since been developed, although they are not all available to all programs and to all processing chips.

Using Extended Memory to Break the Memory Barrier

The most obvious solution to memory constraints is to increase the amount of memory available in the system. If memory were easily added without limit, then such techniques as those discussed in the previous section would be unnecessary. Entire data files and program files supporting an enormous range of features could, regardless of their size, be easily loaded into memory.

Even though memory is becoming increasingly inexpensive, simply adding memory chips or boards is not the answer. Physical availability of memory on a system is not enough. The processing chip must be able to address that memory, and the operating system must also be able to gain access to the program code and data stored in that memory; the application programs themselves may need to modify their addressing techniques to make effective use of the new addresses located outside of conventional memory.

Using Protected Mode to Extend Memory Addressability

The 80286 chip from Intel offers a feature called *protected mode*. Whereas the 8088/8086 chips used 20 bits to construct an address (gaining access to 1 megabyte of memory), this chip uses 24 bits for addressing. Those extra 4 bits allow the protected mode of the chip to directly access 16MB of memory ($2^4 = 16$), many times that allowed by earlier chips. Figure F.4 depicts this enhanced feature of the 80286 chip.

The 80286 chip has a split personality. With only a few assembly language instructions, the operating mode of the chip can be changed from real mode to protected mode. In protected mode, the extra address lines on the PC AT and

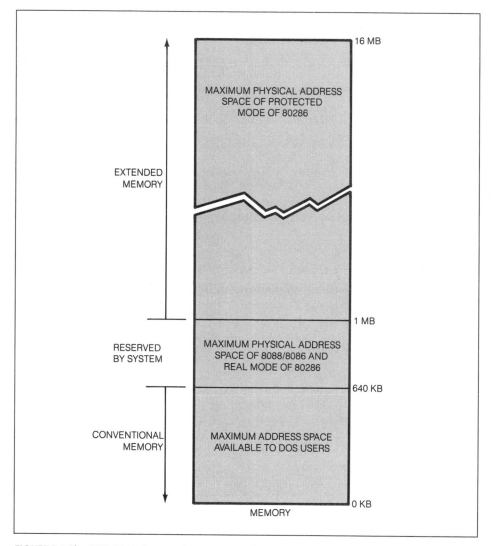

FIGURE F.4: The 8088/8086 chips used in IBM PCs and IBM PC-XTs and all their compatibles were limited to a maximum physical addressability of one megabyte. The real mode of the newer chips is also limited in the same way. However, in IBM PC-ATs and PS/2s and compatibles, the protected mode of the newer 80286 chips allows physical addressability of 16 megabytes.

PS/2 computers allow access to 16 megabytes. This extra memory beyond one megabyte is called *extended memory*.

Unfortunately, most software (including DOS itself) has not been adapted to actually use any of the address space beyond one megabyte. However, DOS 3.X has been able to use this extra memory in the form of a RAM disk (called

VDISK in IBM PC DOS systems). Remember that RAM disks use memory addresses to store files in a special format that emulates the organization and accessibility of a disk drive. This allows disk operations such as on-line overlay transfers to work at memory speeds rather than at the much slower disk speeds.

With a RAM disk, only RAM disk software knows that the data and file access is actually from memory, not from a real disk drive. In fact, earlier RAM disk drivers often created virtual disks from unused memory locations in the conventional memory space below the 640K limit. In either case, however, you must first copy data files or overlay files from their real disk locations to the RAM disk before any programs can access them. After using the data files, you must remember to copy any changes back to their permanent file locations, typically on your hard disk.

Limitations of Extended Memory

Extended memory is just a tool. The 80286 chip provide access to that memory, but DOS is limited in how it uses it. Instruction support in the ROM BIOS is extremely limited, being restricted to determining how much memory is installed and transferring data to and from conventional memory. DOS and the BIOS do not manage this extended memory in any sophisticated way, so it is difficult for multiple programs to use portions of extended memory simultaneously.

DOS still does not directly address the extended memory locations. The newest IBM operating system, OS/2, from Microsoft and IBM, does introduce a sophisticated memory manager that uses this extended memory directly. See my *Essential OS/2* (SYBEX, 1988) for more information about how this mechanism is implemented.

Certainly extended memory can be used as more than just an area for large RAM disk operations. That's just what industry leaders announced in 1985.

USING EXPANDED MEMORY FOR MORE POWERFUL OPERATIONS

The next creative solution to memory constraints was developed in 1985 by Lotus Development Corporation and Intel. In an attempt to further stretch the capabilities of the millions of existing microcomputers, these companies announced a new specification for what they called *expanded memory*. After viewing early presentations of their specifications, Microsoft Corporation joined Lotus and Intel to release the LIM EMS (Lotus-Intel-Microsoft expanded memory specification 3.2.) This common standard became an overnight hit.

Using Bank Switching to Expand Your Memory

Like the size of conventional memory, the size of your desk surface is finite. You can assign a central portion of your desk to papers and folders, selected from a potentially unlimited number of files in your file cabinet. You can have a series of relevant papers on your desk, reserving one area for reference folders you get from and return to your file cabinet (see Figure F.5).

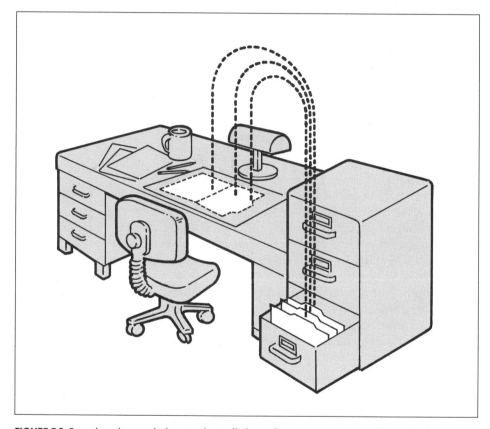

FIGURE F.5: Even though your desktop is physically limited in size, you can use unlimited reference materials by switching among file folders, reserving one portion of your desk as a "switching area." Although your desk may contain a variety of other materials that does not change, you can access 2, 5, or 50 file folders during your own personal information processing, though only one of these folders is open and accessible at any given moment.

Similarly, a computer can reserve a portion of conventional memory as a central "switching area." If this area is analogous to the file folder area in the center of your desk, then any number of similarly sized (or smaller) portions of extended memory can be logically brought into this area. This technique is called *bank switching* (a *bank* of storage addresses in memory is a physically and logically addressable unit). Figure F.6 depicts this approach to memory expansion.

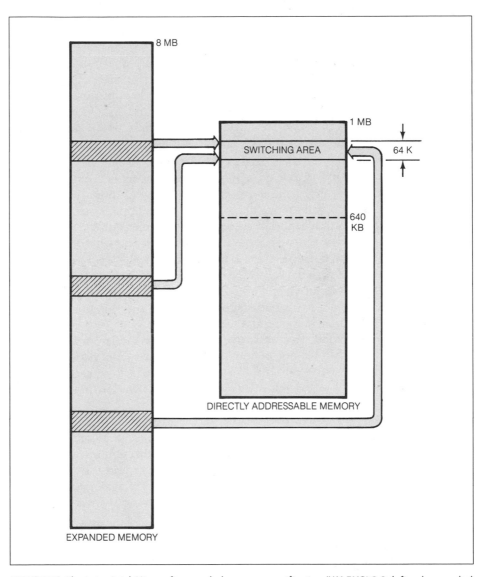

FIGURE F.6: The Lotus-Intel-Microsoft expanded memory specification (LIM EMS) 3.2 defined expanded memory and how it works. In the original specification, up to 8MB of expanded memory could be accessed through one 64K reserved lower memory area. This area was typically carved out of an unused area of contiguous memory located in the sparsely used ROM area at the upper end of addressable memory (below 1MB).

The LIM EMS specification contained many details of expanded-memory management and of the interface between that memory and programs wanting to gain access to it. Many of these details are embodied in a program called the Expanded Memory Manager (EMM.SYS) which expanded memory systems must include as a device driver in the CONFIG.SYS file.

During system booting, when device drivers are installed, EMM.SYS looks for a contiguous, available area of 64KB in the uppermost 256KB of memory reserved for ROM programs. When it finds such an area, EMM.SYS takes control of these addresses and uses them as a window into the separate expanded memory locations. IBM PCs and PC-XTs (and PC-ATs in real mode) can address only up to one megabyte; however, these 64KB address locations are directly addressable by the processing chip.

When a program wants access to the additional memory locations in the expanded memory area, it must make a precisely defined interrupt call to EMM .SYS that provides the uniform interface to any of those locations. EMM.SYS enables this access by providing a unique programming handle to each program using expanded memory. These programs can be single-tasking or multitasking programs, other device drivers, or even carefully written memory-resident programs.

Even though the area reserved by the expanded memory manager is 64KB in size, EMS 3.2 actually called for the banks to be only 16KB in size. Hence, as can be seen in Figure F.7, the EMM must manage the necessary access to up to 8MB of physical expanded memory through the regimen of switching base addresses in units of 16KB at a time.

All expanded memory is treated as a collection of memory banks, divided into 16KB pages. Simple instructions are part of the memory specification, allowing programs to switch new 16KB pages into the 64KB addressable window or to switch existing pages and their data out of the window and back to expanded memory locations.

In total, EMM.SYS provides a variety of services to a requesting program, well beyond the standard initialization and output functions of a standard device driver. EMM.SYS also provides information, through software interrupt 67H, regarding hardware and software module statuses and the current allocation of expanded memory pages. Diagnostic routines are available, as are routines to manage the actual mapping of logical pages into and out of expanded memory into physical pages in the 64KB window.

The LIM EMS specification was the possible groundwork for the next generation of multitasking operating systems. But progress continued in the DOS world with new products from industry competitors.

Enhancing the Expanded Memory Specification

AST Research and Quadram are two of the industry leaders in the production of add-on memory boards, and Ashton-Tate is a major producer of personal

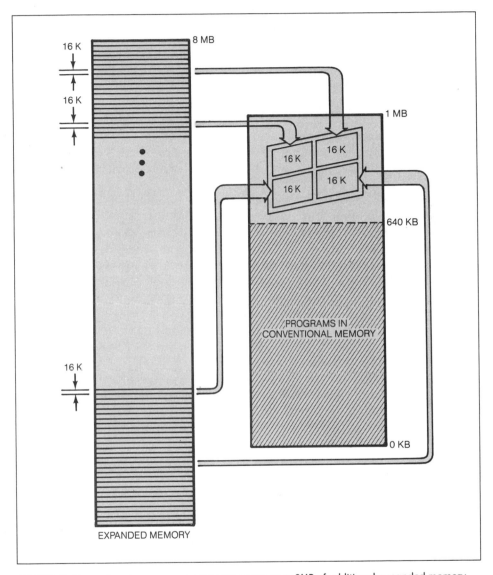

FIGURE F.7: Conventional memory programs can access up to 8MB of additional expanded memory, according to the original expanded memory specification 3.2. They do so through software interrupt calls to the Expanded Memory Manager (EMM.SYS) device driver. EMM.SYS switches banks of 16KB memory addresses. The window into these expanded memory pages is provided and maintained by EMM.SYS in a contiguous block of 64KB, carved out of the 256KB ROM area at the top of the typical 1MB address space.

computer software. Together, these three companies released their own new specifications for expanded memory use. Their enhanced version of EMS was called EEMS (enhanced expanded memory specification).

EEMS was more complex than EMS 3.2 and differed in key ways. Whereas EMS located the switching area above the DOS 640KB program area, EEMS mapped expanded memory into addressable space anywhere under the 1MB address limit. This feature allowed easy switching of memory pages that contain addressable code because they could be switched into the lower memory addresses accessible by DOS programs.

EEMS also offered an expanded mapping window. Whereas EMS allowed the mapping of only four 16KB logical expanded memory pages into physical memory, EEMS allowed the mapping of 64 logical pages (64 × 16KB = 1MB). EEMS also supported a minimum window size of 16KB. In fact, as it turns out, the upper limit on window size was somewhat unrealistic, since much of that 1MB is needed by DOS, application program code, video buffers, and system ROMs. The new EEMS specification did, however, realistically make available all free space: often as much as 20 logical pages.

EEMS also allowed software specification of mapping areas at runtime. Under EMS 3.2, you had to take great care setting the proper switches and jumpers on the memory boards to specify the mapping area. Additionally, EMS 3.2 required one contiguous 64KB memory area. EEMS allowed the use of several areas that are not necessarily physically contiguous.

For a while, it was unclear which of these two heavyweight standards would emerge the winner. Microsoft's Windows used EMS to implement its multitasking strategy, and Quarterdeck's Desqview used EEMS in its more powerful multitasking operating environment. The differing concepts and implementation strategies of these two expanded memory specifications made writing programs that run easily under both specifications difficult. In fact, memory boards conforming to one specification do not necessarily work under the other.

Everyone Wins with the LIM EMS 4.0 Specification

Users of DOS and designers of programs in the DOS environment were gratified in 1987 by the announcement of the latest evolution of the expanded memory specifications. This latest announcement, variously referred to as LIM 4.0 or EMS 4.0, specifies a new set of developer functions that support much larger DOS application programs, as well as multitasking. These new specifications permit the use of these improved features on all DOS machines, even the seemingly more limited 8088/8086 PC and PC-XT models.

EMS 4.0 incorporates all of the best aspects of the earlier EMS 3.2, as well as the improvements made in EEMS, thus reducing confusion among program developers and setting EMS 4.0 apart as a viable standard for future program growth in the DOS world. The AST/Quadram/Ashton-Tate group has accepted the new standard.

The new standard defines more than twice the number of functions and sub-functions (30 versus 15) contained in EMS 3.2. In addition, accessible expanded memory has been increased from a maximum size of 8MB to 32MB. Incorporating some of the EEMS techniques ensures that EMS 4.0 supports the execution of both standard program code as well as TSR (terminate and stay resident, or memory-resident) programs in expanded memory.

EMS 4.0 directly supports multitasking. A requirement of programs when they run concurrently with other programs is that they be able to share data. This new standard also defines how, specifically, common data access and sharing can take place.

The developers of EMS 4.0 clearly state that it is not itself a multitasking operating system. It does, however, provide a formidable array of features that allow applications to perform multitasking in expanded memory. A variety of programs, RAM disks, and print spoolers all can run simultaneously in expanded memory.

The new OS/2 system for IBM computers, on the other hand, is a full-blown multitasking operating system, with significantly enhanced features over both DOS and EMS 4.0. However, if your computer does not run OS/2 or you do not upgrade your system to OS/2, EMS 4.0 can breathe new life into your system. New software will undoubtedly be designed, and certainly much old software will be upgraded, to work in this enhanced DOS programming environment.

Saving Money with Expanded Memory Emulators

If you have no available slots in your IBM PC or PC-XT for a specially designated expanded memory board, or if you choose to avoid the expense of a new expanded memory board, several vendors now offer help. This help may be especially relevant if you've already spent money on an AT-type extended memory board.

Since the expanded memory specification is device independent, the source of the expanded memory is unimportant to applications using it. Therefore, just as surely as a piece of software can cause memory to be perceived as a RAM disk, so a piece of software can cause a disk to be perceived as memory.

In fact, the same concept can be taken one step further. Expanded memory-emulation software can adhere to the EMS requirements, providing memory pages not from an expanded memory board, but from any one of the sources shown in Figure F.8.

If your system already includes extended memory, you can configure the emulation software to use that memory as if it were expanded memory. Naturally, the drawback of this method is the extra software overhead (which can be considerable) required for the emulated access.

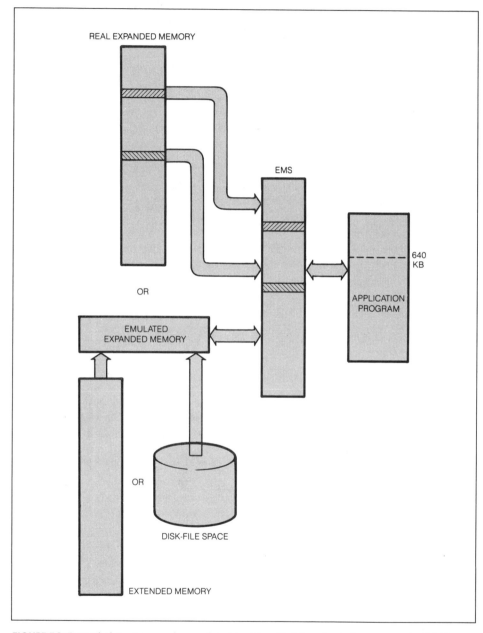

FIGURE F.8: Expanded memory can be emulated in either AT-style extended memory or in disk files created just for this purpose. The emulation software conforms to the expanded memory specifications, so the source of the data is irrelevant to an application program making the proper EMS calls. The source could be a standard expanded memory hardware board, as shown at the top of this figure, or it could be one of the two sources for emulated expanded memory, as shown at the bottom of the figure.

Even if your system has no additional memory installed, you still can run software requiring expanded memory. The emulation routines can create a disk file equal in size to the simulated expanded memory that you need but don't have. The emulator handles the reading and writing of the disk file to obtain the 16KB pages needed by the expanded memory manager. This solution permits you to run software in an expanded memory environment, albeit at significantly reduced speeds because of the relatively enormous disk input/output overhead.

Although emulation may seem attractive, it has some obvious drawbacks. As pointed out, using it is markedly slower than using expanded memory directly. The overhead for the software emulation is considerable, and, if you are using a disk file to emulate expanded memory, the disk I/O overhead further reduces overall system performance. In addition, emulation software is not always completely compatible with programs designed to run using actual hardware boards. So even if you're willing to endure reduced performance, you still may not be able to run your favorite expanded memory program.

INDEX

NOTE: Page numbers in **boldface** type refer to command summaries.   Page numbers in *italics* refer to glossary.

DOS User's Desktop Companion

If you have found *DOS User's Desktop Companion* to be useful, you'll be glad to learn that every one of the batch files in this book is available on a companion diskette. Save time, energy, and money—and avoid the drudgery of typing these excellent programs—by ordering the *DOS User's Desktop Companion Diskette* now.

If you or one of your friends or colleagues would like to begin learning DOS at a more elementary level than this book assumes, you should try the *Introduction to DOS Audio Cassette Training* program. This introductory training guide contains two audio cassettes and an accompanying "Professional Learning Manual" with exercises and learning modules that parallel the tapes. Send in your order for this personal aid to quick and easy understanding of DOS.

Use the order form below to order any of the fine products produced by Judd Robbins. Mail the form with complete payment to Computer Options, 198 Amherst Avenue, Berkeley, CA 94708.

ORDER FORM

_____ copies of *DOS User's Desktop Companion Diskette*   @ $19.95 each = _____

_____ copies of *Introduction to DOS Audio Cassette Training* program   @ $19.95 each = _____

_____ copies of ReComm, the DOS command reissuing utility (see Chapter 20)   @ $19.95 each = _____

_____ Shipping and handling   @ $2.50/product_____

_____ California sales tax (California residents only; add appropriate tax for your city or county)   _____

               TOTAL ORDER: _____

NAME: _____

COMPANY: _____

ADDRESS: _____

CITY, STATE, ZIP: _____

TELEPHONE: _____

SYBEX Computer Books are different.

Here is why . . .

At SYBEX, each book is designed with you in mind. Every manuscript is carefully selected and supervised by our editors, who are themselves computer experts. We publish the best authors, whose technical expertise is matched by an ability to write clearly and to communicate effectively. Programs are thoroughly tested for accuracy by our technical staff. Our computerized production department goes to great lengths to make sure that each book is well-designed.

In the pursuit of timeliness, SYBEX has achieved many publishing firsts. SYBEX was among the first to integrate personal computers used by authors and staff into the publishing process. SYBEX was the first to publish books on the CP/M operating system, microprocessor interfacing techniques, word processing, and many more topics.

Expertise in computers and dedication to the highest quality product have made SYBEX a world leader in computer book publishing. Translated into fourteen languages, SYBEX books have helped millions of people around the world to get the most from their computers. We hope we have helped you, too.

For a complete catalog of our publications:

SYBEX, Inc. 2021 Challenger Drive, #100, Alameda, CA 94501
Tel: (415) 523-8233/(800) 227-2346   Telex: 336311
Fax: (415) 523-2373

SUMMARY OF DOS COMMANDS*
(continued from inside front cover)

COMMAND AND SYNTAX	DESCRIPTION	PAGE
[D:Path]**LABEL** [D1:][String]	Defines or changes existing volume label.	140
LASTDRIVE = D	In a CONFIG.SYS file, specifies the highest drive letter.	330
MD[D:Path]	Creates a new subdirectory. Can also be entered as MKDIR.	141
[D:Path]**MODE** LPTx: [CPL][,[LPI][,P]]	Defines attributes for all ports and	368, 403
[D:Path]**MODE** LPTx: = COMy	code pages.	
[D:Path]**MODE** COMy[:]Baud[,[Parity][,[Bits][,P]		
[D:Path]**MODE** Type		
[D:Path]**MODE** [Type], Shift [,T]		
[D:Path]**MODE** Device CODEPAGE PREPARE = ((CP) FileSpec)		
[D:Path]**MODE** Device CODEPAGE PREPARE = ((CPList) FileSpec)		
[D:Path]**MODE** Device CODEPAGE SELECT = CP		
[D:Path]**MODE** Device CODEPAGE[/STATUS]		
[D:Path]**MODE** Device CODEPAGE REFRESH		
[D:Path]**MORE**	Pauses the display of long files.	531
[D:Path]**NLSFUNC** [FileSpec]	Loads in routines for code pages and the CHCP command.	370
PATH [D1:Path1][;D2:Path2...]	Defines search list for .EXE, .COM, and .BAT files.	142
[D:Path]**PRINT** [/D:Device][/B:BuffSize][/U:BusyTicks] [/M:MaxTicks][/S:TimeSlice][/Q:QueueSize][/C] [/T][/P][FileSpec,...]	Queues files for printing.	487
PROMPT [String]	Changes the system prompt.	172
[D:Path]**RECOVER**[D1][FileSpec]	Rescues damaged files.	630
REN OldFile NewFile	Changes the name of a file. Can also be entered as RENAME.	102
[D:Path]**REPLACE** SourceFile [Dest][/A][/P][/R][/S][/W]	Copies, adds, and updates programs.	631

*Commands used only by assembly-language programmers are outside the scope of this book. The EDLIN subcommands are presented in Chapter 6 and the batch-file subcommands in Chapter 8.